ASKING
THE LAW
QUESTION

Thomson Legal & Regulatory Australia
100 Harris Street Pyrmont NSW 2009
Tel: (02) 8587 7000 Fax: (02) 8587 7100
LRA.Service@thomson.com
www.thomson.com.au
For all customer inquiries please ring 1300 304 195
(for calls within Australia only)

INTERNATIONAL AGENTS & DISTRIBUTORS

NORTH AMERICA
Thomson Legal & Regulatory
North America
Eagan
United States of America

ASIA PACIFIC
Thomson Legal & Regulatory
Asia Pacific
Sydney
Australia

LATIN AMERICA
Thomson Legal & Regulatory
Latin America
São Paulo
Brazil

EUROPE
Thomson Legal & Regulatory
Europe
London
United Kingdom

ASKING
THE LAW
QUESTION

by

MARGARET DAVIES

BA, LLB (Adelaide), MA, DPhil (Sussex)
Professor of Law
Flinders University, Adelaide

Third Edition

LAWBOOK CO. 2008

Published in Sydney by

Thomson Lawbook Co.
100 Harris Street, Pyrmont, NSW

First edition 1994
Second edition 2002
Third edition 2008

National Library of Australia
    Cataloguing-in-Publication entry

Davies, Margaret (Margaret Jane)
    Asking the law question / author, Margaret Davies.

3rd ed.
9780455222912 (pbk)
Includes index.
Bibliography.

Law — Philosophy.

340.1

Editor: Corina Brooks
Publisher: Robert Wilson

Typeset in Legacy Sans and Legacy Serif, 10 on 12 point, by RE Typesetting, Woy Woy, NSW
Printed by Ligare Pty Ltd, Riverwood, NSW

PREFACE

This book was first published 14 years ago, with a second edition appearing six years ago. The first edition was written in a spirit of great enthusiasm and with a sense of urgency generated by radical change in legal theory. The (then) new influences of feminist legal theory, critical legal studies, critical race theory, and postmodernism posed fundamental challenges to established forms of legal theory, adding huge variety to a field dominated by the distinction between natural law theory and positivism. These new critical approaches to law raised questions about the neutrality and objectivity of law, the meanings and interpretation of law, the relationship of law to systemic forms of power such as gender, and law's location in the social and cultural setting.

In the second edition, published in 2002, I simply tried to consolidate and improve upon the earlier material, and to fill in significant gaps. This edition was subtitled "the dissolution of legal theory", indicating that it was no longer possible to see legal theory as a single distinct area of academic inquiry. Legal theory had become, and remains, plural: it cannot be reduced to a core set of questions with a defined number of possible responses. Rather, different theoretical traditions approach law from different angles and with different disciplinary influences.

In keeping with the 2002 edition, I have tried in this edition to continue the process of improving the original text, while updating sources and themes where necessary. In the process of rewriting, I have been faced with some interesting decisions about which theoretical views and examples remain significant. Since the approach of the book has always been transparently personal, these decisions about content are inevitably entangled with my own development as an academic and legal theorist. The book is not comprehensive, but it is increasingly layered in an architectural sense: the structure and basic plan were laid in 1994, and subsequent versions have tried to refresh and refashion the material without completely reconceptualising it. In brief, I have tried to keep one eye on the past (and *my* past) in legal theory while keeping the other eye on the present and future (including, of course, my own current preoccupations).

I have many people to thank for their encouragement, inspiration, practical suggestions, and continuing support. First, all of those people who have engaged with the book over the years, by recommending it in reading lists, referring to it, writing reviews of it (both positive and negative), and otherwise, have given the book its continuing life as a legal theory book — without this interest, it would undoubtedly have remained a single edition. Secondly, several people provided valuable feedback about the second and third editions, including Myint Zan, Reetvinder Randhawa, Irene Watson, Peter Fitzpatrick, Åsa Gunnarsson, Joanne Conaghan, and Greta Bird. I would also like to repeat my thanks (of 2002) to those in Sweden and Finland who organised and supported visits to universities in Umeå, Gothenburg and Helsinki, where some of the writing for the second edition was undertaken. Revisions for the third edition were commenced while I was a visiting scholar at the Research Centre for Law, Gender, and Sexuality at the University of Kent in June and July 2007, and I am grateful to members of the Centre and the Kent law school community generally for their collegiality, their friendship, and their interest in my work and this book. Debbie Bletsas, Christina Son and Rose Polkinghorne have provided research assistance at different stages of the third edition, and I have appreciated their timeliness, diligence, and attention to detail in what is an increasingly complicated task. I would also like to thank the team at Thomson Legal and Regulatory Limited, in particular Corina Brooks, Dana Poulos and Robert Wilson, for their commitment to this book and their motivational emails. And Liz Rawlings continues to be encouraging, sympathetic, and very patient.

Finally, I repeat (with minor amendments) the final paragraph of the Preface to the second edition: I would like to thank all of those who contributed to the first and second editions, especially Mary Heath, who has had a substantial and most valuable input for the whole life of this book. My colleagues at Flinders University School of Law are collectively very co-operative and friendly, making this a most productive environment in which to work. Finally, the first and second editions were dedicated to Ngaire Naffine in appreciation of her intellectually engaging and inspiring friendship over the past 16 years, and I would (once again) like to reaffirm that dedication for this edition.

MARGARET DAVIES

Adelaide
January 2008

ACKNOWLEDGMENTS

The following extracts attributed herein were reproduced with the kind permission of:

Allen & Unwin: www.allenandunwin.com
- Rosi Braidotti, "Ethics Revisited: Women and/in Philosophy" in Pateman and Gross (eds) *Feminist Challenges: Social and Political Theory* (1986).

American Journal of Jurisprudence (by Notre Dame Law School Indiana)
- JB Crozier, "Legal Realism and a Science of Law" (1984) 29 *American Journal of Jurisprudence* 151.

Athlone Press (by the Senate House Library, University of London)
- Carl Stychin and Didi Herman (eds) *Sexuality in the Legal Arena* (2000).

Australian Feminist Law Journal (by the Australian Feminist Law Foundation Inc)
- Irene Watson, "Power of the Muldarbi, the Road to its Demise" (1998) 11 *Australian Feminist Law Journal* 28.
- Irene Watson, "Indigenous Peoples' Law-Ways: Survival Against the Colonial State" (1997) 8 *Australian Feminist Law Journal* 39.

Blackwell Publishers: www.blackwellpublishing.com
- Robert Bernasconi, "Who Invented the Concept of Race?" in Robert Bernasconi (ed) *Race* (2001).
- Anthony Arblaster, *The Rise and Decline of Western Liberalism* (1984).
- David Sugarman, "Legal Theory, the Common Law Mind, and the Making of the Textbook Tradition" in William Twining (ed) *Legal Theory and the Common Law* (1986).

Borderlands e-journal: www.borderlands.net.au
- Suvendrini Perera, "What is a Camp...?" (2002) 1(1) *Borderlands e-journal*.

Boston College Third World Law Journal (©2000 Boston College Law School)
- Reginald Leamon Robinson, "The Shifting Race-Consciousness Matrix and the Multi-racial Category Movement: A Critical Reply to Professor Hernandez" (2000) 20 *Boston College Third World Law Journal* 231.

British Journal of Law and Society (by Blackwell Publishers UK): www.blackwellpublishing.com
- C Veljanovski, "The Economic Approach to Law: A Critical Introduction" (1980) 7 *British Journal of Law and Society* 158.

Buffalo Law Review (the University of Buffalo, Law School): www.buffalolawreview.org
- David Fraser, "Truth and Hierarchy: Will the Circle Be Unbroken?" (Fall 1984) 33(3) *Buffalo Law Review* 729.

Cambridge University Press, Cambridge: www.cup.cam.ac.uk
- Sir John Davies, *Irish Reports* (1612) in Frederick Pocock, *The Ancient Constitution and the Feudal Law* (1957).
- Allan Hutchinson, *Evolution and the Common Law* (2005).

Columbia Law Review (by the Columbia University): www.columbialawreview.org
- Felix S Cohen, "Transcendental Nonsense and the Functional Approach" (1935) 35 *Columbia Law Review* 809.

Connecticut Law Review (by the University of Connecticut, School of Law): connecticutlawreview.org
- Derrick Bell, "Racial Realism" (1992) 24 *Connecticut Law Review* 363.

Cornell Law Quarterly
- John Dewey, "Logical Method and Law" (1924) 10 *Cornell Law Quarterly* 17.

Cornell University Press (by Cornell University): *www.cornellpress.cornell.edu*
• Charles B Mills, *The Racial Contract* (1987).

J M Dent & Sons (Orion Publishing Group, UK): *www.orionbooks.co.uk*
• Aristotle, *The Politic* (1931).

The Federation Press, Sydney: *www.federationpress.com.au*
• Jennifer Clarke, "Law and Race: The Position of Indigenous People" in Bottomley and Parker (eds) *Law in Context* (2nd ed, 1997).

Firebrand Books, Ithaca, New York
• Ruthann Robson, *Lesbian (Out) Law: Survival Under the Rule of Law* (1991).

The Flinders Journal of Law Reform (Flinders University, South Australia)
• Margaret Davies, "The De-capitalisation of a Discipline, or How Legal Theory Lost its Head" (2000) 4(1) *Flinders Journal of Law Reform* 127.

Fontana Press London
• JS Mill, "On Liberty" in JS Mill *Utilitarianism* (1962).
• Roland Barthes, *Image Music Text* (1977).

Free Press (div of Simon & Schuster, Inc): *www.simonsays.com*
• Dinesh D'Souza, "Ignoble Savages" from *The End of Racism: Principles for a Multi-racial Society* (1995). Reprinted in Delgado and Stefancic (eds) *Critical White Studies*.
• St Thomas Acquinas, *Summa Theologica Part II* from Dino Bigiongiari (ed) *The Political Ideas of St Thomas Aquinas* (1953).

Harcourt Brace, New York: *www.harcourt.com*
• Dwight Bolinger, *Aspects of Language* (1975).
• Oliver Wendell Holmes, "The Path of the Law" in *Holmes Collected Legal Papers* (1920).

HarperCollins (UK): *www.harpercollins.co.uk*
• Ursula Le Guin, *The Dispossessed* (1974).

Harper & Row, San Francisco (div of HarperCollins): *www.harpercollins.com*
• Caroline Merchant, *The Death of Nature: Women, Ecology and the Scientific Revolution* (1980).

Harvard Civil Rights — Civil Liberties Law Review: *www.law.harvard.edu/students/orgs/crcl/*
• Patricia J Williams, "'Alchemical Notes' Reconstructing Ideals from Deconstructed Rights" (1987) 22 *Harvard Civil Rights — Civil Liberties Law Review* 401. © 1987 The President and Fellows of Harvard College and the Harvard Civil Rights — Civil Liberties Law Review.
• Harlon Dalton, "The Clouded Prism" (1987) 22 *Harvard Civil Rights — Civil Liberties Law Review* 435. © 1987 The President and Fellows of Harvard College and the Harvard Civil Rights — Civil Liberties Law Review.
• Richard Delgado, "The Ethereal Scholar: Does Critical Legal Studies Have What Minorities Want?" (1987) 22 *Harvard Civil Rights — Civil Liberties Law Review* 301. © 1987 The President and Fellows of Harvard College and the Harvard Civil Rights — Civil Liberties Law Review.

Harvard Law Review: *www.harvardlawreview.org*
• Roscoe Pound, "The Call for a Realist Jurisprudence" (1930-31) 44 *Harvard Law Review* 697.
• Karl Llewellyn, "Some Realism About Realism — Responding to Dean Pound" (1931) 44 *Harvard Law Review* 1222.

Harvard University Press: *www.hup.harvard.edu*
• Rudolphe Gasché, *The Tain of the Mirror: Derrida and the Philosophy of Reflection* (1994).©1986 The President and Fellows of Harvard College.
• Catharine A Mackinnon, *Feminism Unmodified: Discourses on Life and Law* (1987) ©1987 The President and Fellows of Harvard College.
• The Works of William James, "Pragmatism" edited by Fredson Bowers (1975) ©1975 The President and Fellows of Harvard College.

Harvester Wheatsheaf, New York (div of Pearson Education): *www.pearsoned.com*
• Monique Wittig, "The Category of Sex" in Monique Wittig, *The Straight Mind and Other Essays* (1992) ©1992 Monique Wittig.

MSG Haskell House
- PJ Proudhon, *General Idea of the Revolution in the Nineteenth Century* (1969). Translation John Beverley Robinson (1969).

Hill & Wang, New York (division of Farrar, Straus and Giroux): *www.fsgbooks.com/hillandwang.htm*
- Roland Barthes, *Elements of Semiology* (1968). Translated by Annette Lavers and Colin Smith. Translation ©1967 by Jonathan Cape Ltd.

Holt Rinehart & Winston: *www.hrw.com*
- Samuel Johnson, *Rasselas, Poems and Selected Prose* (1958).
- Harry Jones, "Legal Inquiry and the Methods of Science" in Harry Jones (ed) *Law and the Social Role of Science* (1958).

Indiana University Press, Bloomington: *www.iupress.indiana.edu*
- Maria Lugones, "Playfulness, 'World'-Travelling, and Loving Perception" (1987) 2(2) *Hypatia* 3.
- Matthew Kramer, *Legal Theory, Political Theory and Deconstruction: Against Rhadamanthus* (1991).

Journal of the Society of Public Teachers of Law (published by LexisNexis Butterworths London for the Society of Legal Scholars in the United Kingdom and Ireland (formerly the Society of Public Teachers of Law)): *www.lexisnexis.co.uk*
- Lord Reid, "The Judge as Lawmaker" (1972) 12 *Journal of the Society of Public Teachers of Law* (NS) 22.

Kessinger Publishing LLC: *www.kessinger.net*
- John Bowring (ed), *The Works of Jeremy Bentham* (1962).

Knopf Publishing Group (a subsidiary of Random House, Inc): *www.randomhouse.com*
- Friedrich Wilhelm Nietzsche, *Beyond Good and Evil* (1955).

Law Quarterly Review (by Sweet & Maxwell UK): *www.sweetandmaxwell.co.uk*
- Frederick Pollock, "Oxford Law Studies" (1886) 8 *Law Quarterly Review* 453.
- CC Langdell, "Harvard Celebration Speeches" (1997) 9 *Law Quarterly Review* 123.
- Hans Kelsen, "The Pure Theory of Law: Its Method and Fundamental Concepts", Part 1 (1934) 200 *Law Quarterly Review* 474.

Legal Education Review: *www.ler.edu.au*
- Graeme Cooper, "Inevitability and Use" (1989) 1 *Legal Education Review* 29.
- Frank Easterbrook, "The Inevitability of Law and Economics" (1989) 1 *Legal Education Review* 3.

Les Éditions de Minuit, France: *www.leseditionsdeminuit.com*
- Jacques Derrida, *Positions* (1981).

LexisNexis Butterworths Australia: *www.lexisnexis.com.au*
- Australian Law Reports (ALR).

LexisNexis Butterworths UK: *www.lexisnexis.co.uk*
- Roger Cotterrell, *The Politics of Jurisprudence: A Critical Introduction to Legal Philosophy* (1989).

Manchester University Press: *www.manchesteruniversitypress.co.uk*
- Jean-François Lyotard, *The Differend: Phrases in Dispute* (1988).

Martinus Nijhoff Publishers (by Brill Academic Publishers): *www.brill.nl*
- Mary Ellen Waithe (ed), *A History of Women Philosophers* (1987 c1995).

MacGibbon and Kee, London:
- Frantz Fanon, *Black Skin, White Masks* (1968).
- Frantz Fanon, *The Wretched of the Earth* (1965).

Methuen Publishing, London: *www.methuen.co.uk*
- "Reflection by the Lord Chief Justice Hale on Mr Hobbes His Dalogue of the Lawe" in Holdsworth (ed) *A History of English Law* (1924).

The Michigan Law Review: *www.michiganlawreview.org*
- B Flagg, "The Transparency Phenomenon, Race-Neutral Decision-Making, and Discriminatory Intent" in "Was Blind, But Now I See: White Race Consciousness and the Requirement of Discriminatory Intent" (1993) 91 *Michigan Law Review* 953.

Modern Law Review (by Blackwell Publishing): *www.modernlawreview.co.uk*
- Julius Stone, "The Ratio of the Ratio Decidendi" (1959) 22 *Modern Law Review* 34.

Monash Law Review (Monash University, Faculty of Law): *www.law.monash.edu.au/monlr/*
- Anthony Mason, "Future Directions in Australian Law" (1987) 13 Mon L Rev 149.

Northwestern University Press, Evanston: *http://nupress.northwestern.edu/*
- Jacques Derrida, "Letter to a Japanese Friend" in Wood and Bernasconi (eds) *Derrida and Difference* (1988).

Oxford Journal of Legal Studies (by the Oxford University Press): *www.oup.com*
- A Hunt, "The Critical Legal Studies Movement" (1986) 6 *Oxford Journal of Legal Studies* 1.
- Matthew Kramer, "The Rule of Misrecognition in the Hart of Jurisprudence" (1988) 8 *Oxford Journal of Legal Studies* 407.

Oxford University Press: *www.oup.com*
- HLA Hart, *The Concept of Law* (1961).
- HLA Hart, *The Concept of Law* (2nd ed, 1994).
- GWF Hegel, *The Philosophy of Right*. T M Knox translation (1967).
- J Finnis, *Natural Law and Natural Rights* (1987).
- Hans Kelsen, *General Theory of Norms* (1961).

Pan Macmillan Publishers, London: *www.panmacmillan.com*
- Umberto Eco, "Lumbar Thought" in *Travels in Hyper-Reality: Essays* (1987).

Pearson Education, Inc: *www.pearsoned.com*
- Robert Cooter and Thomas Ulen, *Law and Economics* (1988).

Penguin Group (UK): *www.penguin.com*
- Angela Carter, *The Infernal Desire Machine of Doctor Hoffman* (1972).
- Aristotle, *The Ethics* (1976).
- David Hume, *A Treatise of Human Nature* (1969).
- Jonathan Swift, *Gulliver's Travels* (1967).
- Edward Said, *Orientalism* (1978).
- Simone de Beauvoir, *The Second Sex* (1972).
- Sophocles, *The Theban Plays* translated by EF Watling (Penguin Classics, 1947) © 1947 EF Watling.
- Benjamin Franklin, "Observations concerning the increase of mankind and the peopling of countries" (1751) in Benjamin Franklin, *Autobiography and Other Writings* (2003).

Philosophical Library, New York: *www.philosophicallibrary.org*
- Ferdinand de Saussure, *Course in General Linguistics* (1959).

Pollinger Limited London and the Estate of Frieda Lawrence Ravagli: *www.pollingerltd.com*
- DH Lawrence, *Study of Thomas Hardy and Other Essays* (1985).

Princeton University Press: *http://press.princeton.edu*
- Søren Kierkegaard, "Rotation of Crops" in *Either/Or Part 1* (1987).

Random House Group Ltd (UK): *www.randomhouse.co.uk*
- Roland Barthes, *Image Music Text* (1977).
- Simone de Beauvoir, *The Second Sex* (Jonathan Cape, 1972).

Routledge (New York): *www.routledge-ny.com*
- Charles Yablon, "Forms" in Drucilla Cornell, Michel Rosenfeld & David Gray Carlson (eds) *Deconstruction and the Possibility of Justice* (1992).
- Luce Irigaray, *I Love to You*. Alison Martin translation (1996).
- Judith Butler, *Gender Trouble: Feminism and the Subversion of Identity* (1990).
- Jacques Derrida, "Force of Law: The Mystical Foundation of Authority" in Drucilla Cornell, Michel Rosenfeld & David Gray Carlson (eds) *Deconstruction and the Possibility of Justice* (1992).
- Sneja Gunew, *Feminist Knowledge: Critique and Construct* (1990).
- Freidrich Wilhelm Nietzsche, *Nachgelassene Fragmente* (1885) in Sarah Kofman "Descartes Entrapped" in Cadava Connor and Nancy (eds) *Who Comes After the Subject?* (1991).

- Drucilla Cornell, *The Philosophy of the Limit* (1991).
- Michelle Fine, "Witnessing Whiteness" in Michelle Fine, Lois Weis, Linda Power & L Mun Wong (eds) *Off White: Readings on Race, Power, and Society* (1997).
- Friedrich Nietzcshe, *Human, All Too Human* (1964).

Routledge (UK): *www.routledge.co.uk*
- Collette Guillaumin, *Racism, Sexism, Power and Ideology* (1995).
- Richard Dyer, *White* (1997).
- Michel Foucalt, *The Order of Things: An Archaeology of the Human Sciences* (1970).
- Hélène Cixous and Mireille Calle-Gruber, *Helene Cixous, Rootprints: Memory and Life Writing* (1994) Eric Prenowitz translation.

Rowman & Littlefield Publishers, Inc: *www.rowmanlittlefield.com*
- Alison Jaggar, *Feminist Politics and Human Nature* (1988).

Russell & Russell, New York:
- Hans Kelsen, *General Theory of Law and State* (1961).

Social Text (by Duke University Press): *www.dukeupress.edu*
- Sarah Franklin, "Making Transparencies: Seeing Through the Science Wars" (1996) 46/47 *Social Text* 141.

Stanford Law Review (Stanford University)
- Allan Hutchinson and Patrick Monahan, "Law, Politics and the Critical Legal Scholars: The Unfolding Drama of American Legal Thought" (1984) 36 *Stanford Law Review* 391.
- Peter Gabel and Duncan Kennedy, "Roll Over Beethoven" (1984) 36 *Stanford Law Review* 1.

State University of New York Press: *www.sunypress.edu*
- Amartya Sen in Feiwel (ed) *Issues in Contemporary Microeconomics and Welfare* (1985).

The Sydney Morning Herald (by Fairfax Group): *www.smh.com.au*
- "O'Shane's Full Address to the Court", *Sydney Morning Herald*, March 20 1993, p 39 ©1993 Pat O'Shane.

Tavistock Publications UK (by Sweet & Maxwell): *www.sweetandmaxwell.co.uk*
- Alan Sheridan, *Michel Foucault: The Will to Truth* (1980).

Thomson Carswell, a division of Thomson Canada Limited: *www.carswell.com*
- Allan Hutchinson, *Dwelling on the Threshold* (1988).

Thomson Legal & Regulatory Limited: *www.thomson.com.au*
- Vattel, *Law of Nations*, Bk 1 Ch 8, reprinted in Alex Castles and J H Bennett, *A Source Book of Australian Legal History* (1979).
- Commonwealth Law Reports (CLR).

UCLA Law Review (by the University of California Los Angeles): *www.uclalawreview.org*
- Richard Abel, "A Critique of Torts" (1990) 37 *UCLA Law Review* 785. ©1990 The Regents of the University of California.

University of Chicago Press: *www.press.uchicago.edu*
- Gerald Postema, *Bentham and the Common Law Tradition* (1988).
- Sir Matthew Hale, *The History of the Common Law of England* (1971).
- Thomas Hobbes, "Dialogue Between a Philosopher and a Student of the Common Laws of England", Part 1, *Of the Law of Reason* (1971).
- Thomas S Kuhn, *The Structure of Scientific Revolutions* (2nd ed, 1990).
- Catharine MacKinnon, "Feminism, Marxism, Method and the State: Toward Feminist Jurisprudence" (1983) 8(4) *Signs* 635.
- Deborah King, "Multiple Jeopardy, Multiple Consciousness: The Context of a Black Feminist Idealogy" (1988) 14(1) *Signs* 42.

University of Miami Press (by the University of Miami)
- Emile Benveniste, *Problems in General Linguistics* (1971).

University of Minnesota Press (by the University of Minnesota): *www.upress.umn.edu*
- Trinh T Minh-ha, "Not You/Like You: Postcolonial women and the interlocking questions of identity and difference" in A McClintock, A Mufti & E Shohat (eds) *Dangerous Liaisons: Gender, Nation and Postcolonial Perspectives* (1997).
- Jean-François Lyotard, *The Postmodern Condition: A report on knowledge* (1984).

University of Queensland Press (Queensland, Australia): *www.uqp.uq.edu.au*
- Alan Chalmers, *What is This Thing Called Science?* (2nd ed, 1982).
- Aileen Moreton-Robinson, *Talkin' Up to the White Woman: Indigenous Women and Feminism* (2000).

University of Western Australia Law Review (The University of Western Australia): *www.lawreview.law.uwa.edu.au/*
- Valerie Kerruish, "Philosophical Retreat: A Criticism of John Finnis' Theory of Natural Law" (1983) 15 *University of Western Australia Law Review* 224.

Vintage Books (div of Random House, Inc London): *www.randomhouse.co.uk*
- Jeanette Winterson, *Sexing the Cherry* (1988).
- Kwame Ture and Charles Hamilton, "Black Power: It's Need and Substance" from *Black Power and the Politics of Liberation* (1992). Reproduced in Martin Bulmer and John Solomos (ed) *Racism*.
- Robin Morgan (ed) *Sisterhood is Powerful: An Anthology of Writings from the Women's Liberation Movement* (1970).

Washington Law Review (by the University of Washington, School of Law): *www.law.washington.edu/WLR/*
- George Smith, "Dr Bonham's Case and the Modern Significance of Lord Coke's Influence" (1966) 41(2) *Washington Law Review* 297.

Weidenfeld and Nicolson (div of Orion Publishing UK): *www.orionbooks.co.uk*
- John Austin, *The Province of Jurisprudence Determined*, Lecture 1 (1954).

William Heineman (by Pearson Education): *www.pearsoned.co.uk*
- Cicero, *De Republica* (1970).

Women's Rights Law Reporter (Newark, New Jersey): *http://pegasus.rutgers.edu/~wrlr*
- Mari Matsuda, "When the First Quail Calls: Multiple Consciousness as Jurisprudential Method" (1988) 11 *Women's Rights Law Reporter* 7.

Yale Law Journal Company & William S Hein Company: *http://yalelawjournal.org*
- Allan Freeman, "Truth and Mystification in Legal Scholarship" (1981) 90 *Yale Law Journal* 1229.
- Mark Tushnet, "Critical Legal Studies: A Political History" (1991) 100 *Yale Law Journal* 1515.
- Drucilla Cornell, "Sexual Difference, the Feminine, and Equivalency: A Critique of MacKinnon's 'Toward a Feminist Theory of the State'" (1991) 100 *Yale Law Journal* 2247.
- William Kenner, "Methods of Legal Education" (1982) 1 *Yale Law Journal* 143.

Zed Books (London): *www.zedbooks.co.uk*
- Tariq Modood, "'Difference', Cultural Racism and Anti-Racism" in Pnina Werbner and Tariq Modood (eds) *Debating Cultural Hybridity: Multi-cultural Identities and the Politics of Anti-Racism* (1997).

Thomson Lawbook Co. and the author are grateful to the publishers, agents, authors and copyright owners who have allowed us to use extracts of their work in this book. While every care has been taken to establish and acknowledge copyright, Thomson Lawbook Co. tenders its apology for any accidental infringement. The publisher would be pleased to come to a suitable agreement with the rightful owners in each case.

TABLE OF CONTENTS

FOUR LEGAL SCIENCE

FIVE CRITICAL LEGAL STUDIES: THE BEGINNINGS OF A DISSOLUTION

for
Ngaire Naffine

ONE
ASKING THE LAW QUESTION (WHAT IS IT?)

[105] On one level, this book is about legal theories. It aims to describe the theories about law, and approaches to law, which have been adopted by some of the scholars in the field. On another level, the book is an attempt to provide a critical understanding of all of these approaches to law.[1] The term "critique" in this context simply refers to the process of attaining an understanding of the foundations of any approach, theory or system of thought. This involves not only a consideration of what a particular writer consciously relied upon as the foundations for her or his theory, but also a close analysis of the unstated assumptions which are associated with the way we see the world.

This introductory chapter will not address the substance of the theories to be described in the rest of the book: rather than attempting such a difficult task, it will simply introduce some of the elements of a critical approach to law. There is a philosophical reason for proceeding in this fashion: as will become apparent, my view of law is very closely connected to my view of the way we perceive the world. Reflecting upon the founding assumptions of our theories reveals much about our selves, our culture and the reasons we think the way we do about the law. This will be explained further in the course of this chapter.

In addition to this general purpose, this chapter aims (quite modestly) to demonstrate four philosophical theses: (1) Jurisprudence is boring; (2) the Earth is (also) flat; (3) We are not cabbages; and (4) Legal theory has been decapitated (but is not dead).

On Jurisprudence and Being (Boring)
First philosophical thesis: Jurisprudence is boring

[110] When we talk about the philosophy of law or about jurisprudence, we are usually talking about the philosophical questions which are asked about legal systems — either real or ideal ones. In itself, this is an

---

1   The opening section of Chapter 5 considers the term "critical", and its relationship to so-called "traditional" theories.

1

inexpressibly boring way of thinking about the subject. Can we get out of this boredom? Søren Kierkegaard thought the whole world was boring.[2]

> Since boredom advances and boredom is the root of all evil, no wonder then, that the world goes backwards, that evil spreads. This can be traced back to the very beginning of the world. The gods were bored; therefore they created human beings. Adam was bored because he was alone; therefore Eve was created. Since that moment, boredom entered the world and grew in quantity in exact proportion to the growth of population. Adam was bored alone; then Adam and Eve were bored together; then Adam and Eve and Cain and Abel were bored *en famille*. After that, the population of the world increased and the nations were bored *en masse*. To amuse themselves, they hit upon the notion of building a tower so high that it would reach the sky. This notion is just as boring as the tower was high and is a terrible demonstration of how boredom had gained the upper hand. Then they were dispersed abroad, just as people now travel abroad, but they continued to be bored.

All things are boring; jurisprudence is a thing; therefore jurisprudence is boring. Jurisprudence is boring because everything is. (Thesis supported by Kierkegaard and a rather boring syllogism.)

What have we got so far? (1) Jurisprudence is boring because it is philosophy about law. This is hardly a satisfactory result, because: a) the premise is not very precise — law *can* be interesting, it has that potential, if not very often the actuality; and b) if I insist upon it too strongly I will not be very popular with my colleagues. (2) Jurisprudence is boring because everything is boring. This really only holds if we subscribe to the notion that everything which is not boring is, in fact, only a deflection of boredom — such as watching television for something to do. It looks like the thesis will either have to be abandoned, or proven via another route.

Actually, the really boring thing is exactly what Kierkegaard has done here — to say that there is an underlying reason for things, a first cause, which explains the world. I find philosophy which attempts to make the world or any part of it into a static system or structure very depressing, and think it ought to be avoided for that reason. This book is also an attempt to show that it should be avoided for being wrong. (To be fair to Søren K this is not at all what he was about.) Our world is a dynamic and in many ways incoherent place, and to attempt to confine it to an analytical stasis may not only be to limit our current perception of it, but also to limit our view of what it has the potential to become. As Hélène Cixous said,[3]

---

2   Søren Kierkegaard, "Rotation of Crops" in *Either/Or Part I* (Princeton University Press, Princeton, 1987), p 286. See also Amir Baghdadchi, "On Academic Boredom" (2005) 4 *Arts and Humanities in Higher Education* 319.

3   Hélène Cixous and Mireille Calle-Gruber, *Hélène Cixous, Rootprints: Memory and Life Writing* (Eric Prenowitz trans, Routledge, London, 1994), p 4.

> Each object is in reality a small virtual volcano. There is a continuity in the living: whereas theory entails a discontinuity, a cut, which is altogether the opposite of life ... [Theory] is indispensable, at times, to make progress, but alone it is false. I resign myself to it as a dangerous aid. It is a prosthesis. All that advances is aerial, detached, uncatchable.

Cixous seems to be suggesting here that theory entails a death, or a separation, from the living and dynamic objects of the world. (Or, to put it another way, "what many believe is academic rigour is actually rigor mortis".[4]) In one sense this is undoubtedly true: theory does attempt to catch hold of the uncatchable, and to reduce it to a form which can be reproduced and conveyed from one mind to another. (As I am doing now in my efforts to describe theory as an object.) In this sense, theory is, as Cixous says, a "dangerous aid" — it is dangerous because it risks the calcification of its objects, but it is an aid because without it we cannot understand these objects. On the other hand, a theory need not be regarded as a static and dead description or analysis, but rather an activity or process which participates in the life of its object. Suppose a legal theory was not regarded merely as an analysis or description of law, but rather as a player in the legal arena, even in legal practice. Suppose that a theory actually interacted with law and influenced its character. In fact, the history of legal theory suggests that this is precisely what it does do: rather than being a boring description of foundations or axioms, theory really does influence legal culture and thus the "law itself". (Assuming such a thing exists as a separate entity.) All of the theories "described" in this book have at different historical times influenced the cultural concept, the practice and the content of law — making it rather absurd to say that theory merely reflects or describes law.

But do we have to be so certain about what is boring and what is not? Jurisprudence is boring, as I have said, but failed so far to prove. But what is it to be boring? In a short, and philosophically off-beat seminar paper, Charles Yablon said this:[5]

> The papers that have preceded me have all been extremely original and interesting.
>
> I must provide the missing Derridean supplement. I must be boring.
>
> This is not difficult for me. I am a lawyer.
>
> I know many boring things.
>
> Many very, very boring things.

---

4   Bernard Lane, "Mutually Assured Boredom" *The Australian*, 14 December 2005, p 25, commenting on Baghdadchi "On Academic Boredom", p 323.

5   Charles Yablon, "Forms" in Cornel, Rosenfeld and Gray Carlson (eds), *Deconstruction and the Possibility of Justice* (Routledge, New York, 1992). The missing Derridean supplement will remain missing in this book, though the work of Derrida will appear in Chapters 7 and 8.

I must be boring. I must bore. But in another sense, to bore is to dig, to probe under the surface, to uncover that which has been hidden, to view that which has not previously been seen.

In that sense, the papers that have preceded me have been very boring indeed, and I may truthfully say that I hope I may be only half as boring as those who have preceded me.

Yablon's boring subject is a form — literally. It is a blank summons from a United States District Court. So what? Yablon uses the form, which is empty of content (already a philosophical distinction here, between form and substance), to make some profound observations about the impossibility of avoiding the form — it is a legal instrument, indeed the *form of law* itself, which imposes itself on its recipient. In Yablon's analysis the boring lawyers' object has become philosophically, as well as legally, boring. Like the form of law, jurisprudence bores.

Law and Order

[115] All of which is an example of how we should not take anything philosophical at face value. After all, if it only has face value, then philosophically it may not be much good. When I talk about jurisprudence I am (trying my best always to bore) talking about everything — from literature to science to everyday experience. The whole world is structured by laws of one sort or another. The law is a form we cannot avoid, whatever its substance. We think and act in relation to laws. There are laws of social behaviour, laws of language, laws relating to what counts as knowledge and what doesn't, and laws which say that well really, law is actually something different from all of these other things. In other words, there are laws which say that law itself must be clearly distinguished from other sorts of inquiry, such as what god is (if she exists), how I as a person am constituted, what a relationship is, how language works, or whether Nietzsche was a misogynist. This law of exclusion, which protects law school law from the world, has always been a particular problem for me since I am inclined to view all laws as contingent in one way or another. The jurisprudential tradition tends to assume that the proper subject of study for legal philosophers is what Austin called laws "properly so called" (that is, the boring sort). We frequently assume that law is separate and distinct from other aspects of our social existences. Even critical legal theorists, who have challenged the positivist idea of a separate law, often take it as a starting point in their efforts to subvert the conventional understanding of law. But how can law be even conceptually separate from its context? How can it be conceptually separate from the human lives who have created it, who apply it, who criticise it, and who relate to it?

I want to make it absolutely clear right now that saying all laws are contingent does not imply that they can therefore be safely discarded or ignored. This is one of the most widespread misunderstandings of those who (like me) either characterise themselves or are characterised by others as "postmodern".[6] If we think that knowledge is something which must have certain and absolute foundations, then to say that it is based on laws which are contingent *would* mean that we would end up by saying that if something is not absolutely justified, then we can ignore it. If, on the other hand, we do not regard the foundations of knowledge as fixed, then saying that laws are contingent means not that we can simply eliminate them, but rather that we will be more interested in questioning the reasons for their existence. We will be interested in trying to discover why we perceive things as we do. Laws are necessary to existence — without them we would have no knowledge, no reason, no understanding of anything. But that is not to say that we have to accept unquestioningly the laws we have, nor does *that* mean that the laws we have are not real. There are some who try to argue that because certain types (like me) think that our way of viewing the world, and indeed our very beings, are socially determined, we must therefore also reject the very ideas of truth, reality, and knowledge. But my point is that it is only possible to think *that* if knowledge, truth, and reality are seen in the first place as fixed, or coming from somewhere else (outside ourselves and society) altogether.

This "somewhere else" altogether presents a real problem for the way we think. There is an idea in sociology about social determinations which makes it seem as though there are patterns into which people fit. The laws or patterns are first, and people are fitted into them. In a similar way we tend to think of the laws in a legal system as transcendent, meaning that cases are fitted into them in one way or another. The case falls within the rule, or something like that. First the rule, then the case, which either does or doesn't fit. A non-compliant case might demand the creation of a new rule, so that it too has its place in a transcendent scheme. Knowledge is often seen as similar in that we think that there is some place that it comes from which is external to ourselves. It is "out there". Thinking like this allows us to abdicate the responsibility of wondering about why we think the way we do, why we act the way we do, and why we decide legal problems the way we do. If the patterns for life and law are all "out there" somewhere, then there is nothing we can do about them, right? We just go along with them. Now, against this I would like to suggest, like Oliver Wendell Holmes,[7] that there are no rules out there in the sky. Law and knowledge exist only in everyday reality, and are a product of the processes of life and culture. In other words, we continually create and transform rules as we exist. There is no absolute place where they are all fixed, and to which we can refer to find their authentic form. Law is embodied and in process, just as we are, and denying this is only a way

---

6   Postmodernism is the subject of Chapter 8.

7   Justice Oliver Wendell Holmes said, "The common law is not a brooding omnipresence in the sky, but the articulate voice of some sovereign": *Southern Pacific Co v Jensen* (1916) 244 US 205 at 222.

of making life and law easier by pretending that rules are an absolute justification. Another way of saying this is by reference to the existential slogan, "existence precedes essence".[8] Human existence (and practices of language, social action, relating to others) is logically prior to the universals (law, meanings, "human nature") we construct.

Second philosophical thesis: The Earth is (also) flat

[120]   The earth is round and flat at the same time. This is obvious. That it is round appears indisputable; that it is flat is our common experience, also indisputable. The globe does not supersede the map; the map does not distort the globe.[9]

A minimal, and reasonably non-controversial, definition of law is that it is something devised by humans to create order within our society. Law regulates human behaviour, and the relationships between members of a society. Beyond this, of course, it may attempt to enshrine certain ideals, such as equality, freedom, and justice. Hans Kelsen, a legal philosopher whose work I will consider in more detail in Chapters 3 and 4, said that the "norm functions as a scheme of interpretation".[10] The term "norm" is one which will recur frequently in this book. It simply refers to a rule, standard, law or principle, and is related to the word "normal". The crucial issue for Kelsen's argument is that an event or a fact, such as the killing of a human being, does not of itself carry a legal significance. The *legal* meaning of an act cannot be perceived by the senses. Any legal significance or meaning which an event has is not the result of the act itself, but the result of viewing the act through a legal system.

Thus if I drive at 80 kph on a road where the speed limit is 40 kph, the illegality of my act is not something which can simply be seen.on its face value. The illegality is the result of seeing the act through the filter of the *Road Traffic Act 1934* (SA) and its associated regulations. Similarly, to use Kelsen's example, interpreting "an act as the execution of the death penalty rather than as a murder ... results from a thinking process: from the confrontation of this act with the criminal code and the code of criminal procedure".[11] In other words, an act derives its legal significance only from the law, and the law is a scheme of interpretation, because it orders acts into categories like legal or illegal, tortious or criminal, creation, performance, or breach of a contract, and so on. And the law orders not only acts, but also experience and our relation to the world, through legal concepts such as property, reasonableness, and consent.

---

8   Jean-Paul Sartre, "Existentialism" in *Existentialism and Human Emotions* (Philosophical Library, New York, 1957), pp 13-15.

9   Jeanette Winterson, *Sexing the Cherry* (Vintage, London, 1989), p 81.

10   Hans Kelsen, *Pure Theory of Law* (University of California Press, Berkeley, 1967), p 4.

11   Kelsen, *Pure Theory of Law*, p 4.

The important idea behind Kelsen's view of law as a medium of interpretation is that laws themselves are recognised as having a cognitive, as well as a prescriptive, function. By this I mean that law orders the way we perceive the world, as well as our actions. Put more strongly, law imposes order on what would otherwise be legally meaningless acts, experiences and relationships. The law is one huge system of categorisation. Those of us who have studied law know, however, that the "legal" definition of an act often clashes with the popular definition, or the common sense definition, so we are often compelled to be somewhat Janus-faced in our interpretations.

What, as a layperson, we would see as an act of carelessness or even simply as an accident may become for us, as lawyers, the commission of the tort of negligence with several elements. Was there a duty of care owed, a breach of that duty, causation etc? Or, was a sexual act legally a rape? Was it a sexual assault? In addition, there are various ramifications for the parties, who become, potentially, the plaintiffs, victims, witnesses, defendants. Even the "person" is determined and defined by law. In keeping with his view of law as a system of interpretation, Kelsen regarded the legal person as nothing more than "the unity of a complex of legal obligations and rights".[12] For Kelsen, the legal person is distinct from the human being (as we know from studying the law of corporations) — it is a conceptual unity, not a moral and living entity. Conceptually attractive as this approach may appear to be, however, it neglects the human dimension, as well as the fact that the laws constructing the person are not only legal norms, but a web of social and cultural norms: since these norms also interact with each other, it is rather difficult to separate out one "person" and call it "legal" and another which we identify as "natural". Nonetheless, the basic point is clear enough. Law — broadly understood — orders the way we view the world: it shapes our perception, and therefore cannot be identified merely as an "object" of our perception. It enters into the process of cognition.

In saying that the "norm functions as a scheme of interpretation", Kelsen was extrapolating the philosophy of Immanuel Kant, a German philosopher writing at the end of the 18th century. Kant's thought was crucial in the history of philosophy. Instead of starting with the proposition that knowledge must conform to its objects, Kant argued that our perception of objects conforms to certain conditions of knowledge which exist in the mind.[13] Just as Copernicus achieved better results in astronomy by thinking of the spectator as moving and the

---

12 Kelsen, *Pure Theory of Law*, p 173. See generally Margaret Davies and Ngaire Naffine, *Are Persons Property? Legal Debates About Property and Personality* (Ashgate, Aldershot, 2001), Ch 3; Ngaire Naffine, "Who are Law's Persons: From Cheshire Cats to Responsible Subjects" (2003) 66 *Modern Law Review* 346.

13 See Immanuel Kant, "Prolegomena to any Future Metaphysics" in Lewis White Beck (ed), *Kant: Selections* (Scribner/MacMillan, New York, 1988) and *The Critique of Pure Reason* (MacMillan, Hampshire, 1929), especially the Introduction.

stars as fixed, rather than the other way around, Kant proposed that a more definitive knowledge of the processes of understanding could be achieved by reversing the traditional emphasis on experience and examining instead the conditions of knowledge.[14] What does this mean? In essence what Kant argued was that there are certain laws of the understanding which order our experience. We cannot know things in themselves (*noumena*); we can only know the appearance of things (*phenomena*). This does not mean that there is nothing outside the mind; rather that we do not know things as they are prior to their appearance to the mind.[15] Knowledge of the world is not gained simply by receiving unmediated impressions of it or by having sensations entering our minds. Rather, knowledge of the world is filtered by the laws of the understanding. The basic point I want to emphasise is that the processes of the understanding are seen to be structured by laws which order, and make sense of, experience. As Kant points out, normally we do not separate these laws or concepts from our experience, we simply assume their existence — or rather, they provide the structure of knowledge itself.[16] The universal laws of the mind provide the conceptual structure of experience. And it is on the basis of these laws that we can make objective judgements about our experience and the world.

Thus Kant saw the basic concepts of the mind as laws which order experience. Cognitive order is the product of the laws of the understanding, just as social order is traditionally seen as the product of the laws of our legal system. As I have said, Kelsen saw the laws of a legal system as cognitive, in that they provide a framework for the interpretation of certain acts. The reason I am emphasising this point is to reinforce what I said in the last section about the subject matter of jurisprudence not being simply the laws of a legal system which prescribe behaviour and order society. It is clear that the idea of law extends far beyond such things into, for instance, the structure of truth and the interpretations we have of the world. Limiting jurisprudence to the idea of law in a legal system is therefore only reinforcing the artificial distinction between law and non-law.[17]

---

14 The analogy with Copernicus is made by Kant in the Preface to the second edition of the *Critique of Pure Reason*, at Bxvi-Bxvii. (The mode of citation employed for the *Critique of Pure Reason* refers to the two editions prepared by Kant which differ substantially. The editions are marked by "A" and "B" followed by the original page numbers.)

15 Kant, "Prolegomena to any Future Metaphysics", s 13, remarks II and III. Kant talks about both "concepts" and "laws" which order experience. In the *Critique of Judgement* (Oxford University Press, Oxford, 1957) Kant refers explicitly to the legislative function of *a priori* (that is, necessary) concepts, using the analogy of a state or realm which has authority over a particular territory to illustrate the point: see Introduction, "II The Realm of Philosophy".

16 Kant, "Prolegomena to any Future Metaphysics", ss 18 and 19.

17 One philosopher who does not limit law in this way is Michael Detmold. See *The Unity of Law and Morality: A Refutation of Legal Positivism* (Routledge Kegan Paul, London, 1984).

Kant saw the basic structures of the mind as universal: in other words, they are the same for all people. In this sense, the laws of the understanding are *natural*. The distinction between the ideas of natural law and posited laws is an important one, which has several different dimensions. At its simplest, natural law theory attempts to elucidate a system of laws, for instance laws of morality or religion, which exist regardless of whether any human agency has laid them down. Natural law theory can also be taken to refer to the idea that the laws of a legal system must conform in some way to these "natural" laws. Whether or not they believe in such a system of "natural" laws, positivists assert that the validity of a law has nothing to do with its morality or existence in a higher place: law is simply that which has been authoritatively laid down or "posited".

This is only a simple sketch of the natural law/positivism distinction. The theories of natural law and positivism will be explained more fully in Chapter 3. I have introduced them here only in order to clarify what I meant by saying that Kant's laws of the understanding are "natural". They are universally existing laws which lay the basis for objective knowledge. Knowledge can be objective because everyone has the same fundamental structure in their minds.

We can contrast this idea with more recent thought which, while not entirely dispensing with the idea of objectivity, challenges the notion that the conditions of understanding are structured in the same way for everyone. In a famous passage at the beginning of *The Order of Things*, Michel Foucault contemplates the fundamental laws of order which determine our perception of the world. The preface begins, appropriately, with a laughter-inspired transgression of the established boundaries of thought:[18]

> This book first arose out of a passage in Borges, out of the laughter that shattered, as I read the passage, all the familiar landmarks of my thought — *our* thought, the thought that bears the stamp of our age and our geography — breaking up all the ordered surfaces and all the planes with which we are accustomed to tame the wild profusion of existing things, and continuing long afterwards to disturb and threaten with collapse our age-old distinction between the Same and the Other. This passage quotes "a certain Chinese encyclopaedia" in which it is written that "animals are divided into: (a) belonging to the Emperor, (b) embalmed, (c) tame, (d) sucking pigs, (e) sirens, (f) fabulous, (g) stray dogs, (h) included in the present classification, (i) frenzied, (j) innumerable, (k) drawn with a very fine camelhair brush, (l) *et cetera*, (m) having just broken the water pitcher, (n) that from a long way off look like flies". In the wonderment of this taxonomy, the thing we apprehend in one great leap, the thing that, by means of the fable, is demonstrated as the exotic charm of another system of thought, is the limitation of our own, the stark impossibility of thinking *that*.

---

18   Michel Foucault, *The Order of Things: An Archaeology of the Human Sciences* (translated from the French originally published as "Les mots et les Choses" Paris Gallimard 1966 Tavistock, London, Routledge, 2001), Preface, p xv.

The last sentence here is particularly important. Foucault says that the especially wonderful thing about being confronted with a system of classification (or "taxonomy") like the one of Borges' fictional Chinese encyclopaedia, is that it makes us realise that our own system of thought is limited, even though we take it for granted and see it as natural. And in the first place, it is limited because it is impossible to think *that* — it is impossible to think this (admittedly fictitious) Chinese system of classification in our logical and reasoned way. Thus, if there are laws forming our understanding, according to Foucault and other contemporary writers, they are not universal, natural, or eternal, but historically and linguistically specific. The way we perceive something is influenced by our language, culture, gender, race, class, and so on. Just as importantly, for Foucault, the conditions of what is traditionally accepted as knowledge are the effects of power, and of structures laid down by those with an institutionalised authority.[19] Thus the laws of what counts as knowledge in any particular field are posited by those with the authority to do so.

This book is a good example of Foucault's statement. I have organised it along what I think are fairly traditional lines, with the inclusion of some novel, but not unexpected, classifications: for instance the chapter on legal science includes some disparate things which I thought could be usefully placed in the same context. It could have been organised otherwise, but on the whole it just seemed to fall into place in a particular way. Well, it did not exactly *fall*: at times it was squeezed, entreated, even forced into shape. The problem is (and will always be) that the topics of jurisprudence *could* be treated as distinct entities: positivism could have been put by itself, as could other things, but that would be rather artificial. However when one begins to draw connections, the thing turns out to be (like the law) a seamless web, even when the new theoretical approaches are taken into account. So we begin to draw lines, to categorise, in order to gain some understanding of the material at hand. Now on the one hand this organisation of the world allows us to understand it: after a while we even think that our way of seeing is "natural". On the other hand, it excludes other possibilities, limits our perception, crystallises the world into a certain form from which it may be very difficult or impossible to escape. The content and structure of the book is shaped just as much by what it leaves out, as it is by its positive content.

In the end, as I have said, the book has been organised along fairly traditional lines. Even chronologically. This was not intentional: in the beginning, I intended to put natural law after positivism, realism with critical legal studies, and feminism throughout. The last goal has perhaps been partially achieved, but otherwise the material seems to have re-organised itself into a jurisprudential narrative. This is perhaps

---

19   See Michel Foucault, *Power/Knowledge* (Harvester Press, Brighton, 1980). These ideas will be discussed in more detail in Chapter 8.

not a mistake — perhaps I am not as much in control of the concepts as I would like to be. Moreover it is certainly important, and this is a constant theme in the book, to explain what is sometimes called the "historicity" of ideas. In other words, it is important to see ideas as part of social and political environments, for the very simple reason that the people who have and generate ideas are part of their environments, and are immersed in their political, cultural, and intellectual institutions.

This is a basic point, but one which is often overlooked, because our archetype of knowledge in the Western world relies upon the idea that there is a distance between the subjects and objects of knowledge, between the person who has knowledge, and the knowledge itself. The "subject" itself is a very important element of philosophical thought. It simply refers to the "I" in any situation. I am the subject of this sentence. If I write a sentence in which I am not the grammatical subject, like "a boat is sailing past my window", I am still the knowing subject of the statement, since I am the one doing the observing. But I can make what I write look "objective", meaning that it is only concerned with objects of knowledge, and not with me as a subject in a particular environment, by, for instance, eliminating the use of "I" and adopting the language of rationality instead of the language of emotion or impression. This is the dominant mode of academic writing because, as I have said, the paradigm of knowledge in our systems of thought is one which is detached from any particular person. However, as I will explain, in many contexts objective language is often little more than a door opening onto a whole wardrobe full of unstated and often conservative assumptions about the world. For instance, part of the Western intellectual heritage is that the subject of knowledge, the person doing the knowing (the "I"), has traditionally been figured as male and white, while the objects of knowledge have often been represented as "other" by reason of their gender and/or their racial and cultural heritage.[20] (And it is true that until very recently, those occupying the authoritative "knower" positions in the Western world — intellectuals, policy-makers, judges, business leaders, and so forth, were almost exclusively privileged white males.) We are never going to eliminate our assumptions altogether, but I think that theorists do have an obligation to be as clear as possible about where they are coming from.

Which brings me to one of the most important introductory points about this book, which is that in many ways it represents my own personal view of jurisprudence as a topic, and I have not attempted to disguise this fact behind the language of detachment. Many readers will perhaps be a little uncomfortable by my frequent and quite unashamed

---

20 This is nowhere more clear than in the metaphors used to describe the scientific subjugation of nature. Science is hard and rational, while nature is a disorderly woman needing to be controlled. See Caroline Merchant, *The Death of Nature: Women, Ecology and the Scientific Revolution* (Harper and Rowe, San Francisco, 1980); Genevieve Lloyd, *The Man of Reason: "Male" and "Female" in Western Philosophy* (2nd ed) (Routledge, London, 1993).

use of "I", and it is true that this could have been avoided in nearly all cases. But the pretence that my thoughts are not mine would be not only dishonest, it would also undermine one of the theoretical stances I take in the book. This theoretical approach is a variation on the feminist saying that "the personal is political". I would say also that the personal is theoretical. If we accept (as I will argue in Chapter 8) that "subjectivity", that is, the condition of being a thinking, knowing identity, is constructed by our social and linguistic environment, it is important to understand and build on the fact that we are not entities distinct from an external world. The world acts upon us, just as we act upon it. Putting the two phrases together, of course, we get "the theoretical is political", a position which I will explain further in Chapters 6 and 8.

All of which is to suggest that although the world is indeed flat, and that we have begun to recognise its multidimensionality, we nonetheless have an obligation to continue the process of discovery for ourselves ("or failing that", as Monique Wittig says,[21] "invent").

The Outside and the Inside

[125]   Like all walls it was ambiguous, two-faced. What was inside and what was outside it depended upon which side of it you were on.

Ursula Le Guin *The Dispossessed*

One of the most influential of all 20th century English legal thinkers, HLA Hart, said that rules have both an internal and an external aspect to them. The external aspect refers to the process of describing behaviour from the position of an external observer. The internal aspect is essentially the attitude which a person has to her behaviour and the rules which guide her. In the first instance Hart used this distinction to differentiate between "habits" and "social rules".[22] Hart says that habits are just things that we do, without thinking about it, and therefore have an "external" aspect only. Habits can be described from the position of an observer, but it is not essential that those who behave in a habitual manner realise this or characterise their behaviour as such. In contrast, Hart says that rules have both an external and an internal aspect. It is possible to describe the behaviour which people adopt when following a rule from the external position of someone who does not accept the rule. It is also, according to Hart, necessary for some of the people who follow the rule to have an internal "critical" or "reflective"

---

21   "You say there are no words to describe this time, you say it does not exist. But remember. Make an effort to remember. Or, failing that, invent." Wittig, *Les Guerillères* (Owen, London, 1971), p 89.

22   HLA Hart, *The Concept of Law* (2nd ed, Clarendon Press, Oxford, 1994), pp 56-57. The internal/external points of view are discussed by Sandra Berns in *Concise Jurisprudence* (Federation Press, Sydney, 1993), Ch 1.

attitude to it. What this means is that at least some people must recognise that there is a general standard of behaviour. We do not merely move the Queen in a certain manner in a chess game out of habit. We understand that it is a rule of the game that we do so, and, reflecting upon this rule, either follow it or not, as the case may be.

Later in *The Concept of Law* Hart uses the distinction in a slightly different way to refer to the different attitudes which people can take in relation to a legal system. The external point of view again refers to the attitude of an observer of a legal system, who either does not participate in the system, or does so only out of choice, rather than from a feeling of actually being obliged. The external point of view is that of a social observer who takes an anthropological stance towards the legal system, or that of a dissident who does not accept the legal system as authoritative but may nonetheless abide by certain aspects of it having regard to the consequences of not doing so. In contrast, the internal attitude is that adopted by those who accept the obligations which a legal system imposes. This distinction is elaborated in the following passage.

HLA Hart

The Concept of Law[23]

[130]   When a social group has certain rules of conduct, this fact affords an opportunity for many closely related yet different kinds of assertion; for it is possible to be concerned with the rules, either merely as an observer who does not himself accept them, or as a member of the group which accepts and uses them as guides to conduct. We may call these respectively the "external" and the "internal points of view". Statements made from the external point of view may themselves be of different kinds. For the observer may, without accepting the rules himself, assert that the group accepts the rules, and thus from outside refer to the way in which *they* are concerned with them from the internal point of view. But whatever the rules are, whether they are those of games, like chess or cricket, or moral or legal rules, we can if we choose occupy the position of an observer who does not even refer in this way to the internal point of view of the group. Such an observer is content merely to record the regularities of observable behaviour in which conformity with the rules partly consists and those further regularities, in the form of the hostile reaction, reproofs, or punishments, with which deviations from the rules are met. After a time the external observer may, on the basis of the regularities observed, correlate deviation with hostile reaction, and be able to predict with a fair measure of success, and to assess the chances that a deviation from the group's normal behaviour will meet with a hostile reaction or punishment. Such knowledge may not only reveal much about the group, but might enable him to live among them without unpleasant consequences which would attend one who attempted to do so without such knowledge.

---

23   Hart, *The Concept of Law*, pp 89-91.

If, however, the observer really keeps austerely to this extreme external point of view and does not give any account of the manner in which members of the group who accept the rules view their own behaviour, his description of their life cannot be in terms of rules at all, and so not in the terms of the rule-dependent notions of obligation or duty. Instead, it will be in terms of observable regularities of conduct, predictions, probabilities, and signs ...

The external point of view may very nearly reproduce the way in which the rules function in the lives of certain members of the group, namely those who reject its rules and are only concerned with them when and because they judge that unpleasant consequences are likely to follow violation. Their point of view will need for its expression, "I was obliged to do it", "I am likely to suffer for it if ...". But they will not need forms of expression like "I had an obligation" or "You have an obligation" for these are required only by those who see their own and other persons' conduct from the internal point of view. What the external point of view, which limits itself to the observable regularities of behaviour, cannot reproduce is the way in which the rules function as rules in the lives of those who normally are the majority of society. These are the officials, lawyers, or private persons who use them, in one situation after another, as guides to the conduct of social life, as the basis for claims, demands, admissions, criticism, or punishment, viz, in all the familiar transactions of life according to rules. For them the violation of a rule is not merely a basis for the prediction that a hostile reaction will follow but a *reason* for hostility.

At any given moment the life of any society which lives by rules, legal or not, is likely to consist in a tension between those who, on the one hand, accept and voluntarily co-operate in maintaining the rules, and so see their own and other persons' behaviour in terms of the rules, and those who, on the other hand, reject the rules and attend to them only from the external point of view as a sign of possible punishment. One of the difficulties facing any legal theory anxious to do justice to the complexity of the facts is to remember the presence of both these points of view and not to define them out of existence.

[135]   The distinction between the inside and the outside is one which is absolutely fundamental to law: in fact I think that law *is* this distinction, in the sense that it is law which defines the limit of acceptable behaviour. Law operates as a boundary which claims that some types of behaviour are legal or legitimate and others are illegal or illegitimate. It is therefore intrinsically exclusionary — it establishes an inside of acceptable conduct and an outside of unacceptable conduct. The same can be said of social norms, which define zones of acceptability. And I think the same is true of what Kant called the laws of the understanding and what Foucault saw as "discursive regularities":[24] there is an inside way of seeing which is seen to be either universal or culturally imposed (depending on whose view you accept) and an outside way, which may be seen by the insiders as wrong, mad,

---

24   The term is used by Foucault in *The Archaeology of Knowledge* (translated from the French by AM Sheridan Smith, Tavistock, London, 1972), Part I.

distorted, or biased. Traditionally, the laws of understanding as understood by and associated with white Western men have constituted the inside, while it is everyone else's explanations which have been wrong, mad, distorted, or biased. So the first thing to note about the inside/outside distinction is that it operates on many levels, in relation to all sorts of laws and signs. And importantly, as Hart argues, the inside/outside distinction applies not only to the rule itself and the behaviour it governs, but also to the attitudes which people have in relation to these rules, principles, and conventions.

Law, Knowledge, and Identity

[140]   Hart talks about people (especially the men who observe) simply adopting an internal or external point of view to the system of rules in question. Hart's level of analysis is confined to the rational and independent individual who simply situates *him*self either inside or outside. This is arguably the view of a liberal thinker who sees himself as a free agent relating to a world of discernible analytical structures, and thinks that this is the condition of everyone. There are several issues which complicate this view. First, even assuming we are free in the required sense, we may adopt an internal point of view to some rules, like those which define serious crimes, but an external attitude to others, like the traffic code, which we may follow only through fear of punishment. For some purposes we might have an internal attitude to a rule such as that prohibiting trespass on Commonwealth "prohibited areas", while for other purposes, such as when we wish to protest the fact that an area has been appropriated from its Indigenous owners and used as a United States missile tracking station, we might well adopt an external attitude to such a rule.[25] In relation to many of the rules we may have no particular attitude since we are unaware of their existence. I myself adopt a completely uninformed and uninterested attitude to the Commonwealth corporations power, and the rules relating to the appropriate conduct of dinner parties. As well as specific components of a system of norms, we might adopt an internal attitude to the system in general (while disagreeing with some of its elements), or we might take an external attitude, and characterise ourselves as a dissident or conscientious objector. And sometimes we may find that we have a more or less internal point of view to two systems which, however, require us to follow different paths. We may wish to be integrated, law-abiding citizens of our nation but also be required to follow religious observances which are either prohibited by law or which lead to other legal or social disadvantages.

Secondly, however, people may not be free in the sense which Hart assumes is possible. Sometimes there is no choice about where we start

---

25   See the first (pp 16-18) or the second (pp 20-22) edition of this book for an extended discussion of the ambiguities of the Commonwealth prohibited area at Nurrungar in March 1993.

from because the rules exclude us from the beginning. Even if we wish to adopt an internal attitude, we may not be able to. For instance, there is an expectation that people are "normally" heterosexual, meaning that most people do not choose this condition, but simply assume it as their own identity. Any other version of sexuality is seen as a distortion or unnatural. Not only do lesbians and gay men start from a position which is outside mainstream society — they are forced into an outsider position — they are also more often than not excluded from the benefits of whole areas of the law, such as those relating to marriage, adoption and reproductive technologies. This is a lack of freedom defined by the law, designed specifically to advantage some people. People may also be excluded from society and law because of their race, gender, or class. Such exclusions, leading to what is known philosophically as the condition of "otherness", may result in an attempt to be included, a critique of the system in its entirety and the formation of other counter-insides,[26] or, more usually, strategic negotiations from both inside and outside positions.

Therefore we may not simply be able to choose a position "outside" mainstream society or law. And whether we choose or are excluded from the "inside", we are normally not allowed the option of total disengagement. We should not forget that people (say, Indigenous Australians) who are often excluded from the benefits and protection of the law, are not ordinarily excluded from its criminal implications, and indeed, it may often be said that they are given special attention in this area. Similarly, being excluded from the inside of mainstream society does not mean that a person or group will be excluded from its judgement. And conversely, there are those respectable, wealthy, and powerful people who epitomise the aspirations of mainstream society, are easily within it, and can claim the full protection of the law, but are nonetheless somehow outside or above the criminal law, unless of course, the media decides for whatever reason to intervene. And then there are women, who, being inside the home, have traditionally been regarded as outside the protection of State law and incompetent to benefit from it on our own behalf, instead being "protected", defined, and provided for by their husbands. Thus a person can be inside for some purposes and outside for others.

As indicated above, critical theorists have argued that knowledge is not "objective" — that is, it does not inhere in objects — but is a construct of social, cultural and linguistic contexts and the mechanisms of power associated with these contexts. It has also been argued that knowledge is a product of the position of the knowing subject within

---

26 Diana Fuss encapsulates some of the complexities of outsider status in "Inside/Out". She says "To be out, in common gay parlance, is precisely to be no longer out; to be out is to be finally outside of exteriority and all of the exclusions and deprivations such outsiderhood imposes. Or, put another way, to be out is really to be in — inside the realm of the visible, the speakable, the culturally intelligible." *Inside/Out: Lesbian Theories, Gay Theories* (New York, Routledge, 1991), p 4.

her or his context. For instance, feminist theorists have used the terms "standpoint epistemology" and "situated knowledge" to refer to the ways in which social hierarchies influence our perceptions of the world. The condition of "otherness", according to standpoint epistemology, gives rise to a special type of knowledge — the "view from below" as opposed to the allegedly objective "view from nowhere".[27] According to this argument, those who are in a disempowered position in relation to some other social group (for instance, women in relation to men, people with a disability in relation to those without a disability) are able to gain a better or more complete view of the oppressive nature of dominant discourse. This "epistemic privilege", according to Terri Elliott, arises from the fact that the person at the bottom of the hierarchy sees the obstacles which the oppression creates, whereas the person who is relatively powerful does not automatically see such obstacles. Elliott gives the example of a flight of steps leading to a doorway to a building, which most would see as an entrance and an opportunity to gain access, but which a person in a wheelchair would see as a barrier and an obstacle to gaining access. Similarly, we might say that those with the means to assert their legal rights, might see the law as an opportunity or a tool which advances their desires, whereas those without sufficient means might see it as an obstacle, which neither protects nor assists them.

While this argument appears convincing, standpoint epistemology has also been criticised. The strongest criticism of feminist standpoint epistemology has been from those who have argued that it assumes that a defined group generally share the same experiences and the same types of oppression, which simply neglects other significant social hierarchies which intersect any given social grouping.[28] Women are not just women, but also defined in relation to race, sexuality, religion, class, disability and so forth. If a standpoint is to be valued as giving rise to some privileged knowledge, it can only be very localised and specific. It cannot be regarded as more "objective" than a dominant perspective, nor can it be over-generalised (as the category of "women" is an over-generalisation). This critique of the assumption that the experience of gender is universal has given rise to the concept of "multiple consciousness" (as opposed to the dual consciousness of standpoint epistemology). Can we ever be said to have simply one "identity" which conforms to the norms of a culture or subculture? Would it not be

---

27 On standpoint epistemology and its feminist applications, see Sandra Harding, *The Science Question in Feminism* (Open University Press, UK, 1986); Catharine MacKinnon, *Toward a Feminist Theory of the State* (Harvard University Press, Cambridge, Mass, 1989), p 120; Alison Jaggar, *Feminist Politics and Human Nature* (Rowman & Littlefield, New Jersey, 1983), p 28; Donna Haraway, *Simians, Cyborgs and Women: The Reinvention of Nature* (Routledge, New York, 1991); Terri Elliott, "Making Strange What had Appeared Familiar" (1994) 77 *The Monist* 429. For an overview, see Margaret Davies and Nan Seuffert, "Knowledge, Identity and the Politics of Law" (2000) 11 *Hastings Women's Law Journal* 259. On the "view from nowhere", see Thomas Nagel, *The View from Nowhere* (Oxford University Press, Oxford, 1986).

more accurate to say that a person is so affected by their context that we have quite different perceptions, and therefore different identities, depending on where and how we are located at any moment?

The insides and outsides formed by the interweaving of culture and law, are not only a theoretical matter relating to the nature of a person's identity, but have serious practical consequences: being consigned to outsider status as an Indigenous person in Australia or as a member of an ethnic minority in many areas of the world often means being consigned to a lifetime of racism, poverty, and/or ill-health. Being a lesbian anywhere means either living in a closet, having your ("abnormal") sexuality on display to the world, or adopting a compromise between the two extremes. Everywhere is outside, but the outside itself can be formed into an inside. What this means is that for many people the question is not a simple choice of being inside or outside a system of norms, but rather a complicated negotiation within multiple contexts, social codes, and legal systems of inclusion and exclusion. Mari Matsuda has put this problem of "multiple consciousness" like this:[29]

> There are times to stand outside the courtroom door and say "this procedure is a farce, the legal system is corrupt, justice will never prevail in this land as long as privilege rules in the courtroom." There are times to stand inside the courtroom and say "this is a nation of laws, laws recognising fundamental values of rights, equality, and personhood." Sometimes, as Angela Davis did, there is a need to make both speeches in one day. Is that crazy? Inconsistent? Not to Professor Davis, a Black woman on trial for her life in racist America. It made perfect sense to her, and to the twelve jurors good and true who heard her when she said "your government lies, but *your* law is above such lies."

Professor Davis's decision to use a dualist approach to a repressive legal system may very well have saved her life. Not only did she tap her history and consciousness as a Black, a woman, and a communist, she did so with intent and awareness. Her multiple consciousness was not a mystery to her, but a well-defined and acknowledged tool of analysis, one that she was able to share with the jury.

---

28 A second criticism has been offered by Wendy Brown. She argues that standpoint theories are based on a feeling of moral superiority of being in the position of the victim, a position which does not necessarily lead to a more complete knowledge. See Wendy Brown, *States of Injury: Power and Freedom in Late Modernity* (Princeton University Press, New Jersey, 1995).

29 Mari Matsuda, "When the First Quail Calls: Multiple Consciousness as Jurisprudential Method" (1988) 11 *Women's Rights Law Reporter* 7 at 8. Angela Davis is an anti-racism activist who, in 1970 was wrongly accused of murder, kidnapping and criminal conspiracy. At the time she was a member of the Black Panthers, a group of activists who were subjected to harassment and violence because of their anti-racism campaigns. See Kum-Kum Bhavnani, "Complexity, Activism, Optimism: An interview with Angela Y Davis" (1989) 31 *Feminist Review* 66.

In a similar spirit of destabilising our settled notions of identity, Trinh T Minh-ha has written of the subversive potential of adopting a position which moves from inside to outside:[30]

> The moment the insider steps out from the inside she's no longer a mere insider. She necessarily looks in from the outside while also looking out from the inside. Not quite the same, not quite the other, she stands in that undetermined threshold place where she constantly drifts in and out. Undercutting the inside/outside opposition, her intervention is necessarily that of both not quite an insider and not quite an outsider.

In the process of interpreting and acting in the world, we may sometimes have to consciously adopt a position internal to the ruling ideology in order to survive or compete. We may often have to be *seen* to be internal, even though our sympathies are elsewhere. Or, being an insider to one set of cultural norms, it may be valuable to try to move outside and ask what our "inside" might look like to someone who does not share our position. Only by adopting such a critical, reflective attitude to our own context and normality are we able to begin to understand its limitations.

To complicate the picture even more, there is the problem of how to think about social rules which we all internalise in various ways, and which are therefore not chosen or adopted in any meaningful way. The social standards and expectations associated with being a particular sex are often of this order, though that does not mean that they are not part of a legal structure. Monique Wittig wrote:[31]

> For the category of sex is a totalitarian one, which to prove true has its inquisitions, its courts, its tribunals, its body of laws, its terrors, its tortures, its mutilations, its executions, its police. It shapes the mind as well as the body since it controls all mental production. It grips our minds in such a way that we cannot think outside of it.

I have mentioned the perceived normality of heterosexuality: conformity to this norm is socially and ideologically compelled in many ways, meaning that the ideas of "choice" and "preference" are never totally free or undetermined. The condition of not being heterosexual carries with it many violent social sanctions. It has been argued that heterosexuality is an institution (a social structure), not a natural state of affairs, because it is bound by all sorts of rules, standards, and expectations far exceeding the fairly minimal acts which make

---

30   Trinh T Minh-ha, "Not You/Like You: Postcolonial Women and the Interlocking Questions of Identity and Difference" in McClintock, Mufti, and Shohat (eds), *Dangerous Liaisons: Gender, Nation, and Postcolonial Perspectives* (University of Minnesota Press, Minneapolis, 1997), p 418.

31   Wittig, "The Category of Sex" in *The Straight Mind and Other Essays* (Harvester Wheatsheaf, New York, 1992), p 8. Concrete evidence of the terrors, tortures, and mutilations of the category of (the female) sex is to be found in Naomi Wolf, *The Beauty Myth* (Vintage, London, 1990).

reproduction possible.[32] (Nonetheless, as Angela Carter writes, there is nothing "natural" about sex — we take the world to bed with us, since we take ourselves, and all of our assumptions, expectations, and self-definitions.[33]) Even where this is recognised, can there ever be said to be a "choice" to be heterosexual, when the social valuation of it is so compelling? If we *could* decide to be wealthy or poor, and decide on wealth, is this a "choice"? On the other hand, would it be a "choice" to decide on poverty, if that were highly valued by a religious or moral system? On the whole, in cases like this it is difficult to be certain that we freely choose an internal or an external attitude to a norm: our perceptions of the possibilities are limited by the way that our ideology works, meaning that we frequently do not even realise that there may be a choice.[34] Our "freedom" is constrained by social and cultural norms, whether or not we are aware of them. We may feel strongly one way or the other, and regard that feeling as natural, but maybe the "natural" feeling is nothing more than one which is very strongly felt, for whatever reason. Either way, we need to appreciate that there are norms of various sorts determining the way we see the world and the way we act, but that sometimes we do not recognise them as norms, meaning that the inside/outside question does not arise for us except insofar as it affects our judgement of others.

This situatedness of seeing means that the view which is purely "external" in Hart's sense does not exist, except as the internal position of some other set of standards. There is no absolute outside to this complicated web of insides and outsides. Hart wrote at a time when it was still assumed that the objective anthropological observer who only described the regularities of a society's behaviour was a possibility. Subsequently much has been written on this "objective observer" perspective which turned out to be the observational position of educated white people bringing their own assumptions and pre-occupations into their readings of non-Western cultures. This will be considered further in Chapters 6 and 7.

The other really interesting thing which complicates and, in some ways, subverts all of these matters beyond our wildest dreams is the question of how any "inside" and "outside" dichotomy is constituted in the first place. This is another matter for Chapter 8, but I would like to make a few observations here. As I have indicated, I think that law and the outside/inside structure it sets up is like a sign which at the very least, defines a category of things. Some things are inside the category "dog" and others are outside. Now, what Ferdinand de Saussure (who is

---

32 Adrienne Rich, "Compulsory Heterosexuality and Lesbian Existence" (1980) 5 (4) *Signs: Journal of Women in Culture and Society* 631; Wittig, *The Straight Mind and Other Essays*.

33 Angela Carter, *The Sadeian Woman: An Exercise in Cultural History* (Virago, London, 1979), "Polemical Preface".

34 See Rich, "Compulsory Heterosexuality and Lesbian Existence".

usually described as a Swiss linguist) said was that signs are defined relationally. What this means is basically that the "inside" is what it is only in contrast to its "outside", that is, in relation to all the other things which it is not. The idea is essentially that the "inside" position is the creation of what it excludes. For instance, it is often observed that "masculinity" (which is a set of norms, cultural expectations, and signs) is defined in relation to what it is not, femininity. Masculinity defines and protects itself by insisting at every juncture that it is not feminine.[35] The feminine is the excluded "other". Similarly, as Diana Fuss explains in her Introduction to *Inside/Out*, heterosexuality defines itself by excluding or repressing its threatening outside, homosexuality.[36] Homosexuality gets its outsider position by being excluded from the "norm" of heterosexuality. More recently, it has been noted that in political discourse the "citizen" with her or his "national identity" is constituted by reference to a variety of excluded others — notably asylum seekers and those who because of their racial or cultural heritage do not easily "assimilate" (ie, become the same as the mythic ideal citizen).[37] Such distinctions draw upon and entrench what have come to be known as "binary oppositions", the basic building blocks of our (Western) thought.

"Postmodern" writers have argued that such binary oppositions are never pure, never complete and, indeed, always break down at some crucial point. Such distinctions have served as laws to order the world but, in fact, make our thinking processes static, fixed on structures rather than dynamic processes of being. This sort of dilemma can be seen at work in law, which defines itself continually in relation to non-law: the discipline of law is set against an outside of morality or politics which is not law. As much as lawyers attempt to exclude an outside, it is always there *in* the law, for instance in the assumptions lawyers make about society, in the "policy" reasons which lawyers find so hard to eliminate from legal decision-making (and which I think are impossible to distinguish from the law itself), and in the process of transformation within the law. The fact that the outside is actually in the inside (and vice versa) is now being recognised in legal education, where "outsider" perspectives are being brought formally into law school curricula. The question which will have to be continually renewed is whether this is merely an expansion of our essentially closed legal borders or a genuine attempt to open them?

35   Luce Irigaray, *Je, Tu, Nous: Toward a Culture of Difference* (Routledge, London, 1993), p 71.

36   Fuss (ed) *Inside/Out*, p 2.

37   See generally the various essays in Peter Fitzpatrick and Patricia Tuitt (eds), *Critical Beings: Law, Nation and the Global Subject* (Ashgate, Aldershot, 2004).

A multiplicity of boundaries

[145]   We did our best to keep what was outside, out, and what
           was inside, in: we built a vast wall of barbed wire round the
           city, to quarantine the unreality ... But, if the city was in a
           state of siege, the enemy was inside the barricades, and lived
           in the minds of each of us.[38]

In short, there are a multiplicity of ways in which subjects can be defined
as internal or external to some normative system. We may choose an
internal perspective to some laws but not others. We may be involun-
tarily constructed as external by the law or by the cultural setting which
informs the law. Some laws or codes may be essentially inscribed on our
being as assumptions or irrevocable prescriptions. All perspective is
situated and can never be simply "external". We may choose to move in
and out of laws and rules for political purposes. And finally, the inside
and the outside are mutually constitutive and often ambiguous.

But there is yet more that can be said about this fascinating topic.
Specifically, the terminology of internal/external and inside/outside
invokes a specifically *spatial* metaphor of law. Saying that we have an
internal or external attitude to law essentially means that we visualise
ourselves as standing inside or outside some boundary or frontier
representing the territory of law. Similarly, when people are described,
or describe themselves, as social or political insiders or outsiders, it is
as though a mental space is drawn in which some people belong in a
specific area while others do not. Often, this mental space has some
correlation with physical space. In the short extract above, for instance,
Mari Matsuda highlights the connection between physical and mental
space by talking about protesting outside the courtroom doors and
insisting upon one's rights inside the court. Stepping inside the
courtroom, one's location, identity, and attitude changes. But the
connection between our mental and geographical frontiers exists in a
variety of scales or locations: local, national and international. Most
obviously, the spatial limits of law are defined by the association of law
with the state, the nation, and a specific geographical territory.[39] Seeing
law as essentially State law, and State law as exclusively definitive of law
in a bounded space, necessarily precludes the recognition of "other"
experiences of law within a territory, for instance Indigenous law.[40]

---

38   Angela Carter, *The Infernal Desire Machine of Doctor Hoffman* (Penguin, Harmondsworth,
     1972), p 12.

39   See Richard T Ford, "Law's Territory (A History of Jurisdiction)" (1999) 97 *Michigan Law
     Review* 843.

40   Irene Watson, "Aboriginal Laws and the Sovereignty of Terra Nullius" (2002) 1 *borderlands
     e-journal*. See also Sangeetha Chandra-Shekeran, "Challenging the Fiction of the Nation
     in the 'Reconciliation' Texts of *Mabo* and *Bringing Them Home*" (1998) 11 *Australian
     Feminist Law Journal* 107, 123; Irene Watson, "Indigenous Peoples' Law-Ways: Survival
     Against the Colonial State" (1997) 8 *Australian Feminist Law Journal* 39; Michael Detmold,
     "Law and Difference: Reflections on Mabo's Case" (1993) 15 *Sydney Law Review* 158.

The formal limits of law, state, and territory are, however, also intersected by cultural, racial, religious, gender, and class differences with their own topographies. For instance, the white Australia policy, which governed immigration into Australia for the better part of the 20th century, mapped a notion of Australian-ness as whiteness onto the geo-political terrain designated "Australia". A similar mindset forced many Indigenous people into camps and reserves for their "protection" and promoted assimilation through physical removal of children from their families and communities. The space "Australia" was to be governed by British-derived law and occupied by white, European people. Such policies of physical segregation continue, though in a more subtle, more complex and less overtly racist form. In fact, over the past 15 or so years, a significant literature dealing with questions surrounding national and cultural borders has emerged. Where borders were once seen simply as the limits of a social and national territory, they are now seen in more complex terms.[41] There is not just one boundary to a state, but many, and of varying types. These boundaries intersect, are often politically contested, paradoxical, or ambiguous, and are significant in shaping both cultural and individual identities.

Some of these matters are illustrated in the following extract. It begins by referring to a photograph of the infamous migration detention centre at Woomera in South Australia. This detention centre was one of a number of such centres which provided mandatory detention for asylum seekers in Australia. The centre was finally closed in 2003 after allegations of poor living conditions, inadequate staffing and other resources, overcrowding, human rights violations, and high rates of mental illness among detainees. Suvendrini Perera explicitly draws out the symbolism of the centre as a link between historical and contemporary approaches to the boundaries of the nation, its law and culture.

Suvendrini Perera
What is a Camp...?[42]

[150]   1. "Woomera Detention Centre" is an image of another world: a landscape of the known, yet chillingly alien. In this photograph the postcard familiarity of the Australian desert — dust, sand, open horizons, empty skies — is both affirmed and overturned. The outback as prison is confined, sequestered, uncannily ordered space; but still vacant of life, extraterrestrial in its emptiness. The photograph shows a place that is, and yet is not, Australia.

2. In "Woomera Detention Centre" [the photographer] Annette McGuire realises visually a place Bernard Cohen described in 1992, when asylum seekers first became subject to compulsory, indefinite detention on our

---

41   James Anderson, Liam O'Dowd, and Thomas Wilson, "Why Study Borders Now?" (2002) 12 *Regional and Federal Studies* 1.

42   (2002) 1 (1) *borderlands e-journal*. The photograph of Woomera Detention Centre referred to in the piece is unfortunately no longer available on the Internet.

shores: *There are foreign people in Australia thinking foreign thoughts. Some are locked up in Villawood, at the detention centre. Some are restrained in Perth. In those places, you see, they are not really in Australia. They are in the empty ungoverned space of their bodies, I guess, confined within not-Australia.*

3. Not-Australia is a place of strange oxymorons and uncanny repetitions. Here, space confines and vastness isolates. The desert and the ocean alike become prisons. More than two hundred years after the convict ships the Pacific is again imagined as a penal zone. In the centenary year of Federation [ie, 2001] Fortress Australia stages a victorious return. 'Border Protection' becomes (again) the order of the day.

4. In not-Australia Australia's history reappears in unfamiliar yet still recognisable guises. Indigenous Australians remember other internment camps from the not-too-distant past: children's dormitories encased in chicken wire; grids of regulation housing cutting through complex inter-weavings of kin, language and place.

5. Echoing the Dickensian hulks of imperial times, the government considers hiring large ships as holding pens for asylum seekers. *Not-Australia* too has its aspirations to empire. It expands from the mainland camps to swallow Christmas Island, the Cocos islands and Ashmore Reef: by an act of legislation asylum seekers who arrive here will be deemed not to have arrived. They find themselves nowhere but in not-Australia. Outside our national borders not-Australia establishes neo-colonial outposts on Nauru and Papua New Guinea; it attempts forays into a Fijian former leper colony, to an uninhabited island of Kiribati, into East Timor, Tuvalu, Palau — This initiative is termed, apparently without an ear for inauspicious resonances, the Pacific Solution.

6. The inmates of not-Australia are, in official phraseology, unlawful non-citizens. They are Not-Australian and unAustralian; the stuff of contraband: traffic; illegals; human cargo. Non-people. In Tony Birch's phrase, they are unpeopled: the ones whose human suffering may not be seen or recognised.

[155] The detention centre is a place within Australia, yet symbolically designated not-Australia, a place for "foreign people ... thinking foreign thoughts". Just beyond the mainland are other frontiers: areas which are Australia, but which do not count as such for arriving asylum seekers, as well as areas which are not Australia but which are drawn into the frontier zone as "processing centres".[43] In this scenario (combining nightmare and reality), territorial boundaries are deliberately manipulated to reinforce political and ideological objectives.

All of which illustrates several interrelated points about the mapping of law and other norms onto physical space. Despite the commonplace observation that the world is shrinking and that its borders are disappearing, this really depends on who you are and where you come from. Legal/territorial frontiers are sometimes open and sometimes

---

43   See also Tara Manger, "A Less than 'Pacific' Solution for Asylum Seekers in Australia" (2004) 16 *International Journal of Refugee Law* 53.

closed.[44] Concerns for physical safety may be the only deterrent to free movement for some people, whereas for others even extreme and immediate physical risk cannot secure "legal" movement across a border. Similarly, capital, culture, and even law flows freely in some directions and hardly at all in others. The same boundary can mean quite different things to different people (like the "entrance" for the person with a disability). At the same time, borders are not in themselves necessarily precise, but may be ambiguous or even politically manipulated. In a place such as a detention centre or prison camp, ordinary legal principles and rights are often suspended or deliberately blurred. According to Giorgio Agamben, the concentration camp was "a piece of land which is placed outside the normal juridical order, but it is nevertheless not simply an external space". It represented a "zone of indistinction between outside and inside, exception and rule, licit and illicit, in which the very concepts of subjective rights and juridical protection no longer made any sense".[45] (And while modern detention centres cannot be compared to Nazi concentration camps in terms of the scale and horror of human abuse involved, there are symbolic parallels.) The camp is the other side of modern nationalism and its "borderphobia"[46], in a similar way that — according to Foucault — the asylum represented the other side of reason and the Enlightenment (on which see further below, Chapter 8). Thus, the frontiers which define our lives and our existence in relation to law are not only incredibly complex and irreducible to clear spaces, but dynamic and defined according to a variety of overlapping registers.

The multiple intersections of the boundaries of law, religion, culture, place, and identity are perhaps most vividly illustrated (and extensively theorised) by reference to the ongoing process of Europeanisation.[47] Europe is sometimes characterised as a "fortress", meaning that the internal borders are becoming softer and easier to cross, while the external borders are becoming more resistant to outsiders. However, as

---

44   See generally Anthony Burke, "Borderphobia: the politics of insecurity post 9/11" (2002) 1 *borderlands e-journal*; Anderson et al, "Why Study Borders Now", pp 9-10; Fiona Allon, "Boundary Anxieties: Between Borders and Belongings" (2002) 1 *borderlands e-journal*. Allon illustrates the context-specific nature of borders by quoting Margaret Thatcher: "we joined Europe to have free movement of goods — I did not join Europe to have free movement of terrorists, criminals, drugs, plant and animal diseases and rabies and illegal immigrants" para 29.

45   Giogio Agamben, "The Camp as Nomos of the Modern" translated by Daniel Heller-Roazen in Hent de Vries and Samuel Weber (eds), *Violence, Identity, and Self-Determination* (Stanford, Stanford University Press), pp 109 and 110.

46   The word comes from the inaugural edition of the *borderlands e-journal* (2002).

47   See generally David Newman and Anssi Paasi, "Fences and Neighbours in the Postmodern World: Boundary Narratives in Political Geography" (1998) 22 *Progress in Human Geography* 186; Anderson et al, "Why Study Borders Now?"; Gerard Delanty, "Borders in a Changing Europe: Dynamics of Openness and Closure" (2006) 4 *Comparative European Politics* 183.

several scholars have pointed out,[48] the real picture is far more complicated and there are many more layers and locations of Europe's boundaries than simply those defining the old nation states and their present external frontier. "Europe" can be defined in different ways. It consists of a variety of regions with cultural and ethnic histories constantly in transition as a result of internal and external migration. It also contains political alliances and enmities, economic zones, and religious divisions. Within the geographical space various empires and numerous conflicts have left scars on the landscapes and the inhabitants,[49] while beyond it colonialism and contemporary global economic and political relationships impact upon the "internal" spaces and frontiers. It is "in reality — a complicated mosaic of multiple interacting borders".[50]

The Limits of Law: Anarchist Objections to Law and State

[160]   Laws, decrees, edicts, ordinances, resolutions, will fall like hail upon the unfortunate people.[51]

Third philosophical thesis: We are not cabbages

[165]   All of which is to say that, beyond being boring, jurisprudence is about the ways that all sorts of laws which define our society, our political agendas, our sexuality, our visions of reality, and our day-to-day struggles intersect. Is law, then, simply a repressive agent from which we need to be freed in order to recover, or discover, our true selves? As I noted, one of the interesting things about Foucault's Chinese encyclopaedia is that it demonstrates to us the limitations of our own thought processes. Is law only a distortion or reduction of what could otherwise be? Does it suppress our individuality and freedom? DH Lawrence thought so. In his *Study of Thomas Hardy*, he wrote that under the influence of too many laws people are like "the regulation cabbage" — going rotten at the centre instead of blooming.

---

48   Allon, "Boundary Anxieties"; Delanty, "Borders in a Changing Europe".

49   I say "scar" deliberately, having recently visited Berlin and seen the area known as the Topography of Terror where the Gestapo and SS had their headquarters. This unreconstructed part of the city is described in official literature as an "open wound".

50   Delanty, "Borders in a Changing Europe", p 190.

51   PJ Proudhon, *General Idea of the Revolution in the Nineteenth Century* (John Beverley Robinson trans, New York, Haskell House Publishers, 1969), p 132.

DH Lawrence
Study of Thomas Hardy[52]

[170]   [Making laws] is like protecting the well-being of a cabbage in the cabbage-patch, while the cabbage is rotting at the heart for lack of power to run out into blossom. Could you make any law in any land, empowering the poppy to flower? You might make a law refusing it liberty to bloom. But that is another thing. Could any law put into being something which did not before exist? It could not. Law can only modify the conditions, for better or worse, of that which already exists.

But law is a very, very clumsy and mechanical instrument, and we people are very, very delicate and subtle beings. Therefore I only ask that the law shall leave me alone as much as possible. I insist that no law shall have immediate power over me, either for my good or for my ill. And I would wish that many laws be unmade, and no more laws made. Let there be a parliament of men and women for the careful and gradual unmaking of laws.

... we are like the hide-bound cabbage going rotten at the heart. And for the same reason that, instead of producing our flower, instead of continuing our activity, satisfying our true desire, climbing and clambering till, like the poppy, we lean on the sill of all the unknown, and run our flag out there in the colour and shine of being, having surpassed that which has been before, we hang back, we dare not even peep forth, but, safely shut up in bud, safely and darkly and snugly enclosed, like the regulation cabbage, we remain secure till our hearts go rotten, saying all the while how safe we are.

[175]   There may be much value in what Lawrence says. Insofar as laws (of society, thought, the legal system) provide us with a way of existing without giving too much thought to what comes next, and without having to make difficult decisions or reflect upon the assumptions we are making, they can be a deadening influence which both capitalise on our desire for safe answers and encourage complacency.[53] But, as we have seen, law is also arguably the basic condition of meaning: law defines, categorises, and sets conditions for communication.

Lawrence's sentiments raise the question of whether law is necessary to human society at all, and — supposing that it is necessary — what form it should take. These are questions which have not traditionally been central to legal theory, so persuaded are we that law is a necessary and

---

52   In DH Lawrence, *Study of Thomas Hardy and Other Essays* (Cambridge, New York, 1985), pp 10-11. It is interesting to observe that the laws which Lawrence was specifically targeting were those proposed by the suffragists, who he says are "certainly the bravest, and ... most heroic party amongst us": p 10. Although he sees the goals of the early feminists as worthy, insofar as these goals involve making more laws, they are, according to Lawrence, somewhat missing the point. Such laws only regulate the sick. Lawrence's suggestion seems to be that there is no point in adding regulation to an already sick society — that only exacerbates the illness. Something other than increased regulation needs to be attempted.

53   See also Jerome Frank, *Law and the Modern Mind* (Bientano's, New York, 1930); Detmold, *The Unity of Law and Morality*.

(probably) a positive element of social existence. However, political philosophers and, in particular, anarchists, have challenged the traditional acceptance by Western cultures of the state and its associated concept of law imposed by a sovereign. Although anarchist thought has never been regarded as "belonging" to legal philosophy, it does in my view offer some interesting contributions to an understanding of law.

This neglect of anarchist thought is hardly surprising: law is typically regarded by legal theorists as imposing order on a society, while anarchism is frequently associated with chaos and disorder. However, while the "anarchist" label is sometimes adopted by people wishing to reject order altogether, that is not the primary use of the term in political philosophy. Anarchist theory does not reject order as such, but it does reject order imposed on a society by a centralised hierarchical authority such as a state. The political motivations behind this rejection vary considerably between anarchists: broadly speaking, some are libertarians or anarcho-capitalists who see the state as an obstacle to radical individualism or a completely free market; others hold communitarian ideals, and regard the state as a violent institution which creates inequalities between people (through institutions such as private property), which prevents people from taking responsibility for ordering their own communities, which obstructs human potential and mutual co-operation, and which perpetrates more violence and war than it prevents.[54]

Early anarchists tended to identify the concept of law with state-based authority, meaning that their rejection of the state also entailed a rejection of law. For instance, Peter Kropotkin observed that law is seen to be remedy for all evils: "Instead of themselves altering what is bad, people begin by demanding a law to alter it. ... A law about fashions, a law about mad dogs, a law about virtue, a law to put a stop to all the vices and all the evils which result from human indolence and cowardice."[55] In placing our reliance on laws given to us by the state, according to Kropotkin, we fail to exercise our own judgement and initiative in ordering our existences, and become subservient to both the law and the state. Reliance on the state prevents us placing reliance on ourselves and from forming co-operative relationships with others. Similarly, Leo Tolstoy, a Christian anarchist, defined laws as "rules, made by people who govern by means of organised violence for non-compliance".[56] Rather than representing the will of the majority, for

---

54   For an account of strategies designed to minimise state violence, see Brian Martin, "Eliminating State Crime by Abolishing the State" in Ross (ed), *Controlling State Crime: An Introduction* (Garland, New York, 1995).

55   Peter Kropotkin, "Law and Authority" in Roger N Baldwin (ed) *Kropotkin's Revolutionary Pamphlets: a Collection of Writings* (Dover Publications, New York, 1970 c 1927), pp 196-197.

56   Leo Tolstoy, "The Slavery of Our Times" in *Essays from Tula* (Sheppard Press, London, 1948), p 112. See also April Carter, *The Political Theory of Anarchism* (Routledge and Kegan Paul, London, 1971), pp 41-46.

Tolstoy, law represents the subjective wishes of a few privileged people, who create laws which serve their own interests and protect their private property. Tolstoy argued that the violence of law cannot be justified: if people are irrational and need violence to exist, then everybody must have the right to use violence, not just the few who have power; if, on the other hand, people were (as he thought) rational, "then their relations should be based on reason, and not on the violence of those who happen to have seized power".[57]

Any anarchist rejection of law is, however, tied to its rejection of the state. Anarchism does not entail a rejection of law as such, as long as it is possible to disengage the concept of law from the presence of a state.[58] In other words, law may be acceptable, necessary, and even positive for anarchists, as long as it is not arbitrarily imposed by a superior and oppressive institution such as the state. Such a non-state law may be difficult for modern Western lawyers to envisage: after all, our very concept of law tends to assume the existence of state coercion. But anarchists have argued that we do not need to think of law as a hierarchical institution which forces its subjects into compliance. Nor should law necessarily be regarded merely as a set of rules or static limits. Rather, it might be "a design, an experiment, and a learning process".[59] More practically, it could be created and enforced by consensus and with the co-operation of all members of a society. Such a law may seem idealistic, impracticable, even impossible. (Though when we think that something is impossible it is important first to remember Foucault's Chinese encyclopaedia. Is the object impossible, or are we simply limited in our imagination?) Clearly, a greater awareness of the law of non-Western and indigenous cultures has led in recent years to some acceptance of broader concepts of law, which are not based upon the presence of centralised state authority. In many ways, jurisprudence is no longer asking what *the* concept of law is, but rather what concepts of law exist, and what law might become.

---

57   Leo Tolstoy, "The Slavery of Our Times", p 119.

58   See T Holterman and H van Maarseveen (eds), *Law and Anarchism* (Black Rose Books, Montreal, 1984), in particular, the following essays: H van Maarseveen, "Anarchism and the Theory of Political Law"; C Cahn, "Kropotkin and Law"; R Descallar, "Anarchism and Legal Rules".

59   T Holterman, "Anarchist Theory of Law and the State" in Holterman and van Maarseveen (eds), *Law and Anarchism*, p 20.

A Little History of "Ferment and Trouble" in Legal Theory[60]

[180]   We behold all things through the human head and cannot
         cut off this head; while the question nonetheless remains
         what of the world would still be there if one **had** cut it off.[61]

Fourth philosophical thesis: Legal theory has been decapitated (but is not dead)

[185]   Finally, what then is the state of legal theory at the opening of the
21st century? What are the recent trends in the history of legal ideas,
and what may we expect for the future? The following comments are
an overview and evaluation of the material presented in the rest of
this book.

Here is my first comment: legal theory has been decapitated, it has lost
its distinct identity, its subjectivity, and its focus upon the essential
nature, spirit, or rationale of law. At the same time, legal theory has
also lost its head by going mad (figuratively speaking) — no longer one,
but many, legal theory has no idea who it is, what it is, or where it is
going. It has become mutable, malleable, inessential, and infinitely
dispersed. Indeed, we could even ask whether it exists at all.

I am not here to praise legal theory, but nor do I want to bury it, so let
me be clear about the matter: I am not saying that jurisprudence is a
mess or even that it has surrendered to its own decapitation, but rather
that its contradictions, silences, and doubts are finally being given the
attention they deserve. The paradox of the decapitation of legal theory
is that it has not ended in a simple death, but rather a proliferation of
life forms — new species, not mere clones. Although I have cast the
matter somewhat negatively, the decapitation of legal theory is not such
a bad thing: with or without its head, legal thought is on a journey of
self-discovery — the results are not always pleasant (much less pretty),
but will hopefully lead to a more sensitive, politically aware and
responsible legal attitude.

This book is an attempt to encapsulate some of the complexity of
modern legal theory as it exists in the Western world, particularly in
the common law world. In some instances, the effort to describe current
thinking involves reaching a long way back into the history of ideas:
this is most evident in Chapter 2, which deals with common law
thought, and the section in Chapter 3, concerning natural law theory.

---

60   The following section is a modified version of the first sections of Margaret Davies, "The
      Decapitation of a Discipline, Or How Legal Theory Lost Its Head" (2000) 4 *Flinders
      Journal of Law Reform* 127.

61   Friedrich Nietzsche, *Human, All Too Human* (Russell & Russell, New York, 1964),
      section 9.

But it would not be overstating the case to say that much (if not most) 20th and 21st century jurisprudence began in the early 19th century (if not before). At that time, legal theory was developing into a philosophy which excluded any question of natural law or positive morality and confined jurisprudence to what Austin called laws "properly so called".[62] As we will see in Chapter 3, Austin insisted that jurisprudence only describes and analyses existing law, and that existing law is only positive law imposed by a political superior onto a political inferior: ultimately, law consisted of the commands of a sovereign.[63] According to Austin, the province of jurisprudence was institutionally validated law and nothing else, a position which gathered strength throughout the 19th century and was very popular at the opening of the 20th century.[64] It is difficult to think of a notion of law which is more oriented towards the head, both of the body politic and of the enlightened theorist:[65] not only was Austin's concept of law described as originating from the position at the head of the political hierarchy, but legal theory itself thereby asserted its rationalist and scientific credentials. No longer associated with the mystical, the spiritual, the transcendental, or with everyday custom (an outlook which might be seen as more organic, holistic and bodily), law and legal theory were firmly planted in the realm of mind and of reason.

In fact, as David Sugarman has explained in a justly famous article,[66] the overwhelming approach of late 19th and early 20th century legal academics was to emphasise the *scientific* nature of law: in particular, they went to great lengths to justify their existence by expounding the general principles upon which the apparently chaotic realm of legal practice was founded. Sugarman says this:[67]

> They showed that the grubby, disorderly world of the court room and law office could, in fact, be regarded as "science in action". The law was ultimately governed by principles akin to the laws of natural sciences and was, thus a subject worthy of a place in the university firmament.

---

62   John Austin, *The Province of Jurisprudence Determined* (Weidenfeld & Nicholson, London, 1954), Lecture 1.

63   John Austin, *The Province of Jurisprudence Determined* (Weidenfeld & Nicholson, London, 1954), Lecture 1.

64   However, for a more detailed exposition of the early 20th century forms of legal theory see JM Kelly, *A Short History of Western Legal Theory* (Clarendon Press, Oxford, 1992), Ch 9.

65   Though Hobbes' *Leviathan*, as an important predecessor to legal positivism, also emphasises the pivotal place of the earthly sovereign. See Thomas Hobbes, *Leviathan* (first published 1651, Cambridge University Press, Cambridge, 1991), Chs 17-20.

66   David Sugarman, "Legal Theory, the Common Law Mind, and the Making of the Textbook Tradition" in Twining (ed), *Legal Theory and the Common Law* (Basil Blackwell, Oxford, 1986).

67   David Sugarman, "Legal Theory, the Common Law Mind, and the Making of the Textbook Tradition" in Twining (ed), *Legal Theory and the Common Law* (Basil Blackwell, Oxford, 1986), p 30.

In contrast to the more idealistic approach to law and its underlying principles which was evident in Britain, North American jurists were beginning to emphasise the empirical study of law — starting with decided cases, rather than general principles, the idea was that it was possible to extract the principles scientifically by detailed study and investigation.[68] Whatever the methodology, law was overwhelmingly approached through the rationalist values of order, coherence, general intelligibility, and abstract reasoning.

However, it would be simplistic to characterise early 20th century Anglo-American legal theory as unified in its positivism. At the turn of the century in the United States the early signs of legal realism were arising from a new pragmatic philosophy which emphasised the logic of experience, rather than that of principles and rules.[69] In Great Britain a historical study of law had gained some recognition[70] while — outside the formal academic study of law — sociologists, socialists, anarchists and other political philosophers were developing distinctive views about the way in which law operates, and its socio-political role. The study of law itself was fairly well protected from the more radical of these views until quite recently, correlating to the degree that the disciplinary boundary between law and non-law was maintained.[71] Therefore, while there were certainly other rumblings to be heard from time to time, positivism and formalism were undoubtedly the strongest influences affecting the legal theory of a century ago.

In this way, legal theory began the 20th century with a reasonably clear direction, and an appreciable, if somewhat self-defensive identity. In other words, you might say that in general terms the legal conscience was relatively unified: legal theory had a mind, a rationality, a subjectivity. It was placed firmly within the "modernism" which "post" modernism has supposedly supplanted,[72] albeit in a partial and fragmentary fashion. (See Chapter 8 for a discussion of postmodernism and its application to law.) And more importantly, legal theory was

---

68   William Keener, "Methods of Legal Education" (1892) 1 *Yale Law Journal* 143; Russell Weaver, "Langdell's Legacy: Living with the Case Method" (1991) 36 *Villanova Law Review* 517.

69   See in particular OW Holmes, "The Path of the Law" in Holmes, *Collected Legal Papers* (Harcourt, Brace & Howe, New York, 1920); William James, *Pragmatism* (first published 1907, Harvard University Press, Cambridge, Mass, 1975).

70   Henry Maine, *Ancient Law* (Murray, London, 1888); see the exposition of Maine's ideas and influence in Roger Cotterrell, *The Politics of Jurisprudence: A Critical Introduction to Legal Philosophy* (London: Butterworths, 1989).

71   See Margaret Thornton, *Portia Lost in the Groves of Academe Wondering What to Do about Legal Education* (La Trobe University Legal Studies, Melbourne, 1991).

72   Positivist legal thought is "modernist" because it is an attempt to provide law with a "metanarrative", that is a universal explanatory framework or theory which is located outside the history or context of the discipline. Jean-François Lyotard, *The Postmodern Condition: A Report on Knowledge* (University of Minnesota Press, Minneapolis, 1984).

reasonably sure about its own identity and destiny.[73] The Enlightenment had asserted itself in jurisprudence.

Since then, we have seen a great chasm open and partially close. On the one hand, as we will see in Chapters 3 and 4, legal positivism reached its height with the works of Kelsen and Hart, and has indeed become the presumed standard of legal thinking — the one to which we have all been trained to turn as if by instinct. Although their approaches take a different form from Austin's positivism, both Hart and Kelsen still emphasised the rational and scientific model of legal theory, and its attempt to discover an essence or driving principle of law's legitimacy located within law itself.[74] Indeed, the ongoing success of positivism is that it has ensured a solid appreciation of the institutional facticity of law — whatever its blindnesses, its political colouring, or its theoretical failures, the discourse of a separate, objectifiable, and institutionally certain law still provide our framing conception of liberal regulation.

On the other hand, multitudes of anti-positivist approaches have recently flourished. The first obvious signs of the proliferation of legal theories this century are to be found in the realist movement, which was especially strong in the twenties and thirties.[75] (As I have mentioned, the origins of realism occur somewhat earlier in the writings and judgements of Oliver Wendell Holmes[76] and in the pragmatic philosophy of William James.[77]) Karl Llewellyn described the situation of growing dissatisfaction with legal abstractions as a "ferment" — a reaction to the lifeless formalism of dominant legal paradigms which situated the "law" in mere words, abstract concepts, and intangible relationships:

> The ferment is proper to the time. The law of schools threatened at the close of the century to turn into words — placid, clear-seeming, lifeless, like some old canal. Practice rolled on, muddy, turbulent, vigorous. It is now spilling, flooding, into the canal of stagnant words. It brings ferment and trouble. So other fields of thought have spilled their waters in ...[78]

---

73   Of course I say this with the simplification of hindsight, which is unfortunately the fate of any history.

74   This is less clear in the case of Hart, but the later chapters of *The Concept of Law* — despite his stated intention of pursuing a Wittgensteinian approach to the use of the word "law" — are basically an attempt to derive a concept of law from observation and rational argument.

75   A very helpful collection of realist writings is Fisher, Horwitz, and Reed (eds), *American Legal Realism* (Oxford University Press, New York, 1993).

76   "The life of the law has not been logic: it has been experience ... The law embodies the story of a nation's development through many centuries, and it cannot be dealt with as if it contained only the axioms and corollaries of a book of mathematics." OW Holmes, *The Common Law* (Little, Brown, Boston, 1881), p 1. See also Holmes, "The Path of the Law" (1897) 10 *Harvard Law Review* 457.

77   James, *Pragmatism*.

78   Karl Llewellyn, "Some Realism about Realism — Responding to Dean Pound" (1931) 44 *Harvard Law Review* 1222.

As a definable movement legal realism was fairly short-lived, but its long-term influence should not be understated. It invigorated legal theory by breaking from the tradition of abstract formalism, and inspired future generations of legal theorists in its sceptical attitude to legal dogma. Legal realism is perhaps as important for its symbolism as for its intellectual contribution to legal theory — it represented a critical departure from the 19th century and a break in the onward march of positivist and formalist approaches to law. Thus, although realism is arguably more characterised by its enthusiasm than by its theoretical rigour, it has had a marked effect on the terrain of late 20th century legal theory.

The other development of the first part of the century worth noting is the resurgence of natural law thought. Since Austin, natural law had all but disappeared from jurisprudence, and it was not until the atrocities of the Second World War called for a non-legalistic response that natural law began to recapture a significant place in jurisprudence.[79]

Despite the onslaught promised by legal realism and the apparent cracks in the positivist outlook revealed by the war, jurisprudence appeared to settle down in the middle decades of the century into an easily recognisable debate between natural law and positivism. Only 30 years ago legal theory still largely consisted of a seemingly invincible positivism which was contrasted to a resurgent, but never predominant, natural law approach. This division was interrupted only occasionally by mention of American and Scandinavian realism, with the Australian version embodied in the person of Julius Stone. Realism was regarded with some scepticism by most scholars, and did little to undermine the relative clarity of the natural law/positivism divide.[80] In the seventies Ronald Dworkin's work began to upset the seemingly neat division between the natural lawyers and the positivists, and he has inspired something of a revolt even among mainstream legal theorists. Although Dworkin did not defend the natural law belief in objective moral principles, he insisted that the law could not be separated from community values, and thus challenged the positivist view of the separability of law and morality. No longer did natural law and positivism cover the jurisprudential field.

---

79   See JM Kelly, A Short History of Western Legal Theory, pp 374-380. The work of Gustav Radbruch, Lon Fuller, and (later) John Finnis is generally associated with this revival of natural law theory. See HLA Hart, "Positivism and the Separation of Law and Morals" in Ronald Dworkin (ed), The Philosophy of Law (Oxford University Press, Oxford, 1977); Lon Fuller, "Positivism and Fidelity to Law — A Response to Professor Hart" (1958) 71 Harvard Law Review 630; John Finnis, Natural Law and Natural Rights (Clarendon Press, Oxford, 1980).

80   An interesting perspective on the apparent closure of the natural law/positivist debate in the early 20th century is to be found in Stanley Paulson's Introduction to Hans Kelsen, Introduction to the Problems of Legal Theory (Translation of the First Edition of the Reine Rechtslehre or Pure Theory of Law) [1934] (Bonnie Litschewski Paulson and Stanley Paulson trans, Clarendon Press, Oxford, 1992), pp xix-xxix.

These changes have gathered momentum in the past few decades. We have witnessed the development of a range of more radical counter-movements which cannot be accommodated within the traditional terrain of legal theory. By and large these counter-movements do not share the language of law's separateness, autonomy, neutrality, or internal rationality, and tend to see such claims not as innocent theoretical analysis, but as an apology for the legal *status quo*. The Critical Legal Studies movement, which is the subject of Chapter 5, stood on the back of legal realism.[81] A multitude of feminist legal theories has grown out of the technical expertise of feminist lawyers combined with the insights of second and third wave feminist theory and practice. We have a thriving law and literature movement, postmodernist accounts of law, psychoanalytical approaches, critical race studies, gay and lesbian legal theories, queer legal theories, and a growing indigenous intervention.[82] The sociology of law, and the law and economics movement are practically disciplines in their own right. All of these areas are growing in interest, dealing with themes as diverse as embedded discrimination, legal mythology, the sacred in law, and the textuality of law. There is really no way to keep track of it all, and nor is there any way to predict what is going to happen next. Legal theory is not nearly as unified or as clearly identifiable as it once was. The disciplinary boundaries of law are being policed less stringently, and the theoretical enterprise is the beneficiary of a flood of ideas from the social sciences and humanities.

So, what is going on in legal theory, and can any sense be made of it? And do the so-called "critical movements" simply represent the other end of a new dualism? Have we transcended natural law and positivism simply to replace it with mainstream and resistance legal thought? Does legal theory currently fall into two streams — on the one hand traditional and universalist, and on the other critical, postmodern, deconstructive? Or are the lines of influence and connection more complex than this? The rest of this book is an attempt to unravel some of these questions, and to illustrate that although it has been decapitated in the sense that it no longer has a distinct disciplinary identity, legal theory has become a much more vibrant and multi-dimensional creature.

---

81   Mark Tushnet, "Critical Legal Studies: A Political History" (1991) 100 *Yale Law Journal* 515; Mark Tushnet, "Post-Realist Legal Scholarship" (1980) 15 *Journal of the Society of Public Teachers of Law* 20.

82   In the Australian context see in particular the work of Irene Watson: "Indigenous People's Law-Ways: Survival Against the Colonial State" (1997) 8 *Australian Feminist Law Journal* 39; "Power of the Muldarbi, The Road to Its Demise" (1998) 11 *Australian Feminist Law Journal* 28.

TWO

CLASSICAL COMMON LAW THEORY

Introduction

[205] In Chapter 1, I made some observations about logic and law and quoted a passage from Michel Foucault's *The Order of Things*. Foucault writes about a story by Borges which quotes a fictional Chinese encyclopaedia. This encyclopaedia uses a system of categorisation or "taxonomy" which is distinctly foreign to our way of thinking, dividing animals into categories like "(a) belonging to the Emperor, (b) embalmed, (c) tame, (d) sucking pigs, (e) sirens, (f) fabulous, (g) stray dogs, (h) included in the present classification, (i) frenzied, (j) innumerable, (k) drawn with a very fine camelhair brush, (l) *et cetera*, (m) having just broken the water pitcher, (n) that from a long way off look like flies".[1]

As I explained, Foucault's comment about this remarkable passage is not that the classification invented by Borges is illogical, though that is certainly how we perceive it, but rather that in being faced with a system which is clearly alien to our way of thinking, we are confronted with the limitations of our own thought processes. It is almost impossible for us to see the logic of such a system, but that is not because the system *doesn't* have some basis in logic or reason, rather, it is because we are viewing the Chinese encyclopaedia in terms of our own ideas about what is logical or reasonable. And such constructs are, by definition, limited.

I am mentioning this again because I think it is necessary to bear it in mind when we start thinking about legal theories, and, especially, about theories or concepts of law which are not readily comprehensible to Western people in the late 20th century. It is not just that different systems have different rules, doctrines, or principles, or even totally different systems of classifying substantive law: there are ways of understanding law which simply cannot be explained in the terms of modern Western legal theory. As Irene Watson has explained in relation to an indigenous concept of law,[2]

---

1   Michel Foucault, *The Order of Things: An Archaeology of the Human Sciences* (translated from the French originally published as "Les mots et les Choses" Paris Gallimard 1966 Tavistock, London, London, Routledge, 2001), p xv.

2   Irene Watson, "Indigenous Peoples' Law-Ways: Survival Against the Colonial State" (1997) 8 *Australian Feminist Law Journal* 39 at 39.

Our voices were once heard in light of the law. The law transcends all things, guiding us in the tradition of living a good life, that is, a life that is sustainable and one which enables our grand-children yet to be born to also experience a good life on earth. The law is who we are, we are also the law. We carry it in our lives. The law is everywhere, we breathe it, we eat it, we sing it, we live it.

Watson suggests that "law" is not simply an external influence on a pre-existing subject, but is rather a spiritual construct and, as such, is part of the person, as well as inhering in what a non-Indigenous person might call the "environment". From the Western point of view such a concept of law is difficult to comprehend. Western tradition demands that we view law as something imposed by human beings that is separate from any individual and separate from the physical world.[3] Our law is enshrined in particular institutions which we just assume to be the repository (if not the source) of what we understand to be "law".

I will not discuss the various non-Western concepts of law: it would be presumptuous to attempt to describe something which lacks clear comparative analogies to Western theories of law.[4] I simply wanted to point these out so that we are aware that theories about what law *really* is, especially those which include descriptions of non-Western systems as deficient systems of law, are an attempt to subordinate every system which doesn't look like our own, to the ideological supremacy of so-called "developed" law.[5] This is nothing more than a philosophical imperialism — an attempt to capture the world's diverse meanings within the cage of our own system.

Common law theory represents another way of viewing the law as a type of custom. This view of law, despite its historical significance, is tangential to current perspectives about law and its relationship with society. (And, if classical common law thought is tangential to the modern common law mind, it must appear quite incomprehensible even to civil lawyers, let alone to those raised in a non-Western legal tradition. In this sense, like Borges' Chinese encyclopaedia, it can, at the very least, hopefully cast some light on modern Anglo-centric presuppositions concerning law.)

---

3   Patrick Parkinson, *Tradition and Change in Australian Law* (3rd ed, Law Book Company, Pyrmont NSW, 2005); Margaret Davies "Legal Separatism and the Concept of the person" in Tom Campbell and Jeffrey Goldsworthy (eds), *Judicial Power, Democracy and Legal Positivism* (Ashgate, Aldershot, 2000).

4   But see generally, Bryan Hanks and Peter Keon-Cohen (eds), *Aborigines and the Law: Essays in Memory of Elizabeth Eggleston* (Allen and Unwin, Sydney, 1984); Heather McRae, Garth Nettheim, and Laura Beacroft, *Indigenous Legal Issues* (3rd ed, Law Book Company, 2003); Irene Watson, "Power of the Muldarbi, The Road To Its Demise" (1998) 11 *Australian Feminist Law Journal* 28.

5   Instances where writers have identified the concept of law with the characteristics of modern Western law are numerous. For instance, in his *An Introduction to English Legal History* (4th ed, Butterworths, London, 2002) JH Baker notes the lack of a distinction in pre-Conquest English law between administrative, adjudicative and legislative functions, concluding that such a system is "not quite the same as 'law'", p 1. Such a view assumes that law necessarily distinguishes between these functions.

By "Common Law Theory" I do not mean modern theory about the common law, or theory emanating from common law jurisdictions. Rather, I am referring to the conception of law which was held by those eminent British men of the 16th to 18th centuries,[6] who are still revered by some as the "Fathers" of modern common law — in particular, Edward Coke, William Blackstone, and Mathew Hale. (If I sound slightly irreverent about these great men it is for two reasons: (a) whatever we end up with, a Constitution or a whole system of law, and, in spite of whether it is any good, we sometimes exhibit a blind tendency to revere our Fathers; (b) in this instance our Fathers fathered not only the common law system but also certain unfortunate but resistant features of it. Hale, for instance, is well known for his ideas about rape — for example, that it is easy to allege and hard to deny — which have been influential in the development of rape laws, evidence rules and adversarial culture, which have had the practical effect of making rape very difficult to allege and simple to deny.[7])

With these qualifying thoughts in mind, I wish to outline a few of the features of classical common law theory, in order to illustrate that even within a single jurisdiction (in this case England) vastly different ways of perceiving the law can predominate at different historical stages. This may seem obvious, especially since we now have so many different ways (and "perspectives") of seeing the law. However, I think that there is something paradigmatically different about classical common law thought: of course we still have important foundational ideas derived from it,[8] but it seems clear that there was a very significant shift in the

---

6   Gerald Postema writes: "From the perspective of comparative law, Anglophone legal systems are dominated by 'common law' even today. That is to say, conceptions of law and structures of legal argument typical of Anglophone nations have been decisively influenced by the fact that their legal systems developed not from the Romans, or Civil traditions, but out of English Common Law. Of course, this tradition goes back much farther than the seventeenth century. But it was in the late sixteenth and early seventeenth centuries that a distinctive Common Law jurisprudential theory developed. With the term 'classical Common Law theory', then, I wish to pick out a body of thought about the nature of law which begins to take distinctive shape with Coke. It is to be distinguished from contemporary views of Common Law practice and from earlier notions of the law of England — which may have been more directly and explicitly influenced by the natural law tradition." *Bentham and the Common Law Tradition* (Clarendon Press, Oxford, 1989), p 3 fn 1.

7   Hale wrote: "it is true rape is a most detestable crime, and therefore ought severely and impartially to be punished with death; but it must be remembered, that it is an accusation easily to be made and hard to be proved, and harder to be defended by the party accused, tho' never so innocent" *History of the Pleas of the Crown* (revised ed, T Payne et al, London, 1778) vol 1, p 635. These sentiments were until recently reproduced by judges and textbook writers: see Ngaire Naffine, "Windows on the Legal Mind: The Evocation of Rape in Legal Writings" (1992) 18 *Melbourne University Law Review* 741. Hale was also, incidentally, an active participant in the persecution of "witches".

8   Brian Simpson develops a modern theory of the common law in "The Common Law and Legal Theory" in William Twining (ed), *Legal Theory and the Common Law* (Basil Blackwell, Oxford, 1986): of particular significance is his explanation of how modern theories, especially positivism, fail properly to conceptualise precedent.

Anglo-American jurisprudential paradigm towards the end of the 18th century. Most of our modern perspectives, however radical and critical they may appear to be, tend in various (though not always obvious) ways to reinforce — or at least take as a point of departure — the positivist view of law. That is, they presume that law consists of rules and principles laid down in an authoritative manner by an institution with law-making authority (whether that be a court or a legislature), and that it is therefore conceptually separable from morality, custom, religion, and social norms. Though pervasive, positivism is comparatively recent as a paradigm for understanding law and, while a multiplicity of theories about law now exists, it is arguable that no paradigm shift has occurred since the positivist revolution of the early 19th century.[9] Thinking about classical common law theory therefore illustrates the inter-relationship between the history of law and the philosophy of law.[10]

Finally, by way of introduction, it should be noted that although this chapter is divided into several sections, each dealing with an aspect of classical common law thought, these divisions should not be taken as definitive of its characteristics, nor as conceptually separable. I have chosen to deal with these matters under separate headings partly for the sake of clarity and partly to suggest certain modern parallels. However, the understanding of law under consideration is truly organic, in the sense that none of its central characteristics can be meaningfully separated from the others. This is especially so of the matters discussed in the following three sections of the chapter.

Law and Declaration

[210]   "Classical common law theory" is, as I have said, a way of describing the view of law held by the common law theorists of the 16th to 18th centuries. Gerald Postema describes this conception of the law as arising from the political situation in England at the time:[11]

---

9   There is some difficulty even with a proposition as banal as this. To say that no fundamental shift in paradigm has occurred neglects three related matters, which are nevertheless unresolvable: the first is whether we are not in fact in the middle of a fundamental shift in paradigm, but simply not able to recognise it as such, since there is no way to rationalise or totalise our own ideological environment; secondly, any such description of a generally held conception of law fails in any case to account for the complexity of individual views and approaches which are set up as alternatives; thirdly, is it ever possible to claim that a conceptual revolution is "complete" at a particular point in time? Even now the residue of classical common law thinking in modern common law jurisprudence is clear.

10   See generally, Patrick Parkinson, *Tradition and Change in Australian Law*.

11   Gerald Postema, *Bentham and the Common Law Tradition*, pp 3-4; cf Frederick Pocock, *The Ancient Constitution and the Feudal Law* (Norton, New York, reprinted 1967), pp 51-52. The general nature of this "deeper reality" of the common law will be considered in detail below at [250], under the heading "Artificial Reason".

> Common Law theory arose, in part, in response to the threat of centralized power exercised by those who proposed to *make* law guided by nothing but their own assessments of the demands of justice, expediency, and the common good. ... Common Law theory reasserted the medieval idea that law is not something made either by king, Parliament, or judges, but rather is the expression of a deeper reality which is merely discovered and publicly declared by them.

One of the central conflicts of jurisprudence has indeed revolved around the distinction between, on the one hand regarding law as created by human beings, and on the other, as existing separately from deliberate human intervention.[12] However, as will become apparent, in the case of common law theory the distinction is not always easy to draw. According to the classical common law thinkers, the common or customary law was not laid down by anyone, as statutes were. The judges, according to this view, did not make the common law — they declared it. Yet this does not necessarily mean that the common law was not regarded as the product of human action. For although it was not deliberately created by a single act or series of acts (such as those undertaken by a legislature or monarch) it was nevertheless the result of accumulated social and political custom rather than a naturally existent system of norms. Thus common law was not regarded as an ideal existing somewhere quite separate from human agency, nor was it reducible to any specific political or historical origin.

In his *Commentaries on the Laws of England*, Blackstone wrote that judges are the "living oracles" of the law. Judges do not *decide* what the law is, nor do they exercise any *personal* judgment in determining what the proper principle to apply to a case is. The judges are regarded simply as the mouthpiece of the law, and thus each *as an individual* is irrelevant to the development of the law. Note the important argument made by Blackstone towards the end of the extract: a judicial pronouncement which misrepresents the law does not result in *bad* law, it is simply not law (and therefore not to be followed in subsequent cases). According to this view, the common law is authoritatively evidenced, but not determined, by judicial decisions. The law is therefore different from mere decisions: this feature of common law thought led Jeremy Bentham in the early 19th century to characterise the common law itself as a fiction and as non-existent.[13]

12　See the sections on positivism in Chapter 3, and Chapter 4.

13　For an analysis of Bentham's thought on this point see Brian Simpson, "The Common Law and Legal Theory" in Twining (ed), *Legal Theory and Common Law*, pp 8, 16-18.

William Blackstone
Commentaries on the Laws of England[14]

[215]   Some have divided the common law into two principal grounds or foundations: 1. Established customs; ... and 2. Established High rules and maxims. ... But I take these to be one and the same thing, For the authority of these maxims rests entirely upon general reception and usage: and the only method of proving, that this or that maxim is a rule of the common law, is by shewing that it hath always been the custom to observe it.

But here a very natural, and very material, question arises: how are these customs or maxims to be known, and by whom is their validity to be determined? The answer is, by the judges in the several courts of justice. They are the depositaries of the laws; the living oracles, who must decide in all cases of doubt, and who are bound by an oath to decide according to the law of the land. Their knowledge of that law is derived from experience and study; ... and from being long personally accustomed to the judicial decisions of their predecessors. And indeed these judicial decisions are the principal and most authoritative evidence, that can be given, of the existence of such a custom as shall form a part of the common law. ... For it is an established rule to abide by former precedents, where the same points come again in litigation; as well to keep the scale of justice even and steady, and not liable to waver with every new judge's opinion; as also because the law in that case being solemnly declared and determined, what before was uncertain, and perhaps indifferent, is now become a permanent rule, which it is not in the breast of any subsequent judge to alter or vary from, according to his private sentiments: he being sworn to determine, not according to his own private judgement, but according to the known laws and customs of the land; not delegated to pronounce a new law, but to maintain and expound the old one. Yet this rule admits of exception, where the former determination is most evidently contrary to reason; much more if it be clearly contrary to the divine law. But even in such cases the subsequent judges do not pretend to make a new law, but to vindicate the old one from misrepresentation. For if it be found that the former decision is manifestly absurd or unjust, it is declared, not that such a sentence was *bad law*, but that it was *not law*; that is, that it is not the established custom of the realm, as has been erroneously determined.

[220]   It is fairly clear that these ideas have had a very profound impact on legal thought and are still relied upon by judges who see their role as impartially applying and, where appropriate, extending settled principles of law, but not as doing anything which diverges sufficiently from the past to amount to an act of judicial creation.[15] For instance, in the classic case of *SGIC v Trigwell*[16] Barwick CJ (of the High Court of

---

14   William Blackstone, *Commentaries on the Laws of England* (15th ed, T Cadell and W Davies, London, 1809), vol I, pp 68-70.

15   An exposition of the declaratory theory in modern jurisprudence appears in Peter Wesley-Smith, "Theories of Adjudication and the Status of Stare Decisis" in Laurence Goldstein (ed), *Precedent in Law* (Clarendon Press, Oxford, 1987).

16   (1978) 26 ALR 67.

Australia) echoed, two centuries later, Blackstone's views about the relationship between the law and the judicial process:[17]

> Where the law has been declared by a court of high authority, this court if it agrees that that declaration was correct when made, cannot alter the common law because the court may think that changes in the society make or tend to make that declaration of the common law inappropriate to the times ... It can, of course, decide that that declaration was erroneous when made and itself declare what the common law ought properly be held to be.

We still tend to see the judicial function as one of acting impartially and objectively and only in accordance with established law, while political and inventive actions are taken by Parliament. There has been a great deal of jurisprudential debate over this point,[18] the central issues being the nature of judicial discretion, and whether (and to what extent) it is, in any case, possible for rules to be determinately followed.[19] It is no longer radical to claim that judges "make" law, even though there is still widespread community and political criticism of any legal decision which is perceived to extend too far the boundaries of established legal principle. Interestingly, as Lee Godden has argued, some judges may recently have given new life to the declaratory theory.[20] She suggests that the "judicial activism" in the Australian native title cases of *Wik* and *Mabo*, can be understood not as wholesale reinvention of law, but rather as a fresh declaration of law based upon changed perceptions of history. According to this view, the judges did not simply invent new law in order to accommodate changed notions of social justice, but rather re-declared it so that it took better account of historical circumstances.

Although most common law thinkers, and notably Hale (whose arguments I will summarise shortly), recognised that the common law developed over time, any changes were seen to be a product of the general process of legal reasoning manifested in the entire body of precedent and never the work of an individual judge. We can contrast this with the more modern approach which sometimes regards

---

17 (1978) 26 ALR 67 at 70. See also the contrasting position put by Murphy J at 91-92. Another famous rejection of judicial legislation is that of Lord Esher in *Willis v Baddeley* [1892] 2 QB 324 at 326: "There is, in fact, no such thing as judge-made law, for the judges do not make the law, though they frequently have to apply existing law to circumstances as to which it has not previously been authoritatively laid down that such law is applicable." See generally, Wesley-Smith, "Theories of Adjudication and the Status of Stare Decisis", pp 73-87.

18 See, for instance, HK Lücke, "The Common Law: Judicial Impartiality and Judge-Made Law" (1982) 98 *Law Quarterly Review* 29 at 33ff; Michael McHugh, "The Law-making Function of the Judicial Process — Part 2" (1988) 62 *Australian Law Journal* 116; MDA Freeman, *Lloyd's Introduction to Jurisprudence* (7th ed, Sweet & Maxwell Ltd, London 2001).

19 MDA Freeman, *Lloyd's Introduction to Jurisprudence*; HLA Hart, *The Concept of Law* (Oxford University Press, New York 1972, c1961), ch 7.

20 Lee Godden, "Wik: Legal Memory and History" (1997) 6 *Griffith Law Review* 123.

individual judges as being instrumental in the development of certain doctrines or whole areas of law. One obvious example is Lord Atkin's "neighbour principle" which has been taken as central to the decision in *Donoghue v Stevenson*.[21]

As Roland Barthes argued some decades ago, the "Author" was an invention of the Enlightenment and of Western individualism, and has not always enjoyed a position of authority (and still does not in many cultures).[22] Similarly, Martha Woodmansee argues that "the writer of the Rennaissance and neoclassical period [in literature] is always a vehicle or instrument": this notion of the author as medium for a message which came from the tradition or from a supernatural source was replaced in the 18th century by the idea that the author was an original genius, personally responsible for his or her own creations.[23] The postmodern proclamation of the "death of the author" indicates a departure from this belief in individual authorial intention. As Barthes famously declared, "it is language which speaks, not the author".[24] The parallel idea in the early common law thought might well be that it is the law which speaks, not the judge: the judge merely passes on the law. I will return to the matter of the author in Chapter 8. For the time being, it is important to note that the emphasis placed in certain types of modern legal thought upon authorial intention, whether of judges or legislatures, is derived from a world-view which emphasises the autonomy of individual actors, not their place within a communal or discursive system.[25]

The declaratory theory is one of the ways in which the common law has defended itself against the accusation that the law is political. Although the judicial process may result in alteration of the law, this is seen to be the work of the judiciary at large and not the result of individual bias. In recent years however, the critics of traditional jurisprudence, and in particular feminists and scholars of the critical legal studies movement, have argued at length that judicial decision-making is unavoidably political, in the sense that it is influenced by systems of power within our society. Law is not only political because

---

21   [1932] AC 562.

22   Roland Barthes, "Le most d'auteur", *Mantéia*, V, 1968 translated by Stephen Heath as "The Death of the Author" in Roland Barthes, *Image Music Text* (Flamingo, London, 1984). In "What is an Author", Michel Foucault commented that the "coming into being of the notion of 'author' constitutes the privileged moment of individualization in the history of ideas": in Josué Harari, *Textual Strategies: Perspectives in Post-Structuralist Criticism* (London, Methuen, 1980), p 141.

23   Woodmansee, "The Genius and the Copyright: Economic and Legal Conditions of the Emergence of the 'Author'" (1984) 17 *Eighteenth-Century Studies* 425 at 427.

24   Barthes "The Death of the Author", p 143.

25   See also Margaret Davies, "Authority, Meaning, Legitimacy" in Jeffrey Goldsworthy and Tom Campbell (eds), *Legal Interpretation in Democratic States* (Ashgate, Aldershot, 2002).

judges tend to be privileged white men (who hold a powerful position in society) and typically represent mainstream views. Law is also political because it is simply not possible to exclude social or ideological influences from the process of judging. In fact, law is political simply by virtue of the role it plays in ordering society.[26] Judges cannot escape their position of power within the legal system and society, just as they cannot escape their social conditioning, though they may attempt to shelter themselves from public criticism by invoking the myths of impartiality and objectivity. Thus the "politics" of law is not the result of individually biased judges, but is "systemic", that is, built into the very institutions of law which present themselves as neutral. These matters will be discussed briefly at the end of this chapter, and again in Chapters 5 and 6.

Unwritten Law and Time Immemorial

[225] One further reason for this change in the perception of the role of the individual judge was the fact that, as Roger Cotterrell puts it, the law in the 17th century was still considered to be largely unwritten, allowing "individual innovation to be forgotten, subsumed in the image of a changeless collective legal knowledge."[27] The subsequent development of a sophisticated body of legal writing, manifested as statutes, reports, and commentaries by jurists, forced the individual judge or writer to become visible in the process of legal development.

Lex non scripta

[230] The "unwritten" character of the common law may on one level be regarded as a fiction designed to perpetuate the idea that judges themselves did not make the law: clearly the law was written to a certain degree in reported decisions, as well as in the writings of jurists such as Glanvill, Bracton, Coke and Blackstone. But the common law was said to be "unwritten", and therefore distinguished from legislation, because it did not have its *origin* in writing (and could not therefore be the original work of any single author). The common law was said to have originated in custom and in immemorial usage, in contrast to statutes, which are inherently written and derive their force from the written form.

---

26 JAG Griffith, *The Politics of the Judiciary* (Fontana, London, 1985), chs 8 and 9. See the comments I have made on law and order in Chapter 1.

27 Roger Cotterrell, *The Politics of Jurisprudence: A Critical Introduction to Legal Philosophy* (Butterworths, London, 1989), p 29.

Matthew Hale
The History of the Common Law of England[28]

[235]   The Laws of England may aptly enough be divided into two Kinds, *viz Lex Scripta*, the written Law; and *Lex non Scripta*, the unwritten Law: For although ... all the Laws of this Kingdom have some Monuments or Memorials thereof in Writing, yet all of them have not their Original in Writing; for some of those Laws have obtain'd their Force by immemorial Usage or Custom, and such Laws are properly called *Leges non Scriptae*, or unwritten Laws or Customs.

Those Laws therefore, that I call *Leges Scriptae*, or written Laws, are such as are usually called *Statute Laws*, or Acts of Parliament, which are originally reduced into Writing before they are enacted, or receive any binding Power, every such Law being in the first Instance formally drawn up in Writing, and made, as it were, a *Tripartite Indenture*, between the King, the Lords and the Commons; for without the concurrent Consent of all those Three Parts of the Legislature, no such Law is, or can be made: But the Kings of this realm, with the Advice and Consent of both Houses of Parliament, have Power to make new Laws, or to alter, repeal, or enforce the Old. And this has been done in all Succession of Ages.

Now, *Statute Laws*, or Acts of Parliament, are of Two Kinds. *viz* First, Those Statutes which were made *before Time of Memory*; and Secondly, Those Statutes which were made *within* or *since Time of Memory*; wherein observe, That according to a juridical Account and legal Signification, *Time within Memory* is the Time of Limitation in a Writ of Right; which ... was settled, and reduced to the Beginning of the Reign of King Richard I ... who began his Reign the 6th of July 1189, and was crown'd the 3rd of September following: So that whatsoever was before that Time, is *before* Time of Memory, and what is since that Time is, in a legal Sense, said to be *within* or since the Time of Memory.

And therefore it is, that those Statutes or Acts of Parliament that were made before the Beginning of the Reign of King Richard I and have not since been repealed or altered, either by contrary Usage, or by subsequent Acts of Parliament, are now accounted Part of the *Lex non Scripta*, being as it were incorporated thereinto, and become a Part of the Common Law; and in Truth, such Statutes are not now pleadable as Acts of Parliament, (because what is *before* Time of Memory is supposed without a Beginning, or at least such a Beginning as the Law takes Notice of) but they obtain their Strength by meer immemorial Usage or Custom.

[This first part of Hale's treatise concludes with a description of the statutes made both before and within time of memory. The second part deals with the common law.]

---

28   Matthew Hale, *The History of the Common Law of England* (Edited and with an Introduction by Charles M Gray, University of Chicago Press, Chicago, 1971) "Concerning the Distribution of the Laws of England into Common Law, and Statute Law. And First, concerning the Statute Law, or Acts of Parliament", pp 3-4. The last paragraph of the extract is from the second part of the work, "Concerning the Lex non Scripta, ie The Common or Municipal Laws of this Kingdom", p 16.

> And when I call those Parts of our Laws *Leges non Scriptae*, I do not mean as if all those Laws were only Oral, or communicated from the former Ages to the later, merely by Word. For all those Laws have their several Monuments in Writing, whereby they are transferr'd from one Age to another, and without which they would soon lose all kind of Certainty: For as the Civil and Canon Laws have their ... Canons, Decrees, and Decretal Determinations extant in Writing; so those Laws of England which are not comprized under the Title of Acts of Parliament, are for the most part extant in Records of Pleas, Proceedings, and Judgements, in Books of Reports, and Judicial Decisions, in Tractates of Learned Men's Arguments and Opinions, preserved from ancient Times, and still extant in Writing.

[240] The continuity between the common law and an oral or quasi-oral customary tradition, is evident here in the distinction between law which, though set down in writing, did not originate in writing, and that, such as Statute law, which did originate in writing and is formally defined by a particular set of words.[29] The distinction between two different types of origin is interesting because, as will be explained shortly, identifying a specific and formal origin was not considered to be crucial to the validity of a law. In contrast, the theory of legal positivism is founded upon the idea that in order to be valid a legal principle must have an identifiable origin — it must have a formal "pedigree" which is its condition of validity. Custom cannot simply be *created* by a legislative act, though Hale makes it clear that any statute passed before time immemorial is regarded as part of the unwritten law.

Immemorial usage

[245] Note that Hale states at the beginning of the passage that the unwritten laws have "*obtain'd their Force*" by immemorial Usage or Custom". In other words, the common law is law, it is legitimate, not because it has been laid down by someone with the authority to act, but rather because of its age. Because the common law has endured and been developed over such a long period of time, it is, according to this view, imbued with the experience and wisdom of its age, giving it an unquestionable superiority over statutes, which by comparison are devised in the heat of the moment.

It is therefore, according to Hale and others, the timelessness of the common law which gives it its authority. A similar sentiment was expressed by Blackstone: "in our law the goodness of a custom depends upon its having been used time out of mind; or, in the solemnity of our legal phrase, time whereof the memory of man runneth not to the contrary. This it is that gives it its weight and authority".[30] As Gerald Postema points out, the word "goodness" here has a double meaning: a

---

29 TFT Plucknett discusses an earlier and less formal conception of the relationship between custom and statutes in the first chapter of *Legislation of Edward I* (Clarendon Press, Oxford, 1949).

30 William Blackstone, *Commentaries on the Laws of England* (15th ed, T Cadell and W Davies, London, 1809), vol I, p 67.

custom is "good" in the sense of being valid or authoritative because it has been used "time out of mind", and it is also "good" in the sense of being just or reasonable because of its age.[31] The way of proving that a custom is part of the common law is to demonstrate that it has been used since time immemorial. If it has been so used, then it must be reasonable, otherwise it would not have endured. The relationship between timelessness, custom and law, and the superiority of customary law to written law, are more fully explained in the following passage.[32]

> For a Custome taketh beginning and groweth to perfection in this manner: When a reasonable act once done is found to be good and beneficiall to the people, and agreeable to their nature and disposition, then do they use it and practise it again and again, and so by often iteration and multiplication of the act it becometh a *Custome*; and being continued without interruption time out of mind, it obtaineth the force of a *Law*.

> And this *Customary Law* is the most perfect and most excellent, and without comparison the best, to make and preserve a Commonwealth. For the *written Laws* which are made either by the Edicts of Princes, or by Councils of Estates, are imposed upon the Subject before any Triall or Probation made, whether the same be fit and agreeable to the nature and disposition of the people, or whether they will breed any inconvenience or no. But a Custome doth never become a Law to bind the people, untill it hath been tried and approved time out of mind, during all which time there did arise no inconvenience: for if it had been found inconvenient at any time, it had been used no longer, but had been interrupted, and consequently it had lost the virtue and force of a Law.

For all practical purposes "time immemorial" was deemed (by an Act of Parliament) to commence with the reign of Richard I.[33] The "goodness of a custom", in other words, depended upon its having been used since before 6 July 1189.

In this way, "time immemorial" was thought of as a justification for law, for, as Coke explained in *Calvin's Case*:

> we are but of yesterday, (and therefore had need of the wisdom of those that were before us) and had been ignorant (if we had not received light and knowledge from our forefathers) and our days upon the earth are but as a shadow, in respect of the old ancient days and times past, wherein the laws have been by the wisdom of the most excellent men, in many successions of ages, by long and continual experience, (the trial of right and truth) fined and refined, which no one man, (being of so short a time) albeit he had in his head the wisdom of all the men in the world, in any one age could ever have affected or attained unto. And therefore it is ... no man ought to take upon him to be wiser than the laws.[34]

---

31 Note the comments made by Postema in *Bentham and the Common Law Tradition*, p 5.

32 Sir John Davies Irish Reports (1612), as quoted in JGA Pocock, *The Ancient Constitution and the Feudal Law* (Norton, New York 1957 reprinted 1967), p 33.

33 Hale, *History of the Common Law of England*, p 4. This passage appears in the extract above at [235].

34 *Calvin's Case* (1608) 7 Co Rep 1 at 3b.

Because the experience of each individual on the earth is so short and the knowledge attained so limited, we must, according to Coke, submit our own personal ideas and judgment to the wisdom of the law, which represents the entire experience, authority and reason of the past.

Artificial Reason

[250]   Common law theory is a way of thinking which rests on the idea that there is something inherently *necessary* and right about the process of legal reasoning which emerges in decided cases: this clearly contrasts with the arbitrariness of decisions made for political reasons by Parliament. In *Dr Bonham's Case,* Coke made it clear that he considered the common law to be superior to Acts of Parliament:[35]

> And it appears in our books, that in many cases, the common law will control Acts of Parliament, and sometimes adjudge them to be utterly void: for when an Act of Parliament is against common right and reason, or repugnant, or impossible to be performed, the common law will control it, and adjudge such Act to be void.

What is especially interesting about Coke's view of the *reasoning* inherent in common law is his distinction between *natural* reason, which every individual may possess, and *artificial* or legal reason, which is only gained by extensive study of the common law.[36] It is this artificial legal reason, and not natural reason, which underlies the common law's authority.[37] The common law cannot be deduced according to ordinary notions of reason, though this does not make the common law inferior in any way. Indeed, as is made clear by Hale,[38]

---

35   (1610) 8 Co Rep 114 at 118b (spelling regularised). See George Smith, "*Dr Bonham's Case* and the Modern Significance of Lord Coke's Influence" (1966) 41 *Washington Law Review* 297.

36   See generally, Pocock, *The Ancient Constitution and the Feudal Law,* p 35; Postema, *Bentham and the Common Law Tradition*, pp 30-31; DEC Yale, "Hobbes and Hale on Law, Legislation, and the Sovereign" (1972) 31 *Cambridge Law Journal* 121 at 124-126; John Underwood Lewis, "Sir Edward Coke: His Theory of 'Artificial Reason' as a Context for Modern Basic Legal Theory" (1968) 84 *Law Quarterly Review* 330 at 334-338.

37   It is important to remember at this stage that the jurists under consideration are essentially those of the 17th to 18th centuries. Earlier common law writers, such as Fortescue, St German, Yelverton, and Littleton appear to have relied more on the notion of natural law. (See generally Barbara Singer, "The Reason of the Common Law" (1983) 37 *University of Miami Law Review* 797.) In *Doctor and Student* (The Selden Society, London, 1974) for instance, Christopher St German asserts that the first ground of the law of England is the law of reason, by which he means natural reason. The second to sixth grounds are respectively, the law of God, general customs (which are neither against the law of God or against reason), maxims, local customs, and statutes: First Dialogue, chs 5-11. The law of reason is not, according to St German, sufficient to account for all English law, but it is nevertheless the primary standard for determining the law.

38   See the extract from his "Reflections by the Lord Chiefe Justice Hale on Mr Hobbes his Dialogue of the Lawe" in Holdsworth (ed), *A History of English Law, Volume V, Appendix III* (Methuen, London, 1936-1974), below at [265].

the use of natural reason, in the absence of any legal education, would only lead to a multiplicity of conflicting views about what the appropriate laws should be. Legal reason, in contrast, has been accumulated over a very long period of time, and has attained certainty and stability through its development in the customs of the courts. Legal reason, therefore, is essentially an artificial construct underlying the particular laws and can be understood only by individuals who have undertaken a thorough education in the law. This principle was applied on one occasion when James I purported to settle a dispute over land between some of his subjects. The controversy was recorded by Coke in his *Twelfth Reports*:[39]

> A controversy of land between parties was heard by the King, and sentence given, which was repealed, for this, that it did belong to the common law: then the King said, that he thought the law was founded upon reason, and that he and others had reason, as well as the Judges; to which it was answered by me, that true it was, that God had endowed his Majesty with excellent science, and great endowments of nature; but his Majesty was not learned in the laws of his realm of England, and causes which concern the life, or inheritance, or goods, or fortunes of his subjects, are not to be decided by natural law reason, but by the artificial reason and judgement of law, which law is an act which requires long study and experience, before that a man can attain to the cognizance of it; and that the law was the golden met-wand and measure to try the causes of the subjects; and which protected his Majesty in safety and peace: with which the King was greatly offended, and said, that then he should be under the law, which was treason to affirm, as he said: to which I said, that Bracton saith, *quod Rex non debet esse sub homine, sed sub Deo et lege* [that the King is under no man, but under God and the law].

Some of the basic ideas about the nature of the "reason" which was said to underlie the common law are expounded and rejected in the following extract, in which Thomas Hobbes contrasts his own positivist views about the nature of law with those of a common lawyer. The views of the lawyer in Thomas Hobbes' *Dialogue* are substantially those of Coke.[40]

---

39   Coke, *Prohibitions del Roy* 12 Co Rep at 65.

40   The first statement made by the lawyer is a verbatim quotation from Coke's *Institutes of the Laws of England* (15th ed, E and R Brooke, London, 1744), First Part, 97b, s 138. See generally Yale, "Hobbes and Hale on Law, Legislation and the Sovereign".

Thomas Hobbes

A Dialogue Between a Philosopher and a Student of the Common Laws of England[41]

[255]   *La[wyer]* ... this is to be understood of an artificial perfection of Reason gotten by long Study, Observation and Experience, and not of every Mans natural Reason; for *Nemo nascitur Artifex* [no-one is born an artisan]. This Legal Reason is *summa Ratio* [supreme Reason], and therefore if all the Reason that is dispersed into so many several heads were united into one, yet could he not make such a Law as the Law of *England* is, because by so many successions of Ages it hath been fined and refined by an infinite number of Grave and Learned Men.

Ph[ilosopher] ... that the Reason which is the Life of the Law, should be not Natural, but Artificial I cannot conceive. I understand well enough, that the knowledge of the Law is gotten by much study, as all other Sciences are, which when they are studyed and obtained, it is still done by Natural, and not by Artificial Reason. I grant you that the knowledge of the Law is an Art, but not that any Art of one Man, or of many how wise soever they be, or the work of one and more Artificers, how perfect soever it be, is Law. It is not Wisdom, but Authority that makes a law. Obscure also are the words Legal Reason; there is no Reason in Earthly Creatures, but Humane Reason; but I suppose that he [Coke] means, that the Reason of a Judge, or of all the Judges together (without the King) is that *Summa Ratio*, and the very Law, which I deny, because none can make a Law but he that hath the Legislative Power. That the Law hath been fined by Grave and Learned Men, meaning the Professors of the Law is manifestly untrue, for all the Laws of *England* have been made by the Kings of *England*, consulting with the Nobility and Commons in *Parliament*, of which not one of twenty was a Learned Lawyer.

La[wyer] You speak of the Statu[t]e Law, and I speak of the Common Law.

Ph[ilosopher] I speak generally of Law.

[260]   In the next section, Hobbes puts forward his views about the nature of sovereignty and the origin of legal authority. After the lawyer has restated Coke's arguments about the gradual refinement of the common law and its "artificial perfection of reason", the philosopher continues with an argument which places the King at the pinnacle of the legal hierarchy. The judges derive their judicial authority from the sovereign, as does the legislature. It is therefore the reason of the king, rather than that of the judges, which animates the law.

Hobbes' view of law, here presented as that of the philosopher, is essentially positivist. Later in the *Dialogue*, law is defined as "the Command of him, or them that have the Soveraign Power, given to

---

41   Thomas Hobbes, *A Dialogue Between a Philosopher and a Student of the Common Laws of England* (University of Chicago Press, Chicago, 1971), Pt I "Of the Law of Reason", p 55. It is interesting to compare the views expressed here by Hobbes' philosopher and lawyer to those expounded by a modern natural law thinker such as John Finnis. Finnis' work will be discussed in Chapter 3.

those that be his or their Subjects, declaring Publickly, and plainly what every of them may do, and what they must forbear to do."[42] It is the King's reason which is behind the law. After all, as the philosopher points out, the judges, including Coke, have all been appointed by the King, and any authority they have is derived from him. Judges are not made by their faculty of reason, but by the King.[43] The reason of the law cannot be left to individuals, since every person, according to Hobbes, has his or her own view of what is reasonable.[44] The sovereign (whose reason is equally subjective) therefore takes over the function of determining the laws and general institutions:[45]

> Would you have every Man to every other man alledge for Law his own particular Reason? There is not amongst Men an Universal Reason agreed upon in any Nation, besides the Reason of him that hath the Sovereign Power; yet though his Reason be but the Reason of one Man, yet it is set up to supply the place of the Universal Reason.

What this argument tends to overlook is the classical common law view that it is not *individual* judges who determine the law: although the law is expounded and incrementally developed by the accumulated decisions made by individuals, personal opinions are not the source of the law. Indeed, Hale argues in his *History of the Common Law of England*, that it is not really even sensible to speak of an *origin* of the common law.[46]

In a reply to Hobbes' *Dialogue*,[47] Matthew Hale offered a complex defence of the conception of common law as artificial reason: the focus of Hale's argument, some of which is extracted below, is the difference between the study of law and that of other "sciences".[48] Hale begins with a consideration of reason generally and its use in the various areas of knowledge, conceding that the "same faculty of reason" operates in

---

42   Hobbes, *A Dialogue Between a Philosopher and a Student of the Common Laws of England*, p 71.

43   This point is discussed by Gerald Postema in "Some Roots of our Notion of Precedent" in Goldstein (ed), *Precedent in Law* (Clarendon Press, Oxford, 1987), p 13. This article is a very convenient reduction of parts of Postema's much longer work, *Bentham and the Common Law Tradition*.

44   On this point see Postema, *Bentham and the Common Law Tradition*, pp 48-51, 54-55; Sandra Berns, "Judicial Decision Making and Moral Responsibility" (1991) 13 *Adelaide Law Review* 119 at 122.

45   Thomas Hobbes, *A Dialogue Between a Philosopher and a Student of the Common Laws of England*, p 67. See also Hobbes, *Leviathan* (Cambridge University Press, Cambridge, 1991), XVIII, p 88.

46   A relevant extract appears below at [280] (under the heading "Legal Change") and is contrasted with the views of Coke which, on this point, were substantially different from those of Hale.

47   Hale, *Reflections by the Lord Chiefe Justice Hale on Mr Hobbes his Dialogue of the Lawe*.

48   Good expositions of the conflicting positions put by Hobbes and Hale appear in Postema, "Some Roots of our Notion of Precedent", and Yale, "Hobbes and Hale on Law, Legislation and the Sovereign".

different spheres, including law.[49] However, he continues, the use of human reason will not be of much use in the construction of a universally acceptable system of law, simply because moral and political philosophers can never reach sufficient agreement on the characteristics of such an ideal system. The most appropriate way of governing a society cannot be mathematically deduced and any attempt to do so simply results in a multiplicity of different opinions, all of which can be criticised on some ground or other. According to Hale, it is the role of law to bring certainty and stability to government, even though the price to be paid for certainty is often injustice in particular instances.

Hale continues by advancing an argument which can be recognised as the cornerstone of conservative politics: that the test of long experience should ordinarily be preferred to new theories.[50] A law which has withstood the test of time is to be preferred to a law which has simply been devised in a particular era. Although the reasoning in the common law may not be immediately obvious, because it is "the production of long and iterated experience", it cannot simply be discarded or replaced with something which an individual thinks reasonable at a given time. This is not to discount the possibility of legal change: Hale, like later conservative thinkers, viewed change as an incremental process — rather than occurring through arbitrarily imposed laws, it was the result of continuous, but slight, modifications to the common law.[51] The "reason" of the common law, is therefore not comprehensible to those who simply exercise their faculty of reasoning without any other training: it is accessible only to people who have had a long education in the law.

---

49 A modern parallel appears in David Derham, Francis Maher, and Louis Waller, *An Introduction to Law* (7th ed, Law Book Company, NSW, 1995), p 161: "Read a judgement of the High Court of Australia or a textbook on criminal law. You will find that the thinking goes along much the same lines as would be convincing in a theologian's treatise on the Trinity, a scientist's arguments for the acceptance of a new theory, or an historian's estimate of the causes of the Second World War. All use processes of reasoning to draw inferences from principles and facts". The authors continue by considering the specific features of legal reasoning.

50 In considering this part of Hale's argument, Holdsworth cites a passage from the conservative thinker Burke: "The science of government being therefore so practical in itself, and intended for such practical purposes, a matter which requires experience, and even more experience than any person can gain in his whole life, however sagacious and observing he may be, it is with infinite caution that any man ought to venture upon pulling down an edifice which has answered in any tolerable degree for ages the common purposes of society, or on building it up again, without having models and patterns of approved utility before his eyes." Edmund Burke, *Reflections on the Revolution in France and On the Proceedings in Certain Societies in London Relative to That Event* (Penguin Books, Harmondsworth, 1968), p 152. See also Pocock, *The Ancient Constitution and the Feudal Law*, pp 34-35.

51 See Matthew Hale, *History of the Common Law of England*; Edmund Burke, *Reflections on the Revolution in France*, p 106.

Matthew Hale

Reflections by the Lord Chiefe Justice Hale on Mr Hobbes his Dialogue of the Lawe[52]

[265]   In morals and especially with relation to laws for a community, though the common notions of just[ice] and fit are common to all men of reason, yet when persons come to a particular application of those common notions to particular instances and occasions we shall rarely find a common consent or agreement between men though of great reason, and that reason improved by great study and learning — witness the great disagreement between Plato and Aristotle, men of great reason, in the framing of their laws and commonwealth, [and] the great difference in most of the States and kingdoms in the world in their laws, administrations, and measures of right and wrong, when they come to particulars. ...

...

... There are many things especially in laws and governments [which] ... are reasonable to be approved, though the reason of the party doth not presently or immediately and distinctly see its reasonableness. For instance, it is reasonable for me to prefer a law made by a hundred or two hundred persons of age, wisdom, experience, and interest, before a law excogitated by myself ... though I discern better the reason of that law that I have thought of than the reason of the law of those wise men.

Again it is a reason for me to prefer a law by which a kingdom hath been happily governed four or five hundred years, than to adventure the happiness and peace of a kingdom upon some new theory of my own, though I am better acquainted with the reasonableness of my own theory than with that law. Again, I have reason to assure myself that long experience makes more discoveries touching conveniences or inconveniences of laws than is possible for the wisest council of men at first to foresee. And that those amendments and supplements that through the various experiences of wise and knowing men have been applied to any law must needs be better suited to the convenience of laws, than the best invention of the most pregnant wits not aided by such a series and tract of experience.

...

And this adds to the difficulty of a present fathoming of the reason of laws, because they are the production of long and iterated experience which, though it be commonly called the mistress of fools, yet certainly it is the wisest expedient among mankind, and discovers those defects and supplies which no wit of man could either at once foresee or aptly remedy ... And [it is] a foolish and unreasonable thing for any to find fault with an institution because he thinks he could have made a better, or expect a mathematical demonstration to evince the reasonableness of an institution or the self evidence thereof ... Now if any the most refined brain under heaven would go about to enquire by speculation, or by reading of Plato or Aristotle, or by considering the laws of the Jews, or other nations, to find out how lands descend in England, or how estates are there transferred, or transmitted among us, he would lose his labour, and spend his notions in vain, [un]til he acquainted himself with the laws of England, and the reason is because they are institutions introduced by the will and consent of others implicitly by custom and usage, or explicitly by written laws or Acts of Parliament.

And upon all this that hath been said it appears that men are not born common lawyers, neither can the bare exercise of the faculty of reason give a man a sufficient knowledge of it, but it must be gained by the habituating and accustoming and exercising that faculty by reading, study and observation to give a man a complete knowledge thereof. ...

[270] We can contrast this idea of there being an accumulated artificial reason which underlies the law with theories of law which see it as being, in some sense, authorised by natural reason.[53] A law informed by natural reason could be derived simply by the thinking process — by thinking about what is right or necessary in society. As Hale points out, many political philosophers have thought that they could derive good systems of law and political organisation simply by utilising their faculty of reason. But, of course, they have come up with many different and widely divergent perceptions about law.[54] Arguably modern natural lawyers have had no better results. However, the existence and widespread acceptance of principles of human rights does provide an appearance of some agreement on fundamental norms, despite debate over the heritage and interpretation of these norms. In the arguments which have been outlined above, the failure of natural reason to provide any common agreement about law has led, alternatively, to recognising artificial legal reasoning as the basis of law and putting a single authority, such as a sovereign or legislature, in a position to make judgements for individuals. Artificial reason is seen to provoke less controversy than natural law because it is based on a body of settled principle and therefore leaves no room for the subjective opinions of a particular person.

In common law countries "legal education" still means (at least in part) education in "legal reasoning" since, as Hale put it, "men are not born Common Lawyers" — simply developing a capacity for rational thought will not give any insight into the common law (precisely the opposite, you may think). Only legal education, to use the modern term, can facilitate the capacity to think like a lawyer.[55] Of course, we need seriously to reflect upon what "thinking like a lawyer" means in a wider social and philosophical context. Legal education has been criticised as

---

53   I will discuss some of these theories in Chapter 3.

54   Hale, *Reflections by the Lord Chiefe Justice Hale on Mr Hobbes his Dialogue of the Lawe*, p 503; Hobbes *Dialogue*, p 54

55   Hale, *Reflections by the Lord Chiefe Justice Hale on Mr Hobbes his Dialogue of the Lawe*, p 505. See generally Sugarman, "Legal Theory, the Common Law Mind, and the making of the Textbook Tradition" in William Twining (ed), *Legal Theory and the Common Law Mind* (Basil Blackwell, Oxford, 1986).

a "training for hierarchy"[56] or a simple legitimation of the existing ideology and power relations of legal practice. There can be little doubt that much legal education has indeed been directed at reproducing established approaches to law, its relation to society and the role of the lawyer. In this way, legal reasoning itself can be seen to conserve past legal structures: this conservatism is amply evidenced in Coke's and Hale's attitude to the legal past.

Legal Change

[275]   One of the problems for common law thought which has endured into 20th century jurisprudence relates to how the process of legal change can adequately be described. There are several different aspects of this question. In the first place, there would seem to be some difficulty with conceptualising legal change itself. If judicial decisions are primarily determined by a complex configuration of past decisions (increasingly modified by legislation) then how can we theorise meaningful and lasting change through the common law process?[57] To put it in the context of this chapter, if that which is old is valued primarily because of its age, then how can new principles or areas of law develop which have a comparable legal value? If judges only declare a law which represents a collective, immemorial wisdom, then how does the law change?[58] These questions may seem a little artificial at the present time, when we take it for granted that judges will deliberately examine, distinguish, alter, or reject precedents, and in this way achieve change incrementally or, at least in the case of a superior court, with a rapidity which is sometimes legislative in its effect.[59] In fact, it is perhaps because we are so accustomed to legislation, that we no longer have the attitude that the age and endurance of a common law principle is testimony to its value. The modern controversy is focused on the proper balance

---

56   Duncan Kennedy, "Legal Education as a Training for Hierarchy" in Kairys (ed), *The Politics of Law: A Progressive Critique* (revised ed, Pantheon Books, New York, 1990); Margaret Thornton, *Portia Lost in the Groves of Academe Wondering What to do About Legal Education* (La Trobe University Legal Studies, Melbourne, 1991).

57   See Freeman, *Lloyd's Introduction to Jurisprudence* on the question of balance between judicial innovation and determinism. For a modern view, see Alan Hutchinson, *Evolution and the Common Law* (Cambridge University Press, Cambridge, 2005).

58   See Roger Cotterrell, *The Politics of Jurisprudence*, pp 26-30; Pocock, *The Ancient Constitution and the Feudal Law*, p 36.

59   A multitude of Australian High Court cases from the 1990s demonstrates this spirit of innovation, directed partly by the court's sense of responsibility to the community; some obvious recent cases include *Mabo v Queensland (No 2)* (1992) 175 CLR 1; *R v L* (1991) 103 ALR 577; *Commonwealth v Tasmania (The Dams Case)* (1983) 158 CLR 1. See generally Brian Galligan, *The Politics of the High Court* (UQ Press, St Lucia, 1987).

between certainty and innovation.[60] Nevertheless, the paradox inherent in the common law is that it is essentially conservative of its own being, but at the same time reliant on innovation; however the source of that innovation is theorised. The law is always received by the judge, yet only the judge has the capacity to determine the law for a particular case.

A further aspect of the problem concerns the relationship between the development of the common law and its social environment. In *SGIC v Trigwell*[61] several High Court judges stated explicitly that the court could not alter the common law simply because of social change.[62] Again, this attitude seems somewhat outdated: in the last two decades of the 20th century judges were much more explicit about the public policy grounds of their decisions. A slightly more philosophical question is whether the contemporary common law system is essentially the same system as that which prevailed in 13th century England. This is an interesting theoretical question because an answer will depend on how the identity of the object, in this case the law, is conceptualised. If there is virtually nothing of the substance and very little of the form of 13th century common law left in modern common law systems, can we meaningfully say that the system itself has endured? Well, that depends primarily on how the identity of a legal system is perceived — not only the identity through time (to what extent is modern British law continuous with its past?) but also across jurisdictions (where does Australian law stop and British, US, or Canadian law start?) Is there a "common law" identity, not merely derived from the fact of a shared heritage, but also derived from cross-jurisdictional influences?

To some extent, such questions hold little interest in a context where an analysis of concepts of law is perceived as less significant than studies examining the connections between law and its social context. Nevertheless, we need to remember that questions like these have been raised relatively recently, for instance, by Julius Stone, a fact which reveals some continuity between modern jurisprudence and classical common law theory. (It is also crucial to remember that the judiciary, at least in common law jurisdictions, is potentially, though not always actually, a very powerful agency for law reform.) In "The Ratio of the Ratio Decidendi" Stone begins by articulating what he sees as the fundamental paradox or mystery at the centre of the common law — that its essentially conservative emphasis on the past is itself the vehicle of legal development.

---

60 A very good example of this debate appears in (1992) 15 *University of New South Wales Law Journal*: Patrick Atiyah, "Justice and Predictability in the Common Law" (1992) 15 *University of New South Wales Law Journal* 448. Atiyah's article is followed by a reply by Michael Kirby, "In Praise of Common Law Renewal" (1992) 15 *University of New South Wales Law Review* 462.

61 (1978) 26 ALR 67.

62 See, for instance, the comments made by Barwick CJ at 70. A quotation from this judgment appears above at [220], in the section entitled "Law and Declaration".

Julius Stone
"The Ratio of the Ratio Decidendi"[63]

[280]   Poor, indeed, must be the common lawyer who has not paused to ask, with Lord Wright, how the "perpetual process of change" in the body of common law "can be reconciled with the principle of authority and the rule of *stare decisis?*" Beneath the dry and niggling distinctions, the flat frustrating contradictions, behind the bold dynamic precept suddenly emasculated or the mouldering precedent revivified by a new constellation of facts, behind the wavering alternations of judicial caution and judicial valour, coyness and courage, the lawyer of imaginative intelligence must be conscious of the elements of a perennial mystery. He is challenged to ask what magic at the heart of the system of *stare decisis* can transform a symbol of immobility into a vehicle of change? And the challenge confronts him in the dimension both of space and time. In the dimension of space the English common law continues to spread, independently of the powers of political sovereignty, over substantial parts of the globe, and even amidst the uncertainties of our age, its place as a major legal heritage of all mankind seems assured. In the dimension of time this corpus juris already approaches its second millennium of traceable history as a living system of law.

It remains a common assumption among most of us, even today, that the present common law is somehow still one with that common law whose origins we trace back into the early centuries of the modern world. We think of it as a single system of law, somehow linked into unity throughout time. And it is perhaps in this assumed link that we should look for the deepest seat of mystery ...

...

The doctrine of *stare decisis*, in addition to whatever it may enjoin upon the intellect, certainly evokes an atmosphere and a mood to abide by ancient decisions, to follow the old ways, and conform to existing precedents. It suggests a condition of rest, even of stasis, a system of law whose content is more or less settled, the past content by past decisions, and the present and future content because they too are controlled by those past decisions. It implies the stability of the legal system along the stream of time, that despite all the vast social, economic and technological changes of the last eight or nine hundred years, society remains nevertheless in some meaningful sense under the governance of the same system of law.

[285]   Stone's "mystery" — that a developing system of law is governed by a principle of conservation — may not, as I have indicated, seem particularly profound in an environment where so much scholarly interest is centred on the social effects of law. What is significant here is that the mystery is centred on a conception of law as retaining its identity through time and across jurisdictions. Stone highlights the unity of the legal domain and its evolutionary characteristics, rather than that which makes it different, even radically different, from its own earlier versions.

63   Stone, "The Ratio of the Ratio Decidendi" (1959) 22 *Modern Law Review* 597 at 597, 597-598.

I have dwelt on these matters primarily because the question of legal change is one which clearly distinguishes the two principal common law jurists whose work has been outlined in this chapter. So far, I have described the ideas of Hale and Coke together and it is true that they converge on the basic matters which I have described. But there is an essential difference between their views, which relates to the notion of legal change. Put briefly, Coke wished to preserve both the formal and substantive identity of the common law, arguing that it had an ancient origin and that the minor changes which had occurred were degenerative, rather than progressive. In contrast, Hale pointed out that no single origin of the common law, either ancient or otherwise, could be satisfactorily identified, and that it had grown and developed in accordance with the requirements of society.

Coke

[290]   Coke, and several others of his era,[64] insisted that the common law had originated in ancient times, before the Norman Conquest, and that it had continued virtually in an unchanged form since that time. The common law, in other words, had always existed from ancient times in much the same form in which Coke found it in the early 17th century, it was "the presence of God in England, an antique language dressed in a sacramental language of its own, existent outside history and beyond memory".[65] (This idea is sometimes referred to as the doctrine of the "ancient constitution".[66]) Fortescue had claimed that English law was of great antiquity, having survived invasions by the Romans, Saxons, Danes, and Normans. Fortescue's proof of the goodness of the laws was that even the Romans had kept them, who otherwise would have replaced English law with their own, as they had done everywhere else.[67] Coke also took literally the idea of law as immemorial wisdom: in the context of 17th century England it was important to emphasise the non-political nature of law and its agents,[68] and arguing that the existent law was of an ancient or immemorial origin was one way of escaping the charge that the judiciary had merely arbitrarily invented it from time to time according to political necessity. It was also a means

---

64   For details, see Peter Goodrich, *Oedipus Lex: Psychoanalysis, History, Law* (University of California Press, Berkeley, 1995), especially pp 81-89. See also generally Peter Goodrich, *Languages of Law: From Logics of Memory to Nomadic Masks* (Weidenfeld and Nicolson, London, 1990), pp 83-90.

65   Goodrich, *Languages of Law*, p 84. On this point see also Cotterrell, *The Politics of Jurisprudence*, p 27; Pocock, *The Ancient Constitution and the Feudal Law*, p 37; Charles Gray, "Editors Introduction" in Hale, *The History of the Common Law of England*, p xxiii.

66   In *Wallyng v Meger* (1470) 47 Selden Society 38, Catesby is reported to have said, "Common law has existed since the creation of the world". See generally Pocock, *The Ancient Constitution and the Feudal Law*, especially ch 2 "The Common Law Mind: Custom and the Immemorial".

67   John Fortescue, *De Laudibus Legum Angliae* (Sweet and Maxwell, London, 1917), ch 17.

68   See Cotterrell, *The Politics of Jurisprudence*, p 27.

of defending English law against what Coke saw as the treason of importing foreign (especially Roman) ideas into common law. As Peter Goodrich argues, the myth of the origin of the common law "lends an identity to a tradition that is otherwise and self-evidently polyglot, partial, and impermanent."[69]

That Coke was able to hold such an extreme view in the face of much written and unwritten evidence of dramatic legal change and deliberate innovation, especially after the Norman Conquest, seems quite remarkable, and he went to considerable lengths to furnish historical proof of his ideas.[70] Coke habitually took literally somewhat dubious sources which tended to support his thesis or provide evidence of an ancient precedent. One such discredited source was the *Mirror of Justices*, which Coke accepted as a record of King Arthur's law. Maitland commented "It would be long to tell how much harm was thus done to the sober study of English legal history".[71] Indeed Pocock describes Coke's sense of history as "founded on the presumption that any legal judgement declaring a right immemorial is perfectly valid as a statement of history."[72]

Notwithstanding the apparent historical naivety of Coke's thought, it is important not to simplify or reduce his ideas to the obviously indefensible belief in a legal system which had for centuries remained identical to its original form in some remote era. As Gray points out, Coke "did not inhabit a fool's eternity, where the law of 17th-century England looked simply indistinguishable from Anglo-Saxon law."[73] Gray explains that Coke saw legal change as essentially either "degenerative" or "restorative". In other words, by taking existence from time immemorial as the proper standard of legal validity any departure from an immemorial principle would generally represent a degeneration of the legal system. However, given that some such degenerative changes had inevitably occurred, change could also be aimed at restoring the original state of the law.[74] The idea that the common law, in its true, original form would eventually conquer all false diversions, was evidently part of Coke's general epistemological views. In the following passage, Coke contrasts Truth and falsity, arguing that Truth is such that she will in the end prevail. Coke posits a clear, though untheorised, division between Truth and falsity, or Error — a dichotomising habit of mind which is still not uncommon. (It is interesting that both Truth and Error in their metaphysical conflict are attributed the female gender, while mortal men of "great capacity and excellent parts" struggle continually to attain Truth.)

---

69   Goodrich, *Oedipus Lex*, p 81.

70   Pocock, *The Ancient Constitution and the Feudal Law*, pp 35-45.

71   Introduction to the *Mirror of Justices* (1893) 7 Selden Society.

72   Pocock, *The Ancient Constitution and the Feudal Law*, p 38.

73   Gray, "Editor's Introduction", p xxiii.

74   Gray, "Editor's Introduction", pp xxiv-xxv. See also Yale, "Hobbes and Hale on Law, Legislation, and the Sovereign", pp 127-128.

Edward Coke
Preface to the Fifth Reports

[295]   It is truly said (good reader) that Error (Ignorance being her inseparable twin) doth in her proceeding so infinitely multiply her self, produceth such monstrous and strange chimaeras, floateth in such and so many uncertainties, and sucketh down the poison from the contagious breath of Ignorance, as all such into whom she infuseth any of her poisoned breath, she dangerously infects or intoxicates; and that which is wonderful, before she can come to any end, she bringeth all things (if she be not prevented) by confusion to a miserable and untimely end; ... On the other side, truth cannot be supported or defended by any thing but by truth herself, and is of that constitution and constancy, as she cannot at any time, or in any part or point be disagreeable to herself; she hateth all bombasting and sophistication, and bringeth with her certainty, unity, simplicity, and peace at the last ... Error and falsehood are of that condition, as without any resistance they will in time of themselves fade and fall away: but such is the state of truth, that though many do impugn her, yet will she of herself ever prevail in the end, and flourish like the palm tree; she may peradventure by force for a time be trodden down, but never by any means whatsoever can she be trodden out. There is no subject of this realm, but being truly instructed by good and plain evidence of his ancient and undoubted patrimony and birthright, (tho' he hath for some time by ignorance, false persuasion, or vain fear, been deceived or dispossessed) but will consult with learned and faithful counsellors for the recovery of the same: the ancient and excellent laws of England are the birthright, and the most ancient and best inheritance that the subjects of this realm have, for by them he enjoyeth not only his inheritance and goods in peace and quietness, but his life and his most dear country in safety. And for that I fear that many of my dear countrymen, (and most of them of great capacity and excellent parts) for want of understanding of their own evidence, do want the true knowledge of their ancient birth-right in some points of greatest importance.

[2100] Truth (and the ancient legal order) is certain, simple, constant and pure, while Error is a loathsome monster sucking poison and reproducing herself infinitely.

This figuration of Error and Truth, which, not coincidentally, dichotomises femaleness into either vile monstrosity or pure goodness,[75] was not peculiar to Coke. The first book of Edmund Spenser's *Faerie Queene* allegorises, in similar terms, the conflict between goodness and error. The scene is set with the knight "Holiness" who is "pricking on the plaine" apparently in furtherance of an adventure given to him by "greatest Gloriana" (Queen Elizabeth I). Holiness is followed by a pure white lady riding a (less) white ass, and leading a (milky) white lamb. Very pretty. The lady, needless to say, is pure, innocent, and of royal stock. The interesting part begins when, on entering a mysterious wood, they stumble on Error's den. Error is cast as an

---

75   See Andrea Dworkin, *Woman Hating* (EP Dutton, New York, 1974), Pt 1 "The Fairy Tales".

> ugly monster plaine,
>
> Halfe like a serpent horribly displaide,
>
> But th'other halfe did womans shape retaine,
>
> Most lothsome, filthie, foule, and full of vile disdain. (bk I, canto I, 14)

Like Coke's Error, she breathes poison and is surrounded by a multitude of ugly offspring. In true manly style (and more afraid of being shamed than physically harmed), Holiness overcomes Error. Truth may be trodden down, but will never be trodden out. It is interesting to note the lengths to which "Truth" or "her" representatives will go to insult "Error" and "her" offspring, while relying on "her" own purity and obvious moral superiority.

Some centuries later, in a reflective spirit which was to pre-empt some of the themes of postmodernism, the German philosopher Friedrich Nietzsche attacked the simplistic dichotomy between truth and lies, arguing that truth itself is conventional (that is, determined by convention). If, as Nietzsche claimed, truths "are illusions which we have forgotten are illusions" and are laid down by common ways of speaking, then the distinction between truth and lies is rather difficult to define satisfactorily for "to be truthful means to employ the usual metaphors" and "to lie according to a fixed convention".[76] Truth, in other words, is only possible within a framework of conventions, none of which themselves can be said to be "true", since they are just norms which govern what counts as truth. I will return to the matter of the conventional nature of truth (including legal truth, legal theory, and indeed any theory) in Chapter 8.

Hale

[2105] In contrast to Coke, Hale possessed what DEC Yale characterises as a "truly historical sense".[77] Hale saw the common law as a tradition which could not be described definitively, or frozen at a particular point of time, and he emphatically rejected the notion that there had been a single and identifiable source of the common law. He pointed out (and the argument does seem irrefutable to the modern mind) that, in fact, English law had come from several sources, including Danish, Norman, Saxon, and ancient British customs and that these elements had been indistinguishably mixed in the process of legal development. Hale saw the common law as a movement which changed through time: though continually developing, the common law retained its identity because

---

76 FW Nietzsche, "On Truth and Lies in a Nonmoral Sense"; FW Nietzsche, *Philosophy and Truth: Selections from Nietzsche's Notebooks of the Early 1870s*, Breazeale (ed) (London, Humanities Press, 1979), pp 79, 84. See also Jacques Derrida, "White Mythology: Metaphor in the Text of Philosophy" in *Margins of Philosophy* (University of Chicago Press, 1982), p 207.

77 Yale, "Hobbes and Hale on Law, Legislation, and the Sovereign", p 121.

of its continuity with the past. In his *History of the Common Law of England*, Hale compares the common law with the ship of the Argonauts which, it was said, was altered and underwent so many repairs that when it returned it didn't contain any of its original materials. The philosophical question is, is it the same ship? Hale answers that it is. Or, he says, the common law is like a human body: although the material elements may change entirely in the course of a seven-year period, the body is still that of the same person. Even if there is nothing at all left of the original material of the common law,[78] it retains its identity and also its significance as the representative of national unity and security, because of the continuation through time of the common law tradition.

Sir Matthew Hale

History of the Common Law of England[79]

[2110]   The Kingdom of England being a very ancient Kingdom, has had many Vicissitudes and changes (especially before the coming in of King William I.) under several either Conquests or Accessions of Foreign Nations. For tho' the Britains were, as is supposed, the most ancient Inhabitants, yet there were mingled with them, the Romans, the Picts, the Saxons, the Danes, and lastly, the Normans; and many of those Foreigners were as it were incorporated together, and made one Common People and Nation; and hence arises the Difficulty, and indeed Moral Impossibility, of giving any satisfactory or so much as probable Conjecture, touching the Original of the Laws, for the following Reasons, *viz*.

First, From the Nature of the Laws themselves in general, which being to be accommodated to the Conditions, Exigencies and Conveniencies of the People, for or by whom they are appointed, as those Exigencies and Conveniencies do insensibly grow upon the people, so many Times there grows insensibly a Variation of Laws, especially in a long Tract of Time; and hence it is, that tho' for the Purpose in some particular Part of the Common Law of England, we may easily say, That the Common Law, as it is now taken, is otherwise than it was in that particular Part or Point in the time of Hen[ry] 2. when Glanville wrote, or than it was in the time of Hen[ry] 3. when Bracton wrote, yet it is not possible to assign the certain Time when the Change began ... But tho' those particular Variations and Accessions have happened in the Laws, yet they being only partial and successive, we may with just Reason say, They are the same English Laws now, that they were 600 Years since in the general. As the Argonauts Ship was the same when it returned home, as it was when it went out, tho' in that long Voyage it had successive Amendments, and scarce came back with any of its former Materials; and as Titius is the same Man he was 40 Years since, tho' Physicians tells us, That in a Tract of seven Years, the Body has scarce any of the same Material Substance it had before.

---

78   As Postema points out, "This is surely the message of the figure of the Argonaut's ship": *Bentham and the Common Law Tradition*, p 22.

79   Hale, *The History of the Common Law of England*, "Touching the Original of the Common Law of England", pp 39-43.

...

> *Secondly*, the 2d Difficulty of the Discovery of the Original of the English
> Laws is this, That this Kingdom has many and great Vicissitudes of People
> that inhabited it, and that in their several Times prevail'd and obtain'd a
> great Hand in the Government of this Kingdom, whereby it came to pass,
> that there arose a great Mixture and Variety of Laws: In some Places the
> Laws of the Saxons, in some Places the Laws of the Danes, in some Places
> the Laws of the ancient Britains, in some Places the Laws of the Mercians,
> and in some Places, or among some People (perhaps) the Laws of the
> Normans: ... so that altho' the Body and Gross of the Law might continue
> the same, and so continue the ancient Denomination that it first had, yet
> it must needs receive diverse Accessions from the Laws of those People that
> were thus intermingled with the ancient Britains or Saxons, as the Rivers of
> Severn, Thames, Trent, &c tho' they continue the same Denomination which
> their first stream had, yet have the accession of divers other Streams added
> to them in the Tracts of their Passage which enlarge and augment them.
> And hence grew those several Denominations of the Saxon, Mercian, and
> Danish Laws, out of which (as before is shewn) the Confessor extracted his
> Body of the Common Law, and therefore among all those various
> Ingredients and Mixtures of Laws, it is almost an impossible Piece of
> Chymistry to reduce every *Caput Legis* to its true Original, as to say, This is
> a Piece of the Danish, this of the Norman, or this of the Saxon or
> British Law ...

[2115] This approach is the one which prevailed in common law theory,[80] possibly because the rapid increase of legal writing and with it the evidence of substantial and ongoing legal change would eventually have made the belief in a static "ancient constitution" impossible.

Critiques of Common Law Theory and Practice

[2120] Jonathan Swift was not very impressed by the common law system as it operated in 18th century England. His satirical account of it in *Gulliver's Travels* has a peculiarly timeless quality, attacking as it does both the notion of an artificial reason which leads to obscurity and injustice and the use of precedents, which it seems can be used for anything:

---

80 For instance, a similar view was put much later by the legal historian Frederic William
    Maitland, who wrote: "Hardly a rule remains unaltered, and yet the body of law that now
    lives among us is the same body that Blackstone described in the eighteenth century,
    Coke in the seventeenth, Littleton in the fifteenth, Bracton in the thirteenth, Glanvill in
    the twelfth." "Outlines of English Legal History 560-1600" in Fisher (ed), *The Collected
    Papers of Frederic William Maitland* (Cambridge University Press, Cambridge, 1911), Vol II,
    p 418. See also the comments made by Julius Stone in the extract above at [280].

Jonathan Swift

Gulliver's Travels[81]

[2125] I said there was a society of men among us, bred up from their youth in the art of proving by words multiplied for the purpose, that white is black, and black is white, according as they are paid. To this society all the rest of the people are slaves. For example, if my neighbour hath a mind to my cow, he hires a lawyer to prove that he ought to have my cow from me. I must then hire another to defend my right, it being against all rules of law that any man should be allowed to speak for himself. Now in this case, I who am the true owner lie under two great disadvantages. First, my lawyer, being practised almost from his cradle in defending falsehood, is quite out of his element when he would be an advocate for justice, which as an office unnatural, he always attempts with great awkwardness, if not with ill-will. The second disadvantage is, that my lawyer must proceed with great caution, or else he will be reprimanded by the Judges, and abhorred by his brethren, as one who would lessen the practice of the law. And therefore I have but two methods to preserve my cow. The first is to gain over my adversary's lawyer with a double fee, who will then betray his client by insinuating that he hath justice on his side. The second way is for my lawyer to make my cause appear as unjust as he can, by allowing the cow to belong to my adversary; and this if it be skilfully done will certainly bespeak the favour of the Bench.

Now, your Honour is to know that these Judges are persons appointed to decide all controversies of property, as well as for the trial of criminals, and picked out from the most dexterous lawyers who are grown old or lazy, and having been biased all their lives against truth and equity, lie under such a fatal necessity of favouring fraud, perjury, and oppression, that I have known several of them refuse a large bribe from the side where justice lay, rather than injure the *Faculty* by doing anything unbecoming their nature or their office.

It is a maxim among these lawyers, that whatever hath been done before, may legally be done again: and therefore they take special care to record all the decisions formerly made against common justice and the general reason of mankind. These, under the name of *precedents*, they produce as authorities to justify the most iniquitous opinions; and the Judges never fail of directing accordingly.

In pleading, they studiously avoid entering into the *merits* of the cause; but are loud, violent and tedious in dwelling upon all *circumstances* which are not to the purpose. For instance, in the case already mentioned; they never desire to know what claim or title my adversary hath to my cow, but whether the said cow were red or black, her horns long or short; whether the field I graze her in be round or square, whether she were milked at home or abroad, what diseases she is subject to, and the like; after which they consult *precedents*, adjourn the cause from time to time, and in ten, twenty, or thirty years come to an issue.

---

81 Jonathon Swift, *Gulliver's Travels* (Harmonsworth Penguin, 1967) bk 4, ch 5.

> It is likewise to be observed that this society hath a peculiar cant and jargon of their own, that no other mortal can understand, and wherein all their laws are written, which they take special care to multiply; whereby they have wholly confounded the very essence of truth and falsehood, of right and wrong; so that it will take thirty years to decide whether the field, left me by my ancestors for six generations, belong to me or to a stranger three hundred miles off.

> In the trial of persons accused for crimes against the state the method is much more short and commendable: the Judge first sends to sound the disposition of those in power, after which he can easily hang or save the criminal, strictly preserving all the forms of law.

[2130] It was probably the work of Jeremy Bentham and, in particular, the forceful nature of his critique of common law thought, which effected a significant (though not total, as I have indicated) break with that tradition.[82] Bentham criticised virtually every facet of common law jurisprudence for its general obscurity, inaccessibility, and illogicality. He was especially critical of the system of precedent, arguing that it perpetuates unjust legal doctrines, is susceptible to manipulation by corrupt judges and is inherently incapable of revealing with sufficient clarity the state of the law. He saw precedent as productive of many overly technical and incoherent doctrines (many of which are still with us), as being therefore quite inaccessible except to those who have sufficient legal training and as utilising an essentially retrospective method of adjudication. In relation to this final point, he called common law "dog law", because it treats legal subjects like animals in need of training:[83]

> When your dog does anything you want to break him of, you wait till he does it, and then beat him for it. This is the way you make laws for your dog: and this is the way the judges make law for you and me. They won't tell a man beforehand what it is he *should not* do ... they lie by till he has done something which they say he should not *have done*, and then they hang him for it.

And further:[84]

> [*ex post facto* law] is an abomination interwoven in the very essence of that spurious and impostrous substitute, which, to its makers and their dupes, is an object of such prostrate admiration, and such indefatigable eulogy, under the name of *common* or *unwritten* law.

Assuming that the declaratory theory is not supportable, the logical conclusion is indeed that the common law method is inherently retrospective. If judges make law and, in the same instance, apply it to the case before them, they are in effect determining retrospectively the legal relationship between the parties. Yet such retrospectivity is

---

82   See generally Postema, *Bentham and the Common Law Tradition*.

83   John Bowring (ed), *The Works of Jeremy Bentham* (Russell and Russell, New York, 1962), Vol 5, p 235.

84   Bowring (ed), *The Works of Jeremy Bentham*, Vol 4, p 460.

arguably unavoidable in any case: even statutes require interpretation and, in that sense, their effect can never be determined in advance.

Bentham saw nothing good about the common law. Far from being rational or based on an immemorial wisdom, he saw it as an incoherent conglomeration of technical rules, a "shapeless heap of odds and ends" or "prodigious mass of rubbish", made in an arbitrary fashion by judges according to whatever moral or political whim they felt like applying. He described the function of judges as resting on "power everywhere arbitrary, with the semblance of a set of rules to serve as a screen to it."[85] Interestingly, this sort of criticism has resurfaced in modern critiques of law, in particular those of the realists and the critical legal studies movement.[86] The aims and effect of these critiques are, however, somewhat different. But it is interesting to note that although positivism has become the major theoretical perspective of philosophers and jurists in the 20th century, legal systems based upon the common law do not seem to have become any less obscure or technical, or more rational (though that may depend on what we mean by "rational"). The criticism of law as being alien to the people it is supposed to govern is still relevant.

Bentham's aim in criticising the common law tradition was to have it replaced by a comprehensive legal code, based on the principle of utility (ie, maximising happiness — the details of what this involves in Bentham's thought are far too complex to consider here). In 1811, Bentham even wrote to the President of the United States, James Madison, offering to draft such a code for the United States, arguing that until the common law was abolished entirely it would corrupt any law created by the legislature.

Modern criticisms have tended to be directed towards the inherent conservatism of the classical common law approach, or at the notion that judges only declare the law. In "The Path of the Law" Oliver Wendell Holmes said:[87]

> It is revolting to have no better reason for a rule of law than that so it was laid down in the time of Henry IV. It is still more revolting if the grounds upon which it was laid down have vanished long since, and the rule simply persists from blind imitation of the past.

This statement has been fairly influential, especially in the United States where the doctrine of precedent is more flexible than it is in Australia or the United Kingdom. Yet, even an increasingly open attitude to precedent has not made Holmes' argument redundant. In an uncomfortably recent US Supreme Court decision, *Bowers v Hardwick*, where the constitutionality of a Georgia statute making homosexual

---

85   Bowring (ed), *The Works of Jeremy Bentham*, Vol 4, p 460.

86   See Chapters 4 and 5, below.

87   Oliver Wendell Holmes, "The Path of the Law" in *Collected Legal Papers* (Harcourt, Brace and Howe, New York, 1920), p 187.

sodomy a criminal offence was being considered, Justice White, in the majority, cited the supposedly "ancient" roots of the prohibition of homosexual behaviour (a claim which, whatever else it is, ignores certain historical facts).[88] Where convenient, it is still possible for judges to use ancient authority or their own constructions of it in support of their views. In dissent, Justice Blackmun quoted Holmes and rejected White's reliance on the past and present existence of certain statutes as a method of reading the US constitution.[89]

As indicated earlier, one of the most frequent controversies associated with the residue of classical common law thought in the twentieth century concerns its supposed reliance on a view of law as somehow exterior to, and separate from, social and political contingencies.[90] It is as though the law is really "out there" somewhere, existing in an ideal place, waiting to be discovered and declared by the judges. Oliver Wendell Holmes attacked this idealistic notion in his famous statement that "law is not a brooding omnipresence in the sky".[91] Equally evocative are Lord Reid's comments in "The Judge as Lawmaker":[92]

> There was a time when it was thought almost indecent to suggest that judges make law — they only declare it. Those with a taste for fairy tales seem to have thought that in some Aladdin's cave there is hidden the Common Law in all its splendour and that on a judge's appointment there descends on him knowledge of the magic words Open Sesame. Bad decisions are given when the judge has muddled the pass word and the wrong door opens. But we do not believe in fairy tales any more.

In defence of common law theory, it should be pointed out that Holmes and Reid appear both to have put a modern interpretation on the idea that judges merely declare the law. According to this modern view, if the individual judge, or any individual, could not deliberately alter the law, the law would be a brooding omnipresence in the sky, associated more with the idea of a natural law which exists independently of human agency. Of course it would be inappropriate, and somewhat naïve, to suggest today that individual judges do not have a role in determining the future direction of the law. But that does not mean that the common law thinkers were similarly naïve. As I have attempted to explain, the situation is somewhat more complex and cannot be

---

88 *Bowers v Hardwick* (1986) 478 US 186 at 192-194.

89 Good critiques of this decision have been written by Drucilla Cornell, "Law Dressed up as Justice" in Cornell, *The Philosophy of the Limit* (Routledge, New York, 1991) and Rhonda Copelon, "A Crime Not Fit to be Named: Sex, Lies, and the Constitution" in Kairys (ed), *The Politics of Law: A Progressive Critique*.

90 The definition of a "Higher Law" used by John Dickinson in "The Law Beyond Law: Part 1" (929) 29 *Columbia Law Review* 113 at 114 is "a system of independently existing and inherently valid law having its source wholly outside government".

91 *Southern Pacific Co v Jensen* (1916) 244 US 205.

92 Reid, "The Judge as Lawmaker" (1972) 12 *Journal of the Society of Public Teachers of Law* (ns) 22 at 22.

reduced to modern jurisprudential analysis. The dominant view of English common law was that it represented an accumulation of communal wisdom, and was, in that sense, customary. Far from being "out there" or external to the human dimension, social relations over the ages were its real source. It was not simply a set of principles imposed on a society, which is how we presently tend to regard the law, but part of the fundamental structure of the community and thus indistinguishable from it. So while belief in an "Aladdin's cave" is certainly somewhat unrealistic in these individualistic times, it does not accurately reflect the common law consciousness.

Common Law and Modern Jurisprudence

[2135] It is clear from this outline of common law theory that in many ways its legacy is still with us — in the way we think about legal development in the common law, about the process of judicial reasoning, and in the distinction between making law and deciding particular disputes. This latter distinction remains with us even though the doctrine of precedent relies upon the possibility of extracting general and often novel principles from decided cases. Without a doctrine of precedent the distinction between making general rules as a legislative, creative function and deciding particular cases as a judicial function is not particularly problematic, because decisions are never attributed any *meaning* which can survive the effect on the parties to the dispute. The doctrine of precedent, on the other hand, presupposes a wider meaning (such as a *ratio decidendi*) which is read into a decision and which then becomes applied in later cases. According to our current understanding, the doctrine of precedent means that the judicial function is essentially mixed, inasmuch as it involves both laying down general propositions of law and applying pre-existing law to a fact situation. I say that this is our view now because, as I have explained, this was not the perception of the classical common lawyers. For them there was no contradiction in the judicial function, partly because the doctrine of precedent was not as clearly established as it is now, but also because they viewed any general propositions made by a judge as being merely a declaration of existing law.

Another fundamental difference between the classical and the modern views is that modern legal philosophers tend to see law as largely a matter of *positive* rules, doctrines, or other standards which can at any time be reasonably clearly stated by anyone sufficiently educated in the law, and afterwards applied to fact situations. To say that something is seen to be a *positive* legal principle means that it has been created by someone — by a legislative body, or by the courts. I will have more to say about this in the next chapter. In contrast, the classical common lawyers thought that the law which they were declaring pre-existed and was therefore superior to merely created law.

Dworkin, legal change and evolution

[2140] Ronald Dworkin has developed a modern version of the theory that judges do not make law, but rather determine the outcomes of cases by applying existing legal principles. One of the positivist objections to the common law view that judges only declare the law was that, in some cases at least (so-called "hard cases"), there is no clear rule of law to apply so the judge must determine one and apply it to the case, effectively legislating retrospectively. The judge has a broad discretion to create legal standards in order to decide the case before her. Dworkin objects to this argument on several grounds. His first objection is that the positivists assume that law is a system of rules whereas it is clearly composed not only of rules, but also of less formal principles, policies and standards.[93] Dworkin's argument on this point has been criticised on the grounds that even positivists do not characterise law as composed only of rules. As Joseph Raz and others have pointed out, reliance on a formal concept of rules is not at all essential to positivism.[94] Secondly, Dworkin builds on the understanding of law as composed of principles to argue that the law is in fact a "seamless web", or should be regarded that way by judges. Dworkin's aim is to minimise the emphasis on discretion by arguing that there is always, notwithstanding the absence of explicit legal principles on a matter, a right way of deciding a case. Even where there is no previous decision on a matter, the decision is generated by an attempt to act coherently within the web of principles. Dworkin relies both on the critique of judge-made law as unjustly retrospective, and on the ideal that in a democratic society the law should be made by elected representatives. Yet it is hard to see why, when the state of the law is unclear, the injustice of retrospectivity is avoided by Dworkin's theory. It will not matter whether there really was, at the time of a dispute arising, a right accruing to one party if no-one but a subsequent judge knows about it. What difference does a jurisprudential theory that there is always a right in a legal conflict make to the parties, when it is still up to the judge to discover and declare the law? The injustice of retrospectivity and the injustice of legal obscurity and uncertainty are surely not going to look very different to the parties.

In *Law's Empire*, Dworkin attempted to take on board the failure of the earlier versions of his theory to account for the necessity for interpretation of both statutes and common law in judicial decision-making. In this work Dworkin accepts that there is substantial disagreement about what the law "really" is, and that the production of meanings is achieved by the interaction of the interpreting subject and the object of interpretation. Yet Dworkin's major concern here, as previously, is to limit the scope of judges for reaching contradictory decisions, and

---

93   See Ronald Dworkin, *Taking Rights Seriously* (Harvard University Press, Cambridge Mass, 1977), ch 2, especially p 22ff.

94   Joseph Raz, "Legal Principles and the Limits of Law" (1972) 81 *Yale Law Journal* 823.

thus to restore faith in the objectivity and fairness of the judicial process. The way Dworkin does this, after commencing from a potentially subversive position, is to combine the common law ideal of an institutional history which determines to a certain degree (because many cases are clear) the outcome of litigation with his "aesthetic hypothesis". The duty of a judge (and other interpreters), he argues, is to interpret the law's institutional history in its "best light", that is, to render a meaning for the law which is properly integrated with what has gone before and with general community values. Dworkin calls this approach to legal interpretation and decision-making "law as integrity", an approach enshrined in his hypothetical ideal judge, Hercules. Dworkin proposes an analogy between law and a chain novel written by several authors, each of whom has to put the best (most coherent, most plausible) interpretation possible on the preceding chapters.[95] Dworkin's judges are not purely individuals: though he does not deny their private individuality, as judges their role is not to further their personal opinions, but rather to decide cases in a way which best accords with accepted legal and community standards. Thus, while Dworkin does not reproduce the ideal that judges merely declare the law, he is certainly concerned to minimise the idea of individual judicial creativity as a way of theorising the relationship between law and decision-making. In keeping with traditional readings of common law change, he claims that "law works itself pure" through the method of law as integrity: that is, when working correctly, the legal process ensures that the best rules and principles are extracted from the available legal material.

Dworkin's theory of law has generated a good deal of literature, both supportive and critical, which is far too extensive to summarise satis-factorily here. Without entering into what is often a technical and unsatisfying debate, several broad comments may be made. First, Dworkin's theory undoubtedly offers a reasonably contemporary understanding of the common law in that it recognises the centrality of interpretation of the past in law and the role played by community values in reshaping the content of law. In this sense his theory is more realistic than that of natural law or positivist theorists who, for different reasons, minimise or exclude socially-formed morality and values from the central definition of law. On the other hand, Dworkin's theory unifies community values in a way which is completely unrealistic and suppresses the plurality and dissonance within social groups which is characteristic of contemporary globally-situated communities. His theory is also problematic in its support for the notion that legal process and change is a means of purifying law: this presupposes some deep internal coherence and design which is neither

---

95   Ronald Dworkin, *Law's Empire* (Fontana, London, 1986), pp 228-238. In *Concise Jurisprudence* (Federation Press, Sydney, 1993), Sandra Berns provides a detailed critique of Dworkin's view of community and the assumptions he makes about legal interpretations; see especially pp 47-58.

supported by the evidence of existing law (which is often messy and contradictory, not just at the margins) or theoretically defensible given that it calls upon an idealistic layer of legal meaning inaccesible to all but a non-existent super-judge.[96]

Contributing to the debate and in keeping with contemporary critical suspicion of grand, idealistic theories, Allan Hutchinson has argued that common law can be seen as evolutionary. According to Hutchinson, common law is not evolutionary in the popular and traditional sense of continually improving and refining itself from rough origins. There is no "inherent logic" to the common law (just as there is no end point of evolution). Rather, law may be evolutionary in the non-normative sense of being an experimental adaptation to changing conditions:[97]

> the common law is a messy, episodic, and experimental effort to respond and adapt to the contingent demands that the political and social milieu places upon it. If there is a method to the common law's madness, it is to be found in its participants' diverse and unorchestrated attempts to adapt to changing conditions and shifting demands. Nature and the common law, like all efforts to explain and understand them (including this one) are works in progress: They are the revisable result of manifold compromises between variability and stability in which present utility is always a give and take between past promise and future potential.

Rather than seeing the law as having some internal design known only to the most adept judges who are also in tune with the community, Hutchinson asks us simply to recognise what is before our eyes: the dissonance, the plurality, the compromise and the real effort judges, lawyers, scholars and others make to adapt law to changing environments. A historical understanding of the common law should not take it outside or beyond this environment to some better or purer form, but rather situate it entirely in its practical context.

Conclusion

[2145] The final point I want to make about classical common law theory is that it seems to me to represent a much more organic perception of the law than the one we have now.[98] What I mean by this is that the modern view of law is that it is external to us — law is something which is simply imposed on us from outside and though we may feel that a particular law is essential to social life, or, on the other hand, that a law is basically

---

96 See generally Allan Hutchinson, *Evolution and the Common Law*, 75-81.

97 Hutchinson, *Evolution and the Common Law*, p 273.

98 Postema notes: "It is no accident that whereas organic metaphors dominate the writings of Common Lawyers, mechanical metaphors dominate the writings of their positivist critics from Hobbes to Bentham.": *Bentham and the Common Law Tradition*, p 10. An intriguing mix of organic and mechanical references is to be found in the extract from Julius Stone's "The Ratio of the Ratio Decidendi", above at [280].

immoral, on the whole we see these as moral feelings unconnected with the way the law really is. Law remains a sort of regulation over and above our individual persons. Those who wrote about the common law prior to the 19th century, on the other hand, took seriously the idea that law was essentially common to the people, and represented a customary reason: law was not just something external to people, it was part of their existence in a community.

One way of explaining this is by emphasising that classical common law theory viewed law essentially as an unwritten customary tradition, where the legal truth was handed down and developed gradually over generations. It is as though the law were an oral narrative, passed from generation to generation, without an identifiable author or source, but which nevertheless changed gradually. In an early work, *Just Gaming*, Jean-François Lyotard describes the narrative tradition of the South American Cashinahua Indians in terms which I think illuminate some of the characteristics of classical common law thought. Lyotard begins by comparing the "heteronomous" state of the Cashinahua's narrative to the modern emphasis on autonomy and science.[99] The term "heteronomous" in this context refers to the fact that it is not possible to reduce the tradition of the narrative to a single origin, or explain it by a single law. This is contrasted to the modern attitude to a tradition (or an institution like law, or a theory), which involves trying to identify an authoritative origin and unify the whole by reference to some over-arching principle.

In some ways this distinction is very similar to that between classical common law thought and the philosophical attitude to law which developed in the early 19th century. Like common law judges, narrators within the Cashinahua have a formal place in the community: moreover, they are not primarily autonomous individuals who invent stories to relate, but regard themselves as being in the first place imbued with the customs relating to the narration. The Cashinahua narrator always claims to have heard the story first, asserting also that the telling is a faithful transmission of the story, "even if the narrative performance is highly inventive".[100] The narrator, in other words (like the common law judge), is always regarded as the mouthpiece of the story. Only at the end of the story do the narrators attach their own names to it. Each narrator is thus narrated (in the sense of being given an identity within the narrative) by the story, as well as the creator of an original version of it. The narrative is therefore neither merely an

---

99   Jean-François Lyotard and Jean-Loup Thébaud, *Just Gaming* (University of Minnesota Press, Minneapolis, 1985), "Second Day". Lyotard discusses the Cashinahua in several texts, *Just Gaming*, *The Postmodern Condition: A Report on Knowledge* (University of Minnesota Press, Minneapolis, 1984), and *The Differend: Phrases in Dispute* (Manchester University Press, Manchester, 1988). In the latter work his formulation of the idea of narrative and its relation to "pagan" discourses is somewhat different from that presented in the two earlier works.

100   Lyotard, *The Postmodern Condition*, p 20.

imitation of past performances, nor a totally new invention, but a re-invention, or re-animation of the customs of the community. The life of the narrative is in the dynamic interaction of the past, the present, and the future, which emerges in the process of the oral performance. Most importantly, the origin of the narrative is forgotten in its ongoing and unstoppable life: the tradition is always a relay, and can never be reduced to a static content or an original authoritative source.

Thinking about the common law as an oral narrative may in some respects be seen as encouraging an inherently conservative under-standing of law, since part of the idea of the narrative is that the past is conserved in the flow of the legal story. Sudden innovations are not possible in this schema. Conversely, it may also be that thinking about the common law in this way can provide a basis for a more dynamic understanding of the law; one that is not constrained by any particular form or content, but merely by the inexorability of change over time.

THREE
NATURAL LAW AND POSITIVISM

Introduction

[305]   The authority of the common law, according to the classical common law jurists, was derived from the fact that it had existed from time immemorial. As Sir John Davies observed, once a custom had been observed time out of mind, it obtained the status of law. This view meant that the authority of the law was not derived from a single source, but rather from a multitude of practices which developed over time. Indeed, as I explained, one of the important elements of Hale's version of classical common law thought was the insistence that the law has no absolute identifiable origin. English law, he said, developed from England's diverse social and political history. Thus law was seen to be both a dynamic and a conservative institution: changing in response to social needs, and conserving that which was useful.

The idea that the authority of the law is to be found with the passing of time is one which has been lost in modern jurisprudence. From the early 19th century, when Jeremy Bentham attacked the common law, jurisprudential debate has centred on locating the authority of the law at some fixed point. Thus, rather than seeing the basis of the legal system as continually shifting, the contemporary natural law and positivist theorists have tried to isolate the static underlying reasons founding laws generally.[1] Their argument is that legal authority does not move with time: rather, legal change is explained by an underlying reason or authority which is itself stable.

Debates about natural law and positivism have traditionally occupied much of the territory of legal theory. However, the fact that a great deal of space has been devoted to these matters does not demonstrate that these theories are crucial to our understanding of law. It merely illustrates the dominance of certain jurisprudential paradigms within

---

1   As Roger Cotterrell remarks, the "concern which links positivist analytical jurisprudence and natural law theory is a concern with the nature of legal authority; with identifying its sources and its limits": *The Politics of Law: A Critical Introduction to Legal Philosophy* (Butterworths, London, 1989), p 125. In contrast to common law theory, the natural law and positivist approaches have concentrated on identifying grounds which either remain the same for all legal systems, or which are the identifiable and static outer limit of a legal system.

academia. In fact, most contemporary theory does not even accept that there is any clear debate between natural law and positivism.[2] Many contemporary theorists have situated themselves somewhere between natural law and positivism, while others have tried to move beyond these categories altogether. The relationships between law and power, meaning, ideology, and society are often the focus for legal theory, rather than the attempt to identify the essence or basic concepts of law. Nonetheless, theories of natural law and positivism are important because of their place in Western legal heritage. An understanding of positivist theory is particularly important, since it still underpins much mainstream and critical analysis of law. With this in mind, the following discussion of natural law and positivism is intended to perform two functions: first, to provide a basic exposition of some of the fundamental features of natural law and positivism, and secondly, to indicate, where possible, some of the wider theoretical issues raised by these approaches.

Antigone

[310] A classical statement about the antagonism between human law and non-human law appears in Sophocles' play *Antigone*. The action takes place in and around Thebes, a Greek city ruled by Creon. Antigone has two brothers who have just killed each other in a battle for the city. The brother who was defending the city, Eteocles, has been buried with full religious rites, but Creon has ordered that the body of the invading brother, Polynices, be left to rot on the battlefield, an ignominious end which is against religious law. Antigone tries to convince her sister Ismene to help her bury the body according to holy rituals, but since Ismene refuses to disobey the edict of Creon, Antigone buries the body herself. Creon confronts Antigone, and accuses her of disobeying his law, to which Antigone replies:[3]

> That order did not come from God. Justice,
>
> That dwells with the gods below, knows no such law.
>
> I did not think your edicts strong enough
>
> To overrule the unwritten unalterable laws
>
> Of God and heaven, you being only a man.
>
> They are not of yesterday or today, but everlasting,
>
> Though where they came from, none of us can tell
>
> Guilty of their transgression before God
>
> I cannot be, for any man on earth.

---

2   See, for instance, the essays collected in Robert P George (ed), *The Autonomy of Law: Essays on Legal Positivism* (Oxford, Clarendon Press, 1996).

3   From Sophocles, *The Theban Plays* "Antigone" (Penguin, Baltimore, 1947).

Antigone's defiance of the law of Creon is based on the existence of a "higher" law, in this instance a religious law, which overrules any laws made by Creon who is "only a man". The higher, universal law is here in direct conflict with the positive law in the shape of Creon's orders. "Positive" law usually refers to law which is "posited" or laid down by a human agent. However, in relation to this example, it should also be pointed out that religious law can also be considered to be positive. *Antigone* should not be read as though it involves a clash of natural law and positive law. As I will explain shortly, Aquinas distinguished four types of law: natural law, human law, eternal law, and divine law. The law of god is not "natural" in the sense of being part of a natural order to which humans can have immediate access. For those who believe in it, divine law is law which has been laid down by god, and which does not necessarily flow from the nature of things.

The question in *Antigone* can be framed as one of personal obedience to conflicting legal orders — Antigone has the choice to obey the law of Creon or the law of god; man's public law or the laws of family and personal relationships. She chooses the latter and faces the consequences of her disobedience. This is a difficulty which is perhaps not unusual — should we obey an unjust law or a law which conflicts with our fundamental principles? Should a judge apply an unjust law? How unjust must a law be before we are morally justified in disobeying it? Is a morally objectionable rule even law? Thus *Antigone* may be regarded as depicting two different legal systems — one non-human and one human — which are in conflict over a specific issue and the resulting tragedy is the consequence of the unresolvable clash between them.[4] Maybe Antigone herself is saying that Creon's edict is not law because it is against the laws of god, while Creon is saying that the mere fact that he has commanded something means that it is law. On the other hand Antigone could simply be asserting that as a matter of her individual moral conscience she cannot obey the positive law, a position which does not necessarily entail that Creon's order is not law, just that she is unable to follow it in this instance. Unfortunately for Antigone, the difference is academic.

The German philosopher GWF Hegel saw *Antigone* as enshrining the conflict between man's law and woman's law. In his *Philosophy of Right* he wrote:[5]

> ... man has his actual substantive life in the state, in learning, and so forth, as well as in labour and struggle with the external world and with himself ... Woman, on the other hand, has her substantive destiny in the family, and to be imbued with family piety is her ethical frame of mind.

---

4   Michael Detmold writes in *The Unity of Law and Morality: A Refutation of Legal Positivism* (Routledge Kegan Paul, London, 1984), that tragedy is created by the clash of absolutes, pp 144-145, 249.

5   GWF Hegel, *The Philosophy of Right* (Knox trans, Oxford University Press, London, 1967), para 166 and remark.

For this reason, family piety is expounded in Sophocles' *Antigone* — one of the most sublime presentations of this virtue — as principally the law of woman, and as the law of a substantiality at once subjective and on the plane of feeling, the law of the inward life, a life which has not yet attained its full actualization; as the law of the ancient gods, "the gods of the underworld"; as an "everlasting law, and no man knows at what time it was first put forth". This law is there displayed as a law opposed to public law, to the law of the land. This is the supreme opposition in ethics and therefore in tragedy; and it is individualized in the same play in the opposing natures of man and woman.

This view raises a number of interesting issues. For it is certainly the case that positive law is by and large the law of men: as feminist scholarship continues to point out, the law has on the whole been made by men, it tends to reflect and reward stereotypically male attitudes and values and, has traditionally, taken the male as the basic unit of the political and social structure.[6] As feminists have argued, the citizen presumed by law reproduces male characteristics and, as male, is affiliated with the institutions of culture and civilisation.[7] Hegel is contrasting this public, male law of the state to what he sees as the private and family-directed law of women, who have traditionally been associated with everything "natural". Unlike Antigone, Hegel sees the male law as superior since it is "actualised" (that is, made concrete) in the state. In a fairly orthodox philosophical gesture, then, Hegel accepts as given the distinction between the private, family-oriented world of women, and the public, political world of men.[8] This distinction is, however, one of the primary objectives of modern feminist critique. Women have been politically associated with a private sphere, the existence and nature of which is itself the result of social conventions. If, as a result of their subordination, women have developed a set of norms and standards distinct from masculine norms, can we speak of a "women's law"? Would such a law simply be a reflection of what men desire in women, would it be subversive of masculine agendas,[9] or, in a completely restructured legal world, would women's law and men's law

---

6   See Chapter 6, below. See also the feminist accounts of *Antigone* and of Hegel's interpretation: Luce Irigaray, *Speculum of the Other Woman* (Gillian Gill trans, Cornell University Press, Ithaca, NY, 1985), pp 214-226; Luce Irigaray, *To Be Two* (Monique Rhodes and Marco Cocito-Monoc trans, Athlone, London, 2000), ch 9 "She Before the King"; Judith Butler, *Antigone's Claim: Kinship Between Life and Death* (Columbia University Press, New York, 2000).

7   Margaret Thornton, "Embodying the Citizen" in *Public and Private: Feminist Legal Debates* (Oxford University Press, Melbourne, 1995); Elizabeth Kingdom, "Citizenship and Democracy: Feminist Politics of Citizenship and Radical Democratic Politics" in Susan Millns and Noel Whitty (eds), *Feminist Perspectives on Public Law* (Cavendish, London, 1999).

8   This is not to say that the relationship between the two spheres is unproblematic in Hegel's work. See Drucilla Cornell, Michel Rosenfeld and David Gray Carlson (eds), *Hegel and Legal Theory* (Routledge, New York, 1991).

9   Catharine MacKinnon has argued that the "different voice" of women's moral reasoning is in fact a reflection of male desires. See Carol Gilligan, *In a Different Voice: Psychological Theory and Women's Development* (Harvard University Press, Cambridge Mass, 1982); Ellen du Bois et al, "Feminist Discourse, Moral Values, and the Law — A Conversation" (1985) 34 *Buffalo Law Review* 11.

complement each other (as Luce Irigaray has argued)?[10] How can we negotiate this difficult terrain between reflection and subversion? And how do oppressions which are different from gender oppression intersect with the masculine/feminine dichotomy?

These questions will be addressed in Chapter 6, but it is interesting to raise them here because of the seeming fixity of the spheres of natural and positive law. Ordinarily "natural" law is taken to exist in one place (the "natural", universal, and eternal world), while "positive" law is taken to exist in another place, the "human" world. As I will explain shortly, conflicts may arise over the relationship between the two spheres, the proper domain of jurisprudence, and whether natural law exists at all. But what if the distinction between the natural and the human is, like that between the public and the private (and arguably that between male and female), a construction? What if, for instance, the way we see the "natural" — what is "natural" and what is not — is already a result of our social conditioning? What if there are laws or structures of the understanding which are not themselves "natural" but are the result of a complex cultural and linguistic environment? Is not then the "natural" the product of society? Some of these matters have been raised in Chapter 1, and will surface again in Chapters 5, 6, 7, and 8.

The relation between natural law and positive law

[315] The relationship between the concepts of positive and natural law has been the subject of much debate and, it must be said, of confusion and misunderstanding. Natural law theory is sometimes seen to be totally incompatible with positivism, but this is not necessarily the case — it all depends on what view of natural and positive law is taken. Someone who takes the view that an immoral "law" created by a human legal system is not really law is putting a view which is incompatible with the view that law obtains its legal status *only* through being authoritatively laid down by prescribed legal institutions. A person who defends the idea of objective morality is putting a view which is directly inconsistent with the view that all talk of such a moral order is nonsensical, arbitrary, or politically motivated. But these are not the only ways that the relationship between natural law theory and positivism can be understood.[11] The following description is a

10   Luce Irigaray, *Je, Tu, Nous: Toward a Culture of Difference* (Routledge, New York, 1993), esp "Why Define Sexed Rights?"; Luce Irigaray, *I Love to You: Sketch of a Possible Felicity in History* (Routledge, New York, 1996); see generally Burke, Schor, and Whitford (eds), *Engaging With Irigaray* (Columbia University Press, New York, 1994). Irigaray's theory of sexed rights will be further considered in Chapter 6.

11   On this point see John Finnis, *Natural Law and Natural Rights* (Clarendon, Oxford, 1980), Ch 2; Deryck Beyleveld and Roger Brownsword, "The Practical Difference Between Natural-Law Theory and Legal Positivism" (1985) 5 *Oxford Journal of Legal Studies* 1; Neil MacCormick, "Natural Law and the Separation of Law and Morals" in Robert P George (ed), *Natural Law Theory: Contemporary Essays* (Clarendon Press, Oxford, 1992); Robert Moles, "Law and Morality — How to Do Things With Confusion" (1986) 37 *Northern Ireland Legal Quarterly* 29; Tan, Seow Hon, "Validity and Obligation in Natural Law Theory: Does Finnis Come Too Close to Positivism" (2003) 15 *Regent University Law Review* 195; Mark Murphy, "Natural Law Jurisprudence" (2003) 9 *Legal Theory* 241.

simplified account of the various positions which have been adopted. More detail is provided in the discussions of individual writers.

From the perspective of natural law writers there are essentially two types of claim about the relationship of natural law to positivism, according to whether or not the maxim "lex iniusta non est lex", is accepted. The maxim *lex injusta non est lex* means "an unjust law is not law". This was the view of Cicero, who I will quote below.[12] Cicero writes that the Roman Senate cannot do anything against the natural law: the Senate has authority to make laws, but not to make unjust laws. In other words, unjust or immoral statutes or court pronouncements are not law. Law ultimately owes its validity to god or to a higher moral reason, so anything which contravenes this higher order cannot be said to be law. There can be no real conflict between the natural law and the positive law, because the latter, if in conflict with the former, is just not law. There can be no such thing as an "evil law", because if a norm is evil, it is not law. This is a very difficult point of view to appreciate since it is quite different to our normal conception of laws as being capable of being just or unjust. Modern Western conceptions of law have been based on a theoretical separation of the state and state authority from religion, morality, and systems of justice. So it seems obvious to us that we can call something both a "law" and "immoral". However, this separation has not always been so clear (and still is not, in some societies) meaning that something which was held out to be a "law", but which contradicted a moral prescription, would not have been considered to be a law. Clearly this view of the natural law is in direct conflict with positivist theory, which claims that the only criteria for calling something a "law" is whether it has been created according to legal processes.

A second version of the relationship between natural law and positive law from the point of view of the natural lawyer is that unjust laws are laws, but that the natural law *ought* to be implemented. There is no *necessary* relationship between law and morality, natural reason and the commands of god, but conformity is strongly recommended. The existence of a natural law of some sort is defended, but it is also accepted that it may be in conflict with positive laws: positive laws are therefore seen as defective insofar as they do not accord with moral criteria. In some cases, an individual may have a moral justification for refusing to obey the law.[13] This sort of natural law theory is not incompatible with positivism, since it is accepted that the two systems can co-exist as laws.[14] It is just that the natural law is seen as ultimately superior and in need

---

12   Cicero, *De Re Publica*, bk III, xxi (Harvard University Press, Cambridge Mass, 1928, 1977 reprint).

13   Tan, "Validity and Obligation in Natural Law Theory: Does Finnis Come Too Close to Positivism", pp 205ff.

14   Neil MacCormick is particularly clear on this point in "Natural Law and the Separation of Law and Morals" in Robert P George (ed), *Natural Law Theory: Contemporary Essays* (Clarendon Press, Oxford, 1992).

of implementation. This sort of natural law perspective is defended by John Finnis, who does not deny the validity of duly enacted positive laws: what he suggests is that natural law principles should be used to improve or restructure the laws created by people.

Positivists tend either to discount the possibility of natural law altogether, or to argue that although it has nothing to do with the validity of law, it might provide a useful guide for the content of positive legal systems. HLA Hart, for instance, recognised that there should be some "minimum content" of a system of law if it is properly to fulfil its function as the primary means of maintaining order in society. Hart suggests that there must be some limitation on violence, some recognition of "approximate equality", and some mechanism for ensuring a distribution of resources.[15] (Not necessarily a *fair* distribution, but some distribution.)

A "middle way" between natural law theory and positivism has been proposed by Ronald Dworkin. Dworkin has strongly criticised the positivist view, especially that of HLA Hart, for being too reliant on the concept of the rule. Dworkin is not a natural law theorist since he does not defend a notion of an objective moral order. However, he does attempt to articulate the relationship between the political life of a community and its law, rather than assuming or defending a separation between the two.[16] Dworkin's ideas have been extraordinarily attractive for those who have desired a more realistic approach than either natural law or positivism, that is, an approach which does not rely upon the existence of an eternal moral system, which is sensitive to historical factors, but which recognises that legal decision-making may quite properly rely upon "moral" factors. On the other hand, Dworkin's account is also seen by many to be quite unrealistic in its appeal to moral consensus, and in its defence of the notion that every case has a single correct decision.

Natural Law

[320]   Theories of natural law concentrate on an idea of law as being *not* created by any person or culture, but as having an existence independent of the individual or collective will. Natural law is something which

---

15   HLA Hart, *The Concept of Law* (2nd ed, Clarendon, Oxford, 1994), pp 193ff. For a more recent commentary, see Richard Epstein, "The Not So Minimum Content of Natural Law" (2005) 25 *Oxford Journal of Legal Studies* 219; Rachel Patterson, "The Minimum Content of Law: A Critique of Hart's Descriptive Theory of Positive and Natural Law" (2005) 8 *Canberra Law Review* 9.

16   But see especially RM Dworkin, *A Matter of Principle* (Harvard University Press, Cambridge Mass, 1985); "Is Law a System of Rules" in RM Dworkin (ed), *The Philosophy of Law* (Oxford, Oxford University Press, 1977); and *Law's Empire* (Fontana, London, 1986); Joseph Raz, "Legal Principles and the Limits of Law" (1972) 81 *Yale Law Journal* 823; WJ Waluchow, "The Weak Social Thesis" (1989) 9 *Oxford Journal of Legal Studies* 23; "Herculean Positivism" (1985) 5 *Oxford Journal of Legal Studies* 187; Robert Westmoreland, "Dworkin and Legal Pragmatism" (1991) 11 *Oxford Journal of Legal Studies* 174.

is said to exist whether or not any person, judge, or legislature has ordained what the law is. The concept of a natural law implanted in human reason is an ancient one: in *De Re Publica* Cicero said:[17]

> True law is right reason in agreement with nature; it is of universal application, unchanging and everlasting; it summons to duty by its commands, and averts from wrongdoing by its prohibitions ... It is a sin to try to alter this law, nor is it allowable to attempt to repeal any part of it, and it is impossible to abolish it entirely. We cannot be freed from its obligations by senate or people, and we need not look outside ourselves for an expounder or interpreter of it. And there will not be different laws at Rome and at Athens, or different laws now and in the future, but one eternal and unchangeable law will be valid for all nations and for all times, and there will be one master and ruler, that is, God, over us all, for she is the author of this law, its promulgator, and its enforcing judge. Whoever is disobedient is fleeing from himself and denying his human nature, and by reason of this very fact he will suffer the worst penalties, even if he escapes what is commonly considered punishment.

A few different claims about natural law are made here. Some that are noteworthy, and common to natural law theories,[18] are that natural law is "right reason in agreement with nature", that this law is superior to the laws created by a state, that the natural law is universal in the sense that it applies to everyone, whether you live in Rome or in Athens, and that natural law is unchanging.

In the first place, then, natural law is usually said to be discoverable by reason, *natural* reason — as Cicero says, "we need not look outside ourselves for an expounder or interpreter of it". We can contrast this to the idea in common law thinking that the reason of the law is artificial, rather than natural. Artificial reason, that is, the established ways of thinking developed by common law jurists, was seen to be more certain than natural reason, the use of which could lead to many different versions of law. This matter has been discussed in Chapter 2. An example of the idea that the basis of law is to be found in human nature is to be found in a work called *On Human Nature*, of which only a fragment remains. The author,[19] Aesara of Lucania wrote that the

---

17   Cicero, *De Re Publica*, bk III, xxi. Dr Peter Kelly has pointed out to me that the text of *De Re Publica* exists only in fragments, supplemented by quotations by other authors. This passage is missing from the manuscript, but was ascribed to Cicero by Lactantius, a Christian writer who lived in the 3rd and 4th centuries: it may be that Cicero himself would not have referred to a God, but rather to the gods. The author "Cicero", then, may be a construct of the texts, rather than the constructor of them. (By the way, the word "she" in the penultimate sentence is a recent textual corruption of unknown origin.)

18   In the following text I have followed Harris, who has usefully summarised three characteristics of classical natural law theory: it is "universal and immutable", a "higher" law, and discoverable by reason: JW Harris, *Legal Philosophies* (2nd ed, Oxford University Press, Oxford, 2004), p 7.

19   Aesara was a "late Pythagorean", meaning that she lived sometime between 425 BC and 100 AD: see Mary Ellen Waithe (ed), *A History of Women Philosophers* (Martinus Nijhoffs, Dordrecht, 1987 c1995), vol 1, p 19.

nature of the human soul provides the basis for understanding law and social order. She divides the soul into three parts, mind, high spirit, and desire, arguing that order or justice in the soul is to be found in the proportionate existence of these elements.[20]

> Human nature seems to me to provide a standard of law and justice both for the home and for the city. By following the tracks within himself whoever seeks will make a discovery: law is in him and justice, which is the orderly arrangement of the soul. Being threefold, it is organised in accordance with triple functions: that which effects judgement and thoughtfulness is [the mind], that which effects strength and ability is [high spirit], and that which effects love and kindliness is desire.

Secondly, natural law is a "higher" law, meaning that it is superior to any law created by people. This is also the view put by Antigone: the conflict between religious law and Creon's law was resolved by Antigone in favour of the religious law. The question remaining for natural law is *on what level is the conflict resolved?* Certainly as a matter of individual conscience natural law is said to prevail over positive law. For Antigone, the natural law prevailed. However, as I have indicated, not all natural law theorists have gone as far as to argue that where there is a conflict, the positive law is invalid or inoperative. Natural law might just provide a strong model for positive law.

Thirdly, natural law is "universal" because it applies generally, to all people whether they live in Rome or Athens (or even more remote places). It is "immutable" because it cannot be changed by human intervention: natural law is generally considered to be, if not eternal, at least ahistorical, which means that it does not change over time, but remains the same regardless of historical events or social attitudes and opinions. This is something which is, for instance, asserted by John Finnis, a modern natural law theorist. Finnis notes that although there is clearly a history of natural law theories, which vary over time, "of natural law itself there could, strictly speaking, be no history".[21] Although the theory may change, the subject matter remains the same.

The other crucial claim made by Cicero is that it is god who is the source of natural law — it is god who gives the natural law its validity. I will come back to god shortly, but for the moment it is sufficient to note that as author, promulgator, and enforcing judge all rolled into one (legislature, executive, and judiciary?) god does not enshrine the doctrine of the separation of powers. On the other hand, she is a fine example of an indivisible sovereign.

Beyond these generalities natural law theories are very diverse, so I have selected a few writers who have been important to legal theory in order to illustrate some of the central themes. The main aim of this section

---

20 Mary Ellen Waithe (ed), *A History of Women Philosophers* (Martinus Nijhoffs, Dordrecht, 1987 c1995), vol 1, p 20.

21 Finnis, *Natural Law and Natural Rights*, p 24; see also Finnis, "The 'Natural Law Tradition'" (1986) 36 *Journal of Legal Education* 492 at 492.

is simply to elaborate the basic ideas of natural law theory, not to provide an exhaustive account of its history and diversity.[22]

Aristotle and St Thomas Aquinas

[325] In *The Politics*, Aristotle put the view that "man is by nature a political animal", which means, essentially, that it is human nature to associate in political ways. The end or *telos* of human nature is political association, and the "nature" of something is the end goal towards which it is directed. It is in the "nature" of a gumnut to grow into a gum tree,[23] or more traditionally, of an acorn to grow into an oak. "Nature" is taken by Aristotle to mean the natural and perfect end which is inherent in something: that towards which it strives. This view of "nature" is in contrast to the view that takes behaviour as the criterion for determining what is natural. On the one hand "nature" is an ideal, on the other it is a fact.[24] According to Aristotle the association of people in a state is a natural entity, because it is in "men's" nature to form political groupings:[25]

> the city-state is a perfectly natural form of association, as the earlier associations from which it sprang were natural. This association is the end of those others and its nature is itself an end; for whatever is the end-product of the perfecting process of any object, that we call its nature, that which man, house, household, or anything else aims at being ...
>
> ...
>
> It follows that the state belongs to a class of objects which exist in nature, and that man is by nature a political animal; it is his nature to live in a state.

The "natural" state does not grow, in Aristotle's view, from a gumnut, though we may all be better off if it did, considering what Aristotle thinks is natural. Rather, what it grows from is the natural formation of men and women into pairs, and the natural distinction between rulers and those ruled. So the state's equivalent of the gumnut is the association of men with women and slaves, a grouping which constitutes the household. A couple of points need to be observed about this: first, slaves are not men, but secondly, nor are they women. Aristotle insists that women and slaves are distinguished by nature according to their different functions, even though according to Aristotle, some "non-Greek communities fail to understand this and

---

22   For a more extensive overview of the natural law tradition, see MDA Freeman, *Lloyd's Introduction to Jurisprudence* (7th ed, Sweet and Maxwell, London, 2001), Ch 3.

23   To be really pedantic, of course, it is in the nature of the seeds inside the gumnut to grow into gum trees.

24   See Dennis Lloyd, *The Idea of Law* (Penguin, London, 1964), pp 76-77; HLA Hart, *The Concept of Law*, p 189.

25   Aristotle, *The Politics*, bk 1, c 2 (Penguin Books, Harmondsworth, 1981).

assign to female and slave exactly the same status".[26] This failure to distinguish between women and slaves is, for Aristotle, sufficient evidence of the non-existence of "men" or rulers in these communities, meaning that they are all, male and female, actually slaves, and subject to the natural rule of the Greeks. The claim that all this is "natural" may now seem somewhat far-fetched, but as a statement of the underlying political structure of modern patriarchal, paternalistic and imperialist states, Aristotle's version seems remarkably timeless.[27]

Thus Aristotle thinks that states are "natural" in the sense that they are the end product of man's nature. Of "political justice", which is defined in relation to law, Aristotle wrote in *The Ethics*:[28]

> There are two sorts of political justice, one natural and the other legal. The natural is that which has the same validity everywhere and does not depend upon acceptance; the legal is that which in the first place can take one form or another indifferently, but which, once laid down, is decisive: eg that the ransom for a prisoner of war shall be one mina, or that a goat shall be sacrificed and not two sheep; and also that any enactments for particular circumstances, such as the sacrifices in honour of Brasidas [a Spartan general], and decisions made by special resolution ...

Rules of justice established by convention and on the ground of expediency may be compared to standard measures; because the measures used in the wine and corn trades are not everywhere equal: they are larger in the wholesale and smaller in the retail trade. Similarly laws that are not natural but man-made are not uniform because forms of government vary; but everywhere there is only one natural form of government, namely, that which is best. "Natural" justice is the same everywhere , regardless of whether it has been accepted as such, whereas "legal" justice is that which has been laid down in any particular society. Therefore the significant question raised above, of whether one goat or two sheep should be sacrificed, is one which is to be determined by human acceptance and not nature.

Aristotle's ideas that the state is a natural association, and that, within it, laws are both natural and positive, formed part of the basis for the thought of St Thomas Aquinas, a Dominican thinker who lived in the 13th century. In the *Summa Theologica*, Aquinas considered the nature of law, dividing it into four types: the eternal, the natural, the human and the divine. The eternal law is, roughly, god's eternal plan for the universe; natural law is that part of the eternal law which is discoverable by reason and which is to be found in the human mind; human law is the law created by humans on the basis of natural reason; and divine law is that law revealed in scripture.

---

26   HLA Hart, *The Concept of Law*, p 26.

27   See, for instance, Carole Pateman, *The Sexual Contract* (Polity Press, Cambridge, 1988) and Catharine MacKinnon, *Towards a Feminist Theory of the State* (Harvard University Press, Cambridge, Mass, 1989).

28   Aristotle, *The Ethics*, bk 5, vii, 1134b-1135a (Penguin Books, Harmondsworth, 1976).

Two crucial aspects of Aquinas' approach should be emphasised. First, natural law is discoverable by reason, and inherent in humanity: it is a "participation of the eternal law in the rational creature".[29] Secondly, a human law which contradicts the natural law is not a law in the central sense of that term,[30] but that does not mean that all human law directly reflects the natural law. Aquinas distinguishes two methods by which one thing may be said to be derived from another. In the first place, there is the straightforward deduction: for instance the proposition that we should not kill other human beings can be deduced from the principle that we should not harm them. Some human laws can therefore be simply deduced from natural principles. The modern Roman Catholic Church has insisted on the possibility of making such deductions from natural law. For instance, although they have not asserted that there is a natural law which specifically prohibits the use of contraceptives, those with power in Rome have claimed that such a principle can be deduced from natural law: "The Church, calling men back to the observance of the norms of natural law, as interpreted by her constant doctrine, teaches that each and every marriage act must remain open to the transmission of life".[31] The Church doctrine, apparently derived from natural law, that sex must "remain open to the possibility" of pregnancy, is presented as absolute, transcending any social contingencies (such as the sexual exploitation of women, over-population, and the spread of sexually-transmitted disease) which might make contraception desirable. It would seem that the human situation has absolutely nothing to do with this use of a natural law argument — the "law" simply overrides everything.

Secondly, general principles may be particularised to certain forms in human law. What Aquinas means by this is that the natural law is a form which does not necessarily cover every contingency within society. It often exists only as general principles providing guidance to the legislator. The exact content of human law will therefore need to be determined by the application of natural reason to practical situations. Aquinas compares this sort of derivation to the process used by a craftsperson building a house: she needs to "determine the general form of a house to some particular shape". Or we could say that there are natural principles which need to be taken into account when knitting a jumper so that it does not fall apart. But that does not make all jumpers the same: in fact the knitter has, according to the level of his skill, quite a lot of discretion as to shape, style, colour, thickness, and

29 St Thomas Aquinas *Summa Theologica*, question 91, article 2; in Bigongiari (ed), *The Political Ideas of St Thomas Aquinas: Representative Selections* (Hafner, New York, 1969, c1953), p 13.

30 That is, it is not a law derived from natural reason. See the comments on this made by Finnis in *Natural Law and Natural Rights*, pp 363-366.

31 From the Papal encyclical *Humanae Vitae* (1968), reprinted in Harris *Legal Philosophies*, pp 9-10.

so on. Similarly, the human ruler has discretion as to how the natural law takes shape in society for the common good. These matters are explained in the following passages.

St Thomas Aquinas
Summary Theologica Part II[32]

[330] Question 90 ... Law is a rule and measure of acts whereby man is induced to act or is restrained from acting; for *lex* (law) is derived from *ligare* (to bind), because it binds one to act. Now the rule and measure of human acts is the reason, which is the first principle of human acts, as is evident from what has been stated above, since it belongs to the reason to direct to the end, which is the first principle in all matters of action, according to the Philosopher [Aristotle].

...

Question 95 ... As Augustine says, "that which is not just seems to be no law at all"; wherefore the force of a law depends on the extent of its justice. Now in human affairs a thing is said to be just from being right according to the rule of reason. But the first rule of reason is the law of nature ... Consequently, every human law has just so much of the nature of law as it is derived from the law of nature. But if in any point it deflects from the law of nature, it is no longer a law but a perversion of law.

But it must be noted that something may be derived from the natural law in two ways: first, as a conclusion from premises; secondly, by way of determination of certain generalities. The first way is like to that by which, in the sciences, demonstrated conclusions are drawn from the principles, while the second mode is likened to that whereby, in the arts, general forms are particularized as to details: thus the craftsman needs to determine the general form of a house to some particular shape. Some things are therefore derived from the general principles of the natural law by way of conclusions, eg, that "one must not kill" may be derived as a conclusion from the principle that "one should do harm to no man"; while some are derived therefrom by way of determination, eg, the law of nature has it that the evildoer should be punished; but that he be punished in this or that way is not directly by natural law but is a derived determination of it.

Accordingly, both modes of derivation are found in the human law. But those things which are derived in the first way are contained in human law, not as emanating therefrom exclusively, but having some force from the natural law also. But those things which are derived in the second way have no other force than that of human law.

[335] Thus, according to Aquinas, when Aristotle says that positive justice is originally indifferent, this does not mean that it has no connection to natural law. Yet, although positive law is rationally derived from natural law, it is not, according to Aquinas, wholly determined by natural law. It is a sort of supplement to natural law, which cannot deal with every social variation. This is an important feature of the theory of natural law developed by Aquinas, and one which, according to Finnis, has

---

32 From Bigongiari (ed), *The Political Ideas of St Thomas Aquinas*, pp 4 and 58-59.

been misunderstood.[33] Aquinas forwards another reason for the existence of human law in addition to the natural law, which is that some people need to be coerced in order to act in accordance with law. Positive law is therefore necessary to lay down and enforce punishments for wrongdoers.[34]

As Harris comments, Aquinas "threw over positive law a halo of moral sanctity".[35] In the legal thought of Aquinas, the authority of the positive law is derived from the natural law through the application of reason, giving it a moral dimension which it would not otherwise have: as the jurist Christopher St German commented in *Doctor and Student*, "in every law positive well made is somewhat of the law of reason and of the law of god".[36] A well-made positive law is derived from the law of reason, and commands obedience accordingly. Positive law is justified in some sense by its connection with natural law.

Finnis: Natural law and natural rights

[340]   "This will never do, my friend; you are not obeying the universal rule of Reason; you have misjudged the occasion."

"Bloody hell," replied the other. "I am a sailor and was born in Batavia. I have had to trample on the crucifix four times in various trips I've been to Japan. I'm not the man for your Universal Reason."

Voltaire *Candide*

Seven centuries and a great many philosophical men after Aquinas, John Finnis returned to his ideas in an attempt to formulate a modern theory of natural law. Finnis explains the conception of natural law which operates in his work as follows:[37]

---

33 See Finnis, *Natural Law and Natural Rights*, pp 28-29.

34 Aquinas, *Summa Theologica*, question 95, article 1, in Bigongiari (ed) *The Political Ideas of St Thomas Aquinas*, pp 56-57.

35 Harris, *Legal Philosophies*, p 10.

36 St German, *Doctor and Student* (The Selden Society, London, 1974), p 27. St German follows the division of laws adopted by Aquinas.

37 Finnis, *Natural Law and Natural Rights*, p 23. See also Finnis, "On the Incoherence of Legal Positivism" (2000) 75 *Notre Dame Law Review* 1597. Much has been written on Finnis' conception of natural law. The following is a selection of relevant articles: Valerie Kerruish, "Philosophical Retreat: A Criticism of John Finnis' Theory of Natural Law" (1983) 15 *University of Western Australia Law Review* 224; Ian Duncanson, "Finnis and the Politics of Natural Law" (1989) 19 *University of Western Australia Law Review* 239; Ruth Gavison, "Natural Law, Positivism, and the Limits of Jurisprudence: A Modern Round" (1982) 91 *Yale Law Journal* 1250; Neil MacCormick, "Natural Law Reconsidered" (1981) 1 *Oxford Journal of Legal Studies* 99; Jeremy Shearmur, "Natural Law Without Metaphysics? The Case of John Finnis" (1990) 38 *Cleveland State Law Review* 123; Robert Scavone, "Natural Law, Obligation and the Common Good: What Finnis Can't Tell Us" (1985) 43 *University of Toronto Faculty of Law Review* 90.

There is (i) a set of basic practical principles which indicate the basic forms of human flourishing as goods to be pursued and realized, and which are in one way or another used by everyone who considers what to do, however unsound his conclusions; and (ii) a set of basic methodological requirements of practical reasonableness (itself one of the basic forms of human flourishing) which distinguish sound from unsound practical thinking and which, when all brought to bear, provide the criteria for distinguishing between acts that ... are reasonable-all-things-considered ... and acts that are unreasonable-all-things-considered, ie between ways of acting that are morally right or morally wrong — thus enabling one to formulate (iii) a set of general moral standards.

One of the positivist criticisms of natural law theory has been that it attempts to derive an "ought" from an "is". What this means is that, according to some positivist writers, natural law theory starts with a description of the natural world (an "is"), but somehow ends up by supporting normative propositions about what law *ought* to be.[38] I will come back to this in more detail towards the end of the chapter. Finnis circumvents this positivist criticism of natural law by arguing, again in the footsteps of Aquinas, that the principles of natural law are *not derived from anything*. They are self-evident.[39] Thus, in the first place, according to Finnis, there are a number of human "goods" or forms of flourishing which are not derived from descriptions of the world, but are understood (or at least used) by everyone.

One of these goods is practical reason. By "practical reason" Finnis means the type of reasoning we use in order to make decisions about how to act and how to order our lives.[40] It is fairly clear that some notion of practical reasoning is an important part of legal theory, which is not only (or even primarily) about abstract notions of law, but the practical application of legal ideas. Practical reasoning is reasoning about our practices, and, according to Finnis, is fundamental to the concept of natural law.[41] However, it is obvious that in order for there to be a connection between "practical reason" and natural law, the standards of practical reasonableness must themselves be universal and natural.[42] The practical reason of natural law cannot be culturally specific, or dependent on experience, language, class, gender, or race.

---

38   An example of an invalid derivation of a norm from a description might be: in order to reproduce, sexual contact between one male and one female is necessary (an "is" statement); it follows that sexual contact between members of the same sex is un-natural and should be prohibited (an "ought" supposedly derived from the "is"). Obviously there are some steps in argumentation missing here.

39   Finnis, *Natural Law and Natural Rights*, pp 33, 85.

40   Finnis, *Natural Law and Natural Rights*, Ch 5; see also Finnis, "Natural Law and Legal Reasoning" in George (ed), *Natural Law Theory: Contemporary Essays*.

41   Thus, as I see it, practical reason is also theoretical. See the comments made in the Introduction to Chapter 6 on the theory/practice distinction in feminism.

42   Finnis says that the requirements of practical reason are a "natural law method" for determining a moral law: *Natural Law and Natural Rights*, p 103.

Now, without wishing to foreclose entirely the possibility of such a universal "reason", I think we should be aware of the implications of making such an argument. If "practical reason" is given a content which applies universally, we are entitled to ask *whose* idea of reason it represents, and whose idea it excludes.[43] Surely it is not the case that I will necessarily approach the practical questions of my life in the same way as those whose material conditions and culture are substantially different from mine. Western individualism does not of necessity contribute a great deal to the styles of reasoning employed by those who live in more community-oriented cultures. What gives credibility and political purchase to Western "practical reason" is not *necessarily* its moral superiority over other ways of understanding the world, but rather its political and ideological superiority. Importantly, this is not to claim that all moral systems are equally valid, or that no evaluation can be made of an evil political regime: such debate and evaluation, based on firmly-held moral beliefs, will always be possible and necessary. However, it remains the case that cultural differences are reflected in approaches to "practical reason", and that the superiority of Western reason in this regard is more a consequence of ideological domination than of philosophical justification. Hence, as we will see in Chapters 6 and 7, gender and race have become important points of departure for theorists wishing to critique claims of theoretical objectivity and rationality.

In other words, I do not think that the question of "practical reason" can be isolated from the value system of a society, and giving a formal content to practical reasonableness (as exists, for instance, in the concept of the reasonable man[44]) may well result in the exclusion of ways of approaching problems which do not fit within the tradition of reason.[45] Finnis may think that natural law has no "history" because it is eternal and unchanging, but it is nevertheless the case that what has counted as "reason", "good" or "right" has been determined by historical factors, and has changed over the centuries. How are we to distinguish this history from that which is, in Finnis' view, *eternally* "reasonable", "good" or "right"? For instance, "reason" as a concept has historically reflected norms which are socially male, Eurocentric

---

43   A comprehensive critique of the politics behind Finnis' use of the idea of practical reasonableness is Duncanson, "Finnis and the Politics of Natural Law".

44   See Genevieve Lloyd, "The Man of Reason" (1979) 10 *Metaphilosophy* 19; Lucinda Finley, "A Break in the Silence: Including Women's Issues in a Torts Course" (1989) 64 *Notre Dame Law Review* 886; Leslie Bender, "A Lawyer's Primer on Feminist Theory and Tort" (1988) 38 *Journal of Legal Education* 3; Caroline Forell, "The Reasonable Woman Standard" (1992) 11 *University of Tasmania Law Review* 1; Robyn Martin, "A Feminist View of the Reasonable Man: An Alternative Approach to Liability in Negligence for Personal Injury" (1994) 23 *Anglo-American Law Review* 334; Elizabeth Handsley, "The Reasonable Man: Two Case Studies"(1996) 1 *Sister in Law* 53.

45   For a critique of Finnis' conception of practical reason on its own terms see Scavone "Natural Law, Obligation and the Common Good: What Finnis Can't Tell Us".

and white.[46] What has traditionally counted as being "reasonable" are characteristics culturally associated with white masculinity. This is not in itself an argument against having a notion of practical reason: as I have said, it is necessary to reflect about our actions and their implications within a social context. However, it is equally necessary to be attentive to the way, and according to whose point of view, any concept of reason is formulated. It is particularly important to be aware of the effects that differences in power have on what counts as reasonableness. Arguments from a fairly specific and often dogmatic idea of what counts as reasonable, frequently operate to suppress and render illegitimate other notions of reason.

In addition to practical reason, Finnis identifies six self-evident "goods" which can be grasped by a process of introspection: this basically involves asking whether something is in itself a good.[47] According to Finnis the "goods" are life, knowledge, play, aesthetic experience, sociability, practical reasonableness, and religion. Any other goods, he argues, fall within one of these categories, or within a combination of two or more of the fundamental goods.

In itself, the list appears to be fairly benign, although we could easily quibble with details. For instance, Finnis offers a broad definition of "religion", focused not specifically on a belief in some divinity, but in the recognition that there is "an order of things 'beyond' each and every man?"[48] (Well yes there is, actually — billions of women.) Finnis asks whether it is "reasonable to deny that it is ... peculiarly important to have thought reasonably and (where possible) correctly about these questions of cosmic order and of human freedom and reason".[49] Frankly, I do not see it as being at all essential to have thought reasonably or correctly about *cosmic* order when there is so much oppression and hatred in the world. It is important to think about freedom and interpersonal relationships, but is that necessarily a question of religion? Finnis might say that it is, since in thinking about these things I am recognising that there is an order or orders beyond each and every woman/man. (They're called patriarchy, racism, capitalism, and heteronormativity — but I do not think that these are quite the sort of orders Finnis has in mind.) Of course, many people accept the value of thinking about order, cosmic or otherwise. However, such thought comes in many forms — sociology, legal theory, philosophy, science — and is not necessarily to be characterised as "religion".

---

46   See Genevieve Lloyd, *The Man of Reason: "Male" and "Female" in Western Philosophy* (Methuen, London, 1984).

47   Finnis, *Natural Law and Natural Rights*, p 85ff.

48   Finnis, *Natural Law and Natural Rights*, p 90.

49   Finnis, *Natural Law and Natural Rights*, p 90.

Finnis seems here to be thinking about the possibility of an order or set of principles which transcends human society. But if this "order" is not divinely inspired, and if it arises from modes of human interaction as such, then how can we say that it is either "transcendent" or "orderly"? If what we think is "beyond" our selves is still entrenched in the material conditions of human existence, it is not essentially different from those conditions, and cannot be described as transcendent. And if our analysis of our condition is contextual — that is to say concentrates on a particular time, place, and set of power relationships — then "order" will not be general and transcendent, but materially located and specific.

The really significant question about Finnis' set of "goods" is how does he know that these forms of good are those which are basic? According to what or whose criteria has he articulated them?[50] What gives him the authority to say so (except perhaps, the fact that he is a reasonable man)? Now, Finnis does not say that this is the only possible way of formulating such a list — others will disagree. But he does say that they are, more or less, descriptive of areas of existence which are in themselves "good", and which are self-evidently so.[51] I have said that they are unobjectionable, but that does not mean that I think they are basic. They are unobjectionable because they are vague.[52] But why basic? A "good" like sexual contact may fit within life (if one is heterosexual and intending to reproduce), play (if one is not heterosexual or not intending to reproduce) or, I suppose, sociability. But why is it not "basic" in itself? What makes "aesthetic experience" more basic than physical experience? How do we know that knowledge is not a form of sociability? Or derivative of religion? How do we know that everything is not a form of play, or conversely, a deflection of boredom?[53]

More importantly, is not much of what we consider to be "good" actually reliant on our own experience rather than on a universal structure of goodness? Finnis is fond of situating his arguments within a (selective) reading of the Western philosophical tradition, but surely this tradition (as well as the natural law element of it) is itself contingent, and surely his reliance upon it is a consequence of his own life experience. There are many other traditions and many dimensions to the Western tradition. So is it not reasonable to relate our perceptions and articulations of "goodness" to individual experience (which includes our cultural heritages)? For instance, in a patriarchal

---

50   On the list of "goods" see the critiques of *Natural Law and Natural Rights* by Valerie Kerruish, "Philosophical Retreat: A Criticism of John Finnis' Theory of Natural Law" (1983) 15 *University of Western Australia Law Review* 224 and MacCormick, "Natural Law Reconsidered".

51   See the comments made by Finnis in *Natural Law and Natural Rights*, pp 90-94.

52   See also Lord Lloyd and Michael Freeman, *Lloyd's Introduction to Jurisprudence*, p 133; Kerruish, "Philosophical Retreat: A Criticism of John Finnis' Theory of Natural Law".

53   See the beginning of Chapter 1.

society where the experiences and existences of women are undervalued and bound by patriarchal convention, is it not reasonable that some women identify lesbian existence as a basic form of good, as well as a political strategy and survival mechanism?[54] Finnis in fact sees same-sex relationships as a violation of natural law,[55] and I suspect he would argue that any *perception* of "good" attached to them is not self-evident and natural, but rather derived from the nature of society (which clearly deviates from natural law in many respects). These issues raise the problem of the nature of evidence and in particular self-evidence. Am I *ever* evident to myself? If so, which bits? And how do I account for that in myself which I cannot have evidence of?[56] More worryingly, how did whatever it is that is evident get there in the first place? (As I indicated in Chapter 1, maybe heterosexuality is no less constructed and no more "naturally good" than other forms of sexuality.) How am I to interpret the evidence, assuming I can obtain it? Is so much introspection really "good"? As MacCormick says, the "Scottish verdict of 'not proven' must be returned in relation to the claim about self-evidence."[57]

---

54   In *Lesbian Ethics: Toward new Value* (Institute of Lesbian Studies, Palo Alto, 1988), Sarah Lucia Hoagland attempts to outline an anti-patriarchal ethic in detail. See also Ruthann Robson, *Lesbian (Out)Law: Survival Under the Rule of Law* (Firebrand Books, Ithaca, 1992); Ruthann Robson, *Sappho Goes to Law School* (Columbia University Press, New York, 1998).

55   In a fascinating sequence of events in 1993, both Finnis and feminist philosopher Martha Nussbaum found themselves acting as expert witnesses (on opposite sides) in a legal challenge to an amendment to the Colorado constitution: see *Evans v Romer* (Colo 1994) 8 P 2d 1335, aff'd 517 US 620. The amendment made it illegal for state instrumentalities to give any special protection (for instance by way of anti-discrimination rules) to lesbians, gays, or bisexuals. The point of Finnis' testimony was to show "the presence in the Western legal and philosophical tradition of a non-biblical civic antipathy toward the practice of homosexual congress": Randall Baldwin Clark "Love in a Colorado Courtroom: Martha Nussbaum, John Finnis, and Plato's *Laws* in *Evans v Romer*" (2000) 12 *Yale Journal of Law and the Humanities* 1 at 3. Finnis called upon the views of various ancient Greek philosophers to support his case. In contrast, Nussbaum sought to show that these same philosophers — Aristotle, Plato, and Socrates — were not hostile to homosexuality. Subseqent to the case, both Finnis and Nussbausm separately expanded upon their views. See, for instance, Finnis, "Law, Morality, and 'Sexual Orientation'" (1994) 69 *Notre Dame Law Review* 1049; "The Good of Marriage and the Morality of Sexual Relations: Some Philosophical and Historical Observations" (1997) 42 *American Journal of Jurisprudence* 97; Martha Nussbaum, "Platonic Love and Colorado Law: The Relevance of Ancient Greek Norms to Modern Sexual Controversies" (1994) 80 *Valparaiso Law Review* 1515.

56   In his *Tractatus Logico-Philosophicus* (Routledge and Kegan Paul, London, 1922), Ludwig Wittgenstein wrote: "If I wrote a book 'The world as I found it', I should also have therein to report on my body and say which members obey my will and which do not, etc. This then would be a method of isolating the subject or rather of showing that in an important sense there is no subject: that is to say, of it alone in this book mention could not be made ... The subject does not belong to the world but is a limit of the world.": ss 5.631-5.632. In other words, there is a point at which "I" am not evident to myself: something about me escapes my own scrutiny. See also the comments about subjectivity made in Chapter 8.

57   MacCormick, "Natural Law Reconsidered", p 107.

For Finnis, the standards of natural law developed through the process of applying practical reason provide criteria for deriving and evaluating the laws of a legal system. Finnis argues that positive law is a necessary medium for the expression of natural principles and for the development of a communal environment in which the "goods" are attainable. Thus, according to his view, natural law theory is not primarily directed at providing a moral justification for every principle of positive law. It is instead intended to elaborate on the requirements of practical reasonableness in relation to law; requirements which in his view have demonstrated a number of things:[58]

> [The concern of the natural law tradition] has been to show that the act of "positing" law (whether judicially or legislatively or otherwise) is an act which can and should be guided by "moral" principles and rules; that those moral norms are a matter of objective reasonableness, not of whim, convention, or mere "decision"; and that those same moral norms justify (a) the very institution of positive law, (b) the main institutions, techniques, and modalities within that institution (eg separation of powers), and (c) the main institutions regulated and sustained by law (eg government, contract, property, marriage, and criminal liability). What truly characterises the tradition is that it is not content merely to observe the historical or sociological fact that "morality" thus affects "law", but instead seeks to determine what the requirements of practical reasonableness really are, so as to afford a rational basis for the activities of legislators, judges, and citizens.

Law is not regarded by Finnis as invalid if it contradicts natural reason and, in fact, he sees the proposition *lex injusta non est lex* (an unjust law is not law) as only a secondary concern of natural law theories.[59] For Finnis, natural law provides a rational basis for the determination of positive law, as well as a set of criteria for individual judgement about whether or not to obey a law. An unjust law may not be binding on the individual conscience even though it is law in the sense that it has been laid down by a person or institution with authority to do so. Finnis goes on to argue, however, that circumstances may demand that an unjust law be obeyed because to disobey it would weaken the legal system as a whole. The "degree of compliance will vary according to time, place, and circumstance" but "in some limiting cases (eg of judges or other officials administering the law) the morally required degree of compliance may amount to full or virtually full compliance, just as if the law in question had been a just enactment."[60] In other words, the mere fact that a law has been authoritatively created gives it some weight in moral terms: the purpose of the legal system is to further the common good, and the existence of the legal system merits protection. A disobedient act which tends to weaken the legal system may therefore be unjustified.

---

58   Finnis, *Natural Law and Natural Rights*, p 290.

59   Finnis, *Natural Law and Natural Rights*, Ch XII.

60   Finnis, *Natural Law and Natural Rights*, p 361.

Finnis has been criticised for reproducing a bourgeois liberal ideology in his theory of natural law and for being blind to the political and social realities of law.[61] As I have indicated, there are a great many uncertainties in both the fundamentals and the details of his theory, meaning that those matters which he does assert with clarity and precision, are just that — assertions, often of a dogmatic nature. Jeremy Shearmur comments on the "unfortunate tendency in Finnis' work to present his ideas as if he were reading them off the very fabric of the universe".[62] The values upon which Finnis' work is based no doubt appeal to many, but is this enough? Moreover, abstract theorising about the nature of human existence neglects what may fairly be called in this instance "reality" — the material reality of oppression, for instance, as the abstract from Valerie Kerruish's critique of Finnis' work suggests:

Valerie Kerruish
"Philosophical Retreat: A Criticism of John Finnis' Theory of Natural Law"[63]

[345]   The Philosopher rose early and having breakfasted, was carried down the hill to a place on the banks of the river. The eight men who carried his sedan chair set it down gently. He thanked them politely. They nodded deferentially.

Then each of the eight took an armalite rifle and a bag of hand grenades from the back of the sedan and formed a semi-circular guard from the river's diameter. Setting up his chair and easel, for it was his day of rest and he intended to spend it in painting the reflections on the river's surface, the Philosopher stood to attention as each guard unfurled a banner. The first banner carried the inscription LIFE, the second KNOWLEDGE, the third PLAY, the fourth AESTHETIC EXPERIENCE, the fifth FRIENDSHIP, the sixth PRACTICAL REASONABLENESS, the seventh RELIGION. The Philosopher's self-portrait was on the eighth. He was no mean artist. It was well done.

As the day progressed, an aerial view of the riverbank showed that others too had formed arenas, with armed guards and fluttering banners. Between them a dense mass of people struggled to preserve a foothold against the crush of other bodies. With arms which must surely have ached, they held aloft placards reading POVERTY, MALNUTRITION, UNEMPLOYMENT, TORTURE, WAR, CORRUPTION, RACISM, HOMELESSNESS, STARVATION, OPPRESSION.

The Philosopher sighed as he saw these signs and turned away.

"Man is made in the image of God, and this implies, as St John of Damascus said, that man is intelligent and free in judgement and master of himself," he murmured to himself.

---

61   Kerruish, "Philosophical Retreat: A Criticism of John Finnis' Theory of Natural Law"; Duncanson "Finnis and the Politics of Natural Law".

62   Shearmur, "Natural Law Without Metaphysics? The Case of John Finnis". Finnis defends himself against Shearmur in "Concluding Reflections" (1990) 38 *Cleveland State Law Review* 231.

Natural law and modern politics

[350]   The attraction of natural law in the modern era is its ideal of providing a system of universal moral values according to which atrocities — war and other abuses of human rights — can be objectively condemned. Many modern constitutions contain a statement of fundamental rights framed in universal language, against which domestic legislation can be measured. Similarly, the International Covenant on Civil and Political Rights declares a number of basic principles of human rights, which are increasingly recognised as minimum standards for law. Although the concept of human rights is often taken for granted, there is extensive controversy about both the content of human rights and about their normative foundation. As I will explain in Chapter 5, some critical legal scholars have argued that abstract rights are liberal constructs designed to protect the already-privileged individuals of the world community. In addition, the meaning of specific rights is often vague and ambiguous, making them subject to manipulation. This has been countered by others who argue that rights are nonetheless important ideals which provide the basis for improvement in the condition of oppressed groups. The way that rights have been interpreted and applied in concrete situations has also been criticised, for instance by non-Western scholars, who have argued that human rights have historically been constructed around Western concepts of rights. Feminists have criticised the failure of the global human rights regimes to address harms done specifically to women, such as rape.[64] Much has been done in recent years to highlight and correct these inadequacies.

On a different level altogether, there is an ongoing debate about the nature and source of human rights: is it still possible to argue that human rights are "natural"? Natural law is sometimes seen as the most secure and incontrovertible foundation for human rights. But do rights inhere in the nature of things generally or are they to be understood and interpreted in relation to existing legal and cultural contexts?[65] Since there is little agreement about what would be part of natural law (supposing it to exist at all), perhaps a more pragmatic and less controversial foundation for human rights comes from positive law. As Rory O'Connell aptly asks, "Do We Need Unicorns When We Have Law?"[66]

---

63   Kerruish, "Philosophical Retreat: A Criticism of John Finnis' Theory of Natural Law" at 224.

64   See, for instance, Shelley Wright, "Human Rights and Women's Rights" (1993) 18 *Alternative Law Journal* 113; Hilary Charlesworth, "Feminist Methods in International Law" (1999) 93 *American Journal of International Law* 379; J Oloka-Onyango and Sylvia Tamale, "'The Personal is Political,' or Why Women's Rights are indeed Human Rights: an African Perspective" (1995) 17 *Human Rights Quarterly* 691; see also the extract from Olympe de Gouges in Chapter 6.

65   Ernest Weinrib, "Natural Law and Rights" in George (ed), *Natural Law Theory: Contemporary Essays*.

66   Rory O'Connell, "Do We Need Unicorns When we Have Law" (2005) 18 *Ratio Juris* 484. See also Costas Douzinas, "The End(s) of Human Rights" (2002) 26 *Melbourne University Law Review* 445.

During the 1990s, natural law also made a curious appearance in the party-political arena. In the 1993 Australian Federal election, the Natural Law Party diverted people's attention, but not their votes, away from the main contestants. At about the same time, numbers of Natural Law Parties were established throughout the world, and, by the end of the millenium there were dozens of national Natural Law Parties. After about a decade of enthusiastic promotion of natural law, however, most of the parties disbanded. They were organised under a central umbrella organisation (the Maharishi International Council of Natural Law Parties) and advocated a cosmic understanding of natural law:[67]

> Natural Law is the intelligence and infinite organising power that silently maintains and guides the evolution of everything in the universe. The activity of every grain of creation and of every level of nature — from the tiniest sub-atomic particle to the vast galaxies — is governed by Natural Law with perfect efficiency so that everything in the universe functions with perfect precision and is in perfect co-ordination with everything else.
>
> ...
>
> The infinite variety of problems facing the life of the individual and the different fields of national administration results from violation of the laws of nature. When we do not act in accordance with Natural Law, the automatic result is stress, frustration, sickness, crime, violence, and all the other forms of negativity that beset society.

Natural law is nature's "intelligence", but unlike the mainstream Western philosophical tradition of natural law, this version emphasises the physical world, the planet, and the cosmos. Natural law, according to this view, consists of the unified principles upon which human consciousness *and* the natural world are organised. It is not merely a system of objective moral principles. Use of the term "law" to refer to the physical world seems to be at odds with using it to refer to norms of human action. It is not possible to contravene a law of nature: I may not fully understand the law of gravity, but I am not able, through an act of will, to transgress it. I cannot, no matter how hard I try, fly (except in my imagination). It is true, that, should I (like superman) jump off a building in an attempt to fly, I will inevitably suffer the judgement of the natural law. It is also arguable that extensive interference with "nature", for instance by genetically modifying naturally-occurring species or continuing to generate hazardous volumes of environmental pollutants, will have unpredictable and unhealthy results on human individuals, on the species, and on the planet. (As if we haven't interfered enough already.) More controversial is the notion that the problems facing human communities are a direct result of violation of natural laws, and that reassertion of natural law (assuming it to be evident) will solve humanity's woes. It is this argument that the Natural Law Parties were seeking to promote.

---

67 http://www.natural-law-party.org.uk/misc/what-is-natural-law.htm. On file with the author.

It should be emphasised that it may not be possible to understand the position of the Natural Law Parties properly without an understanding of the eastern (Vedic) philosophy upon which the ideas are based. On the one hand, there does seem to be an irreconcilable difference between two types of law: first a concept of natural law which flows from nature, with its concern that attempts to swim against the tide (or master nature) will have adverse results for the planet and for human societies; secondly, the concept of human law with its emphasis upon rules and principles laid down for ordering social interaction, with any adverse consequences flowing directly to the individual in cases of transgression. On the other hand, what these two types of law have in common is the notion of order and the consequences flowing from transgression: laws order nature, just as they order society and, human thought.

Natural law methodology, according to the Natural Law Party, is not practical reasonableness, but Transcendental Meditation (TM), a process through which we are apparently enabled to attain an internal harmony. It is not so much a question of deriving norms from the natural world so that society may be ordered politically, but of living in harmony with ourselves, with each other and with nature. Ideals are fine (though clearly they can also be dangerous), but the question which will invariably present itself concerns the material particulars of life in harmony with nature. What *is* it to live in accordance with nature? The problem is nicely illustrated in this passage from Samuel Johnson's *Rasselas*, in which a philosopher explains to Rasselas the fundamentals of a happy life:

Samuel Johnson

Rasselas[68]

[355] "The way to be happy is to live according to nature, in obedience to that universal and unalterable law with which every heart is originally impressed; which is not written on it by precept, but engraven by destiny, not instilled by education, but infused at our nativity. He that lives according to nature will suffer nothing from the delusions of hope, or importunities of desire: he will receive and reject with equability of temper; and act or suffer as the reason of things shall alternately prescribe. Other men may amuse themselves with subtle definitions, or intricate ra[t]iocination. Let them learn to be wise by easier means: let them observe the hind of the forest, and the linnet of the grove: let them consider the life of animals, whose motions are regulated by instinct; they obey their guide and are happy. Let us therefore, at length, cease to dispute, and learn to live; throw away the incumbrance of precepts, which they who utter them with so much pride and pomp do not understand, and carry with us this simple and intelligible maxim, that deviation from nature is deviation from happiness."

---

68   From Samuel Johnson, *Rasselas, Poems, and Selected Prose* (Holt Rinehart and Winston, New York, c1958).

When he had spoken, he looked round him with a placid air, and enjoyed the consciousness of his own beneficence. "Sir, said the prince, with great modesty, as I, like all the rest of mankind, am desirous of felicity, my closest attention has been fixed upon your discourse: I doubt not the truth of a position which a man so learned has so confidently advanced. Let me only know what it is to live according to nature."

"When I find young men so humble and so docile, said the philosopher, I can deny them no information which my studies have enabled me to afford. To live according to nature, is to act always with due regard to the fitness arising from the relations and qualities of causes and effects; to concur with the great and unchangeable scheme of universal felicity; to co-operate with the general disposition and tendency of the present system of things."

The prince soon found that this was one of the sages who he should understand less as he heard him longer. He therefore bowed and was silent, and the philosopher, supposing him satisfied, and the rest vanquished, rose up and departed with the air of a man that had co-operated with the present system.

[360] The rhetoric associated with the natural world is certainly powerful, but as I have indicated, exactly what constitutes "nature" is a matter of some controversy.

Positivism

[365] "Positivism" has two primary meanings in relation to philosophy. In the first place, "positivism" refers to positivist philosophy or positivist science.[69] The so-called "founder" of modern scientific positivism was Auguste Comte (1798-1857). Comte saw human knowledge as developing through three states: (a) the theological state, where all phenomena and knowledge are presumed to be derived from a supernatural entity; (b) the metaphysical state, where abstract ideas, or a single all-encompassing Idea (like Nature as a concept) are substituted for the supernatural entities; (c) the positive state, where laws of knowledge and existence are derived from a close observation of all "positive" phenomena (that is, general laws are derived from *facts* which exist in the world).[70] Positivism in this sense refers to a methodology which takes facts or empirical data to be primary in the search for knowledge, and tries to base any general deductions solely on the observation of such facts. For instance, positivist sociology or criminology is based on the collection of empirical data — social facts — as the basis of social knowledge. Such data is collected in a statistical or quantitative form.[71] Non-positivist sociology, in contrast, is more

---

69   As I will explain in Chapter 4, "philosophy" and "science" are not always seen to be different.

70   Auguste Comte, *The Positive Philosophy* (AMS Press, New York, 1974), Ch 1.

71   For an extended discussion of positivism in sociology and its relationship to science see Robert van Krieken et al *Sociology: Themes and Perspectives* (3rd ed, Pearson-Longman, NSW, 2006), pp 600-612.

likely to look at qualitative forms of information, which takes into account the motives, consciousness, beliefs, and ideas of social actors.

Legal positivism shares with scientific and sociological positivism the belief in objectively observable facts; in this case, facts about law. However, legal positivists do not generally adopt a method which involves structured or rigorous observation of legal facts.[72] Rather, "legal positivism" refers to ideas about legal systems and their origins. The idea behind "positivism" as a legal philosophy is that legal systems are "posited", that is, *created*, by people, rather than having a natural or metaphysical existence. Positivists emphasise that the law of legal systems is made by human acts, posited or imposed on people, and that the proper role for legal philosophy is not to speculate about the morality of the system or particular parts of it, but to come to an understanding about the nature of legal systems. This is not to say that morality is not important, but that it is not a necessary element of the concept of law and can thus be excluded from the analytical study of law.

There are therefore several important features of positivist legal philosophy which can be briefly summarised. First, law is created by human beings: it is part of society, and does not transcend it. It is possible to tell whether something is a law by asking whether it has been created within the framework of social rules specified within a society for the establishment of law. And anything not created in the correct way is not a law.[73] This is sometimes referred to as the "pedigree" requirement — if a rule has the right legal pedigree, then it is a "law", and if not, it isn't. The broader set of claims about the place of law *within* society is also known as the social thesis.[74] Secondly, this focus on law as created within a particular framework means that there is no *necessary* connection between law and morality. Law is a posited system of norms, which may accord with moral standards, but will still be law if it doesn't. As Hart has explained, morality is not considered to be part of the *definition* of law as the positivists see it.[75] The validity of law is a matter which is independent of the content of law. Legal positivism claims to study what *is*, not what *ought to be*. This claim, or variations on it, is generally referred to as the separation thesis.[76] The "separation thesis" is obviously at odds with some versions of natural law theory, but it also stands in contrast to the common law approach which views the two things (law as it is and as it ought to be) as

---

72 For a notable recent attempt to apply a "social scientific" method to legal positivism, see Brian Tamanaha, *A General Jurisprudence of Law and Society* (Oxford University Press, Oxford, 2001), especially Ch 6 "A Socio-Legal Positivist Approach to Law".

73 This is to say that the fact of creation according to law is a necessary and sufficient condition of calling a rule a "law".

74 Andrei Marmor, "Legal Positivism: Still Descriptive and Morally Neutral" (2006) 26 *Oxford Journal of Legal Studies* 683, p 686.

75 HLA Hart, *Law, Liberty and Morality* (Oxford University Press, Oxford, 1963), p 2.

76 Marmor, "Legal Positivism", p 686.

inextricable — the fact that a legal doctrine had supposedly existed from time immemorial meant that it was a good doctrine and shouldn't be interfered with. Roughly, law *ought to be* what it *is*, and if "it" is not what it ought to be, then it is not really law, because the law is what ought to be. (Clear?)

The positivist emphasis on the objective facts of posited laws, which exist regardless of what ought to be, rather than on debatable matters like moral standards, underpins positivism's claim to be scientific in its outlook. I will come back to the is/ought question at the end of the chapter, but first will note that it is possible to question the distinction which is frequently made between description and prescription. A descriptive statement may in itself contain very strong, but usually unstated prescriptions. The attempt to describe law as it is, rather than as it ought to be and the confinement of the matter of jurisprudence to positive law, are the bases of positivism's claim to scientificity. Legal positivism arose in an age where the spirit of science was well advanced in its occupation of many intellectual fields.[77] I will discuss the scientific aspirations of positivism in Chapter 4.

These basic aspects of positivism may seem to be absolutely indisputable and, in a sense, they are. They may *seem* indisputable because, after all, modern legal education and practice is based on positivist foundations — this is how we have all been trained to think and so it is rather difficult to think differently. One problem with positivism (apart from the fact that it tends simply to reinforce the legal status quo) is that it relies only on law in order to explain law. If we ask why a law is valid, positivists can only point to another law and not to anything more fundamental. But if we keep asking, we reach a paradox because eventually there has to be some non-legal reason for saying that something is law: it appears that mere political or ideological force distinguishes a legal rule from any other.[78] The people who are dominant in society, who really have the means of social control, are those who dictate the laws. In fact, on one level we know this to be the case, but positivists have avoided stating the logical conclusion of their position this bluntly — they tend to reflect the position of the reasonable lawyer who likes to concern himself with formal structures, and excludes politics and morality altogether. The basic point is that positivism is a theory of positive (ie, created) law, and that it tends to close off legal analysis from other considerations. Positivism has been extremely influential over the past two hundred years or so, and we can see the effect it has had both on judicial reasoning and legal education, which have often been restricted to purely legal doctrines and not their social and political context.

---

77 See Lloyd, *The Idea of Law*, pp 105-109.

78 See also David Dyzenhaus, "Why Positivism Is Authoritarian" (1992) 37 *American Journal of Jurisprudence* 83, for an argument concerning the authoritarian aspects of positivist ideas about adjudication.

John Austin

[370]   Modern positivism has several founders. The early positivist who has had the greatest influence on jurisprudence as a discipline is John Austin. Austin's predecessor, Jeremy Bentham, has had less influence, though it is not always clear why, since a good deal of Austin's work is influenced by Bentham's.[79] It is true, though, that Austin concentrated solely on the description of positive law, an aim which is central to modern positivism, while Bentham diluted his work in this area by writing a good deal about law reform. Thomas Hobbes was an intellectual predecessor of both, but has, however, had even less of a formal place in the tradition of legal philosophy than Bentham.[80] Again, this is a curious fact, though one which I think is explicable by the self-definition of jurisprudence as based on reasoning very closely associated with existent legal systems.[81]

As I have said, Austin was an intellectual successor of Bentham, and is generally regarded as the true founder of modern positivist jurisprudence. Although Austin derived much of his study of the law from Bentham, he confined his writings to just that — a description of the law as it is, and did not engage in speculation about what the law ought to be. (It would perhaps not be too far off the mark to think of Bentham as the first and last great advocate of law reform among the positivist thinkers, although recent positivist theory has attempted to recapture the radical and "ethical" origins of positivism.[82]) In stressing this distinction — between law as it is, and law as it ought to be, or between what became known as the science of jurisprudence and the science of legislation — Austin entrenched what has become the most fundamental distinction in legal philosophy, that between law and morality. Although Bentham had also relied upon this distinction (which as I will explain is derived from the thought of David Hume), Austin really made it the cornerstone of his theory.

Austin wrote an introductory jurisprudential work entitled *The Province of Jurisprudence Determined*, and this title indicates that Austin's project consisted essentially of confining law to its own pure domain, the domain of positive law. Austin begins by attempting to distinguish the proper sphere of jurisprudence (positive law) from various other usages of the concept of law, for instance the law of God ("natural law"), the laws of morality, and the norms associated with social behaviour.

---

79   For a discussion of the nature and reasons for the limitations of Bentham's influence see Philip Schofield, "Jeremy Bentham and Nineteenth-Century English Jurisprudence" (1991) 12 *Journal of Legal History* 58.

80   But see Dyzenhaus, "Why Positivism Is Authoritarian".

81   I have made some observations about the work of both Hobbes and Bentham in Chapter 2, and will not elaborate on them further.

82   For instance Tom Campbell's theory of "ethical positivism", which I will discuss briefly towards the end of the chapter, argues that positivism ought to be accepted on the ethical grounds that it assists clarity in law-making and supports democracy. See Campbell, *The Legal Theory of Ethical Positivism* (Dartmouth, Aldershot, 1996).

There is no *law* which says you must form a queue at the post office, but accepted standards of social behaviour nevertheless make pushing in at the front unacceptable. There is no legislatively posited rule that women have to shave their legs, but it is nonetheless a social convention with which many women comply. The difference between these sorts of rules and legal rules has sometimes been problematic for jurisprudence, but seems usually to be resolved by the type of sanctions or punishment which applies. Infringement of a social rule will result in anything from slight disapproval to being treated as a social outcast, while infringement of "legal" rules results in certain "legal" consequences (fines, damages awards, injunctions, imprisonment etc) determined by courts and other legally empowered tribunals. Austin calls social standards "positive morality".

Austin characterised law "properly so called" as *general commands made by a sovereign*. The features of a command, according to Austin, are (a) that it is a wish or desire of one rational being directed at another rational being; (b) that this intention is communicated; and (c) that if the command is not obeyed a punishment of some sort will result. The command is backed up by state coercion.[83] Thus the Austinian notion of law is sometimes said to turn on the presence of "orders backed by threats". The apparent arbitrariness of the law on this definition is qualified somewhat by the other aspect of Austin's view of positive law, namely that the commands must emanate from a political superior or sovereign which is habitually obeyed by its subjects and which does not itself obey a superior.

Although this is a very reduced and simplified summary of Austin's position, some criticisms of it are obvious. In the first place, Austin relies on the notion of there being a determinate intention to create a particular law: there must be a rational being who can be identified as a sovereign and who commands subjects to act in a particular way. This idea does not accord very well with modern legal practice, which is much more complex than the notion of a simple vertical relationship between a sovereign and subject implies: for instance it is ordinarily the case that those who create the law are themselves bound by it. Secondly, the notion of a command does not adequately describe legal rules which confer power on someone — the idea behind a command backed by threats is that legal subjects *must* do something, whereas there are many laws which simply enable or empower people to act, but do not punish them if they don't. We can still characterise something as law even though it does not involve any element of coercion. So although the command theory may have something to say about criminal laws, it does not adequately describe all law. Thirdly, Austin insisted that the sovereign is a determinate and rational being who can be identified in any legal system — the problem with this is that it appears to rely heavily on a monarchical model of government where the sovereign is the

---

83   John Austin, *The Province of Jurisprudence Determined* (Weidenfeld and Nicholson, London, 1954), Lecture 1.

person at the top of the legal hierarchy. It does not take into account, for instance, a federation governed by a constitution where "sovereignty" is vested in a number of legislative bodies, none of which can override the constitution (which is itself therefore also "sovereign").[84]

HLA Hart

[375]   One of the major positivist theorists of the 20th century is HLA Hart.[85] In 1961, he published an influential work, *The Concept of Law*, which used the ideas of Austin as a springboard for the development of a more sophisticated version of positivism. Hart rejected the notion of sovereignty as being in itself a necessary feature of a legal system. Instead he divided laws into two basic groups, which are joined and made coherent by a superior rule. The first group, "primary rules", are more or less what we would term rules of substantive law. For instance, road rules, the law relating to negligence, and laws which generally regulate behaviour in a social context are all "primary rules". The second group, "secondary rules", are rules about rules which "specify the ways in which the primary rules may be conclusively ascertained, introduced, eliminated, varied, and the fact of their violation conclusively determined".[86] Secondary rules then, are fundamentally the rules which enable primary rules to be changed and enforced, and include constitutional laws and rules of procedure. According to Hart, "primitive" legal systems are composed only of primary rules. Rather than a real legal system, "primitive" societies only have a set of standards for living which, if not entirely static, do not change except over time, and which cannot be enforced in an authoritative fashion. (It is interesting to note that Hart did not actually look at any "primitive" communities to support his claims.) "Advanced" (British) legal systems on the other hand combine rules about conduct with rules about rules. In the final section of this chapter I will examine more closely the justification for Hart's analysis of some legal systems as "primitive" and others as "developed".

This combination of primary and secondary rules is not, however, sufficient to characterise a system of rules as a "legal system". Rather than a "system" a combination of primary and secondary rules may just be a loosely associated set of standards. And far from being associated specifically with law or legal obligation such a combination of rules would also be found in a game of cricket. In order for cricket to be distinct from law, it is necessary to have some ultimate limitation, something which distinguishes legal rules from non-legal rules. So to the primary and secondary rules Hart adds an overarching "rule of

---

84   All of these criticisms are to be found in Hart, *The Concept of Law*, Chs 1-4; see also Lloyd and Freeman, *Lloyd's Introduction to Jurisprudence*, pp 242-254 for a comprehensive summary of the criticisms of Austin.

85   For an excellent and fascinating biography of Hart see Nicola Lacey, *A Life of HLA Hart: The Nightmare and the Noble Dream* (Oxford University Press, Oxford, 2004).

86   Hart, *The Concept of Law*, p 94.

recognition" which is the basic source of legal authority in any system. For instance, prior to joining the European Community,[87] the rule of recognition in the United Kingdom *might* have been something like "whatever the Queen in Parliament enacts is law".[88] (This is not, of course an adequate statement of the actual position since it does not take account of what the courts do — but the courts' ability to make legal pronouncements may be said to be derived from the Queen in Parliament.) *Exactly* what the content of the rule of recognition is, is not always clear in Hart's writings: what is clear is that it is not necessarily a rule which can simply be stated, but is actually a more complex set of attitudes held by legal officials (judges, legislators etc) about what constitutes law. Such a rule may, of course, also exist in normative systems which are not law. A game of cricket may have a "rule of recognition" in the form of scoring conventions: the players and officials do not articulate such rules in the course of the game, but they are nonetheless basic to its progress.[89]

Now, the next question which arises from this scheme is fairly obvious. What makes the rule of recognition valid? Hart's answer is basically that the rule of recognition is used or assumed by the officials of the legal system. The rule of recognition is ascertained by reference to the attitude of legal officials, by their assumptions and actions:[90]

> In the day-to-day life of a legal system its rule of recognition is very seldom expressly formulated as a rule ... For the most part the rule of recognition is not stated, but its existence is shown in the way in which particular rules are identified, either by courts or other officials or private persons or their advisers.

In other words, the existence and identity of the rule of recognition relies upon the attitude of the system's officials. But who or what makes the officials official? Surely it can only be the rule of recognition, which is the fundamental source of all things legal. As several commentators have pointed out, this looks suspiciously circular.[91] The officials recognise the rule which recognises them as officials:[92]

---

87   For a discussion of the rule of recognition after the United Kingdom joined the European Community, see Neil MacCormick, *Questioning Sovereignty: Law, State, and Nation in the European Commonwealth* (Oxford University Press, Oxford, 1999), Ch 6, in particular pp 81-91.

88   See Hart, *The Concept of Law*, pp 102 and 106-107.

89   See Hart, *The Concept of Law*, p 102.

90   See Hart, *The Concept of Law*, p 101.

91   Matthew Kramer has written a lengthy exposition of circularity in Hart. See *Legal Theory, Political Theory, and Deconstruction: Against Rhadamanthus* (Indiana University Press, Bloomington, 1991), pp 115-124. See also Ian Duncanson, "The Strange World of English Jurisprudence" (1979) 30 *Northern Ireland Legal Quarterly* 207; Neil Simmonds, *Central Issues in Jurisprudence: Justice, Laws and Rights* (Sweet and Maxwell, London, 1986), pp 77-95; Morton Horwitz, "Why Is Anglo-American Jurisprudence Unhistorical?" (1997) 17 *Oxford Journal of Legal Studies* 551 at 573-576.

92   Kramer, *Legal Theory, Political Theory, and Deconstruction*, p 120.

In describing whose behaviour is given shape by the rule of recognition, Hart claims that the foundational rule is immanent in official practices. But "officials" can be identified as such only when a framework of laws has come into existence already.

As Kramer points out, this is rather like the logical gap which Jacques Derrida identifies in the American *Declaration of Independence*. The *Declaration* claims to speak in the name of the people, that is, to be a product of the people's word, yet it is the *Declaration* itself which constitutes the people *as* a people.[93] In both cases the purported foundation of authority proves to be no foundation at all, leaving us to wonder whether there *can* be a logically watertight foundation. Would it not be preferable to admit that it really depends on who or what institution has the power at a particular moment to enforce their word?[94] Such power to define and enforce the law does not necessarily take the form of physical force, but — in modern democracies — is more likely to be found in the accumulated and dynamic practices, assumptions, and conventions surrounding law. Such a "foundation" cannot be defined as a single rule, but is instead dispersed throughout society and therefore inherently pluralistic.

The other matter which is important to note about Hart's concept of law is that "natural" principles are not altogether excluded from it. Hart does not go so far as to say that the relationship between law and some basic social principles (whether we call these "morality" or not) is totally contingent. Law cannot have any content at all if it is to provide a reasonable foundation for the continued existence of the human race. As a practical necessity, in order to provide the conditions for social survival, Hart accepts that law has a "minimum content", including basic prescriptions against killing and causing bodily harm, a minimal form of private property, and a way of ensuring compliance with legal order.

Hans Kelsen

[380] The legal philosophy of Hart is supposedly empirical, although, as I will explain in Chapter 4, its credentials on this score are a little wobbly. In contrast, Hans Kelsen structured his theory of law around the idea of a "pure" science. A "pure" science of law, according to Kelsen, would be one which was conceptual in its approach, meaning that it aimed at describing the fundamental conceptual system of law, excluding in the process approaches and values derived from other disciplines, such as sociology, economics, history, or politics. For Kelsen legal science could only be "pure" if it limited the analysis of law to law itself. I will come back to this in Chapter 4.

---

93   Kramer, *Legal Theory, Political Theory, and Deconstruction*, pp 120-121.

94   Jacques Derrida explains the relationship of law and force in some detail, and with particular attention to the question of justice, in "Force of Law: the 'Mystical Foundation of Authority'" in Drucilla Cornell, Michel Rosenfeld, and David Gray Carlson (ed), *Deconstruction and the Possibility of Justice* (Routledge, New York, 1992). I will come back to this in Chapter 8. Further uncertainties in the rule of recognition are conveniently summarised in Lloyd and Freeman, *Lloyd's Introduction to Jurisprudence*, pp 337-345.

What I want to focus on here is how Kelsen explained legal validity. As has become apparent throughout this chapter, the common thread in the debate between natural law and positivism is the concern with validating laws produced authoritatively. The basic questions have been — what is the source of the legitimacy of law? What makes a law valid? For the positivists these questions have been related to the sytematic nature of the legal system — the fact that the laws of a legal system are bound together in some way and are related to each other as parts of a system. The following extract from one of Kelsen's major works is a clear exposition of some of his ideas on these matters. Kelsen argues here that the reason for the validity of a norm can only be another norm: in asking where the validity of a norm originates, we can only go to a higher norm in the system. Eventually, says Kelsen, we will get to a highest norm, the "basic norm", from which all norms in the system derive.

Hans Kelsen
General Theory of Law and State[95]

[385]   The legal order is a system of norms. The question then arises: What is it that makes a system out of a multitude of norms? When does a norm belong to a certain system of norms, an order? This question is in close connection with the question as to the reason of validity of a norm.

In order to answer this question, we must first clarify the grounds on which we assign validity to a norm. When we assume the truth of a statement about reality, it is because the statement corresponds to reality, because our experience confirms it. The statement "A physical body expands when heated" is true, because we have repeatedly and without exception observed that physical bodies expand when they are heated. A norm is not a statement about reality and is therefore incapable of being "true" or "false", in the sense determined above. A norm is either valid or non-valid ...

The reason for the validity of a norm is not, like the test of the truth of an "is" statement, its conformity to reality. As we have already stated, a norm is not valid because it is efficacious. The question why something ought to occur can never be answered by an assertion to the effect that something occurs, but only by an assertion that something ought to occur. In the language of daily life, it is true, we frequently justify a norm by referring to a fact. We say, for instance: "You shall not kill because God has forbidden it in one of the Ten Commandments"; or a mother says to her child: "You ought to go to school because your father has ordered it". However, in these statements the fact that God has issued a command or the fact that the father has ordered the child to do something is only apparently the

95 Hans Kelsen, *General Theory of Law and State* (Russell, New York, 1961), pp 110-111. See also *Pure Theory of Law*, pp 193-195; Iain Stewart, "The Critical Legal Science of Hans Kelsen" (1990) 17 *Journal of Law and Society* 273; Iain Stewart, "Kelsen Tomorrow" (1998) 51 *Current Legal Problems* 181-204; Paulson and Litschewski Paulson (eds), *Normativity and Norms: Critical Perspectives on Kelsenian Themes* (Oxford, Clarendon Press, 1998); Stanley Paulson, "Four Phases in Hans Kelsen's Legal Theory? Reflections on a Periodization" (1998) 18 *Oxford Journal of Legal Studies* 153; Sylvie Delacroix, *Legal Norms and Normativity: An Essay in Genealogy* (Hart, Oxford, 2006), Ch 2.

reason for the validity of the norms in question. The true reason is norms tacitly presupposed because taken for granted. The reason for the validity of the norm You shall not kill, is the general norm, you shall obey the commands of God. The reason for the validity of the norm, You ought to go to school, is the general norm, Children ought to obey their father. If these norms are not presupposed, the references to the facts concerned are not answers to the questions why we shall not kill, why the child ought to go to school. The fact that somebody commands something is, in itself, no reason for the statement that one ought to behave in conformity with the command, no reason for considering the command as a valid norm, no reason for the validity of the norm the contents of which corresponds to the command. The reason for the validity of a norm is always a norm, not a fact. The quest for the reason of validity of a norm leads back, not to reality, but to another norm from which the first norm is derivable in a sense that will be investigated later ...

A norm the validity of which cannot be derived from a superior norm we call a "basic" norm. All norms whose validity may be traced back to one and the same basic norm form a system of norms, or an order. This basic norm constitutes, as a common source, the bond between all the different norms of which an order consists. That a norm belongs to a certain system of norms, to a certain normative order, can be tested only by ascertaining that it derives its validity from the basic norm constituting the order ... [T]he reason for the validity of a norm is a presupposition, a norm presupposed to be an ultimately valid, that is, a basic norm. The quest for the reason of validity of a norm is not — like the quest for the cause of an effect — a *regressus ad infinitum*; it is terminated by a highest norm which is the last reason of validity within the normative system, whereas a last or first cause has no place within a system of natural reality.

[390]   Normative systems are systematic because of the presupposition of a highest norm which binds the various parts of the system together. All norms, which have their ultimate reason for validity in the same basic norm, are part of the same system. We could say, for instance, that the norms of a game of hockey are all derived from the sport's governing body, and that while we are playing, we presuppose them to be valid. We presuppose, in other words, a norm to the effect that "whatever the governing body has laid down is valid". Without the presupposition, we could argue with the umpires not only regarding their application and interpretation of the rules, but also about the content, utility, and desirability of the rules themselves, as well as about the authority of the umpires to control the game. (Personally, however, I never argue.) For the purposes of playing, we situate ourselves inside the established rules, and presuppose them to be valid.[96]

Kelsen applies this reasoning to systems of norms generally. The same considerations apply to legal systems, as the following passage illustrates. Kelsen considers in the first place the "positivity" of law (that is, its non-reliance on moral precepts) and secondly the reason for the

---

96   This should be qualified by the observations made in Chapter 1 about the possibility of being entirely "inside" or "outside" a normative system.

validity of law. Note that Kelsen says the "validity" of a law cannot be measured against moral or political principles. This is not the same thing as saying that the content of the law cannot be measured by reference to morality.

Hans Kelsen

General Theory of Law and State[97]

[395]   The system of norms we call a legal order is a system of the dynamic kind. Legal norms are not valid because they themselves or the basic norm have a content the binding force of which is self-evident. They are not valid because of their inherent appeal. Legal norms may have any kind of content. There is no kind of human behaviour that, because of its nature, could not be made into a legal duty corresponding to a legal right. The validity of a legal norm cannot be questioned on the ground that its contents are incompatible with some moral or political value. A norm is a valid legal norm by virtue of the fact that it has been created according to a definite rule and by virtue thereof only. The basic norm of a legal order is the postulated ultimate rule according to which the norms of this order are established and annulled, receive and lose their validity.

...

The derivation of the norms of a legal order from the basic norm of that order is performed by showing that the particular norms have been created in accordance with the basic norm. To the question why a certain act of coercion — eg, the fact that one individual deprives another individual of his freedom by putting him in jail — is a legal act, the answer is: because it has been prescribed by an individual norm, a judicial decision. To the question why this individual norm is valid as part of a definite legal order, the answer is: because it has been created in conformity with a criminal statute. This statute, finally, receives its validity from the constitution, since it has been established by the competent organ in the way the constitution prescribes.

If we ask why the constitution is valid, perhaps we come upon an older constitution. Ultimately we reach some constitution that is the first historically and that was laid down by an individual usurper or some kind of assembly. The validity of this first constitution is the last presupposition, the final postulate, upon which the validity of all the norms of our legal order depends. It is postulated that one ought to behave as the individual, or the individuals, who laid down the first constitution have ordained. This is the basic norm of the legal order under consideration. The document which embodies the first constitution is a real constitution, a binding norm, only on the condition that the basic norm is presupposed to be valid. Only upon this presupposition are the declarations of those to whom the constitution confers norm-creating power binding norms. It is this pre-supposition that enables us to distinguish between individuals who are legal authorities and other individuals whom we do not regard as such, between acts of human beings which create legal norms and acts which have no such effect.

---

97   Kelsen, *General Theory of Law and State*, pp 113-115.

[3100] Kelsen goes on to consider the limitations in time of a legal order. He says that one legal order may be replaced by another by a revolution (which is taken to include a *coup d'état*). A revolution "occurs whenever the legal order of a community is nullified and replaced by a new order in an illegitimate way, that is in a way not prescribed by the first order itself".[98] The new legal order will have a new basic norm and a new constitution: Kelsen notes that frequently many of the norms of the old system will remain in force, but the reason for their validity will have changed. That is to say, after a revolution, many of the old laws will remain, but the reason for their validity becomes the new constitution, not the old one.

Kelsen's theory has been criticised on the grounds that the basic norm cannot be verified,[99] since it is just a presumption or a hypothesis, and its form is only vaguely identified.[100] Such a criticism may be the result of empirical tendencies in Anglo-American jurisprudence. An inability to identify precisely the legal hierarchy and basic norm in an existing legal system leads to scepticism about the value of the theory. However, as I have explained, Kelsen was not attempting to achieve an empirically grounded explanation of law, but rather an understanding of the conceptual aspects of law. Identifying an actual basic norm in a legal system is not the point, according to this approach.

In my view, the status of the basic norm as an abstract feature of a legal system is one of the more interesting aspects of Kelsen's system. It is, in the first place, the limit of law: in other words, it is the basic norm which separates everything which is in the legal system from everything which is not. The basic norm establishes the notional closure of law. Secondly, the basic norm is not derived, but presupposed. Every legal norm can be derived clearly and logically from a superior norm: legal norms are valid by virtue of the conditions of their creation. The basic norm, in contrast, is simply the conceptual point at which the process stops. It is the place at which the potentially infinite regression ceases. Thirdly, as the underived condition of law, and of its unity and coherence as a system, the basic norm is not itself law. It is not itself part of the legal system. Thus the basic norm is in a paradoxical position. It is not itself law, but it is the basic definition of what is law. It would seem at once to be both inside and outside the legal system. This is hardly surprising, since it is the limit of law. A limit is neither inside nor outside that which it defines. My windows are the limit of one side of my office, but they are neither inside nor outside the building. I have discussed the matter of insides and outsides in

---

98   Kelsen, *General Theory of Law and State*, p 117.

99   Graham Hughes, "Validity and the Basic Norm" (1971) 59 *California Law Review* 695 at 699-700.

100   Julius Stone, "Mystery and Mystique in the Basic Norm" (1963) 26 *Modern Law Review* 34. See also Kelsen's reply, "Professor Stone and the Pure Theory of Law" (1965) 17 *Stanford Law Review* 1128, and Lloyd and Freeman, *Lloyd's Introduction to Jurisprudence*, pp 290-293.

Chapter 1 and will come back to them in Chapter 8. Basically what this paradox indicates to me is the artificial nature of legal closure, and the impossibility of drawing absolute limits of law.

Kelsen tried to deal with these matters more fully in his later work. In *General Theory of Norms*, which was not published in English until 1991, he claimed that the basic norm is a fiction.[101] The reason for this is a little complicated. In the first place, Kelsen says that a valid norm is a statement whereby the subjective meaning of an act of will is also its objective meaning. This is not a particularly helpful way of explaining anything, but what Kelsen seems to mean is that a purely subjective statement cannot be a norm. If I say, "you must hand in a 3000 word essay", this is not in itself a norm. It might just be a joke, or I might say it to my sister who would probably laugh at me. In order for this to be a valid norm it must be supported by a reason which makes it more than a purely subjective wish on my part. The statement becomes "objective" in Kelsen's terminology if it is grounded by some reason beyond my subjective will. In this case, the norm is "objective" because it has as its reason for validity the assessment scheme in a university subject, which lays down certain requirements. Kelsen goes on to point out that this style of reasoning seems to lead to an infinite regression. For you can also demand that the assessment scheme be justified. The assessment scheme must itself be more than an arbitrary and unauthorised act of will in order to have normative force. All of this is really a more complicated way of saying what Kelsen had already written some years earlier, that we need a norm to validate a norm. The question is how do we get out of the infinite regression?

Hans Kelsen
General Theory of Norms[102]

[3105]   ... the Basic Norm of a positive moral or legal system is not a positive norm, but a merely thought norm (ie a fictitious norm), the meaning of a merely fictitious, and not a real, act of will. As such, it is a genuine or "proper" fiction ... whose characteristic is that it is not only contrary to reality, but self-contradictory. For the assumption of a Basic Norm ... not only contradicts reality, since there exists no such norm as the meaning of an actual act of will, but is also self-contradictory, since it represents the empowering of an ultimate moral or legal authority and so emanates from an authority — admittedly a fictitious authority — even higher than this one.

---

101   Hans Kelsen, *General Theory of Norms* (Michael Hartney trans Oxford University Press, Oxford, 1991). On the issue of the basic norm and its role at the limit of law, see Iain Stewart, "Closure and the Legal Norm: An Essay in Critique of Law" (1987) 50 *Modern Law Review* 908.

102   Kelsen, *General Theory of Law and State*, p 256. The work referred to by Kelsen in this passage has been translated into English as Hans Vaihinger, *The Philosophy of As-If: A System of the Theoretical, Practical, and Religious Fictions* (Routledge Kegan Paul, London, 1965). This work has also been relied on extensively by Lon Fuller in *Legal Fictions* (Stanford University Press, California, 1967).

> According to Vaihinger, a fiction is a cognitive device used when one is unable to attain one's cognitive goal with the material at hand ... The cognitive goal of the Basic Norm is to ground the validity of the norms forming a positive moral or legal order, that is, to interpret the subjective meaning of the norm-positing acts as their objective meaning (ie as valid norms) and to interpret the relevant acts as norm-positing acts. This goal can be attained only by means of a fiction. It should be noted that the Basic Norm is not a hypothesis in the sense of Vaihinger's philosophy of As-If — as I myself have sometimes characterized it — but a fiction. A fiction differs from a hypothesis in that it is accompanied — or ought to be accompanied — by the awareness that reality does not agree with it.

[3110] This passage raises a number of very interesting points, the most startling of which is that the legal system is based on a fiction (and not only any fiction but a "genuine" fiction). The basic norm is a fiction because it contradicts reality — that is, it does not actually exist. It is a *genuine* fiction because it also contradicts itself: it is ultimate, but at the same time, would seem to hold out the promise of a higher system from which it is derived. It is the end of the road, so to speak, but the fact that an end has been reached still seems to imply some beyond. (We cannot help but wonder what came before the Big Bang.[103])

Writers generally tend to think that contradiction in theory demonstrates it to be flawed in some way, but I do not believe this to be the case. What Kelsen has said is that, in the end, validity is indemonstrable. What I find especially interesting about this is the sense it gives of the constructed nature of law, while at the same time conveying an impression of certainty in the legal system. Everything that is legal "reality" is so only because of a fiction which is the final ordering principle of law. All of our legal norms, and the associated perceptions of the world, rely for their force on something analogous to the law of the father — a totally arbitrary and oppressive way of defining legal authority, but one which proves particularly difficult to eject from our consciousness. The law is "logocentric" in the Derridean sense: this means that it derives all of its authority and meanings from a single original source. Here, however, Kelsen has gone as far as to admit that the logos (or basic norm) is self-contradictory. It is just something that we assume to be the case.

Contemporary positivism

[3115] In 1994, when the first edition of this book was published, legal theory was expanding rapidly in terms of both the volume of scholarship devoted to legal theory and the diversity of theoretical approaches. The rate of expansion has possibly increased since that time. Much of the new legal theory has been anti-positivist in its motivation and some

---

103 Dennis Lloyd comments about the basic norm: "It is rather like the idea of the world supported on an elephant, the rules not permitting you to ask what supports the elephant"; *The Idea of Law*, p 194.

of this work will be considered in Chapters 5 to 8. However, positivism itself has also enjoyed a revitalisation, as indicated by several major works published from the mid-1990s to the present.[104] WJ Waluchow goes so far as to suggest that the differences between positivists are now sufficiently significant that it may be more accurate to speak of "positivisms" rather than a single theory of positivism.[105]

It is not possible to consider all of the variants on positivism, some of which are intended to clarify the considerable confusion now existing over whether it is even possible clearly to delineate theories of natural law, positivism, and the various "in-betweens" (most notably that of Dworkin). A bewildering and not always helpful terminology has grown-up around these various efforts at clarification.[106] Some new versions of positivism have moved beyond the traditional field of analytical jurisprudence and brought other disciplinary perpectives to bear on positivism. For instance, the sociology of law and legal philosophy have often been seen as distinct approaches to law, the former emphasising the social facts and social groundedness of law; the latter emphasising the theoretical nature of law. Brian Tamanaha's "socio-legal positivism" is one attempt to bring the two perspectives together and to take seriously Hart's unrealised vision of a legal theory which was "an essay in descriptive sociology".[107] Tamanaha's approach involves identifying law through social practices, usages, and meanings, rather than through the theoretical definitions of philosophers and social scientists.[108] In this sense, it is a notion of law grounded in social usage, not in philosophy.

Another interesting new version of legal positivism, advanced by Tom Campbell, attempts to highlight the moral/political basis for the

---

104 These include the following: a second edition of Hart's classic work, *The Concept of Law*; WJ Waluchow, *Inclusive Legal Positivism* (Oxford, Clarendon Press, 1994); Tom Campbell, *The Legal Theory of Ethical Positivism* (Aldershot, Dartmouth, 1996); Stephen Guest (ed), *Positivism Today* (Aldershot, Dartmouth, 1996); Robert P George (ed), *The Autonomy of Law: Essays on Legal Positivism* (Oxford, Clarendon Press, 1996); Anthony Sebok, *Legal Positivism in American Jurisprudence* (New York, Cambridge University Press, 1998); Tom Campbell and Jeffrey Goldsworthy (eds), *Judicial Power, Democracy, and Legal Positivism* (Aldershot, Dartmouth, 2000); Matthew Kramer, *In Defence of Legal Positivism: Law Without Trimmings* (Clarendon Press, Oxford, 1999); Brian Tamanaha, *A General Jurisprudence of Law and Society*; Kaarlo Tuori, *Critical Legal Positivism* (Ashgate, Aldershot, 2002). In addition to these books, a large number of articles concerning positivism have been published, especially in journals such as the *Oxford Journal of Legal Studies*, and *Ratio Juris*.

105 WJ Waluchow, "The Many Faces of Legal Positivism" (1998) 48 *University of Toronto Law Journal* 387 at 390.

106 Terminology which includes the following: soft and hard legal positivism; inclusive and exclusive legal positivism; ethical positivism; conventionalism: see, for instance, Eleni Mitrophanous, "Soft Positivism" (1997) 17 *Oxford Journal of Legal Studies* 621.

107 See HLA Hart, *The Concept of Law*, Preface; see Brian Tamanaha, *General Jurisprudence of Law and Society*, Ch 6, in particular, pp 134-135.

108 Tamanaha, *General Jurisprudence of Law and Society*, pp 162-170, and Chs 6 and 7.

notion that law is separate or separable from morality.[109] Campbell does not argue that law and morality/politics are, in fact, separate (the "separation thesis"). Instead, he argues that, for ethical reasons, we should strive for an understanding and practice of law which achieves as much separation as possible (the "separability thesis"). Where 20th century positivisms have tended to be "descriptive" in that they attempt to advance a description of law that corresponds to some conceptual or empirical truth of the separation of law and morals, Campbell's theory is "prescriptive" because it prescribes such a separation on ethical grounds. Put simply, Campbell does not think that all versions of positivism are always true as a description of law (they may or may not be), but he does think that certain legal and political goals would be strengthened if we aspired to a positivistic separation of law and morality. To this end, legal rules ought to be as identifiable and as determinate as possible (they should be rules, and not vague principles or standards), and decisions determining the content of the law should, as far as possible, be made by a legislature, and not by those who apply the law.

Insofar as it advances ethical grounds for the separation of law and political/moral considerations, Campbell's work "goes back to the real roots of the positivist tradition, to the reforming impulses of Jeremy Bentham and his disciples."[110] In fact, Campbell argues that most positivists have some ethical, moral, or political motivation behind their theories, but that these have frequently been implicit or "submerged".[111] (And a general point might be made that all theories at some point have an ideological or value-laden basis: whether the theorist is aware of the moral/political ends she or he wishes to advance, or whether it is simply embedded in a substratum of cultural value, there is arguably never an entirely descriptive theory.)

In order for "ethical positivism" to be a viable approach, a separation between law and morality must be both possible and desirable. Whether or not real legal practice will ever be able to separate law from non-law completely, it must at least be possible to envisage such a separation: otherwise legal practice will not know what it is aspiring for. As MacCormick says: "Fairyland might be a nice place in theory, but there is no point in planning to live in fairyland or launching political programmes aimed at setting it up as a framework for human society."[112] Therefore one crucial matter for Campbell's theory is whether it is possible to construct laws in such a way as to eliminate (or at least minimise) the potential for non-legal sources to creep into

---

109 See generally Tom Campbell, *The Legal Theory of Ethical Positivism*, especially Ch 1.

110 Neil MacCormick, "Ethical Positivism and the Practical Force of Rules" in Campbell and Goldsworthy (ed), *Judicial Power, Democracy and Legal Positivism*, p 37. See Campbell, *The Legal Theory of Ethical Positivism*, pp 73-75.

111 Campbell, *The Legal Theory of Ethical Positivism*, p 74.

112 MacCormick, "Ethical Positivism and the Practical Force of Rules", p 38.

legal decision-making. Is it possible, in creating and framing laws, to eliminate all of the following: difficulties in identifying law, controversies in their interpretation, exercises of judicial discretion, and the use of broad policies to contextualise application? For reasons which will be discussed in Chapters 5 to 8, critical legal scholars have thought that such absolute clarity is not possible. In particular, they have pointed to the inevitable need for interpretation flowing from the use of language. Of course, even supposing that determinate rules are possible, the question remains whether they are desirable: does minimising the discretion of decision-makers really promote justice?[113]

Some Critical Comments

[3120] As indicated above, the legal theorist whose critique of positivism has received the most attention is Ronald Dworkin. Given that so much scholarly space has been devoted to the debates between Dworkin, and the proponents of natural law and positivism, I do not wish to pursue his work here. However, I would like to point out that together, Dworkin, natural lawyers, and positivists constitute the core of a tradition in legal theory which presupposes a unitary and static notion of "law" — one which is capable of objective theorisation and which is conceptually distinct from mere legal practice. (Although Dworkin does concentrate on judicial action and interpretation rather more than the positivist writers, it is from the point of view of an ideal judge, Hercules, who draws upon idealised legal and social sources in order to construct an "integrated" picture of the law.[114]) The tradition thus constituted holds a position of dominance within the legal academy.

In contrast, jurisprudential dissidents have challenged both the theoretical stance and the theoretical conclusions of this tradition. For instance, feminist legal theory has rejected the idea that law is or can be "autonomous" from social, moral, cultural and political factors. As Nicola Lacey points out, feminist theory "seeks to reveal the ways in which law reflects, reproduces, expresses, constructs and reinforces power relations along sexually patterned lines."[115] Rather than isolating an ideal concept of law, the dissidents to the jurisprudential tradition have indicated the complicity of law with systems of social power, such as gender, culture, and race. Indeed the very ideology of the separation of law is said to disguise and, therefore, perpetuate inequalities.[116]

---

113 See Martin Krygier, "Ethical Positivism and the Liberalism of Fear" in Campbell and Goldsworthy (eds), *Judicial Power, Democracy, and Legal Positivism*.

114 Ronald Dworkin, *Law's Empire* (Fontana, London, 1986), p 239ff.

115 Nicola Lacey, "Feminist Perspectives on Ethical Positivism" in Campbell and Goldsworthy (eds), *Judicial Power, Democracy and Legal Positivism*, p 95.

116 Margaret Davies, "Lesbian Separatism and Legal Positivism" (1998) 13 *Canadian Journal of Law and Society* 1; "Legal Separatism and the Concept of the Person" in Campbell and Goldsworthy (eds), *Judicial Power, Democracy, and Legal Positivism*, pp 115-137.

Is and ought

[3125] One of the major controversies between natural law theorists and positivists concerns the apparently illicit deduction from "is" statements to "ought" statements which positivists have accused natural law writers of making. Positivists have insisted that it is not logically possible to derive a prescription for human action (an "ought") from a description of the natural world (an "is"). As Lloyd and Freeman observe, the attractions of being able to make such a deduction are obvious:[117] since scientific observations about the world are verifiable, if we could derive moral prescriptions from them, we would be able to attain the same degree of certainty in moral reasoning as in science. On the other hand, science is itself arguably political. This is because its "objective" point of view is based on the power of the scientific establishment, because what counts as "verified" will always be a consequence of acceptable conventions within the scientific community and because the doing of science cannot be dissociated from the political purposes for which it is done. If this is the case, then we are entitled to have doubts about the claims of science to epistemological authority.[118]

The positivist perception of natural law theory has often been that it tries to derive legal propositions from facts in the world. "Oughts" can only be derived from other "oughts". This argument is based on that made by David Hume in Book 3 of *A Treatise of Human Nature*. Hume wrote:[119]

> In every system of morality, which I have hitherto met with, I have always remark'd, that the author proceeds for some time in the ordinary way of reasoning, and establishes the being of a God, or makes observations concerning human affairs; when of a sudden I am surpriz'd to find, that instead of the usual copulations of propositions, *is*, and *is not*, I meet with no proposition that is not connected with an *ought*, or an *ought not*. This change is imperceptible; but is, however, of the last consequence.

Hume continues by cautioning readers to be attentive to the use of this transition, observing that such attention would "subvert all the vulgar systems of morality".[120] Subsequently, legal writers took up the argument in an attempt to eliminate altogether questions of morality from jurisprudence. The following famous statement, made by John Austin, reflects the positivist view:[121]

> The existence of a law is one thing; its merit or demerit is another. Whether it be or be not is one enquiry; whether it be or be not conformable to an assumed standard, is a different enquiry. A law, which actually exists is a law, though we happen to dislike it ...

---

117 Lloyd and Freeman, *Lloyd's Introduction to Jurisprudence*, pp 90-91.

118 Some of these matters will be discussed in Chapter 4.

119 David Hume, *A Treatise of Human Nature* (Penguin, Middlesex, 1969), p 521.

120 Hume, *A Treatise of Human Nature*, p 521.

121 Austin, *The Province of Jurisprudence Determined*, p 184.

In consequence, positivists confine themselves to describing the law as it is, not as it ought to be. Or at least, that is their claim. Positivist writers have therefore asserted that their view of law, their concept of jurisprudence, is one which is not based on individual moral or political values — it is merely an analysis of the concept of law as it exists.[122] The description or definition of law is separated from questions of morality, politics and personal ideals. However one very obvious observation about this supposed separation of law from morality is simply that it is in itself a political gesture. The exclusion, and effective suppression, of matters other than those which are determined to be "legal" cannot be politically neutral, although the power of the ideology of "objectivity" is such that in the past it has been viewed in precisely this way, and continues to be. The point is that the separation of law from non-law is a political separation because it sets up an authoritarian notion of jurisprudential correctness. The exclusion of politics is as political as its inclusion.

It is moreover doubtful whether description which is claimed to be "pure" or value free in some sense, is possible. This matter will be discussed in Chapter 4, but some pertinent points about the positivist project should be noted now. In the opening chapter of *Natural Law and Natural Rights* John Finnis points out that much positivist jurisprudence has been based on isolating and describing central cases of law, and distinguishing these central cases from marginal cases. But, as Finnis points out, the process of selecting and interpreting central cases is itself something which is reliant on the judgement of the individual theorist. Value judgements are made as to what counts as central.

I would like to add to what Finnis said, that the interpretation of something as central is actually *political* (value-laden is a fairly weak term for this), because it marginalises the perceptions and experiences of those who do not share the view of the theorist. And it is also *normative*, in that it compels conformity to whatever is seen as central, where that is valued. I do not want to imply that theory should not be political. It cannot fail to be. What I am suggesting is simply what I have already said, which is that we should recognise all theoretical approaches as being political, in the sense of reflecting and centralising certain standpoints. The claim to objectivity has simply been an exceptionally powerful way of centralising a certain style of theory.

A very clear example of the way in which a political judgement forms the basis of a positivist description of the central or typical case of the idea of law appears in Hart's *The Concept of Law*. In that work, as I have explained, Hart describes legal systems as characteristically based on two sorts of rules, primary and secondary, and a "rule of recognition" which is the ultimate criterion of validity. Hart says that legal systems

122 Though note Tom Campbell's suggestion that positivists have derived an "is" (the separation thesis) from an "ought" (that separation will advance good things like the rule of law). See Campbell, *The Legal Theory of Ethical Positivism*, pp 74-75.

which contain these elements are developed, while those that do not are primitive. Primitive legal systems only have primary rules. The "central" cases of the concept of law, are developed legal systems. This characterisation is, in fact, itself very difficult to justify as a pure description. If some cases are central and developed, and others marginal and primitive, then shouldn't the primitive systems be striving to become more like the developed ones? The central "is" of the concept of law has a very strong normative pull to it. This is like making the observation that a woman is not feminine, a "descriptive" statement which is often based on the assumption that women *ought to* strive for some feminine ideal. There is an "ought" contained in the "is". Being "developed" as a legal system is supposedly better than being "primitive".

But how does Hart make this distinction? He has not done any empirical analysis of actual legal systems, some of which might in the 1960s have been designated "primitive" and others "developed" (designations which are, in themselves, political). So his distinction between the centre and the margin is, in the first place, based on mere speculation of what exists in legal systems.[123] We must, moreover, ask how he manages in the first place to characterise one sort of legal system as central to the concept of law and the other as marginal. Surely it can only be on the basis of assumptions he makes about the value of "developed" systems as opposed to "primitive" ones, combined with the value he attaches to the concept of law as he has describes it. Why are the "developed" legal systems more "legal" than "primitive" ones? To this question Hart provides no answer, save for the circular one: "developed" legal systems reflect the characteristics of law as formulated by Hart from his description of "developed" legal systems. We would come to an equally valid argument by taking so-called "primitive" legal systems as central. Such an argument would not, however, be equally convincing, because the power of Western "democracies" is such that our Western political values can be imposed globally.

All this is to suggest that the distinction between "is" and "ought" is one which may not hold in many situations where what is being described is a social institution: the description of that institution may contain assumptions about what ought to be the case. The description of a certain type of legal system as a central type relies on the presupposition that a different type of system is not a proper legal system. The invariable description of people as either female or male presupposes that people ought to be one thing or the other. The same point has also been made in relation to descriptions of nature (sex may be considered to be a description of nature, but as I have indicated in Chapter 1 my view is that it is a social institution):[124]

---

123 Tamanaha, *General Jurisprudence of Law and Society*, pp 150-151.

124 Caroline Merchant, *The Death of Nature: Women, Ecology and the Scientific Revolution* (Harper and Row, San Francisco, 1980), p 4.

It is important to recognise the normative import of descriptive statements about nature. Contemporary philosophers of language have critically reassessed the earlier positivist distinction between the "is" of science and the "ought" of society, arguing that descriptions and norms are not opposed to one another by linguistic separation into separate "is" and "ought" statements, but are contained within each other. Descriptive statements about the world can presuppose the normative; they are then ethic-laden. A statement's normative function lies in the use itself as description. The norms may be tacit assumptions hidden within the descriptions in such a way as to act as invisible restraints or moral ought-nots. The writer or culture may not be conscious of the ethical import yet may act in accordance with its dictates.

As is evident from this argument, it may not be possible to distinguish between "nature" and social institutions. Because descriptions of nature are inevitably framed in language, and language is itself a social institution, any description relies entirely upon the norms of language. In addition, as I have indicated, descriptions may rely on general norms which are assumed by a theorist — such as that which values the model of law of modern Western "democracies" over other, less powerful, models.

In this way one of the central positivist critiques of natural law may be self-defeating: if facts are indeed based on normative assumptions, then the positivist attempt to describe law simply as it is will be reliant on the cultural and linguistic norms within which the description is formulated. Similarly, the view that we should strive for a legal system in which moral norms do not enter into the identification and interpretation of law must also be mistaken because it presupposes that mere description (without interpretation) is possible.

Law and morality

[3130] What happens if you are being asked to obey a law which you really think is unjust? What sort of weight do you give to the mere fact that it is *law*? What should a judge do if she is asked to apply a law she thinks is morally objectionable? What happens if, having obeyed or applied such a law, you are subsequently subjected to legal scrutiny for having done so? How does "morality" intersect with the law? These are some of the perennial problems of jurisprudence, problems which, I would suggest, cannot be answered for all time or all circumstances, but which, in practice, will have to be considered in their own context. I only intend to make a few observations here.

In considering such questions we need to appreciate that we live in a society where dissent is often possible and sometimes effective.[125]

---

125 I do not want to overstate the case: dissent can easily be stifled. According to the *Sydney Morning Herald*, Pat O'Shane thought at length about whether to give reasons for her decision to the court in the Berlei case (which I will discuss shortly) at all, partly because previous dismissals of trivial charges laid against Aboriginal people were not liked by the New South Wales police force and resulted in huge quantities of anonymous hate-mail being sent to her.

What about cases where dissent by officials carries the certainty of serious punishment? One of the most focused issues which has confronted those who defend positivism has been the prosecution for crimes against humanity in cases where the acts complained of were actually performed in pursuance of the formal laws of a legal system. If a person commits an atrocity which is allowed or even required by the positive "law" of a country, should s/he be able to plead that s/he was only acting in accordance with the law? Under Hitler's regime, Germany enacted a great deal of legislation which was acted upon by legal officials, courts, and private citizens. When their actions subsequently came up for scrutiny at the war crimes trials one argument offered in their defence was that they were merely acting in accordance with the law. One approach the tribunals took to this defence was that because Hitler's wartime legislation was in many instances so abhorrent, it was simply not law. Hart, in particular among positivist theorists, has criticised this approach as involving a confusion between law and morality.

One example discussed by Hart concerns the case of a woman who denounced her husband to the authorities for making insulting remarks about Hitler — which was illegal under certain statutes which had been in force since 1934.[126] The husband was sentenced to death, but ended-up being sent to the front instead. After the war the woman was prosecuted under the 1871 German Criminal Code for illegally depriving her husband of his freedom, but she argued that since her husband's imprisonment was carried out in accordance with the 1934 statute, no illegality was involved. But the court held that the later statute was so contrary to justice that it was not law. As Hart points out "this reasoning was followed in many cases which have been hailed as a triumph of the doctrines of natural law and as signalling the overthrow of positivism",[127] a hysterical response, in his view. Hart sees the court's argument as involving a very fundamental confusion between law and morality, preferring instead to say that this was a case where the *law* was clear (because it had been enacted) but too evil to be obeyed. Such an argument would not, of course, help those wishing to prosecute war criminals (who had in fact obeyed the domestic "law", but had transgressed the bounds of morality). Hart offered several alternatives — either accept that what the woman did was lawful and let her off, or introduce a retrospective law to punish her. This latter course he saw as undesirable, but probably to be preferred to the first. In any case, his main argument is that striking down legislation because it is immoral confuses moral and political concerns with the basic

---

126 HLA Hart, "Positivism and the Separation of Law and Morals" in Dworkin (ed), *The Philosophy of Law* (Oxford University Press, Oxford, 1977), pp 32-33.

127 Hart, "Positivism and the Separation of Law and Morals", p 33. A classic critique of Hart's position on these matters is Lon Fuller, "Positivism and Fidelity to Law — A Reply to Professor Hart" (1958) 71 *Harvard Law Review* 630. For a recent evaluation of the effect of World War II on legal theory see Carl Landauer, "Deliberating Speech: Totalitarian Anxieties and Postwar Legal Thought" (2000) 12 *Yale Journal of Law and the Humanities* 171.

nature of law, which is "posited". Hart's argument is confined to a narrow analytical point which is still of relevance. However, it should be noted that since the early 1990s (when South Africa started its transition from racial apartheid to majority rule), debate in the area of "transitional justice" has moved well beyond the issue of individual legal responsibility. Rather than focus on strict legality and retribution for past crimes, attention has moved to the collective (social and political) transitional processes which help to recognise past atrocities and facilitate reconstruction and reconciliation of previously authoritarian, divided and violent societies.[128] Prosecution alone does little to encourage public and widespread acknowledgement of past violence, and may in some cases impede rather than promote reconstruction. Contemporary approaches therefore emphasise the need to balance legal accountability under positive law with the ethical and political imperatives of truth-telling and reconciliation.

I have also discussed briefly the legal theory of John Finnis, and the importance he attaches to the notion of practical reason. As I have said, practical reason is something which we all apply in order to make basic decisions about what we do. What I objected to was the more formal notion of "practical reasonableness" formulated by Finnis, which implies that there is a certain universally accepted "reasonable" way of approaching things which could be used not only as a guide for ethical action, but also as a basis for a legal system. As I noted, people perceive the world in fundamentally different ways, operate according to various systems of values and react to practical situations quite differently. We have to recognise the fact that attempts to articulate a content of "practical reasonableness" can be based (some, including myself, would say are invariably based) on a reinforcement of a particular set of standards and the exclusion of other ways of being and acting. The excluded position is generally in the process devalued.

But Finnis goes on to suggest, as I noted, that judges may have a positive obligation to apply the law, even where it is unjust, in order that the fabric of the legal system not be undermined. Is this right? Under what circumstances should a judge refuse to apply the law? One example of a judge who has challenged a strictly legal approach is Pat O'Shane, an Aboriginal magistrate in New South Wales. Early in 1993 in the Balmain Local Court, O'Shane dismissed charges against four women who had defaced a billboard depicting a woman wearing Berlei underwear being sawn in half. The caption read "You'll always feel good in Berlei" to which the defendants had added "Even if you're mutilated". O'Shane's reasons for dismissing the charges were reported as follows:

---

128 See, for instance, Therese O'Donnell, "Executioners, bystanders and victims: collective guilt, the legacy of denazificaiton and the birth of twentieth-century transitional justice" (2005) 25 *Legal Studies* 627-667; Maryam Kamali, "Accountability for Human Rights Violations: A Comparison of Transitional Justice in East Germany and South Africa" (2001) 40 *Columbia Journal of Transnational Law* 89-14: see generally the essays collected in Scott Veitch (ed), *Law and the Politics of Reconciliation* (Ashgate, Aldershot, 2007).

Pat O'Shane[129]

[3135]   Let me say this. Women are subjected to violence daily, if not hourly, if not by the minute. It is no accident in a society dominated by males that we get this kind of advertising that is depicted in these photographs. It is no accident that we do not see similar depictions of men being disembodied, dismembered and it is no accident therefore, in fact it flows indeed, that we have laws framed ... to protect the property of a male dominated society. The real crime in this matter was the erection of these extremely offensive advertisements. Let nobody be under any misapprehension about it. And what redress does 51 per cent of the population have? Absolutely none. Not only because of that male dominance in the fields that I have just indicated, but also because of the massive power that is exercised through huge financial resources. It is an absolute outrage and I am enraged to find myself in a position where I have to deal with four women who have taken the action which they did on this particular occasion, which they felt justified in taking and I don't for one moment accept that they were misguided in their actions and I don't for one moment accept that they were engaged in some kind of idealistic prank. We have a very, very sorry society indeed when these women can be brought before this court for this sort of thing in the light of the depictions which I find in the photograph of that particular advertisement. We live in a society where at least one and possibly more judicial officers can actually state to the world that the law will condone violence towards women. What sort of world are we creating for ourselves? Ladies, you are excused.

[3140]   In dismissing the charges was O'Shane undermining the structure of the legal system? Was she bringing it into disrepute? Or was she stengthening its commitment to a just society? Is there even a way of answering such questions in advance? O'Shane was certainly criticising the way that the law protects male interests, and in that sense the criticism is a very fundamental one indeed, and one which is essential to the construction of a fair legal regime. Arguably a law which cannot tolerate criticism from within is totalitarian. A law which cannot be sufficiently flexible to allow justice to be done is oppressive to those whose interests are not protected. And legal officials who never reflect upon the established conventions and formalities of the law or society are arguably no better than cabbages.[130] Does this mean that transgression of the law is sometimes necessary to the maintenance of justice? My own opinion is clearly "yes", but I will have more to say on the topic in Chapter 8.

---

129   From *Sydney Morning Herald*, 20 March 1993, p 39. The charge was dismissed under a section of the *Crimes Act* which allowed various factors (health, age, previous record etc) to be taken into account. The judicial officer referred to by O'Shane at the end of her address was a South Australian judge, who said in a rape trial that it is acceptable for a man, in trying to persuade a woman to have sexual intercourse, to use "rougher than usual handling". O'Shane explains the circumstances surrounding the case in (1994) 2 *Australian Feminist Law Journal* 3.

130   See the third philosophical thesis in Chapter 1: "We Are Not Cabbages".

Legitimating authority

[3145]   I indicated at the beginning of this chapter that theories of natural law and positivism have a common desire to locate an absolute ground or foundation for legal authority. Several "grounds" have emerged in the course of the chapter, such as god, practical reason, the common good, the commands of a sovereign, a rule of recognition, and a basic norm. Each of these foundations is supposed to provide a justification for law: each represents a basic principle or point of reference from which legal authority is derived. However, in relation to each (apart from god) I have noted certain problems. In fact, I would say that the attempt to locate such a fundamental principle will always be beset by problems, simply because what is being attempted is the description of law as an abstract totality, when no such monster is possible.[131] Some of the problems have been summarised conveniently by Jean-François Lyotard:[132]

> Attempts at legitimating authority lead to vicious circles (I have authority over you because you authorize me to have it), to question begging (the authorization authorizes authority), to infinite regressions (x is authorized by y, who is authorized by z), and to the paradox of idiolects (God, Life, etc, designate me to exert authority, and I am the only witness of this revelation).

We can recognise in this statement some of the difficulties which have emerged in this chapter, in relation to both natural law and positivism. I suggested, for instance, that John Finnis' explanation of self-evident goods may not be demonstrable, and self-evident only to himself. Is Finnis the only witness of the natural law revelation? And what do we make of the fact that no-one can agree on what constitutes natural law? But nor can the positivists find a satisfactory way of filling in the authority gap. Hart's explanation of the rule of recognition is circular, and Kelsen's theory finds an arbitrary resting point for what would otherwise be an infinite regress. Kelsen, at least, recognised the gap in calling the basic norm a "fiction". All of which is to suggest that, as a matter of logic, authority cannot be legitimised absolutely. In particular, the positivist thesis on the separation of law from non-law breaks down, because the source of this separation (in the shape of a fundamental rule of some sort) can itself never be grounded in law. I will come back to this matter in more detail in Chapter 8. In the meantime, I should also point out that the separation of law from the rest of the world is not only frustrated by this logical difficulty, it is frustrated by what I described in Chapter 1 as the intersections of many levels of normativity. In particular, we cannot dissociate our under-standing of law from our conventional environments — our language, our social existence, and the institutions which structure our lives.

---

131   This point will be discussed further in Chapters 7 and 8.

132   Jean-François Lyotard, *The Differend: Phrases in Dispute* (Manchester University Press, Manchester, 1988), s 203, p 142.

FOUR
LEGAL SCIENCE

Introduction

[405] In the last two chapters several different approaches to the question "what is law?" were described. As we saw in Chapter 2, the common law theorists saw law as custom, authorised by iteration: law was seen to be an accumulated wisdom accessible only by total immersion in legal practice. In contrast, the natural law writers considered in Chapter 3 (some of whom pre-date the common law theorists) saw law as discoverable by "natural" processes or by revelation. The "natural" dimension in natural law theory as we understand it today (usually) refers, however, not to the physical world, but to an understanding of social and moral relationships which is universal and necessary, not contingent. Yet the relation of law to the "natural" world can be cast in a rather different light, as Harry Jones illustrates in the following passage:[1]

> To the mind of the Middle Ages, the world of science and the world of law were not as far apart as they seem to the modern mind. In the world view of the thirteenth and fourteenth centuries, the eternal law, God's ordained and promulgated reason, provided both the government of inanimate nature and the constitution for control of human behaviour and interpersonal relations. The man of science and the man of law were both interpreters: the scientist striving to discern and formulate the eternal laws of nature that explain physical phenomena, the lawyer striving to apprehend and make effective the moral structures of God's natural law for man. It would not have occurred to Thomas Aquinas that there would be any great intellectual or cultural difficulty about inter-disciplinary understanding between scientists and lawyers — he would have said that the scientist and the jurist are, at farthest remove, workers in neighboring vineyards.

> This felt affinity of science and law has disappeared with the theocentric world view that gave it birth. No explicit postulate of divine ordinance supports the logical structure of contemporary science, and law, for its part, is studied and appraised as a product of human will, judgement, and artifice.

---

1   Harry Jones, "Legal Inquiry and the Methods of Science" in Jones (ed), *Law and the Social Role of Science* (Holt, Rinehart and Winston, New York, 1958), p 120.

(Jones overlooks one matter — there were also *women* of science and law working in the various vineyards of the middle ages.)[2] The medieval way of viewing natural phenomena rested on the idea that the natural world was the book of God, and could be read and interpreted as such. As St Bonaventure said: "the creatures of this sensible world signify the invisible things of God; in part because God is the source, exemplar, and end of every creature; in part through their proper likeness; in part from their prophetic prefiguring".[3] An example of this approach is the medieval English *Bestiary*, which describes, among other things, the industry, strength, and foresightedness of the ant as symbolic of the need for humans to prepare themselves well in this life for the next.[4] Of course things have got to the stage these days where, even if we believe in authors, we ("postmodernists", at least) certainly do not believe that their intention (even if the "author" *is* God) is central or even accessible in the quest for meaning. Meaning is not only, or even primarily, a consequence of intention. But that is a story for a later chapter.[5] (A further aside on this question seems, however, necessary: it is that we have now returned in some ways to the paradigm of "reading" the world as a text, even though what we understand "reading" and its consequences to be, are vastly different from the medieval view.)

Now as we have seen, the common law jurists insisted that law was *artificial* reason in some sense, which did not mean that it conflicted with God's plan, but that it was the expression of a wisdom available only to lawyers, rather than to those with a theological training or an

---

2   Peter Kelly has provided me with the following information: "After the dark ages, the study of Roman law was taken up again, initially and principally in Bologna. This began about 1090. The next two centuries were the creative time. With the revived Roman law went the creativity and systemisation of Canon law. The last of the great classical canonists was Joannes Andreae, who was born about 1270 ... He taught at Bologna for years. He had a large family. His wife Melancia was a lawyer. There were three sons and four daughters. The sons were all lawyers, but we do not know much of them ... The youngest child was named Novella after Justinian's work ['Novellae' being the fourth book of Justinian's code]. (Novella is undoubtedly a pretty name; but could you imagine the parents in their zeal naming her Digest or Institutes?) She was a canonist of such high class that she substituted for her father in the lecture halls of Bologna when he was unavailable. Yet so great was her beauty that she had to lecture from behind a curtain so as not to distract the students." Dr Kelly also informs me that, having told this story in a lecture once, he arrived at the next lecture to find that his students had erected a screen in front of the podium. Information about Novella appears in the *Dictionnaire de Droit Canonique*, vol 6, under the entries of "Jean d'Andre" and "Novelle".

3   Quoted in JAW Bennett and GV Smithers (eds), *Early Middle English Verse and Prose* (2nd ed, Clarendon Press, Oxford, 1968), p 164.

4   JAW Bennett and GV Smithers (eds), *Early Middle English Verse and Prose* (2nd ed, Clarendon Press, Oxford, 1968), pp 168-170; a more comprehensive (and readable, since it is in modern English) bestiary is TH White's translation of a 12th century Latin text, *The Book of Beasts: Being a Translation From a Latin Bestiary of the Twelfth Century* (Cape, London, 1954).

5   That is, Chapter 8, on (so-called) "postmodernism", where I will describe current ideas about the social and linguistic specificity of meaning.

interest in the "natural" sciences.[6] If the law applicable to human beings is simply there to be discovered, like the laws of physics, the appropriate stance for a legal theorist to take would be simply that of an external and objective observer whose aim is to describe as accurately as possible the laws which she has discovered. But as I explained, the "discoveries" which the common law jurists made were not like scientific findings, because the reasoning behind the law was seen as artificial, not natural: discoveries could therefore only be made by those with the requisite legal training and judicial capacity. Following the Enlightenment, and especially in the 19th and 20th centuries, knowledge was divided into broad areas and more specific disciplines and it became, for various reasons which will be described below, important to associate law with science or a scientific method. The resulting "legal science" has taken several very different forms and it is the purpose of this chapter to explain and analyse some of these methods. To begin with though, some general remarks about the nature and current significance of scientific knowledge will be made.

Why Science?

[410] Twentieth century values regarding knowledge were centred on the traditional concept of scientific knowledge, which is supposed in certain ways to be *objective* and value free. Taking this view, scientific knowledge is the archetype of knowledge, because it is just there, and is not dependent on the political opinions or other preoccupations of the scientist. We believe in science because it is supposed to provide the truth, or something close enough to it. "Scientific" proof is the standard for all knowledge: it is hard, factual, undeniable, and "proved" in a way that other forms of knowledge can only aspire to. Therefore (it sounds simple) you form a hypothesis and then collect the data to test it. The facts in a sense, speak for themselves. Your own personal views have nothing to do with what you conclude. What could be more objective? In fact, as philosophers of science have argued, the limits of the empirical scientific method are that the "truth" derived from it depends on highly subjective things like how the hypothesis was formulated in the first place, how the data was collected, and very importantly, how it was interpreted.[7] Some modern philosophies of science emphasise that even science relies on particular ways of seeing which are not common to all people, is not based on an absolute and fixed structure of concepts and will change from time to time even

---

6   I am qualifying "natural" in this context because, as explained in Chapter 3, the term is generally taken in opposition to "culture" or an artificial human existence, but is nonetheless of necessity mediated by "culture". In other words, there can be no nature which is just there, pre-existing society, providing its own neutral and objective interpretation. This point will be discussed more fully in the context of science shortly.

7   See Alan Chalmers, *What Is This Thing Called Science?* (3rd ed, University of Queensland Press, St Lucia, 1999), Chs 1-3.

within the scientific community.[8] Science has also been described as a "mythology" in the sense that it provides not only a particular way of organising the world and making statements about truth, but also a system of beliefs for modern society. Science is much more than a way of seeing: it is something for modern Western culture to believe in, a world-view taking the place of religion.[9] Some of these matters will be explained in more detail shortly.

The idea of science is thought of as giving some objectivity (and therefore legitimacy and respectability, since we value objectivity so highly) to what may otherwise be seen as very speculative disciplines. For example, "political science", "social science", "legal science" and economics fall into this category. Alan Chalmers notes that United States universities have taught subjects such as Forest Science, Administrative Science, Dairy Science and Mortuary Science.[10] Many women over a certain age would have encountered "domestic science" as part of their school curriculum. Early last century there was even a move to make literary criticism scientific, by concentrating on the purely formal aspects of literature.[11] It may seem equally strange that law and legal philosophy have, at times, had scientific aspirations, though exactly what would constitute a "science" of law is not always clear, even to those advocating it. As I will explain, in the 19th century the phrase "legal science" was sometimes used to refer to what has become "jurisprudence" (with all its ambiguities) but without much connection to any rigorous scientific method. At the same time jurists in the United States developed ways of understanding law through empirical methods. More recently there has been talk of a "new scientism" in jurisprudence, connected particularly with the schools of law and economics.[12] In some instances, the study of law has been seen as susceptible to rigorous scientific analysis, while in others "science" is more of an analogy used to indicate that law and legal theory are not merely speculative or subjective, but in some sense guided by clear methods. The details of some of these connections between law and science will be explained in the main part of the chapter: for the

---

8   For example Thomas Kuhn's classic and very readable work, *The Structure of Scientific Revolutions* (3rd ed, University of Chicago Press, Chicago, 1996), where the notion of a scientific "paradigm" is introduced.

9   Anthony O'Hear, *Introduction to the Philosophy of Science* (Clarendon Press, Oxford, 1989), pp 202-210. For a critique of the critiques of science see Paul Gross and Norman Levitt, *Higher Superstition: The Academic Left and Its Quarrels with Science* (Johns Hopkins University Press, Baltimore, 1994).

10   Chalmers, *What is this thing called Science?*, pp xix-xx.

11   In *Formalism and Marxism* (Methuen, London, 1979), Tony Bennett describes the formalist approach in literature as resting on the premise that the study of literature should be concerned with literary objects and the concept of literariness, rather than with the multitude of other things with which it had become mixed: pp 48-49.

12   George Priest, "The New Scientism in Legal Scholarship: A Comment on Clark and Posner" (1981) 90 *Yale Law Journal* 1284.

moment it is enough to say that establishing the scientificity of law has at certain times, and for some people, seemed an essential way of reinforcing law's claim to truth.[13]

The limits of science

[415] As I indicated above, science holds a privileged place in the 20th century because of its supposed value-free, non-theological, and objective descriptions of the real world, and because of the popular view that scientific investigations attain some absolute truth through the process of empirical proof. ("Empirical" refers to methods of acquiring knowledge through experience. The application of empirical methods to legal theory will be explained in the next section and in the main part of the chapter.) But there are many different accounts of the role and limitations of science in modern society, and it is very important to have some understanding of these matters when reflecting on the idea of a legal science and what it might mean for jurisprudence. However, I am only going to describe very schematically some of the different views and theories which have been proposed.[14]

One view of science, which Chalmers calls "inductivism", is that scientific knowledge begins with simple observations or facts about the world, which are then reduced to general statements or universal laws.[15] The foundation of scientific knowledge is simple experience, from which certain truths are drawn. Of course, the *quantity* of observations must be appropriate in the circumstances. It would be quite improper for me to draw the conclusion that all cats are grey if I have only ever seen one or two cats. Chalmers expresses the principle of *induction* as follows:[16]

> If a large number of A's have been observed under a wide variety of conditions, and if all those A's without exception possess the property B, then all A's have the property B.

Having arrived at a general law attained in this way from a number of single observations, the scientist can then make predictions by *deduction* about future events or observations. Having seen many things which are not helium-filled balloons fall to the ground when dropped, I can safely predict that if (or when) I throw my computer out of the window it will follow a similar trajectory. As long as I realise first that it is not in fact a helium-filled balloon, I will be in a position to understand to the best of my non-scientific ability, the consequences of my potential action. Having observed that things fall, I can deduce that my computer

---

13   More on the subject of the ways in which law (and science) legitimate their own claims to truth appears in Chapter 8.

14   Most of these theories are summarised in Chalmers, *What is this thing called Science?*

15   See generally Chalmers, *What Is This Thing Called Science?*, Chs 1-4: the classic critique of induction is Karl Popper's *Logic of Scientific Discovery* (Unwin Hyman, London, 1959).

16   Chalmers, *What Is This Thing Called Science?*, p 47.

will too. "Deduction" is a way of logically deriving a conclusion from a set of premises. Again, Chalmers' example is particularly instructive:[17]

1) All books on philosophy are boring.

2) This book is a book on philosophy.

3) This book is boring.

The point about an argument like this is that it is valid, but the conclusion is not *necessarily* true. It is true only if the first two propositions are true. The first statement, which makes a general assertion about philosophy books, could be true by experience, or it could be true of necessity. It would be true by necessity if "all books on philosophy are boring" is a tautology, philosophy being inherently and of necessity boring.[18] The deduction is a way of extending the general law derived from observation of facts to new instances. As AB Wolfe puts it:[19]

> If we try to imagine how a mind of superhuman power and reach, but normal so far as the logical processes of its thought are concerned, ... would use the scientific method, the process would be as follows: First, all facts would be observed and recorded, *without selection* or *a priori* guess as to their relative importance. Secondly, the observed and recorded facts would be analysed, compared, and classified, without *hypothesis or postulates*, other than those necessarily involved in the logic of thought. Third, from this analysis of the facts, generalizations would be inductively drawn as to the relations, classificatory or casual, between them. Fourth, further research would be deductive as well as inductive, employing inferences from previously established generalizations.

The idea here is that a superhuman mind could be objective because no prejudices or assumptions would be incorporated into the processes of making observations and eliciting a meaning from the facts. This position is one which Chalmers calls "naïve inductivism": it is an extreme position, and not one which is defended in this simple form by science philosophers. Nevertheless, it does represent a popular view of the possibilities and actual practices of scientific investigation.

To be brief, this position is "naïve" because it is not, in fact, possible to observe and classify information without having in place some theoretical understanding of the world. If I were to go about observing facts *without selection*, the world would simply be a mass of shapeless and meaningless particulars.[20] I must have in my mind a conception of what

---

17   Chalmers, *What Is This Thing Called Science?*, p 42. It should be noted here, that this sort of reasoning is very important in the process of applying the law to individual cases: it will be discussed in its legal dimensions below at [495], under the heading "Legal Formalism".

18   See Chapter 1 and the hypothesis that jurisprudence is boring.

19   Quoted in Chalmers, *What Is This Thing Called Science?*, p 53.

20   The point will be made in Chapter 8 that the selection is already made for us by language: the world is organised and made meaningful by signs of various sorts, which differ betwen cultures, so it is not possible to claim that observations are made which are either natural or neutral.

is relevant, what is important, what can be compared, distinguished, and so on. Facts do not speak for themselves. Philosophers of science call this difficulty the "theory dependance" of observation.[21] And the way that the "theory" is formulated is itself dependent upon a a world view, a social context, and the conceptual structure of our language. As Sandra Harding says, "when epistemological push comes to shove, we can never tell for sure when we are responding to the compulsions of our language rather than those of our experience."[22] This lack of a clear distinction between theory, language, and observation can be compared to the lack of a clear distinction in law between law and facts. "Facts" for the lawyer are never pure or unmediated: they are always selected and coloured by what the law deems relevant. Law cannot simply be applied to facts without there being already in place a law-dependent interpretation of them. For example, breach of duty in the law of negligence is said to be a question of fact determined in the circumstances of each case: but that the car driven by the defendant was purple instead of green is not relevant to the issue of whether there was such a breach. The "facts" which go to demonstrate breach of duty are never the unmediated particular circumstances but are subject to interpretations of (and by) the law. "Facts" are law-dependent,[23] and law is language-dependent. Moreover, the idea of simple induction gives no explanation of how singular observations can be generalised: even if I have observed a phenomenon on numerous occasions to demonstrate certain properties, that is not to say that it will *always* behave this way. Maybe my computer will float when I throw it out of the window.

Modern philosophers of science have challenged the notion that science simply observes "reality" in a value-free environment and then elicits general laws from these observations. (In fact it should be pointed out that even this way of talking about "science" doing something is symptomatic of the mythology of scientific neutrality: it is *scientists* who observe, experiment, and generalise.) Karl Popper's notion of "falsification", for example, refers to the idea that scientific theories are formed as hypotheses and tested by observation and experimentation: theories can be corroborated or falsified by empirical analysis but never proved conclusively.[24] Scientific theories must be falsifiable, but not actually falsified. Falsified theories give way to new theories which are

21   Chapter 3; O'Hear, *Introduction to the Philosophy of Science*, Ch 5; see also Popper, *The Logic of Scientific Discovery*, pp 93-95.

22   Sandra Harding, *The Science Question in Feminism* (Milton Keynes, Open University Press, 1986), p 37.

23   See, for example, Roscoe Pound, "The Call for a Realist Jurisprudence" (1930) 44 *Harvard Law Review* 697; Zenon Bankowski, "The Jury and Reality" in Nerhot (ed), *Law, Interpretation, and Reality: Essays in Epistemology, Hermeneutics, and Jurisprudence* (Kluwer Academic Publishers, Dordrecht, 1990).

24   Popper, *The Logic of Scientific Discovery*; see also the critique of Popper's critique of inductivism by Hilary Putnam, "The 'Corroboration' of Theories" in Boyd, Gaspar, and Trout (eds), *The Philosophy of Science* (MIT, Cambridge, Mass, 1991).

not yet falsified. In this context Popper contrasts Einstein's theory of relativity, which could be falsified by certain sorts of observations, with psychoanalysis, which — as a myth of the human psyche — cannot be falsified by empirical observations.[25] Psychoanalysis offers interpretations of the psyche which can either be accepted as useful in a clinical environment and informative of cultural constructions, or simply rejected, but never disproved.[26] The theory of relativity is therefore "scientific" while psychoanalysis is not. On the other hand, it could be pointed out that no theory can be conclusively falsified: the explanation for a wayward observation may not be that the theory itself is false, but that something else has not been taken into account. (Maybe the earth *is* flat and all of the contrary evidence could be interpreted another way. Maybe it is all one of God's complex jokes. A very unlikely, but logically possible thesis.)

In *The Structure of Scientific Revolutions*, Thomas Kuhn presented a view of science which concentrates not on the supposedly natural and objective processes of observation and theory-formation, but rather on the different ways of understanding the world which have been dominant at various stages in the history of science. Kuhn's approach helps to explain why science has not, in fact, progressed by either a process of falsification or induction: the really big changes in science occur at moments of crisis when the shared beliefs of a scientific community undergo a fundamental alteration. Scientific knowledge, according to Kuhn, cannot be understood in isolation from the community within which it is developed, and the basic conceptual structures and beliefs of any scientific community constitute what Kuhn calls the "paradigm" of its scientific knowledge at any given moment.[27] The "paradigms" or shared beliefs of a scientific community change very markedly from time to time, during scientific "revolutions", meaning, as Kuhn explains, that the way scientists see the world also changes:[28]

> Examining the record of past research from the vantage of contemporary historiography, the historian of science may be tempted to exclaim that when paradigms change, the world itself changes with them. Led by a new paradigm, scientists adopt new instruments and look in new places.

25   Karl Popper, *Conjectures and Refutations: The Growth of Scientific Knowledge* (3rd ed, Routledge Kegan Paul, London, 1969), pp 33-39.

26   This might also be explained by saying that it is not clear what would constitute falsification of psychoanalysis: saying that little girls don't actually envy the penises of little boys may not be to the point, when the traditional rights and privileges of men are sometimes desired by women. As Luce Irigaray has shown, what is, on one level of Freud's reasoning, pure misogyny, on another level is a cultural commentary which can be subverted to feminists ends. The point is that the "truth" of the theory is demonstrable or falsifiable on several different levels at once: see Luce Irigaray, *Speculum of the Other Woman* (Cornell University Press, Ithaca NY, 1985), pp 11-129.

27   The emphasis on the community structure of science is to be found in the "Postscript" to the 1970 edition of Kuhn, *The Structure of Scientific Revolutions*.

28   Kuhn, *The Structure of Scientific Revolutions*, p 111.

Even more important, during revolutions scientists see new and different things when looking with familiar instruments in places they have looked before. It is rather as if the professional community had been suddenly transported to another planet where familiar objects are seen in a different light and are joined by unfamiliar ones as well. Of course, nothing of quite that sort does occur: there is no geographical transplantation; outside the laboratory everyday affairs usually continue as before. Nevertheless, paradigm changes do cause scientists to see the world of their research-engagement differently. In so far as their only recourse to that world is through what they see and do, we may want to say that after a revolution scientists are responding to a different world.

Kuhn describes the paradigm as not only essential to the identification of a scientific community, but also to the constitution of nature itself: "What were ducks in the scientist's world before the revolution are rabbits afterwards".[29] The perception of the object is relative to the social context in which the perceiving is done. Kuhn's revelations may have come as more of a surprise to Western scientists than to others. As Ziauddin Sardar comments: "Kuhn's analysis shows how science works in one civilisation: the Western civilisation. His insights are hardly new for postcolonial writers on science: the very premise of all non-Western sciences is that science operates and progresses within a world view."[30]

Recent commentators have taken ideas such as these further into the realms of political theory, feminist thought and sociology.[31] For instance, as I have mentioned, Anthony O'Hear describes science as a modern mythology: he sees it as a thoroughly human activity, reliant not only on the paradigms of scientific communities, but on the entire context of social existence, elevating it to its present day status of the archetype of knowledge.[32] And Joseph Rouse has used the work of French thinker Michel Foucault to articulate the relationship between

---

29   Kuhn, *The Structure of Scientific Revolutions*, p 111.

30   Ziauddin Sardar, "Above, Beyond, and at the Center of the Science Wars: A Postcolonial Reading" in Ashman and Baringer (eds), *After the Science Wars* (London, Routledge, 2001), p 130.

31   Generally on this point see Harding, *The Science Question in Feminism*, pp 199-202. The question of scientific objectivity and claims of epistemological relativism were the subject of the so-called "science wars" fought in the 1990s between critics and defenders of science. See in particular the special edition of *Social Text* (1996) dealing with these matters. This edition contains the (in)famous article by Alan Sokal, "Transgressing the Boundaries: Toward a Transformative Hermeneutics of Quantum Gravity". Having had the article published, Sokal revealed that it was a hoax which deliberately but meaninglessly appropriated the language of postmodernism. See also Paul Gross and Norman Levitt, *Higher Superstition: The Academic Left and its Quarrels with Science* (Johns Hopkins University Press, 1994); Alan Sokal and Jean Bricmont, *Fashionable Nonsense: Postmodern Intellectuals' Abuse of Science* (Picador, New York, 1998); Ashman and Baringer (eds), *After the Science Wars*; Keith Parsons (ed), *The Science Wars: Debating Scientific Knowledge and Technology* (Prometheus Books, Amherst, NY, 2003).

32   O'Hear, *Introduction to the Philosophy of Science*, Ch 9.

science and power.[33] As I will explain more fully in Chapter 8, Foucault argued that "truth" is a product of power relations in society.[34] (It is important to understand in this context that, for Foucault, power is not just political power, but arises in complex ways within the network of relations which constitute society.) So, to take a simple example, the "truth" of science is not just there: what counts as proper scientific verification or evidence is determined by the conventions of the scientific community. Knowledge and power are not separate because one group of people, in this case the scientific community, determines what counts as "true" in any given context.[35] (To explain this in any more detail would transgress on the territory of Chapter 8, so I will leave it there, with the comment that at this point we can see a connection between law, science, and knowledge generally through the idea of legitimation: just as positive law must comply with certain criteria of legitimation, so in order to count as "knowledge" a theory, statement, or observation must conform to the criteria laid down by the scientific community.)

Now it may seem that making this sort of claim about science (ie, the observation of facts is dependent on a scientist's pre-existing perspective) destroys claims of scientific objectivity or neutrality. It can certainly no longer be said that there is just a reality out there which scientists (above and before all others) can gain direct access to. Their understanding of nature is mediated by conceptual structures which organise the world. But this certainly does not mean that scientific knowledge is all relative, or simply not "true". If we understand "truth" itself to be a product of certain ways of perceiving the world, and not simply pre-existing any interpretation of "reality" (however that is defined) then scientific paradigms are simply highly developed methods of perception, which help us to understand natural phenomena. The problem of scientific imperialism arises when the cultural and discursive limitations of science are not properly understood, and it is taken as providing an absolutely objective and real description of the world.[36] In other words, critiques of science do not show it to be wrong, but rather, like all forms of knowledge, limited in certain respects. Indeed, the scientific emphasis on objectivity can be said itself to *produce* partial perspective within scientific disciplines, rather than eliminate it, as Sarah Franklin explains:[37]

33   Joseph Rouse, *Knowledge and Power: Toward a Political Philosophy of Science* (Cornell University Press, Ithaca NY, 1987).

34   Michel Foucault, "Truth and Power" in Foucault, *Power/Knowledge* (Harvester Press, Brighton, 1980).

35   The classical statement of these matters in the context of postmodernism is that of Jean-François Lyotard in *The Postmodern Condition: A Report on Knowledge* (University of Minnesota Press, Minneapolis, 1984). This work will be discussed in Chapter 8.

36   See the comments made by O'Hear in *Introduction to the Philosophy of Science*, p 204.

37   Sarah Franklin, "Making Transparencies: Seeing Through the Science Wars" (1996) 46/47 *Social Text* 141-155.

To know a thing in itself is the equivalent of radically decontextualising it. The scopic instruments of scientific investigation depend upon the limitation they impose on their field of vision: the microscope, the telescope, the laparoscope, the endoscope. The effect is of looking through a toilet paper tube: it has the effect of being radically blinkered. Disciplinarity is defined by what is excluded, and so is detached, objective observation. The idea is that you see through a tunnel to the thing itself, the object to be known ... Both tunnel vision and disciplinarity rely on not seeing "the rest of the picture" so it does not distract from the object in question. Like objectivity, disciplinarity is about screening things out.

Looking at the object "itself" requires methods for excluding things which are irrelevant or not part of the object as judged by the scientist and her community of peers. It is obvious that such an observer (or any observer) is not presented with a picture of everything that might be known about the object. She obtains a limited representation of the picture, though obviously having a certain utility and truth as framed by the conditions of observation.

If the most that can be said about scientific objectivity is that it is constructed within a particular (Western) frame of reference, then clearly mainstream science will be vulnerable to critical theories which question the relationship between the subject of knowledge (such as the scientific observer) and the object. It is easy, in a liberal context which believes in the rational and independent individual, to think of the observer as neutral and as able to put their personal predilections aside. It is equally easy to dismiss critique as being merely concerned with the possibility of personal bias, a problem which may be minimised by the adoption of appropriate scientific protocols such as peer review. Science does, after all, have its own in-built mechanisms for self-critique. Thus, some critiques may serve the scientific ideal of objectivity by highlighting instances where it has not been followed — such critiques may suggest methods of strengthening scientific method and objectivity. However, the critique of science goes beyond any mere perception of possible bias: it is also concerned not with individual subjects, but rather with that which is systemic, institutional, and cultural. The critique of the rational and autonomous liberal subject brings with it a critique of the notion that this subject can "know" independently of others, and independently of a cultural context. Feminist and postcolonial critics of science, for instance, have challenged the alleged universality of Western science, by showing that its very structure is embedded in a cultural and patriarchal context which *could* operate by different norms (and thus produce different knowledge): the message is that science is not a "universal" knowledge, but one knowledge among many forms of knowledge, each of which may be suited to different contexts and different purposes.

In explaining feminist critiques of science, for instance, Evelyn Fox Keller identifies a number of ways in which the practice and ideology of science may be said to reproduce masculine values and bias.[38] Some of these critiques merely concern poorly designed scientific practices, while others concern the standard of objectivity itself. First, Fox Keller notes that the institution of science is male dominated, and has been subjected to a liberal feminist critique aimed at promoting equal opportunity in a field not traditionally welcoming to women. Secondly, she points out that this "predominance of men in the sciences has led to a bias in the choice and definition of problems" and that this criticism "is most frequently and most easily made in regard to the health sciences".[39] The prioritising of scientific problems may be made by individuals or teams, but it may also be set by the funding agencies and governments, which decide where resources are to be deployed. Thirdly, Keller notes that feminists sometimes claim that the male is taken as the standard of the human (and other) species, a fact perhaps illustrated most obviously in anatomical charts depicting the male body. Such "androcentrism" may affect the interpretation of empirical observations: a group of several female primates mating with one male is sometimes classified as a "harem" rather than as a practical reproductive arrangement where the male input is reduced to the essential minimum.[40] In addition to these illustrations of bias, some feminists have argued that — as a culture — science has been gender specific in its symbolism and recognition of subjects as holders of knowledge. The position of the knower has been identified as masculine, while the object of knowledge — frequently "nature" — has been identified as feminine.[41]

Critics of science have identified similar problems with the racial and ethnocentric assumptions made by science. For instance, Ziauddin Sardar argues that the contributions and distinctive nature of Islamic, Indian, and Chinese science are generally ignored by Western science. Western science has appropriated much from these traditions, a fact which is not traditionally acknowledged in science education. According to some, Western science continues to regard traditional and indigenous knowledge as vast uncharted territories, a repository of potential "discoveries", while devaluing the scientific status of such

---

38   Sandra Harding's work, especially *The Science Question in Feminism*, is particularly useful because she engages with mainstream philosophies of science, particularly that of Kuhn.

39   Evelyn Fox Keller, "Feminism and Science", in Boyd, Gaspar, and Trout (eds), *The Philosophy of Science* (MIT Press, Cambridge Mass, 1991), p 280. See also Sandra Harding, *Whose Science? Whose Knowledge? Thinking From Women's Lives* (Cornell University Press, Ithaca NY, 1991), Ch 5; Sylvia Walby, "Against Epistemological Chasms: The Science Question in Feminism Revisited" (2001) 26 *Signs* 485; Sandra Harding, "Comment on Walby's 'Against Epistemological Chasms: The Science Question in Feminism Revisited': Can Democratic Values and Interests Ever Play a Rationally Justifiable Role in the Evaluation of Scientific Work" (2001) 26 *Signs* 511.

40   Keller cites the work of Jane Lancaster on this issue: Jane Lancaster, *Primate Behaviour and the Emergence of Human Culture* (New York, Holt, Rinehart and Winston, 1975).

41   Carolyn Merchant, *The Death of Nature: Women, Ecology, and the Scientific Revolution* (Harper and Rowe, San Francisco, 1980).

knowledge.[42] Seemingly, knowledge cannot count as "scientific" until it has been published in a peer-reviewed journal, and subjected to the kind of analysis expected by the Western scientific institution. The fact that a traditional body of knowledge may have been accumulated and developed over generations does not guarantee its acceptance by science. Similarly, there are many examples of ethnocentrism in science, where the human norm in biology, social life, and culture is assumed to be European.[43] These types of bias are what Ann Cudd calls "cognitive mistakes" — they do not necessarily undermine science as such, and acknowledgement that they have been made should lead to a more objective scientific enquiry. Identification and elimination of such mistakes leads to better science.[44]

However, critiques of science have not only identified ways in which science fails in its objectivity. They also, as indicated above, may question the very possibility of scientific objectivity. Or, they may emphasise that science itself is not singular, but can take many different cultural forms. Beyond the liberal critiques outlined above, Keller mentions the "truly radical critique that attempts to locate androcentric bias even in the 'hard' sciences, indeed in scientific ideology itself."[45] That is, as indicated above, some critics have questioned whether there is any knowledge which is independent of social context and language. Perhaps "science" is only one knowledge among many possibilities. And perhaps "objective" knowledge can only be formulated in relation to the context of the "subjects" who hold the knowledge. Both Sandra Harding and Donna Harraway have accepted the possibility of "objectivity", while attempting to re-fashion what is meant by the term: Harding speaks of the "strong objectivity" which results from acknowledging the standpoint of the "other",[46] while Haraway sees objectivity as residing in a "joining of partial views and halting voices into a collective subject position".[47]

It is not very difficult to observe parallel developments in the critique of law: as we will see in Chapters 5 to 8, critics have identified bias in the application of law; a phenomenon which may flow from the white, male, middle-class dominance of the legal profession. The fundamental

---

42 Vandana Shiva, *Biopiracy: The Plunder of Nature and Knowledge* (Green, Dartington, 1997).

43 Some examples are provided by Ann Cudd, "Objectivity and Ethno-Feminist Critiques of Science" in Ashman and Baringer (eds), *After the Science Wars* (London, Routledge, 2001), p 80.

44 See also Keller ,"Feminism and Science", p 281.

45 Keller, "Feminism and Science", p 281.

46 Harding, *Whose Science? Whose Knowledge? Thinking From Women's Lives*, p 123ff.

47 Donna Haraway, *Simians, Cyborgs, and Women: The Reinvention of Nature* (New York, Routledge, 1991), p 196.

values upon which law is sometimes said to rest have also been critiqued — in particular, the ability of lawyers to identify and apply the law in a neutral and objective fashion. Just as the scientific insistence on neutrality and universality may provide an easy target for critics who can show only too clearly many instances of bias, so the legal claim of objectivity has provoked a reaction from feminists and others who can point to a multitude of cases where a male or ethnocentric norm has prevailed. In the case of both science and law, however, something more significant than mere bias is at stake — the very values upon which the discipline is built. This is not to say that acceptance of the critical approach will destroy either science or law, merely that the claims of objectivity and neutrality may need to be re-evaluated. Most importantly, as with any area of knowledge, there is a need for ongoing critique and reflection about fundamental presuppositions.

Law and science

[420] What complicates the picture for law is that when people make claims about law as a "science" they are sometimes talking only very generally about the possibility of objectivity, neutrality, and finding a "right" answer, while at other times they mean literally that the study of law can follow a scientific methodology. Sometimes they mean that law as an object of study is to be treated as a closed system whereby certain fundamental principles can be scientifically deduced, while sometimes they mean that already established "sciences" like social science, formal logic, or economics can be applied to the law. Moreover, the idea that science operates at several different levels of legal analysis can be used in various ways: it can be used to talk about the "formal" (and objective) nature of legal reasoning; it can be used as a method to answer the philosophical question "what is law?"; it has been applied very extensively by law and economics writers to substantive legal doctrines; and, in the trial process, it has become an important feature of establishing the facts of a particular case.

The understanding of science by jurisprudence has been basically either *empirical* ("inductive" — drawing conclusions and wider explanations from observed data) or *conceptual* (meaning in this case that fundamental concepts are used to explain law). The essential difference is that in purely empirical jurisprudence the observed facts about law are supposed to lead to general truths or at least hypotheses about the nature of law, while conceptual jurisprudence is based on the idea that we have to impose a structure of concepts on our experience before we can understand it. The distinction between formal or conceptual science and empirical science is explained by Crozier in terms of the distinction between *a priori* thought ("self-evident truths") and a process of abstracting general statements from observed data.

JB Crozier
"Legal Realism and a Science of Law"[48]

[425] Formal, pure science is seen as an analysis of nature which flows from the application of an abstract system of postulates. The postulates, which typically have the status of self-evident truths, give rise to *a priori* knowledge of nature through a process of hypothetico-deductive reasoning. Probably the most well-known example of such a scientific system is that of Euclidean geometry. Here, we find an autonomous body of propositions which seemingly deduce the properties of physical space. Of course, now we can say "seemingly", for by the mid-nineteenth century we find the emergence of non-Euclidean geometries, and with them the realization that even pure, formal science involves the trial-and-error application of relative, rather than absolute principles.

In contrast to formal science, empirical science is inductive in its scope. With its genesis in knowledge gained by sensory observation, it only secondarily proceeds to a level of abstract theorizing. But, in the realm of descriptive science, this level of abstraction functions largely as a conceptual summarization for the observations, and does not have the immutable status characteristic of the pure, formal perspective. The focus of such a descriptive science is the chronology of antecedent and consequence events, and their subsequent demonstration through replication.

[430] In other words, empirical science proceeds through using observed facts, either to construct new hypotheses or to test existing ones.

In the dominant tradition of common law legal philosophy, the empirical methodology has been by far the more important. As Roger Cotterrell points out, this may have something to do with the fact that common law is itself based on the idea of reasoning about law from decided cases.[49] However, before understanding anything about a case we have to exercise a great deal of personal judgement in interpreting and categorising the case. The case does not speak for itself, and it would be idealistic to suggest that even if an "objective" reader (assuming such a person is plausible) had read all the common law cases, a coherent order would emerge. (This point could, of course, be debated endlessly.)

48   JB Crozier, "Legal Realism and a Science of Law" (1984) 29 *American Journal of Jurisprudence* 151 at 162. The term "hypothetico-deductive reasoning" here used in conjunction with "formal" science is confusing: "hypothetico-deductive" systems typically involve an empirical scientific methodology, beginning with hypotheses rather than simple observation. On the conceptual/empirical distinction, see also Hessel Yntema, "The Rational Basis of Legal Science" (1931) 31 *Columbia Law Review* 925 at 927-929; Roscoe Pound, "Law and the Science of Law in Recent Theories" (1934) 43 *Yale Law Journal* 525; Roger Cotterrell, *The Politics of Jurisprudence: A Critical Introduction to Legal Philosophy* (Butterworths, London, 1989), Ch 4; Charles Barzun, "Common Sense and Legal Science" (2004) 90 *Virginia Law Review* 1051.

49   Cotterrell, *The Politics of Jurisprudence: A Critical Introduction to Legal Philosophy*, pp 106-107.

There have been several distinctly different attempts to apply an empirical method to the study of law. One of the most famous and influential (at least in the United States) is that instituted at the Harvard Law School last century by Christopher Columbus Langdell. Langdell argued that the primary data of the law is decided cases, and that a scientific understanding of law could be gained by a detailed examination of such cases in isolation from other aspects of the law. Some decades later in the United States the Realists, many of whom were very critical of Langdell's method,[50] broadened the category of observable data in law by insisting that the law must be studied in its social and political dimensions. The North American Realists saw the proper object of study to be the behaviour and values of actors in the law in its wider institutional sense, not simply the derivation of general propositions about law from decided cases.[51]

Rather than following strictly an empirical method like that employed by mainstream science (which might involve hypothesis formulation, construction of an experimental environment, and experimentation), empirical legal philosophy has seen itself as scientific in the sense of being a precise body of thought which *observes and describes* the way law really operates. Langdell saw the materials of legal observation to exist essentially in reported cases. But empiricism in law has not always been so clearly defined, as is evident by a consideration of methodology in the work of HLA Hart. As we saw in Chapter 3, Hart attempted to discover principles which apply to legal systems generally, by describing things which he thought existed in actual legal systems and, in particular, the linguistic practices of legal officials. Such an enquiry goes well beyond Langdell's attention to decided cases. Thus Roger Cotterrell argues that Hart instituted a new type of empiricism in law: one in which the "observable reality" of the law was the practices and linguistic usages of people in relation to law.[52] Hart actually describes *The Concept of Law* as "an essay in descriptive sociology",[53] a claim which Cotterrell disputes because of the absence of empirical evidence. The nature of Hart's methodology is in fact highly problematic, as Cotterrell argues.

---

50   See generally Wai Chee Dimock, "Rules of Law, Laws of Science" (2001) 13 *Yale Journal of Law and the Humanities* 203.

51   See Crozier, "Legal Realism and a Science of Law"; Levit, "Listening to Tribal Legends: An Essay on Law and the Scientific Method" (1989) 58 *Fordham Law Review* 263 at 277-280; Karl Llewellyn, "The Theory of Legal Science" (1931) 44 *Harvard Law Review* 697.

52   Cotterrell, *The Politics of Jurisprudence: A Critical Introduction to Legal Philosophy*, pp 87-92.

53   HLA Hart, *The Concept of Law* (2nd ed, Clarendon Press, Oxford, 1994), p v. For an extended discussion of Hart's claim and its relevance to current jurisprudential projects, see Nicola Lacey, "Analytical Jurisprudence Versus Descriptive Sociology Revisited" (2006) 84 *Texas Law Review* 945.

Roger Cotterrell
The Politics of Jurisprudence[54]

[435]   The root of the problem is this: Hart seeks to provide a general explanation of the character of law on an empiricist basis — in other words, the concepts which he seeks to link theoretically are to be drawn from actual experience or observation of law. But he rejects the idea that legal doctrine itself provides the empirical materials for theory, because there is no necessary fixity of meaning of legal ideas. They do not necessarily represent anything consistently so theory cannot concern itself exclusively with their meaning and the logic of their relationships in legal doctrine. Therefore, the empirical reality to be reflected in theory is the reality of people's (linguistic) practices — the way they talk and think around notions such as "obligation". But this should involve actually finding out how people talk and think and such an inquiry is not normative legal theory but sociology or social psychology. As long as empiricist approaches in normative legal theory were satisfied with analysing legal doctrine (the concept of "corporate personality", for example) as the relevant empirical reality (asking what is a "corporation"), they did not lead normative legal theory's inquiries into a study of society at large. But Hart's empiricist approach leads in just such a direction. There is a kind of sociological drift (but no serious sociology) in Hart's normative legal theory.

[440]   One of the problems with Hart's method was that the system he described was basically the English one, so any principles he discovered were of necessity limited in their descriptive power. For instance he described certain legal systems which failed to fulfil all the conditions of what he thought was a legal system as "primitive". But it seems obvious that if we describe something we know as a model of law, then anything which doesn't fit the description entirely will be seen to be deficient. Legal systems derived from those of Europe could also be seen to be "primitive" in a great many ways. Moreover, as Cotterrell notes, Hart didn't actually do any substantial empirical study of the existing practices of legal officials within a legal system, and even though this was not his primary objective, the nature of his claims concerning the study of law through linguistic practice suggest it should have been a methodological necessity.

The other sort of legal science is "conceptual", and proceeds not only by description of actual systems, but by thinking about the nature of law and the meanings attached to it. Hans Kelsen emphasised something which is often overlooked by theorists relying on a purely empirical method, which is that the mere occurrence of any act is distinguishable from its legal meaning. An act of killing a person could be *legally* a number of things, such as a lawful execution or a murder: this meaning is not derived from our perception of the act, but from the meaning which is given to it by the law: "The qualification of a certain act as the execution of the death penalty rather than as a murder — a qualification that cannot be perceived by the senses — results from

54   Cotterrell, *The Politics of Jurisprudence: A Critical Introduction to Legal Philosophy*, p 96.

a thinking process: from the confrontation of this act with the criminal code".[55] The science of law was, according to Kelsen, a way of organising the legal system: "Just as the chaos of sensual perceptions becomes a cosmos, that is, 'nature' as a unified system, through the cognition of natural science, so the multitude of general and individual legal norms, created by the legal organs, becomes a unitary system, a legal 'order', through the science of law."[56]

Unlike more recent legal scientists (such as the law and economics writers) Kelsen insisted on the "purity" of legal science, that is, its non-moral, non-political, non-ideological, and non-natural character. Kelsen was very clear about the need for purity in legal science.

Hans Kelsen
"The Pure Theory of Law"[57]

[445]   1. The Pure Theory of Law is a theory of the positive law. As a theory it is exclusively concerned with the accurate definition of its subject-matter. It endeavours to answer the question, What is the law? but not the question, What ought it to be? It is a science and not a politics of law.

That all this is described as a "pure" theory of law means that it is concerned solely with that part of knowledge which deals with law, excluding from such knowledge everything which does not strictly belong to the subject-matter law. That is, it endeavours to free the science of law from all foreign elements. This is its fundamental methodological principle. It would seem a self-evident one. Yet a glance at the traditional science of law in its nineteenth and twentieth century developments shows plainly how far removed from the requirement of purity that science was. Jurisprudence, in a wholly uncritical fashion, was mixed up with psychology and biology, with ethics and theology. There is to-day hardly a single social science into whose province jurisprudence feels itself unfitted to enter, even thinking, indeed, to enhance its scientific status by such conjunction with other disciplines. The real science of law, of course, is lost in such a process.

2. Law is a social phenomenon. Society, however, is something wholly different from nature, since an entirely different association of elements. If legal science is not to disappear into natural science, then law must be distinguished in the plainest possible manner from nature. The difficulty about such a distinction is that law, or what is generally called law, belongs with at least part of its being to nature and seems to have a thoroughly natural existence. If, for instance, we analyse any condition of things such

---

55   Hans Kelsen, *Pure Theory of Law* (University of California Press, Berkeley, 1967), p 4. See also Kelsen, "On the Theory of Interpretation" (1990) 10 *Legal Studies* 127.

56   Kelsen, *Pure Theory of Law*, p 72.

57   Kelsen, "The Pure Theory of Law: Its Method and Fundamental Concepts, Part 1" (1934) 200 *Law Quarterly Review* 474 at 477-481. Iain Stewart makes the important point that Kelsen's "science" is a pure theory of law, not a theory of pure law, in that it is an attempt to set rigorous conditions for understanding law. Stewart, "Kelsen Tomorrow" (1998) 51 *Current Legal Problems* 181 at 183; see also Stewart, "The Critical Legal Science of Hans Kelsen" (1990) 17 *Journal of Law and Society* 273.

as is called law — a parliamentary ruling, a judicial sentence, a legal process, a delict — we can distinguish two elements. The one is a sensible act in time and place, an external process, generally a human behaviour; the other is a significance attached to or immanent in this act or process, a specific meaning. People meet together in a hall, make speeches, some rise from their seats, others remain seated; that is the external process. Its meaning: that a law has been passed. A man, clothed in a gown, speaks certain words from an elevated position to a person standing in front of him. This external process means a judicial sentence. One merchant writes to another a letter with a certain content; the other sends a return letter. This means they have concluded a contract. Someone, by some action or other, brings about the death of another. This means, legally, murder.

...

8. In delimiting law from nature, the Pure Theory of Law at the same time draws the line of demarcation between Nature and Idea. The science of law is a mental and not a natural science.

[450]   According to Kelsen then, the scientificity of legal theory flows in the first place from its purity as an intellectual discipline, and secondly from its attempt to reach an understanding of the conceptual structure of law rather than its sociological, historical, moral, or political dimensions. A more detailed appraisal of Kelsen's theory has been considered in Chapter 3.

Another, more everyday, connection between law and science which I am going to briefly mention is associated with the trial process. In this context, the use of science in the legal process is in issue, rather than conceiving of and studying law scientifically. Science is merely there to help establish the facts relied upon by law for decision making. Trials have become more reliant upon science in the last few decades as a result of the rapid development of those sciences (and notably forensic science) which have an impact on the evidence which is presented in a case. As I mentioned at the beginning of this chapter, "proof" is typically regarded as scientific proof — science is supposed to be objective and value-free, and reliant only on facts, which are there for everyone to see. There are, of course, problems associated with this tendency to rely on scientific demonstration in the legal process, not least of which is that non-expert judges and juries are being asked to evaluate evidence which is frequently too complex for them to understand.[58] Another obvious difficulty is that — even if it were faultless — forensic evidence can be (and has been) manipulated. It is also clear that a certain sort of expert evidence has often been preferred by courts. The people considered to be "expert" by the court (and who therefore possess the requisite knowledge according to the law) are those who have the right formal qualifications — doctors, psychiatrists, forensic experts, anthropologists, and so on. "Objective" knowledge is that learned at a distance, as an

---

58   See also Chris Corns, "The Science of Justice and the Justice in Science" (1992) 10 *Law in Context* 7; Howard Markey, "Jurisprudence or 'Juriscience'?" (1984) 25 *William and Mary Law Review* 525.

observer rather than a participant, and within the right institutional framework, for instance. A person who has extensive experience in a rape crisis centre but no formal qualifications is unlikely to be considered an expert on the question of how rape victims behave immediately after they have been raped. An anthropologist may be preferred to a member of an Indigenous community.[59] The "scientific" evidence is selective, participating as it does in the idea that what has been scientifically learned is superior knowledge.

Moreover, in many jurisdictions the courts have also been resistant to admitting evidence from experts in the social sciences, a tendency which may be seen as protecting the process of proof from anything which is not "hard" science (and thus apparently not sufficiently certain), or as a way of protecting the disciplinary boundaries of law itself — from politics, morality or society. The result is that home-spun (and very traditional) views of "social realities" with no social scientific backing, for instance the "realities of sex",[60] can be retained by the law, since there is no way of countering the assumptions made by judges, jurors, and counsel on these matters.[61] None of this is to say that expert or scientific evidence is pointless (on the contrary, it is often crucial), rather that it is necessary to understand its limits and limitations.

One fundamental matter which must be raised about the "scientific" process of establishing evidence is that the trier of fact is being asked to accept as truth something which may very well be open to various interpretations, especially when what is being accepted as "science" falls into a very narrow category premised on the exclusion of what may well be very useful areas of knowledge. And because the triers of fact are not themselves experts, it is impossible for them to enquire into the assumptions which underlie the evidence. Legal education generally ensures that lawyers and judges have a reasonably homogeneous outlook on the world (although this homogeneity is at last under threat): the power of this homogeneity, in turn, ensures that other views or alternative interpretations are marginalised. The "science" of law, which involves the self-legitimating idea of law as a closed logical system is supposedly reliant on none of the contiguous areas of knowledge, and protects its own identity not only through juris-prudential exclusion, but in the trial process.

---

59   See Irene Watson, "Indigenous People's Law-Ways: Survival Against the Colonial State" (1997) 8 *Australian Feminist Law Journal* 39 at 49-54.

60   See, for instance, comments made by White J in *R v Egan* (1985) 15 A Crim R 20 at 25-26.

61   The mandatory warning to be given by judges to juries that it is unsafe to convict a defendant of rape on the uncorroborated evidence of the victim could not have lasted as long as it did if social scientific evidence on the behaviour of rape victims had been considered. Rather than checking the facts, the law has simply rested on the assumption that women lie about sex. Even now, the warning is discretionary in many jurisdictions, giving judges the opportunity to feed in their own prejudices about this matter.

[455]   The rest of this chapter examines specific examples of legal thought where an attempt has been made to apply scientific ideals and methods to law. In the first instance I will explain briefly two ways in which the ideal of achieving a legal science was implemented in the 19th century. These matters are important because of the profound effect they have had on legal education and the way law has been understood, throughout the 20th century and into the 21st century. The third section of the chapter looks at legal formalism, which may be described as the attempt to apply scientific values (such as closure in the legal system, and logical deduction), though not necessarily a scientific method, to the process of analysing and applying the law. The fourth section will return to a consideration of the uses of empirical science in the work of the North American Realists, and the fifth section is a very brief account of the way in which an existing science — economics — has been applied to legal thought. Another major dimension of legal science is, of course, positivism, especially the thought of Hans Kelsen: I have considered the substance of positivism in Chapter 3, and discussed some issues about its scientific aspirations in the first section of this chapter.

The 19th Century: Textbooks and Casebooks

[460]   In the first instance, it will be helpful to put the desire for legal "scientificity" in the context of the development of law as a respectable object of study within universities.

Law texts

[465]   The classical common law theorists, as I explained in Chapter 2, defended a notion of the "artificial reason" of the law: an under-standing of the underlying reason of the common law was seen by jurists, like Coke and Hale, to be acquired only through a long process of practical study. The law was seen to have its foundation in custom, and the basis of its authority was immemorial wisdom, meaning that the exposition of the law was entirely within the domain of lawyers who had sufficiently imbued themselves in legal practice. "Natural" reason was seen to be an inadequate explanation or source of the law since, as Hale pointed out, different thinkers inevitably come to different conclusions about the demands of natural reason.[62] Unfortunately, the result was that the law was generally seen to be a tangle of illogical and often incoherent details which could be manipulated by lawyers and

---

62   See especially Matthew Hale "Reflections by the Lord Chiefe Justice Hale on Mr Hobbes his Dialogue of the Lawe" in Holdsworth *A History of English Law*, Volume V, Appendix III (Methuen, London, 1924), extracted in Chapter 2.

judges to achieve their own ends.[63] Jeremy Bentham went as far as to argue that the common law needed to be scrapped altogether in favour of a comprehensive legislative code. And as we saw in Chapter 3, the early positivists, especially Bentham and Austin, attempted to develop general theories of law based on a relatively simple legislative model.

In the later 19th century, when law became the object of systematic study at British universities, it was necessary to improve somewhat this image of the law: an obscure and illogical mass of technical rules or "shapeless heap of odds and ends" (as Bentham put it) was not considered to be an appropriate basis for a university education. At the same time, the approaches of Bentham and Austin (who were seen as respectively destructive of the common law ideal and neglecting its internal structure) were regarded by some at least to have hindered the exposition of the law originally begun by Blackstone. Pollock, for instance, claimed:[64]

> The crabbed involution of Bentham's own later manner, and the still more repulsive formlessness of his successor Austin, who could never forgive Blackstone for writing good English, deprived a later generation of these advantages [ie, of Blackstone's work]. In following the technical divisions of the law (with partial amendments, not always felicitous) Blackstone was at any rate intelligible to lawyers. The terminology of Bentham and Austin inflicted on us a mass of new technicalities, little better in themselves, if at all, than Blackstone's, and intelligible to nobody.

The object of the study of law was, according to Pollock, to gain a clear and scientific understanding of the generalities which underlie the detail of the substantive law: the "art" or practice of law would then be revealed to the practitioner in all of its true beauty. If that sounds extreme (and it does to me) consider seriously, if you can, Pollock's view of the "joy" to be discovered in legal analysis and application:[65]

> As a painter rests on the deep and luminous air of Turner, or the perfect detail of a drawing of Leonardo; as ears attuned to music are rapt with the full pulse and motion of the orchestra that a Richter or a Lamoureux commands, or charmed with the modulation of the solitary instrument in the hands of a Joachim; as a swordsman watches the flashing sweep of the sabre, or the nimbler and subtler play of opposing foils; such joy may you find in the lucid exposition of broad legal principles, or in the conduct of a finely reasoned argument on their application to a disputed point.

As David Sugarman writes in the following extract, the concern of the new law teachers was to demonstrate that the study of law could be regarded as a science, and its practice as an application of a science.

---

63   See "The Critique of Common Law Theory" section in Chapter 2.

64   Frederick Pollock, "Oxford Law Studies" (1886) 8 *Law Quarterly Review* 453 at 457.

65   Pollock, "Oxford Law Studies", p 462.

David Sugarman
"Legal Theory, the Common Law Mind, and the Making of the Textbook Tradition"[66]

[470]   It was only during the period c 1850-1907 that professional law teachers were appointed to universities in any number. For many of these classical legal scholars, the major intellectual task was to transcend the "chaos and darkness" of contemporary legal education and scholarship and to create a world of "order and light". This was also essential if they were to establish themselves as one of the many new professions that arose in the latter half of the nineteenth century. In other words, for Dicey, Bryce, Pollock, Anson, Holland, Salmond, and other classical law dons, their desired professional legitimacy in the eyes of sceptical universities and a largely hostile profession required the assertion of a special body of expertise which jurists monopolized. What was this special expertise?

     The argument espoused by most classical law dons was that law may appear chaotic but is, in fact, internally coherent. This cohesion derives from the fact that law is grounded upon relatively few general principles. The legal scholar was in a unique position to tease out the general principles underlying the law and impart this sense of cohesion through the teaching of general principles and the systematization of those principles in law textbooks. They were, therefore, uniquely useful to the profession. They showed that the grubby, disorderly world of the court room and law office could, in fact, be regarded as "science in action". The law was ultimately governed by principles akin to the laws of natural sciences and was, thus, a subject worthy of a place in the university firmament. Here then was the *raison d'être* of the new professional jurist and university legal education.

[475]   It was important, then, for law to be regarded as "scientific" in some way, though, as Sugarman goes on to note, for both Dicey and Pollock "this seems to have meant little more than that law was clear, rational, internally coherent and systematized".[67] Law was seen to be scientific simply because it could be explained by a few basic principles which informed the detail of substantive law. For the growing class of legal academics, an important aspect of the "scientific" study of the law involved the reduction of areas of common law to textbooks which illustrated the elementary principles of the law in a unified and coherent fashion. This process of exposition of the common law is described by Sugarman in the following terms:[68]

---

66   David Sugarman, "Legal Theory, the Common Law Mind, and the Making of the Textbook Tradition" in Twining (ed), *Legal Theory and the Common Law* (Basil Blackwell, Oxford, 1986), pp 29-30. See also Jerome Frank, *Law and the Modern Mind* (Brentano's, New York, 1930), Ch 11 "Scientific Training"; Dimock "Rules of Law, Laws of Science", pp 206-208.

67   Sugarman, "Legal Theory, the Common Law Mind, and the Making of the Textbook Tradition", p 30.

68   Sugarman, "Legal Theory, the Common Law Mind, and the Making of the Textbook Tradition", p 50.

The circumstances in which the classical jurists found themselves seemed to require textbooks that conceived of the law as unitary and principled and which verged on the "dogmatic". Pedagogically, their ultimate *raison d'être* was simplicity of exposition, orientation and standpoint. They did their best to ignore the "exceptions" and "aberrations"; they concentrated on the principles and "the general part" of the law. They emphasized the "best law", that is, they were highly selective in the cases they cited and deliberately eschewed the enumeration of numerous authorities which was the hallmark of practitioner texts.

This view of the law might seem to be more appropriately applied to civil law systems, where legislative codes, rather than precedents built up in a piecemeal fashion, form the basis of the substantive law. And, in fact, it was lawyers from civil law jurisdictions who developed a "geometric" understanding of law, based on the idea that law can form a coherent and complete system, and that deductions from these first principles could account for every possible case.[69] However, this understanding of law appears to have taken a normative form: the claim was not made that *existing* law is comparable to geometry, but rather that law can be like this, and that it ought to be reconstructed so that sound logic could predominate in legal reasoning, rather than judicial whim and archaic custom.[70] It is just such a process of rationalisation which was undertaken by Bentham and Austin in the early 19th century.

The development of the case method

[480]   Thus in Britain the push to have law accepted as a respectable and worthy object of university study took the form of an assertion that it could be studied "scientifically" because, like other sciences, it was based on axioms or general principles which served as an organising framework for the mass of technical details with which practising lawyers were confronted. The methodical exposition of these principles took the form of written texts which aimed to explain clearly and simply the coherence of any area of law. In the United States at around the same time the place of law in universities was also in the process of being established and, as in Britain, demonstrating the "scientificity" of law was a crucial part of its acceptance as a proper object of academic study.[71]

However the "scientific" nature of the study of law took a somewhat different form in the United States than it did in Britain, and one which was explicitly centred on an inductive scientific method.[72]

---

69   A very useful account of the pre-Langdellian view of law as a deductive science is MH Hoeflich, "Law and Geometry: Legal Science from Leibniz to Langdell" (1986) 30 *American Journal of Legal History* 95; see also Barzun, "Common Sense and Legal Science".

70   Hoeflich, "Law and Geometry: Legal Science from Leibniz to Langdell", p 102.

71   Russell Weaver, "Langdell's Legacy: Living with the Case Method" (1991) 36 *Villanova Law Review* 517 at 529-531.

72   See the explanation of induction above and Levit, "Listening to Tribal Legends: An Essay on Law and the Scientific Method" (1989) 58 *Fordham Law Review* 263 at 275-277.

Christopher Columbus Langdell, Dean of the Harvard Law School, has ordinarily been attributed with the introduction of an empirical approach to the study of law,[73] and it is Langdell's name, above all others, which is associated with "legal science" in Anglo-American jurisprudence. Langdell pointed out that the primary sources of the common law are to be found in decided cases, and he believed that a scientific understanding of the law could be gained from detailed attention to cases. This excluded specifically political, moral, or religious concerns from the study of law. The law, then, is considered to be comparable to natural phenomena, and susceptible to a similarly methodical and empirical analysis through a process of induction:[74]

> the library is the proper workshop of professors and students alike; ... it is to us all that the laboratories of the universities are to the chemists and physicists, the museum of natural history to the zoologists, the botanical garden to the botanists.

The practical consequence flowing from this view of the law was that legal education, in order to instil in students a scientific approach to the law, had to proceed primarily, if not entirely, by studying cases: the "case-method" which was thereby established has since been the dominant approach to legal education in the United States.[75] The rationale behind the case-method of teaching law was explained in more detail by the Dean of Columbia College Law School.[76]

William Keener
"Methods of Legal Education"

[485]   The case system consists in putting into the hands of the students a number of cases on any given subject, taken not at haphazard but selected by the professor with a view to developing the law on that subject. The theory on which this proceeds is that it is only by regarding law as a science that one can justify its being taught in a university, and regarding it as a science, the student should not only be encouraged to investigate the law in its original sources, but should be distinctly discouraged from regarding as law, what is, in fact, simply the conclusions of writers whose opinions are based upon the material to which the student can be given access.

The case system then proceeds on the theory that law is a science and, as a science, should be studied in its original sources, and that the original sources are the adjudged cases and not the opinions of text writers, based

---

73   Weaver notes that "there is some disagreement about whether Langdell originated the [case] method": "Langdell's Legacy: Living with the Case Method", pp 520-521; see also Stephen Spiegel, "John Chipman Gray and the Moral Basis of Classical Legal Thought" (2001) 86 *Iowa Law Review* 1513; Dimock, "Rules of Law, Laws of Science".

74   Christopher Columbus Langdell, "Harvard Celebration Speeches" (1997) 9 *Law Quarterly Review* 123 at 124.

75   An extremely interesting account of the origins and history of the case method is Weaver "Langdell's Legacy: Living with the Case Method".

76   William Keener, "Methods of Legal Education" (1892) 1 *Yale Law Journal* 143 at 144-145.

upon the adjudged cases. But the law is an applied science and therefore to appreciate thoroughly the principle involved in a given topic the student should deal with it in its application, and as he learns these principles in their application they are not a mere abstraction, but have assumed to him a concrete form, and he is prepared to apply them in mastering new problems. Instead of reading about principles he is studying and investigating the principles themselves. Under this system the student is taught to look upon law as a science consisting of a body of principles to be found in the adjudged cases, the cases being to him what the specimen is to the mineralogist.

[490] I explained above some of the problems associated with the belief in simple induction. In particular, I mentioned the argument that observations are "theory dependent": it is not possible to observe phenomena without prior selection and categorisation of the relevant facts, and it is not possible to interpret facts without some theoretical preconceptions. Langdell's approach would seem to suffer from similar difficulties, since in order to be at all practical, the case method must rely upon a prior selection and organisation by a person who has already been imbued with certain theoretical views of the law. It is not therefore absolutely correct to say that the student studies law in its "original" sources (which would include every case decided on a question): the sources have already been selected and categorised by the teacher in order to make them intelligible in the wider framework.[77] The "facts" upon which the study of law are based must therefore already be dependent upon some theory of what the law is. Of course, this does not mean that the case method (any more than the idea of induction) is pointless. Like any science or "objective" knowledge it is, however, limited by the conditions which frame or determine the act of observation.

Legal Formalism

[495] Legal formalism (also known as "doctrinalism" or "legalism") is an approach to legal reasoning which emphasises the specifically *legal* dimension of a dispute. The formal approach to determining a legal issue assumes that the law is a closed logical system: this means that it is considered to be the law alone — relations between legal concepts and the facts of a case — and not anything outside the law, which resolves legal questions. An initial objection to such a position might be that in some instances there is not a clear legal rule to determine a dispute, so the judge must have regard to other considerations in deciding the case. But the formalist position ordinarily goes beyond the claim that existing rules are simply applied deductively to facts: modern formalists also argue that law has an internal rational structure which generates

---

77   This point is made by Edwin Patterson in "The Case Method in American Legal Education: Its Origins and Objectives" (1951) 4 *Journal of Legal Education* 1 at 11; see also Weaver, "Langdell's Legacy: Living with the Case Method", p 531; Patrick Kelley, "Holmes, Langdell and Formalism" (2002) 15 *Ratio Juris* 26 at 39.

legal interpretations of, and solutions for, novel fact situations.[78] Such an approach is supposed to preserve the objectivity and independence of the law. Thus, formalism is related to the idea of legal science, indeed has been seen as the archetype of legal science in the practice of law, basically because it treats the law as a "closed" system, and in doing so lays claim to the possibility of objective determination of disputes.[79] And since the idea of formalism also refers to the possibility of applying a strictly deductive process of reasoning in many cases, and to the fundamentally rational structure of law, it is seen, in addition, to have a particularly strong grounding in logic. I will come back to some criticism of formalism at the end of this section, but will begin with two illustrations.

In an episode from Shakespeare's *Merchant of Venice*, Portia takes first an anti-formalist then a formalist approach. The merchant Antonio has made a contract with Shylock providing that Shylock will lend Bassanio (a friend of Antonio) a sum of money, with Antonio acting as guarantor for the loan, Antonio's capital being, at that time, literally "all at sea" (in the form of various merchant shipping ventures). The agreement or "bond" between Antonio and Shylock provides that if the debt is not paid within a certain date a "forfeit" will become due, which is a pound of Antonio's flesh. When none of Antonio's ventures come to fruition, Shylock claims the forfeit, and the case is heard before Portia (who has since married Bassanio) disguised as a doctor of laws. In a famous speech Portia contrasts mercy and justice (justice here is understood roughly as law), pleading with Shylock to be merciful, to take three times the original debt (which Bassanio has since obtained through his marriage to Portia) and renounce the forfeit. Portia's initial, non-formal, approach is therefore to take into account something other than law in order to resolve the dispute — mercy. But when Shylock refuses to be merciful towards Antonio, she gives him law, and law alone:[80]

> This bond doth give thee here no jot of blood,
>
> The words expressly are "a pound of flesh":
>
> Take then thy bond, take thou thy pound of flesh,
>
> But in the cutting it, if thou dost shed
>
> One drop of Christian blood, thy lands and goods
>
> Are (by the laws of Venice) confiscate
>
> Unto the state of Venice. (Act IV, Scene i, 302-308)

---

78   Ernest Weinrib, "Legal Formalism: On the Immanent Rationality of Law" (1988) 97 *Yale Law Journal* 949; Weinrib, "Why Legal Formalism" in George (ed), *Natural Law Theory: Contemporary Essays* (Clarendon Press, Oxford, 1992).

79   See, for example, Richard Posner, *The Problems of Jurisprudence* (Harvard University Press, Cambridge Mass, 1990), Ch 1 "Law as Logic, Rules, and Science".

80   There is an anti-Semitic element to the story, emphasised by Portia's mention of "Christian" blood — Shylock is Jewish.

Shylock realises fairly quickly that he is not going to get very far with this claim so he decides that Portia's original suggestion — to be merciful — is a decent second choice. But Portia by that stage has determined that he will have nothing but justice, and reinforces her original pronouncement that a pound of flesh doesn't include any blood, with the statement that a pound of flesh means exactly a pound of flesh, not more or less:

> Shed thou no blood, nor cut thou less nor more
>
> But just a pound of flesh: if thou tak'st more
>
> Or less than a just pound, be it but so much
>
> As makes it light or heavy in the substance,
>
> Or the division of the twentieth part
>
> Of one poor scruple, nay if the scale do turn
>
> But in the estimation of a hair,
>
> Thou diest, and all thy goods are confiscate. (IV, i, 321-328)

The point which I want to emphasise about this instructive story is condensed into the pun which Portia makes on the word "just". In the first instance, "just a pound of flesh" means *only* a pound of flesh. Next, it means *exactly* a pound ("a just pound": "just" is here used in what is now an archaic way, to mean "exact" — this usage is retained in one meaning of the modern French word "*juste*"). But "just" also of course refers to what Portia is applying — "justice", and in this instance, as she stresses, justice requires exactitude. The just solution is the exact one, the one which flows directly from a literal interpretation of the legal document in question. Evidently Portia's own original advice to temper justice with mercy does not apply to her, and so she gives a literal and formal decision, a decision which rests on nothing other than the exact determination of the legal issue. The decision is "just" because it is exact and because it is in accordance with the law. In a general sense this sort of approach — the meeting of law and precision, to the exclusion of what is perceived to be outside the legal interest — is what is termed "legal formalism". The formal solution is the one which adheres to the law as stated, and is not qualified by anything vague or soft like mercy. The formalist approach in jurisprudence sees law as both self-contained and coherent: law, in other words, is separate from both politics and morality, and is thus seen by some as representing a scientific approach to legal reasoning. The formal solution, since it doesn't rely on the subjective values of the individual judge but only on the rational coherence of the law, is defended as a disinterested and value-free solution.

We need to be careful to keep a couple of things in mind about the terms used here. Portia opposes mercy and justice, but the usual modern jurisprudential (and formalist) distinction is between justice and law, or more broadly, between everything which isn't law, and law itself, which is supposed to be a closed and internally logical space.

Justice is usually considered in our modern terminology to be a moral and political thing, while law is just law (or rather law is not necessarily *just* law — it is *only* law!). The legal solution, in other words, may not always be what we call the just one, and the formalist argument in particular is that the legal solution can and should be determined without having regard to justice or morality.[81] It is up to Parliament to change the law if it is no good, but it is after all the law and that is apparently what we are all, as lawyers, supposed to be applying. In general then, formalism relies on the idea of objectivity and rationality inherent in law, emphasising in particular that the application of the law is quite distinct from any social, moral, or policy considerations. This view reflects at the level of legal norms Kelsen's insistence on the "purity" of legal science:[82] if law is to be studied as a science, it must be distinguished rigorously as an intellectual discipline. Secondly, within the logic of the play the legal solution (Portia's "justice") is arguably more just than allowing Shylock to cut off a pound of Antonio's flesh,[83] but a formalist approach would endorse such a solution regardless of its justice. Of course, where "justice" lies is debatable: while it might be unjust for the bond to be paid, Antonio did enter into the contract freely and, moreover, has reportedly abused and spat on Shylock earlier in the play. Antonio is hardly a saint, while Portia's subsequent actions in removing Shylock's property and allowing Antonio to force his conversion to Christianity border on being malicious. [84]

(And a final word about Portia, while I am on the topic. Some feminists have adopted Portia as a symbol of women as lawyers. But Portia's solution is ambivalent — she proposes first a non-formal, then a formal resolution of the dispute — which some would identify with, respectively, a socially feminine and a masculine approach (both socially constructed, rather than biological).[85] Similarly her gender as a lawyer is ambivalent — she is a woman, but the persona of the judge is definitely male. Portia has to reproduce the masculinity of the law,

---

81 The law/justice distinction will be considered again in Chapter 8, in the context of deconstruction. It should be noted, however, that Kelsen was not a formalist when it came to matters of interpretation.

82 See Kelsen, "The Pure Theory of Law": a relevant section is extracted at [445] in the first section of this chapter.

83 On the other hand, the just solution may have been that which Portia calls "merciful", giving Shylock the option of accepting the bond three times over, and relinquishing the claim to the pound of flesh. Such a solution would, at least, have been less viciously directed against Shylock.

84 Daniel Kornstein goes further, saying "In addition to [Portia's] hypocrisy and vindictiveness, we see her as a bigot, and not just a minor-league bigot, but a world-class, equal opportunity hate monger". Kornstein, *Kill All the Lawyers? Shakespeare's Legal Appeal* (Princeton University Press, New Jersey, 1994).

85 See, for instance, Carol Gilligan, *In a Different Voice: Psychological Theory and Women's Development* (Harvard University Press, Cambridge Mass, 1982), and the huge literature generated by her research.

but in doing so destabilises its gendered character.[86] Portia is a much more interesting and provocative character than the simple model of a female judge.)

Allan Hutchinson provides the following example of formalist reasoning:[87]

> A year or so ago, a swimming meet took place at the University of Toronto. Most of the races proceeded as planned. But, at the end of one race, there was a challenge to the winner of the race. The appropriate group of officials convened. The deliberations were lengthy and tense. After much argument and poring over the rules, a decision was announced: the winner had been disqualified and the second swimmer was acclaimed the victor. The referee took the unusual course of offering a brief justification of the committee's decision — "the rules were clear ('The winner is the first swimmer to touch the side of the pool with both hands') and, if this regrettable outcome is to be avoided in the future, it will be necessary to change the rules". The winning swimmer had only one arm.

This example might indicate one reason why, when law prevails over justice, formalism is one of the most criticised concepts in legal theory. As Bottomley and Bronitt comment, "The point of this story ... is presumably that formalism can descend into the mindless application of rules which appear, in a crude literal sense, to be relevant to the dispute. The story points to the need for other values to be invoked in legal reasoning to control the actual outcome."[88] On the other hand, it is sometimes said that the occasional injustice is outweighed by the need for certainty in the law, and that the formalist approach aids certainty. The "virtues" of formalism have been described by Anthony Mason in the following terms:[89]

---

86   Catherine Belsey comments: "Portia's right to exercise her authority depends on her lawyer's robes, and the episode can be seen as making visible the injustice which allows women authority only on condition that they seem to be men. Even while it reaffirms patriarchy, the tradition of female transvestism challenges it precisely by unsettling the categories which legitimate it.": Belsey, "Disrupting Sexual Difference: Meaning and Gender in the Comedies", in Drakakis (ed), *Alternative Shakespeares* (Methuen, London, 1985), p 180. For a thorough analysis see also Ian Ward, "When Mercy Seasons Justice: Shakespeare's Woman Lawyer" in McGlynn (ed), *Legal Feminisms: Theory and Practice* (Ashgate, Aldershot, 1998).

87   Allan Hutchinson, *Dwelling on the Threshold* (Carswell Company, Toronto, 1988), p 23. The example is also discussed in some detail by Stephen Bottomley and Simon Bronitt, *Law in Context* (Federation Press, Sydney, 2006), pp 70-71.

88   Bottomley and Bronitt, *Law in Context*, p 72.

89   Anthony Mason, "Future Directions in Australian Law" (1987) 13 *Monash University Law Review* 149 at 156: taken out of context this statement may suggest that Mason is defending formalism, which is certainly not the case. John Gava has, however, keenly and vigorously defended formalism. See the following two articles: Frank Carrigan, "A Blast from the Past: The Resurgence of Legal Formalism" (2003) 27 *Melbourne University Law Review* 163; Gava, "Another Blast from the Past or Why the Left Should Embrace Strict Legalism: A Reply to Frank Carrigan" (2003) 27 *Melbourne University Law Review* 186.

The virtues of legal formalism are continuity, objectivity and absence of controversy, attributes calculated to induce public confidence in the administration of justice and respect for the law. Legal formalism provides a mantle of legitimacy for the non-elected judiciary in a democratic society. If the principles of law are deducible from past precedents, there is no place for the personal predilictions and values of the individual judge, and there is less scope for controversy about the law that the judge is to apply. What the law should be is a matter not for the courts but for Parliament ... In its most extreme form legalism required a complete separation of law from politics and policy, partly on the ground that the law is a self-contained discipline and partly on the ground that exposure to politics and policy would subject the law to controversy.

The realist and critical legal studies movements both developed partly in response to this idea of the separation of law from politics. I will consider the approach of these movements in some detail in their turn,[90] but some of the more obvious objections to formalism can be briefly stated. In the first place, it seems fairly clear that many judgements are *in fact* based on policy, changing notions of public morality, and expediency, rather than purely on legal reasons:[91] this is the case even though the language of the law may be used to give a legal flavour to a decision. In itself though, this fact is not sufficient to rebut the formalist approach — since it may be that judges who decide their cases on non-legal grounds are simply not doing their job properly.

A stronger argument is that no matter what judges actually do, or think they are doing, it is logically, socially, or humanly *impossible* to make a strict distinction between legal and non-legal reasons. There are several reasons for this. One concerns the social and human dimension of the judge: judges are people not machines, so it is impossible for them to exclude their social conditioning. There will come a point when a judge must rely on assumptions or stereotypes in interpreting both the facts of a case and the law which is applicable to it (to use, for a moment, the problematic fact/law distinction). The stance of judicial neutrality therefore takes on a quite different meaning — the claim to objectivity is no longer a simple or disinterested application of law to the facts, but rather a way of reinforcing a dominant legal and political ideology.[92] Making judges aware of the effect their socialisation has on the outcome of a case would arguably make them more receptive to other perspectives, but will not make the process more "objective".

---

90   Realism forms the subject of the next section of this chapter, while critical legal studies will be considered in Chapter 5.

91   See Frank, *Law and the Modern Mind*; David Kairys, "Legal Reasoning" in Kairys (ed), *The Politics of Law: A Progressive Critique* (Pantheon Books, New York, 1990); Roberto Mangabeira Unger, *The Critical Legal Studies Movement* (Harvard University Press, Cambridge Mass, 1983); JW Harris, "Unger's Critique of Formalism in Legal Reasoning: Hero, Hercules, and Humdrum" (1989) 52 *Modern Law Review* 42.

92   For instance, Allan Hutchinson and Patrick Monahan, "Law, Politics and Critical Legal Scholars: The Unfolding Drama of American Legal Thought" (1984) 26 *Stanford Law Review* 199 at 206.

It is therefore not only unrealistic but also impossible to expect judges to apply "objective" legal reasoning to their cases, simply because no such thing exists, at least not in the traditional form. Instead of thinking about law as a system which is logically closed, and about legal reasoning as being mechanically determined by pre-existing formulae, we should be studying law as a social phenomenon.[93] (However, as I will argue in Chapter 8, this does not mean that any conclusion can be justified. On moral grounds one decision may be better than another.)

Another reason why it is logically impossible to enforce a purely formal view of the law is that it is not expressed in mathematical symbols, but in language, which is often (some would say intrinsically) unclear. Law is not a logical system, and it does not have any intrinsic order.[94] If it is not possible to enshrine a legal meaning precisely in a legal instrument or judgement, then there must always be some room for conflicting interpretations. And especially where the language used is manifestly vague or ambiguous, the notion that there is a correct legal answer or even a "better view" (as I sometimes say in lectures or tutorials myself) simply represents a false pretence that the law itself can resolve such an ambiguity. The more radical writers in critical legal studies have denied that there is ever any legal compulsion to determine a dispute in a particular way, while others have argued that legal meanings must be understood within their social and historical context.[95]

On the other hand, it is perhaps true that objections such as these themselves rely on taking the formalist propositions somewhat too literally. While it may not be the case that there is a correct legal solution to every question, lawyers have to work on the assumption that there is one in the vast majority of cases. The "cases" we actually read in the reports represent only a fraction of the issues actually dealt with through legal mechanisms and probably distort our view of legal reasoning: most "legal" questions can be, and are, decided relatively simply, in accordance with the law. Moreover, it would seem that the idea of legal reasoning is intelligible, if only up to a certain point,

---

93   See especially Roscoe Pound's famous essay on this question, "Mechanical Jurisprudence" (1908) 8 *Columbia Law Review* 605. Pound was a leading exponent of sociological jurisprudence in the United States: this is an aspect of "legal science" which I will not be considering in this chapter, but see Dimock, "Rules of Law, Laws of Science", pp 213-218. Although Pound was also a critic of legal realism, many of his insights were used by the realists. See Karl Llewellyn, "Roscoe Pound" in Llewellyn, *Jurisprudence: Realism in Theory and Practice* (University of Chicago Press, Chicago, 1962).

94   David Trubeck, "Where the Action Is: Critical Legal Studies and Empiricism" (1984) 36 *Stanford Law Review* 575 at 578.

95   Elizabeth Mensch writes, "no interpretation or application of language can be logically required by the language itself. Words are created by people in history, and their definition inevitably varies with particular context and with the meaning brought to them by the judges who are asked to interpret them. That act of interpretation is, in every instance, an act of social choice"; "The History of Mainstream Legal Thought" in Kairys (ed), *The Politics of Law: A Progressive Critique*, p 28; see also Robert Gordon, "Critical Legal Histories" (1984) 36 *Stanford Law Review* 57 at 125.

because it takes as its major focus legislation and judicial decisions. It therefore must be different in some way, if not absolutely, from moral or political arguments. Finally, there must be some degree of determinacy in language, because otherwise we would not be able to communicate. The effect of the objections to formalism, therefore, can perhaps only be used to reject the *absolute* separation of legal reasoning from other sorts of reasoning. There *is* form, there *is* law, and there *is* meaning. What has to be considered is: what is the nature of form, of law and, of meaning? Are we simply talking here about "fuzzy edges", or something more fundamental?

The formal view of legal reasoning can never describe an absolute legal truth. Rather it describes a legal "truth" which has gained that status through its political dominance (and which subsequently takes on the status of an absolute truth because, if it has the power to convince people that it is the only truth, then the alternatives will not seem at all credible).[96] Other perspectives on the legal process, other views of the world generally, are excluded by the formal approach, because this is what it requires. Formalism capitalises on the interpretations which are accepted, central, "plain" (though we should always ask, in whose eyes?). A view which seems marginal is not just ridiculed, it is simply not believed, because it does not accord with the "objective" (dominant) version.

Realism

[4100] In a sense the advent of realism marks the beginning of the modern critique of law in the Anglo-American context, though it is by no means the first theoretical movement which had critique and reform as its basic aims. Although we now see the positivist theory initiated by Jeremy Bentham as representing the dominant legal orthodoxy, like realism, it began as a very strong reaction against what were perceived to be the mysteries and uncertainties of common law jurisprudence. The main difference between previous critical writings and those of the 20th (and now 21st) century is that the latter tend not to be consolidated into definite and coherent theoretical systems, which is why they are termed "movements" rather than "theories". Even at the beginning, positivism took the form of a theory which attempted to say something general about law. Like later movements, realism grew out of a dissatisfaction with aspects (and sometimes the entirety) of accepted legal doctrines and practices.

Before continuing, I should point out that "realism" is, in fact, two distinct schools of thought, originating in Scandinavia and the United States. I am going to focus on the latter school here, because it

---

96 The political dimensions of "law's truth" have been analysed by (among others) Carol Smart in *Feminism and the Power of Law* (Routledge, London, 1989). I will come back to this theme in Chapter 8, so will not pursue it here.

has more relevance to the context of Anglo-centric jurisprudence, which is the central concern of this book, and because it has been influential in the developments of later critical movements. However, a few points of comparison can be briefly made. Like US realism, Scandinavian realism — led by figures such as Axel Hägerström,[97] Karl Olivecrona,[98] and Alf Ross — has had a considerable influence on the concept and practice of law in its "home" jurisdictions, primarily Sweden and Denmark. Both schools of thought were motivated by a desire to eliminate "transcendental nonsense", including moral debate, religious or semi-religious concepts and other non-"real" elements from the study and understanding of law. Olivecrona, for instance, wrote a highly influential work entitled *Law as Fact*, in which he argued that positivism relied upon reconstructed natural law concepts (such as the derivation of law from a general will), and that law should be regarded merely as an actually existing factual phenomenon: we do not know the origins of law, we cannot justify its existence without recourse to metaphysical ideas, it is just there — law is fact, and nothing more.[99] It has no inherent relationship to justice and cannot be said to represent a general will, or will of the sovereign, since there *is* no general will or will of the sovereign.[100] Whereas the effect of US realism was to produce a less formalistic, more policy-oriented approach to legal decision-making, Scandinavian realism was associated with an approach which was highly doctrinal.

Pragmatism and realism

[4105] The realist thinkers were, however, thoroughly immersed in the ideology of science which, as I have explained, was a major feature of legal theory in the 19th and early 20th centuries. The "science" of the realists was centred on neither the empirical analysis of decided cases (as in the methods established by Langdell), nor the exposition of the law as a closed order of formal or rational doctrines. Indeed, if one generalisation can be made about realism, it is that it frequently takes the form of a reaction against formalism and particularly against the idea that law is simply a set of doctrines which are the sole determinants of legal issues. As Oliver Wendell Holmes asserted, "the actual life of the law has not been logic: it has been experience".[101]

---

97   Axel Hägerström, *Inquiries into the Nature of Law and Morals* (CD Broad trans, Almqvist and Wiskell, Stockholm, 1953). For a succinct account of Hägerström's thought in relation to other Scandinavian realists and positivists such as Kelsen, see Jes Bjarup, "The Philosophy of Scandinavian Legal Realism" (2005) 18 *Ratio Juris* 1. See also Mauro Zamboni, "Legal Realisms: On Law and Politics" (2006) 12 *Res Publica* 295.

98   Karl Olivecrona, *Law as Fact* (2nd ed, Stevens and Sons, London, 1971).

99   For in-depth analysis and critique, see Dennis Töllborg, "Law as Value" (1998) 4 *Archiv für Rechts und Sozialphilosophie* 489.

100 Töllborg, "Law as Value", p 496.

101 Oliver Wendell Holmes, *The Common Law* (Little, Brown, Boston, 1881), p 1.

The real nature of the law cannot be explained by formal deductive logic, only by its empirical and historical existence and the social ends towards which it is directed. For Holmes, legal "science" therefore pays attention to the practical dimensions and purposes of the law, an empirical exercise requiring improved methods of legal analysis.[102] The work of Holmes paved the way for much Realist thought, even though his own work predated the movement.

Legal realism was part of a larger empirical trend in science and philosophy which directed the quest for understanding away from a metaphysical search for truth to an understanding of truth grounded only in experience and practical relations. William James explained the central aims of philosophical "pragmatism" in the following terms:[103]

> Pragmatism represents a perfectly familiar attitude in philosophy, the empiricist attitude, but it represents it, as it seems to me, both in a more radical and in a less objectionable form than it has even yet assumed. A pragmatist turns his back resolutely and once for all upon a lot of inveterate habits dear to professional philosophers. He turns away from abstraction and insufficiency, from verbal solutions, from bad *a priori* reasons, from fixed principles, closed systems, and pretended absolutes and origins. He turns towards concreteness and adequacy, towards facts, towards action and towards power. That means the empiricist temper regnant and the rationalist temper sincerely given up. It means the open air and possibilities of nature, as against dogma, artificiality, and the pretence of finality in truth.

From this perspective, the boundary between science and philosophy is broken down, because, like the scientist, the philosopher evaluates "truth" only in relation to what can be empirically verified or corroborated.[104]

This approach was applied by John Dewey in a famous article on logic and law.[105] Dewey contrasted the traditional mechanical notion of logic, which has as its paradigm the syllogism,[106] with the pragmatic understanding of logic as the consequence of experience. In commenting upon Holmes' view of law as the product of experience, rather than logic, Dewey notes that Holmes had in mind a particular view of logic — that it is formal and deductive.[107] The life of the law does not exist in the application of pre-existing rules to concrete cases, but rather in the development through experience of legal principles. Yet if logic is

---

102 See generally Holmes, "Law in Science and Science in Law" in Holmes, *Collected Legal Papers* (Harcourt, Brace and Howe, New York, 1920).

103 William James, *Pragmatism* (Harvard University Press, Cambridge Mass, 1975), p 51.

104 William James, *Pragmatism* (Harvard University Press, Cambridge Mass, 1975), pp 200-201.

105 John Dewey, "Logical Method and Law" (1924) 10 *Cornell Law Quarterly* 17; see also Jay Wesley Murphy, "John Dewey — A Philosophy of Law for Democracy" (1960) 14 *Vanderbilt Law Review* 291.

106 That is, 1. All men are mortal; 2. Socrates is a man; 3. therefore Socrates is mortal.

107 Dewey, "Logical Method and Law", p 21.

understood to be experimental, rather than mechanical, then the law does proceed by a logical method. Dewey saw logic as an experimental process of "search and discovery", where the premises of an argument are always themselves only hypotheses, not absolute pre-existing principles, which must be tested and modified in the practical process of making decisions. Logic is not immutable, but subject to experience-based development. In this sense, the process of law is logical. Legal "hypothesis testing" consists in measuring the "hypothesis" or rule of law against the present concrete situation: this is an ongoing process, because of the inadequacy of existing legal principles to deal with changing social circumstances.[108]

Dewey pointed out that what this means for legal logic is that it can never be sufficient to ennumerate existing principles, or antecedent legal premises. Legal logic must be directed at consequences, at predictions based on working hypotheses:[109]

> ... either ... logic must be abandoned or ... it must be a logic *relative to consequences rather than to antecedents*, a logic of prediction of probabilities rather than one of deduction of certainties.

A logic based only on deduction "sanctifies the old": this tendency is especially regressive in law, which needs to be sensitive to society.[110] Thus Dewey advocates regarding all legal principles as working hypotheses or adaptable tools, since even views reflecting a current social ethos which become enshrined in law will, if understood to be immutable antecedent formulae, in their turn become outmoded.

This emphasis on prediction as the basis for legal science reinforced something which Holmes had said two decades earlier and which has sometimes been taken (not altogether accurately) as one of the hallmarks of realist thought. What Holmes said was this:[111]

> Take the fundamental question, What constitutes the law? You will find some text writers telling you that it is something different from what is decided by the courts of Massachusetts or England, that it is a deduction from principles of ethics or admitted axioms or what not, which may or may not coincide with the decisions. But if we take the view of our friend the bad man we shall find that he does not care two straws for the axioms or deductions, but that he does want to know what the Massachusetts or English courts are likely to do in fact. I am much of his mind. The prophecies of what the courts will do in fact, and nothing more pretentious, are what I mean by the law.

---

108 Dewey, "Logical Method and Law", pp 26-27.

109 Dewey, "Logical Method and Law", p 26 (emphasis in original).

110 Arguments such as this also became common among the critical legal scholars: see, for instance, Duncan Kennedy, "Legal Education as a Training for Hierarchy" in Kairys (ed), *The Politics of Law: A Progressive Critique*.

111 Holmes, "The Path of the Law" (1897) 10 *Harvard Law Review* 457 at 460-461.

Holmes' "bad man" is the person who decides what to do only on the basis of the likely consequences of any action, and not on the basis of whether it is the legal or moral thing to do. Being a "bad woman", I decide occasionally to ride my bicycle on the footpath because it generally seems unlikely that I will be caught and prosecuted. Having regard only to the formal rules in the traffic code, I really ought never to do this. In a situation which may attract a claim for compensation by an injured party, the "bad person's" (or corporation's) question is not whether the risk of injuring someone is morally or legally justified, but what the probability of having to pay damages is:[112] in many circumstances it may be more profitable to take the risk, regardless of the legal obligations. The law then, is what the courts do, not what they did two centuries ago (except insofar as it is a guide to what they will do now), or an abstract set of doctrines.[113]

The philosophical and legal context for realism was therefore based on the general perception of law as a social instrument which ought to be directed at achieving specific goals, and not at the adoration of rules and formal reasoning. This general approach took several forms. Roscoe Pound, for instance, who was not a realist himself, advocated a sociological approach to jurisprudence which would be empirically scientific.[114] Pound's work paved the way for more recent sociological studies of law. And Cassius Keyser saw human behaviour as part of the natural world, and judicial behaviour as merely a special type of human behaviour. "Legal science" in his view was simply the study of this special category of behaviour.[115] In the following short outline of some aspects of realist thought, I concentrate on the question of what constitutes the "real" for realism, and how this relates to law.

Transcendental nonsense v the "real"

[4110] The main themes of realism can be summarised quite simply, even though the realists, like critical legal scholars, feminists, law and economics theorists and many other 20th century legal thinkers did not uniformly develop and support a single theory.[116] They preferred to call themselves a "movement", and the word is particularly apt since

---

112 See Peter Cashman, "Toxic Torts: The Bottom Line — How Corporate Counsel Condemn Consumers and Create New Forms of Forensic Farce for Litigation Lawyers" in Beerworth (ed), *Contemporary Issues in Product Liability Law* (Federation Press, Sydney, 1991).

113 One criticism of this view of law is that it is not complete, taking into account essentially only the point of view of the pragmatists in the legal world. William Twining discusses this point in detail in "The Bad Man Revisited" (1973) 58 *Cornell Law Review* 275.

114 Pound, "Mechanical Jurisprudence".

115 Cassius Keyser, "On the Study of Legal Science" (1929) 38 *Yale Law Journal* 413 at 416.

116 See Frank, *Law and the Modern Mind*, Preface to 6th ed; Llewellyn, "Some Realism About Realism — Responding to Dean Pound" (1931) 44 *Harvard Law Review* 1222; William Twining, *Karl Llewellyn and the Realist Movement* (Weidenfeld and Nicolson, London, 1973), pp 73-83.

most critics see themselves as stirring up the stagnant pool which is legal orthodoxy. (Although the critics may not always develop a viable alternative or even propose realistic reforms, arguably the mere fact of moving what was previously fixed is an important aim.) As you will notice, many of these arguments about law re-appear in later critical writings. In response to Roscoe Pound's critique of realism,[117] Karl Llewellyn wrote a defence of the movement, outlining fairly clearly its general scope and social and political context.

Karl Llewellyn

"Some Realism About Realism —
Responding to Dean Pound"[118]

[4115]   Ferment is abroad in the law. The sphere of interest widens; men become interested again in the life that swirls around things legal. Before rules, were facts; in the beginning was not a Word, but a Doing. Behind decisions stand judges; judges are men; as men they have human backgrounds. Beyond rules, again, lie effects: beyond decisions stand people whom rules and decisions directly or indirectly touch. The field of Law reaches both forward and back from the Substantive Law of school and doctrine. The sphere of interest is widening; so, too, is the scope of doubt. *Beyond rules lie effects* — but do they? Are some rules mere paper? And if effects, what effects? Hearsay, unbuttressed guess, assumption or assertion unchecked by test — can such be trusted on this matter of what law is *doing?*

The ferment is proper to the time. The law of schools threatened at the close of the century to turn into words — placid, clear-seeming, lifeless, like some old canal. Practice rolled on, muddy, turbulent, vigorous. It is now spilling, flooding, into the canal of stagnant words. It brings ferment and trouble. So other fields of thought have spilled their waters in: the stress on behaviour in the social sciences; their drive toward integration; the physicists' re-examination of final-seeming premises; the challenge of war and revolution. These stir. They stir the law. Interests of practice claim attention. Methods of work unfamiliar to lawyers make their way in, beside traditional techniques. Traditional techniques themselves are re-examined, checked against fact, stripped somewhat of confusion. And always there is this restless questioning: what *difference* does statute, or rule, or court-decision, make?

Whether this ferment is one thing or twenty is a question; if one thing, it is twenty things in one. But it is with us. It spreads. It is no mere talk. It shows results, results enough through the past decade to demonstrate its value.

And those involved are folk of modest ideals. They want law to deal, they themselves want to deal, with things, with people, with tangibles, with *definite* tangibles, and *observable* relations between definite tangibles — not with words alone; when law deals with words, they want the words to represent tangibles which can be got at beneath the words, and observable relations between those tangibles. They want to check ideas, and rules, and

---

117   Pound "The Call for a Realist Jurisprudence".

118   Llewellyn, "Some Realism About Realism — Responding to Dean Pound", pp 1222-3.

formulas by facts, to keep them close to facts. They view rules, they view law, as means to ends; as only means to ends; as having meaning only insofar as they are means to ends. They suspect, with law moving slowly and the life around them moving fast, that some law may have gotten out of joint with life. This is a question in first instance of fact: what does law *do*, to people or for people? In the second instance, it is a question of ends: what *ought* law to do to people, or for them? But there is no reaching a judgment as to whether any specific part of present law does what it ought, until you can first answer what it is doing now. To see this, and to be ignorant of the answer, is to start fermenting, is to start trying to find out.

[4120] The passage is interesting because it demonstrates a clear frustration on Llewellyn's part with the abstract, purely conceptual, nature of the study of law, which he sees as distracting us from its real purpose. Llewellyn emphasises the material basis of legal institutions: rules are preceded by facts, the beginning was an action, not a word, and it is judges who make decisions. Most importantly, the law should be concerned with "observable relations between definite tangibles": that is, law should relate to the way things are, not only to its own abstractions.

This emphasis on the "real" operation of law led to several sorts of claims made by the realists. One claim which has had a lasting effect is that law is not separate from politics, as formalists and positivists assert. First, law is not an end in itself, but a means to an end — we have law for purposes of social regulation, and it must be studied as such, not in isolation from society.[119] Treating legal propositions as "working hypotheses" which can be tested and altered according to political and social conditions gives the law an in-built mechanism for reform. Secondly, judges are men and therefore, their political and moral convictions inevitably influence their decisions. The realists liked to talk about "real" men. (Of course, I should also point out that because judges, lawyers, legal academics and others associated with the law *are* predominantly privileged in terms of gender, race, and class, law is not only not separate from politics, it is also not separate from the power which its personnel have over less privileged people.)

Thus the realists refused to separate law from politics, arguing that law must be seen as connected to existing political processes and institutions. Related to this argument about the political nature of law is the perception that the law is indeterminate. The dominant trend in traditional legal thought, as the realists perceived it, was to view law as consisting of fairly clear rules and principles which could be applied to particular cases. The realists did not entirely disagree with this view, though they saw the actually existent law as being somewhat too opaque, vague, and contradictory to be fully determinate. In addition, they argued that law cannot be determinate because of its political character: if the law is reliant for its existence, interpretation and direction on social institutions, it cannot be exact at any one time.

---

119 See also the comments I made about "law and order" in Chapter 1.

It is not that judges make decisions arbitrarily, but that because each case is new, and because the social context is continually changing, there will always be a degree of novelty or unpredictability: the formal law does not totally determine the outcome.

In *Law and the Modern Mind* Jerome Frank, a prominent realist, described "The Basic Myth" of legal certainty and attempted to explain its psychological hold on lawyers and the general population.[120] Frank argues that people, including lawyers and judges, have a childish fear of indeterminacy — we like things to have the certainty of a child's "father-controlled world". If we think about this we may come to a different conclusion — that it is children who are adventurous and delight in novelty, while adults prefer stability. (But I have no expertise in this matter at all.[121]) Rules in particular, according to Frank, are a sort of safe haven into which we can retreat to recapture the law of the father and dispel the lack of control which we sense when we do not have a definite rule to apply. This is an interesting (if somewhat unsophisticated) early identification of the formalist concept of law with patriarchy. Frank's argument is that it is about time we grew up, and learnt to see and exploit the productive, indeterminate side of law. Frank coined the term "Bealism" (after Joseph Beale, a Harvard professor) to describe the approach which idealises legal formalism.

In this way, one of the major themes which links most of the realists is the idea that law and the study of law is an inherently practical activity and must be associated with the "real" world. Law is to be seen as something which has a practical effect in the concrete world, and not merely as a body of abstract rules and doctrines. This approach can be contrasted with that taken by the earlier legal writers who had tended to consider law and legal philosophy as primarily abstract — based on fundamental principles which could be articulated without any particular reference to the way these principles interact with society, the economy, or the political context. Felix Cohen's "heaven of legal concepts", describing a dream of the German jurist Von Jhering, illustrates the emphasis in law on abstraction and formality and the dissociation of legal theory from the real world.

Felix Cohen
"Transcendental Nonsense and the Functional Approach"[122]

[4125]   Some fifty years ago a great German jurist had a curious dream. He dreamed that he died and was taken to a special heaven reserved for the theoreticians of the law. In this heaven one met, face to face, the many

---

120   Frank, *Law and the Modern Mind*, Chs 1-8.

121   Though it has been pointed out to me, a fact which I had almost forgotten, that I too was once a child.

122   Felix Cohen, "Transcendental Nonsense and the Functional Approach" (1935) 35 *Columbia Law Review* 809 at 809.

concepts of jurisprudence in their absolute purity, freed from all entangling alliances with human life. Here were the disembodied spirits of good faith and bad faith, property, possession, *laches*, and rights *in rem*. Here were all the logical instruments needed to manipulate and transform these legal concepts and thus to create and to solve the most beautiful of legal problems. Here one found a dialect-hydraulic-interpretation press, which could press an indefinite number of meanings out of any text or statute, an apparatus for constructing fictions, and a hair-splitting machine that could divide a single hair into 999,999 equal parts and, when operated by the most expert jurists, could split each of these parts again into 999,999 equal parts. The boundless opportunities of this heaven of legal concepts were open to all properly qualified jurists, provided only they drank the Lethean draught which induced forgetfulness of terrestrial human affairs. But for the most accomplished jurists the Lethean draught was entirely superfluous. They had nothing to forget.

[4130] Cohen's article is an attempt to deny the reality (and thus the utility — in Realist terms) of some of the basic concepts of the common law. There are many legal concepts, as Cohen points out, which are simply legal constructs or plain fictions, such as the idea of the "corporation" as a legal person. Corporations do not actually exist in the natural world: the corporation is simply a legal fiction or supernatural concept designed to allow groups of people to have a legal identity *as* a group, and not just as numerous individuals. The concept is scientifically unverifiable, because it simply does not exist in the "real" world. Cohen argues that "any word that cannot pay up in the currency of fact, upon demand, is to be declared bankrupt, and we are to have no further dealings with it".[123] Such a demand, although perhaps not without its superficial attractions, would seem to be impossible to fulfil — not only would it deprive us of most of our legal concepts, but also of much of our language and social values, which are conceptual in nature. For instance, if it is not possible to speak of a corporation, which doesn't actually exist except as a legal construct, how could we talk about a contract, which is simply an agreement of a more specific nature? Although the contract is supposed to represent the agreed will of the parties, what the contract is according to the law and what each party thinks she has agreed to may be different things. The contract is a legal construct which does not necessarily correspond to anything in the "real" world. The point is simply that legal meaning is different from what we perceive around us. This is unavoidable if we are to have legal meanings at all.

The problem as I see it is that Cohen, and other realists, tended to think of the "real" as being only that which is available to sensual experience, that is, the concrete world in which people live and form relationships. To put it roughly, this view doesn't accept any "reality" in fictions or in "metaphysical" concepts (that is, a concept which relates to something which is not merely physical. Some examples of such concepts are

123 Cohen, "Transcendental Nonsense and the Functional Approach", p 823.

identity, and existence considered in the abstract.). The realists started with the perfectly clear aim of cleansing the law of the unnecessary and unwieldy aspects of its dogma, and this included reference in legal propositions to anything which was not connected to the real world. However, at least in Cohen's case, this was not accompanied by an understanding of "reality" which could account for the ways in which an organisation of the real world is, of necessity, conceptual. Cohen seems to believe that we can have direct access to facts and that the facts will organise themselves in a rational way: rather than seeing the rules, based on abstract concepts, as tools (which, as I explained above, was the view of Dewey), he wanted to eliminate them altogether from the law. This looks suspiciously like a reversion to the naïve empiricism which I discussed at the beginning of this chapter,[124] a point illustrated by the following passage from Roscoe Pound's critique of realist thought:[125]

> There is nothing upon which the new realist is so insistent as on giving over all preconceptions and beginning with an objectively scientific gathering of facts. As the analytical jurist insisted on the pure fact of law he seeks the pure fact of fact. But facts occur in a multifarious mass of single instances. To be made intelligible and useful, significant facts have to be selected, and what is significant will be determined by some picture or ideal of the science and of the subject of which it treats. Thus preconceptions will creep in and will determine the choice of pure fact of fact as they determined the pure fact of law of the analytical jurist. The new realists have their own preconceptions of what is significant, and hence of what juristically must be.

The difficulty then with this faith in facts, is that facts are never themselves entirely innocent of theory or of pre-existing assumptions about what law is and how it operates.

This emphasis on "reality", then, is obviously problematic because even the physical side of our existence is structured in fundamental ways by ideas which are not "true" in the sense of being absolute for all times and places. For instance, the law of torts requires us to see certain human actions as fitting into the categories of trespass, negligence, or whatever. These categories are fictions and unreal in the sense that they are not naturally occurring in the world — and other legal systems structure things differently — but that doesn't mean that they have nothing to do with reality.[126] The law of torts is a conceptual apparatus which constitutes our legal reality by giving meaning to physical things. Torts is perhaps not the best example, because it is *so far* removed from the way most people see the world, but the basic point is that "reality" consists of ideas and meanings as well as the concrete world, and that

---

124 See the discussion of Cohen in Cotterrell, *The Politics of Jurisprudence: A Critical Introduction to Legal Philosophy*, p 187.

125 Pound "The Call for a Realist Jurisprudence", p 700.

126 I have discussed matters relating to the "legal" ordering of the world in Chapter 1.

not everybody has the same ideas about things (which means not that some people are wrong, just that there is not a natural or correct way of seeing. "Reality" doesn't just come from experience — it is a meeting of meanings with the world.) However, it is only fair to add that the realists were not, on the whole, concerned with formulating a philosophically sophisticated analysis of the law.

In recent years, law and society scholars, especially those who work in the United States where realism was most influential, have discussed and consolidated the movement towards a "new legal realism". Like the "old" realism, this movement emphasises a pragmatic and non-formalist, non-positivist understanding of law within the social environment. However, the new realism is based on a more sophisticated conception of, and relationship with, social science methodology. For instance, in an introduction to a symposium on this new realism, Howard Erlanger and others emphasised four method-ological points of departure. First, it should be a "bottom-up" rather than simply a top-down approach, meaning essentially that it should be "supported by [empirical] research at the 'ground' level".[127] Secondly, that it should be reflective about the difficulty of translating between social science and legal methods: "an important initial step — is for scholars to communicate more cautiously across these disciplinary divides, in order to make each other aware of divergent assumptions, epistemologies, or goals." Thirdly, without predetermining the issue of whether knowledge can be objective, the new realism — like all social science research — must remain conscious of this as a fundamental issue for research. Fourthly, the new realism (unlike the old) takes a global and transnational perspective in its approach to policy and the law-society nexus.

It is easy to sympathise with the realist aim of achieving a socially relevant way of understanding the legal system and particular legal doctrines: initially, this aim was a reaction to the formal and positivist study of law which was preoccupied with the abstract exposition of prevailing doctrines. The "old realism" emphasised that law is not a "brooding omnipresence in the sky" and does not exist somewhere out there in its own heavenly conceptual world, separate from human existence. Recent "new realist" scholarship is attempting to flesh out this perception with extensive empirical research leading to new insights into law at both a general and a doctrinal level. In addition to the recent turn to social science by legal researchers, realism was, in essence, a practical attempt to deal with law as a social and political phenomenon. It may therefore also be regarded as the intellectual precursor of current "critical" movements in jurisprudence.

---

127   Howard Erlanger et al, "Is it Time For a New Legal Realism?" (2005) *Wisconsin Law Review* 335 at 339-345. See also Sally Engle Merry, "New Legal Realism and the Ethnography of Transnational Law" (2006) 31 *Law and Social Inquiry* 975.

Law and Economics

[4135]   ... one cannot ignore the impact the Legal Realists had in cracking the edifice of doctrinalism: and, with the edifice cracked, a void had been created for others to fill[128]

Realism paved the way for a range of social sciences to be seen as relevant in the study of law. Probably the most widespread and influential of the modern social-scientific approaches to law is law and economics. In a recent article, Thomas Ulen went so far as to claim that "law and economics (or the economic analysis of law) is the default style of legal scholarship".[129] Many would doubt this claim, but it is certainly true that, especially in the United States, economic analysis of law has become extremely widespread. In general terms law and economics began as an attempt to make the study of law scientific insofar as it applies an existing "science" (if we accept that economics is scientific) to law. As Gary Minda explains, however, "second generation" law and economics (which began in the mid-1980s) moved away from the scientific paradigm in favour of more localised, more practical, and often specifically progressive, analysis of law.[130] Like other contemporary movements in legal theory, law and economics is not a single theory: beyond the basic aim of applying economic concepts and analysis to law, there is a great deal of diversity in both the types of economic thought utilised and the way these are brought into legal thinking.

The main approach which I am going to describe is the early, "neo-classical" economics, which as I will explain, involves assumptions of human rationality, utility maximisation, and the moral and social value of efficiency. As this is a book on legal theory, not economics, I will concentrate on the basic aspects of this early law and economics from a legal theory perspective.[131] What I am going to describe is introductory,

---

128   Nicholas Mercuro and Steven Medema, *Economics and the Law: From Posner to Post-Modernism and Beyond* (2nd ed, Princeton University Press, Princeton, 2006), p 19.

129   Thomas Ulen, "Book Review: Law's Order: What Economics Has to Do With Law and Why it Matters" (2001) 41 *Santa Clara Law Review* 643 at 643.

130   Gary Minda, *Postmodern Legal Movements: Law and Jurisprudence at Century's End* (New York University Press, New York, 1995), p 87. For other recent evaluations of the directions of economic analysis of law see Richard Epstein, "Law and Economics: Its Glorious Past and Cloudy Future" (1997) 64 *University of Chicago Law Review* 1167; Gregory Crespi, "Review Essay: Does the Chicago School Need to Expand its Curriculum?" (1997) 22 *Law and Social Inquiry* 149.

131   Of course, a book on legal theory can include all sorts of things, but my other reason for looking at law and economics from a legal theory perspective is that I am not an economist, at least not in the formal sense of the term, having had no training. Good introductions to law and economics are: George Stigler, "Law or Economics?" (1992) 35 *Journal of Law and Economics* 455; Jules Coleman, "Economics and the Law: A Critical Review of the Foundations of the Economic Approach to Law" (1984) *Ethics* 649; Cento Veljanovski, "The Economic Approach to Law: A Critical Introduction" (1980) 7 *British Journal of Law and Society* 158; Bottomley and Bronitt, *Law In Context*, Ch 11. An excellent technical critique of economic theory is Steve Keen, *Debunking Economics: The Naked Emperor of the Social Sciences* (Pluto Press and Zed Books, NSW and London, 2001).

and should not be taken as representative of the whole of the field of law and economics because there is no single way of understanding this field.[132] Law and economics has, for instance, often been understood as presenting a "scientific" mask for what is, in fact, a very conservative political agenda. There is some truth in such claims, but only insofar as they apply to certain types of economic analysis. Other streams of law and economics are not inherently conservative.

Law's *terra nullius* — settled or conquered?

[4140]   "Economists are imperialists", says Frank Easterbrook.[133] Most people would not these days readily admit to having an imperialist outlook on life: *explicit* imperialism as a political ideology is somewhat outmoded. Post-World War II imperialists are somewhat more discreet about their motives. But some, if not all, neo-classical economists do not have any such political sensitivity about bluntly admitting that their aim is simply to colonise other "softer" disciplines which have not developed the technical (by which is meant mathematical and quantitative) capacity of economics. Cooter and Ulen write:[134]

> This aggression against softer subjects has been called the "imperialism of economics." One recent beneficiary, or victim, is the law. Left to its own devices, the law stood no more chance of developing quantitative methodology than Australia stood of independently developing the rabbit.

The words "beneficiary" and "victim", given as alternatives (depending on whose side you are on) are notably void of moral content here. What seems to be important to the authors is simply who can win the desired territory with "superior" methods of analysis. Economics has more powerful guns than law, and more ammunition. *Some* economists at least, do not actually consider whether guns are morally justified, or they simply take efficiency to be the primary moral value.[135]

---

132   In particular I am not going to explain in any detail the Coase theorem, which has been very influential in economic analysis of law. There has been a huge amount of writing on this subject, which is quite impossible to reduce intelligibly to such a short space. For an introduction to later law and economics, see Gary Minda, *Postmodern Legal Movements: Law and Jurisprudence at Century's End*, pp 95-105; Robin Malloy and Christopher Braun (eds), *Law and Economics: New and Critical Perspectives* (Peter Lang, New York, 1995); Mercuro and Medema, *Economics and the Law: From Posner to Post-Modernism and Beyond*; Robin Malloy, *Law in a Market Context: An Introduction to Market Concepts in Legal Reasoning* (Cambridge University Press, Cambridge, 2004); Megan Richardson and Gillian Hadfield (eds), *The Second Wave of Law and Economics* (Federation Press, Sydney, 1999).

133   Frank Easterbrook, "The Inevitability of Law and Economics" (1989) 1 *Legal Education Review* 3 at 24.

134   Robert Cooter and Thomas Ulen, *Law and Economics* (Harper and Collins, USA, 1988), p 8. It may be that "imperialism" in this context means nothing more than what others mean by an "interdisciplinary approach", but that is not how I read it. See also CAE Goodhart, "Economics and the Law: Too Much One-Way Traffic" (1997) 60 *Modern Law Review* 1 at 2.

135   Maybe we can compare economists who fail to examine the moral implications of their work to scientists who argue that the morality of certain types of scientific research is not their business: knowledge is the primary goal.

(Aggression and "developing the rabbit" in Australia are presented as morally neutral, or even as morally desirable.) What is important for these writers is simply that the scientific void apparent in any discipline employing what are seen as fuzzy concepts gives economics not only the opportunity but also the *right* to inhabit any *terra nullius* it can find.[136] Subjects which are soft, defenceless, and, in this sense, primitive in comparison to economics, deserve their fate. Law is an obvious target, not only because it fulfils the required criteria in terms of its perceived technological barbarity, but because it is already a powerful element of any society, and is seen as being an extremely lucrative prize. Moving into English literature or philosophy would just not be the same. Cooter and Ulen continue their explanation of the law and economics phenomena as follows:[137]

> Watching law respond to economic analysis is rather like watching an ecological system rearrange itself after the release of an exotic animal. Like the rabbits in Australia, economists have discovered an unoccupied niche in legal scholarship, specifically, the absence of quantitative reasoning, and are moving quickly to fill it.

Cooter and Ulen seem to regard the process of colonisation simply as an interesting phenomenon, but for those of us who regard the introduction of rabbits into Australia as an unmitigated ecological disaster, the comparison is an unhelpful one.[138] Fortunately, law and economics has started to move beyond this imperialistic approach in which "economics, the active part, analys[es] law, the passive part."[139] As Gillian Hadfield puts it:[140]

> to do true law and economics means to recognise that law has its own knowledge, and that knowledge has to be respected alongside economics. Law and economics is about a partnership, rather than a hierarchy.

Asking the economy question

[4145] Neo-classical economists tend to divide their work into two broad approaches, both of which have been applied to law. Predominantly, economics is used as a tool for interpreting the economic interactions which take place in the world, and predicting behaviour on the basis of this description. Such description is based on empirical observation, hypothesis formulation and hypothesis testing and is called "positive"

---

136   The definition of *terra nullius*, of course, is in the eye of those with the power to behold: that is, the conquerors, who can say what counts as truth.

137   Cooter and Ulen, *Law and Economics*, p 9.

138   In a broader sense, "colonisation" is itself a euphemism for what has usually in fact been a disastrous application of brute imperial force to native people, cultures, wildlife, and landscape. Perhaps it does after all, in spite of itself, tell us the truth about some aspects of the economic invasion of law.

139   Hadfield, "The Second Wave of Law and Economics: Learning to Surf" in Richardson and Hadfield (eds), *The Second Wave of Law and Economics*, p 54.

140   Hadfield, "The Second Wave of Law and Economics: Learning to Surf", p 54.

or "predictive" economics. Economic forecasting is essentially about formulating hypotheses concerning a future state of affairs, based on observation and interpretation of past and present situations. This sort of economics is "positive" in the sense outlined in Chapter 3 in relation to positive scientific methodology.[141] Applied to law, positive economics can be deployed to study the effects of legal doctrines on people's behaviour. Mercuro and Medema give the following examples, among others: "Does the rule of negligence in force induce those who can undertake precautionary activities at the lowest cost to do so? To what extent does the law of contracts facilitate or inhibit the movement of resources into areas where they are most highly valued?"[142]

"Normative economics" on the other hand is an attempt to *determine*, not merely predict, a future state for the world, based on an economic theory. To take the most simple example, if an optimal allocation of resources can theoretically be obtained in a free market economy (and if our aim is efficiency), then we ought to deregulate and privatise as much as possible. Or, if a particular form of legal regulation is proved by whatever means to be more efficient than that employed at present, then according to some economists, that more efficient form of regulation ought to be adopted. Normative law and economics is directed at law reform and, in the neo-classical version, usually takes the line that existing laws or legal doctrines need to be altered because they are inefficient. Recent, more critical, law and economics scholarship has moved away from using efficiency as the sole criterion by which to evaluate law and advocate reform.[143]

An infamous early example of this style of economic analysis can be found in "The Economics of the Baby Shortage" written by Richard Posner and Elisabeth Landes. Posner and Landes write about the shortage of babies for adoption and the surplus of unwanted children in foster homes or institutions, and consider this "market disequilibrium" to be an effect of excessive government regulation on adoption. In their view the "baby market" ought to be deregulated so that adoption agencies (which are the primary facilitators of adoption in the US) could charge the "demanders" (childless couples) a market price for the "product" (babies), and, in turn, the "suppliers" (mothers) could charge a market price for their product, based on its quality. Consider the following statement: "In a legal and competitive baby market, price would be equated to the marginal costs of producing and

---

141 That is, positive economics is "positive" in the sense proposed by Auguste Comte, insofar as it is based on observation, hypothesis formulation, and prediction. See the section on positivism in Chapter 3.

142 Mercuro and Medema, *Economics and the Law: From Posner to Post-Modernism and Beyond*, p 46. See also Michael Trebilcock, "The Value and Limits of Law and Economics" in Richardson and Hadfield (eds), *The Second Wave of Law and Economics*, pp 12-22.

143 Minda, *Postmodern Legal Movements*, p 95.

selling for adoption babies of a given quality".[144] According to the authors (who provide plenty of graphs and equations to support their view), the effect of such a deregulation would be to achieve an efficient equilibrium in the baby market.

Both positive and normative economics as they are applied to law usually involve the analysis of substantive legal doctrines from an economic perspective. A third type of economics which is perhaps more closely allied with the concerns of legal theory is often referred to specifically in relation to law and economics.[145] "Descriptive" law and economics uses economic concepts to describe either substantive law or the legal system generally. Law is described through the filter of economics: for instance, a legal doctrine is explained in economic terms as promoting efficiency, or the legal system is described as an economy. Richard Posner's *Economic Analysis of Law* is probably the best-known example of descriptive law and economics. In this work Posner describes common law doctrines as forming an economic system: the common law is to be understood as an institution which promotes efficiency in human transactions.[146]

The main assumption of neo-classical economics is that human beings are rational utility maximisers. That is, when faced with a choice people will choose the alternative which produces for them the greatest personal satisfaction or "utility". For instance, when faced with a decision about whether to buy something, the economically rational person will ask whether the cost of the purchase is worth its benefits. (And in this context what is also taken into account is the so-called "opportunity cost", that is, the opportunities which have to be given up in order to take the proposed course of action. The cost of a particular course of action is not just, for instance, the immediate financial cost — it is also the cost of giving up an alternative.) As Easterbrook points out, saying that people are "rational" does not mean that we are computers.[147] And saying that we maximise "utility" does not mean that we are only concerned about money or things which can have a monetary value attached to them. "Utility" is not necessarily only money, though in economic terms it must be something to which some sort of value can be (subjectively) attached, making it capable of being measured or balanced against other aspects of one's utility. So the point is not that we try to maximise wealth, but that in the ordinary course of events we do try to weigh up the costs and benefits of a particular course of action. This perhaps reflects what most non-economists would assume that economics is about.

---

144 Elizabeth Landes and Richard Posner, "The Economics of the Baby Shortage" (1978) 7 *Journal of Legal Studies* 323 at 339.

145 Bottomley and Bronitt, *Law In Context*, p 338

146 Richard Posner, *Economic Analysis of Law* (3rd ed, Little, Brown, Boston, 1986), pp 21 and 229. See also Stigler, "Law or Economics?"; Cento Veljanovski, *Economic Principles of Law* (Cambridge University Press, Cambridge, 2007), pp 12-17.

147 Easterbrook, "The Inevitability of Law and Economics", pp 5-6.

As an example of a neo-classicist, take Judge Frank Easterbrook, who introduces the interface between economics and the law in the following manner.

Frank Easterbrook
"The Inevitability of Law and Economics"[148]

[4150]   Economics is the study of rational behaviour in the face of scarcity. Economics and law are, therefore, inseparable. The legal system too, is about coping with scarcity. If there were an abundance of every good thing, there would be no need for law, no need for a state. Life would also be boring.

Like economics, the legal system assumes rational behaviour. It seeks to influence by the threat of sanctions, such as imprisonment or civil damages. The coercive aspect of law assumes that persons care about consequences; "a legal duty so called is nothing but a prediction that if a man does or omits certain things he will be made to suffer in this or that way by judgement of the court", a penalty set to influence the behaviour of the "bad man" who looks only to consequences — for other sorts, the law is less important anyway. Legislatures and judges believe that people will respond to these threats by modifying their behaviour so as to minimise the sum of compliance and sanction costs; the state, for its part, tries to minimise the sum of the enforcement costs and the residual harms caused by non-compliance with law — subject to a budget constraint and the desire to equate marginal returns on the many activities in which the state is involved.

The world of the economist starts with free trade and the world of the lawyer with regulation; the two disciplines often come up with different prescriptions for social interactions. But both are about self-interested behaviour in a world of scarcity. Take away scarcity, and both professions have no reason to exist. If there is scarcity, law cannot be understood apart from economic thought. Neither teaching nor practice nor judging can disregard the subject.

[4155] Easterbrook says that without scarcity, the legal system would not be necessary. The obvious question which this raises is whether human conflict is largely the consequence of scarcity of some resource or another? What is the "scarcity" which leads to domestic violence, sexual assault, or pornography? Does shoplifting always involve a choice made by someone to face the risk of being caught in order to satisfy a personal desire or need for a material good? Or can it involve other factors, having nothing to do with scarcity?[149] I raise these questions because they seem to me to lead in many directions. For instance Richard Posner, an influential legal-economist judge in the United States, some of whose views I can really only describe as bizarre (although his views have clearly changed over the decades), argued that

---

148   Easterbrook, "The Inevitability of Law and Economics", p 3. The quotation is from Holmes, "The Path of the Law", pp 460-461.

149   As Mary Heath has pointed out to me, poverty in our society has nothing to do with scarcity.

rape occurs because of a scarcity of sex: sex is relatively costly, so men have to rape to get it.[150] According to Posner, rape is not about the sexual subordination of women by men, or what MacKinnon has called the "eroticisation of dominance".[151] Rape for Posner is simply about male desire, and finding substitutes for consensual sex.[152] This may appear to be an extreme application of economics to an area of human activity, however, feminist economists have argued that it is not necessarily the use of economic analysis in this context which is problematic "but rather that the economic analysis used to defend socially conservative, and anti-feminist, political views was not good economic analysis."[153] In any event, the classic approach is to see social order imposed by law as a system of costs and benefits about which people can make rational choices. This is, after all, basically what the idea of deterrence relies upon.

Veljanovski clarifies the notion of the rational "man" by pointing out that the assumption of rationality is not intended to be an empirically true statement applied to all individuals. It is, instead, an "average" for men in society. (I use the word "men" deliberately.)[154]

> The economic approach does *not* contend that all individuals are rational nor that these assumptions are necessarily realistic. The economist's model of man as a rational actor is a "fiction", but one that has proved extremely useful in analysing the behaviour of groups. Although much of economics is framed in terms of individual behaviour there is no belief among economists that all people behave in this way. Rather economic man is some weighted average of the individuals under study in which the non-uniformities and extremes in behaviour are evened out. The theory allows for irrationality but argues that *groups* of individuals behave *as if* their members are rational. Related to this *as if* approach is that the utility maximising postulate is not one concerned with the psychology of man or

---

150 Posner, *Sex and Reason* (Harvard University Press, Cambridge Mass, 1992); see the critique by Martha Fineman, "The Hermeneutics of Reason: A Commentary on Sex and Reason" (1993) 25 *Connecticut Law Review* 503. Jeanne Schroeder has undertaken a sustained critique of Posner's views on rationality. See Jeanne Schroeder, "Just So Stories: Posnerian Methodology" (2001) 22 *Cardozo Law Review* 351; "Rationality in Law and Economics Scholarship" (2000) 79 *Oregon Law Review* 147. An excellent economic critique of Posner's book is Gillian Hadfield, "Flirting with Science: Richard Posner on the Bioeconomics of Sexual Man" (1992) 106 *Harvard Law Review* 479.

151 See generally Catharine MacKinnon, *Feminism Unmodified* (Harvard University Press, Cambridge Mass, 1987). MacKinnon's views will be discussed further in Chapter 6.

152 Posner comments: "Contrary to a view held by many feminists, rape appears to be primarily a substitute for consensual sexual intercourse rather than a manifestation of male hostility toward women or a method of establishing or maintaining male domination": *Sex and Reason*, p 384. This argument forms part of Posner's larger analysis of sex and sexuality as an economy: the regularities of sex can, according to Posner, be explained in terms of the costs and benefits attaching to particular sexual choices.

153 Gillian Hadfield, "Learning to Surf", p 53.

154 Veljanovski, "The Economic Approach to Law: A Critical Introduction". For a thorough critique see Keen, *Debunking Economics: The Naked Emperor of the Social Sciences*, Ch 2.

his actual decision making process. It does not assert that individuals consciously calculate the cost and benefits of all actions only that their behaviour can be "explained" as if they did so. Admittedly this is *not* the only view of rationality either in economics or generally, but it is the one that forms the basis of what is known as the positive or predictive economic approach.

Thus, according to the economic model, individuals may (and do) behave irrationally, but the behaviour of *groups* of people can be explained by assuming that an average member behaves rationally. So apparently arguing that the assumption of rationality is unjustified because not all people are rational does not quite hit the mark. The assumption is not that all people are rational, but that average behaviour is.

Nonetheless, I think it is still possible to criticise the assumption on the basis that it assumes and values a certain type of behaviour historically and culturally associated with a very specific social group: educated white men. Like the reasonable man, the rational man is, in the end, envisaged as a man.[155] This has a couple of fairly clear consequences. First, the theory of economics focuses on a paradigm of humanity which is, in fact, a stereotypical *male* of a certain culture and social background.[156] The values associated with women and with non-European cultures are devalued by the theory and not taken into account in its description of social interaction. The result is evident in the way that economic thought has traditionally been applied: in constructing a reality of a particular type, activities traditionally undertaken by women are not seen as part of the market place.[157] Housework, for instance, is not "economically productive" even though it is obvious that it is work and that it contributes in many ways to the material well-being of a society. A further criticism, levelled some time ago by Amartya Sen, is that the concept of the rational person is far too simplistic as a model: maximisation of utility may be one motivation for behaviour, but it is hardly the only one: "The *purely* economic man is indeed close to being a social moron. Economic theory has been

---

155   The "reasonable man" standard is discussed in Leslie Bender, "A Lawyer's Primer on Feminist Theory and Tort" (1988) 38 *Journal of Legal Education* 3; Lucinda Finley, "A Break in the Silence: Including Women's Issues in a Torts Course" (1989) 41 *Yale Journal of Law and Feminism* 41; Caroline Forrell, "Reasonable Woman Standard of Care" (1992) 11 *University of Tasmania Law Review* 1.

156   Wanda Wiegers, "Economic Analysis of Law and 'Private Ordering': A Feminist Critique" (1992) 42 *University of Toronto Law Journal* 170. Wiegers comments: "While recognizing that 'economic man' is an abstraction, the classical model of competetive individualism that emerged in the nineteenth century clearly failed to describe or reflect the reality of women. Historically, women have been assumed and expected to be all that 'economic man' is not — emotional, vulnerable, passive, empathic, caring, and nurturant. The central ideas in neoclassical economic theory were formulated by men and were intended to explain behaviour in traditional markets that have always been male-dominated", p 170.

157   See, for instance Marilyn Waring, *Counting for Nothing: What Men Value and What Women Are Worth* (Allen and Unwin, Wellington NZ, 1988).

much preoccupied with this rational fool decked in the glory of his *one* all-purpose preference ordering."[158] In particular, Sen argued that if a person has a commitment to a goal, the attainment of which will however result in a decrease of her or his well-being, an action in pursuance of the goal cannot be interpreted as within the normal one-dimensional definition of "rationality". (And clearly a group, as well as an individual, may have a commitment or a complex of commitments affecting their group choices.)

A second argument of this brand of economics is that this pattern of behaviour — rationally maximising utility — will, in the ideal market situation, lead to a situation of equilibrium which is efficient in the sense that it minimises total costs and maximises total benefits.[159] Economists talk about several types of efficiency, but one of the most commonly used term is "Pareto efficiency" (or Pareto optimality), which describes that state of equilibrium where it is impossible to increase the welfare of one individual without adversely affecting the welfare of another.[160] It has been pointed out that describing something as "Pareto optimal" does not necessarily indicate that it is a socially desirable state:[161]

> A state in which some people are starving and suffering from acute deprivation while others are tasting the good life can still be Pareto optimal if the poor cannot be made better off without cutting into the pleasures of the rich — no matter by how small in amount. Pareto optimality is faint praise indeed ...

It would seem clear from this that describing something as "efficient" in economic terms is not an indication of its social desirability, and may, in fact, totally neglect the distributional effects of a particular policy or state of affairs.

Nonetheless, Pareto optimality is defended by some economists as a way of judging, in moral terms, the probable consequences of a transaction. For instance, Judge Frank Easterbrook argues that because human beings are free individuals working to optimise their utility, any transaction reached between adults will "satisfy the Pareto criterion",

---

158 Amartya Sen, "Rational Fools: A Critique of the Behavioural Foundations of Economic Theory" (1977) 6 *Philosophy and Public Affairs* 317 at 336. See also Neil Siegel, "Sen and the Hart of Jurisprudence: A Critique of the Economic Analysis of Judicial Behaviour" (1999) 87 *California Law Review* 1581.

159 For a re-examination of the notion of equilibrium see Lawrence Boland, *Methodology for a New Microeconomics: The Critical Foundations* (Allen and Unwin, Boston, 1987); Keen, *Debunking Economics: The Naked Emperor of the Social Sciences*, pp 168-178.

160 For a general critique see Jeffrey Harrison, "Piercing Pareto Superiority: Real People and the Obligations of Legal Theory" (1997) 39 *Arizona Law* Review 1; for a brief account of law and optimality, see Mercuro and Medema, *Economics and the Law: From Posner to Post-Modernism and Beyond*, pp 26-27.

161 Sen, quoted in Feiwel (ed), *Issues in Contemporary Microeconomics and Welfare* (State University of New York Press, Albany, 1985), p 3.

meaning that it will not reduce overall well-being: it will in all likelihood be a transaction which increases the utility of all parties.[162]

> Economics treats people as autonomous, able to decide for themselves. Certainly these were the premises on which the founders of Australia, New Zealand and the United States operated. The moral basis of economic analysis is the Pareto criterion: any transaction that improves at least one person's lot and makes no-one worse off is desirable. There is widespread agreement on this as an ethical rule, and it describes the sorts of voluntary exchanges with which economic inquiry is concerned. (If the exchange does not make at least one party better off, why do we observe it? If it makes one party worse off, that party would balk. Hence voluntary transactions between adults satisfy the Pareto criterion, and likely make all participants better off.) Although transactions often leave someone worse off in retrospect (the buyer of stock who is disappointed when the price falls; the spouse disappointed by the chosen partner), they are beneficial ex ante, which is the right time frame. One cannot do much about the way things turn out without stifling agreements that everyone desires at the outset.

There are some obvious difficulties with seeing the way people relate to each other solely in terms of autonomy and rationality. Easterbrook implies that transactions which would make one party worse off will be rare, since parties made worse off would decline to enter into such an agreement. This assumes, in the first place, that a party made worse off by a transaction is actually a party to the transaction — but we can think of many instances where a transaction between two or more people will make a third person, or group of people, worse off. A transaction between the Australian government and a mining company may well be a transaction between two autonomous individuals, but that it not to say that a third group of people, the traditional owners of an area of land, will not be disadvantaged by it. Obviously people do not always have a choice about what others do to them.

Secondly, even assuming that we can talk about closed transactions between two people, Easterbrook's analysis clearly fails even to take note of the effects of power differentials in relationships. Such power differentials *may* be confined to a particular relationship, and simply be the product of the different personalities involved, but they may

---

162 Easterbrook, "The Inevitability of Law and Economics", p 24. Easterbrook mentions the "ex ante" time frame as the right one, explaining this by contrasting the two functions of pie-slicer and pie-enlarger. There is a tendency in litigation, he suggests, to focus on slicing the pie, that is, distributing a loss or imposing a sanction after the event which has led to litigation. An economic approach, in contrast, will take into account not only the relationship between the parties to a dispute, but also the probable consequences of deciding it in a particular way, consequences which should be taken into account by the judge in making her decision. Looking at a legal doctine ex ante will enable the decision-maker to make a prediction about the likely effects of deciding in one way or another. As Easterbrook points out, this is "also called policy analysis". Easterbrook distinguishes the type of policy analysis which is common in law from economic analysis, which he says is more consistent (lawyers only think about ex ante effects when it suits them) and in being more rigorous in thinking through the likely effects of a decision or legal doctrine. See also Coleman, "Economics and the Law: A Critical Review of the Foundations of the Economic Approach to the Law", pp 649-652.

also be part of a social hierarchy which gives certain groups of people more persuasive power in a range of situations: in relation to poor people the wealthy have a far greater social power; men and women are socialised to regard the relations between the sexes in a particular way which gives men power over women; whites in Australia are socialised to regard Aboriginal people as inferior. In other words, the assumptions of autonomy and rationality leave out of the picture the effects of power in society. Differences in power may be systemic, not just individual, in which case the assumption of a particular average person is clearly problematic.

This brings me to a further introductory point about economic modelling, which is that it is precisely that — modelling. It is not intended to be an absolutely accurate representation of the way the world is. It reduces relationships so that they can be generalised and provide the basis for predictions.

Substantive analysis

[4160] One of the "soft" concepts of the law is that of the reasonable person. The standard of care in torts is that of the reasonable person in the position of the defendant. But, Cooter and Ulen ask *"exactly how much care is 'reasonable'?"*[163] The very question seems to assume that reasonableness can be quantified, whereas most lawyers would see reasonable care as a flexible standard which depends on the facts of a particular case. The economic approach is to replace this "vague" (unquantifiable) concept with something which can be given a number and ranked alongside other examples of taking care.

One clear example of the application of economic reasoning to a legal question is to be found in the formula proposed by Judge Learned Hand in *United States v Carroll Towing Co* (7th Circuit 1947) 159 F2d 1022. The Hand formula is that if the actual cost of *preventing* an accident (B) is less than the economically determined "expected cost" of the accident, then the person who in law caused the accident is liable in negligence. The "expected cost" is an economic term which represents a sort of prediction about the probable cost of an accident before it has occurred. In formal terms, the "expected cost" is the *probability* (P) of an accident occurring multiplied by the *loss* which will eventuate if the accident actually occurs (L). So if B<PL then the defendant who owes a duty of care to the plaintiff is to be liable for breach of duty. To attach some numbers to the formula: if the probability of an accident occurring is 1/100, and the loss which will be suffered if the accident does happen is $100 000, the "expected cost" is $1 000. If the cost of avoiding the accident in the first place is less than $1 000, the defendant is liable, if it is more than $1 000, he or she

---

163 Cooter and Ulen, *Law and Economics*, p 328 (emphasis added); see also, for a contrasting approach, Jennifer Arlen, "Reconsidering Efficient Tort Rules for Personal Injury: The Case of Single Activity Accidents" (1990) 32 *William and Mary Law Review* 41.

is not. This is obviously a very simplistic account — it will become more complex shortly. It is clear from the outset here that what is being attempted is a substitution of the legal notion of reasonableness by an economic notion of "rationality".

The immediate criticisms which arise from this sort of quantification of a legal concept are that it totally disregards the human factor, it is quite incapable of taking into account the justice of a particular case, it reduces a dangerous situation to cold calculation, and (if you think that last statement was a little emotive) encourages those who frequently create potentially dangerous circumstances to weigh the physical well-being of others against profit. It encourages people to take risks with the safety and well-being of others when the profit to be gained from the risk outweighs any costs to victims. For instance there is no liability if the "expected cost" of an accident is $1 000, and the cost of prevention is $1 100. But what about the cost to the *victim*, who may have suffered a permanent and significant loss of amenity? If we remember that the concept of "expected cost" includes an *actual* cost to the victim which is generally significantly higher than the cost of prevention, the injustice of the formula is immediately apparent. The "expected cost" of $1 000 may mean that the victim in fact suffers a loss evaluated at $1 000 000. And despite statements which appear in every introductory chapter that utility means more than wealth, a test like this can only work if a monetary value is put on every element of the costs involved: otherwise the different parts of the equation would simply be incommensurable. Putting a monetary value on a victim's loss is a necessary evil when an assessment of damages has to be made: doing it before the event so the creators of dangerous situations can maximise their profit while they minimise their liability is a different matter altogether.

What this test says, in effect, is that if manufacturers of goods have done their sums properly, they will always escape liability: simply, if they have correctly evaluated the "expected cost" to be less than the cost of avoidance, then — *because they have taken the efficient course of action* — they are to be rewarded by not being liable for any accidents they have caused. Conversely, if they have taken the inefficient course of action, then they are to be punished with liability. The liability rule is formulated *only* to encourage efficiency. Either way, the effect on the victim is irrelevant — what matters for determining liability is simply whether the defendant took the correct action to reduce costs. Whether it is actually *fair* that the victim of an accident should have to bear the loss is not considered. On a more pragmatic level, a test like this assumes that full and reasonably precise information about the gravity of a harm and the probability of its occurrence is available. But I think that this practical objection is insignificant against the moral ones. And it is precisely the "vagueness" of the legal concept of reason-ableness which, despite its other shortcomings, allows at least some attention to be paid to the merits of the individual case. (Even if I don't think the reasonable person (man) standard is always fair, it is certainly far preferable to a standard of economic rationality.)

Economists have criticised the Hand formula, but not necessarily because of its neglect of what is individual, or unjust, or difficult about a specific case. The Hand formula has been criticised because it presents the options as being black and white: either the manufacturer can take a precaution or she should not. But it has been pointed out that the formula is economically simplistic because it only takes into account total costs and benefits, not marginal costs and benefits.[164] It assumes that the choice facing the defendant was between avoiding the accident completely or taking no precaution at all. But what if the risk of an accident occurring could be substantially reduced at relatively little cost? The revised Hand formula takes into account that "the costs of precaution increase as more of it is taken",[165] and sets the optimal level of precaution (beyond which there will be liability) at the point where *less* precaution will result in the cost of accidents being too high, and *more* precaution will not be justified because it is too costly when compared with the expected cost of an accident. This more complex version of the formula is an improvement only in the sense that it corrects the economic faults of the simple test. It does not address the other problems: in particular it remains the case that it takes only the perspective of those who are potential injurers and ignores the perspective of the victim.

In "Inevitability and Use" Graeme Cooper compares the Hand formula to an explanation of the standard of care offered by Mason J in *Wyong Shire Council v Shirt*:[166]

> The perception of the reasonable person's response calls for a consideration of the magnitude of the risk and the degree of probability of its occurrence along with the expense, difficulty and inconvenience of taking alleviating action.

Cooper comments:[167]

> That is an economic test. It tracks very closely the test called the Learned Hand test in the *Carroll Towing* case which is the basis from which the economic analysis of negligence proceeded in the United States. The Australian version has everything but the algebra.

I disagree. Not having the algebra is not a minor difference, but a crucial one. The so-called "negligence calculus", involving a consideration of the magnitude of the risk, its probability, and the possibility of avoiding or minimising the risk, is a flexible test which cannot be reduced to numbers. It is an "economic" test in the sense that it weighs up costs

---

164 Stephen, *The Economics of the Law*, p 136; Bottomley and Bronitt, *Law in Context*, pp 191-193; Posner, *Economic Analysis of Law*, p 320ff.

165 Cooter and Ulen, *Law and Economics*, p 347.

166 (1980) 146 CLR 40 at 47-48.

167 Graeme Cooper, "Inevitability and Use" (1989) 1 *Legal Education Review* 29 at 31. See also Ian Malkin and Joan Wright, "Product Liability under the Trade Practices Act — Adequately Compensating for Personal Injury?" (1993) 1 *Torts Law Journal* 63 at 65.

and benefits, but it does this with a large degree of sensitivity to the particular facts of each case, the relative positions of the plaintiff and defendant, and the nature of the duty of care which was owed. There is certainly no way of making the application of this test absolutely consistent and nor, I would argue, should there be.

Another important feature of the economic analysis of substantive law which I should briefly mention is the Coase theorem, which has been central to much law and economics analysis.[168] Coase argued that if the costs of bargaining are ignored (that is, assuming "zero transaction costs"), the economically efficient solution will prevail, regardless of where a legal doctrine places liability as between individual parties. This is because (in a free market situation) legal rights can be bought and sold: the right to do something which injures somebody else can be "bought" by the person injured. If X has a right to carry out an activity which injures Y, then Y can pay X to desist. This will occur (according to the theory) if Y values X not doing the activity more than X values doing it. Conversely a prohibition against injuring somebody can be turned into a right, if the prohibited person is willing to pay the person(s) who will be injured by the activity. If X is prohibited from doing something which would injure Y, then X can pay Y so that X can carry out the activity. Again, this will occur if X values her ability to carry out the activity more than Y values the absence of the injury. Therefore (the theory goes) the efficient solution will eventually be reached: the parties will negotiate and formulate an agreement which maximises the utility of each.

The Coase theorem has been taken up in a fairly major way by the law and economics theorists at the University of Chicago (and their followers elsewhere). Often, it was used as an argument against government regulation — this only adds to transaction costs and makes it more difficult to achieve the efficient solution.[169] This type of economic analysis suffers from the same general moral objections as the application of the Hand formula. It has been pointed out by Polinsky that "although the choice of the legal rule does not affect the attainment of the efficient solution ... it does affect the distribution of income".[170] The question of income distribution is not one which is very seriously considered in Chicago-style law and economics theory. Quite apart from this problem, it is assumed that there is in the first

---

168 I am not going to explain the Coase theorem in detail here, but good explanations appear in several texts. See especially RH Coase, "The Problem of Social Cost" (1960) 3 *Journal of Law and Economics* 1; Veljanovski, *Economic Principles of Law*, pp 41-42; Mercuro and Medema, *Economics and the Law: From Posner to Post-Modernism and Beyond*, pp 110-113.

169 Veljanovski comments that "at one level the Coase Theorem was interpreted as a market manifesto; at another that the common law had an underlying economic logic ... . That Coase did not actually say or mean either mattered little to the debate which subsequently raged." *Economic Principles of Law*, p 5.

170 Polinsky, *An Introduction to Law and Economics* (1989), in Bottomley and Bronitt, *Law in Context*, p 343.

place available income on both sides which can be distributed. But what if the victim of the injury-causing activity is in no position, either financially or politically, to negotiate? What is being assumed here is not only that people are rational utility-maximisers, but also that they are equal in terms of their financial, physical, and psychological ability to contend with the world. (An assumption which, in turn, rests on the idea that the world deals equally with every individual — regardless of race, sex, class, physical and mental ability, age, and one's capacity and willingness to conform with the rest of the sheep.) It will be objected here that the economic model assumes an ideal situation, and that I am confusing the model's claims about what *would* happen in the perfect market situation with the real world. Maybe I am. But until the model starts taking account of the way people are, in fact, dealt with by their external environment, it should be treated on its own terms, as a set of ideas which are limited in their practical applicability. In fact, such a model is only likely to entrench existing inequalities, because those who have bargaining power will be able to use and magnify it, while those who don't will simply have to take what they get and have no options about maximising their utility.

Conclusion

[4165] Science, as I explained at the beginning of this chapter, is the predominant paradigm of 20th and 21st century knowledge. Science is seen to be objective, politically neutral, and certain. What I have attempted to illustrate in this chapter is that science is none of these things (and cannot be), but is rather a perspective, or way of seeing the world, which is particularly powerful in its interpretations of reality. The power of scientific ideals is such that attaining the status of a science, or at least approximating or assuming some of its trappings (like the language of objectivity), has been an important goal for many intellectual areas, including, as I have explained, law. As I will explain further in Chapter 8, science is (like law-school law) a self-defining institution — what counts as proof, for instance, or verification, or falsification of a theory is determined by convention. The scientific community has a self-defined standard of "scientificity". Science itself is therefore defined and constrained by its own conventions — a system of standards, categories, norms, assumptions, models, and rules, all of which are the result of a particular historical development. It is this quasi-legal framework which determines the nature of the scientific "product". A critique of these rules and assumptions does not of necessity discredit the product, though it may do so. Rather, recognising that the scientific truth is also constructed within a particular context, allows us to see that it is also a *perspective*, and that its claim to "truth" must be understood in this light.

FIVE
CRITICAL LEGAL STUDIES: THE BEGINNINGS OF A DISSOLUTION

Introduction

[505]   The term "critical legal studies" can be understood in a broad or a narrow sense. In a broad sense, "critical legal studies" refers to all modern and postmodern critical scholarship which has been flourishing for over two decades. These critical approaches include such diverse perspectives as feminist legal theory, critical race theory, critical historical scholarship, psychoanalytical theory, postmodernism (in its various manifestations), the law and literature movement, and queer legal theory. In this broad sense, "critical legal studies" is impossible to define, because it is composed of so many different theoretical stances. Indeed, any attempt to define the broad phenomenon of critical legal studies would limit it and thus contradict its critical commitment to open and interdisciplinary theory.

Having said that, there are a few ways of differentiating this broad concept of "critical" legal theory from its other, "traditional" legal theory. For a start, most of those (myself included) who regard themselves as engaged in some form of critical scholarship wish to critique, and sometimes reject, the "traditional" notions of legal objectivity and legal neutrality. The idea that law can be studied in isolation from its social, moral, and political context is challenged by critical legal theories. In consequence, critical legal theories also frequently (but not always) highlight the complicity of "traditional" legal theory with the politics of race, sex, and class. Critical legal theory aims to be reflective, in a philosophical sense, meaning that it considers the fundamental conditions of knowledge and being. It questions the assumptions upon which "traditional" theory is based. For instance, a critical legal scholar might ask how the individual is positioned and constructed in society and language, rather than taking the notion of the individual for granted.

As Max Horkheimer[1] explained, "critical" theory regards the individual as a part of the web of social and historical relationships within which both observable facts and theoretical ideas are situated. In Horkheimer's account, "traditional" theory sees facts as objective, and therefore as separate from any theory which is constructed about them, as well as separate from the free-standing thinking individual who constructs the theories. "Critical" theory, in contrast, sees the thinking individual as embedded within a network of social and historical relationships. In this view, the individual, the theory, and the objects of theory, are all inter-connected. It is the role of critical theory to understand this connection, but at the same time to be self-reflective: since critical theory rejects the separation of facts, thinking subject, and theory, it clearly must not only apply its critical methodology to show the social constructedness of "traditional" theory, but also to illustrate its own premises and positioning within the social context. To put it very simply, critical theory sees theory and the theorist as socially and culturally situated, rather than objective and universal.

However, to claim that "critical" legal theory is "critical" while traditional legal scholarship is not, might be overstating the extent to which critical legal studies "owns" critique: in terms of its repeated questioning of the assumptions of theory, "traditional" theory *may* be just as critical as "critical" legal studies. I will have more to say about the characteristics of critical thought in later chapters.

This chapter is not concerned so much with "critical legal studies" in its broad sense, but rather with the relatively distinct "Critical Legal Studies" (CLS) movement. In this narrow sense, CLS has a definable historical location (late 1970s and 1980s), as well as a geographical centre (the United States).[2] CLS was the first of the late 20th century critical approaches to law (in Anglo-American jurisprudence, at least), and it served to inspire and influence later critical movements. Unlike the various arms of recent critical scholarship which I will consider in later chapters, Critical Legal Studies as a distinct movement flourished briefly before a rather swift decline. In the first edition of this book, written in 1994, I asked whether CLS was "dead, or worse, assimilated".

---

1   Max Horkheimer was a leading member of the Frankfurt school of critical theory. He wrote a series of essays on critical thought in the 1930s, collected and published in English in 1968 as *Critical Theory: Selected Essays* (Continuum, New York, 1968). See in particular "Traditional and Critical Theory". For further commentary on the meaning of critical theory see Loïc Wacquant, "Critical Thought as Solvent of *Doxa*" (2004) 11 *Constellations* 97; Julia Chryssostalis, "The Critical Instance 'After' the Critique of the Subject' (2005) 16 *Law and Critique* 3; Costas Douzinas, "Oubliez Critique" (2005) 16 *Law and Critique* 47; Costas Douzinas and Adam Geary, *Critical Jurisprudence: The Political Philosophy of Justice* (Hart Publishing, Oxford, 2005), p 36ff; George Pavlich, "Experiencing Critique" (2005) 16 *Law and Critique* 95.

2   For a comparison of US and British critical legal studies see Douzinas, "Oubliez Critique", pp 58-63, and Douzinas and Geary, *Critical Jurisprudence*, p 239ff.

It is now clear that whatever else it is, there is no doubt about the death of CLS as a defined movement, although its legacy remains significant. One optimistic commentator has, however, compared CLS to Kenny in the cartoon series *South Park*, in a (rather hopeful) effort to argue that it may yet be revived.[3] (Kenny, incoherent to all but his friends, dies unexpectedly in each episode only to reappear in the next one.) Given that the (narrowly-defined) CLS movement has dissipated, most of the chapter is written in the past tense. Although many of the central figures of CLS are still engaged in critical legal scholarship,[4] the movement no longer has an identity as a distinct form of legal theory. Indeed, I think it is accurate to say that historically CLS is located at the beginnings of the "dissolution" or "disintegration" of legal theory: as I noted in Chapter 1, theory has moved from a somewhat closed activity, into a multitude of legal theories which are loosely held together by the focus upon law, but which do not always seriously engage with each other. CLS helped to precipitate some of these critical movements. This is not to say that without CLS we would have no feminism, race theory, or postmodernism. On the contrary, CLS simply represents one highly publicised, influential, and *early* element of critical scholarship, the existence of which may (or may not) have eased the infiltration of other critical movements into the legal academy (and not only in the US, but also in other Anglocentric legal cultures). Clearly, however, these other critical movements have achieved a vibrant life of their own, and have outlived the influence of the CLS movement. Having said that, it is useful to consider the CLS movement as a historical moment in legal theory. Not only did it raise many themes which were generally taken up by critical approaches, it also generated extensive debate. Critique of CLS came from conservative commentators but also from radical scholars who felt that elements of CLS did not sufficiently take into account the position of socially marginalised groups. These tensions and blind spots in critique remain generally instructive.

---

3   E Dana Neacsu, "CLS Stands for Critical Legal Studies, If Anyone Remembers" (2000) 8 *Journal of Law and Policy* 415. Douzinas and Geary argue that "the defining feature of CLS … is an anxiety towards its own constitution. In American CLS, the repeated announcements of its own death have marked this unique anxiety." *Critical Jurisprudence*, p 229. See also Mark Tushnet, "Critical Legal Theory (Without Modifiers) in the United States" (2005) 13 *Journal of Political Philosophy* 99.

4   In particular, see Duncan Kennedy, *Critique of Adjudication [Fin de Siecle]* (Harvard University Press, Cambridge Mass, 1997). See also Peter Goodrich, "Duncan Kennedy as I Imagine Him: The Man, the Work, his Scholarship and the Polity" (2001) 22 *Cardozo Law Review* 971; Joanne Conaghan, "Wishful Thinking or Bad Faith: A Feminist Encounter with Duncan Kennedy's Critique of Adjudication" (2001) 22 *Cardozo Law Review* 721.

CLS: A Brief History of the Movement

[510] CLS[5] originated in the United States in the late 1970s as a response to what was widely perceived as an increasing political and legal conservatism. The movement brought together a range of disenchanted left-wing legal academics, who saw their task to be one of "demystifying" and "delegitimating" liberal legalism. Supporters of CLS have defined themselves loosely around their left-ish position on the (United States) political spectrum and by virtue of the fact that many of them are legal academics who have in common aspects of their intellectual and political backgrounds. But just as there is no single theory of feminism, law and economics, critical race theory, or realism, there was never a single CLS theory. CLS writing was similarly diverse — infuriatingly obscure and jargonistic, passionate, funny, insightfully critical of legal ideology, intimate, provocative, or vague. Sometimes an article managed to be all of these things at once. Not surprisingly then, reactions to CLS also varied a great deal — from the infuriated and defensive to the intimate and humorous.

The "Movement"

[515] Although CLS did not take on any definite identity until the first formal meeting of the Conference on Critical Legal Studies in 1977,[6] its intellectual and political origins arose somewhat earlier. In the first place, CLS marked a return to certain themes of legal realism, in particular, the opposition to formalist styles of legal reasoning, and the belief in the political nature of both legal institutions and legal processes generally. Secondly, the radical student politics of the late 1960s provided the political impetus for the later consolidation of the movement. In "Critical Legal Studies: A Political History", Mark Tushnet, one of the movement's founders and leading exponents, explains these origins in what he calls "The Dark Ages" of the Yale Law School in the late 1960s and early 1970s, a period during which the faculty at that law school fired six junior academics.[7] According to

---

5   It seems appropriate here to quote an atypical CLS first footnote: "At this point, it is *de rigeur* to list much of the work of one's friends, all of one's own past work, most of what one has recently read, virtually everything one should have read, or all of the above. I won't." Aviam Soifer, "Confronting Deep Strictures: Robinson, Rickey, and Racism" (1985) 6 *Cardozo Law Review* 865 at 865, note 1.

6   In Madison, Wisconsin. See generally John Henry Schlegel, "Notes Toward an Intimate, Opinionated, and Affectionate History of the Conference on Critical Legal Studies" (1984) 35 *Stanford Law Review* 391 at 396. For a recent retrospective on CLS see Richard Abel, "Ideology and Community in the First Wave of Critical Legal Studies" (Book Review) (2003) 54 *Journal of Legal Education* 201.

7   Mark Tushnet, "Critical Legal Studies: A Political History" (1991) 100 *Yale Law Journal* 1515 at 1530. The six were Richard Abel, Lee Albert, John Griffiths, Robert Hudec, Larry Simon, and David Trubeck: Tushnet, "Critical Legal Studies: A Political History", p 1530, note 60. They also became known as the "Radical Yale Law School in Exile 'Mafia'", led by David Trubeck: see Schlegel, "Notes Toward an Intimate, Opinionated, and Affectionate History of the Conference on Critical Legal Studies", p 392.

Tushnet, a student at Yale at the time, the dismissals had little to do with the official reasons given (raising standards for granting tenure), but were rather political lynchings by a conservative core of senior legal academics. Tushnet describes the environment of Yale as one where the junior academics were influenced by the radical politics of the time, a situation which caused some tension in the faculty, and its political polarisation. In any case, it was in this context that a group of students and academics formed some close political ties. In the early 1970s a similar political bonding was taking place at the Harvard law school.[8]

One of the Yale students who subsequently led the charge at Harvard was Duncan Kennedy, who became a foremost, if somewhat eccentric, figure in the movement. The crucial event in CLS history seems to have taken place in 1976, when Kennedy and David Trubek, one of the ex-Yale academics, decided to form a group of similarly-minded legal academics.[9] While the precise historical origins of CLS may seem marginal to a theoretical discussion, it is important to note that the movement grew out of a narrow base of privileged white male academics from elite United States law schools. It is possible that this original elitism explains its downfall as a movement with any broad appeal: at least, as Peter Goodrich has cogently argued, the elitism of CLS certainly undermined its claim to radicalism.[10] Having said that, it is true that CLS did enjoy a period as an influential and diverse intellectual movement, not confined to either the United States or white men.[11]

In fact the lines of intellectual influence, of the history and the disintegration of CLS, are very complex. Critical Legal Studies has been associated with "postmodernism" and "deconstruction",[12] though there

---

8   Louis Schwartz, "With Gun and Camera Through Darkest CLS-Land" (1984) 36 *Stanford Law Review* 413 at 415.

9   Tushnet, "Critical Legal Studies: A Political History", p 1523; Schlegel, "Notes Toward an Intimate, Opinionated, and Affectionate History of the Conference on Critical Legal Studies", pp 392-403.

10   Peter Goodrich comments that, "The radicalism of American CLS ... does not threaten the institutional safety, tenured security, economic comfort, or frequently elite status of the critics." "Sleeping With the Enemy: An Essay on the Politics of Critical Legal Studies in America" (1993) 68 *New York University Law Review* 389 at 398. Goodrich is also critical of the self-adoption of the outsider status by some CLS writers — "It is as though the greatest injustice known to the world were the indignity of being fired from Yale, refused tenure at Harvard, or barred from promotion at Stanford or Pennsylvania." "Sleeping With the Enemy", p 399.

11   Some feminist scholars, for instance Clare Dalton, Elizabeth Mensch, and Diane Polan, have been identified as critical legal scholars.

12   See, for instance, Christine A Desan Husson, "Expanding the Legal Vocabulary: The Challenge Posed by the Deconstruction and Defence of Law" (1986) 95 *Yale Law Journal* 969; JM Balkin, "Deconstructive Practice and Legal Theory" (1987) 96 *Yale Law Journal* 743; David Fraser, "What a Long, Strange Trip Its Been: Deconstructing Law from Legal Realism to Critical Legal Studies" (1990) 5 *Australian Journal of Law and Society* 3, and "The Owls Are Not What They Seem: David Lynch, The Madonna Question, and Critical Legal Studies" (1993) 18 *Queens Law Journal* 1; Neil MacCormick, "Reconstruction After Deconstruction: A Response to CLS" (1990) 10 *Oxford Journal of Legal Studies* 539.

was much in CLS which did not sit easily with either of these labels, in spite of their proven flexibility.[13] CLS also originally drew upon the "Frankfurt school" of critical theory, including its emphasis upon Marxist thought.[14] In the 1980s there was some talk of "fem-crit theory," but feminism quickly became a distinct and vigorous movement in its own right, often in alliance with other critical movements. "Critical race theory" also emerged in the late 1980s, partly as a response to the inadequacies of CLS in dealing with issues of race, but also because an independently vocal group of racial minority scholars began to develop their own distinct critique of legal scholarship. More recently, a splinter group of "Lat-Crit" theorists has emerged in the United States. While Critical Legal Studies was a point of departure for both feminist legal theorists and race theorists, arguably these movements, both supported by flourishing social movements, would have developed quite independently of CLS.

So what was CLS? As I have said, CLS was not a theory. Its followers were more likely to describe it as a "movement", though Mark Tushnet called it a "political location", "where people with a wide but not unlimited range of political views can come together for political education, sustenance, and activity".[15] Given this range of political views, the question of exactly *who* was a critical legal scholar has always been a difficult one. Mark Kelman suggests that self-identification was the central criterion,[16] while Alan Hunt notes that intellectual influence may be as good an indicator as any: "It is not entirely flippant to notice that a preliminary test of whether an article or book is to be regarded as falling within the critical movement is whether it carries an attribution to Duncan Kennedy".[17] Given the narrow origins of CLS at Harvard and Yale, it is not surprising that early practices of citation revolved around a closely-knit core group.

Alan Hunt also summarised the identity of CLS by saying that it "exhibits both homogeneity and diversity".[18] CLS was homogeneous

---

13 This is basically my reason for separating CLS from postmodern approaches. I see them as sufficiently distinct (though overlapping in certain ways) as to merit separate consideration.

14 See generally Jason Whitehead, "From Criticism to Critique: Preserving the Radical Potential of Critical Legal Studies Through a Reexamination of Frankfurt School Critical Theory" (1999) 26 *Florida State University Law Review* 701.

15 Tushnet, "Critical Legal Studies: A Political History", p 1515, note 2.

16 Mark Kelman, "Trashing" (1984) 36 *Stanford Law Review* 293 at 299, note 13. Kelman goes on to describe some of the difficulties in defining CLS by reference to the type of work being undertaken by a scholar, making it clear that some of the work done by people who are not part of the movement may have more in common with aspects of CLS than other CLS work. Since this is the case, the only reasonable way of defining CLS is by self-identification.

17 Alan Hunt, "The Theory of Critical Legal Studies" (1986) 6 *Oxford Journal of Legal Studies* 1 at 2, note 5.

18 Hunt, "The Theory of Critical Legal Studies", p 2.

because it was established by a group of individuals with close political and personal ties, a fact which has been reflected in citation practices, and in the continued reappearance of certain scholars in what became a well-defined canon of critical works. On the other hand, CLS also achieved a remarkable level of theoretical diversity, a fact largely due to its lack of a distinct intellectual heritage. Although it is true that CLS in broad terms took up and continued the realist project, as Hunt says "the theoretical inspiration and roots that inform [CLS] writing reveals a remarkably wide trawl of twentieth-century radical and revisionist scholarship".[19]

Within CLS, two major strands were identified, one based on a broad critique of legal ideology, and one which has been termed "nihilist".[20] The former strategy situated legal doctrine within its historical and ideological context and, in this way, attempted to to demystify it. For instance, showing that a legal doctrine or decision is better understood as a response to a particular political situation than as some mysteriously rational way of ordering human affairs is a way of showing that it is contingent — that is, that it *could* be otherwise, but is not for historical and ideological reasons.[21] Or showing that an aspect of legal ideology (for instance, that people are free and equal) masks the oppressive operation of legal doctrine (the protection of private property involves protecting the power which some people have over others), is a way of challenging the perception that law is impartial and, on the whole, fair.[22]

The other strand of CLS was "nihilist" in a very broad sense:[23] it attempted to show the contradictions, indeterminacy, and incoherence of existing legal doctrine. Arguments of this nature tend to suggest either that legal thought is *necessarily* incoherent and indeterminate, an argument against formalism, or that existing liberal legal thought is

---

19 Hunt, "The Theory of Critical Legal Studies", p 3.

20 Frank Munger and Caroll Seron, "Critical Legal Studies versus Critical Legal Theory: A Comment on Method" (1984) 6 *Law and Policy* 257; William Forbath, "Taking Lefts Seriously" (1983) 92 *Yale Law Journal* 1041. Munger and Seron call the two strands "totalistic" and "nihilistic" while Forbath calls them "neo-Marxian" and "neo-realist". The label "nihilist" really only applied to a few critical legal scholars, such as Joseph Singer and Gary Peller.

21 Elizabeth Mensch, "The History of Mainstream Legal Thought" in Kairys (ed), *The Politics of Law: A Progressive Critique* (revised ed, Pantheon, New York, 1990); Robert Gordon, "Critical Legal Histories" (1984) 36 *Stanford Law Review* 57, and "Historicism in Legal Scholarship" (1981) 90 *Yale Law Journal* 1017; Morton Horwitz, "The Historical Contingency of the Role of History" (1981) 90 *Yale Law Journal* 1057.

22 Roger Cotterrell, "Power, Property, and the Law of Trusts" in Fitzpatrick and Hunt (eds), *Critical Legal Studies* (Basil Blackwell, Oxford, 1987).

23 The term "nihilist" is usually used negatively by detractors of CLS, although some writers such as Joseph Singer have themselves assumed this label; see Joseph Singer, "The Player and the Cards: Nihilism and Legal Theory" (1984) 94 *Yale Law Journal* 1; general discussions and rejections of the "nihilist" position have been written by Daniel Chow, "Trashing Nihilism" (1990) 65 *Tulane Law Review* 221, and John Stick, "Can Nihilism be Pragmatic?" (1986) 100 *Harvard Law Review* 332.

indeterminate, and should be rejected or reconstructed for that reason.[24] These strands of CLS were never entirely separate, and nor is this an exhaustive description of CLS strategies. The political and nihilist classifications do, however, provide a useful overview of most CLS scholarship.

These two elements of the CLS project are explained by Allan Hutchinson and Patrick Monahan in the following terms:[25]

> Like traditional scholars the Critical scholars are obsessed with the judicial function and its alleged central importance for an understanding of law in society. Yet, while they share this infatuation, they adopt a radically different view of the judicial process. All the critical scholars unite in denying the rational determinacy of legal reasoning. Their basic credo is that no distinctive mode of legal reasoning exists to be contrasted with political dialogue. Law is simply politics dressed up in different garb; it neither operates in a historical vacuum nor does it exist independently of ideological struggles in society. Legal doctrine not only does not, but also cannot, generate determinate results in concrete cases. Law is not so much a rational enterprise as a vast exercise in rationalization. Legal doctrine can be manipulated to justify an almost infinite spectrum of possible outcomes. Moreover, a plausible argument can be made that any such outcome has been derived from the dominant legal conceptions. Legal doctrine is nothing more than a sophisticated vocabulary and repertoire of manipulative techniques for categorizing, describing, organizing, and comparing; it is not a methodology for reaching substantive outcomes. As psychiatrists create "a monologue of reason about madness" so, the CLSers claim, do lawyers establish a fake rationalistic discourse out of the chaos of political and social life.

In the first place, CLS refuses to distinguish law from politics. Law is political, and legal reasoning is a technique used to rationalise in legal jargon the political decisions that are actually made. As I have said, this matter was central to CLS thinking, and has become so to some proponents of feminist and race scholarship. Secondly, Hutchinson and Monahan describe a fairly radical version of the "indeterminacy thesis". This thesis basically states that legal doctrines do not and, in fact, cannot be determinate: they cannot, in other words, determine absolutely the outcome of a case. The manipulability of legal doctrines means that any number of outcomes could be justified in any particular case. Not all of the "crits" (as they call themselves) supported this "indeterminacy thesis" in such a strong form. I will come back to it later in the chapter.

---

24   Sometimes it is not altogether clear what is being suggested: if legal doctrine is *necessarily* indeterminate, it is not much of a criticism of liberal legalism to say that it is indeterminate. Indeterminacy could be a good thing, since it provides the conditions under which flexibility and change are possible. See Hunt, "The Critical Legal Studies Movement" in Fitzpatrick and Hunt (eds), *Critical Legal Studies*, p 36.

25   Allan Hutchinson and Patrick Monahan, "Law, Politics, and the Critical Legal Scholars: The Unfolding Drama of American Legal Thought" (1984) 36 *Stanford Law Review* 199 at 206. The quotation concerning psychiatry in the last sentence is from Michel Foucault's *Madness and Civilisation: A History of Insanity in the Age of Reason* (Tavistock, London, 1967).

Despite the fact that it is arguably no longer quite the movement it once was,[26] CLS holds a crucial place in the recent history of critical legal thought. CLS was the first of the critical approaches to become institutionalised in legal theory: this is perhaps not surprising when we consider that, like other approaches (especially feminism and critical race theory), CLS is indebted in some ways to the political struggles of the late 1960s. As I have suggested though, as an identifiable movement with identifiable members, CLS has outlived itself, and has been overtaken in its importance as a "political location" by feminism, minority scholarship, and other more loosely-aligned critical approaches. However, this is not to say that the types of critique practised by the critical legal scholars are dead: critiques of law have become much more widely understood and practised in recent years, and this growth area of legal theory has certainly been at least partly due to the influence of CLS.

The place of CLS in current legal thought is, therefore, complicated. In order to avoid the worst of these complications (and to keep the chapter reasonably brief), the following description of CLS concentrates on the "central" characters in the early CLS drama — Kennedy, Gabel, Tushnet, Abel, Freeman, and Trubek.

Beyond Realism

[520] CLS was obviously the intellectual successor of realism, though it is also clear that in several crucial respects CLS has moved beyond realism. The perception of early CLS writers was that, although realism had had an effect on legal thinking, it had been assimilated into mainstream law as "policy" analysis, which remained marginal to doctrinal arguments. Examining the policy underlying a doctrine in the law of torts certainly challenges the idea that the law is free from such things, but it does not necessarily lead to the suggestion that the law is inevitably political. Thus one of the aims of CLS was to revive the radical realist edge, and insist that the social and political dimensions

---

26 CLS has become more institutionalised, a fact which has raised questions about its anti-authoritarian and anti-hierarchical credentials. In "Psycho-Social CLS: A Comment on the Cardozo Symposium" (1985) 6 *Cardozo Law Review* 1013 Duncan Kennedy discusses the institutionalisation of CLS; see also the critique of Kennedy's sexism written by Robin West, "Deconstructing the CLS-Fem Split" (1986) 2 *Wisconsin Women's Law Journal* 85. In "Critical Legal Studies: A Political History", Mark Tushnet examines the state of CLS in the early 1990s, concluding that it "may not be a growth field" and that it "is likely to remain one element in the pluralistic universe of the legal academy, but not much more", pp 1541 and 1543.

of law be understood.[27] CLS therefore revived "rule-scepticism" and the critique of "formalist" and "objectivist" modes of reasoning and focused on the function of legal doctrine and the role of policy. Critical legal writers devoted a great deal of time to "debunking", "demystifying", "delegitimating", "deconstructing", or "trashing" the idea of formalism, both on the grounds that law doesn't in fact work like that (judges simply can't step outside their own social conditioning), and that even if we were all amoral automata able to apply the law in a vacuum, the ideal of rationality and coherence in law is in any case unattainable because the language in which rules are expressed can never be sufficiently precise. Since interpretation relies very much on how we see the world, a single "objective" understanding of the law is impossible. Some criticisms of formalism, together with what I have offered as a little common sense on the matter, are to be found in Chapter 4: I will have more to say about CLS strategies regarding formalism later in this chapter.

Like realism, CLS also insisted on a view of law and a program of reform which better reflect "reality" and the needs of society. CLS produced an extensive critique of the abstract nature of formal legal doctrine, and the way it is separated in the legal mind from the real world. For instance, as I will explain, one eminent critical legal scholar, Peter Gabel, emphasised the way that law and legal rights are "alienating" for individuals.[28] Gabel's approach was in some ways similar to that of Felix Cohen who, as I explained in Chapter 4, attacked the "transcendental nonsense" of abstract legal concepts.[29] However the object of Gabel's critique was not just abstract legalism, it is *liberal* legalism: Gabel's attack was not simply directed at the ideals of mainstream legal thought, but of the entire political and social context within which law is situated.

One of the assumptions underlying both CLS and realist critiques of legal abstraction and its separation from reality is that we would all be a lot better off if lawyers would only drop the pretence of objective, non-political, legal reasoning. Such an assumption may not be entirely

---

27   See Tushnet, "Critical Legal Studies: A Political History", pp 1532-1533, and Mark Tushnet, "Post-Realist Legal Scholarship" (1980) 15 *Journal of the Society of Public Teachers of Law* 20; Robert Gordon, "Critical Legal Studies as a Teaching Method, Against the Background of the Intellectual Politics of Modern Legal Education in the United States" (1989) 1 *Legal Education Review* 43; Frederic Kellogg, "Legal Scholarship in the Temple of Doom: Pragmatism's Response to Critical Legal Studies" (1990) 65 *Tulane Law Review* 15; a contrasting view is held by Jeffrey Standen, who argues that CLS and realism are fundamentally opposed, see "Critical Legal Studies as an Anti-Positivist Phenomenon" (1986) 72 *Virginia Law Review* 983. Peter Goodrich has written that "CLS is the 'leftist' inheritor of Legal Realism": Goodrich, "Sleeping With the Enemy", p 390. The "rightist" inheritor would presumably be the law and economics movement.

28   Peter Gabel, "The Phenomenology of Rights-Consciousness and the Pact of the Withdrawn Selves" (1984) 62 *Texas Law Review* 1563.

29   Felix Cohen, "Transcendental Nonsense and the Functional Approach" (1935) 35 *Columbia Law Review* 809.

justified, since it neglects the way that marginalised groups in society actually rely on the power of law while being oppressed by it. We may not believe in the rule of law but others do, and it is certainly strategically necessary from time to time to use legal arguments to gain whatever ground is possible.[30] The degree to which those within CLS accepted the idea of legal reform varied: many took the view that reform simply endorses the status quo and should be rejected as a way of changing the system. The preliminary goal, before any reform can take place, involves a process of consciousness-raising and consciousness-changing. On the other hand, as some have pointed out, definite reform may be preferable to the mere chance of radical change: "A court order directing a housing authority to disburse funds for heating in subsidized housing may postpone the revolution, or it may not. In the meantime, the order keeps a number of poor families warm ... It smacks of paternalism to assert that the possibility of revolution later outweighs the certainty of heat now, unless there is evidence for that possibility".[31]

CLS also moved beyond realism insofar as it made extensive use of a concept of ideology to explain and demystify legal doctrine and applied its techniques to legal history. The main addition to realism made by CLS writers in this context was their concentrated exposure of the political and ideological motivations which underlie the operation of the law. While the realists saw that law could not be analytically separated from politics considered generally, CLS writers analysed the relationship between the law and a specific form of political thought — liberalism — and deliberately attempted to break the hold which liberal thought has on legal doctrine and judicial decision making. As I have indicated, part of the CLS project in this area was historical analysis.

Themes and Strategies

[525] The central features of early CLS writings are difficult to disentangle from each other, since they are all part of the central goal of constructing a fundamental critique of liberal legalism. In this part of the chapter I am going to concentrate on some of the ways in which CLS writers attempted to further this end, describing briefly along the way some of the basic objectives of the critique. In the next section I will concentrate on some specific examples of the analysis of liberal ideology.

---

30 See Mari Matsuda, "When the First Quail Calls: Multiple Consciousness as Jurisprudential Method" (1988) 11 *Women's Rights Law Reporter* 7 at 8; Patricia Williams, "Alchemical Notes: Reconstructing Ideals from Deconstructed Rights" (1987) 22 *Harvard Civil Rights — Civil Liberties Law Review* 401.

31 Richard Delgado, "The Ethereal Scholar: Does Critical Legal Studies Have What Minorities Want?" (1987) 22 *Harvard Civil Rights — Civil Liberties Law Review* 301 at 307-308.

Theory and politics: Intersubjective zap

[530]   I have said that there was no CLS "theory" as such, though there are
certain themes and approaches which recur in the literature. Before
getting to this, it is important to understand that some CLS writers
rejected entirely the notion of theory as simply dead intellectual
"bullshit". A good example appears in "Roll Over Beethoven", which
was for some time an influential dialogue between two of the American
critical gurus, Duncan Kennedy and Peter Gabel. The piece is a
somewhat obscure debate about the place of theory in political and
social change. Gabel begins with the following formula: "The project is
to realise the unalienated relatedness that is immanent within our
alienated situation."[32] Kennedy counters Gabel's claim with an equally
irrefutable argument:[33]

> What I'm saying is, that that does not sound to me like an evocation which
> can fulfill the legitimate functions of communication, of language and
> knowledge, because it's abstract bullshit, whereas what we need is small-
> scale, microphenomenological evocation of real experiences in complex
> contextualized ways in which one makes it into doing it.

Using the Marxist concept of alienation, Gabel is essentially saying that
people have lost touch with themselves and each other, and that we
need to find ways to rediscover a non-alienated existence. Kennedy, on
the other hand, argues that localised action is needed, not more theory.
Throughout the dialogue, Kennedy argues that theoretical abstractions,
such as those concerning unalienated relatedness, must be eliminated
from the CLS project. In particular, he sees theory in general as inviting
a "takeover" of radical politics by "pods". (In the 1956 movie *Invasion of
the Body Snatchers* pods containing aliens come down to earth and take
over human bodies.) Conceptualisation of the project is rejected for a
number of reasons. For a start, it is itself personally and politically
alienating. Theory alienates us from our true selves and our true
political motives. According to Kennedy, abstract concepts distract us
(as scholars) from the real thing, which is political action. Theory
reinforces the ivory tower syndrome of academia, effecting a certain
distance between the law and real people. Equally important, however,
is that Kennedy sees theory as simply false. Theory does not describe
reality, it turns people into pods.[34] Abstractions, in other words, are
inevitably distortions of real social conditions. Thus, for Kennedy, what
is needed is not theory, but a way of tapping into the political energy
of a community, a process which involves refusing to describe social and
political relations in theoretical terms. In order to describe such a

---

32   Peter Gabel and Duncan Kennedy, "Roll Over Beethoven" (1984) 36 *Stanford Law Review* 1
      at 1; see also, for a much more lengthy account, Peter Gabel, "The Phenomenology of
      Rights-Consciousness and the Pact of the Withdrawn Selves", p 1563.

33   Gabel and Kennedy, "Roll Over Beethoven", p 3.

34   See also the comments by Hélène Cixous in Hélène Cixous and Mireille Calle-Gruber,
      Hélène Cixous, Rootprints: Memory and Life Writing (Eric Prenowitz trans, Routledge,
      London, 1994), p 4. A short quotation appears above in Chapter 1, at note 3.

process in a non-theoretical way Kennedy coins the phrases "making the kettle boil" (to describe the energy of real political action) and "intersubjective zap". Of "intersubjective zap" Harlon Dalton comments: "This CLS buzz phrase can freely be translated as a sudden, unexpected, electric moment of shared intuition. Only a Crit would load down a zippy word like 'zap' with a brain-deadener like 'intersubjective'".[35]

Kennedy seems to be assuming here that it is not only desirable, but also possible to separate theory and politics. We can readily appreciate his reasons for doing so, in particular the perception that academic theorising frequently takes place within a confined circle of initiated intellectuals, and therefore has only a marginal impact on concrete social change. Kennedy argued that it is necessary to break out of this circle, and this is certainly an ongoing tension for those of us who do believe that change is necessary. What I am not certain about is the way he proposed to do this. Is breaking out of the circle and leaving it behind altogether the best thing to do? Is it possible? In my view, accepting the dichotomy between theory and practice or politics, and simply reversing it, so that practice becomes more important than theory, is not a very convincing way of challenging the established order. It should, rather, be possible to attempt to break down the distinction: to insist on a practice which is theoretical or reflective, and on a theory which is in itself practical, that is, which achieves something. "Making the kettle boil" is all very well, but in order to achieve anything, we do need to communicate and agree on certain things, a process which invariably involves some sort of abstraction from the here and now. We must be able to say, for instance, what needs changing and why. Theory may "distort" me, but then so do social conventions, laws, and other relationships. Maybe these are not really distortions of my true self, but things which actually define the way I am. If this is the case, "I" am the theories and relationships which surround me: there is no pre-existing self to be in tune with.[36]

Despite Kennedy's views about abstract theorising, CLS did not develop a reputation for active political involvement. In fact, as I have indicated, the perception is rather that CLS writing was obscure, overly-theoretical, and frequently of little relevance to real social problems. In 1987 Patricia Williams observed a "disproportionately low grass-roots membership in or input to CLS",[37] the implication of which is that it indeed failed to overcome its ivory tower origins. She offers the following story as an illustration of the political insularity of CLS.

---

35   Dalton, "The Clouded Prism" (1987) 22 *Harvard Civil Rights — Civil Liberties Law Review* 435 at 441.

36   This point will arise again later in the chapter, but it is dealt with more fully in Chapter 8. Traditional liberal thought tends to see the individual as a free and autonomous agent, who may be influenced, affected, or distorted in some ways by society. In contrast, some contemporary thinkers on the matter have challenged the idea of a "true" and unitary self, thinking of the "subject" (that is, the "I") more in terms of being a position in a complex network of relationships.

37   Patricia Williams, "Alchemical Notes", p 402.

Patricia J Williams

"Alchemical Notes: Reconstructing Ideals from Deconstructed Rights"[38]

[535]   THE BRASS RING AND THE DEEP BLUE SEA

A. The Meta Story

Once upon a time, there was a society of priests who built a Celestial City whose gates were secured by Word-Combination locks. The priests were masters of the Word, and, within the City, ascending levels of power and treasure became accessible to those who could learn ascendingly intricate levels of Word Magic. At the very top level, the priests became gods; and because they then had nothing left to seek, they engaged in games with which to pass the long hours of eternity. In particular, they liked to ride their strong, sure-footed steeds, around and around the perimeter of heaven: now jumping word-hurdles, now playing polo with the concepts of the moon and of the stars, now reaching up to touch that pinnacle, that fragment, that splinter of Refined Understanding which was called Superstanding, the brass ring of their merry-go-round.

In time, some of the priests-turned-gods tired of this sport, denounced it as meaningless. They donned the garb of pilgrims, seekers once more, and passed beyond the gates of the Celestial City. In this recursive passage, they acquired the knowledge of undoing Words.

Beyond the walls of the City lay a Deep Blue Sea. The priests built themselves small boats and set sail, determined to explore the uncharted courses, the open vistas of this new and undefined domain. They wandered for many years in this manner, until at last they reached a place that was half-a-circumference away from the Celestial City. From this point, the City appeared as a mere shimmering illusion; and the priests knew that at last they had reached a place which was Beyond the Power of Words. They let down their anchors, the plumb lines of their reality, and experienced godhood once more.

B. The Story

Under the Celestial City, dying mortals called out their rage and suffering, battered by a steady rain of sharp hooves whose thundering, sound-drowning path described the wheel of their misfortune.

At the bottom of the Deep Blue Sea, drowning mortals reached silently and desperately for drifting anchors dangling from short chains far, far overhead, which they thought were life-lines meant for them.

[540]   In Chapter 3, I quoted a similar story written by Valerie Kerruish as a parody of natural law thinking. Just as Kerruish implies that natural law is insular, paternalistic, and idealistic, so Williams sees CLS as neglecting, in its heated and complex theoretical deliberations, the fact of real need by oppressed people. In both cases a select group of religious figures is portrayed as having power over the theoretical domain, with little practical effect. Thus it may be that the negative side of the movement, rather than its contribution to social change, may be its most important dimension.

---

38   Patricia Williams, "Alchemical Notes", pp 401–402.

Alienation and trashing

[545]   One of the most widespread criticisms of CLS is that although it devoted a great deal of attention to the defects in modern liberal legal theory, it totally failed to deliver any plausible alternative.[39] CLS is usually perceived to be a "negative" movement which rejected a great deal, and — with the exception of Roberto Unger[40] — offered no solutions. This "problem" with CLS has been taken to be quite destructive of its credentials as a movement aiming for radical change. However, what the critics of CLS appear to be assuming here is that it is necessary, if an approach to legal thought is to be valid, for it to replace one world view with another, and more concretely, one model of law with another. Is such an assumption justified? Why do we think that a single "alternative" is readily available? How can one group come up with a monolithic solution for a pluralistic society?

It may be that CLS played a useful role in establishing the conditions under which change is possible. Challenging, and eventually breaking down established modes of thought may have been the most effective way for those centrally involved in CLS to contribute to broad political change. In other words, because it was fundamental to CLS that it is not only a change of law which is required, but also a change of consciousness and ideology, attacking it on the grounds that it did not come up with an alternative rather misses the point.

The CLS approach to how individuals relate to their social and legal environments provides an interesting example. One of the dominant ideas in early CLS writings was that in modern liberal society we are all "alienated" from our true selves by liberal ideology. I have already quoted Peter Gabel making some observations on this point. I will come back to liberal theory in more detail in the next section of this chapter: for the present it is enough to comment that the liberal emphasis on individuals and their formal legal rights was seen by many CLS writers as an illusion which deflects people from realising their true connectedness with others. In a sense then, we are already pods, but there is a human somewhere in there trying to break its way out.

One of the ways CLS writers tried to break the hold liberalism has on everyone's lives was by what they called "trashing", which basically meant showing that the dominant legal doctrines do not work, are not

---

39   See, for instance, Dalton, "The Clouded Prism"; Robert Gordon, "New Developments in Legal Theory" in Kairys (ed), *The Politics of Law: A Progressive Critique* (rev ed, Pantheon Books, New York, 1990). In "The Question That Killed Critical Legal Studies" (1992) 17 *Law and Social Inquiry* 779, Richard Michael Fischl considers the question of positive political action from a perspective sympathetic to CLS.

40   In *The Critical Legal Studies Movement* (Harvard University Press, Cambridge Mass, 1986), Roberto Unger proposes a model of transformation towards a post-liberal society and legal system: the transformation is "internal" because it does not involve a revolutionary rejection of the existing system and the construction of another, but rather the expansion and development of existing principles.

coherent or consistent, are "fundamentally contradictory" (to use one of Duncan's earlier phrases[41]), and not supported by "reality". This process of "delegitimation" is achieved by demonstrating that liberal theory is contradictory or incoherent in fundamental ways, or that its main purpose in our system is to mask the reality of widespread and systemic oppression. "Delegitimation" was a term often used by critical legal scholars to indicate that what they were doing was undermining the ideological and legal bases upon which legitimacy is constructed. Sometimes, however, there is a slip from the process of *delegitimation* to the claim that something is *illegitimate*:[42] in the absence of a clear standard of moral or social legitimacy, such a claim is confusing — in order for a doctrine or area of law to be illegitimate there must be a pre-existing standard of legitimacy against which it can be measured.

Similarly, the reason for arguing that liberal legal thought is incoherent and irrational is not always entirely clear, as Alan Hunt has pointed out:[43]

> We need to ask a naive question: precisely what does it prove to demonstrate an incoherence or contradiction in an intellectual position? It is a well established feature of rationalist epistemology that the pursuit of internal coherence constitutes a major form of intellectual legitimation. But since critical theory disputes the very claims of rationalist epistemology in its pursuit of logically gapless intellectual constructs, it is puzzling why the shout of triumph should ring out when incoherences or contradictions are demonstrated.

Put very simply, why do we have to regard an incoherent or inconsistent legal doctrine as a flaw in the system, especially if we are also arguing that law is *necessarily* inconsistent or contradictory? Hunt suggests that the exposure of contradiction and incoherence in legal systems emphasised by critical legal theorists has formed the basis of several types of argument.[44] In the first place, coherence-analysis revives the contentions of realist rule-scepticism in that inconsistencies are taken to be evidence of law's indeterminacy. Secondly, contradiction is said to be a symptom of the larger incoherences of liberal thought. Thirdly, demonstrating incoherence in the law is a challenge to the self-definition of liberal legal thought. One of the central ideals of liberal legalism is that the law is relatively rational and coherent: showing that this is not the case is more than an internal criticism — it is a fundamental challenge to the ideological basis of the law.

---

41   Duncan Kennedy, "The Structure of Blackstone's Commentaries" (1979) 28 *Buffalo Law Review* 205. In "Roll Over Beethoven", Kennedy rejected the "fundamental contradiction" arguing that it had outlived its usefulness, having become frozen into yet another abstract concept.

42   Alan Freeman, "Truth and Mystification in Legal Scholarship" (1981) 90 *Yale Law Journal* 1229; Kennedy, "The Structure of Blackstone's Commentaries".

43   Hunt, "The Critical Legal Studies Movement", p 33; see also Kress, "Legal Indeterminacy" (1989) 77 *California Law Review* 235.

44   Hunt, "The Critical Legal Studies Movement", pp 32-35.

The fourth aim of (in)coherence analysis is, according to Hunt, to free the territory of legal thinking from its liberal chains: exposing contradictions, and thereby demystifying the law, creates a potential for seeing it differently. I will come back to this shortly. Finally, it has been suggested that the inconsistencies in the law can be exploited in a very directed way: Roberto Unger has argued that inconsistencies in legal doctrine are evidence of a "countervision" of human association implicit in the law.[45] In other words, legal doctrine contains *within itself* the potential for radical transformation: although at present this potential is masked by legal ideology, accentuating the contradictions (a process which Unger calls "deviationist doctrine") will reveal the post-liberal possibilities of the law.

As I have emphasised at various stages of this book, I see the aim of "critique" to be a detailed analysis of the foundations of the way we understand the things we think about, whatever they are. Critique is useful and necessary to all forms of theory, because it exposes the assumptions we make as being not natural or neutral but, rather, associated with our particular position in the world. Critique can therefore enable us to understand, at least, that our own view is partial. Is this essentially the project of trashing in its fourth manifestation? In "Truth and Mystification in Legal Scholarship", Alan Freeman says this about trashing:[46]

> The point of delegitimation is to expose possibilities more truly expressing reality, possibilities of fashioning a future that might at least partially realize a substantive notion of justice instead of the abstract, rightsy, traditional, bourgeois notions of justice ... One must start by knowing what is going on, by freeing oneself from the mystified delusions embedded in our consciousnesses by the liberal legal worldview. I am not defending a form of scholarship that simply offers another affirmative presentation; rather, I am advocating negative, critical activity as the only path that might lead to a liberated future.

In other words, in order to achieve real reform, according to Freeman, it is necessary first to break out of the liberal world view which at the moment determines the way we think and theorise. This means understanding "what is going on": if we have as good an understanding as possible of why the law is like it is and whose interests it serves, rather than just accepting it like it is or being blinded by its mystifications (like the concept of the rule of law, perhaps), then we have a chance of gaining a better understanding of legal ideology. Secondly, the idea is to destroy or at least break open the system of ideas which constitutes legal thinking.

It is important to contrast this strategy to the alternative, which is simply to present a different theory about law. In presenting a different

---

45   Unger, *The Critical Legal Studies Movement*, Ch 2. See also David Jabbari, "From Criticism to Construction in Modern Critical Legal Theory" (1992) 12 *Oxford Journal of Legal Studies* 507.

46   Freeman, "Truth and Mystification in Legal Scholarship", pp 1230-1231.

positive view of law, it may be that the theorist is less able to eliminate or minimise the assumptions which constitute the political context of theory (such as the ideas of individualism and freedom). The negative strategy, while it may not immediately be able to come up with an alternative system or theory, at least makes a start by aiming to get rid of, or bring to light, some of those things which influence the way we see the world. This is what is "critical" about the analysis — not so much the trashing, but the attempt to explain the ideological foundations of liberal legal thinking.

However, whether or not the aim of exposing "possibilities more truly expressing reality"[47] is realistic depends on what view we take of our ideological context. If, as many of the early CLS writers assumed, we think ideology is an alienation or distortion of a *more true* reality — if for instance liberal thought operates only to disguise or distort reality — then trashing law and legal theory will help us get closer to reality. If we are looking at the world through a pair of glasses which change the shape of everything, then we will be able to see a more true reality by taking them off. This is the possibility which many early CLS writers envisaged — demystifying the law in order to get closer to the truth. On the other hand, we might need the glasses — what if it is ideology which allows us to "see" in the first place?[48] What if we can't just get rid of ideology? Maybe we can't do without it, meaning that there is no more "true" reality outside our ideological constructs. In other words, perhaps we are so thoroughly socialised that there is no sense in which we can speak of a "truth" outside what we learn from our cultural contexts. If this is the case, then we can think of there being a *better* ideology or way of seeing the world — one which does not oppress women for example — but not one which is absolutely true and non-ideological. Failure to appreciate the complexities of the relationship between our perception of reality and our ideological environment was something of a problem for the early CLS movement — the assumption was often simply that ideology is false,[49] and that we can achieve a non-ideological view of the truth. This may not be the case.

47   Freeman, "Truth and Mystification in Legal Scholarship", p 1230.

48   For an analysis of the different ways in which the term "ideology" can be understood, see Slavoj Zizek, "The Spectre of Ideology" in Zizek (ed), *Mapping Ideology* (Verso, London, 1994), pp 1-33. A simplified summary of Zizek's account appears in Margaret Davies, "Legal Separatism and the Concept of the Person" in Tom Campbell and Jeffrey Goldsworthy (eds), *Judicial Power, Democracy, and Legal Positivism* (Ashgate, Aldershot, 2000), pp 128-130.

49   For instance, Duncan Kennedy has written: "To say that law school is ideological is to say that what teachers teach along with basic skills is wrong, is nonsense about what law is and how it works; that the message about the nature of legal competence, and its distribution among students is wrong, is nonsense; that the ideas about the possibilities of life as a lawyer that students pick up from legal education are wrong, are nonsense": "Legal Education As Training For Hierarchy" in David Kairys (ed), *The Politics of Law: A Progressive Critique* (rev ed, Pantheon Books, New York, 1967), p 38. The idea that ideology is wrong in the sense that it does not reflect some prior truth is, at best, a limited understanding of the power of ideas — which construct, as well as describe, reality.

However the critique of ideology in CLS also specifically emphasised the fact that liberal ideology works by covering up the oppressive, alienating, and contradictory structures of society. Liberal ideology, in other words, prevents us from seeing the way that oppression is entrenched in our social, political, and legal environments. Highlighting the distance between ideology and the way the system actually operates to protect already privileged people is a way of seeing through the thought system which is central to liberalism.

Notwithstanding the criticism that Freeman does appear to be contrasting a "false" political system to an unspecified "true" one, I would say that I think that he is on the right track by saying that *simply* proposing an alternative theory will not work. At least with his method we have some chance of arriving at new possibilities for seeing the world. In order to achieve fundamental change (if that is what we are after, and most feminists, critical race theorists, and left-leaning scholars, in general, are pursuing basic social change) then orthodox preconceptions need to be challenged. The question is really how we decide to resolve the tension between simply criticising everything and not positively deciding to build a better future, and making positive reform proposals which risk slipping back into liberal assumptions. What the crits appear to have assumed is that the time will come when trashing is no longer needed, since liberal mythology will have totally disintegrated. Then we will have a clear vision of what to do. Such a perception of the possibilities rests on a number of further assumptions, such as: there is life without ideology; we have "true" or "authentic" selves; and consensus can be achieved about social goods. Yet as I have suggested, if we accept that as individuals we are inevitably constructed by our social environments and cannot simply "escape" such constructions (indeed they are the condition of our "subjectivity"), then all reforms at all times will be contingent. It is idealistic in the extreme to think that a final state of harmony can be achieved. Surely it is better, rather than wait for the impossible, to begin to push for a better society, better legal system, better political understanding *now*, even if our efforts cannot withstand intense theoretical scrutiny. This does not necessarily mean that we need a grand plan for the revolution. But it does mean working in a positive, reflective, and interactive way with whatever we can. In fact, I would say that despite the lack of a positive program, the crits helped to create the conditions under which change and further critique is possible. This is a good start.

Harlon Dalton has made a similar point in his critique of CLS, arguing that trashing or delegitimation is a useful strategy, but needs to be balanced by an ongoing program of reform:[50]

---

50   Dalton, "The Clouded Prism", p 436, note 4.

I share the concern that we risk undermining ourselves by moving ahead with a positive program before the critique has adequately altered our consciousness. I also recognize the utility of and even necessity of delegitimation. I am convinced, however, that the movement can and must proceed on two tracks simultaneously. Despite the risk of replicating the tried and untrue path, we must create even as we reenvision. In my view, negative critique and positive program are, or at least can be, symbiotic; the former launches the latter and keeps it on course, whereas the latter saves the former from petulance and self-parody.

We can recall in this context something which Mari Matsuda said about the relationship of political dissent to the legal institution, and which I discussed in Chapter 1. Matsuda commented that there are times to stand outside the courtroom to protest the system as a whole, and times to stand inside to defend one's rights.[51] Assuming that there is nowhere *absolutely* outside the law, this would seem to be our only available strategy. It is certainly the only practical strategy, given that as subjects of a particular legal order (a matter we do not have any real choice about) it is always necessary to deal with the system rather than simply reject it.

It is not possible to leave the topic of trashing without mentioning the related strategy practised by David Fraser, which he called "moral terrorism". Here it is, in his very own words:[52]

> Moral terrorism seeks to avoid reform at all costs. For example, in the academy, rather than encouraging our students and colleagues to engage in left-wing study groups, where they can escape from the mysteries of trespass and case to the inherent clarity of Derrida's *Of Grammatology*, we should encourage them to learn a socially useful trade — playing the piano, for example — and to abandon law school forever. We can disrupt faculty meetings with various acts of civil or, preferably, uncivil disobedience. We can engage in subversion by memorandum. The possibilities are limited only by the available concepts of the absurd.

> Several objections could be raised against this version of moral terrorism; especially that it is juvenile. This is true. It is juvenile. The very point of moral terrorism is to permit us to recapture the halcyon days of our youth, when freedom was an unquestioned component of our daily existence. A perpetuation of childhood or adolescence can have a highly liberating effect. Besides, it really bothers the liberals.

I can't help but sympathise with Fraser's call for more pianists and fewer lawyers and Derrideans. However his "freedom" to terrorise is one which, like many others, can be practised only by those with relative power and privilege. Untenured academics and others without strong job security would not feel that moral terrorism within the academy is a viable strategy.

---

51   Matsuda, "When the First Quail Calls", p 8.

52   Fraser, "Truth and Hierarchy: Will the Circle Be Unbroken?" (1984) *Buffalo Law Review* 729 at 773, note 156. Derrida's *Of Grammatology* is notoriously obscure.

The Critique of Liberal Ideology

[550] Modern critiques of law attack the surrounding political ideology as much as individual theories about law. This is as true of CLS as it is of most feminist approaches as well as those which have come to be characterised as "postmodern". This surrounding political ideology, by which is meant the dominant or conventional way of viewing and analysing the public relationships of people in society, has been identified as "liberalism", and in order to understand the nature of any modern critical approach, it is also necessary to understand some of the basic features of liberal thought.[53]

While it is not claimed that liberal thinking has been the *only* political ideology which has shaped the way we view law, it is said to be the dominant Western ideology of the twentieth century. It is clear, for instance, that legal analysis, and ultimately legal philosophy, owes a great deal to the classical common law tradition which I described in Chapter 2. Elements of this tradition, like its attachment to the past at the expense of the present, have had a very profound effect on legal thinking and do not easily fit into liberal political thought. Moreover, although liberal thought can reasonably be reduced to a broad set of propositions, it is composed of a variety of conflicting theories. Within liberal thought, considered as the wider context of social and political analysis, there are many disagreements about things such as how individual freedom is best recognised, what constitutes justice, and how law ought to go about regulating society. For instance liberal feminism has been described as being "on the progressive edge of liberal thought", and posing a challenge to some of the basic liberal principles.[54] It would therefore be simplistic to assume that liberal thought is a unified theoretical system which can be identified in a clear way with mainstream jurisprudence. It would be better to say that it is the context — and a very complex one at that — within which legal analysis has come to be situated.

The most fundamental element of liberal thought is its emphasis on the concept of civil freedom or "liberty". Exactly what constitutes civil liberty is a matter of some complexity, but the central idea is fairly clear: for most liberals "freedom" is the absence of interference, and typically systematic interference by the State, with the individual's capacity for self-determination. Liberty in this sense is taken to be the fundamental value of political organisation: this has been explained as involving a shift from power to rights as the absolute principle of social

---

53 There are many in-depth analyses of the phenomenon of liberalism. One which is particularly good, and useful in a discussion of legal theory, is Stephen Bottomley and Simon Bronitt, *Law in Context* (3rd ed, Federation Press, Sydney, 2006), Ch 2.

54 Alison Jaggar, *Feminist Politics and Human Nature* (Rowman and Littlefield, New Jersey, 1983), p 28. I will have more to say about liberal feminism in Chapter 6.

organisation.[55] The liberal view is therefore that the individual, and the individual's liberties (not the arbitrary power of a sovereign monarch or legislature) lie at the heart of society.

The basic question for liberalism therefore, is — what degree of state interference is justified? Given that some interference by the state is necessary, simply in order to achieve a minimal regulation of society, where is the frontier between "legitimate" and "illegitimate" interference to be drawn? A classic formulation of a liberal principle on this matter is John Stuart Mill's "harm principle":[56]

> ... the sole end for which mankind are warranted, individually or collectively, in interfering with the liberty of action of any of their number, is self-protection. That the only purpose for which power can be rightfully exercised over any member of a civilised community, against his will, is to prevent harm to others. His own good, either physical or moral, is not a sufficient warrant.

"Liberty" has been generally seen as reliant on a balance between state intervention and social co-existence. Classical liberal thought recognises that any individual's liberty is limited by the autonomy of others. The obvious difficulty with such a view is that it leaves entirely open the definition of what counts as harm to others, and who is empowered to define harm. What one person may see as encouraging social degeneration, another may see as a necessary element of social change and regeneration. What one person may regard as an "other" (an embryo or an animal), another may not. Many harms may be indirect to greater or lesser extents, while some may in fact be encouraged by the prevailing system (such as economic harm to another caused by capitalist competition).

One of the ways in which modern liberal "democracies" have given a more concrete form to the concept of individual liberty is through the creation of specific legally protected rights. Rights formalise the limitations of state intervention and of interference between individuals. Some obvious and familiar rights defend the individual's equality, life, property, freedom of speech, freedom from oppression, and privacy. Whether the ultimate source of these rights is seen to be nature, god, morality, the demands of political co-existence or something else, is not as crucial as their formal recognition. The legal protection of such "rights" is seen by many liberal theorists to be

---

55 In one of the classics of 20th century liberalism "Two Concepts of Liberty", Isaiah Berlin explains the concept of liberty by distinguishing between negative liberty or *freedom from*, and positive liberty, or *freedom to*. It is negative liberty which provides the fundamental framework of liberal thought — negative liberty corresponds with the ideal of freedom from external interference. Berlin thus speaks of an "area of non-interference" within which the individual is free to act without impediment from the law or any other source. Isaiah Berlin, *Four Essays on Liberty* (Oxford University Press, Oxford, 1969), p 165.

56 John Stuart Mill, "On Liberty" in Mill, *Utilitarianism* (12th ed, Routledge, London 1895), Ch 1 "Introductory".

the necessary precondition for the pursuit of individual goals within society.[57]

The idea of legal rights was one of the major focal points for the CLS critique of liberal ideology.[58] There are several different elements of this critique. Rights have been seen as an abstract diversion from true political needs: they are "alienating" because they are mere ideals which do not reflect people's real needs. Rights have also been criticised as ideals which protect the interests of the privileged in society: in a capitalist legal world where the ability to defend one's rights is reliant on the ability to pay, those who effectively have rights are the wealthy. Liberal ideals generally operate as a screen hiding the true nature of oppression in society. In addition, rights are seen by CLS writers to be historically determined and unstable: the instability of rights means in effect that they are used for conservative political purposes.

In "Roll Over Beethoven" Peter Gabel, whom we have already met, argues that rights are part of the abstract ("reified") and alienating structure of the law. Rights should be abandoned because they have nothing to do with social reality, but operate to alienate individuals from their social and political environment.[59] Talking about rights to solve political problems, moreover, involves utilising the very form of legalistic consciousness which ought to be the target of critique:[60]

> This is one way I would now put the problem with rights. At New College, people are constantly trying to figure out how to make legal arguments to support their political aims. Now, these are intensely political people — people who want to transform the society, to bring about real equality, real democracy, shared control over the workplace, more love and connection — all of that. This is what they want in their hearts ... But because they're going to "become lawyers", they think they have to somehow transform these feelings into "good legal arguments" ... So what happens is people start translating their political feelings into unconscionability arguments or right-to-privacy arguments without realizing that there is a weird dissociation taking place, as if it were inevitable that you had to take your true needs and desires and translate them into one or other of these available arguments. This is the essence of the problem with rights discourse. People don't realize that what they're doing is recasting the real existential feelings that led them to become political people into an ideological framework that coopts them into adopting the very consciousness they want to transform.

---

57   See, for instance, Ronald Dworkin, *Taking Rights Seriously* (Harvard University Press, Cambridge Mass, 1977). A useful summary appears in Bottomley and Bronitt, *Law in Context*, pp 32-35.

58   Major articles on this subject include: Mark Tushnet, "An Essay on Rights" (1984) 62 *Texas Law Review* 1363; Allan Hutchinson and Patrick Monahan, "The 'Rights' Stuff: Roberto Unger and Beyond" (1984) 62 *Texas Law Review* 1477.

59   See also Gabel, "The Phenomenology of Rights-Consciousness and the Pact of the Withdrawn Selves".

60   Gabel and Kennedy, "Roll Over Beethoven", p 26.

Rights, then, are seen as abstractions which distort the true nature of people's political feelings. Rights do not adequately encapsulate political needs and can actually encourage people to become complicit with a system which they wish to overturn. Later, Gabel makes the point even more clearly by stating that rights are not the same as objectives, but rather a diversion from real politics:[61]

> Exactly what people don't need is their rights. What they need are the actual forms of social life that have to be created through the building of movements that can overcome illusions about the nature of what is political, like the illusion that there is an entity called the state, that people possess rights. It may be necessary to use the rights argument in the course of political struggle, in order to make gains. But the thing to be understood is the extent to which it is enervating to use it. It's a diversion from true political language, political modes of communication about the nature of reality and what it is that people are trying to achieve ...

Gabel is suggesting that *formal* rights do not produce substantive justice. This is an argument which is also familiar to feminists: although women have achieved formal rights in most spheres over the last century, this does not mean that we have achieved substantive equality. In fact, the existence of formal equality is used to mask real inequality — women can consume pornography (rape, harass, be elected to parliament) just as men can, so what's the problem? On this level, the CLS critique attempts to unmask the false hopes promised by rights and the way they can be used to entrench established inequalities. However, Gabel goes further to say that, although there may be strategic reasons for doing so, buying into rights discourse is simply a distraction from real political action — selling out to the liberals, so to speak.

The strongest criticism of CLS on the question of rights has come from African-American scholars and activists. The essence of the criticism is that rights have been a source of empowerment for minorities and have provided them with both a point of solidarity for their struggle against white oppression and a crucial tool for negotiation. Some of the problems have been summarised by Richard Delgado.

Richard Delgado

"The Ethereal Scholar: Does Critical Legal Studies Have What Minorities Want?"[62]

[555] The CLS critique of rights and rules is the most problematic aspect of the CLS program, and provides few answers for minority scholars and lawyers. We know, from frequent and sad experience, that the mere announcement of a legal right means little. We live in the gap between law on the books and law in action. We have no difficulty imagining a better world; for us, eliminating racism would be a good start.

61　Gabel and Kennedy, "Roll Over Beethoven", p 33.

62　Delgado, "The Ethereal Scholar", pp 304-305. See also Daria Roithmayr, "Left Over Rights" (2001) 22 *Cardozo Law Review* 1113.

Even if rights and rights-talk paralyze us and induce a false sense of security, as CLS scholars maintain, might they not have a comparable effect on public officials, such as the police? Rights do, at times, give pause to those who would otherwise oppress us; without the law's sanction, these individuals would be more likely to express racist sentiments on the job. It is condescending and misguided to assume that the enervating effect of rights talk is experienced by the victims and not the perpetrators of racial mistreatment.

Second, CLS scholars are often hazy about what would provide minorities comparable protection if rights no longer existed. The CLS positive program, or Utopia ... is both far from adequate, and far off in time.

Third, Crits argue that rights separate and alienate the individual from the rest of the human community. This may be so for the hard-working Crits who spend much of their lives in their studies and law offices. For minorities, however, rights serve as a rallying point and bring us closer together. On the other hand, any distance rights place between us and others may be beneficial; there is at least safety in distance.

One explanation for the CLS position on rights may be that the average Crit, a white male teaching at a major law school, has little use for rights. Those with whom he comes in contact in his daily life — landlords, employers, public authorities — generally treat him with respect and deference. Rarely is he the victim of coercion, revilement, or contempt. In the mind of the average Crit, rights offer relatively little security, while they promote a shrunken, atrophied, and unsatisfying social existence.

[560] One clear conclusion to be drawn from Delgado's critique of CLS is that in contrast to their stated desire to uncover the realities of the operation of the law, what the crits have actually done with rights analysis is to look at it in the abstract, and from their own rather insular and privileged point of view.

Some of the matters raised by Delgado are illustrated by Patricia Williams in a very immediate way, through a story about herself and Peter Gabel. Williams tells how at about the same time they were each looking for an apartment in New York, having both recently moved from California. Gabel, according to Williams, handed over a substantial cash deposit to strangers, did not sign a lease, or obtain a receipt: the "handshake and the good vibes were for him indicators of trust more binding than a distancing form contract".[63] Williams, however, had friends who owned a building, and who found her an apartment in it. She signed "a detailed, lengthily-negotiated, finely-printed lease".[64] In analysing the significance of their different experiences, Williams concentrates on their different social positions, and their different relationships to the law. As a white male in a relatively powerful position, Gabel found it desirable to eliminate formalities as much as possible, finding them an obstacle to establishing a relationship of trust between himself and the lessors. In contrast, as a Black woman, part of

---

63 Williams, "Alchemical Notes", p 406.
64 Williams, "Alchemical Notes", p 407.

a category of people generally regarded as "unreliable, untrustworthy, hostile, angry, powerless, irrational, and probably destitute",[65] Williams sought the formal contractual relationship: for her this was a way of ensuring that she would be regarded as an autonomous trustworthy individual with rights. In other words, social position has an impact on the way we relate to the legal system and the rights it establishes. Some people can take their rights for granted because they are regarded by the prevailing ideology as the typical holders of such rights. It is easy enough, when you are the paradigm case, to cast aside formalities. Discarding the formalities will, however, affect less privileged people in a different way.[66]

A CLS strategy which is related to the critique of formal rights emphasised the effects of liberal mythology generally on the law. This argument, which is still very frequently made, points out that a certain aspect of liberal ideology underlies a legal doctrine, but operates, in fact, not to further the aims of the liberal ideal, but to obscure the reality of an inequitable social situation.

Such an argument has been made in relation to many areas of law. For instance, the liberal ideals of freedom and equality have a considerable effect on the substantive doctrines of the law of contract. Individuals are idealised in the law of contract as autonomous individuals who have powers of self-determination, and utility-maximisation. But because these ideals do not represent the reality of society, contract law may, in many situations, reinforce the power of those who are already socially privileged.[67] Power relations in society, and especially those created by wealth differentials, mean that some people are able to capitalise on liberal ideals at the expense of others. The liberal myth or ideal of equality is enshrined in contract law, which in turn obscures the reality which is structured by capitalism, not ideals. In other words, contract doctrine pretends to speak a truth about social relations, and, in doing so, perpetuates an ideology which is not only not representative of social relations, but which also operates to keep oppressed people in their place.[68]

---

65 Williams, "Alchemical Notes", p 407.

66 Delgado, "The Ethereal Scholar", p 306, note 35.

67 Gabel and Feinman say, "contract law today constitutes an elaborate attempt to conceal what is going on in the world. Contemporary capitalism bears no more relation to the imagery of contemporary contract law than did nineteenth-century capitalism to the imagery of classical contract law"; "Contract Law as Ideology" in Kairys (ed), *The Politics of Law: A Progressive Critique* (rev ed, Pantheon Books, New York, 1990), p 183. See also Gerald Frug, "A Critical Theory of Law" (1989) 1 *Legal Education Review* 43.

68 The question is whether contract doctrine can be rectified in some respects by reform in areas like consumer protection: it may be that the CLS writers would argue that it cannot be, because it is the fundamental structure which is at fault — mere reform will not do. Nonetheless, as both a practical necessity (since a wholesale change in the capitalist consciousness seems unlikely) and as a step towards a more fair system, a reformist approach may be inevitable. See the comments made by Richard Delgado in "The Ethereal Scholar", pp 307-308.

Or, as Roger Cotterrell has argued, the concept of private property as we know it is based on an ideological separation of persons from the things they own. We can own property (or not) and according to liberal ideals we are all still free and equal individuals. But the liberal concept obscures the real effect of private property, which is to vest those who have it with a great deal more political power (in both public and private) than those who don't. So the ideological separation of persons from the things they own ends up by reinforcing the practical inequalities in property ownership: property rights are supposed to enshrine our freedom and equality, but their effect is, in fact, to preserve and intensify existing inequalities.[69]

In "A Critique of Torts", Richard Abel applies similar sorts of arguments to the liberal underpinnings of the law of torts. Abel argues that tort law is historically related to industrialisation and the growth of capitalist economies which turned a community-based existence into liberal societies composed of (potentially) warring, but essentially disconnected, individuals. For example, capitalist enterprise necessitates that profit be balanced against individual safety and that a monetary value be placed on physical injuries. People are commodified by torts, both in the evaluation of what constitutes an acceptable risk, and in the determination of the cost of an injury in assessing damages.[70] Torts also rests on the liberal assumption of individual autonomy and equality, its doctrines masking, as far as the law is concerned, the fact that in this sphere at least, relatively few people (such as manufacturers) are actually in control of the fate of many others (such as workers and consumers).

What is perhaps most obnoxious, according to Abel, is the way that recovery of damages in torts actually strengthens existing distributions of wealth: for a multitude of structural and doctrinal reasons already wealthy people are more likely to recover large payouts for their injuries than others.[71] What this means is that those who create the risks will take fewer precautions to protect such people:[72]

---

69   Cotterrell, "Power, Property, and the Law of Trusts". See also Margaret Davies, *Property: Meanings, Histories, Theories* (Routledge-Cavendish, Abingdon, 2007).

70   See my discussion of this matter in the section on law and economics in Chapter 4.

71   For instance, victims of crime, who are disproportionately from non-privileged groups, are unlikely to be able to recover damages in tort, and therefore rely on criminal injuries compensation schemes, which are much less generous than tort damages; similarly workers compensation schemes, where damages are also limited, are generally designed to compensate lower income workers: Abel, "A Critique of Torts" (1990) *University of Los Angeles Law Review* 785 at 798-799. In most Australian jurisdictions complaints of sexual harrassment are heard by equal opportunities tribunals where awards of damages are much lower than they are in the various courts.

72   Abel, "A Critique of Torts", pp 809-810. I have not reproduced the footnotes to this paragraph, but they do contain some very interesting information about the Bhopal disaster and the location of toxic waste dumps.

... tort liability necessarily translates unequal recoveries ... into unequal exposure to risk. An entrepreneur in a competitive market must spend less to protect those who are less likely to claim or who will recover lower damages — poor, unemployed, young, old, or inadequately educated individuals, racial minorities, noncitizens, and women. Thus, cheap consumer products not only perform less well, but also are more dangerous; low-paid workers suffer more frequent and more serious injuries and illnesses at work; and the underprivileged are exposed to greater environmental pollution. Whether or not the Bhopal disaster was an "accident", it was no accident that its victims were among the poorest in the Third World. Nor is it chance that toxic waste dumps are concentrated in black ghettoes in the United States.

Abel's article is somewhat unusual for CLS because he does actually propose concrete reforms to the torts system in order to resolve some of its most obvious inequities.[73] For instance, Abel envisages a legal regime which treats all accident victims equally, regardless of whether or not their injuries were caused by the fault of another. At the same time he insists that tortfeasors should have to accept moral responsibility for their wrongs. Some of Abel's proposals are simply reforms to the law, while others rely on a fundamental change in social vision: for instance he suggests that a preferable world would be one where the community responds to the personal (not only material) needs of the victim.

Is It Dead? (Or Worse, Assimilated?)

[565] In 2003, Duncan Kennedy summarised the state of CLS in this way: "although critical legal studies as a political movement has been dead for a number of years, critical legal studies as a legal academic school of thought is very much alive".[74] It is certainly the case that CLS is no longer quite the "movement" or "political location" that it was in the early 1980s. What happened to it? Did it die because of its inability to provide realistic alternatives to the dominant legal world-view?[75] Was it overtaken as a politicised critical movement by feminism and critical race theory? Did it just run out of steam? Did it diversify? Was it, like realism, assimilated into the legal academy in a depoliticised form?[76] Did its (often reactionary) critics actually win the argument?

There may be an element of truth to all of these suggestions and, in the end, it is not possible to provide a definitive description of changes in critical theory. As an interesting case of assimilation, however, consider the following reflections.

---

73 Abel, "A Critique of Torts", pp 819-831.

74 Kennedy, "Two Globalizations of Law and legal Thought: 1850-1968" (2003) *Suffolk University Law Review* 631 at 631. See also Tushnet, "Critical Legal Theory (Without Modifiers) in the United States".

75 Fischl, "The Question that Killed Critical Legal Studies".

76 Tushnet, "Critical Legal Studies: A Political History", pp 1538-1539.

Mark Tushnet
"Critical Legal Studies: A Political History"[77]

[570] The cls critique of legalism has, in my view reached a point where it may be difficult to develop substantial political energy from its continuation. The point may be made by imagining that we have developed a measure of the determinacy of a set of legal rules, the "determinile". A completely determinate legal system would measure 100 determiniles, while a completely indeterminate one would measure zero. Cls adherents at present defend the position that the proper measure of legal systems is probably between five and fifteen; that is, no system is completely indeterminate, but the level of determinacy is relatively low. Mainstream legal theorists at present defend the position that the proper measure of well-functioning legal systems like that of the United States is somewhere between forty and sixty; that is, such systems have a substantial amount of indeterminacy, but not nearly as much as the cls position claims. The positions differ, as is suggested by the existence of a gap between the "most determinate" position of the cls position and the "least determinate" one of the main-stream position. In addition, among cls adherents there is disagreement about the primary reason for the degree of determinacy that there is: power relations associated with gender differences, race differences, and class differences are all candidates of some. Yet at this point we are simply arguing over a mere detail, the question of degree.

[575] Tushnet is attempting to explain one of the reasons for the apparent decline in CLS political fervour. His argument is that CLS has been assimilated to a certain degree into the legal academy: the idea that law is politics has been more or less accepted. Not having anything substantial to argue over then, except the question of degree, the CLS debate with the academy has been defused.

The passage is also illuminating for a totally different reason. Tushnet postulates a measure of determinacy, the "determinile", and argues that the essential difference between CLS and mainstream scholars on the determinacy issue is where they would place a legal system on the scale. Crits suggest a measure between five and 15 out of 100, while mainstream scholars suggest between 40 and 60. Power differences associated with gender, race and class are all potential contributors to the *degree* of indeterminacy. Tushnet assumes that there can be a determinate place from which to judge determinacy. In even postulating the possibility of such measurement is it Tushnet who buys into the mainstream position, rather than the mainstream position which accepts part of the CLS argument? (Positivists, for instance, clearly accept that there is a penumbra of uncertainty in rules, and did so before the establishment of CLS.[78]) In other words, what Tushnet has revealed is his ultimate belief in a determinate and objective position from which to measure determinacy. There is a determinate "outside" to the law.

---

77 Tushnet, "Critical Legal Studies: A Political History", p 1538. See also Tushnet "Critical Legal Theory (without Modifiers) in the United States", p 100.

78 See, for instance, HLA Hart, *The Concept of Law* (2nd ed, Clarendon Press, Oxford, 1994), pp 124-132.

212 Asking the Law Question

Moreover, for Tushnet, power differences only contribute to the measure of indeterminacy, whereas for many feminists and race theorists, the law is all too determinate in its self-protection and in its protection of privilege. The effect of a power differential is to reinforce a dominant position and naturalise it: in other words, what is itself only a "perspective", that of the privileged academic knower (and stereotypically a white man), is seen to be the standard case or neutral position in comparison to which others are mere deviations. I would have thought that the point about indeterminacy to be derived from issues of power differences is that there is simply no outside, no way of measuring which is not itself also a perspective. Epistemologically, there is no "view from nowhere", but this does not mean that one cannot be set up politically and ideologically: indeed we know that privileged meaning-systems are relentless in their domination of the cultural, political, and legal environments. Tushnet's lapse into an assumption of determinacy (where crits and liberals argue over the effects of race, class, and gender) is only one illustration of the power of predominant meanings.

Even if aspects of CLS have been assimilated into the legal academy, it is also true to say that the critical movement in law generally has grown a great deal since the early days of CLS. In the next three chapters I will consider some areas of critique which have become central to contemporary legal theory — feminism, queer theory, critical race theory, postcolonialism, and postmodernism.

SIX
FEMINISMS AND GENDER IN LEGAL THEORY

Introduction

[605]   Representation of the world, like the world itself, is the work
of men; they describe it from their own point of view, which
they confuse with the absolute truth.

Simone de Beauvoir *The Second Sex*

[610]   So far this book has been largely concerned with forms of jusris-
prudence and legal theory developed by male scholars who have
worked within male-dominated scholarly environments.[1] This is on the
whole (with a few exceptions) as true of Critical Legal Studies (CLS) as
it is of positivism, law and economics, and common law theory. With
the exception of the chapter on CLS, the book has also been about
theories which assume that knowledge is independent of broad social
categories such as gender and race, and uninfluenced by the social
location of the person who knows. Of course, I have not been entirely
uncritical of these positions, and have attempted where possible to
indicate the possibility of thinking otherwise. It is only recently in
Western history that inroads have been made into this cultural and
ideological insistence on neutral knowledge. This chapter represents a
departure from the earlier chapters because it introduces feminist
approaches to law which aim to show that the supposed gender-blind
approach to legal scholarship is problematic, since the claim of
neutrality is often a cover-story for male-oriented and discriminatory
legal knowledge and policy.

Feminist legal theory has changed significantly since the first edition
of the book (1994), especially in terms of the diversification of interests
and theoretical approaches adopted by feminist scholars. Though the

---

1   A useful and accessible account of the masculine character of the liberal state is Wendy
Brown, "Finding the Man in the State" in Brown, *States of Injury: Power and Freedom in Late
Modernity* (Princeton University Press, Princeton, 1995). See also Margaret Thornton,
"Embodying the Citizen" in Thornton (ed), *Public and Private* (Oxford University Press,
Melbourne, 1995); Elizabeth Kingdom, "Citizenship and Democracy: Feminist Politics of
Citizenship and Radical Democratic Politics" in Millns and Whitty (eds), *Feminist
Perspectives on Public Law* (Cavendish, London, 1999).

changes since the second edition (2002) are perhaps more subtle than those which occurred throughout the late 1990s, they nonetheless consolidate earlier developments. At the present time, there is considerable interest in the relationship of questions of feminism and sexuality to religion, which parallel but are are not reducible to debate about the intersection of gender with culture and race. Western feminism has become more global in its outlook and has started giving more recognition to feminist or woman-centred scholars from the majority world.[2] And for several years, a resurgence of materialist feminism has been foreshadowed:[3] the meanings of "materialism" vary, but it generally involves attention to the everyday conditions of women's lives; particularly in relation to work, reproduction, and caring responsibilities. These developments indicate that feminism is far from a settled terrain. Indeed, this is one of the strengths of feminism thought — that it is self-critical, flexible, and responsive to change. My objective in this chapter, as elsewhere, is to balance history with current debates: the chapter therefore does devote some space to scholars and theories which have waned in popularity. Understanding the recent history of feminism is important because it has strongly influenced the current shape of feminist thought.[4] At the same time, feminist legal scholarship remains a vibrant and highly dynamic discipline and is constantly developing new directions. Where possible, I try to take account of these developments.

The claim that common law theory or positivism are underpinned by a male theoretical orientation may not be immediately obvious: it is one of the aims of this chapter to elucidate such ideas, as well as to indicate some of the specific focal points of feminist thinking as it relates to jurisprudence. In essence though, to say that Western jurisprudence and law are gendered means several inter-related things.[5] In the first place, it is empirically true that law and legal theory have been (and still are) the province of men.[6] Very simply, it is mainly men who have

---

2   Because of its association with Western thought, the term "feminism" is not always acceptable to those who come from a non-Western perspective. For instance, women working with gender equality in Islamic contexts have been divided over whether to characterise their research and activism as "feminist".

3   Susan Boyd, "Family, Law and Sexuality: Feminist Engagements" (1999) 8 *Social and Legal Studies* 370.

4   For an interesting and thoughtful piece about feminist history see Clare Hemmings, "Telling Feminist Stories" (2005) 6 *Feminist Theory* 115.

5   As in other instances, I am directing my remarks to Western law and jurisprudence, and, in particular, the Anglo-American conceptions of law which have been considered in other chapters. Here, as elsewhere, I make no pretensions to speak globally about law.

6   Kate Millet wrote "our society, like all other historical civilizations, is a patriarchy. The fact is evident at once if one recalls that the military, industry, technology, universities, science, political office, and finance — in short, every avenue of power within the society, including the coercive force of the police, is entirely within male hands": *Sexual Politics* (Abacus, London, 1972 c1970), p 25. Thus "patriarchy" refers on one level to the empirical fact of the control of society by men, but more importantly, to the cultural values which reinforce this domination.

written the law and theories about the law. Austin's "province of jurisprudence" is a terrain dominated by men. (Not all men, of course, but educated white men.) If you believe that social and legal truth is singular and that the identity of the "knower" is irrelevant, then this would not be a problem. Whatever the "knowers" said would be true for all of us, whatever our culture, our sexuality, our religion, or our gender. But many people (myself included) take a different view — that knowledge cannot be disentangled from social meanings and that personal history does influence what you know and how you know it. (Note — this is different from being completely determined by your social background.)

Secondly, law and jurisprudence reflect values conventionally associated with the liberal male. Men have made the legal world in their own image, confusing it, as de Beauvoir says, with the absolute truth. For women, and other marginalised groups, it is not only the over-representation of one group in legal decision-making and theorising which is the problem. A much deeper difficulty lies in the value systems of law and culture, which reinforce in various ways oppressions of gender, race, class, sexuality, and so on. When certain values (such as rationality and reasonableness, independence and autonomy, objectivity, authority and neutrality[7]) are culturally associated with white, middle-class men and masculinity at the same time as they are valued by the law, it is hardly surprising that the law seems to "speak" to men within this dominant culture in a way in which it does not speak to women or to other marginalised groups. This general ideological form of patriarchy is repeated in the law itself, where substantive legal categories often overlook, trivialise, or marginalise the concerns of women.[8] Feminist legal scholars have analysed virtually every area of substantive law — torts, contract, property, constitutional law, human rights and so forth — to show how ideas about gender are deeply embedded in law.[9]

The masculine values embedded in law are reinforced by a view of legal theory which assumes that it is possible to achieve a general explanation or description of law: in the process of constructing such a description, legal theory excludes knowledges emanating from non-dominant experiences and cultures. The idea that such general

7   For a succinct account of the feminist critique of legal positivism see Nicola Lacey, "Feminist Perspectives on Ethical Positivism" in Campbell and Goldsworthy (eds), *Judicial Power, Democracy and Legal Positivism* (Ashgate, Aldershot, 2000).

8   See Regina Graycar and Jenny Morgan, *The Hidden Gender of Law* (2nd ed, Federation Press, Annandale NSW, 2002), Ch 1; Tove Stang Dahl, *Women's Law: An Introduction to Feminist Jurisprudence* (trans by Ronald L Craig, Norwegian University Press, Oslo, 1987); Lucinda Finley, "Breaking Women's Silence in Law: The Dilemma of the Gendered Nature of Legal Reasoning" (1989) 41 *Yale Journal of Law and Feminism* 41.

9   For an excellent overview of the recent state of feminist legal theory, its achievements and challenges, see Joanne Conaghan, "Reassessing the Feminist Theoretical Project in Law" (2000) 27 *Journal of Law and Society* 351.

explanations are possible is not politically innocent, but is rather imposed on us as a way of stifling dissent or different points of view. If there is a "neutral" or "objective" way of seeing things, then those of us who do not share it are more likely to accept the characterisation of our own views as distorted or biased, and consequently attempt to fit them into the dominant mould. The fact that the law might look totally different to people whose main experience of it is as an instrument of oppression or exclusion cannot easily be accommodated by mainstream thinkers. Nor can the complicating fact that many people will in any case have internalised the official message about law and culture, simply because of the power of prevailing ideologies.

Feminism, Politics, and Knowledge

Theory and practice

[615] Feminism is not only theory, though nor is it only a political practice. Although it is always problematic, the distinction between theory and practice is usually considered to be fundamental to our way of doing things. We find a theory to explain an experience or a phenomenon: concrete things are explained by universal laws. Conversely, we develop a theory, and then apply it so that it has practical results. Theoretical physics is turned into technology, for instance. Philosophy is "applied" in medical ethics. As lawyers, we often think that a theory must be directed towards a practical end such as law reform, and that if there is no concrete solution to a problem, then the theory which identifies it is not much good. For instance, as I explained in Chapter 5, critical legal studies has frequently been criticised for failing to develop a strategy to change the world. As I pointed out, such a criticism is itself based on a rather narrow view of what constitutes change: helping to produce the conditions in which change can occur may itself be an important contribution to the process. One prevalent idea on the matter is that theory and practice are different, though related through the notions of application or explanation. More broadly, abstraction is different from practical things, either facts or actions.

Questioning this common distinction between theory and practice is important for an understanding of feminist politics.[10] In the first place, it is clear that theory of some sort is always essential to our understanding of the world. In Chapter 4, I considered what has been

---

10   Some articles on this topic include bell hooks, "Theory as Liberatory Practice" (1991) 4 *Yale Journal of Law and Feminism* 41; Catharine MacKinnon, "From Practice to Theory, or What is a White Woman Anyway?" (1991) 41 *Yale Journal of Law and Feminism* 13; Phyllis Goldfarb, "A Theory-Practice Spiral: The Ethics of Feminism and Clinical Education" (1991) 75 *Minnesota Law Review* 1599; Naomi Cahn, "Defining Feminist Litigation" (1991) 14 *Harvard Women's Law Journal* 1; Martha Fineman, "Challenging Law, Establishing Differences: The Future of Feminist Legal Scholarship" (1990) 42 *Florida Law Review* 25 at 27-34; Liz Stanley and Sue Wise, "But the Empress Has No Clothes!" (2000) 1 *Feminist Theory* 261.

called the "theory dependence" of observation — the recognition that it is not possible simply to observe the world in a value-free environment. Observation is always dependent on theory in a broad sense: for instance we are not able to say "the carpet is red" without a pre-existing conception of what a carpet is, and what redness is. The categories of carpets and redness are abstract notions, and ones which differ according to cultural and linguistic context. It is therefore possible to say that the theory/fact distinction is *never* entirely pure: facts are already invested with a theoretical understanding of the world. Similarly, social practices are not just "facts": people do not naturally organise themselves and relate to each other in predetermined ways. Social practices are thoroughly imbued with conventions and culture, and in the case of Western countries, this means the theory, ideology and practices of liberalism. And the distinction between law and fact, which mirrors the general/particular and theory/practice distinctions, cannot be absolute. As I have explained, "facts" are characterised within a prior legal structure.

The reason that a law is never a pure universal is probably not as easy to grasp as the reason that facts are never purely material. The practicality of the law, the fact that law is practice and not merely abstract, can be seen in a similar light to the practicality of feminist theory, which, as I will explain, normally has some transformative purpose. Such "transformation" should be understood very broadly. A transformation in the way that the world is perceived is as important as getting more women and minorities into parliament. Similarly, in order to have any meaning as a law, a norm must have some effect in the world. Law itself is never static, but forever changing. And we should not forget the argument put forward by some of the Realists that law is only what happens in practice. (How can we *know* law except insofar as it arises from practice?) In a similar vein, as I will explain in Chapter 8, postmodern theorists have argued that our "universals" are in fact the effect of our practices: repeated performances, actions, and habits, are the basis for our norms. As we will see towards the end of this chapter, Judith Butler has argued that gender is the effect of our performances as female or male. How we *do* "femininity" or "female" is the basis for how we conceptualise these ideas. (Which is to put it simplistically — I will come back to this later.)

Thus the distinction between theory and practice, like the distinctions between fact and value and fact and law, never actually works in a pure way. It is simply a way of talking about the world, and dividing it into different levels of understanding (the general and the particular). Saying that the distinction does not work and that it is important to challenge it, however, does not mean that it will simply go away. Like many of the fundamental building-blocks of our way of seeing the world, the theory/practice distinction is very difficult to eliminate from our minds: we keep on using it, just as we are intent upon challenging it. This challenge has become a central theme in much feminist writing, partly, I would say, because it has become evident that in order to change social practices and the external circumstances of women's lives, it is also necessary to change the way we see the world.

It is true on one level that the world hits women in the face (some more than others).[11] Even after decades of feminist activism and theory, on both a local and a global scale women are still the targets of discrimination and violence. However, this does not mean that a feminist understanding of the world is unmediated by theory. In fact it has been crucial for feminists to be able to say not only that this or that woman has been discriminated against, trafficked, sexually assaulted, marginalised, excluded or harrassed, but also that these are things which, on the whole, are symptoms of a culture which tolerates gender inequality, violence and discrimination. It is not that men do not get discriminated against, raped or excluded, but rather that the gendered pattern of discrimination and violence is generally of women by individual men and by a male-dominated culture which has not yet done enough to stop this behaviour. The particular women who have been hit in the face by the world of gender-based oppression are not alone, or accidental cases, but are on the receiving end of a pattern of exclusion which is manifested in many ways.

Women's "reality" is not just there, but is rather already highly conditioned by a complex network of cultural structures which often naturalise and legitimate male domination. For instance, the unquestioning tendency we have to divide the social world into public and private spheres has often been used as a way of legitimating (or at least masking) violence which takes place in "private". Violence against women — domestic assault, rape, sexual abuse, incest — has often been defined as private and beyond state intervention, meaning simply that women have traditionally been less protected by the criminal law than men. The reality of this sort of violence is structured by the association of women and women's issues with the private sphere, and the reluctance of the liberal state to intervene in so-called "private" matters.[12]

Feminist practice therefore does rely on theoretical understandings of the world, and in particular of the complex expressions of gender difference and subordination, but it is always practical and political in

---

11   Catharine MacKinnon wrote: "Women know the world is out there because it hits us in the face. Literally. We are raped, battered, pornographed, defined by force, by a world that begins ... entirely outside us": *Feminism Unmodified: Discourses on Life and Law* (Harvard University Press, Cambridge Mass, 1987), p 57. Although this may look as though MacKinnon is arguing for the existence of an unmediated experience, elsewhere in her writings it appears that this is not her intention. See the section on MacKinnon below at [650]-[680].

12   The reluctance is formal and ideological, rather than substantive: as Katherine O'Donovan has argued, the family is also constructed by law: *Sexual Divisions in Law* (Weidenfeld and Nicolson, London, 1985). See also Nicola Lacey, *Unspeakable Subjects: Feminist Essays in Legal and Social Theory* (Hart Publishing, Oxford, 1998), Ch 3.

the sense that it aims for a transformation of social relationships. Unlike most of the theories considered so far in this book (with the exception of the race-conscious critiques of CLS), feminism is primarily a broadly-based political and social movement. Feminism is an ongoing political struggle and for that reason alone can never be seen as simply an abstraction or purely theoretical. At the same time, it has been important for the practice of feminism to be reflective: that is, it has not been simply an unthought reaction against a male-controlled world, but is directed towards certain ends and must therefore continually question and develop its theories and strategies.

Conversely, it is important to see feminist theory as practical. Academic feminism has at times been rightly criticised as having no political effect, as having no particularly positive consequences in women's struggle for justice.[13] It has been seen as having no direction or a misguided one,[14] and as therefore being a distraction from the "real" feminist agenda. And it is certainly true that there is much theory which is obscure and alienating for the majority of its readers, and which has no clear political purpose. This criticism has in particular been directed in recent years against postmodern feminism. However, it should be emphasised that transformative theory is as important for feminists as transformative politics. It is as important to change the way we understand the world as it is to change the practical ways in which the world is organised.

In this way, feminist theory and practice cannot be usefully separated. Transformative theory *is* transformative politics. For instance, it has become obvious to feminists that simply changing the law of rape has not eliminated rape or even secured more convictions of rapists.[15] Feminist-inspired reforms — by themselves — have had little, if any, effect on either the incidence of rape or the number of successful prosecutions. It is clear that it is also necessary to alter the way in which sexual relationships are viewed by society. Ideas such as that romantic love happens between a strong and conquering man, and a submissive woman who needs to be convinced to engage in sex, or who doesn't know her own mind, or who is deliberately (but dishonestly) resistant,[16] seem hopelessly outdated. These are nonetheless still common social narratives and can therefore be easily drawn upon in legal contexts. Even outdated social stereotypes affect our evaluation of many

---

13   See, for instance, hooks, "Theory as Liberatory Practice", p 5; MacKinnon, "From Practice to Theory, or What is a White Woman Anyway?".

14   Controversies over postmodern feminism have concerned, precisely, whether it has a strategy which is useful for feminism.

15   There is much statistical evidence which demonstrates that of the number of rapes which are reported, only a small proportion are prosecuted, and of these the number of convictions is minimal.

16   Ngaire Naffine, "Possession: Erotic Love and the Law of Rape" (1994) 57 *Modern Law Review* 10.

situations: it is therefore critical to continue to educate judges, counsel, juries, and all people about such matters. What this means is that feminism has become a project which is not directed only at substantive "women's issues" or gender discrimination. It also poses a challenge to the fundamental structure of the law itself. It is a challenge, in other words, to the substantive law, to the ordering concepts of the law (such as the "reasonable person/man"), to the liberal ideology of the law, as well as to its conceptual self-image.

In short, it is possible to say that feminist practice is theory, and also that feminist theory is practice. The two things are inextricable, since the aim of feminism is always transformation, which is both a practical and a theoretical process.

"Feminisms"

[620] So far I have been speaking of "feminism" as though the word itself were relatively unproblematic, which is not the case. This chapter often refers to "feminisms" in the plural, because the word "feminism", in the singular, tends to suggest that there is a common theoretical approach shared by those of us who believe that women are marginalised and devalued in society and that we must work towards the eradication of such disadvantage and oppression. Feminism is a political agenda which can be reasonably broadly and uncontroversially defined insofar as it has as its aim a social and political environment in which women and men of all ethnicities, class backgrounds, sexualities, and abilities are equally valued and empowered.[17] However, as soon as we start talking about the theory which underlies feminist beliefs, why women experience inequality on the basis of gender, what the characteristics and dimensions of gendered thinking are, and what to do about it, it becomes not only reductive, but meaningless to talk about "feminism" as though it is a single body of thought — just as it is meaningless to speak of "women" as though we are all the same.

This can be most clearly illustrated by a consideration of the ways that different forms of social exclusion and discrimination intersect. I said above that it is important for feminists to be able to develop theory from our perceptions of discrimination and violence so that an understanding of the nature of our gendered world can be attained: such a theoretical understanding is the basis of both practical and conceptual change. But any process of generalisation is of necessity limited by the context from which it is drawn. Theory developed by white middle-class heterosexual women from developed countries may in many important

---

17   For some helpful reflections on what constitutes feminist theory, see Sara Ahmed, "Whose Counting?" (2000) 1 *Feminist Theory* 97; Bronwyn Winter, "Who Counts (Or Doesn't Count) What as Feminist Theory? An Exercise in Dictionary Use" (2000) 1 *Feminist Theory* 105; Elizabeth Ermath, "What Counts as Feminist Theory?" (2000) 1 *Feminist Theory* 113.

respects be specific to such women. It certainly should not be taken to explain the condition of women who are from another racial group, from a religious minority, from developing countries, or who identify as lesbian. As a white gentile woman I cannot possibly know what it is like to be systematically oppressed because of my race, ethnicity, or religious beliefs so it would be presumptuous to assume that whatever I have to say about women applies indifferently to Indigenous, Black, or Jewish women. Race is not something which can simply be added on to my theory: as women of colour have pointed out, being a member of an oppressed race does not only make the oppression *more*, it makes it *different*.[18] To be an African-American woman in the United States or an Indigenous woman in Australia is not just to be in a worse position than a white woman in relation to the dominant culture: it is to be in a qualitatively different position. So when white women develop theories of feminism which do not recognise this sort of difference we are perpetuating the self-centredness which de Beauvoir identified in relation to men's representations of the world, as descriptions of it from their own point of view confused with the absolute truth.[19] In relation to other women, privileged white heterosexual women are a powerful group: putting such voices in the place of those who are less powerful repeats the patriarchal gesture of disenfranchising an oppressed group by taking over their right to speak. Our understanding of the world is affected by our place in it: our experience affects what and how we see. We therefore need to recognise the perspectives of others (and that dominant ways of seeing are also perspectives).[20] Thus, even talking generally about "patriarchy", male dominance, or gendered power differences as all-encompassing dimensions of society neglects the fact that for many women there are other types of oppression than those based on gender divisions. Speaking of gender as *the* fundamental system of disempowerment begins to look like a denial of the significance of racism and other systems of oppression.[21]

None of this, however, should be taken to suggest that we can simply abdicate responsibility for recognising and challenging the heterosexism, classism or racism in our societies and our selves. As Barbara Smith defines feminism, it is "the political theory and practice that struggles to free all women: women of color, working-class women, poor women, disabled women, lesbians, old women — as well

---

18   Angela Harris, "Race and Essentialism in Feminist Legal Theory" (1990) 42 *Stanford Law Review* 581 at 596; Barbara Smith, "Toward a Black Feminist Criticism" in Showalter (ed), *The New Feminist Criticism: Essays on Women, Literature, and Theory* (Virago, London, 1986). See generally the section on feminism and race, below at [690]-[6140].

19   Elizabeth Spelman, *Inessential Woman: Problems of Exclusion in Feminist Thought* (Beacon Press, Boston, 1988), p 160.

20   Philipa Rothfield, "Alternative Epistemologies, Politics and Feminism" (1991) 30 *Social Analysis* 54.

21   See the comments made by Gemma Tang Nain in "Black Women, Sexism and Racism: Black or Antiracist Feminism?" (1991) 37 *Feminist Review* 1 at 3-8.

as white, economically privileged, heterosexual women. Anything less than this vision of total freedom is not feminism, but merely female selfaggrandizement."[22]

Race, class, religion, and sexuality are not the only sources of diversity within feminist theory. Many different ways of understanding the condition of women, and of theorising and subverting cultural notions of femininity and womanhood, have been developed. This has often, but not always, occurred in response to "liberal" feminism, the perspective which has undoubtedly been the major force behind many substantive legal reforms, but which, as I will explain, is not acceptable to many feminists as a world-view. A variety of feminisms has therefore emerged, all of which challenge the liberal view in one way or another. These challenges are themselves by no means reducible to a single body of thought, having concentrated on different aspects, experiences, and representations of women's lives.

If we regard theory in the traditional light as attempting to provide an over-arching explanation of some aspect of the world, then this diversity in feminist thinking may seem to be an obstacle to feminist progress. Indeed some feminists have presented their own theory as an authentic statement of feminism, implying that any departure from it is not "real" feminism, or not feminism at all.[23] However, the demand for a general statement of feminism ignores not only the fact that the condition of women is not uniform, but also that feminism is a process: attempts to reduce it to a static theory neglect its dynamic nature. Transformation which is based on the continuing evaluation and modification of a complex material and ideological environment cannot be reduced to a scientific theory of change, like those of evolution or the half-life of radioactive substances. As I have said, practical change occurs within a climate of serious reflection, and diversity of opinion is in my view absolutely essential as a stimulus to theory.

A final point which deserves some attention here relates to the classification of feminisms. In this chapter I have used some of the standard categories as they have been constructed and used through recent feminist history — liberal, radical, African-American, Indigenous, lesbian, postcolonial, and postmodern — but have been conscious that the use of such classifications usually leads to some degree of caricature. This is because the boundaries are not in fact all that clear (and are certainly not analytically pure), and are becoming less so as feminists continue to question our own theoretical presuppositions. As I will explain, liberal feminism has in the past been defined as that branch of feminism which is centrally concerned with the attainment

---

22   Barbara Smith, "Racism and Women's Studies" in Anzaldúa (ed), *Making Face, Making Soul: Haciendo Caras* (Aunt Lute Books, San Francisco, 1990), p 25.

23   This is the unavoidable implication of some of Catharine MacKinnon's statements on the matter. Her "feminism unmodified" can look as though it is being presented as some sort of "pure" feminism.

of equal rights and opportunities, especially in employment and education, as the primary way of promoting the individual potential of women to the same degree as is already enjoyed by men. However, liberal feminism has broken the boundaries of traditional liberal thought insofar as it recognises the need to think about the social structures which reinforce the inequality and discrimination.[24] Similarly, radical feminism was originally centred on the belief that sex is the basic division and oppression in society. More recently it has had to come to terms with the existence of other exclusive divisions, such as those based on race, sexuality, class, age, and physical ability. With the present emphasis on elaborating the ways in which different systems of power intersect, and the recognition that variations according to the cultural and political context are crucial, it is clear that some of the larger theoretical movements of feminists are tending to move towards a more detailed cultural critique.

Thus, whereas it was once possible to divide feminist theory into a few fairly clear categories, this is no longer the case: it is much more likely that scholars will draw on a variety of theoretical tools and traditions. Moreover, the complexity of feminist and feminist-related issues has been developed to a stage where it is impossible to make very solid generalisations. For instance, feminist international lawyers have recently emphasised the special situation of women in post-conflict "transitional" societies:[25] being a useful scholarly or activist "ally" in these circumstances may bring into play familiar issues of women's rights and resisting subordination, but also raise "intersectional" concerns of religion, culture, nation, and ethnicity together with a need to be self-reflective and resist ongoing (feminist) imperialism all within the context of a gendered understanding of international law and politics. This is not a feminist analysis which can be reduced to a theory, but is heavily context-dependent, though obviously also highly theoretically informed.

This tendency in recent feminism is in line with what Jean-François Lyotard called "the postmodern condition", which is, as I will explain in more detail in Chapter 8, a general movement away from large theoretical explanations, to the examination of more localised "discourses".[26] Thus, rather than attempt to develop grand theories

---

24   Zillah Eisenstein, *The Radical Future of Liberal Feminism* (Longman, New York, 1981).

25   Hilary Charlesworth, "Building Justice and Democracy After Conflict" (2007) 2 *Academy of the Social Sciences in Australia, Occasional Papers* 1; Katherine Franke, "Gendered Subjects of Transitional Justice" (2006) 15 *Columbia Journal of Gender and Law* 813; Fionnuala Ní Aoláin, "Political Violence and Gender During Times of Transition" (2006) 15 *Columbia Journal of Gender and Law* 829.

26   "Discourse" is a term which is widely used by writers influenced by "postmodern" and "poststructural" thought. It is a non-technical word, used loosely to refer to shared spheres of communication, and the characteristics of any such sphere: thus we can speak generally of feminist discourse, legal discourse, medical discourse, and so on.

which factor in race, class, sexuality, and so on, current feminism focuses upon the specific ways in which systems of oppression and cultural expressions of gender difference relate in various contexts. However, it is not only the insensitivity of grand theory to "intersecting" oppressions which has led to the breakdown of feminist categories. Many writers have recently begun to question the possibility of making anything but provisional and strategically useful classifications. For instance, feminists have pointed out that while in many circumstances it may be politically appropriate to identify with a certain group (such as being a lesbian, a woman, or of a certain race), the identity of such groups is not (cannot and should not be) fixed.[27] Indeed the fixing of such identities by a dominant ideology has always been one of the ways in which power differences are institutionalised. Women have been defined and stereotyped as a group: femininity has come to mean certain things which disempower and silence women, and which further marginalise women who do not conform. It is therefore necessary to question and re-formulate the meaning of "the feminine", "female-ness", and "women" as categories, but to be aware at the same time that simply re-fixing the boundaries may be counter-productive.[28] Modern feminism is also looking beyond the traditional political questions to issues inspired by the linguistic thought which has been so crucial to postmodernism: for instance the ways in which cultural meanings are produced, how they operate, and how they can be altered have all been seen as increasingly significant matters. Some of the ideas associated with "postmodernism" will be explained at the end of this chapter and in Chapter 8.

The object of feminist knowledge

[625] The other important thing to consider in an introduction to feminist thought relates to how we view whatever it is that we think we know. This is a matter which has been given a great deal of attention by many

---

27   An excellent recent essay on the difficult issues of identity, essentialism, and feminist politics is Conaghan, "Reassesing the Feminist Legal Project in Law". Conaghan urges caution in moving away from the traditional woman-centred politics of feminism.

28   A strategy based on a refusal to fix the boundaries of the feminine is central to the work of, for instance, Luce Irigaray, Judith Butler and Drucilla Cornell. See, for instance, Irigaray, *Speculum of the Other Woman* (trans by Gillian C Gill, Cornell University Press, Ithaca, 1985); *This Sex Which is Not One* (trans by Catherine Porter with Carolyn Burke, Cornell University Press, Ithaca 1985); Judith Butler, *Gender Trouble: Feminism and the Subversion of Identity* (Routledge, New York, 1990); Drucilla Cornell, *Beyond Accommodation: Ethical Feminism, Deconstruction and the Law* (Routledge, New York, 1991). Some more accessible works by Irigaray include *Je, Tu, Nous: Toward a Culture of Difference* (Routledge, London, 1993); *I Love to You: Sketch of a Possible Felicity in History* (Routledge, New York, 1996); *Why Different? A Culture of Two Subjects* (Interviews) (Semiotext(e), New York, 2000). Reasonably accessible works about Irigaray include Margaret Whitford, *Luce Irigaray: Philosophy in the Feminine* (Routledge, London, 1991) and Christine Holmlund, "The Lesbian, the Mother, the Heterosexual Lover: Irigaray's Recodings of Difference" (1991) 17 *Feminist Studies* 283.

critical theorists and feminists, especially insofar as the relationship between power and knowledge has been brought into the picture. Traditionally knowledge has been seen as power: to have knowledge is potentially to have access to a form of power. Those who know can use their knowledge to their own ends. More recent thought on this matter, often inspired by the work of Michel Foucault, suggests that the inverse is also the case: that the conditions of what counts as "knowledge" are in fact determined by relations of power.[29] The structures and institutions which control society determine what is "true", and what is not. Feminists have pointed out that predominant systems of meaning tend to be socially (not biologically) male, and that this is related to the empirical fact that men have power over women. It is men who traditionally have taken the position of "knowers", and one of the things men have "known" is women. The point was made by radical feminist Catharine MacKinnon, in *Feminism Unmodified*:[30]

> Objectivity is a stance only a subject can take ... It is only a subject who gets to take the objective standpoint, the stance which is transparent to its object, the stance that is no stance. A subject is a self. An object is other to that self. Anyone who is the least bit attentive to gender since reading Simone de Beauvoir knows that it is men socially who are subjects, women socially who are other, objects. Thus the one who has the social access to being that self which takes the stance that is allowed to be objective, that objective person who is a subject, is socially male. When I spoke with David Kennedy about this earlier, he said that the objective subject didn't *have to be* male, so he didn't see how it was gendered. It *could be* any way at all, he said. Well, yes; but my point is that it *isn't* any way at all; it *is* gendered, in fact in the world. If, in order to be gendered, something has to be [that is, is of necessity] gendered, those of us in the social change business could pack up and go ... where? We would give up on changing gender, anyway. Of course it could be any way at all. That it could be and isn't, should be and isn't, is what makes it a political problem.

The last point is particularly important. The claim is not that "objectivity" is of necessity male. If that were the case there would be nothing we could do about it. Rather, the position of the "knower", and thus of objectivity (since modern knowledge is regarded as good only insofar as it is objective), has been socially and philosophically

29   See especially Michel Foucault, *Power/Knowledge: Selected Interviews and Other Writings, 1972-1977* (trans by Colin Gordon, Harvester Press, Brighton, 1980); a relevant passage from this book will be discussed in Chapter 8. A good exposition of the relevance of Foucault's ideas in the context of feminism is Sneja Gunew, "Feminist Knowledge: Critique and Construct" in Gunew (ed), *Feminist Knowledge: Critique and Construct* (Routledge, New York, 1990), pp 22-23.

30   MacKinnon *Feminism Unmodified: Discourses on Life and Law*, p 55.

associated with the male point of view.[31] It is one of the political tasks of feminism not only to ensure that women get access to the position of the subject, but also that the non-situated, non-subjective, paradigm of knowledge is challenged. Such a challenge is important because the ideal of objective knowledge has, as I indicated above, worked to silence or stigmatise as "subjective" views which do not reflect the orthodox epistemological order. And while MacKinnon's point was originally made in the context of gender relations, it is equally true of other unequal power distributions. For instance, Western scholarship often claims to generate authoritative knowledge about non-Western cultures, sometimes appropriating or devaluing the knowledge such communities have about themselves.[32]

MacKinnon says that objectivity "is a stance only a subject gets to take", which is a succinct way of saying that in any case there *has* to be a subject of knowledge (not a subject matter, but a person who knows), and in this sense, subjectivity is an unavoidable element of knowledge. The further argument relating to this matter is that in the ideal of objective knowledge, the existence of the subject position is minimised, and usually erased altogether. As Lorraine Code points out, for something to qualify as "objective knowledge" the subjects of it must be interchangeable: the idea is that it could be anyone doing the knowing.[33] Knowledge is "out there", and the content is the same no matter who is doing the knowing — except that it is the privileged male position which is seen to be position-less (and hence interchangeable with other similarly neutered beings) while as subjects women and others are visibly sexed or turned into "others", and therefore never neutral enough to be objective. None of this alters the fact that knowledge is not in itself neutral, since it always exists within a particular social and philosophical context. "Neutrality" is only the position which is culturally enabled to deny its positionality — it is the position which is empowered to know.

Before proceeding, there is one final introductory point which may need clarification. Some feminist theory distinguishes between sex and gender: "sex" is the natural or biological category, while "gender" refers

---

31   Again, this is one of the themes of much "postmodern" feminism. See, for instance, Irigaray, "Any Theory of the 'Subject' has Always Been Appropriated by the 'Masculine'" in *Speculum of the Other Woman*; Kathy Ferguson, *The Man Question: Visions of Subjectivity in Feminist Theory* (University of California Press, Berkeley, 1991), Ch 2; Judy Grbich, "The Body in Legal Theory" (1992) 11 *University of Tasmania Law Review* 26. An excellent and accessible article on feminist approaches to truth is Mary Hawkesworth, "Knowers, Knowing, Known: Feminist Theory and Claims of Truth" (1989) 14 *Signs* 533. See also Susan Hekman, "Truth and Method: Feminist Standpoint Revisited" (1997) 22 *Signs* 341; Sylvia Walby, "Against Epistemological Chasms: The Science Question in Feminism Revisited" (2001) 26 *Signs* 486.

32   For the most famous proponent of such an argument, see Edward Said, *Orientalism* (Penguin, Harmondsworth, 1978).

33   See Lorraine Code, "Taking Subjectivity Into Account" in Linda Alcoff and Elizabeth Potter (eds), *Feminist Epistemologies* (Routledge, New York, 1993), p 16.

to the socially constructed expectations aligned with sex, but not totally determined by it. "Woman" is the sex, while "feminine" is a gender characteristic. Using this typology, it is possible to say that a woman has masculine characteristics, or that a man behaves in a feminine way. However, many feminists have rejected the sex/gender distinction.[34] Apart from some rather minimal biological characteristics, what belongs to "sex" and what to "gender" is unclear. A man may not be capable of gestating a baby or breastfeeding it, but does that mean he is "naturally" less capable of being a primary caregiver? In my opinion it means no such thing. If women are currently more suited to certain roles, while men are currently more suited to others, the reason is likely to be that we have been socialised in this way. Even if there were a way of establishing that women and men are naturally different, what purpose would such a proposition serve? We do not live in nature, but in a highly technologised, politicised, socialised order. Moreover, the existence of a clear dividing line between women and men, even on biological grounds, is hard to sustain. Just as some women are stronger, taller and more "rational" than some men; many men are weaker, shorter and more emotionally sensitive than many women. Although there is no similar continuum of reproductive organs, there are many people who are born with an indeterminate sex: the dualistic notion of sex has often resulted in their surgical "correction" so that they become female or male (sometimes with tragic results). In this sense, the dualism is not natural, but enforced. Insisting on such categorisation will only entrench stereotypes which are not universally accurate, and marginalise those who do not naturally fit their category. Even more to the point, and bypassing these arguments about nature and biology, it has been argued that the category of "sex" is just as much a construction of language and culture as "gender". Why do we need to divide people according to sex at all? Does modern law really need such a status category?

Feminists are therefore divided on whether sex is a natural category — perhaps most believe that it is not, but there are a few notable exceptions. In this chapter, I have not adhered to a clear division between the terminology of "sex" and "gender". For the most part, the terms are used interchangeably.

---

34   In "Interpreting Gender" (1994) 20 *Signs* 79, Linda Nicholson outlines the history and rationale of the distinction, and critiques its current use. See also, Myra Hird "Gender's Nature" (2000) 1 *Feminist Theory* 347; Denise Thompson, "The Sex/Gender Distinction: A Reconsideration" (1989) 10 *Australian Feminist Studies* 23.

Feminist Legal Theory — General Views of Sex and Oppression

Liberal feminism

Liberalism

[630] In Chapter 5 I outlined some of the basic features of liberal political philosophy, and in particular its ideals of liberty, rationality, equality, and individuality.[35] Liberal conceptions of social and political "rights" are based on seeing the individual primarily as a rational and autonomous agent who is equal to others and whose freedom must not be interfered with arbitrarily by the state. Human beings are seen to have a natural capacity to reason, and a naturally individual and autonomous character. In this view, the state and society are, in a sense, added on to individuals, who logically pre-exist their environments: thus, according to the liberal world-view, social and political organisation should be directed at promoting individualism, freedom of thought and action, and equality. In particular liberal thought has traditionally defended freedom in the "private" realm, where it is assumed a person's actions will not affect others in the same way that they will in public: the "private", notwithstanding the problems of defining it, must therefore be protected from interference by the state. There are, of course, many variations on these basic liberal themes.

It is important to recall that liberal thought is not only a set of philosophical theories but in fact has come to represent the dominant world view of the West. Liberalism is not a political choice for most people, if for any: it is simply assumed. Anthony Arblaster puts it like this:[36]

> Liberalism in its contemporary form is not so much a set of ideas or doctrines to which people subscribe by conscious choice; it is a way of seeing the social world, and a set of assumptions about it, which are absorbed by the individual in so natural and gradual a manner that he or she is not conscious of their being assumptions at all. Liberalism makes up a large part of the intellectual air we breathe.

Thus the pervasiveness of liberal thought in the West and the fact that it has filtered into our general way of seeing things is not always evident to us because it is part of our very existence. Saying that someone is a critic of liberal thinking does not imply that she is entirely free of liberal assumptions or values: indeed within the West this is unlikely, since such beliefs are built into our world-view. It should also be noted that

---

35 See also Stephen Bottomley and Simon Bronitt, *Law in Context* (3rd ed, Federation Press, Sydney, 2006), Ch 2; Anthony Arblaster, *The Rise and Decline of Western Liberalism* (Basil Blackwell, Oxford, 1984); Harold Joseph Laski, *The Rise of European Liberalism* (Allen and Unwin, London, 1936); Alison Jaggar, *Feminist Politics and Human Nature* (Rowman and Littlefield, New Jersey, 1983).

36 Arblaster, *The Rise and Decline of Western Liberalism*, p 6.

while liberal thought has increasingly become the target of criticism, it remains pervasive.[37] Some of the limitations of liberalism as a framework for political change have been outlined briefly in Chapter 5. These limitations have become critical in the context of feminism, which is, as a movement, directed towards broad political change.

Public participation and the extension of liberal rights

[635]   Liberal feminism can be reasonably simply defined as accepting the liberal world-view, but arguing in addition that all the rights and privileges which men enjoy, as individuals, under a liberal political system should be accorded to women. Women should have the right to own private property, to litigate as independent citizens, to vote, to be educated, to hold public office, and in general to lead separate lives as rational individuals. In short, women's rights and opportunities should mirror men's rights and opportunities. The view of liberal feminists has essentially been that while men are treated by political and social institutions as individuals, women have been (and sometimes still are) treated as a group. In this sense the project of liberal feminism is to make liberalism *more* liberal, or more faithful to the aspirations and philosophy of liberalism. The argument is that liberalism is not fulfilling its goals as a political practice because women have not been treated as individuals but rather as a class — women's roles, aspirations, and characteristics have been judged not according to the liberal criterion of individuality but according to certain ascribed conventions of womanhood. So the fundamental claim of liberal feminism is that the legal and social obstacles to equal rights need to be dismantled.

Liberal feminism can be clearly associated with an agenda of law reform, and in fact feminism has historically been dominated by pressure for law reforms which would institute, formally at least, the demand for equal recognition. Historically, the subordination of women has been very clearly reproduced in the law, for instance in the exclusion of women from political life, from many professions, from educational institutions, from owning private property independently of a husband: thus the law became a primary and obvious target in the struggle for equality.

This is not to say that liberal feminism has confined itself only to legal demands. One of its important and ongoing functions lies in the enormous task of getting recognition for women, and women's achievements, in the face of (often, but by no means always, implicit) persistent misogyny. Beyond legal reform, liberal feminism has concentrated much attention on other, informal, aspects of adverse discrimination, which have limited women's opportunities and conditions, particularly in the spheres of education and employment. One example of this sort

---

37   Arblaster argues that while liberalism may well be in retreat, it is far from dead. The intensity of the attack on liberal thought is evidence of this: see *The Rise and Decline of Western Liberalism*, Ch 1.

of liberal feminism is the work which was begun by feminist literary critics in the 1970s to have the literature of women writers recognised by the male-dominated literary establishment.[38] The tradition of literary "greats" has consisted mainly of male authors and a few women novelists of the 19th century — Jane Austen, Charlotte and Emily Brontë, George Eliot, and (sometimes) Virginia Woolf. Recognising women's literature as a tradition has been an important part of having it accepted and respected by the literary community. Such a project was originally undertaken simply as a way of gaining equal recognition for women writers: in this sense it is a liberal undertaking, since the underlying assumptions of literary criticism were not being challenged. It was initially the "male monopoly" of literature which was coming under scrutiny. However, as in other areas of feminism, what started as a liberal project has broken the bounds of the liberal world view: it has been argued that simply making another tradition does not alter the fundamental assumptions about literature, gender, sexuality, race, and class, which were a large part of the problem in the first place. Thus feminist literary criticism also developed into an analysis of the distinct features of women's writing, and of the heterosexually-oriented, colonialist, and racist nature of some forms of literature and literary criticism. Of course, some of this analysis developed independently of feminism. It also began to develop an understanding of the material conditions of literary production, and of the ways in which gender categories are socially and linguistically constructed, and reproduced and subverted in literature. Feminist literary criticism has required nothing less than a fundamental re-evaluation of traditional literature and criticism as an institution.[39]

I think we can see a similar process at work in legal feminism. Legal feminism, and feminism generally, began very much as a claim for equal status and equal rights. It was premised on the view that women have the same reasoning capacity as men. Liberal feminism assumed a universal standard of humanity, comprising both women and men. Yet liberal feminism, because it was also premised on the fact of women's oppression, has had to deal with women *as* women, and not just as members of humanity. Liberal feminism has had to deal not only with the formal obstacles to equality, but also with social assumptions and stereotypes: it has therefore had to develop an analysis of at least some of the fundamental reasons for women's oppression. I think this has, even within liberal feminism, generated a sense of what lies beyond liberal thought, and of where liberal thought breaks down.

---

38   See, for instance, Elaine Showalter, *A Literature of Their Own: British Women Novelists from Brontë to Lessing* (rev ed, Virago, London, 1982).

39   There are many good collections of essays on the basic questions of feminist literary theory. Some early collections are Showalter (ed), *The New Feminist Criticism*; Gayle Greene and Coppélia Kahn (eds), *Making a Difference: Feminist Literary Criticism* (Methuen, London, 1985); Mary Eagleton (ed), *Feminist Literary Theory: A Reader* (2nd ed, Basil Blackwell, Oxford, 1996).

Alison Jaggar puts it like this:[40]

> The long history of liberal philosophy makes it inevitable that it should contain a number of strands, not all of which are consistent with each other. Liberal theory is unified, however, by certain assumptions about human nature that constitute the philosophical foundation for the theory. Liberal feminism too is built on this foundation. Yet although liberal feminism has always begun from liberal principles, it has operated always on the progressive edge of liberal thought, pushing those ideals to their logical conclusion. In doing so, it has found itself forced to challenge not only the currently accepted interpretation of liberal principles but also liberalism's underlying assumptions about human nature. Thus liberal feminism contains contradictions that threaten ultimately to shatter its own philosophical foundation.

One of the difficulties with liberal theory which liberal feminists have had to deal with concerns the notion of the abstract non-gendered and non-sexed individual who is equal to all others: it has become clear, first, that such a being is in any case culturally seen as male, while women are still socially sexed, gendered, and definitely embodied. It has also become clear that the ideal of "equality" becomes problematic as soon as we recognise that our society is not in fact simply a collection of abstract individuals,[41] but structured around racial, cultural, gender, and other groupings. The starting point for equality is not individuals who are basically similar, but rather people who are identified, and who identify themselves, by complicated cultural alliances.

The basis of liberalism is that human beings are all essentially rational and autonomous individuals, and that all people must therefore be treated as equal and free. Yet the "rational individual" who deserved freedom and equality is, on the traditional liberal world view, male. Saying that liberalism's "rational individual" is male contains two related propositions, which need to be distinguished. First, there is the empirical claim (supported by denigrators of women's rights) that women as a *sex* and for biological reasons are not capable of rational thought, and therefore not deserving of rights. It is perfectly consistent with liberalism to deny rights to women (as well as racial "others", non-humans, children, people with disabilities) if they are not regarded as possessing the human characteristics which form the justification for these rights. Arguments of this nature were consistently set against women's demands for rights throughout the 19th and 20th centuries.[42] The first issue for the liberal feminists therefore concerned the rational capacity of women. For women to be accorded the same rights as men, it had to be shown that women have the same capacities for reason and education.

---

40 Jaggar, *Feminist Politics and Human Nature*, p 28; see also Susan Wendell, "A (Qualified) Defense of Liberal Feminism" (1987) 2 *Hypatia* 65.

41 Ngaire Naffine, *Law and the Sexes: Explorations in Feminist Jurisprudence* (Allen and Unwin, Sydney, 1990).

42 Many examples are discussed in the first chapter of Jocelyn Scutt, *Women and the Law: Commentary and Materials* (Law Book Company, Sydney, 1990).

However the claim that the supposedly ungendered "rational individual" is male, has also been made more recently by feminists in a critique of the basic ideals of liberal thought.[43] In Western ideology, the "rational individual" has been *gendered* as masculine: that is, as an idea it is not, and never has been, gender-neutral, but is rather culturally associated with masculinity. This has a couple of consequences which are important in the critique of liberal feminism, and which I will elaborate on shortly. They are, briefly, that liberal feminism ultimately accepts *male* and not neutral standards and values as appropriate goals for women, and secondly, that it is necessary to combat not only empirical and formal discrimination in order for women to attain full status as individuals, but much more crucially, the cultural association of certain values with men.

The main aim of liberal feminism in its formative stages was to demonstrate that women, like men, possess or can develop the "higher" capacities of human nature.[44] Mary Wollstonecraft put forward such a view in the late 18th century, at a time of revolutionary political change in France and North America. She argued that any differences in the natures of men and women were due not to natural capacity, but to the differences in the social and educational environments of the sexes. Wollstonecraft's *Vindication of the Rights of Women* is an angry polemic against the state to which women had been reduced by their caged existences and lack of educational opportunities. Wollstonecraft did not question the basic liberal system of values, seeing the capacity to reason as the highest human achievement.[45] However, she did call for a fundamental re-organisation of society in order that the relatively novel demands for the rights of man, which were central to the ideology of the French and American revolutions, be also extended to women.[46]

A clear example of the claim by women to men's rights occurred during the French revolution, at around the same time that Wollstonecraft published the *Vindication*. In 1789, the French revolutionaries created a charter of civil rights, the famous *Declaration of the Rights of Man and Citizen*, which proclaimed the liberal ideals of individual liberty, freedom of speech, equality, and the right to own private property. In 1791, Olympe de Gouges published a parallel charter, the *Declaration of the Rights of Woman and Citizen*. The main purpose of *Rights of Woman* is

---

43   The classic work on this is Genevieve Lloyd, *The Man of Reason: "Male" and "Female" in Western Philosophy* (2nd ed, Routledge, London, 1993).

44   Mary Wollstonecraft, *Vindication of the Rights of Women* (2nd ed, Penguin, Harmondsworth, 1978). Two other very important texts in early liberal feminism which I will not discuss here, are Harriet Taylor Mill, *Enfranchisement of Women*, and John Stuart Mill, *The Subjection of Women* which have been published together (Virago, London, 1983).

45   See eg, Wollstonecraft, *Vindication of the Rights of Woman*, p 103.

46   Kate Millet, who was influential in the rise of radical feminism, said of Wollstonecraft's *Vindication*, that it was, "the first document asserting the full humanity of women and insisting upon its recognition": *Sexual Politics*, p 65.

to assert the equality of public rights between men and women. It is clear that de Gouges considers that women's inferior position is due not to nature but to the oppression of women by men. Article Two of *Rights of Man* declares the inalienable rights to be "liberty, security and resistance to oppression". The equivalent article in *Rights of Woman* adds one word, so the rights become "liberty, security, and *especially* resistance to oppression".[47] It is freedom from oppression which is foremost for women, and if men can declare their freedom from the tyranny of a class system, so women can declare their freedom from the tyranny of men, a claim which is as relevant after the revolution as before it. So, Article Four of *Rights of Woman* explains that "the exercise of women's natural rights is limited only by the perpetual tyranny with which man opposes her; these limits must be changed according to the laws of nature and reason".[48] Similarly, Article 6 of the *Rights of Man* declares that

> **VI.** The law is the expression of the general will; all citizens must participate in its expression personally or through their representatives; it should be the same for all, whether it protects or punishes. All citizens being equal in its eyes are equally admissible to all public honours, positions, and employments, according to their capacities and with no distinctions other than those of their virtues and talents.

The equivalent section in Olympe de Gouges' Rights of Woman proclaims equal status for women in public affairs:

> **6.** The law should be the expression of the general will; all female and male citizens must participate in its expression personally or through their representatives. It should be the same for all; female and male citizens, being equal in the eyes of the law, should be equally admissible to all public honours, positions, and employments, according to their capacities and with no distinctions other than those of their virtues and talents.

Needless to say, this declaration was not adopted by the revolutionary National Assembly. As Elizabeth Kingdom points out, its failure testifies to the "conservative nature" of the revolutionary politics being practised at the time.[49] Kingdom is suggesting that it was, after all, men who were largely in control of the revolution and that although their stated goal was to reform the inequities of class in French society, they were not particularly interested in giving up the privileges which they themselves enjoyed *as men*. So while they based their own declaration on the proposition, stated in the preamble of their charter, that public misfortune and corruption of governments were the result of neglect of the rights of *men*, they would not adopt the more radical statement,

---

47   See the comments made by Elizabeth Kingdom on the word in "Gendering Rights" in Arnaud and Kingdom (eds), *Women's Rights and the Rights of Man* (Aberdeen University Press, Aberdeen, 1990).

48   From Elizabeth Kingdom, *What's Wrong With Rights? Problems for Feminist Politics of Law* (Edinburgh University Press, Edinburgh, 1990), pp 143-147.

49   Kingdom, *What's Wrong With Rights?*, p 103.

contained in the preamble to the *Rights of Women*, that the basic cause of public misfortune was the oppression of *women*. Claiming rights for all men was a way of upsetting the established aristocratic order, while claiming rights for women may well have been seen as subverting order (as men knew it) altogether. As Carol Pateman argues, the phrase "liberty, equality, and fraternity" really signifies the freedom *of men*, equality between classes *of men*, and the brotherhood *of men*.[50] For Pateman, the liberal social contract is in reality a sexual contract, ensuring the rights of men and the sexual subordination of women. It is also, according to Charles Mills, a racial contract in which whites gained identity and political and economic superiority by the oppression of non-whites.[51]

It should be pointed out that resistance to feminist claims is a difficulty which many women associated with revolutionary movements have experienced. The idea is that even if women are oppressed under an existing regime, everything will be alright after the revolution: the oppression of women is still seen, even by many "progressive" thinkers and activists, as secondary to capitalist and military oppression. In fact, part of the impetus behind the second wave of feminism which developed in the 1960s was a concern about the marginalisation of women in the peace movement which grew in conjunction with anti-Vietnam war activism and an increasing awareness of the nuclear threat. This point is made very clearly by Robin Morgan in her introduction to *Sisterhood is Powerful*:[52]

> Every time drastic change has shaken the established social order, some drive for women's rights has surfaced — only to be put down, or told to "wait until after", after the revolution or whatever else concerned the men. ... Thinking we were involved in the struggle to build a new society, it was a slowly dawning and depressing realization that we were doing the same work and playing the same roles *in* the Movement as out of it: typing the speeches that men delivered, making coffee but not policy, being accessories to the men whose politics would supposedly replace the Old Order. But whose New Order? Not ours certainly.

The common perception of feminists has been that in many ways male radical political movements have reproduced conservative hierarchies, especially in relation to women.[53] One consequence has been the

---

50 Carole Pateman, *The Sexual Contract* (Polity Press, Cambridge, 1988), Ch 4.

51 Charles W Mills, *The Racial Contract* (Cornell University Press, Ithaca NY, 1997).

52 Robin Morgan (ed), *Sisterhood is Powerful: An Anthology of Writings from the Women's Liberation Movement* (Vintage Books, New York, 1970), p xx. See also Marge Piercy, "The Grand Coolie Damn" in the same anthology, and Andrea Dworkin, *Right-Wing Women: The Politics of Domesticated Females* (The Women's Press, London, 1983), pp 95-97.

53 In *Does Khaki Become You? The Militarization of Women's Lives* (Pluto Press, London, 1983), Cynthia Enloe examines the relation of women to the military, pointing out that military tactics have often been adopted by male anti-militarists. Women's peace groups in contrast have aimed at developing a practice of activism which challenges the concept of militarism without reproducing it.

development of a specifically women's peace movement, manifested in the 1980s at the women's camp at the United States' cruise missile base at Greenham Common in England.[54] A parallel development occurred in the "radical" arm of the legal academy: in response to feminist dissatisfaction with the agenda of the critical legal studies movement, an alternative conference was held in the mid-1980s. Menkel-Meadow comments that "some male critical theorists ... felt the conference had been a 'diversion' from the critical legal studies agenda, and that now that the women had been given a chance to 'do their own thing', we should return to 'critical' work".[55] Women working in the anti-globalisation movement of the present era have reported similar exclusions, and it is also clear that transitional societies are often more concerned with peace-building than gender justice. What this sort of response from male "radicals" and reformers has indicated to many feminists is that ideals formulated as a reaction to a dominant politics may not respond adequately to the ways in which women's oppression is manifested.

The demand for rights is just one example of the sort of claim made by "liberal" feminists. I am calling Wollstonecraft and de Gouges "liberal" because their claims were based on liberal values of humanity, equality, and rights. Yet they are also both good examples of feminists who, to use Alison Jaggar's phrase, were "on the progressive edge of liberal thought".[56] For their time, their arguments were definitely radical in relation to male activists. Both women identified oppression on the basis of sex as the fundamental oppression in society: their arguments that women be given an equality measured according to the position of men must be regarded in that light and in the light of the political context of the times.

Liberal feminism challenges the male dominance of the public sphere, attempting to remove the legal and social impediments to women exercising the same rights, and enjoying the same opportunities, as men. The argument is that women's subordination is not a rational element of the liberal state, and the goal is basically equality to pursue the aspirations of white, middle-class, male individuals. On the formal level, in some areas the battle has been won — legally women *can* own property, occupy public positions, and be educated to the same extent

---

54   Generally on this topic see Adrienne Harris and Ynestra King (eds), *Rocking the Ship of State: Toward a Feminist Peace Politics* (Westview Press, Boulder, 1989); Barbara Harford and Sarah Hopkins (eds), *Greenham Common: Women at the Wire* (The Women's Press, London, 1984); Jill Liddington, *The Long Road to Greenham: Feminism and Anti-Militarism in Britain since 1820* (Virago, London, 1989); Victoria Davion, "Pacifism and Care" (1990) 5 *Hypatia* 90.

55   Carrie Menkel-Meadow, "Feminist Legal Theory, Critical Legal Studies, and Legal Education or 'The Fem-Crits Go to Law School'" (1988) 38 *Journal of Legal Education* 61 at 65; see also Robin West, "Deconstructing the CLS-Fem Split" (1986) 2 *Wisconsin Women's Law Journal* 85.

56   Jaggar, *Feminist Politics and Human Nature*, p 28.

as men, even though some things remain part of the most sacred domains of male right — such as combat roles in the defence forces, the central positions in many religions, and (*de facto*) the status of sporting hero. Men are very reluctant to give up their status as the ultimate guardians of society and religious truth. But the fact that women still *do not* own property, occupy public positions or wield social influence to the same extent as men indicates that the struggle for formal legal rights was only the beginning — and only the easy part at that, since it was in the beginning fairly clear what needed doing. Liberal feminism therefore continues its campaign to have areas of the public domain opened up to women.

A short critique of liberal feminism

[640]   Liberal feminism accepts the fundamental premises of liberal political theory. It accepts that people are or should aim to be rational, independent, and free individuals. It generally implies that the highest ambition for any person, male or female, is the attainment of a public role in life — to become a legal practitioner, hold public office, be elected to parliament, engage generally in public affairs. The most fundamental critique of liberal feminism then is that it is simply telling women that they should aspire to those characteristics which liberalism has always held out as the proper goals of men — to be rational, autonomous, individualistic.[57] While accepting that there is a division between the values conventionally associated with women and those associated with men, rather than criticising or attempting to alter this value system, liberal feminism is simply trying to invest women with the opportunities and values of men, trying to alter the character of law and other public institutions as a "male monopoly".[58] What liberal feminism does not confront is the liberal world-view itself, and the way society is accordingly organised.

Although, as I have said, the law reform inspired by liberal feminism has been far-reaching, it has certainly not resulted in substantive equality, nor a major revision of the social value-system. In the first place, concentrating attention on the potential public role of women does not alleviate the problems in areas where women are most vulnerable — in the home and in everyday contacts with men.

One of the most important critiques of liberal feminism has concentrated on the public/private distinction which is central to liberal thought. There are several elements of this critique which I will only

---

57   For an analysis of the ongoing relationship between liberal thought and feminism in political philosophy see Pauline Johnson, "Feminism and Liberalism" (1991) 14 *Australian Feminist Studies* 57. For some recent works defending liberal feminism see Gal Gerson, "Liberal Feminism: Individuality and Oppositions in Wollstonecraft and Mill" (2002) 50 *Political Studies* 794; Ruth Groenhout, "Essentialist Challenges to Liberal Feminism" (2002) 28 *Social Theory and Practice* 51.

58   See Naffine, *Law and the Sexes: Explorations in Feminist Jurisprudence* , pp 3-6.

mention here.[59] First, it reinforces the gendered division of labour and fails to value the work traditionally done by women. Secondly, it encourages the repetition in private of male dominance in public through the liberal unwillingness to interfere in private affairs. The traditional reluctance of the police to hear and respond to complaints of domestic violence is only the most clear example of this. Liberal thought has been blind to harms perpetrated in private (the "private" having been constructed as precisely that place where harm does not happen), and the victims of these harms are typically women and children. Feminist critiques of liberal thought have pointed out that the family is one of the central spheres of women's oppression.[60] Thirdly, it has been argued that that the so-called "private" sphere is as regulated as the "public": the boundaries of the private are not natural, but created by the limits of legal interference.[61] In many instances, the distinction may be quite impossible to draw: can it be said that the consumption of pornography is ever private when it is based on the portrayal of women as a group as mere flesh available for abuse?[62] The point is fundamentally that gendered meanings cross the boundary between public and private, and it is important for feminism to take account of this fact. And finally, despite its emphasis upon tolerance of difference, liberal thought can often seem insensitive to cultural difference: assuming that the good life is to be obtained by treating everyone as rational individuals, for instance, when this is not a universally-shared world view.

A further important point to be made about liberalism is that the issues faced by feminism do not just turn on the fact that women have been denied civil rights and real opportunities to determine our own lives. The more fundamental point is that there is a dominant value-system within which all social relations are situated. Arguing that the legal system itself is gendered does not just mean that it is on the whole men who run it. The legal system stands for certain values — rationality, individualism, adversarial dispute resolution, civic personality, independence — which have been associated with men. The system

---

59 Two excellent works on this topic are Margaret Thornton, "Feminism and the Contradictions of Law Reform" (1991) 19 *International Journal of the Sociology of Law* 453 and Lacey, *Unspeakable Subjects: Feminist Essays in Legal and Social Theory*, Ch 3; see also Margaret Thornton, "Feminist Jurisprudence: Illusion or Reality" (1986) 3 *Australian Journal of Law and Society* 5; Nadine Taub and Elizabeth Schneider, "Women's Subordination and the Role of Law" in Kairys (ed), *The Politics of Law: A Progressive Critique* (Pantheon Books, New York, 1990); Alan Freeman and Elizabeth Mensch, "The Public-Private Distinction in American Law and Life" (1987) 36 *Buffalo Law Review* 237.

60 MacKinnon, *Toward a Feminist Theory of the State* (Harvard University Press, Cambridge Mass, 1989), Part I, "Feminism and Marxism"; Andrea Dworkin, "Woman-Hating Right and Left" in Leidholt and Raymond (eds), *The Sexual Liberals and the Attack on Feminism* (Pergamon Press, New York, 1990).

61 O'Donovan, *Sexual Divisions in Law*, Ch 1; Mensch and Freeman "The Public-Private Distinction in American Law and Life".

62 See Dworkin, "Woman-Hating Right and Left", p 32.

therefore "speaks" to men (and in particular privileged men), while it more often may alienate and exclude women. For instance, assuming that victims of domestic violence are partly to blame because they could simply have left a violent relationship is a clear application to women of masculine standards of independence, economic power, and self-determination. Ironically in some instances, such as cases of rape, women are also considered partly to blame if they *do* follow the masculine norms of independence such as walking alone on the street at night. So a further problem with liberal feminism is that it doesn't take account of the fact that the law uncritically reflects gendered social standards.

Moreover, and this point seems obvious, there are more than simply formal impediments to equality. Part of the problem is with the very notion of equality, since it is clear that measuring such a thing is very difficult indeed, if not impossible. Merely enshrining a principle of equality in the law will not solve the much more profound inequalities entrenched in cultural perceptions, economic status, and biological difference. Thus the idea of equality has been very closely scrutinised: if women are expected to be like men in order to be treated equally, if women will only be treated equally insofar as we *are* like men, equality itself can seem to be a repressive ideal.[63] An "equality" defined according to male standards will only benefit women who can or do conform to that standard.[64] More importantly, we do not have any meaningful understanding of equality if men are always the referent. And obviously we do not have equality if it is men who have the power to determine what the measurement of equality is to be (that is, themselves). It has also been argued that some positive improvement in the legal relationships of people could be achieved by integrating into it some of the values culturally associated with women. One example of this sort of argument applied to the law of torts is Leslie Bender's proposal that the standard of the reasonable person/man be replaced with a more "feminine" standard which emphasises the need to show care and concern for others.[65]

Although these criticisms of liberal feminism are well-founded, and raise real questions about what feminists consider to be important in social and legal reform, they certainly do not invalidate the liberal

63   See the comments made by Catharine MacKinnon in Ellen DuBois et al, "Feminist Discourse, Moral Values, and the Law — a Conversation" (1985) 34 *Buffalo Law Review* 11 at 23.

64   Although the debate about equality has been central to much legal feminism, I do not wish to examine it in any detail here. An excellent summary of the various positions appears in Graycar and Morgan, *The Hidden Gender of Law*, pp 44-55.

65   Leslie Bender, "A Lawyer's Primer on Feminist Theory and Tort" (1988) 38 *Journal of Legal Education* 3 at 28-37. See the brief commentary on Gilligan below at [685], and see generally Carol Gilligan, *In a Different Voice: Psychological Theory and Women's Development* (Harvard University Press, Cambridge Mass, 1982); Mary Jeanne Larrabee (ed), *An Ethic of Care: Feminist and Interdisciplinary Perspectives* (Routledge, New York, 1993).

feminist approach.[66] As I have said, all feminisms are part of an ongoing process of restructuring: even where an argument does involve what might be seen as a problematic characterisation of women's position in society (which is probably the case with most feminist theories), the continuing process of questioning and discussion of conflicting views provides the general environment in which positive reforms can be made and their effects evaluated. Liberal feminism may not in itself be the whole answer, but it is nevertheless important in the sense that it continues the struggle for women to be represented in society: even gaining some degree of public representation in itself poses a challenge to the association of women with the private sphere.

It is probably the case that the liberal feminist claim for equal rights and a strengthened individualism has been a necessary starting point: no matter how much those of us in privileged positions disparage the liberal concepts of rational individualism and abstract rights, for people who culturally or politically have little ability to exercise their individual autonomy or rights they may be very significant.[67] As we saw in Chapter 5, one of the fundamental objections to the CLS critique of the liberal concept of rights has come from minority scholars pointing out that rights are a necessary focus for racial justice, as well as a concrete way of curbing abuses of power.[68] As Catharine MacKinnon points out about the "upper-class white men [who] repudiate rights as intrinsically liberal and individualistic and useless and alienating" — "they have them in fact even as they purport to relinquish them in theory".[69] On the other hand, it is just as clear that although equal "rights" have been formally enshrined in the law, it is generally those who are already socially or economically privileged in some way who are able to take the most advantage of them. It is white middle-class women who have most benefited from the liberal version of women's liberation. Generally speaking, "rights" can be best utilised and defended by those with means: a right to free speech is far more useful to media owners than it is to most workers, much less to those who are disenfranchised by their social position or silenced by the weight of liberal ideology. I can't do as much with my freedom of speech as a

---

66 Johnson, "Feminism and Liberalism"; Wendell, "A (Qualified) Defense of Liberal Feminism".

67 See the comments made by Carol Smart in *Feminism and the Power of Law* (Routledge, London, 1989), p 139. See also Martha Nussbaum, "The Feminist Critique of Liberalism" in Martha C Nussbaum, *Sex and Social Justice* (Oxford University Press, New York, 2000); Anne Phillips, "Feminism and Liberalism Revisited: Has Martha Nussbaum Got It Right?" (2001) 8 *Constellations* 249.

68 Patricia Williams, "Alchemical Notes: Reconstructing Ideals from Deconstructing Rights" (1987) 22 *Harvard Civil Rights — Civil Liberties Law Review* 401; Richard Delgado "The Ethereal Scholar: Does Critical Legal Studies Have What Minorities Want?" (1987) 22 *Harvard Civil Rights — Civil Liberties Law Review* 301.

69 MacKinnon, *Toward a Feminist Theory of the State*, p xiv. Cf Wendy Brown, "Suffering Rights as Paradoxes" (2000) 7 *Constellations* 230.

media owner (although as an academic I have more opportunities to be heard than many). So it is important to realise that, although rights might originally have been formed as individual rights, they are in the modern world often exercised within the framework of corporate, political, or economic power. "Rights" cannot be separated from the political, cultural, and economic context in which they are set.

Radical feminism

[645] "Radical" means "going to the root or origin: fundamental".[70] In this context "origin" means not only first in time, but more importantly, the source from which a thing is derived. "Radical feminism" is feminism which sees oppression on the basis of sex as the fundamental or original oppression.[71] Rather than assuming that existing social structures and values simply need to be reformed to cater for women, it has located the basis of subordination within those structures, and aimed at a much more fundamental transformation in the balance of power.

I mentioned in the section on liberal feminism that one of the problems which has faced women associated with so-called "radical" political movements has been the sexism inherent in male-dominated institutions, a difficulty which "progressive" organisations have failed to rectify. Politically, modern radical feminism was partly inspired by the failure of the activist organisations of the 1960s and 1970s to take any serious notice of women, and of demands for sexual equality. In the face of arguments that equality could wait until the more important issues were resolved, early radical feminism took oppression on the grounds of sex as *the* fundamental oppression,[72] and attempted to elaborate the nature and dimensions of the sex hierarchy. As a strategic move this was probably necessary at the time to counter claims that sex oppression was secondary or non-existent. Beyond this point though (which has not remained fixed) the label "radical feminism" has encompassed an extraordinarily diverse range of views which have, however, often been caricatured as a unitary thesis for the purposes of criticism.[73] I am going to focus on the early work of one radical feminist, Catharine MacKinnon, who has been extremely influential in

---

70 This is the primary *Macquarie Dictionary* definition.

71 Catharine MacKinnon says "the molding, direction, and expression of sexuality organises society into two sexes — women and men — which division underlies the totality of social relations": "Feminism, Marxism, Method, and the State: An Agenda for Theory" (1983) 7 *Signs* 515 at 516.

72 See Morgan (ed), *Sisterhood is Powerful: An Anthology of Writings from the Women's Liberation Movement*; Shulamith Firestone, *The Dialectic of Sex* (The Women's Press, London, 1979).

73 I do not think that this tendency is confined to attacks on radical feminism: postmodernism, and postmodern feminism, have also suffered from being characterised in overly simplistic ways. One of the connections between radical feminism and postmodernism is that both approaches require the reader to question some of her fundamental assumptions about the way that the world is "naturally" ordered.

feminist legal theory. MacKinnon's influence waned in the 1990s, and her work was critiqued on a number of grounds; however the insight she provided in the formative stages of feminist legal theory cannot be disputed. I focus on the early work here for two simple reasons: first, *Feminism Unmodified* and *Toward a Feminist Theory of the State* are clearly the most influential and definitive of MacKinnon's works, and secondly, the later works, while clearly of significance within the US context, have made less of an impact elsewhere.[74]

Catharine MacKinnon and unmodified feminism

[650] As a radical feminist, Catharine MacKinnon has emphasised the necessity of centralising women's experiences and interpretations of the world, and challenged masculinist ideology in a variety of ways. Like earlier radical feminists, MacKinnon perceived the failure of Marxist theory to take account of gender oppression as a clear indication that feminism needed to start from a basis other than that of a male-centred political theory. I do not wish to explain MacKinnon's views in any detail here: the best introduction to them is *Feminism Unmodified*.[75] What I do want to indicate is that despite many adverse critiques of MacKinnon's work, it is necessary to approach it in a careful and considered way. Her views are not as simplistic as they are sometimes represented to be (though nor, as we will see in the section on post-modernism, are the views of others quite as simple as MacKinnon sometimes characterises them). This is not to say that I do not see any problems with her ideas, just that I think that we need to be cautious about fixing them down too quickly. In the following extract, MacKinnon makes a number of important assertions about feminism generally, and radical feminism in particular.

Catharine MacKinnon

"Feminism, Marxism, Method, and the State: Toward Feminist Jurisprudence"[76]

[655] Feminism does not begin with an unpremised audience because there is no such audience. Its project is to uncover and claim as valid the experience of women, the major content of which is the devalidation of women's experience.

This defines our task not only because male dominance is perhaps the most pervasive and tenacious system of power in history, but because it is

---

74   Though see MacKinnon, *Only Words* (Harvard University Press, Cambridge Mass, 1993); Judith Butler, *Excitable Speech: A Politics of the Performative* (Routledge, New York, 1997).

75   See also "Feminism, Marxism, Method, and the State: An Agenda for Theory"; "Feminism, Marxism, Method and the State: Toward Feminist Jurisprudence" (1983) 8 *Signs* 635; cf Mary Heath, "Catharine MacKinnon: Toward a Feminist Theory of the State?" (1997) 9 *Australian Feminist Law Journal* 45.

76   MacKinnon, "Feminism, Marxism, Method and the State: Toward Feminist Jurisprudence", pp 638-640.

metaphysically near perfect. Its point of view is the standard for point-of-viewlessness, its particularity the meaning of universality. Its force is exercised as consent, its authority as participation, its supremacy as the paradigm of order, its control as the definition of legitimacy. Feminism claims the voice of women's silence, the sexuality of our eroticized desexualization, the fullness of "lack", the centrality of our marginality and exclusion, the public nature of privacy, the presence of our absence. This approach is more complex than transgression, more transformative than transvaluation, deeper than mirror-imaged resistance, more affirmative than the negation of our negativity. It is neither materialist nor idealist; it is feminist ... Women's situation offers no outside to stand on or gaze at, no inside to escape to, too much urgency to wait, no place else to go, and nothing to use but the twisted tools that have been shoved down our throats. If feminism is revolutionary, this is why.

Feminism has been widely thought to contain tendencies of liberal feminism, radical feminism, and socialist feminism. But just as socialist feminism has often amounted to marxism applied to women, liberal feminism has often amounted to liberalism applied to women. Radical feminism — after this, feminism unmodified — is methodologically post-marxist ... Where liberal feminism sees sexism primarily as an illusion or myth to be dispelled, an inaccuracy to be corrected, true feminism sees the male point of view as fundamental to the male power to create the world in its own image, the image of its desires, not just as its delusory end product. Feminism distinctively as such comprehends that what counts as truth is produced in the interest of those with power to shape reality, and that this process is as pervasive as it is necessary as it is changeable. Unlike the scientific strain in marxism or the Kantian imperative in liberalism, which in this context share most salient features, feminism neither claims universality nor, failing that, reduces to relativity. It does not seek a generality that subsumes its particulars or an abstract theory or a science of sexism. It rejects the approach of control over nature (including us) analogized to control over society (also including us) which has grounded the "science of society" project as the paradigm for political knowledge since (at least) Descartes. Both liberalism and marxism have been subversive on women's behalf. Neither is enough.

[660]   MacKinnon says that feminism is the "voice of women's silence" and "the centrality of our marginality". Feminism is thought which tries to *start* with the voices of women. Radical feminism is feminism "unmodified" because it is not a male-authored theory or perspective simply applied to women. MacKinnon has been criticised for assuming that women's experience is pure in some sense, and that all women share the same experience, as though it is *experience* which is "unmodified" and which is essentially *women's* experience.[77] Is she saying this? As I read the passage, MacKinnon recognises that reality is shaped by ideology, and that what women "see" is determined by the "truth" constructed by male power. The starting point seems to be not an authentic women's experience, but rather whatever it is that we,

---

77   Rothfield, "Alternative Epistemologies, Politics and Feminism".

as women, can use. (I do not really like to re-use MacKinnon's phrase, but she does make this clear by saying that feminism has "nothing to use but the twisted tools that have been shoved down our throats".)

The starting point, in other words, is to make audible that which has been silent, and to make central that which has been marginal.[78] Her feminism does not claim to be universal: it does not seek an "abstract theory" or a "science of sexism". But it does seek to uncover the ways in which male dominance defines society, and to legitimate the presently illegitimate perceptions of women. Having said that, it is true that MacKinnon has also been criticised for giving a specific *content* to women's voices, a content which assumes that the fundamental issues of oppression will be the same for non-white women, for lesbians, and for other non-privileged women.[79]

I should point out that, in my view, the word "unmodified" remains a problem: as MacKinnon herself has argued, the situation of women is not unmodified (there is no such thing as an unmodified experience), so a *feminism* based on women's experience cannot really be unmodified either.[80] While feminism may be unmodified in the rather narrow sense of not being answerable to a pre-existing political theory, it can hardly escape the conditions of its own existence. Feminism cannot escape the fact that there is a pre-existing, and continually changing, set of social and philosophical assumptions which create our world, and shape us as sexed individuals. Nor can feminism (any longer) ignore the fact that being a woman is not a separate part of our identities, which include also being white, or Indigenous, or lesbian, or heterosexual, and any number of other things.

Part of the problem may be that MacKinnon does at times appear to suggest that there is an essential women's experience, the experience of being victimised, which is the basis of feminist thinking. Such a suggestion, despite its polemical importance, does lay itself open to the criticism that the world thereby simply divides into two: those with power and those without, male and female, a division which overlooks the complexities of power, ideology, and other fundamental divisions in social organisation, such as those based on race, class, and sexuality. MacKinnon has in particular been criticised for neglecting the difference that racial oppression makes to many women.[81] In fact, I would argue that MacKinnon is not always true to her feminist theory:

---

78 One way of doing this which MacKinnon has advocated very strongly is to give women a legal cause of action against pornographers.

79 See especially Harris, "Race and Essentialism in Feminist Legal Theory".

80 See Cornell, *Beyond Accommodation: Ethical Feminism, Deconstruction and the Law*, Ch 3 "Feminism Always Modified: The Affirmation of Feminine Difference Rethought".

81 See Angela Harris, "Categorical Discourse and Dominance Theory" (1989) 5 *Berkeley Women's Law Journal* 181 and "Race and Essentialism in Feminist Legal Theory"; Larissa Behrendt, "Black Women and the Feminist Movement: Implications for Aboriginal Women in Rights Discourse" (1993) 1 *Australian Feminist Law Journal* 27.

any attempt to minimise the complexity of identity, and reduce it to essential features such as being a woman above all else, neglects one of the most important facets of her feminist politics, listening to the actual voices of women (and not only to academic theorists). As Angela Harris says, "feminist essentialism represents not just an insult to black women, but a broken promise — the promise to listen to women's stories, the promise of feminist method".[82]

As I explained above, the primary project of liberal feminism has been to challenge male domination by demonstrating that there are no fundamental differences between the sexes which ought to make a difference to who gets which social roles. There is nothing in a woman's constitution which makes her unfit to be a member of Parliament. Sex is irrelevant. MacKinnon says something quite different, which is that sex and sexuality are fundamental. It is not that sex is fundamental biologically, but rather that it is fundamental to the structure of male dominance: it *is* the social structure of male dominance.

Before explaining this any further I think it should be pointed out that the liberal argument and MacKinnon's may not in fact be directly opposed. The liberal argument is that, apart from some obvious biologically determined differences, women and men are potentially the same — in intelligence, rationality, parenting capabilities, and so on. MacKinnon's argument bypasses this question of what the pre-given characteristics of the sexes are, for an analysis of what the socially constituted characteristics are, and whose interests they serve. The liberal view takes the individual and individual characteristics as given, and current society as a distortion of the principles of individualism. MacKinnon takes the structural nature of dominance as the central feminist concern. Liberal feminism sees women's true nature as being deformed and weakened by male domination, while MacKinnon deals directly with the way that women are created socially and with the social structure itself as reflecting male, not universal characteristics. Thus liberal feminism is assuming that there is an authentic character in women which must be recovered, so that we can participate in the good society, while MacKinnon is saying that the only basic thing is sex subordination, and that we have to work to eliminate it.

Central to MacKinnon's analysis of male dominance is the view that sex is not a question of sameness or difference. The point is not whether women and men are essentially the same as each other or essentially different. According to MacKinnon sex is a hierarchy formed by a power differential. Men have power and women do not: more specifically, men have power over women, and sex is simply the social meaning of this hierarchy. In other words, the sex difference is meaningful socially only because of the difference in power between men and women. As MacKinnon puts it:[83]

---

82   Harris, "Race and Essentialism in Feminist Legal Theory", p 601.

83   MacKinnon, *Feminism Unmodified: Discourses on Life and Law*, p 51.

Gender here is a matter of dominance, not difference. Feminists have noticed that women and men are equally different but not equally powerful. Explaining the subordination of women to men, a political condition, has nothing to do with difference in any fundamental sense. Consequentially, it has a lot to do with difference, because the ideology of difference has been so central in its enforcement. Another way to say that is, there would be no such thing as what we know as the sex difference — much less would it be the social issue it is or have the social meaning it has — were it not for male dominance. Sometimes people ask me, "Does that mean you think there's no difference between women and men?" The only way I know how to answer that is: of course there is; the difference is that men have power and women do not. I mean simply that men are not socially supreme and women subordinate by nature; the fact that socially they are, constructs the sex difference as we know it.

The origin of gender is not difference between women and men. The origin of gender, and all of the ways in which it is manifested, is the power which men have over women. The division, in other words, is co-extensive with the hierarchy, and integral to the way society is structured.[84] In order to survive, women learn to adopt the position which male power attributes to the feminine. "Feminine" qualities are the product of this power differential, and reinforce it in various ways.

One way in which hierarchy of gender is manifested is in the cultural eroticisation of dominance. The paradigm of heterosexuality in Western culture assumes a strong dominating man, and a weak submissive woman. Women's vulnerability is a marker of femininity, and thus of sexual attractiveness to men. Conversely, men's potency and power to persuade is a marker of masculinity, and therefore of the patriarchal version of what women want. MacKinnon emphasises that this is the dominant version of sexuality which our culture has produced, and in this sense, sexuality, as socially constructed, is on a continuum with rape. The point as I see it is not that MacKinnon thinks that all sex is rape, but rather that the way our society sets the paradigm of sex, makes it impossible to draw a clear line between sex and rape:[85] the patriarchal version is that women cannot be believed when they say "no", are always there to be persuaded, and are objects to be consumed, not listened to. MacKinnon puts it like this:

---

84 Monique Wittig made the point very clearly when she wrote: "For there is no sex. There is but sex that is oppressed and sex that oppresses. It is oppression that creates sex and not the contrary. The contrary would be to say that the cause (origin) of oppression is to be found in sex itself, in a natural division of the sexes preexisting (or outside of) society": "The Category of Sex" in *The Straight Mind and Other Essays* (Harvester Wheatsheaf, New York, 1992), p 3.

85 MacKinnon, *Feminism Unmodified: Discourses on Life and Law*, Ch 7 "Sex and Violence".

Catharine MacKinnon

Feminism Unmodified[86]

[665]   I do not see sexuality as a transcultural container, as essential, as historically unchanging, or as Eros. I define sexuality as whatever a given society eroticizes. That is, sexual is whatever sexual means in a given society. Sexuality is what sexuality means. This is a political hermeneutical view. Hermeneutics concerns matters of meaning. If sexuality is seen in this way, it is fundamentally social, fundamentally relational, and it is not a thing — which by the way, does not mean it is not material, in a feminist sense of materiality. Because sexuality arises in relations under male dominance, women are not the principal authors of its meanings. In the society we currently live in, the content I want to claim for sexuality is the gaze that constructs women as objects for male pleasure. I draw on pornography for its form and content, for the gaze that eroticizes the despised, the demeaned, the accessible, the there-to-be-used, the servile, the child-like, the passive, and the animal. That is the content of the sexuality that defines gender in this culture, and visual thingification is its method.

[MacKinnon continues by explaining that the dominant paradigms in our culture are masculine, and that the masculine standard is taken for the universal one.] ...

Consider the example of faking orgasms... Men have anxiety that women fake orgasms. Take women's orgasms as an example of something about which one can have Cartesian doubt. "How do I know" she's satisfied, right? Now consider *why* women fake orgasms, rather than how too bad it is men can't, so that therefore they're unequal to us. I would bet that if we had the power men have, they would *learn*. What I'm saying is, men's power to *make* the world here is their power to make us make the world of their sexual interaction with us the way they want it. They want us to have orgasms; that proves they're virile, potent, effective. We provide them that appearance, whether it's real for us or not. We even get into it. Our reality is, it is far less damaging and dangerous for us to do this, to accept a lifetime of simulated satisfaction, than to hold out for the real thing from them.

[670]   MacKinnon makes it clear in the first part of this passage that her critique of sexuality is limited to the social view of sexuality. It is a critique of a social meaning, of a dominant social paradigm. For her, sexuality is *only* this social meaning.

Angela Harris comments that "MacKinnon's argument is a powerful antidote for the view that sexuality is somehow natural and free, an island in a sea of inequality and domination".[87] What is important about MacKinnon's views of sexuality and of the structure of gender relations generally is that she, like other writers, has taken an existing social myth and shown that it is a construct forming the basis of unequal gender relations.

---

86   MacKinnon, *Feminism Unmodified: Discourses on Life and Law*, pp 53-54. See also MacKinnon *Toward a Feminist Theory of the State*, Ch 7 "Sexuality".

87   Harris, "Categorical Discourse and Dominance Theory", p 192.

However, MacKinnon's views have been strongly criticised by a number of feminists, including Harris, on two grounds.[88] First, MacKinnon has been criticised for reducing something which is really very complex to a singular narrative which essentialises women's experience, that is, which reduces the experiences of women to a fundamental condition, regardless of their race, class, age, or sexuality. I will come back to the question of intersecting oppressions in the next part of this chapter. Secondly, MacKinnon expresses her argument as universally true, which seems to allow no escape for women. If it is really like this, how can we possibly envisage change? If sexuality is *only* this patriarchal story, then women have no sexuality of our own at all, and no position from which the masculine story can be challenged. MacKinnon seems herself to see this as a puzzle when she says that the "issue is not why women acquiesce but why we do anything but".[89] Yet there are other stories around, other ideas about sexuality, and other sexual practices, some of which do subvert the dominant version.[90] Drucilla Cornell has pointed out that "institutionalised meaning", by which she means the predominant meanings of our society, does not account for the whole, and that it is possible to subvert the established myths and metaphors around which female sexuality has been constructed.

Drucilla Cornell

"Sexual Difference, the Feminine, and Equivalency"[91]

[675]   Simply put, I will argue that women's sexuality cannot be reduced to women's "sex", as sex has been currently defined, once we understand

---

88   Carol Smart identifies two problems with MacKinnon's work, those of "determinism" and "essentialism". It is said that MacKinnon falls into the trap of "determinism" because her view of the power of the gender division seems absolute, as though all that women can have is false consciousness. The charge of "essentialism" relates to the totalistic way in which MacKinnon describes women's experience: as though all women experience the same thing in the same way. See Smart, *Feminism and the Power of Law*, pp 76-82. I think the situation is more complex than Smart's critique allows for, but she does encapsulate what are two very common criticisms of MacKinnon's work. See Harris, "Race and Essentialism in Feminist Legal Theory"; "Categorical Discourse and Dominance Theory"; Cornell, *Beyond Accommodation: Ethical Feminism, Deconstruction and theLaw*, Ch 3 "Feminism Always Modified: The Affirmation of Feminine Difference Rethought"; Jeanne Schroeder, "Abduction from the Seraglio: Feminist Methodologies and the Logic of Imagination" (1991) 70 *Texas Law Review* 109 at 193-200.

89   MacKinnon, *Feminism Unmodified: Discourses on Life and Law*, p 61.

90   One of the threatening elements of the idea of lesbian identity, for instance, is the possibility of defining women's identity and sexuality in a way which does not revolve around male identity and sexuality. See Sarah Lucia Hoagland, *Lesbian Ethics: Toward New Value* (Institute of Lesbian Studies, Palo Alto, 1988), pp 4-5.

91   Cornell, "Sexual Difference, the Feminine, and Equivalency: A Critique of MacKinnon's *Toward a Feminist Theory of the State*" (1991) 100 *Yale Law Journal* 2247 at 2250; see also Harris, "Categorical Discourse and Dominance Theory"; Susan Williams, "Feminism's Search for the Feminine: Essentialism, Utopianism, and Community" (1990) 75 *Cornell Law Review* 700. Cornell's own approach to feminist legal theory provides an original alternative to many of the approaches considered here. See, for instance, Cornell, *The Imaginary Domain* (Routledge, New York, 1995); *At the Heart of Freedom: Feminism, Sex, and Equality* (Princeton University Press, New Jersey, 1998).

> both the limit to institutionalized meaning and the possibility of re-metaphorization which inheres in the rule of metaphor. MacKinnon's understanding of feminine sexuality accepts what Irigaray has called the "old dream of symmetry". Irigaray uses the concept of symmetry to explain the masculine fantasy that our sexuality is symmetrical to that of men. In other words, what men fantasize women want is what they want us to want. In fact, women's sexuality is irreducible to the fantasy that we are only "fuckees". MacKinnon's reduction of feminine sexuality to being a "fuckee" endorses this fantasy as "truth" and thereby promotes the prohibition against the exploration of women's sexuality and "sex" as we live it and not as men fantasize about it.
>
> Men, defined by MacKinnon as sexual beings, may imagine that what they think women want, what they want women to desire, *is* what women desire. However feminine writing on feminine sexuality has recognized the "old dream of symmetry" as just that: a dream and, more specifically, a masculine dream. I want to emphasize the political and personal signif- icance for women of challenging MacKinnon's view of feminine sexuality.

[680] Cornell is arguing that MacKinnon accepts the masculine version of sex, and of women as "fuckees", as the only manifestation of female sexuality. Personally, I do not think that MacKinnon has such a simplistic view of things, but I *do* think that she has not been as unambiguous as she could have been on this matter. In any case, the issues are fairly straightforward, at least at a basic level. One clear way of illustrating that women's sexuality is not simply the sexuality ascribed to women through the dominant order is to reconsider the suggestive example which MacKinnon has herself used to illustrate the power of the masculine version of sex. Women fake orgasms. It is true, as MacKinnon points out, that on one level this is a reinforcement of the male version of sex, and indicative of the male power to determine reality. But this is not all — women are *faking and know it*. The "reality" laid down by the male view is not the woman's reality — it is not *our* sexuality which is being faked, but the male/universal version of sex. What this pretended sexual satisfaction demonstrates is that there are several "realities" here, not one. Men too are left with their "Cartesian doubt": they can never be sure that their version is the right one. Where does this leave heterosexual sex, if not in desperate need of reconstruction?

Thus, MacKinnon's interpretation of faked orgasms highlights the distance between a dominant masculine reality, and seeing things from women's points of view. On the one hand, the masculine view of sex *is* reflected in this practice: faked orgasms reproduce the masculine version of sex. On the other hand, that is not the only level of interpre- tation. It is important as well to see it from a woman's point of view. As I indicated at the beginning of this section, MacKinnon insists that the first thing for feminism is to make central the marginalised voices of women. To see from women's points of view is to subvert the dominant way of seeing the world. Seeing faked orgasms from women's perspectives makes us realise that there is a distance between what women see and the masculine view of sex. Women's sexuality does not *only* reflect the masculine fantasy. If that were the case we would not see it as faking. The imitation would be the only reality. So, as Cornell says, the "old dream of symmetry" is a dream, a masculine dream, and does not encapsulate women's sexuality.[92] It is important to recognise this distance between women's sexuality (whatever form it takes) and the masculine construction of it: this contradiction opens up a space which allows the feminist project to continue.

Here as elsewhere, it is simplistic to argue that MacKinnon characterises all women's consciousness as false consciousness imposed by patriarchal ideology: in fact MacKinnon's work does recognise the importance of developing our understanding of the world through the method of "consciousness raising", which is based on the necessity of understanding the nature of women's oppression, and challenging patriarchal truths.[93] It may be that the problems which have been identified with MacKinnon's arguments stem in part from the polemical style in which they are framed, a style which tends to reduce complexity, and present as a total interpretation something which really only describes one (very powerful) dimension of women's existence.

The distance between the patriarchal version of what women are and the lives of women is not always so easy to perceive. How can we disentangle our selves from the social environment which has made us what we are? In most instances it is not a question of comparing our own version of the world with what a patriarchal story tells us, because, as MacKinnon argues, we live the myth. It has shaped our lives. We reflect patriarchal stories about the world in all sorts of ways (not just during sex), and very often we do not see ourselves as faking, even though we are living in representations of the world made by men. Indeed we are not faking since there is no other reality behind the multilayered contexts which constitute our existences: to some extent patriarchal ideology has shaped our lives and we cannot simply step outside it. That does not mean, however, that we cannot develop a reflective and critical attitude to our lives, and perhaps envisage a different way of being. And it does not mean that there is nothing authentic about our lives and definitions. In fact it is important to recognise that each woman occupies a different position in a network of intersecting social systems, and that there is no formula for reconstruction: the response of each will differ according to her circumstances. To summarise, I think that one of the most important things about the work of MacKinnon is that it raises the questions of how we become what we are, how this fits into the patriarchal structuring of society, and how we conceptualise transformation.

92   Cornell's exposition and critique of MacKinnon is more fully developed in *Beyond Accommodation: Ethical Feminism, Deconstruction and the Law*, Ch 3 "Feminism Always Modified".

93   See MacKinnon, *Toward a Feminist Theory of the State*, Ch 5 "Consciousness Raising"; Harris, "Categorical Discourse and Dominance Theory", pp 183-186.

Women's voices, women's law

[685] Much of MacKinnon's work theorises male dominance in the law, and represents an effort to identify and eliminate the effects of this domination. In this sense, it is conducted, as Irene Watson says, on "a patriarchal horizon"[94], in that it takes as its point of departure a patriarchal legal system rather than a positive construct of a non-patriarchal legal system. Indeed, MacKinnon's point is that we do not, at this stage, understand what a non-patriarchal legal system would look like. In contrast to MacKinnon, some feminists have argued that the differences between the sexes can and should be reflected in the law. In the US context, for instance, the work of Carol Gilligan has been very influential in feminist legal theory. Gilligan was a psychologist who identified a difference in the moral reasoning paradigms of female and male subjects.[95] When confronted with an ethical dilemma, the female subjects in Gilligan's study tended to reason using an "ethic of care" focusing upon relationships, while the male subjects usually used a more logical, rights-based approach. Gilligan's research counteracted previous research in psychology, which indicated that men have a superior ability to use moral reasoning. Gilligan's point was that this "superiority" was in fact assumed by the paradigm of ethical reasoning used in the research, rather than proved by it. She argued that women and men reason using different "voices". Her point was not that this difference was "natural" (as it could be the effect of social construction), but rather that it existed, and should be recognised in patterns of moral reasoning.

Feminist legal theorists have used Gilligan's insights to strengthen their argument that the law tends to reflect masculine values: many of the values around which the law is built, including its assumption of an individualistic "reasonable" person, are those used and valued by men. Some have gone further and argued that recognition of the "different voice" within law might improve its ethical credentials: the individualistic and competitive dimension of law not only reflects the values of only a portion of the population, but it also leads to results which are often inadequate, having been based upon a lopsided view of the world as composed of autonomous individuals. An antidote for the detachment of law would be to include the "ethic of care", and to develop a more relational, less individual rights-based notion of law. Such a strategy may be seen as a positive feminisation of legal values, or simply as an overdue improvement in processes of legal reasoning: as Gilligan herself said some years ago, "if you include both voices you transform the very nature of the conversation".[96]

---

94 Irene Watson, "Power of the Muldarbi, the Road to its Demise" (1998) 11 *Australian Feminist Law Journal* 28 at 36.

95 Gilligan, *In a Different Voice: Psychological Theory and Women's Development*.

96 Du Bois et al, "Feminist Discourse, Moral Values and the Law — A Conversation", p 61.

In a similar vein (but not specifically connected to the Gilligan-inspired dimension of Anglo-centric feminist legal theory) French feminist Luce Irigaray has characterised law as protective of male privileges and rights. Instead of promoting the incorporation of "feminine" values into law, she argues for positively sexed rights, that is, a legal regime which recognises two sexes rather than just one universal sex. Like MacKinnon, Irigaray argues that the legal system presupposes a universal subject, who is in fact male, and that this male subject has constructed a law for men, but not a law for women. However, rather than arguing that the universal subject ought to become more inclusive, and that the law ought to recognise gender difference where relevant, Irigaray argues in favour of a "double subjectivity", and a correspondingly double law. [97]

> The fact remains that we are men and women. And that this constitutes a living universal. It is a universal related to our real person, to his or her needs, abilities, and desires. The particularity of this universal is that it is divided into two. ... It necessitates a law of persons appropriate to their natural reality, that is, to their sexed identity.

Irigaray argues that recognition of sexed rights is an essential component of the process of breaking down the male privilege entrenched in the law. She believes that there is something *necessary* about sexual difference as a significant element of human production and reproduction — in *je, tu, nous* she argues that "Sexual difference is necessary for the continuation of the species",[98] and (somewhat dogmatically) that to "wish to get rid of sexual difference is to call for a genocide more radical than any form of destruction there has ever been in History".[99] "Genocide" is a very strong and historically-loaded term, and is perhaps stretched when applied to the failure to reproduce which Irigaray assumes would be the result of eliminating sexual difference. It is certainly true that reproduction of the species is usually a consequence of sexual relationships between women and men. However, would eliminating the social significance of sex and gender, so that we do not identify people primarily according to their sex, result in the elimination of sexual relationships between women and men? It would, of course, alter the dynamics of sex, but to suggest that sex between women and men would disappear seems to overstate the case.

Moreover, it is not just sexual *difference* which Irigaray regards as essential to survival, but the sexual *dichotomy*: it is *two* genders/sexes which are necessary (not three or more), because they are mutually defining, and because reproduction demands a division into two. Thus,

---

97   Luce Irigaray, *I Love to You: Sketch of a Possible Felicity in History*, pp 50-51. See also "Why Define Sexed Rights" in *Je, Tu, Nous: Toward a Culture of Difference*.

98   Irigary, "The Neglect of Female Genealogies" in *Je, Tu, Nous: Toward a Culture of Difference*, p 15.

99   Irigary, "A Personal Note: Equal or Different?" in *Je, Tu, Nous: Toward a Culture of Difference*, p 12.

Irigaray wishes to preserve and redefine the division of female and male, but to strip masculinity of its social and legal privilege. Gender difference is basic.

> It seems to me that the difference with other Others — for example, the difference with an Other of the same gender — that to me is not the same as the difference with someone who is of another gender.[100]

Certainly in the Western, and most other traditions, an "Other" of the same sex is not an "Other" in the same way as an "Other" of the other sex. Our whole social system is set up to ensure the difference and — as Irigaray elsewhere argues — to ensure that the system revolves around a male symbolic order.[101] Feminism is based upon this perception, and upon the need to challenge it.[102] However, who is to say that the difference between a woman and a man is a more central cultural difference than that between an Indigenous person and someone of Anglo-Saxon origin? And if it is the relation between persons which is important here, why is "otherness" ascribed to the heterosexual partnership? Why does that involve a "different difference" from the lesbian or gay partnership?[103] Moreover, Irigaray claims that sexual difference is a fact of *nature*, it is "ontological" — a claim which many feminists and all queer theorists (including myself) would reject. Drucilla Cornell says:[104]

> I strongly disagree with Irigaray that our sexed identity is a natural reality and that our particularity as a person can be adequately expressed through legally defining gender as a universal. Thus, I reject her conceptualization of sexuate rights, despite the advance she has made by insisting on women's right to a civil identity that recognizes the inviolability of their persons.

In contrast to Irigaray, who imagines a natural sex dichotomy, Cornell proposes instead the concept of an "imaginary domain", where we have "freedom to create ourselves as sexed beings".[105]

Margaret Whitford emphasises that Irigaray's aim is a radical one: "The vision of a transformation of imaginary and symbolic to allow for an other sex, a different subject, is what gives Irigaray's work its utopian and mythical quality but also its reconstructive challenge."[106]

---

100 "Je-Luce Irigaray" in Gary Olsen and Elizabeth Hirsch (eds), *Women Writing Culture* (State University of New York Press, New York, 1995), p 163.

101 In particular in *This Sex Which Is Not One*.

102 An excellent essay on this matter is Elizabeth Grosz, "The Hetero and the Homo: The Sexual Ethics of Luce Irigaray" in Carolyn Burke, Naomi Schor, and Margaret Whitford (eds), *Engaging With Irigaray* (Columbia University Press, New York, 1994).

103 For an excellent evaluation of Irigaray's notion of sexed rights see Lacey, *Unspeakable Subjects*, pp 212-218.

104 Cornell, *At the Heart of Freedom: Feminism, Sex, and Equality*, p 122.

105 Cornell, *At the Heart of Freedom: Feminism, Sex, and Equality*, p ix. See Cornell, *The Imaginary Domain: Abortion, Pornography, and Sexual Harassment* (Routledge, New York, 1995).

106 Whitford, "Reading Irigaray in the Nineties" in Burke, Schor, and Whitford (eds), *Engaging With Irigaray*, p 27.

Yet it is arguably equally radical to imagine a world without sexual difference, as Monique Wittig has done,[107] or alternatively to imagine a world of sexual plurality, as some queer theorists have done. (I will be considering queer theory very briefly below at [6155].)

Race, Culture and Ethnicity

[690] As I stated in the Introduction, one of the most important challenges to mainstream feminist thought has come from women who are disempowered in relation to privileged white heterosexual feminists. One of the assumptions made by some writers is that taking women as a group is a sufficient basis for feminist thought, without being sensitive to other systems of oppression which are not co-extensive with, but do "intersect" with gender oppression. This has been one of the major criticisms of radical feminism, which has taken sex oppression to be fundamental in the sense that it appears in all race and class groups. For instance, I explained above that Catharine MacKinnon appears to base her "unmodified" feminism on the insight that the world is divided into two — male and female. I pointed out that the term "unmodified" is a problem, because it implies that there is some position for feminism to take which is outside cultural conditioning. A further interpretation of the term "unmodified" is that it focuses on feminism *as feminism*, and not mixed up with any other theory or struggle. But whose feminism is this?

The criticism directed at early "second wave" feminism is that it assumes that there is an experience which is essentially female, and takes the position of white heterosexual and privileged women to be the standard case. Elizabeth Spelman explains this as a misguided attempt to hold constant other variables of oppression, such as race and class, in order to isolate the dimensions of sexism.[108] Or, as john a powell has suggested, "unmodified" feminism means feminism unmodified by race. As he says, this perspective fails "to see that White is as much of a racial modifier as Black."[109] The idea is that some women are oppressed solely on account of their sex or, as MacKinnon has written, they "do not share their oppression with any man".[110] The formulation is unfortunate, since it seems to suggest that the oppression of white heterosexual wealthy women is somehow more

---

107 Wittig, *The Straight Mind*.

108 Spelman, *Inessential Woman*.

109 john a powell, "The Multiple Self: Exploring Between and Beyond Modernity and Postmodernity" (1997) 81 *Minnesota Law Review* 1481 at 1494.

110 MacKinnon, "From Practice to Theory, or What is a White Woman Anyway?", p 22. In the next sentence MacKinnon says explicitly that this does not make the white woman's condition any more definitive of what it means to be a woman. At the same time, she does say that the trivialisation of white women's oppression is a "particularly sensitive indicator of the degree to which women, as such, are despised". I am not sure how to reconcile these two statements.

pure than that of other women, oppression on the basis of sex alone. MacKinnon's point seems to be that certain categories of women, in sharing their oppression with men, gain some benefit thereby: "if your oppression is also done to a man, you are more likely to be recognized as oppressed, as opposed to inferior".[111] But the main point of the critique of white heterosexual and middle-class feminism is not that women as such are not oppressed, but that some feminists have not recognised the *privilege* of being in the same dominant social, racial, and (hetero)sexual category as certain men, and have therefore assumed that whatever it is we say about ourselves will apply across the board. Our whiteness is transparent to us, and we often therefore imagine that issues of "race" apply to others, but not ourselves. Yet all the while our whiteness is only too obvious to non-white "others".[112]

Even among white Western feminists, there are considerable cultural differences which can lead to very different perceptions about what is important in feminism. The approaches of radical, liberal, and "difference" feminism may not be particularly relevant where the cultural conditions which have produced these feminisms do not exist, or where they exist in a form different than that experienced in the United States, Britain, Canada, Australia, or New Zealand. White anglo-centric feminism has become dominant with the dominance of the English language, and with US cultural imperialism, but the analysis applied in Australia or the United States may not be appropriate elsewhere. "Western feminism" is itself split in many ways by cultural difference.

The existence of cultural differences between Western feminists is illustrated by a recent collection, *Responsible Selves: Women in the Nordic Legal Culture*.[113] The book indicates that the context of Nordic feminism is quite different from the context of feminism within the US or British context. As Kevät Nousiainen and Johanna Niemi-Kiesiläinen point out, in the Nordic cultures "the polarisation of male and female selves, or masculine and feminine identities, is less marked than in other modern cultures".[114] A feminist analysis which critiques the polarisation and

---

111 MacKinnon, "From Practice to Theory, or What is a White Woman Anyway?", p 22.

112 For a discussion of the transparency of whiteness, see Barbara Flagg, "'Was Blind, But Now I See': White Race Consciousness and the Requirement of Discriminatory Intent" (1993) 91 *Michigan Law Review* 953; see also Richard Dyer, *White* (Routledge, London, 1997); Aileen Moreton-Robinson, *Talkin' Up to the White Woman: Indigenous Women and Feminism* (University of Queensland Press, St Lucia, 2000).

113 Kevät Nousiainen, Åsa Gunnarsson, Karin Lundström, Johanna Niemi-Kiesiläinen (eds), *Responsible Selves: Women in the Nordic Legal Culture* (Ashgate, Aldershot, 2001). See also Eva-Maria Svensson, Anu Pylkkänen and Johanna Niemi-Kiesiläinen (eds), *Nordic Equality at a Crossraods: Feminist Legal Studies Coping with Difference* (Ashgate, Aldershot, 2004); Åsa Gunnarsson, Eva-Maria Svensson, and Margaret Davies (eds), *Exploiting the Limits of Law: Swedish Feminism and the Challenge to Feminism* (Ashgate, Aldershot, 2007).

114 Kevät Nousiainen et al (eds), *Responsible Selves*, "Introductory Remarks on Nordic Law and Gender Identities", p 2.

hierarchisation of genders, such as radical feminism, is not highly compelling in a context where such polarisation is neither extreme nor consistent (as it is elsewhere).[115] Similarly, Anu Pylkkänen shows that in Finland the public/private distinction is neither as strong, nor as gendered, as it is theorised to be in some feminist literature. Moreover, the discourse of liberal individualism, while present in Nordic cultures, is not as significant as it is in other Western countries. "Rights" are not as significant as "responsibilities", and the state — rather than being seen either as a necessary evil (as in classical liberal thought) or simply as a patriarchal institution (as in radical feminism) — is regarded more as the manifestation of the community's collective identity. The self is not absolutely separated from the state, and the state's proper role is to ensure the wellbeing of the individual. In such a context, the liberal insistence on individual rights such as formal equality, may be less important than achieving substantive equality by ensuring the welfare of all citizens. Thus Nordic feminism has focused its efforts more on reforms to the welfare state, than on issues such as discrimination and sexual violence.[116] This is certainly not to suggest that there is no need for a discussion of these issues in Nordic countries, far from it — the authors merely demonstrate that the cultural context influences the shape and role of feminism. One size does not fit all. Clearly feminism is context-specific even within the domain of white Western privilege.

Putting a section on the feminisms of women marginalised in ways other than by gender into this particular chapter may lead to the unfortunate implication that the feminist perspectives developed by women from racial and ethnic minorities, queer theorists and lesbians, constitute subsets of feminist thought. It may also lead to the view that I have simply taken the standard representatives of "difference" and written obligatory but token "minority and queer" sections, which remain, nonetheless, inside the feminist chapter which is inside the work on patriarchal jurisprudence. The impression created by this approach is that the dominant paradigms are larger than the various criticisms which have been developed in response to them: (patriarchal) legal theory is the general category, of which feminism is a subset, of which minority feminisms are further subsets. Such an illusion does tend to reinforce the position of the establishment, rather than emphasising that there exist truly different ways of experiencing, interacting with, and theorising the world.

These are strategic problems which are difficult to avoid, but I have attempted to begin to do so by indicating where possible that what appear as "insides" in more general contexts (such as queer/lesbian

---

115 See also Anu Pylkkänen, "The Responsible Self: Relational Gender Construction in the History of Finnish Law" in Nousiainen, Gunnarsson, Lundström, Niemi-Kiesiläinen (eds), *Responsible Selves*.

116 See, for instance, Åsa Gunnarsson, "The Autonomous Taxpayer and the Dependent Caregiver: The Effects of the Division Between Tax Law and Social Law" in Nousiainen et al (eds), *Responsible Selves*.

jurisprudence inside feminist jurisprudence) have actually been developed by those who begin with an "outsider" status, and are themselves larger than the fairly narrow and one-dimensional story offered by white mainstream discourse.[117] Thus feminist jurisprudence extends well beyond the terrain of conventional jurisprudence, even though it can appear to be inside it as a sub-category.[118] The feminisms of indigenous and other non-white women are in many ways a completely different genre to the feminisms of white women, even though I have placed them as a category within some "general" feminisms. The point of finding a voice as an outsider (and thus to be "in" some political strategy) has never been simply to find a niche within someone else's version of reality, but to challenge its foundations and go beyond its idea of truth. "Outsider jurisprudence" (as Mari Matsuda calls it[119]) is important for precisely this reason. As "standpoint" feminists have argued, the oppressed person may understand aspects of her oppression better than the oppressor, because she has access to knowledge about both the process and forms of oppression, the consequences of oppression, and the extra obstacles she must overcome in order to reach a position of equality.[120] (I have considered the theory and criticisms of standpoint theory more fully in Chapter 1.) According to this view, men cannot understand the nature of oppression on the basis of sex in the same way that women can, because the experience of the oppression is the basis for our understanding of it. And white women cannot fully understand the nature and extent of racial oppression, because we are within the group of the oppressors, and benefit from our position. What this means is that we have a responsibility to educate ourselves about racism and about other forms of oppression in addition to sex and gender oppression.

As Mari Matsuda has argued, there are times to stand outside the courtroom and criticise the legal system, and there are times to stand

---

117 I say "larger than" to indicate simply that feminisms cannot be considered to be a subset of patriarchal jurisprudence. For further thoughts on the outside/inside paradox see Chapter 1, and reconsider the cover of this book.

118 As Teresa de Lauretis puts it, feminism is "at once inside its own social and discursive determinations and yet also outside and excessive to them": "Eccentric Subjects: Feminist Theory and Historical Consciousness" (1990) 16 *Feminist Studies* 115 at 116.

119 Mari Matsuda, "Public Response to Racist Speech: Considering the Victim's Story" (1989) 87 *Michigan Law Review* 2320 at 2323.

120 "Standpoint" approaches have developed into sophisticated analyses of methodology and epistemology particularly in the sciences and social sciences. See Sandra Harding, *The Science Question in Feminism* (Open University Press, Milton Keynes, 1986), Ch 6, and "Rethinking Standpoint Epistemology: 'What Is Strong Objectivity?'" in Linda Alcoff and Elizabeth Potter (eds), *Feminist Epistemologies* (Routledge, New York, 1993); Donna Haraway, *Simians, Cyborgs, and Women: The Reinvention of Nature* (Routledge, New York, 1991), Ch 9, and "Situated Knowledges: The Science Question in Feminism and the Privilege of Partial Perspective" (1988) 14 *Feminist Studies* 575; for an overview see Margaret Davies and Nan Seuffert, "Knowledge, Identity and the Politics of Law" (2000) 11 *Hastings Women's Law Journal* 259.

inside the courtroom and use the law to further one's political goals.[121] The point then is that what appears here under the headings "feminism and race" and "queer theory" are not subsets of feminism, but intersections, sites of difference. The issue is not only that many women have been left out, and now wish to be included, but more fundamentally that the complexity and specificity of particular forms of social difference need to be recognised. The critical approaches presented here suggest that a new understanding of feminism (and of jurisprudence) has been emerging over the past 15 or so years, one which attempts to recognise and use productively the differences between women, rather than see them as a source of political fragmentation.

Feminism and race

[695]   The critique of mainstream feminisms from the perspective of women from racially disadvantaged groups has concentrated on the ways in which white feminism has been, and to some degree remains, elitist and blind to questions of race. This is manifested in a number of ways: in the exclusivity of the political practices of white feminism, and its marginalisation of non-white women;[122] in the idea that sex oppression is more fundamental than other forms of oppression;[123] in the way that some feminism divides the social world into two groups, female and male, without having regard to racial or class differences; in the tendency to make theoretical assumptions and arguments which are racially specific but framed as universal;[124] and in a general ignorance of the nature and extent of oppression on the basis of race.

Exclusion

[6100] The strength of the criticisms of mainstream feminism really began to be felt in legal scholarship about 20 years ago. Since that time many

---

121   Mari Matsuda, "When the First Quail Calls: Multiple Consciousness as Jurisprudential Method" (1988) 11 *Women's Rights Law Reporter* 7 at 8. A short passage from this article is extracted in Chapter 1.

122   Doris Davenport, "The Pathology of Racism: A Conversation with Third World Wimmin" in Moraga and Anzaldúa (eds), *This Bridge Called My Back: Writings By Radical Women of Color* (Kitchen Table, Women of Color Press, New York, 1981); Smith, "Racism and Women's Studies". In general, see Moraga and Anzaldúa (eds), *This Bridge Called My Back: Writings by Radical Women of Color*, and Anzaldúa (ed), *Making Face, Making Soul: Haciendo Caras* (Aunt Lute Books, San Francisco, 1990). See also Susan Arndt, "African Gender Trouble and African Womanism: An Interview With Chikwenye Ogunyemi and Wanjira Muthoni" (2000) 25 *Signs* 709.

123   Elizabeth Spelman discusses the various forms which the claim that sexism is "more fundamental" than racism takes in *Inessential Woman*, pp 116-119. For instance, in *The Dialectic of Sex*, Shulamith Firestone wrote that "racism is a sexual phenomenon" and that "racism is sexism extended", p 106.

124   Tang Nain, "Black Women, Sexism and Racism: Black or Antiracist Feminism?"; Chandra Mohanty, "Under Western Eyes: Feminist Scholarship and Colonial Discourses" (1988) 30 *Feminist Review* 61.

(not all) feminists have developed more inclusive practices, those of us who occupy a relatively privileged social location have hopefully learnt to appreciate the fact, and have come to a much more sophisticated understanding of how power is distributed. Nonetheless, this is no excuse for complacency, and it is worth reiterating the criticisms. First, white feminism has tended to reproduce in relation to racially oppressed women similar strategies of exclusion as those which we have identified as masculine exclusions of women: this has happened, as Deborah King explains, at both a conceptual and a practical level.

Deborah King

"Multiple Jeopardy, Multiple Consciousness: The Context of a Black Feminist Ideology"[125]

[6105] Feminism has excluded and devalued black women, our experiences, and our interpretations of our own realities at the conceptual and ideological level. Black feminists and black women scholars have identified and critically examined other serious flaws in feminist theorizing. The assumption that the family is by definition patriarchal, the privileging of an individualistic worldview, and the advocacy of female separatism are often antithetical positions to many of the values and goals of black women and thus are hindrances to our association with feminism. These theoretical blinders obscured the ability of certain feminists first to recognize the multifaceted nature of women's oppressions and then to envision theories that encompass those realities. As a consequence, monistic feminism's ability to forsee remedies that would neither abandon women to the other discriminations, including race and class, nor exacerbate those burdens is extremely limited. Without theories and concepts that represent the experiences of black women, the women's movement has and will be ineffectual in making ideological appeals that might mobilize such women. Often, in fact, this conceptual invisibility has led to the actual strategic neglect and physical exclusion or non-participation of black women. Most black women who have participated in any organizations or activities of the women's movement are keenly aware of the racial politics that anger, frustrate, and alienate us.

[6110] King argued that mainstream feminism did not take account of the "multifaceted nature of women's oppressions" and therefore offered only a partial view of oppression which is not relevant to many women. Although white feminists are conscious of oppression on the basis of sex, the nature and dimensions of other sorts of oppression have often been neglected: the theories constructed are therefore meaningful only for those who are within a particular dominant racial and class group. For instance, the radical feminist analysis of rape regards it as an exercise of male dominance over women. However, as Kimberle Crenshaw points out, the "singular focus on rape as a manifestation of male power over female sexuality tends to eclipse the use of rape as a

---

125 Deborah King, "Multiple Jeopardy, Multiple Consciousness: The Context of a Black Feminist Ideology" (1988) 14 *Signs* 42 at 58.

weapon of racial terror".[126] Inter-racial rape raises issues not dealt with by the core radical feminist analysis: namely that the experience of rape is not the same for all women, and it can be as much an expression of white dominance as it is of male dominance.

White privilege

[6115] Not only has white feminism excluded or ignored questions of race, it has also suffered from a lack of self-reflectiveness about its own position within a world divided along racial lines. As Aileen Moreton-Robinson has recently argued, there has been a tendency for white feminism to forget that "white" is also a racial marker:

> Whiteness remains invisible in these [feminist] analyses because these women have a consciousness that they live in gendered bodies, but they do not have a consciousness that they live in racialised bodies. Fundamentally this is because they construct their oppression in opposition to white men on the basis of gender. White middle-class feminists utilise race privilege to write about their gendered oppression, but whiteness remains invisible, unnamed, and unmarked in their work. The values and assumptions that make whiteness invisible, unnamed and unmarked to white people in society are enmeshed in the epistemology and knowledge with which white feminists work.[127]

The extent of this critique is far-reaching: not only does white feminism often ignore issues of race, it also ignores its own racial positioning, and is based upon a universalist approach to knowledge — one which is narrowly focused upon Western society, and does not recognise the different knowledges which exist in non-Western cultures. For instance, as Moreton-Robinson suggests, liberal feminism, radical feminism, marxist/socialist feminism, and lesbian feminism have all emphasised a particular dimension of gender oppression (unequal treatment, male power, class division, compulsory heterosexuality) and elevated their observations into a general explanation of such oppression. None of these theories, however, has seriously questioned the influence of race on identity, and none of them have until recently shown any great recognition of the nature and extent of the privilege of whiteness. This does not necessarily invalidate these approaches, which may still provide useful analytical tools as well as powerful strategies for improving the status of women, but it does invalidate any claim they may make about providing a general explanation or theory of gender oppression.

---

126 Kimberle Crenshaw, "Demarginalizing the Intersection of Race and Sex: A Black Feminist Critique of Antidiscrimination Doctrine, Feminist Theory and Antiracist Politics" (1989) *University of Chicago Legal Forum* 139 at 158. See also Janet Galbraith, "Processes of Whiteness and Stories of Rape" (2000) 14 *Australian Feminist Law Journal* 71.

127 Moreton-Robinson, *Talkin' Up to the White Woman*, pp 42-43.

Identity

[6120] Responses to the racist presuppositions and practices of white feminism have been very diverse, extending well beyond critiques of mainstream feminist thought. Some women have argued that racism impacts more immediately on their lives than sexism, and that their primary concern must therefore be with the struggle against racism.[128] The point has not been so much that the sexist nature of societies is irrelevant, but that there are more urgent matters to deal with, concerning in some instances the very *existence* of marginalised cultures. Others, recognising that Indigenous women, Black women and other non-white women have distinct political identities, have worked towards theoretical approaches which recognise this distinct identity.

One of the major concerns of many women has been that white women have assumed that race is simply something which can be *added on* to an analysis of sex oppression, as though being a woman from an oppressed race is essentially the same, but worse, than being a white woman.[129] It has been pointed out that the whole question of which comes first, or is more fundamental, involves an artificial separation of their identities which is part of the problem in the first place. Identity is not something which can simply be separated out into several parts, and analysed according to different power structures. It is, as Patricia Williams says, a "complexity of messages implied in our being".[130]

For instance, white feminists understand that in order to live in a world dominated by men and male values, we have to learn to play the male game:[131] for academic feminists such as myself this means being competitive, individualistic, and learning to give greater value to those things which will lead to recognition in the academic community; being employed means having to organise our working lives according to a model designed for men, and so on. We live in a world which is still male-oriented, and find ourselves having to negotiate our lives accordingly. Our identities may be split by the need to negotiate. For women who do not share the privileges of whiteness,[132] the negotiation operates around several different axes at once.

---

128 Lahrissa Behrendt, "Black Women and the White Lies of the Feminist Movement: Implications for Aboriginal Women in Rights Discourse"; Pat O'Shane, "Is There Any Relevance in the Women's Movement for Aboriginal Women?" (1976) 12 *Refractory Girl* 31.

129 King, "Multiple Jeopardy, Multiple Consciousness: The Context of a Black Feminist Ideology".

130 Patricia Williams, "On Being the Object of Property" (1988) 14 *Signs* 5 at 24. See also María Lugones, "Hispaneando y Lesbiando: On Sarah Hoagland's *Lesbian Ethics*" (1990) 5 *Hypatia* 139.

131 Of course, we are always playing the male game, since its ideology has shaped our lives.

132 These privileges include the privilege of not having to think of oneself as having a "race" and as constantly seeing one's racial group represented in the media, in popular culture, and in the public sphere. I will have more to say about whiteness in Chapter 7.

María Lugones has developed the idea of different (racial, cultural, economic) worlds which exist in society as a way of articulating the way that non-white women interact with each other and in other various contexts, including the dominant White/Anglo culture of the United States.[133] This concept is similar to what others have called "multiple consciousness".[134] Lugones argues that women of colour are "world"-travellers, because they are forced to be flexible about moving between the different "worlds" which exist in a pluralistic society. A "world", according to Lugones, is not necessarily a formal or closed system: it is a social environment operating according to various norms and constructs, which affects the position of a person who lives within it or who comes into contact with it. We are different people in different worlds.[135] Given the complexity of the various aspects of a social existence, outsiders are forced to travel between worlds:[136]

> I think that most of us who are outside the mainstream of, for example, the US dominant construction or organization of life are "world travellers" as a matter of necessity and of survival. It seems to me that inhabiting more than one "world" at the same time and "travelling" between "worlds" is part and parcel of our experience and our situation.

Lugones goes on to emphasise that many worlds are hostile environments, into which a person will clearly not "fit" comfortably, or from which she may be excluded as a participant. Nonetheless, the experience of "world travelling" can be a productive one:[137]

> [T]here are "worlds" that we can travel to lovingly and travelling to them is part of loving at least some of their inhabitants. The reason why I think that travelling to someone's "world" is a way of identifying with them is because by travelling to their "world" we can understand *what it is to be them and what it is to be ourselves in their eyes*. Only when we have travelled to each other's "worlds" are we fully subjects to each other.

The "loving perception" which Lugones refers to in the title is a very important part of her conception of "world travelling". Travelling to a different world (perceiving it, living in it, interacting with it) can be done in an imperial fashion — where the aim is to appropriate, colonise, or objectify what we are seeing, reducing it to a set of our own rules (that is, rules which fit in with our pre-existing understanding). Such an attitude will not lead to self-reflection, only to objectification of the other. Or it can be done with a loving and playful attitude, meaning that we are open to learning new ways of being ourselves,

---

133 María Lugones, "Playfulness, 'World'-Travelling, and Loving Perception" (1987) 2 *Hypatia* 3. See also Lugones, "Hispaneando y Lesbiando: On Sarah Hoagland's *Lesbian Ethics*".

134 Angela Harris, "Race and Essentialism in Feminist Legal Theory"; cf john a powell, "The Multiple Self: Exploring Between and Beyond Modernity and Postmodernity" (1997) 81 *Minnesota Law Review* 1481.

135 Lugones, "Playfulness, 'World'-Travelling, and Loving Perception", p 11.

136 Lugones, "Playfulness, 'World'-Travelling, and Loving Perception", p 11.

137 Lugones, "Playfulness, 'World'-Travelling, and Loving Perception", p 17.

"open to self-construction" as Lugones puts it.[138] Being bound by rules, having an overly legalistic attitude to whatever confronts us, is a deadening existence, whereas being open and playful not only towards others but also towards our understanding of ourselves, is productive and challenging. Personally, I find Lugones' explanation of her concept of loving world travelling very compelling, because it describes an attitude for living which is subversive of our own established structures, and because it indicates that meaningful social change is also personal change: if we are to come to an understanding of the nature of oppression, we have to change both our attitude to others *and* ourselves, a process which will not necessarily lead to a solution, but which will itself be part of one.

Culture, religion and gender[139]

[6125] In its early stages, debate concerning the differences between women tended to focus upon race and sexuality. Since the mid-1990s Western feminism has developed a more global perspective, partly through its strong focus upon women's rights in international and domestic arenas as human rights. One consequence of this globalisation of feminist legal scholarship is a greater awareness by Western feminists of non-Western feminisms: such an awareness is beginning to influence not only feminists who work in international contexts, but also those whose concerns are primarily domestic. One issue brought to the foreground by the more global approach is the apparent contradiction of cultural/religious and gender-based rights, in a context where both equality between cultures and equality of women and men are valued. The issue is of particular interest to feminist lawyers, since the formal delineation of cultural rights and their relationship to gender rights occurs primarily through the medium of law. The point is sometimes made that women are in the impossible position of choosing either cultural equality or gender equality.[140] For instance, special legislative recognition of a culture may bring with it recognition of conventions within that culture which, from a Western (or sometimes any) perspective, are violent, or prejudicial to women's full social participation and equality. Either the culture is recognised, or the woman's equality; but recognition of both seems impossible.

---

138   Lugones, "Playfulness, 'World'-Travelling, and Loving Perception", p 16.

139   This section of three paragraphs was originally published in Margaret Davies, "Unity and Diversity in Feminist Legal Theory" (2007) 2 *Philosophy Compass* 650-664. I thank the journal for permission to reproduce the material in a slightly edited form here.

140   Susan Moller Okin, "Is Multiculturalism Bad for Women?" in Joshua Cohen and Matthew Howard (eds), *Is Multiculturalism Bad For Women?* (Princeton University Press, New Jersey, 1999); Ayelet Shachar, "Group Identity and Women's Rights in Family Law: The Perils of Multicultural Accommodation" (1998) 6 *Journal of Political Philosophy* 285-305.

On the other hand, it may also be superficial to say that cultural rights are in conflict with gender rights. For a start, such assertions seem to presuppose that the framing (Western) culture against which the "other" culture is being measured is neutral and is itself already gender equal. Within a Western context where people are generally not forced by law to dress a particular way, critics of a Muslim woman's decision to wear a *hijab* often see it as an internalisation of the patriarchy of Muslim cultures; while Muslim women may point to the constraining and sexualising fashions chosen by many Western women as evidence of a continuing patriarchy in the West, despite its liberal rhetoric of equality.[141] Perhaps more significantly, arguing that gender equality is in conflict with culture, tends to assume that culture is a singular and non-dynamic entity: it masks the internal divisions and inconsistencies within any culture, and erases dissenting voices who may have an equally "authentic" and more woman-friendly view of their cultural context.[142] For instance, by adopting the simplistic view that Islamic religion and culture is uniformly patriarchal and oppressive of women, we participate in the silencing of women who are attempting to promote notions of gender equality and human rights which are developed from an Islamic, rather than a Western, context.[143] It is preferable to recognise the plurality within cultures, rather than simplify them into uniform normative blocs. Nonetheless, anxiety remains within feminism over cultural relativism (which can seem to undermine the interests and rights of women) and universalism (which can seem to impose Western values on non-Western cultures). In recent years, Western feminism has perhaps become more successful at listening to non-Western feminists and understanding that forms of dissent in non-Western social and political environments may differ from those needed in Western liberal contexts.

In some ways, concern with the status of women within religious contexts mirrors concern over cultural relativism. Like cultures, religions transmit particular practices, world-views, and ways of life through their "subjects". Western feminism has been highly suspicious of the patriarchal manifestations of many, if not most, religions including, of course, Christianity. While mainstream feminism developed a primarily secular identity, there has always been a less visible feminism within

---

141 Azizah Al-Hibri, "Islam, Law, and Custom: Redefining Muslim Women's Rights" (1997) 12 *American University Journal of International Law and Policy* 1 at 4.

142 Sherene Razack, "Imperilled Muslim Women, Dangerous Muslim Men, and Civilised Europeans: Legal and Social Responses to Forced Marriages" (2004) 12 *Feminist Legal Studies*; Robert Post, "Law and Cultural Conflict" (2003) *Chicago-Kent Law Review* 485.

143 Asifa Quraishi, "Her Honour: An Islamic Critique of the Rape Laws of Pakistan from a Woman-Sensitive Perspective" (1997) 18 *Michigan Journal of International Law* 287. See also Ziba Mir-Hosseini, "The Construction of Gender in Islamic Legal Thought and Strategies for Reform" (2003) 1 *HAWWA: Journal of Women in the Middle East and the Islamic World* 1; Irshad Manji, *The Trouble with Islam : A Muslim's Call for Reform in Her Faith* (Random House, NSW, 2003); Saba Mahmood, *Politics of Piety: The Islamic Revival and the Feminist Subject* (Princeton University Press, Princeton, 2005).

religious contexts. Given the heightened awareness of religion in contemporary political debate, it is not surprising that feminism has also recently questioned its relationship to religion. This questioning takes at least two forms of interest to feminist legal scholars. First, in parallel with the debate over cultural rights, there is controversy over whether it is appropriate for law to recognise religious obligations, especially where these have the potential to operate in a discriminatory fashion. Secondly, there is also the more self-reflective implication of trying to understand what secularism really means for feminism: is Western feminism really as secular as it assumes itself to be? Does secularism mean prohibiting certain expressions of religious observance; and what are the limits of feminist/liberal tolerance?[144] What *is* the relationship of secular to non-secular feminism?

Beyond the patriarchal horizon

[6130] We saw above that, within Western feminism, there has in recent years been an attempt to define a concept of "women's law" which would reflect what are perceived or reclaimed as the fundamental differences between the sexes. The possibility of such a law has been criticised within the Western feminist context, because it presupposes something which many Western feminists (in particular within anglo-centric contexts) have argued has no reality outside the context of male dominance — fundamental, natural, or "ontological" sexual difference. For some Western feminists, such an idea has too many resonances with stereotypes perpetuated throughout history, which have justified continuing sexism. However, this is not to say that in a non-Western context the concept of a women's law might have a very different, and more inherently dignified, existence. Irene Watson has written of the existence of such a concept for Indigenous women, suggesting that Western feminism takes place within the "horizon of patriarchy" (this is a point conceded by most Western feminists), and indicating that Indigenous women's law has a distinct character, integrated into the fabric of Indigenous life.

Irene Watson

"Power of the Muldarbi, The Road to its Demise"[145]

[6135] Nunga Mimini's law is from Kaldowinyeri, it comes out of the creation. Always was, always will be, we come from a place of law, a space and a horizon that was always women. In terms of women's law, there is nothing to be discovered that has not always been known to our old people. It is

---

144 Joan Scott, "Symptomatic Politics: The Banning of Islamic Head Scarves in French Public Schools" (2005) 23 *French Politics, Culture and Society* 106; Stewart Motha, "Veiled Women and the Affect of Religion in Democracy" (2007) 34 *Journal of Law and Society* 138.

145 (1998) 11 *Australian Feminist Law Journal* 28 at 36. According to Watson "muldarbi" means "demon spirit". She uses the term to refer to white law and practices. "Ruwe" refers to the land.

useful for me here to distinguish the work of MacKinnon. Her writings are not about a discovery of women's law. They are a response to the void and rape of women's law. MacKinnon writes from a patriarchal horizon, like the sister who got left behind, in the place of men, while the other sisters continued their journey as they had always done. Now, following the rape, there is a long trek in the journey to rediscover women's law for the sister who got left behind. Catharine MacKinnon speaks of a way out of the despair, as being a journey into uncharted waters. But the trek is not as difficult as MacKinnon would have us believe, for the waters have always been known to the indigenous world. There is nothing to be discovered by Aboriginal women that they have not already known. The journey is for our sister who got left behind. MacKinnon herself said maybe white women have no songs, and perhaps the only song she can now sing is of feminism in the struggle to be. But as I write, the songs of Nunga miminis are also quietening as the horizon of patriarchy spreads to encompass all. The songs need to be sung for they are the medicine that will dissolve the muldarbi.

The seven sisters travelled in all directions across the country, giving to the women their laws and ceremonies of ruwe. Aboriginal women come from a continuous history of law. A law which I am not going to describe, because it is not simply an intellectual process, rather it is a spiritual and ceremonial one, one that carries with it onerous obligations. These obligations are to ensure the continuity of law and ruwe, and that the law is handed on for the future of all humanity. The law cannot be freely spoken of because many aspects of law are sacred and secret. In communicating the law it is not simply a process of telling a story. There are laws that guide us in the communication of law. The traditional boss for the story may decide to sanction or not to sanction the teaching of law. Law travels across the country, and unlike most stories the law has no beginning or end. The communication of law is complex, a process of negotiation between "bosses" who hold the law as it crosses into their country. When one is given the opportunity to respect and honour the law, one then begins to know the law of ruwe and that of itself takes on a dimension that is Aboriginal. In coming to learn and to know the law one takes on the obligation of law and ruwe.

[6140] Watson's evocation of a women's law which already exists, which has always existed, and which will continue to exist, stands in marked contrast to the Western feminist dream of a *future* law which would be inclusive of all people, or which would reflect women's concerns. Watson's work is important not only for the critique it offers of Western colonial institutions (including feminism) in the Australian context, but also because it illustrates that concepts of assimilation or even recognition, in truth would constitute a destruction of Indigenous law and culture. Cultures are in an important sense incommensurable, meaning that one culture cannot be incorporated within or reduced to another while retaining its integrity. Even the process of comparing or describing — while necessary to raise levels of awareness about cultural difference — can never adequately capture difference. (This does not necessarily mean that cultures — including Western culture — should never be subjected to moral judgments, rather that such judgments should be extremely cautious, based on awareness of difference and dissent within the culture and on a knowledge of how the culture views itself.[146]) As Watson argues, the only conceivable way out of this trap for Indigenous people is self-determination, where different laws can truly exist as such.

Sexuality and Legal Theory

[6145] Race, culture, religion and ethnicity therefore provide key sites of difference from the white norm in mainstream and feminist scholarship.[147] Another site of difference, this time from the heterosexual norm, relates to sexuality. Historically, there have been some points of tension between feminism and activism/theory concerning sexuality: the marginalisation of lesbians in mainstream feminism in the 1970s and 1980s; the political alliances of lesbians and gay men who have sometimes been little interested in the causes of women's oppression; and the development of "queer" theory and activism, which seemed to undermine the political identity and women's consciousness upon which feminism is based.[148] Broadly speaking, however, there is also a deep affinity between feminist thought and the theory and activism related to sexuality. The relationship between homophobia, the social norms of heterosexuality (or "heteronormativity"), and the structural inequality of women is one source of this connection. Another is the critique of the legal enforcement of social norms relating to sex.

Didi Herman and Carl Stychin have helpfully summarised two trajectories in "law and sexuality" scholarship:

Didi Herman and Carl Stychin
"Introduction"[149]

[6150] On the one hand, there are now many exponents of a positivist, pragmatic approach. These academics tend to assume the importance ... of law in advancing social change, and they can place tremendous faith in law's rationality. This view also generally assumes the naturalness and coherence of sexual identity categories, and pays little attention to the ways in which such categories are variously socially constructed.

---

146 Debates surrounding cultural relativism have of course had a great impact on feminism, particularly in the arena of international law and human rights. See, for example, Martha Nussbaum, "Women and Equality: The Capabilities Approach" (1999) 138 (3) *International Labour Review* 227; Hilary Charlesworth, "Martha Nussbaum's Feminist Internationalism" (2000) 111 *Ethics* 64.

147 This paragraph was originally published in Margaret Davies, "Unity and Diversity in Feminist Legal Theory" (2007) 2 *Philosophy Compass* 650-664 at 661-662. I thank the journal for permission to reproduce the material in a slightly edited form here.

148 Sheila Jeffreys, "The Queer Disappearance of Lesbians in the Academy: Sexuality in the Academy" (1994) 17 *Women's Studies International Forum* 459; Kathy Rudy, "Radical Feminism, Lesbian Separatism, and Queer Theory" (2001) 27 *Feminist Studies* 191; see generally Vanessa Munro and Carl Stychin (eds), *Sexuality and the Law: Feminist Engagements* (Routledge-Cavendish, Abingdon, 2007), pp xi-xvii.

149 In Carl Stychin and Didi Herman (eds), *Sexuality in the Legal Arena* (Athlone Press, London, 2000), p vii.

> The second trajectory of analysis ... encompasses several approaches which might be characterised generally by a more critical, sceptical (but ultimately pragmatic) approach to legal discourse and its relationship to social change. Drawing on a variety of intellectual tools — deconstruction, literary analysis, feminist, queer and critical race theory, post-colonial studies, anthropology, masculinity studies, radical political theory (to name but a few) — this work aims in part to problematise both the idea(l) of law and the dominant, hegemonic construction of sexualities. Thus, for example, work of this type might focus upon law's ability to normalise and discipline the sexual subject while, at the same time, recognising that subject's claim to rights. This approach tends to see sexualities, not as transhistorical, universal categories of identity, but instead as provisional, contested and always produced in relation to other identifications.

[6155] The first trajectory described by Herman and Stychin is basically the familiar liberal one. A liberal approach to sexuality and law accepts that the categories (if not the experience) of sexuality are given and that the law is a neutral and rational medium for promoting change — for instance by granting same-sex couples equal rights to relationship recognition through access to marriage or other marriage-like legal forms such as civil partnerships or unions. The second trajectory incorporates a range of approaches and is more consciously critical and theoretical. It critiques the liberal assumptions that sexual categories are given and that law is a neutral medium of change. This second approach views the categories of sexuality and sexual subjects as produced and constructed by law and by culture generally. It sees the law as necessarily implicated in the forming of sexualised persons. Importantly, this approach may also incorporate claims for rights, but within the context of a critical approach to the basis and nature of such rights. In the area of relationship recognition, for instance, a number of writers have argued that simply and uncritically extending marriage or civil union "rights" to same-sex couples normalises a particular type of relationship, and "render[s] invisible important feminist critiques of marriage, familial ideology and the domestication of lesbian and gay relationships".[150] This does not necessarily mean that liberal equality rights should not be granted, but that we should continue to critique the assumptions upon which such recognition is based and in particular the presumed normality of the heterosexual family form.

In this section of the chapter, I want to focus specifically on queer theory and the earlier lesbian jurisprudence as two specific forms of critical sexuality scholarship. The first edition of this book included a section entitled "lesbian jurisprudence" which considered briefly what appeared, in the early 1990s, to be a new development in legal theory,

---

150   Claire Young and Susan Boyd, "Losing the Feminist Voice? Debates on the Legal Recognition of Same Sex Partnerships in Canada" (2006) 14 *Feminist Legal Studies* 213 at 214. See also Rosemary Auchmuty, "Out of the Shadows: Feminist Silence and Liberal Law" in Munro and Stychin (eds), *Sexuality and the Law*.

spearheaded by Ruthann Robson.[151] Robson was only one of a number of scholars working in the area of sexuality and law at the time, though she was perhaps unusual in her efforts to establish a specifically lesbian approach to legal theory. Robson's work started from the perceived need for a theory developed from the subjectivity and experiences of lesbians, rather than from that of the heterosexual woman who was so often the assumed point of departure for the mainstream feminist legal theory of the time. Like racially marginalised women, lesbians have felt that they, their experiences, and their world-views have been excluded from feminist thought. Mainstream feminism has often assumed that women are heterosexual, and centred its analysis on the situation of women in a heterosexual context.[152] As is the case with the exclusion of the perspectives of non-white women from feminist thought, the silencing of lesbians within feminism indicated a failure of feminism to develop an understanding of the world and of oppression based on the experiences and perspectives of all women.[153] Robson noted therefore that feminism and lesbian theory are "not coextensive,"[154] and that "feminist jurisprudence certainly has failed to incorporate lesbian visions, and to that extent is heterosexist". However, her idea for a lesbian jurisprudence is not, as she says, a "request to be included in the request to be included" (that is, of mainstream feminism in relation to patriarchal jurisprudence). Rather, she emphasised that a lesbian jurisprudence should be based on the distinct experiences and identity of lesbians, such as the experience of invisibility in a heterosexual culture, the experience of coming out, and the experience of life in a woman-centred context. And importantly, like other theorists of marginal identities, Robson refused the attractions of a "paradigmatic" jurisprudence: in other words, her version of jurisprudence is not intended to be all-encompassing or universal, but rather just one approach among many possible approaches. Unlike MacKinnon, Robson rejects the notion of a general theory — in that sense she adopted a postmodern suspicion of the assumption that there is one systematic explanation of law.[155]

---

151 See in particular *Lesbian (Out) Law: Survival Under the Rule of Law* (Firebrand Books, Ithaca, 1992); *Sappho Goes to Law School: Fragments in Lesbian Legal Theory* (Columbia University Press, New York, 1998).

152 Adrienne Rich, "Compulsory Heterosexuality and Lesbian Existence" (1980) 5(4) *Signs: Journal of Women in Culture and Society* 631.

153 Leigh Megan Leonard, "A Missing Voice in Feminist Legal Theory: The Heterosexual Presumption" (1990) 12 *Women's Rights Law Reporter* 39.

154 Robson, *Lesbian (Out) Law*.

155 Robson, *Lesbian (Out) Law*, pp 451-452. Didi Herman has written a critique of Robson's lesbian legal theory in "A Jurisprudence of One's Own? Ruthann Robson's Lesbian Legal Theory" in Wilson (ed), *A Simple Matter of Justice? Theorising Lesbian and Gay Politics* (Cassell, London, 1995).

Any pretense to paradigmatic status on the part of lesbian jurisprudence would be as problematic as the claim to paradigmatic status on the part of patriarchal jurisprudence. Positing one partial view as paradigmatic to replace another partial view solves few problems. Further, the entire concept of paradigmatic thinking is patriarchal. A theory which aspires to be a paradigm, and thus explicative of all else, is a theory which is necessarily hierarchical, hegemonic and hubristic.

As I am imagining lesbian jurisprudence, it does not aspire to paradigmatic status. It does not seek to explain all legal phenomena; it does not seek to limit, encompass or define "jurisprudence". Instead, I would see lesbian jurisprudence as part of an organic whole, co-existing with other juris- prudences: feminist jurisprudence, African-American jurisprudence, disability jurisprudence, and all other types of jurisprudential approaches, including patriarchal jurisprudence shorn of its pretence to paradigmatic status. Thus the process of jurisprudence would not be the process of the "science" of law charting historical shifts from one paradigm to another. Jurisprudential theories would conflict in certain cases; alliances and coalescing concepts would be fluid. It might even be messy.

It is one of the themes of this book that Robson's "messy" juris- prudence has indeed eventuated. (Even the relationship between feminist, lesbian, and queer theories is messy, let alone the rest of jurisprudence. For me, as for Robson, this does not indicate a subject in need of order, but rather a subject with huge potential, with a place for all types of theorists, and in the process of substantial growth.)

As I have said, this rejection of the possibility of a "paradigm" suggests a postmodern critique of "metanarratives", or objective theories. However, Robson's work is not wholeheartedly postmodern. This is particularly evident in the significance she, like MacKinnon, places on the notion of an identity which grounds political action. For Robson, as for other lesbian theorists, the identity "lesbian" is the basis for a lesbian legal theory, just as for MacKinnon the category "woman" is the basis of feminist theory and political activism. Both theorists adopt what has been termed "weak essentialism",[156] meaning that they reject the notion that there is a pre-given and natural concept of "woman" or "lesbian", and accept that these concepts are socially defined in such a way as to reproduce patriarchy and compulsory heterosexuality. However, they argue that by virtue of this social construction, the members of the category (women or lesbians) share similar experiences, and a similar consciousness of their oppression. The construction of theory and activist practice around such an essentialised identity is therefore seen as possible, even though others have argued that it neglects significant differences within a marginalised group, and fails to acknowledge the experience of multiple consciousness or split identities such as that described by Lugones above at [6120].

---

156 See generally Margaret Davies and Nan Seuffert, "Knowledge, Identity and the Politics of Law", pp 277-281; Teresa DeLauretis, "The Essence of the Triangle or, Taking the Risk of Essentialism Seriously" (1988) 1 *differences: A Journal of Feminist Cultural Studies* 3.

In contrast, queer theorists have concentrated not on the essences of identity categories, but rather upon the problems associated with any subjective identity. The term "queer" is intrinsically impossible to pin down and has been deliberately made so by those who use it, but several features can be identified. First, the term "queer" provides an instance of a deliberate reappropriation of a term of abuse as a political strategy to withdraw the power of that abuse: like the lesbian reappropriation of "dyke" it becomes a source of pride, rather than a matter of shame. Secondly, the term "queer" has come to denote an identity, but, as David Halperin says, "one characterized by its lack of a clear definitional content", "an identity without an essence".[157] Thirdly, in relation to sexual normality (often referred to as "heteronormativity"), "queer" offers a place of subversion – not necessarily a place of direct opposition, but perhaps a place where the norms of sexuality are constantly called into question by parody, by obvious or subtle difference, or by practices "at odds with the normal, the legitimate, the dominant".[158] Some have seen this development as an ambush of lesbian and feminist ideals by "queer"-identified persons (who can be transgender, straight, gay, bi-sexual – the list is endless),[159] while others have seen it as a necessary corrective to the identification of increasingly specific, but nevertheless "essentialised" identities. Thus, where lesbian theory tended to emphasise the exclusion of lesbian identity from mainstream feminism,[160] and attempted to construct a theoretical approach around lesbian experiences such as legal invisibility and coming out, queer theory has critiqued the very notion of gender identity, and therefore of any essential lesbian or gay experience.

The difficulty queer theory seems to pose for feminism is that in critiquing the notions of gender and sexed identity it appears to pull the rug out, as it were, from under feminism: with no category "woman" how can feminism claim either a political or a theoretical basis? Surely the feminist goal should be to strengthen the category of "woman", not weaken it or challenge it.[161] As I will explain, however, the critique of

---

157 David M Halperin, *Saint Foucault: Towards a Gay Hagiography* (Oxford University Press, New York, 1995), p 61. For an excellent discussion of queer theory and its relationship to gay and lesbian activism, see Annamarie Jagose, *Queer Theory* (Melbourne University Press, Carlton, 1996).

158 Jagose, *Queer Theory*, p 60.

159 Jeffreys, "The Queer Disappearance of Lesbians: Sexuality in the Academy".

160 See for instance Rich, "Compulsory Heterosexuality and Lesbian Existence"; Leonard, "A Missing Voice in Feminist Legal Theory: The Heterosexual Presumption".

161 There is a considerable critical literature on the relationship between queer theory and feminism: see, for instance, Sally O'Driscoll, "Outlaw Readings: Beyond Queer Theory" (1996) 22 *Signs* 30; Biddy Martin, "Sexualities Without Genders and Other Queer Utopias" (1994) 24.2 *diacritics* 104; Catherine Dale, "A Debate Between Queer and Feminism" (1997) 1 *Critical inQueeries* 145; Suzanna Danuta Walters, "From Here to Queer: Radical Feminism, Postmodernism, and the Lesbian Menace (Or, Why Can't a Woman Be More Like a Fag?)" (1996) 21 *Signs* 830; for several sympathetic accounts of the relationship between feminism and queer see Elizabeth Weed and Naomi Schor (eds), *Feminism Meets Queer Theory* (Indiana University Press, Bloomington, 1997).

identity does not necessitate the elimination of those categories with which we are familiar. It is these categories, after all, which shape our experience of the world, and it is not possible simply to pretend that they do not exist. However, that should not prevent us from questioning how these categories are defined, how they have come into being, what mechanisms reproduce them, and whether they are universally "given". Nor should it prevent us from imagining a world where gender and sexuality are not so constrained. It is possible to hold that a category is a construct of language or merely the effect of repeated behaviours, but still immensely powerful and having real consequences.

Instead of seeing social construction as resulting in reasonably clear categories within which different classes of people become situated, queer theorists have therefore argued that identity is a much more fluid, on-going, and open aspect of our existences. For example, Judith Butler, one of the central figures in queer theory, has argued that gender identity is a performance – not an essential identity category, but a way of being and doing. (In making this argument Butler is adapting the analysis of the linguist John Austin of "speech acts" – performative utterances which bring something into being by a ritualised form of words, such as "I now pronounce you husband and wife" or "I accept your offer to purchase my car for $10 000".[162]) She says:[163]

> In what senses, then, is gender an act? As in other ritual social dramas, the action of gender requires a performance that is repeated. This repetition is at once a reenactment and reexperiencing of a set of meanings already socially established.

Gender is the consequence of repeated acts, and in that sense it is performed in the world: we become our gender by the way we live, move, interact. In other words, rather than seeing our gendered actions and ways of life as mere expressions of a pre-given gender identity, Butler sees repeated action or gender performance as the cause of social notions of gender identity, which therefore can be neither true nor false, but must be recognised as a mere effect of social performances.[164]

> If gender attributes and acts, the various ways in which a body shows or produces its cultural signification, are performative, then there is no preexisting identity by which an act or attribute might be measured; there would be no true or false, real or distorted acts of gender, and the postulation of a true gender identity would be revealed as a regulatory fiction. That gender reality is created through sustained social perfor-mances means that the very notions of an essential sex and a true or

---

162 JL Austin, *How to Do Things With Words* (Harvard University Press, Cambridge Mass, 1962). Generally, see Judith Butler, *Excitable Speech: A Politics of the Performative* (Routledge, New York, 1997).

163 Judith Butler, *Gender Trouble: Feminism and the Subversion of Identity* (Routledge, New York, 1990), p 140. See also Butler, *Bodies That Matter: On the Discursive Limits of Sex* (Routledge, New York, 1993). There are many critiques and discussions of Butler. A recent one is Susan Hekman, "Beyond Identity" (2000) 1 *Feminist Theory* 289.

164 Butler, *Gender Trouble*, pp 140-141.

abiding masculinity or femininity are also constituted as part of the strategy that conceals gender's performative character and the performative possibilities for proliferating gender configurations outside the restricting frames of masculinist domination and compulsory heterosexuality.

Genders can be neither true nor false, neither real nor apparent, neither original nor derived. As credible bearers of those attributes, however, genders can also be rendered thoroughly and radically *incredible*.

Note that Butler says that the performative nature of gender is concealed by "the very notions of an essential sex and a true or abiding masculinity or femininity". We assume that there are gender universals, and this thought conceals the fact that gender is constantly being performed and recreated. Butler's idea of gender is certainly counter-intuitive — it is more normal to assume that there are identities prescribed for us (by nature or by a gendered social context) within which we fit ourselves. The drama described by Butler is rather one in which social meanings are already established, but these only exist by virtue of gender performance — in other words, it is a two-way process, in which we perform an identity by "re-enacting" social norms and signs, and these norms are recreated according to our performances. The clear implication appears to be that social notions of gender can be changed, though not merely by an alteration in ideas. Notions of gender change as the ways in which gender is performed changes. Think of it this way — is the concept of "woman" the same as it was fifty years ago? Certainly not. Why not? One answer, consistent with Butler's notion of gender as performance, is that women are being women differently. Or rather, we are doing "woman" differently. It is not so much that the concept has, through an ideological change, gradually become less restrictive, that there are more ways of being a woman, and so women are comfortable doing things which simply wouldn't have been acceptable half a century ago. Rather, women are performing their gender differently, and the conceptual change flows from this altered performance. And if altered performances can, in time, challenge what is included in one gender concept, then they can challenge the very notion of dualistic, "heteronormative" gender. If there is no truth or falsity to gender, and if it is merely a consequence of the ways in which people act in the world and the interpretations of these actions, then gender can be changed, bent, transformed or, as Butler says "rendered thoroughly and radically incredible". Gender does not need to be divided into two (as Irigaray supposes), it can be many. Such a thought gives rise to the queer vision of a plurality of sex identities and of sexual orientations.

In order to illustrate the way in which gender can be regarded as complex and multiple, rather than simply dualistic, Butler gives the examples of drag, crossdressing, and butch/femme practices. It is possible to see drag as a simple and unthinking adoption of the garb and behavioural characteristics of the gender opposite to one's own. Some feminists have seen the practice of drag as a regressive reproduction of female stereotypes and gender hierarchy which belittles women.[165] Similarly, it is possible to see the adoption of butch/femme identities within a lesbian relationship as an unreflective reproduction of heterosexuality. In contrast, Butler argues that drag and butch/femme are (or at least can be) an ironic imitation of gender difference and norms of sexual preference, which highlights the fact that gender itself is nothing but a performance, and that the categories we normally use are transgressed on a daily basis.[166] After all, a lesbian butch/femme couple is not a heterosexual couple, they are lesbian, but nor are they entirely opposite to or outside heterosexuality.[167] Both butch/femme and drag illustrate the fact that our categories of gender and sexuality can be transgressed and are not stable.[168]

The idea that gender is a performance does not mean simply that we make it up as we go along, or that we can change gender in the way that we might change our residence, our job, our clothes, or our favourite cafe. Gender norms have a certain resistance to change and while it is true that we can stretch and challenge social expectations, we cannot altogether determine the way in which our "transgressive" practices are understood. It is quite common for such practices to be viewed by mainstream culture as mere perversions: rather than threatening the stability of the dominant norms of male, female and heterosexual, non-mainstream sexualities or gender practices are often seen as simply deviant, and irrelevant to the construction of mainstream categories. In a sense, the very idea of queer theory and practice rests upon its transgression of norms — it needs the norms in order to be transgressive in the first place. The visibility of difference in gender identity therefore becomes in itself an important political goal.

Wayne Morgan argues that the queer "strategy of transgression entails 'decentring' law." He says,[169]

165　Jeffreys, "The Queer Disappearance of Lesbians: Sexuality in the Academy", pp 464-465.

166　See Butler, *Gender Trouble*, pp 128-141. Unfortunately I am unable here to reproduce the complexity of Butler's subtle analysis, nor the equally complex critiques which have been made of the notion of performativity as applied to gender.

167　See generally Sally Munt (ed), *Butch/Femme: Inside Lesbian Gender* (London, Cassell, 1998). See also the very clear discussion by Tuija Pulkkinen in *The Postmodern and Political Agency* (SoPhi, Jyväskylä, 2000), pp 153-168 and 186-190.

168　In the context of law, Andrew Sharpe argues that case law relating to transsexualism, while attempting to reassert the norms of sexual identity and heterosexuality, has in fact encountered a number of difficulties resulting in the destabilisation of clear gender identities: See Sharpe, "Institutionalizing Heterosexuality: The Legal Exclusion of 'Impossible' (Trans)sexualities" in Leslie J Moran, Daniel Monk and Sarah Beresford (eds), *Legal Queeries: Lesbian, Gay and Transgender Legal Studies* (Cassell, London, 1998). See also Carl Stychin, *Law's Desire: Sexuality and the Limits of Justice* (Routledge, London, 1995).

169　Wayne Morgan, "Queer Law: Identity, Culture, Diversity, Law" (1995) 5 *Australian Gay and Lesbian Law Journal* 1. See also Carl Stychin, *Law's Desire: Sexuality and the Limits of Justice*; Sarah Zetlein, "Lesbian Bodies Before the Law: Chicks in White Satin" (1995) 5 *Australian Feminist Law Journal* 49.

As law is one of the discourses of homophobic power, queer is in eternal opposition to law's myriad expression of that power. It does not attempt to use law as a strategy in achieving "'rights" — but seeks to have a more directly cultural impact.

Because queer is not an identity as such or, if it is, it has no essence, no absolute content, rights cannot be the goal of queer thought: rights make identities static, and it is the whole point of queer theorising to sit at the margins of identity categories. Rather, the queer approach to law is to understand and challenge its heteronormativity and homophobia,[170] not to achieve rights where the standard assumptions about sexuality can remain firmly in place.

For some, the notion of queer identity provides a vision of a world where gender and sexuality are not associated with natural or social essences, but are more fluid and open to reconstruction. More important perhaps than the vision of a future where multiple gender is generally accepted, queer also illustrates how gender is *not now* confined to a simplistic heteronormative formula, but is lived and performed in a variety of ways. As indicated above, some feminists have seen queer theory as a threat to the categories upon which feminism is built, and in particular the political category of "woman" (a category which has also been seen to be threatened by race theory). Others have argued that the queer challenge to dual gender is completely in keeping with the feminist critique of naturalised gender categories. My own view is that it is possible to adopt, for some purposes, a political identification with others (such as other women), while still working towards a destabilisation and alteration of these identity categories.

Feminism, Postmodernism and Deconstruction

[6160] As I will explain in Chapter 8, "postmodernism" is a term with a fairly flexible meaning.[171] Or, "postmodernism" is a term with no *essential* meaning. And "deconstruction" — although it refers to a type of thought strongly related to postmodernism — has a different, more technical meaning. To put the matter simply, "postmodernism" refers to the loss of faith in "grand narratives" or general theories, while "deconstruction" is the process of destabilising or overturning the binary oppositions upon which Western thought is based. Both types of theorising emphasise the constructed, social, and political nature of knowledge. In what follows I will tend to talk about postmodernism generally, even though much of what I have to say is derived from deconstruction.

---

170 Morgan, "Queer Law: Identity, Culture, Diversity, Law", p 37. For an example in relation to the concept and law of property, see Margaret Davies, "Queer Property, Queer Persons: Self-Ownership and Beyond" (1999) 8 *Social and Legal Studies* 328.

171 For those who do not have some knowledge of postmodernism, the following may not make much sense without looking first at Chapter 8.

Deconstruction has emphasised the binary oppositions or dualisms which underlie much Western philosophy: dominant meanings operate through the exclusion and repression of secondary or inferior meanings. For instance, as I said in Chapter 3, Hart's concept of the developed legal system excludes and represses the concept of the primitive one: in a sense, the developed legal system gets its own meaning from this exclusion. Similarly, the meaning of "masculinity" excludes and represses the feminine: masculinity is not something which exists as a natural and essential conceptual or social category — it is constructed through the exclusion, dominance and repression of the feminine. As I have briefly indicated, theories relating to feminism and race and queer theory are based to some degree upon the postmodern critiques of identity and "grand theory". In the case of queer theory, the relationship is explicit: queer theorists have deliberately taken on various facets of postmodernism and deconstruction in order to question the notion of stable gender identities. The idea that gender is "performed" is an explicit rejection of any concept of gender as a stable category of thought or of the natural world. Some race theorists, in particular those involved in "postcolonial" thought, have also explicitly placed their ideas within a postmodern context, but not all race theory is based on postmodernism.

I will describe postmodernism in some detail in Chapter 8. In this section, I want to consider how postmodern thinking and the "postmodern condition" intersect with feminism.[172] In what senses are postmodernism and feminism divergent, and even in conflict? It has to be said at the outset that there has been some tension between those feminists who think that postmodernism undermines their version of the feminist project, and those who regard it as offering some important strategies and critique for feminism.[173]

"Postmodernism" is sometimes associated with a particular group of founding fathers, who, if they were not themselves French, tended to write in French. They are (need I name them?) Lacan, Barthes, Foucault, Derrida, and Lyotard, among others. It is sometimes assumed that postmodern thought starts with this select group of highly

---

172 Many feminists have tackled this problem in recent years. See, for instance Seyla Benhabib, Judith Butler, Drucilla Cornell and Nancy Fraser, *Feminist Contentions: A Philosophical Exchange* (Routledge, New York, 1995); Paula Moya, "Chicana Feminism and Postmodernist Theory" (2000) 26 *Signs* 441; Katherine Sheehan, "Caring for Deconstruction" (2000) 12 *Yale Journal of Law and Feminism* 85.

173 See, for instance, Catharine MacKinnon, "Points Against Postmodernism" (2000) 75 *Chicago-Kent Law Review* 687; Martha Nussbaum, "The Professor of Parody: The Hip Defeatism of Judith Butler" (1999) 22 *The New Republic*. In response to Robin West's critiques of postmodernism in *Caring for Justice* (New York University Press, New York, 1997), see the excellent essay by Katherine Sheehan, "Caring for Deconstruction" (2000) 12 *Yale Journal of Law and Feminism* 85. As Sheehan points out, critics of postmodernism and deconstruction frequently do not display the same care in understanding these movements as they would ordinarily demand in their scholarship. See generally Linda Nicholson (ed), *Feminism/Postmodernism* (Routledge, New York, 1990).

revered writers,[174] and this assumption, I would suggest, is an illustration of the way that a patriarchal understanding of intellectual influence can reassert itself. I do not want to suggest that these writers are not the originators of many interesting and useful ideas, and some of these will be described in detail in Chapter 8. However, we need to bear in mind not only what the postmodern fathers can do for feminist thought, but more importantly the political and theoretical specificity of feminism. In other words, the emphasis should not only be upon what the fathers can tell us, but how feminisms, insofar as they are attacking one or more of the fundamental systems of oppression in our society, are also crucial to the intellectual challenge which post-modernism presents to us. Postmodern feminism is not a subset of postmodernism: feminist thought is itself a fundamental challenge to intellectual, legal, political and social orders. Thus, I do not wish to pit radical feminists against postmodern feminists, or postmodernism generally against feminism generally. My intention is simply to describe what I see as the potential for fundamental change which the present intellectual climate generates. There are many ways in which post-modern thought (whether that label is adopted or not) furthers or is consistent with the goals of feminism. However, there are also ways in which feminist approaches are politically and intellectually specific. The situation is made more complex by the fact that both feminism and postmodernism present complex, not simple theoretical landscapes. Just as feminism is composed of many different strands, so is postmodernism.

To begin with, I want to go back to radical feminism, and consider how some of the basic themes and arguments presented by Catharine MacKinnon resound with a conceptual challenge compatible with some of the basic themes and ideas of postmodernism. As I have indicated, MacKinnon has been criticised on the grounds of being too rigid in her understanding of gender relations, too reductive, too determinist, too dichotomous, and essentialist. MacKinnon *can* be seen as the representative anti-postmodernist, and indeed she has seen herself that way.[175] However I believe that just as MacKinnon's work is not in direct contradiction to liberal feminism, neither is it in direct contradiction to postmodernism. This may seem to be a startling and counter-intuitive claim, especially given MacKinnon's comprehensive rejection of postmodernism as a theory which aims to "get as far away from anything real as possible."[176] While some of MacKinnon's criticisms may be justified in relation to *some* theory adopting the name of "postmodernism", it is important to recognise the diversity of the

---

174 For an especially reverential approach, see Davies, "Pathfinding: The Way of the Law" (1992) 14 *Oxford Literary Review* 107; "Towards the Common Law? The Limits of Law and the Problem of Translation" (1993) 2 *Asia Pacific Law Journal* 65. I will also be describing the approaches of these men in Chapter 8.

175 Catharine MacKinnon, "Points Against Postmodernism".

176 Catharine MacKinnon, "Points Against Postmodernism", p 702.

movement and to identify those aspects of it which are useful. In my view, postmodernism and radical feminism are not mutually exclusive approaches because the questions being tackled, and the level at which they are addressed differ: although the theories intersect in various ways, the terrain being covered is never identical. For instance, MacKinnon sees feminism as tackling the real, concrete, and specific dimensions of violence against women.[177] In contrast, a postmodern-inspired feminism might, perceiving that gender is produced within "discursive contexts", attempt to show how it is produced, and how it is destabilised and conceptually fragile. None of this denies that gender has brutal effects in the "real" world. Indeed, many postmodernists are only too well aware of the fact that systems of thought, such as the gender system, far from being open to negotiation, are extremely resistant to alteration. This is because they are not in the end built upon logic or reason, but rather upon dogma and convention. What *is* problematic about MacKinnon's work is, as I have explained, its global approach: the idea that feminism and women's experiences can be "unmodified". But MacKinnon's essentialism, which I think is at least in part polemical, is complicated in her work by her own insistence on the non-essential, social, structure of the gender hierarchy.

One of the fundamental elements of MacKinnon's work, as well as that of other radical feminists, concerns the analysis of social meanings. In the first place, power is not only political, social, economic and so forth; power brings the ability to create and define the world. To repeat de Beauvoir, men have had the power to create the world in their own image, to define what counts as truth. This association of power with truth is something which is also important in postmodern thought.[178] What this insight into the nature of meaning indicates is that it is not possible simply to escape a dominant system of thought. We cannot simply step outside and construct a new system, because there is nothing which pre-exists the existing constructions of social meanings. It is necessary then, to work with what we have got, to try to change it, and use it to envisage new meanings. This is a matter which has been discussed at various stages in this book.

One of the central ways in which the association of power with truth appears in both radical feminism and postmodernism/deconstruction is in the idea that meaning is constructed through exclusion and hierarchy. As I have explained, central to MacKinnon's work is the insight that gender is not a matter of essential differences between the sexes, but rather an ideologically supported system of dominance. MacKinnon (like most feminists, although this is not universal) does not accept biological determinism — the view that we are what we are because of our biology. Rather, we are constructed through an opposition. Gender is a violent hierarchy, the dominant term of which, masculinity, oppresses the subordinate term, femininity. The system of

---

177   Catharine MacKinnon, "Points Against Postmodernism", p 702.

178   See Foucault, *Power/Knowledge*; Smart, *Feminism and the Power of Law*, Ch 1.

gender is the social meaning of this dominance. In other words, the social meaning does not correspond to some original differences between men and women. The differences, and the significance of the differences, are produced through the exclusion and devaluation of the feminine. As I will explain in Chapter 8, writers influenced by the linguistic theory developed by Ferdinand de Saussure, have come up with a similar account of how meaning generally works. Words do not have essential meanings: meaning is constructed through systems of oppositions. The way we see and categorise the world is reliant on this system of oppositions, and does not pre-exist language.[179] In particular, our mode of thought is said to be structured around "binary oppositions", which are pairs of meanings or values, one term of which is generally characterised as positive, while the other is characterised as negative. Feminists, whether influenced by post-modernism and deconstruction or not, have focused much attention on the "hierarchised" oppositions which structure our thought (nature/culture; passive/active, emotion/reason etc), noting that they are aligned with the two sides of the heterosexual couple.[180] Western thought is organised around the ideas of the unitary subject (the "I" in its relation to language, culture, the law, etc), reason, and logic, among other things. In particular, Western thought is organised around binary oppositions. The point is not only that Western thought is organised in this way, but that the oppositions work by exclusion and domination. The positive term in the opposition is reliant on the devalued term for its own meaning: the concept of reason is reliant for its own identity on what it is not, emotion, madness, and hysteria. Reason is associated with masculinity, while emotion, madness and hysteria are associated with women. Without the exclusion, reason would not have the significance it does have. Similarly, dominant social meanings of masculinity are often reliant on the exclusion and repression of the feminine. This conceptual, metaphysical structure is repeated in the real relations between men and women. These are violent hierarchies, in much the same way that MacKinnon has said that gender is a violent hierarchy, deriving their significance not from any original or essential difference, but from the fact of domination. A central feature of both feminism and postmodernism is the critique of this dominant mode of Western thought.[181]

Both feminism and postmodernism have also offered strong critiques of objective knowledge, although they have differed in their approach to this issue. I explained that one of the political strategies which MacKinnon employs involves making women's experience central. MacKinnon says that the fundamental method of feminism is

---

179   I can only give a brief version here, but these matters are explained in detail in Chapter 7.

180   Hélène Cixous, "Sorties" in Marks and de Courtivron, *New French Feminisms* (Harvester Press, Sussex, 1981).

181   This point is discussed by Seyla Benhabib in *Situating the Self: Gender, Community and Postmodernism in Contemporary Ethics* (Polity Press, Cambridge, 1992), p 205 and pp 211-213.

consciousness raising, a process claiming the "voice of women's silence, ... the fullness of 'lack', the centrality of our marginality and exclusion, the public nature of privacy, the presence of our absence".[182] Feminism, in other words, involves taking women's experience as central, of making that which has been absent, present and achieving a "truth" about women's experience which does not accord with the dominant truth. Feminism is based on taking the marginalised term in the opposition man/woman as the centre of thought, rather than as secondary to it. This is one of the most fundamental feminist challenges to the established order, posing a challenge not only to the perceived naturalness of the present system, but also to the truth of the world we see. Moreover, this process of centralising that which has been regarded as marginal, has also provided the basis for the critique of feminism from "intersectional" feminisms, leading to a situation where we cannot conceptualise an "essential" feminism, or an "essential" woman. This process, then, has led to a re-evaluation not only of traditional patriarchal thought, but also of mainstream feminism. It should be noted that postmodern theorists have been highly critical of standpoint epistemology,[183] and reject the notions of an essentialised identity and alternative truth upon which it is often based. For some explanation and discussion of standpoint epistemology, see Chapter 1.

As I indicated above, postmodernism also critiques the notion of a dominant truth, but unlike some versions of feminism, it does not replace the prevailing notions of truth with an alternative: rather, it sees "grand narratives" as defunct. And certain feminist theories — radical, liberal, socialist, Marxist — do have a unifying or "grand" explanation of women's oppression, a possibility which has been rejected by feminists inspired by postmodernism. Part of the process of deconstruction (again, as will be explained in more detail), involves looking at the way that binary oppositions operate in systems of thought (for instance philosophy), and showing how the marginalised or subordinate concept is in fact essential to that which is regarded as the central or dominant term. Any concept is not pure or totally autonomous, but has its "other" within its core. (The "other" is that which the "self" — or in this context the concept — endeavours to exclude in order to define its own identity.) This provides a basis for the critique of fixity and essentialism in theory: it emphasises the social nature of meaning (and therefore its mutability) as well as its lack of absolute determinateness. Again, this is a political process which involves destabilising established realities. Like radical feminism, it involves centralising the marginal term, although for deconstruction this is more a process of thought illustrating the instability of philosophy and ideology rather than a political process involving people.

---

182 MacKinnon, "Feminism, Marxism, Method, and the State: Toward Feminist Jurisprudence", p 638.

183 For a response to this critique, see Sandra Harding, "Feminism, Science, and the Anti-Enlightenment Critique" in Nicholson (ed), *Feminism/Postmodernism*.

It may seem that postmodern thought thereby collapses into relativism, or into the theoretical belief in a lack of any stability in interpreting the world. Postmodern thought has at times been taken to be mainly about how interpretation is flexible. A collapse into relativism is certainly not in the interests of feminism, since it remains necessary for feminists to be able to say that gendered structures are not a matter of interpretation, and cannot be changed simply by thinking that they are not what they seem. Women's social, political, and economic disadvantage is only too evident in many places. However, in my view it is a mistake to focus solely on the instability of conceptual systems, as this idea has been developed by postmodern theorists. Postmodernism is not (necessarily) relativism or nihilism, though some have seen it this way. In my view it is more a critique of established, conventional, and naturalised patterns of thought. It is necessary to bear in mind the power and sturdiness of the conceptual hierarchies. Deconstructing an opposition does not make it go away. It demonstrates that it is not immutable, or essential, but it does not magically make it disappear. In fact, the dominant systems of thought just keep coming back at us, no matter how hard we try to circumvent, circumnavigate, or simply destroy them. Achieving lasting conceptual change, and therefore a change in how the world is constructed materially, does not happen overnight. Moreover, categories of thought, however constructed, are absolutely necessary for the organisation and creation of meaning.

A further element of feminist thought which has postmodern resonances relates to the problem of the construction of female identity. Remember what Catharine MacKinnon said about female sexuality: that it is a reflection of masculine desires, masculine assumptions of what constitutes sexuality, and the patriarchal association of women with passivity. Women are constructed according to masculine images, because men have the power to define reality: for radical feminists, this experience grounds a political identity. The insight that the category "woman" is constructed through violent hierarchy has also provided the basis for a postmodern critique of masculinist ideals of femininity: however, this critique is used as a springboard for critique of male/female as a conceptual structure, for critique of the notion that identity is a solid category from which politics or knowledge simply flows, and for a recognition of the complexities of subject-formation.

Despite some points of convergence, radical feminism and postmodernism are clearly not the same thing. As an illustration of the tension between them, consider the question of the establishment of identity within a category. As I have indicated, radical feminism has concentrated its attention on the broad structures of oppression between men and women, and the idea that knowledge and politics flows from this identity. Postmodern feminism tends to be more aligned with queer theory: both have questioned the category "woman" and the idea of "female sexuality", arguing, for instance, in relation to the latter, that the patriarchal definitions of female sexuality do not account for the whole. The "old dream of symmetry" is a *dream*, and female sexuality cannot be confined to patriarchal definitions. Thus we are presented, for instance, with the idea of multiple female sexualities, and multiple masculinities. Female sexuality takes many forms: we are encouraged to think in new, as yet uncharted, ways about what constitutes sexuality. Re-thinking the question of sexuality is in itself a liberating personal and theoretical experience. Yet simply *re-thinking* it does not eliminate the basic structure of sexual oppression, and may in fact only serve to reinforce the dominant stereotypes.[184] It is all very well to say that female sexuality and sexual identity is complex and plural, but we are still confronted with a social environment which stereotypes, objectifies, and demands conformity from women. So there is a tension between the promise of new horizons in our understanding of sexuality and identity, and the recognition that, after all, the fundamental structures of gendered social meaning and power still exist. There is a tension between envisaging fundamental social and conceptual change and the necessity of negotiating with meanings and practices which just keep reasserting themselves. Similarly, postmodern thought has been highly critical of "standpoint epistemology", and the notion that there is an innocent (or more innocent) position from which to understand the world.

I think it is possible, and desirable, to see this "tension" neither as a contradiction since the two approaches are concerned with different questions, nor as requiring a "compromise" since both views are at once equally valid. The tension is a productive one, generating new realms of meaning, and new ways of approaching concrete and theoretical problems. Yet translating between postmodernism and feminism may call for a reconciliation of some sort, a recognition that both perspectives can operate usefully simultaneously.

Conclusion

[6165] It should be evident from this chapter that there are many different varieties of feminist theory. Some would perhaps see this as a problem with the movement, as a fragmenting of feminist identity and political motivations, making solidarity very difficult to achieve. Others, like myself, see diversity as a source of strength in feminism. It is not necessary to adopt a single world-view, or a single theory, in order for feminism to be useful. After all, the world itself is a complex and plural place, and different contexts call for different reactions. Liberal feminism might constitute a powerful argument in some contexts, whereas other contexts call for something different. Queer theory and

---

184 Mia Campioni, "Women and Otherness" (1991) 1 *Journal of Australian Lesbian Feminist Studies* 49; Gayatri Chakravorty Spivak, "Displacement and the Discourse of Woman" in Antony Easthope and Kate McGowan (eds), *A Critical and Cultural Theory Reader* (2nd ed, University of Toronto Press, Buffalo, Toronto, 2004).

postmodernism provide possibilities for far-reaching reconstructions of our very notions of gender, sex, and sexuality, as well as of the entire realm of Western thought: however, a simple "application" of post-modernism is not possible. It is also politically necessary, in a world which divides people according to race, sex or sexuality, that these identities be recognised as a social fact, and mobilised where appropriate. At the same time, moving beyond sex-based oppression will, in my view, involve a transformation in the social perception of sex/gender and, possibly, the recognition of plural, non-hierarchical versions of gender and sexuality.

SEVEN

RACE AND COLONIALISM: LEGAL THEORY AS "WHITE MYTHOLOGY"[1]

Introduction

[705] Chapters 5 and 6 provided an introduction to some of the critical approaches to law which have emerged over the past three decades. In Chapter 5, I introduced Critical Legal Studies (CLS), probably the first self-consciously critical movement of recent times to challenge the predominantly positivist tradition of legal theory. As we saw, CLS opened up the terrain of legal critique. Most "traditional" approaches tended to focus upon developing theories about law as an object, without considering how the position of the "subject" (that is, the person in relation to the law) might affect such knowledge, or how legal ideology might operate to constrain theoretical choices. In contrast to these approaches, CLS saw law as a political instrument which not only shapes our perception of "truth", but which also constructs legal subjects in particular ways. According to CLS, neither the object of law nor the subject constructed by law can be regarded as fixed or stable. Both are open to challenge, and the breaking down of Western (particularly Anglo-American) faith in liberalism was seen to offer the potential of a less hierarchised and more inclusive legal culture. The distinctive character of the legally constructed subject identified by US Critical Legal Scholars was the liberal holder of rights, an entity seen by some as alienated from a more "true" social consciousness.

Similarly, feminist legal scholarship has identified a political dimension to law, and to those legal theories which do not acknowledge (or which downplay) the inherent politics of law. The feminist challenge to law has been carried out in a variety of ways, as we saw in Chapter 6. Suffice it to say here, feminists have moved well beyond an internal critique of discriminatory laws, to an appreciation of how the concepts favoured

---

1   The term "white mythology" was used by Derrida in "White Mythology: Metaphor in the Text of Philosophy" in Derrida, *Margins of Philosophy* (Harvester Press, Brighton, 1982). It has subsequently been coined as the title of a book by Robert Young, *White Mythologies: Writing History and the West* (Routledge, London, 1990). I would like especially to thank Mary Heath, Reetvinder Randhawa and Irene Watson for reading and commenting on this chapter.

by law and by theory purporting to describe law, support a socially embedded notion of masculinity.

As we saw in both chapters, however, the problems of inclusion and exclusion are not confined to "traditional" theories. Critical theorists have themselves perpetrated some of the same mistakes and blind spots of mainstream theory. The idea that rights could be eliminated — a position held by many Critical Legal Scholars — was very effectively criticised by race theorists, who pointed out that rights are only legally and socially insignificant to those who are sufficiently privileged to be able to assume that their rights will normally be respected. Although liberalism clearly has its faults, it is an exceptionally powerful rhetorical tool, which can at times promote the recognition of social and legal outsiders. At the very least, the liberal emphasis upon equality ensures that — if only in some limited ways, such as in the context of formal legal rules — explicit, overt, and legally sanctioned discrimination within the framework of mainstream law is no longer the norm.[2] (Of course this does not even touch upon forms of unconscious bias, nor the fact that "the" law — that is, Western state law — does not recognise competing laws, such as those of Indigenous peoples.) Regardless of whether liberalism provides a satisfactory world-view for the long term, the existence of liberal ideology is an unavoidable fact: progress may consist not only in the destruction of the dominant world-view, but may also at times (as Mari Matsuda has argued[3]) require some degree of engagement. The rejection of liberalism, for those who cannot take its freedoms for granted, must be done cautiously, practically, and with regard to contexts. The early CLS movement tended to neglect such complexities in a quest for a utopia in which individuals were not alienated from their communities and from their true needs (whatever these may be).

Similarly, early legal feminisms (in this context including the feminisms of the 1970s and 1980s) were criticised for their assumption that the standard "woman" was white, middle-class, and heterosexual.[4] In attempting to isolate gender as a point of departure for feminist analysis, feminists failed to consider the issue of race, and also tended to base their analyses upon a white norm.

The blind spots of both the early CLS movement and early feminism in relation to questions of race have added urgency to critical race theory and Indigenous critiques of law. As we saw in Chapter 6, distinct

---

2   See, for instance, Richard Delgado, "The Ethereal Scholar: Does Critical Legal Studies Have What Minorities Want?" (1987) 22 *Harvard Civil Rights — Civil Liberties Law Review* 301.

3   See the discussion of Matsuda in Chapter 1.

4   See, for instance, Aileen Moreton-Robinson, *Talkin' Up to the White Woman: Indigenous Women and Feminism* (University of Queensland Press, St Lucia, 2000); "Troubling Business: Difference and Whiteness Within Feminism" (2000) 15 *Australian Feminist Studies* 343.

forms of feminism, which take intersecting oppressions as a central point of departure rather than as marginal experience, have emerged in response to middle-class white feminism. Postcolonial thought has also arisen as a distinct theoretical perspective concerning the legacies of colonialism, particularly in areas of the world where colonial rule has legally, if not in practice, ended.

There are some parallels between gender oppression and racial oppression. Mostly, these parallels arise because relationships of power, oppression or hierarchy have some consequences which can be observed whatever the nature of the oppression. For instance, a position of social power brings with it an ability to define the world — to influence what is regarded as "truth". In consequence, hierarchy often results in the objectification and commodification of those in less powerful positions, who are not seen as knowledge-bearers or subjects. This generalisation is true of both gender and race-based distributions of power. However, there are also significant differences which overshadow any similarities: for instance, Western women have frequently been commodified by patriarchal culture, and even socially regarded as the property of their fathers and husbands, but this commodification has never been formally recognised by Western law. Women have seldom been enslaved because they are women,[5] but slavery has been closely aligned with white supremacy, especially in the United States.[6] Moreover, the experience of enslaved women, like the position of women of colour today, was qualitatively different from that of either enslaved men or sexually commodified white women. Similarly, colonial expansion was legitimated by the notion that Indigenous peoples throughout the world were uncivilised and inefficient managers of land and other natural resources. In Australia, the colonial state was (and is) based upon an official denial that Indigenous people were governed by law.[7] This type of domination has no parallel. Therefore, while it is possible to say that there are some structural similarities between different types of oppression, the content and character of oppression varies widely.

Theory relating to race, like feminist theory, takes many different forms, and it would be impossible to cover them all adequately. But it is very important to note the range of theoretical concerns which converge around what I have broadly designated "race". Although the key terms and main themes in this chapter are race and colonialism, a large number of issues are brought into play by related literatures:

---

5   The sex slaves of World War II provides one instance where slavery was instituted against women *as* women.

6   This is not to say that slavery is always a direct consequence of racism, merely that racism and slavery became mutually reinforcing in the United States: see Dinesh D'Souza, *The End of Racism: Principles for a Multiracial Society* (Free Press, New York, 1995), pp 36-39.

7   Irene Watson, "Indigenous Peoples' Law Ways: Survival Against the Colonial State" (1997) 8 *Australian Feminist Law Journal* 39.

ethnicity, migration, cultural difference, caste, Western imperialism, national difference, geographical heritage, and increasingly religion.[8] To generalise very broadly, the theoretical basis of these topics is focussed on questions of discrimination and equality, but also more fundamentally considers the mechanisms employed by dominant cultures, ethnicities (etc) to construct and exclude or marginalise "others" who are "different". A point which is frequently made in relation to such constructions is that their core objective is to secure and preserve the identity of those who are in a dominant position.[9] Under the White Australia policy, for instance, Australia could secure its identity as a "white" country only by endorsing naturalist explanations of racial difference accompanied by vigilant exclusion of those regarded as racially "other". These days the exclusions and constructions are undoubtedly more subtle and often hidden behind different rationales, though they can be equally as powerful. But it would be wrong to generalise too much: the point is that all of these issues converge and intersect and cannot be dissociated or studied in isolation. But nor can they all be reduced to a coherent or general set of concerns.

For instance, in Australia, New Zealand, Canada, and the United States there are certain facets to the circumstances surrounding Indigenous peoples and that of non-Indigenous racial groups which can be compared, especially when we try to understand the forces within Western "white mythology" which exclude, stereotype, enslave or try to assimilate the racial (or sometimes "ethnic") "other"[10]. On the other hand, there are certain dimensions of Indigenous experience — such as the experience of being forcibly dispossessed from land, the experience of European failure to acknowledge Indigenous legal orders and, the experience of continuing colonialism — which are distinct and cannot be comprehended merely by considering the issue of race in the

8   There is much literature on these matters, but see, for instance, Ben Berger, "Understanding Law and Religion as Culture: Making Room for Meaning in the Public Sphere" (2006) 15 *Constitutional Forum* 15; Robert Post, "Law and Cultural Conflict" (2003) 78 *Chicago-Kent Law Review* 485; Qudsia Mirza, "Islam, Hybridity and the Laws of Marriage" (2000) 14 *Australian Feminist Law Journal* 1-22. See also Prakash Shah, *Legal Pluralism in Conflict: Coping with Cultural Diversity in Law* (Glasshouse Press, London, 2005); Ihsan Yilmaz, "The Challenge of Postmodern Legality and Muslim Legal Pluralism in England" (2002) 28 *Journal of Ethnic and Migration Studies* 343; Didi Herman, "'An Unfortunate Coincidence': Jews and Jewishness in Twentieth-century English Judicial Discourse" (2006) 33 *Journal of Law and Society* 277.

9   Barbara Hudson, "Beyond White Man's Justice: Race, Gender and Justice in Late Modernity" (2006) 10 *Theoretical Criminology* 29 at 32-33; Catherine Dauvergne, "Making People Illegal" and Sarah Kyambi, "National Identity and Refugee Law", both in P Fitzpatrick and P Tuitt (eds), *Critical Beings* (Ashgate, London, 2004).

10 See Ann Curthoys, "An Uneasy Conversation: The Multicultural and the Indigenous", and Vince Marotta, "The Ambivalence of Borders: The Bicultural and the Multicultural" both in Docker and Fischer (eds), *Race, Colour, and Identity in Australia and New Zealand* (UNSW Press, Sydney, 2000).

abstract.[11] Thus, mainstream policy in New Zealand has adopted the approach of "biculturalism" to recognise the specific relationships between Maori people and the European Pakeha. In contrast, Australia's "multiculturalism" may tend to neglect such differences, reducing all to a situation of ethnic difference.[12] Insofar as both approaches operate within a framework of state policy, they overlook the fact that for many Indigenous people it is not equality which is the primary goal of their legal and political struggles, but rather self-determination. This chapter introduces some central concepts and debates, but of course cannot attempt to cover what is a rapidly expanding and heterogeneous field. Having said that, I have tried to consider both the general question of racism and white domination, as well as the specific issues of colonialism and Western cultural imperialism.

Of course, my comments are also shaped in many respects by my "whiteness" and my privileged position within a colonising and imperialistic culture: in relation to this chapter, above all others, notions of any authorial "authority" which I might have must be tempered by a recognition that I do not have experience of racial oppression or of being colonised though I clearly do have experience of both race and colonialism — that is, the experience of the white Australian.[13] (And for a long time, "Australian" necessarily meant "white", indicating a conflation of nationality and race which is still present for many.[14]) Moreover, because the concept of race and the cultural associations relating to race are embedded in our culture, it would be idealistic to think that I can simply be "not racist". Racism does not only involve conscious bias, or even only unconscious bias: it is reproduced in cultural symbols and values and is frequently systemic

---

11   Of the notion that Indigenous people are "ethnic minorities", Irene Watson says, "This is another lie. It is an attempt to conceal our identity as being the First Peoples of the land." Irene Watson, "Indigenous Peoples' Law-Ways: Survival Against the Colonial State" (1997) 8 *Australian Feminist Law Journal* 39 at 56.

12   See generally Anne Maxwell, "Ethnicity and Education: Biculturalism in New Zealand" in David Bennett (ed), *Multicultural Studies: Rethinking Difference and Identity* (Routledge, London, 1998). Maxwell points out that the policy of biculturalism has in practice tended to rely on an official version of Maori history, "with devastating consequences for tribal identity": p 197. See also Judith Pryor, "Reconciling the Irreconcilable? Activating the Differences in the Mabo Decision and the Treaty of Waitangi" (2005) 15 *Social Semiotics* 81.

13   An excellent and recent analysis of privilege is Sonia Kruks, "Simone de Beauvoir and the Politics of Privilege" (2005) 20 *Hypatia* 178. For an in-depth, though often daunting, discussion of the relationship between power and the ability to "speak" about its effects, see the classic text by Gayatri Chakracorty Spivak, "Can the Subaltern Speak?" in Cary Nelson and Laurence Grossberg (eds), *Marxism and the Interpretation of Culture* (University of Illinois Press, 1988); for further up-to-date commentary see Jill Didur and Teresa Heffernan, "Revisiting the New Subaltern in the New Empire" (2003) 17 *Cultural Studies* 1.

14   Jane Haggis and Susanne Schech, "Migrancy, Whiteness and the Settler Self in Contemporary Australia" in Docker and Fischer (eds), *Race, Colour and Identity in Australia and New Zealand* (UNSW Press, Sydney, 2000).

or institutional as well as individual. Finally, I should note that oppression on the basis of race and ethnicity is obviously not confined to the power of white people and our institutions in relation to a "non-white" other. However, within the white-dominated societies of the Western world (where this book will be read), this is clearly the most widespread and significant form of racial oppression and, therefore, forms the core of my discussion.

Race as Construct

[710]   Abstraction, the tool of enlightenment, treats its objects as did fate, the notion of which it rejects: it liquidates them.[15]

[715]   The category of race is often naturalised, meaning that it is assumed to be a natural and biological characteristic of human beings. It is only too easy to see why this is the case: after all, people originating from different parts of the world can look very different. There seems to be a biological basis to the idea of racial difference, just as there seems to be a biological basis to the concept of sexual difference.

The modern concept of race is, however, now generally regarded as a "discovery" or "invention" of the Enlightenment. I should point out that what is termed "Enlightenment" was a broad movement, comprising a new humanism, increasing secularism, the development of liberalism, the reinvention of democracy, and the rise of the sciences and an "enlightened" — non-superstitious — rational philosophy and world view. It therefore includes a great many features which we in the West today would identify as socially progressive. However, the Enlightenment cannot be characterised as unequivocally good: as Adorno and Horkheimer argued, it was always inherently irrational as well as rational, and produced fascism as well as liberalism.[16] Despite liberalism, Enlightenment values have become associated with a general intolerance to radical pluralism: modern thought, based on an Enlightenment vision of one rational Truth, has not been particularly successful in finding ways of recognising difference without assimilating it into its own grand narratives of science and philosophy.[17] From a position internal to Western culture, it may seem that this singularity of thought has rarely become as extreme as fascism; however, it may not seem that way to the colonised peoples who — like the victims of fascism — have suffered genocide and displacement in the name of progress. In my view, the Enlightenment has not, in fact, produced anything approximating a universal science or philosophy.

---

15   Theodor Adorno and Max Horkheimer, *Dialectic of the Enlightenment* (Verso, London, 1979), p 13.

16   Adorno and Horkheimer, *Dialectic of the Enlightenment*, Ch 1 "The Concept of Enlightenment".

17   See comments made by Dipesh Chakrabarty, "Modernity and Ethnicity in India" in Bennett (ed), *Multicultural States: Rethinking Difference and Identity*, p 93.

(Indeed, as I have indicated elsewhere, it is doubtful whether such a thing is possible.) What the Enlightenment arguably did produce was a mode of thought built upon a solid European cultural base, which could, in turn, promote itself as universal.

From the late 17th century it became common for scholars to divide all of the peoples of the world into four or five broad classifications.[18] Prior to this time, although there was certainly awareness and discussion of cultural and ethnic difference, Western thinkers did not classify people according to presumed biological difference.[19] Several factors are regarded as playing a part in the development of the concept of race. These factors include a desire to make sense of the increasing knowledge of cultures beyond Europe, scholarly attention to human beings as an object of study, the growth in "natural history" and its impulse to discover the rational order of the world, and the perceived need to justify colonial expansion and the slave trade.[20] I will have something to say about colonialism later in the chapter, but will concentrate for the moment on the impact of science on racial classification.

The new emphasis upon rationality in the natural sciences generated a climate of taxonomy, that is, a scholarly context in which the proper purpose of studying the natural world was the orderly categorisation of all things. In nature, everything had its place, and in observing the natural world, places were assigned to all things in a "great chain of being". For instance, Linnaeus (Carl von Linne) was a Swedish scholar who published his *Systema Naturae* in several editions in the 18th century: one of the features of Linnaeus' work was his inclusion of humankind in the classification of the natural world, and — more importantly for this chapter — his division of humankind into several types. Robert Bernasconi summarises Linnaeus' classification in the following manner:[21]

> ... one finds in the tenth edition of 1758, after the feral or wild man, the following classes: *homo Americanus*, who was allegedly obstinate, content, free, and governed by habit; *homo Europaeus*, who was allegedly gentle, very acute, inventive and governed by customs or religious observances ...; *homo Asiaticus*, who was allegedly severe, haughty, covetous, and governed by opinions; and *homo Africanus*, who was allegedly crafty, indolent, negligent and governed by caprice.

---

18   Robert Bernasconi identifies an essay attributed to François Bernier, written in 1684, as one of the first sources both to divide the earth's people into classifications and to use the word "race" in describing the types; Robert Bernasconi, "Who Invented the Concept of Race?" in Bernasconi (ed), *Race* (Blackwell Publishers, Oxford, 2001), p 12.

19   Dinesh D'Souza, *The End of Racism*, pp 39-43; Frank Snowden, *Before Color Prejudice: The Ancient View of Blacks* (Harvard University Press, Cambridge Mass, 1983).

20   See generally Bernasconi, "Who Invented the Concept of Race?"; Philip Curtin, "The Africans' 'Place in Nature'" from Curtin, *The Image of Africa: British Ideas and Actions, 1780-1850* (Macmillan, London, 1965), and Michael Banton, "The Racialising of the World" from Banton, *The Idea of Race* (Tavistock, London, 1977), both extracts reprinted in Bulmer and Solomos (eds), *Racism* (Oxford University Press, Oxford, 1999).

21   Bernasconi, "Who Invented the Concept of Race?", p 15.

Although, as Bernasconi notes, Linnaeus does not explicitly state that the European type is better than the others, it is obvious from the stereotyped descriptions that he felt Europeans possessed superior characteristics. Importantly, at its origins in European science and philosophy, the concept of race was associated with the presumption of white superiority. It is not as though a neutral taxonomy of race was drawn in which people were regarded as "equal but different". Inequality was built into the classification of perceived difference, and further strengthened in the 19th century with the advent of social Darwinism or Spencerism. (This was the view that "stronger" races would inevitably eliminate "weaker" races through the process of natural selection. Such "selection" — in reality genocide — was seen to be positive, because it would only strengthen humanity and eradicate its less successful communities.[22]) The bizarre inclusion of the wild or feral man in the classification further illustrates the inherently hierarchical nature of the system: it apparently derives from a combination of rumour and the idea that the gap between human beings and other primates was too large — the "great chain of being" demanded that more incremental steps between the species be identified.[23]

While Linnaeus is regarded as the first scientist specifically to include racialised humans in a grand scheme of natural classification, the pattern of thought continued to develop and crystallise, despite several important critics.[24] The philosopher Immanuel Kant was the author of a number of statements which would today be regarded as blatantly racist, and he also wrote several strong justifications for the concept of race, dividing humankind into a few types based on skin colour.[25] Indeed, so influential (but so forgotten in modern philosophical analysis) were Kant's statements on race, that he is sometimes (dis)credited with being the "father of racial thought". Charles Mills comments:[26]

---

22   Julie Marcus, *Australian Race Relations, 1788-1993* (Allen and Unwin, Sydney, 1994), Ch 1.

23   Philip Curtin, "The Africans' 'Place in Nature'", *The Image of Africa: British Ideas and Actions, 1780-1850* (Macmillan, London, 1965), p 33.

24   For instance, Robert Bernasconi examines the debate between Kant and Herder, who rejected the reality of race: see Bernasconi, "Who Invented the Concept of Race?", pp 27-29.

25   Bernasconi, "Who Invented the Concept of Race?", pp 27-29. See generally Immanuel Kant, "On the Use of Teleological Principles in Philosophy" (1788) reprinted in Bernasconi, *Race*.

26   Charles B Mills, *The Racial Contract* (Cornell University Press, Ithaca, 1997), p 72. Kant's views on race have not, until very recently, been subjected to even the (fairly minimal) critical scrutiny attracted by Hegel's views on gender. It is most noticeably absent from mainstream analysis. See also Robert Bernasconi, "Who Invented the Concept of Race?"; Emmanuel Eze, "The Color of Reason: The Idea of 'Race' in Kant's Anthropology" in Katherine M Faull (ed), *Anthropology and the German Enlightenment: Perspectives on Humanity* (Bucknell University Press, Lewisburg, 1995).

> ... the embarrassing fact for the white West (which doubtless explains its concealment) is that their most important moral theorist of the past three hundred years is also the foundational theorist in the modern period of the division between *Herrenvolk* and *Untermenschen*, persons and subpersons, upon which Nazi theory would later draw. Modern moral theory and modern racial theory have the same father.

This is not to suggest that without Kant there would have been no concept of race and no racism: prior to Kant, and independently of his views, the concept of race was gathering strength in the scientific literature. Other philosophers held similar views to his about the natural inferiority of African people and of Indigenous peoples, and the natural superiority of Europeans.[27] Kant was, however, one of the first major philosophers to address and defend the concept of race systematically and theoretically.

Although numbers of scientists and philosophers have defended the scientific categorisation of races, the biological classifications were discredited in the second half of the 20th century. For a start, there is an infinite number of human physical differences — why do some count in racial classification while others do not? Moreover, as Steve Fenton has commented, "it proved impossible to sustain any single classificatory system because the degree of variation within postulated races came to be recognised as greater than the variation between them."[28] When confronted with such dilemmas, those who love fixed taxonomies tend to revert to a notion of "pure" or central types and marginal types. An early example of privileging the English as the white race is Benjamin Franklin's characterisation of all peoples, bar the Saxons and the English, as "black", "tawny" or "swarthy":[29]

> All Africa is black or tawny; Asia chiefly tawny; America (exclusive of the newcomers) wholly so. And in Europe, the Spaniards, Italians, French, Russians, and Swedes are generally of what we call a swarthy complexion; as are the Germans also, the Saxons only excepted, who, with the English, make the principal body of white people on the face of the earth. I could wish their numbers were increased.

Franklin's rather rough description of peoples according to skin colour — written in the earliest days of formal racial classification — idealises a defined group as truly white. Subsequently, and with rather less emphasis upon skin colour, the category of whiteness has come to mean different things in different contexts. As several commentators have pointed out, the category of whiteness is in flux, a fact which indicates its contextual and socially constructed nature. The English

---

27 For some examples, see D'Souza, *The End of Racism*, p 28.

28 Steve Fenton, *Ethnicity: Racism, Class and Culture* (Rowman and Littlefield, Lanham, 1999), p 5.

29 Benjamin Franklin, "Observations Concerning the Increase of Mankind and the Peopling of Countries" [1751] in Kenneth Silverman (ed), *Benjamin Franklin/Autobiography and Other Writings* (Penguin Books, New York, 1986).

and some Northern European people, have occupied the core category of whiteness, while Jewish people, the Irish, and Southern Europeans, have, at different historical periods and in different political circumstances, been included in a monolithic category of whiteness, completely excluded, or partially excluded as "white others" or "ethnic whites."[30] (It hardly needs to be pointed out that everybody has ethnicity, so the use of the term "ethnic" as a signifier of difference, exclusion, or otherness, presumes a standard in comparison to which the "ethnic" is other.[31] Such a presumption is one of the ways in which the ethnicity or race of the standard is obscured.)

The nomenclature of race which emerged out of early modern thought can therefore be understood not as a "discovery" of the natural order governing humanity, but rather as a construct which itself did the ordering. A multitude of different peoples were ordered into a few broad groups, and — at the same time — into a hierarchy with the European racial type placed firmly at the top. Of course, the construction of a culture's perceptions is never quite that simple: in all probability those scholars "responsible" for the early scientific and philosophical "description" of different races were simply crystallising in their scholarly works an already-present cultural tendency or, as some have suggested, trying to find a way of justifying what were at the time regarded as the economic necessities of slavery and colonialism.[32] Belief in the inferiority of Indigenous peoples, contempt for their non-institutionalised social organisations and, for their apparent lack of technology, provided a convenient justification for colonial powers intent on expansionism.

At the same time, the mere description of race could never be sufficient to transform it into a social and cultural reality: for this to occur, people must identify themselves and others through the lens of race, and live as though it is more than a mere labelling methodology.

---

30   See Matthew Frye Jacobson, *Whiteness of a Different Color*, p 52; Theodore Allen, *The Invention of the White Race* (Verso, New York, 1994); John Tehranian, "Performing Whiteness: Naturalization Litigation and the Construction of Racial Identity in America" (2000) 109 *Yale Law Journal* 816 at 816-817. For a longer historical view, exploring the existence of white identities outside Europe and before the modern period, see Alastair Bonnett, "Who Was White? The Disappearance of Non-European White Identities and the Formation of European Racial Whiteness" (1998) 21 *Ethnic and Racial Studies* 1029; Joe Pugliese, "Race as Category Crisis: Whiteness and the Topical Assignation of Race" (2002) 12 *Social Semiotics* 149.

31   Werner Sollers, "Who Is Ethnic?" from Sollers, *Beyond Ethnicity: Consent and Descent in American Culture* (Oxford University Press, New York, 1986) extract reprinted in Ashcroft, Griffiths, and Tiffin (eds), *The Postcolonial Studies Reader* (Routledge, London, 1995).

32   For a discussion of the relationship between slavery and racism, see Dinesh D'Souza, *The End of Racism*, pp 36-39. D'Souza argues that slavery did not give rise to racism, nor did racism necessarily result in slavery, as the two institutions are often found separately in history (that is, racism without slavery, and slavery without differentiation on the basis of race). However, clearly in the context of slavery and racism in the United States, the two were mutually reinforcing.

Ideas about race are reinforced and made real by material factors such as slavery and other forms of exploitation, as well as by general social disadvantage.[33] The practical manifestation of racial categories occurs in many ways and includes both the conceptual violence of regarding certain groups as "other" and inferior, the physical violence produced by this perception, the legitimation of the racist world-view through legislation and other types of legal recognition, and strategies of resistance to these forms of domination.

Racial Domination and Anti-racism Strategies

[720] To state that race is a cultural construct does not negate its reality: it is rather to say that it has no "natural" reality, but is firmly entrenched in our psyches, our institutions, our knowledge, and our social practices. This point is of the utmost significance: it would be both naïve and dangerous to believe that the recognition that race is an illusion, a figment of the collective imagination, is sufficient to negate its power. It is difficult to "undiscover" aspects of social ordering which are so firmly embedded in both our world-view and our actual social relations.

Colette Guillaumin
Racism, Sexism, Power, and Ideology[34]

[725] It is not possible to argue that a category which organizes whole states (the Third Reich, the Republic of South Africa, etc), and which is incorporated into the law, does not exist. It is not possible to claim that the category which is the direct cause, the primary means, of the murder of millions of human beings does not exist.

...

... the legal inscription of race and the practices that accompany it certainly do exist. And they are precisely the reality of race. Race does not exist. But it does kill people. It also continues to provide the backbone of some ferocious systems of domination. And in France today it is rearing its ugly head once again. Not in the shameful margins of our society, but behind the honourable mask of 'opinions' and 'ideas'. Let us be clear about this. The idea, the notion of race is a technical means, a machine, for committing murder. And its effectiveness is not in doubt. It is a way of rationalizing and organizing by murderous violence the domination of powerful social groups over other groups reduced to powerlessness. Unless anyone is prepared to claim that, since race does not exist, nobody is or can ever have been repressed or killed because of their race. And nobody

---

33   Richard Delgado, "Two Ways to Think about Race: Reflections on the Id, the Ego, and Other Reformist Theories of Equal Protection" (2001) 89 *Georgetown Law Journal* 2279.

34   Collette Guillaumin, *Racism, Sexism, Power and Ideology* (Routledge, London, 1995), pp 106-107.

> can make that claim, because millions of human beings have died as a result of their race, and millions of others are now dominated, excluded and repressed for the same reason.
>
> No, race does not exist. And yet it does. Not in the way that people think; but it remains the most tangible, real and brutal of realities.

[730] Race does not exist as a natural or biological category, and in this sense it is nothing more than a cultural fiction which has at times been lent legitimacy by science and philosophy. Nonetheless, because it has become so widespread, especially in the Western view of the world, it has, as Guillaumin states, had extremely bloody consequences, and continues to be the basis for all sorts of "domination, exclusion and repression", including physical violence. Thus Racism has become entrenched materially as well as ideologically.[35] Moreover, identities and alliances are formed in relation to the concept of race, and while identities reinforcing white power need to be questioned and dis-aggregated, it may be strategically necessary for resistance movements to use racial identity in order to consolidate their political claims. In this sense, consciousness of race is for the time being an undeniable dimension of social existence in the West. Even those who argue in favour of dismantling race consciousness do not deny that race has practical consequences for the world.[36] It is therefore extremely important to understand the various ways in which racial domination is manifested, as well as the strategies deployed to combat it.

Racism and liberal anti-racism

[735] Unlike concepts such as "nationality", "ethnicity", or "culture", "race" is an attempt to classify the human element of the natural world. "Racism" as we normally understand it is the presumption that race determines characteristics such as intelligence, work ethic, and moral fibre. Specifically, it is usually the presumption that white people are naturally or biologically superior, especially in relation to intelligence and morality. As I explained above, such a perspective has been thoroughly entrenched in Western ideology by science and philosophy and material exploitation. The idea of natural racial difference has also been enforced by law in many countries. For instance, upon the invasion of Australia, the Indigenous people became British subjects, a status which afforded them, however, little and meaningless protection from the law. On the contrary, the history of state violence — including (but not limited to) mass killing — against Indigenous people suggests

---

35   Delgado, "Two Ways to Think about Race".

36   See, for instance, Reginald Leamon Robinson, "The Shifting Race Consciousness Matrix and the Multiracial Category Movement: A Critical Reply to Professor Hernandez" (2000) 20 *Boston College Third World Law Journal* 231; Reginald Leamon Robinson, "'Expert' Knowledge: Introductory Comments on Race Consciousness" (2000) 20 *Boston College Third World Law Journal* 145.

precisely the opposite.[37] As Kenneth Nunn comments in relation to colonialism generally, "Although the European was liberal with his law, he was parsimonious with his rights."[38] Prior to 1967, the Australian states had the power to make laws in relation to Aboriginal people, a power which was exercised in various "protection" statutes. For much of the 20th century these statutes established reserves upon which many Indigenous people were forced to live and work, while being denied wages and citizenship.[39] They also required the removal of "half caste" children from Indigenous communities in order to assimilate them into white society.[40] In the United States, between 1790 and 1952, only "free white persons" could be naturalised as citizens, leading to an extensive jurisprudence on the meaning of whiteness.[41] Although African-Americans were citizens by birth since the passing of the Fourteenth Amendment in 1868, the practice of racial segregation was not regarded as antithetical to the "equal protection" provision until the Supreme Court decision of *Brown v Board of Education* in 1954.[42]

As a result of pressure brought to bear on national governments by race activists,[43] *explicitly* discriminatory laws have generally been dismantled in the Western world. Within the liberal West it has been common in recent decades to regard racism as a problem of individual ignorance or prejudice which, when it exists on a large scale, results in the social disadvantage of specific racial groups. If this were correct, eliminating racial disadvantage should be as simple as eliminating racial prejudice from a reasonable proportion of the population (not practically

---

37   See generally Heather McRae, Garth Nettheim, and Laura Beacroft, *Indigenous Legal Issues* (3rd ed, Lawbook Co., Pyrmont NSW, 2003), pp 36-43; Valerie Kerruish, "Responding to Kruger: The Constitutionality of Genocide" (1998) 11 *Australian Feminist Law Journal* 65.

38   Kenneth Nunn, "Law as a Eurocentric Enterprise" (1997) 15 *Law and Inequality* 323 at 361.

39   Jennifer Clarke, "Law and Race: The Position of Indigenous People" in Stephen Bottomley and Stephen Parker, *Law in Context* (2nd ed, Federation Press, Sydney, 1997), pp 251-257. See also McRae, Nettheim and Beacroft, *Indigenous Legal Issues*, pp 43-50.

40   See *Bringing Them Home*, Report of the National Inquiry Into the Separation of Aboriginal and Torres Strait Islander Children from Their Families (Commonwealth of Australia, 1997). On 13 February 2008, the Australian Parliament finally apologised for the policies and laws which led to the removal of Indigenous children, instantly creating a more hopeful environment for relations between Indigenous and non-Indigenous Australians. Of course, this important symbolic gesture must also be accompanied by effective material, structural, and — within the non-Indigenous community — ideological changes.

41   See Angela Harris, "Equality Trouble: Sameness and Difference in Twentieth Century Race Law" (2000) 88 *California Law Review* 1923.

42   (1954) 347 US 483.

43   In Australia, the Federation for the Advancement of Aborigines and Torres Strait Islanders was at the forefront of efforts to remove power over Indigenous people from state legislatures. See Clarke, "Law and Race", pp 256-257. This activism was built upon a much longer tradition of Indigenous activism and resistance. See Geoffrey Stokes, "Citizenship and Aboriginality: Two Conceptions of Identity in Aboriginal Political Thought" in Stokes (ed), *The Politics of Identity in Australia* (Cambridge University Press, Cambridge, 1997).

"simple", but clear-cut in conceptual terms). The most obvious strategies of an anti-racist agenda are structurally similar to the strategies deployed by liberal feminism, which aimed to show that rationality, intelligence, and morality were not biologically male characteristics, and to eliminate legal discrimination against women. The liberal agenda in the case of racial domination has involved discrediting the biological notion of race, showing that biologically all are equal in the characteristics of a human being, educating people that this is the case, and eliminating any legal classifications which reinforce presumptions of natural difference. "Equality" is the benchmark for such an anti-racist agenda. The Civil Rights movement in the United States is probably the most well-known example of a broad anti-racist movement which aimed to combat the biological notion of race and to ensure equality before the law.

Beyond the liberal discourse of racial discrimination

[740] Clearly, however, modern manifestations of racism go beyond the claim of biological difference and hierarchy. Nor was racism ever entirely a question of individual prejudice or ignorance. In the past decade, scholars of race have noticed the emergence of a new form of racism, labelled "neo-racism" or "cultural racism":[44]

> During the 1980s, several sociologists and anti-racists discerned the growing presence of a British "new racism" — It was argued that, following the Holocaust and the comprehensive discrediting of nineteenth-century scientific racism, racism based upon biological theories of superior and inferior races was no longer intellectually and politically viable as a public discourse. Instead, what had emerged was a racism based upon cultural differences, upon the "natural" preference of human beings for their own cultural group, and the incompatibility between different cultures, the mixing or coexistence of which in one country, it was alleged, was bound to lead to violent social conflict and the dissolution of social bonds.

As Modood points out, this neo-racism was not confined to Britain, but had a lengthy international genesis, gaining a social niche once the crude theory of biological superiority was definitively discredited. Adopting some aspects of the idea of cultural relativism, it claimed that there was a natural (and therefore inevitable) basis to the separation of cultures — essentially that people *naturally* maintain their inherited cultural groups, are intolerant of other mainstream cultural groups and, therefore, it is inviting trouble to try to mix cultures within one society. Such a view would justify, for instance, the dismantling of policies of multiculturalism, the restriction of immigration to those felt

---

44   Tariq Modood, "'Difference', Cultural Racism and Anti-Racism" in Werbner and Modood (eds), *Debating Cultural Hybridity: Multi-Cultural Identities and the Politics of Anti-Racism* (Zed Books, London, 1997), p 154. See also Michel Wievorka, "Is It So Difficult to Be Anti-Racist" in the same volume; David Bennett "Introduction" in Bennett (ed), *Multicultural States: Rethinking Difference and Identity* (Routledge, London, 1998), and Andrew Markus, *Race: John Howard and the Remaking of Australia* (Allen and Unwin, Sydney, 2001).

to be culturally compatible with the dominant group, and the demand for Indigenous people and ethnic minorities to be assimilated and to receive "equal" not "special" treatment. Insofar as "others" are not like "us", they should become so, or go back to wherever they came from. (Sound familiar? If it does, it is because ideas such as these have become widespread throughout the Western world.) It is easy to see that even the term "racist" becomes contested in this context: on the one hand, it is used to characterise those who want to block the special measures designed to level the playing field, at the same time, it is also used against those who defend such measures, on the grounds that they are "anti-white".[45] So entrenched is the liberal rhetoric of formal equality.

In addition to the new cultural racism, critics have also in recent years become more attentive to non-individual and structural forms of racial domination. It should be reasonably obvious from the foregoing discussion that the construct of race in Europe was not culturally neutral, nor a mere scientific observation,[46] it was inherently Eurocentric, meaning that the values associated with human beings were European values: the West created humankind in its own image, and classified those who did not fit the image as inferior. Moreover, the West has gradually gathered the power to enforce this "truth" throughout the world. As a result of colonial expansion, followed by cultural and economic imperialism, the Western world view with its ideal of the rational and autonomous individual, organised in highly institutionalised secular societies, has become prevalent.

I will have more to say on the meaning of "whiteness" and its relationship to a racialised "other" later in the chapter. For the moment, I simply wish to note the systemic, institutional, and material character of modern racial dominance. To say that racism is "systemic" is to recognise that differentiation on the basis of race is not merely a prejudice held by some individuals, whether consciously or unconsciously. It is rather to note that the concept of "race" and its inbuilt hierarchical presumptions are embedded in the Western world-view. Society is structured racially. To say that race is "institutionalised" is to recognise that that this systemic racism runs into and shapes the institutions governing society.

For instance, although law now tends to be formally "race-neutral", and forbids individual racial discrimination (and sometimes vilification), it still presumes a model of the person and a model of law which reflect the values of white, culturally hegemonic, Europe. According to Kenneth Nunn the attributes of Eurocentric thought enshrined in law

---

45   Markus, *Race*, p 3; Wievorka, "Is It So Difficult to Be Anti-Racist" in Werbner and Modood (eds), *Debating Cultural Hybridity*, p 139.

46   There is debate over whether racism (and therefore race) is universal, that is, whether it exists in all societies. As Dinesh D'Souza points out, most societies exhibit some form of ethnocentrism, but not all are racist: D'Souza, *The End of Racism*, pp 33-36. In Western thought, however, ethnocentrism and racism are two sides of the same coin.

include the following: dichotomous reasoning, division of the world into hierarchies, analytical thought, objectification, abstraction, extreme rationalism, and "desacralisation" (that is, a view of the cosmos which is secular and non-spiritual).[47] The positivist separation of law from culture and morality exhibits all of these attributes. Separating law from morality involves the creation of a dichotomy (law, as opposed to morality, whether natural or cultural), which is clearly hierarchical, the product of a rational abstract objectification of law and denies any relevance to law of the spiritual dimension of people and their communities. At a fundamental level, this positivist separation involves a separation of law from the individual. The individual and her law are separate entities, and this separation itself excludes from the very concept of law's methods of social ordering not based on the differentiation of the person from the law. Irene Watson says of Indigenous law, "The law is who we are, we are also the law."[48] Such a notion of law as intrinsically connected to the identity of persons within a community is so foreign to the West that we have for a long time been much more comfortable calling Indigenous laws "culture" or "religion".

Law and the positivist concept of law therefore reflect the cultural values associated with whiteness: given the origins and history of Western law, this is not perhaps surprising, and nor would it *necessarily* be indicative of institutional racism if Western legal systems did not have a tendency to nullify the differences between legal subjects within its borders, and refuse to acknowledge the existence and legitimacy of types of law which do not conform to the Western model. Western legal theory, while purporting to theorise the (universal) concept of law, has singularly failed to consider non-Western concepts of law: it tells its own story of origins and progress, without reflecting upon whether this experience of law is shared by all.[49] Indeed, we (white Westerners) are quite accustomed to speak unreflectively about **the** law, as though it is perfectly obvious what we mean. The Western concept of law — essentially legal positivism — admits only one law, and it is the dominant institutionalised state-based version. This linguistic act of exclusion obliterates other laws: in the case of Australia, for example, it obliterates consciousness and recognition of Indigenous laws.[50]

---

47   Nunn, "Law as a Eurocentric Enterprise", pp 333-338.

48   Irene Watson, "Indigenous Peoples' Law-Ways: Survival Against the Colonial State", p 39. See also Margaret Davies, "Legal Separatism and the Concept of the Person" in Tom Campbell and Jeffrey Goldsworthy (eds), *Judicial Power, Democracy, and Legal Positivism* (Ashgate, Aldershot, 2000).

49   See Set Lee Schmutz, "No Longer Mute" (1997) 3 *Law/Text/Culture* 7.

50   See Irene Watson, "Power of the Muldarbi, The Road to Its Demise" (1998) 11 *Australian Feminist Law Journal* 28 and "Kalsowinyeri — Munaintya — In the Beginning" (2000) 4 *Flinders Journal of Law Reform* 3; see also Ruby Langford Ginibi, "Aboriginal Traditional and Customary Law" (1994) 1 *Law/Text/Culture* 8.

In the context of systemic racism, there is arguably no absolutely clear-cut distinction between individuals who are "racist" and "non-racist" or "anti-racist". Certainly, there are views which we would have no trouble in labelling as individually racist, such as the biological determinism outlined above. However, if racial domination is structural, then individual racist attitudes are only part of the problem. The problem also exists in the relationships of power embedded in our institutions, language, cultural symbolism and distribution of resources.

The various types of racism and the forms of racial dominance and exclusion which they support, are often separated in order to understand more clearly how racism operates. However, it should be said that throughout history, and in the contemporary world, they are often not distinct, but mutually supportive. The plurality of forms of racial dominance calls for a variety of responses, and in the rest of this chapter I aim to focus on scholarship which highlights ongoing racial dominance and which offers some distinct strategies to combat it.

To simplify, I have divided the remainder of the chapter into three further sections, each of which considers a separate aspect of race theory. These dimensions of the scholarship are not comprehensive, nor are they entirely distinct from each other, although they do evoke different traditions in race theory — notably scholarship relating to colonialism, sociological theory of whiteness, and US critical race theory. Briefly, the three sections are as follows:

• *Colonialism and Postcolonialism:* The colonial expansion of the early modern period was underpinned by the view that Indigenous peoples were mere savages, frequently with no attachment to land, and little if any law. Modern critiques of colonialism are interesting for several reasons: in particular, they illustrate the oppositional or dualistic thought (self and other) which is characteristic of racial domination and which is physically manifested in colonial situations; they show the complete arrogance of the Western epistemological mentality which could only see a single form of "Truth"; and some also, most interestingly, demonstrate that colonialism is not a thing of the unenlightened (or imperfectly enlightened) past, but continues to operate in places such as Australia which have never been decolonised. The concept of postcolonialism was developed in the 1980s to describe the complex situation of those living in post-independence states. Neither pre-colonial nor colonial, "postcolonial" refers to a condition of multiple or "hybrid" existence. Postcolonialism describes a certain cultural condition, but it also for some provides a challenge to dualistic thinking about race, ethnicity, and culture — it breaks down the oppositions between subject and object, West and East, and white and non-white.

• *Whiteness:* Theory which objectifies whiteness turns the tables, so to speak, on the self/other, subject/object dichotomies. Western anthropology has often regarded non-Western societies as the "other" to be studied through "objective" Western methods. Whiteness theory objectifies or "anthropologises" white supremacy.[51] It makes white people and white culture the object (although it

---

51   Ali Rattansi and Sallie Westwood, *Racism, Modernity and Identity: On the Western Front* (Polity Press, Oxford, 1994), pp 5-6.

has to be said, a peculiar and somewhat active object — we are not passivised by theory in quite the same way as non-Western others). The point of whiteness studies is to encourage self-reflectiveness about whiteness as a racial category, and to discredit the idea that issues of "race" concern only non-white people. It also aims to dismantle white power and privilege.

• *Race Consciousness:* One of the enduring features of racial thought is the exclusion of the non-white other on the basis of its difference from the white norm. The effect has been to dehumanise and obliterate any subjectivity in this other. The liberal concept of colour-blindness, while intended to ensure that all peoples are equally regarded as subjects, merely reinforces the benchmark white subject. The development of race consciousness and multiple consciousness foregrounds the existence of different identities, and also the differences within any identity.

Colonialism

[745] In hindsight, the fact of widespread colonialism seems at once both extraordinary and mundane. On the one hand it is extraordinary when viewed in the light of modern notions of self-determination and respect for sovereignty: how could any nation think it had the right to enter and appropriate huge areas of the world which were already populated without the permission of the inhabitants?[52] How could any nation feel that it could justifiably exterminate or displace whole populations merely in order to advance its own political or economic needs? The puzzlement is all the greater given that colonialism continued through the age of Enlightenment, when Western humanity was supposedly achieving a more humanist and rational outlook. On the other hand, colonialism is also in a sense depressingly familiar: the context in which it took place was, as I have indicated above, one in which white racial superiority was increasingly regarded as natural and, in the world-wide context, white people were set against inferior racial "others".

The subjects and objects of Western knowledge

[750] Through the age of colonisation, the dualistic thought of the West was aligned with a European/non-European dichotomy so that non-European "others" were mere objects and not political or moral agents. Rousseau's "noble savage" may have been noble but as Charles Mills points out, he or she was still, in the end, savage.[53] Enlightened knowledge was knowledge of, and power over, this objectified world.

---

52   The instructions given to Captain James Cook — that Australia was only to be occupied "with the consent of the natives", or if it was uninhabited — suggest some sense of limitation here, if a minor one, given that the British had the power to define the Indigenous people out of existence, and demonstrated this power by doing it. See Alex Castles, *An Australian Legal History* (Law Book Company, Sydney, 1982).

53   Mills, *The Racial Contract*, Ch 1. See also Robert Williams, *The American Indian in Western Legal Thought* (Oxford University Press, New York, 1990) and "Documents of Barbarism: The Contemporary Legacy of European Racism and Colonialism in the Narrative Traditions of Federal Indian Law" (1989) 31 *Arizona Law Review* 237.

Western knowledge was structured so that if you weren't a subject, you were an object and on a continuum with nature — hence not only women,[54] but also Indigenous people, Africans, and other non-white people were associated with the realm of nature and, like nature, there to be governed, controlled, mastered, and enslaved. I should note that the *Western* concept of nature reduces it to a debased resource to be dominated, mastered, or exchanged for money, but this obviously is not a universal perception.[55]

The oppositional model of knowledge which provided part of the context for the colonisation of areas outside Europe was not only a matter of abstract science or philosophy. (As Adorno and Horkheimer said, abstraction liquidates its objects.[56]) Frantz Fanon was a Black psychiatrist who became a resister to the French colonial regime in Algeria. In the following extract he depicts the dualistic nature of the colonial world: a world in which colonised and coloniser are completely at odds, separated by a line of physical force imprinted on the colonised landscape.

Frantz Fanon
The Wretched of the Earth[57]

[755]   The colonial world is a world cut in two. The dividing line, the frontiers are shown by barracks and police stations. In the colonies it is the policeman and the soldier who are the official, instituted go-betweens, the spokesmen of the settler and his rule of oppression. ... In the colonial countries ... the policeman and the soldier, by their immediate presence and their frequent and direct action maintain contact with the native and advise him by means of rifle-butts and napalm not to budge. It is obvious here that the agents of government speak the language of pure force. ...

The zone where the natives live is not complementary to the zone inhabited by the settlers. The two zones are opposed, but not in the service of a higher unity. ... The settlers' town is a strongly-built town, all made of stone and steel. It is a brightly-lit town; the streets are covered with asphalt, and the garbage-cans swallow all the leavings, unseen and unknown and hardly thought about. The settler's feet are never visible, except perhaps in the sea; but there you're never close enough to see them. His feet are protected by strong shoes although the streets of his town are clean and even, with no

---

54   As I explained in Chapter 6, feminists have noted that women are frequently associated with "nature" rather than "culture", and with "emotion" rather than "reason". As Aileen Moreton-Robinson points out, however, white feminist scholars have effectively appropriated the position of the rational knower whose race and cultural positioning is invisible: see Moreton-Robinson, "Troubling Business: Difference and Whiteness Within Feminism" (2000) 15 *Australian Feminist Studies* 343.

55   See Irene Watson, "Power of the Muldarbi, the Road to its Demise".

56   See the quotation above at [710] under the heading "Race as Construct".

57   Frantz Fanon, *The Wretched of the Earth* (McGibbon and Kee, London, 1965). See also Jean-Paul Sartre, "Colonialism is a System" (2001) 3 *Interventions* 127.

holes or stones. The settler's town is a well-fed town, an easy-going town; its belly is always full of good things. The settler's town is a town of white people, of foreigners.

The town belonging to the colonised people, or at least the native town, the Negro village, the medina, the reservation, is a place of ill fame, peopled by men of evil repute. They are born there, it matters little where or how; they die there, it matters not where, nor how. It is a world without spaciousness; men live there on top of each other, and their huts are built one on top of the other. The native town is a hungry town, starved of bread, of meat, of shoes, of coal, of light. The native town is a crouching village, a town on its knees, a town wallowing in the mire.

[760]   The symbols of the colonising power are everywhere. The colonial world is a "world of statues: the statue of the general who carried out the conquest, the statue of the engineer who built the bridge."[58] (It hardly needs to be pointed out that such symbols need not be statues, but can also be names of streets, cities, buildings, universities, etc.) Because he wrote compellingly about a number of themes raised in postcolonial thought, Fanon is frequently regarded as a writer who, in the 1960s, anticipated the later development of postcolonialism. These themes include the effects of colonisation on the consciousness of both the coloniser and colonised; the colonial construction of the "other" and the adoption of this construction by colonised peoples; and the contested, threatened nature of culture under colonialism and "after" colonialism. (It is a theme of postcolonialism that colonialism doesn't really end except in a legal way, since the effects of colonialism are enduring, both for the colonised and the colonisers.) However, as the extract illustrates, Fanon's point of departure was not a post-independence state where these complexities are given expression by a population which is, at least in legal terms, self-determining and autonomous. Rather, his analysis emphasised the position of the still colonised state where the opposition between the natives and the colonial regime is the paramount consideration.

Terra nullius and continuing colonialism

[765]   The oppositional nature of colonialism is also illustrated in Australia, where there was an attempt to define the Indigenous people out of existence, and numerous attempts to make that definition a practical reality. For two hundred years the colonisation of Australia was justified by reference to the fiction that Australia was "terra nullius" when the first governor planted the British flag and claimed what is now New South Wales, Queensland, Victoria, Tasmania, part of South Australia, as well as adjacent islands, for Britain.[59] The fact that the land was regarded as terra nullius, or belonging to no-one, meant that under international law (allegedly based on natural law) it was available for

58   Frantz Fanon, *The Wretched of the Earth*, p 40.
59   Castles, *An Australian Legal History*, p 25.

settlement, and that British law would automatically operate in the new territory.[60] As Jennifer Clarke notes,[61]

> At this time, this body of law was like a code of honour among thieves. It governed relations between 'sovereign', 'civilised' European nation states, but was not particularly concerned with the relationship between those states and the populations of colonised territories.

The actual existence of the Indigenous people was at best a minor obstacle to the classification of the land as terra nullius. The following passage from Vattel's *Law of Nations* is frequently quoted, but worth repeating for its blunt certainty that European overcrowding justified expansion, and furthermore, that uncultivated land could not really be said to be possessed at all.[62]

> ... in speaking of the obligation of cultivating the earth, ... these tribes cannot take to themselves more land than they have need of or can inhabit or cultivate. Their uncertain occupancy of these vast regions can not be held as a real and lawful taking of possession; and when the Nations of Europe, which are too confined at home, come upon lands which the savages have no special need of and are making no present and continuous use of, they may lawfully take possession of them and establish colonies in them.

Like many others of his time, Vattel claimed that his views represented the natural law (which, as we saw in Chapter 3, comes in so many forms that any claim to "naturalness" is really very suspect). The appeal to natural law, of course, is a very powerful justification, since it carries with it the significance of absolute right, of universal justification, and — for Vattel as for many others — the authority of the Christian god.

According to mainstream legal orthodoxy, the fiction of terra nullius was jettisoned from Australian law by the decision in *Mabo v Queensland*.[63] In that case, for the first time in Australia's Western legal history, the High Court accepted a claim to native title, a decision which involved the formal acknowledgement that terra nullius was a fabrication and that Indigenous people did have a relationship to land recognisable by law. Importantly, however, the decision was qualified by the fact that native title was recognisable within *Australian* (that is,

---

60   See William Blackstone, *Commentaries on the Laws of England*, Vol I (1765), pp 104-105. For an extended and subtle analysis of the law relating to colonialism, see Peter Fitzpatrick, *Modernism and the Grounds of Law* (Oxford University Press, Oxford, 2001), Ch 5 "Imperialism".

61   Clarke, "Law and Race", p 246.

62   Vattel, *Law of Nations*, Bk 1 ch 8 reprinted in Alex Castles and JH Bennett, *A Source Book of Australian Legal History* (Law Book Company, Sydney, 1979), p 251. See also John Locke, *Two Treatises of Government*, Second Treatise (Cambridge University Press, Cambridge, 1967), Ch 5. Locke argued that property was derived from mixing one's labour with natural resources. It seems that where there was no true mixing (by way of appropriating and transforming), just hunting and gathering, there could be no property.

63   *Mabo v Queensland* (1992) 175 CLR 1.

the colonial) law. The decision does not "recognise" Indigenous law, beyond the recognition that it exists. It merely constructs a new fiction — "native title" — within the framework of Western law. Indigenous law is assimilated in a form palatable to the dominant law within Australia. None of the judges were willing to question the legitimacy of the invasion of Australia, and nor, as Brennan CJ said, would they take any action which would rupture the inviolable "skeleton of principle which gives the body of our law its internal shape and consistency".[64] On the contrary, the acts of violence which led to the foundation of Australia's legal system are merely repeated in this decision by the very refusal to question sovereignty, and by the creation of a Westernised version of Indigenous law.[65] As Indigenous legal scholar and activist Irene Watson argues, therefore, terra nullius is still with us.

Irene Watson
"Indigenous Peoples' Law-Ways: Survival Against the Colonial State"[66]

[770]   Many people might argue that terra nullius was put to rest by the High Court in the Native Title decision. This decision was celebrated as being an initiative in reconciliation, when it overturned the application of terra nullius to Australia's law of real property. However the High Court did not fully reject the terra nullius doctrine. This was avoided through their failure to question the legitimacy of the British occupation of Australia. The High Court decided that the invasion and the British Crown's acquisition of sovereignty over the Australian colony was an "act of state" that could not be challenged in any Australian court. In reaching this conclusion the High Court sanctioned colonialism, dispossession and disempowerment of Nungas, as a legitimate "act of state".

---

64   *Mabo v Queensland* (1992) 175 CLR 1 at 29.

65   See generally on the issue of founding violence Sangeetha Chandra-Shekeran, "Challenging the Fiction of the Nation in the 'Reconciliation' Texts of *Mabo* and *Bringing The Home*" (1998) 11 *Australian Feminist Law Journal* 107. For further critical commentary see the collection of essays in (2002) 13 *Law and Critique*, including Shaugnnagh Dorsett and Shaun McVeigh, "Just So: The Law Which Governs Australia is Australian Law", p 289; Peter Fitzpatrick, "'No Higher Duty': Mabo and the Failure of Legal Foundation", p 233; Valerie Kerruish, "At the Court of the Strange God", p 271; Stewart Motha, "The Sovereign Event in a Nation's Law", p 311. Published in the same volume, but written in a different idiom and from a different perspective is Irene Watson's "Buried Alive", p 253.

66   Irene Watson, "Indigenous Peoples' Law-Ways: Survival Against the Colonial State", pp 47-48. "Nunga" refers to the Indigenous people. The article by Paul Coe referred to by Watson is "Mabo-Confirming Dispossession" (1993) *Broadside*, 10 February, p 9. See also Watson, "Buried Alive"; Ginibi, "Aboriginal and Traditional Customary Law"; Jacqui Katona, "'If Native Title Is Us, It's Inside Us': Jabiluka and the Politics of Intercultural Negotiation" (1998) 10 *Australian Feminist Law Journal* 1; Hannah McGlade and Jeannine Purdy, "From Theory to Practice: Or What is a Homeless Yamatji Grandmother Anyway?" (1998) 11 *Australian Feminist Law Journal* 137; Michael Detmold, "Law and Difference: Reflections on Mabo's Case" (1993) 15 *Sydney Law Review* 158; Valerie Kerruish, "Responding to Kruger: The Constitutionality of Genocide" (1998) 11 *Australian Feminist Law Journal* 65.

Indigenous barrister Paul Coe points out the comparative thinking behind
the High Court and the state of Germany during the tyranny rule of Hitler.
The same justification — an "act of state", was used by the Nazis in the
attempted genocide of the Jewish people. The High Court has merely
closeted terra nullius, and to replace it, the court has taken off the hanger
the "act of state" doctrine. The legal theory of terra nullius has remained
intact. The real death of terra nullius would have dismantled the Australian
legal system.

The impact of terra nullius surrounds us: violations of our law, ecological
destruction of our lands and waters, dispossession from our territories and
the colonisation of our being. Terra nullius has not stopped; the violations
of our law continue, the ecological destruction of the earth our mother
continues with a vengeance, we are still struggling to return to the land,
and the assimilator-integrator model is still being forced upon us. This is
terra nullius in its practical and continuing application. There is no death
of terra nullius. Its life is my struggle against extinguishment: the end of
struggle against extinguishment would be the death of terra nullius. The
celebration of the death of terra nullius is a farce: a collective act of schizo-
phrenia, a false-hood, a conspiratorial lie, which has lulled the Australian
psyche into a fantasy myth that there had been in the Native Title decision
an act of recognition of indigenous peoples' rights.

[775] Watson argues that Australia is still governed by a colonial legal system.
As far as the non-Indigenous people are concerned, colonialism ended
at some point between Federation and the Australia Acts in 1986, which
abolished the power of the British legislature to legislate for the
Australian States. Despite the Queen's continuing constitutional
presence (absence?), we non-Indigenous Australians like to think of the
nation as independent.[67] However, for many Indigenous people, this
"decolonisation" is quite meaningless and simply involved a transfer of
colonial power from Britain to the Australian governments. There has
been no decolonisation, no withdrawal of sovereignty from any
territory, no recognition of Indigenous law, and no recognition of the
right to self-determination. The forceful imposition of a colonial
sovereign power remains complete. It has merely naturalised itself by
breaking from its parent sovereign.[68]

---

67 Patrick Parkinson comments "The Australia Acts thus represented an important
symbolic break with Britain, emphasised by the Queen's visit to Australia to sign the
legislation personally.": *Tradition and Change in Australian Law* (3rd ed, Lawbook Co.,
Pyrmont NSW, 2005), p 142. It is unclear to me whether Parkinson is aware of the irony
of his statement: Australia's independence is underlined by a personal visit from the
Queen — as though the authority or legitimacy of the separation was confirmed by the
Queen herself, the very embodiment of dependence.

68 This ongoing colonialism is underlined by the subsequent history of native title claims:
see generally Valerie Kerruish and Colin Perrin, "Awash in Colonialism" (1999) 24 (1)
Alternative Law Journal 3; Ben Golder, "Law, History, Colonialism: An Orientalist Reading
of Australian Native Title Law" (2004) 9 *Deakin Law Review* 41; Kirsten Anker, "Law in the
Present Tense: Tradition and Cultural Continuity in *Members of the Yorta Yorta Aboriginal
Community v Victoria*" (2004) 28 *Melbourne University Law Review* 1.

Considered from the point of view of legal theory, the continuation of terra nullius is easily explained, though not justified. As we saw in Chapters 3 and 4, the prevailing ideology of law in the modern Western world is the concept of positivism, under which law is seen to be singular (one law governs one territory), separable from morality and culture, and institutionalised.[69] The Western *concept* of law excludes other law: it excludes for instance the possibility of law existing outside its domain yet within its "own" territory; it excludes questions about its own existence, presuming instead its own legitimacy, even though this legitimacy is arguably due to nothing more than force (and in the case of many colonised nations, is completely dubious); and it excludes from the idea or concept of law any law which is not institutionalised after a Western model. In this way the racial dominance of Indigenous peoples by law extends well beyond the ways in which the Western legal system treats individual persons. It is also built into the ideological self-justification of Western law.

To my mind, what is called for in this context from Western legal scholars is self-reflectiveness about the philosophical landscape which has facilitated this dominance. This is not a new idea, although it has only recently been taken on board by those in a position of privilege. For decades, non-Western scholars have suggested the urgent need for the West to reflect upon itself. As others have said, Western scholars need to "anthropologise" or objectify our power and our ways of thinking, to put these matters into question, rather than merely assume their validity. One example of the objectification of white dominance is the emerging field of whiteness studies, which I will consider shortly.

Postcolonial thought

[780] The term "postcolonialism" was coined in the 1980s to describe cultures where colonial rule had formally ended, such as India, the Caribbean states, and areas within Africa and Asia. The term does not necessarily imply an end to colonialism, but rather a change in its dynamics. In other words, the "post" here does not simply mean *after* colonialism or *beyond* it in any simple sense, but rather denotes the continuation of colonialism in the consciousness of the formerly colonised people and in the institutions which were imposed in the process of colonisation. Thus, where speaking of "colonialism" implies a clear dividing line between the colonisers and the colonised, "postcolonialism" implies a more complex situation, where the mentality and culture of the (physically departed) colonisers has been brought to bear on the colonised people. Thus the term recognises that decolonisation does not result in a return to a pre-colonial state, but rather movement into a "postcolonial" state, where the effects of colonialism have become an inextricable part of the culture and of its

---

69   For a more extensive analysis of positivism see Margaret Davies, "Legal Separatism and the Concept of the Person".

legal, educational, and political institutions, and where the colonial state still serves as a reference point in local discourse.

To the extent that there may be said to be a core or original denotation of the term "postcolonial" then, it is that it refers to the study of the continuing effects of colonial power in post-independence societies. However, the term has expanded well beyond this original sense, and is now used (or over-used) to characterise the condition of all groups affected in one way or another by a past or present colonialism or imperialism:[70] this includes peoples from former colonies who have migrated to Western colonising powers, as well as white Western people whose identities have been formed, in part, by the discourse of colonialism (in particular its notions of racial and cultural superiority). However, a few qualifications need to be offered. First, arguably this global reach of the term is inappropriate to certain situations. For example, if, as Irene Watson argues, Australia remains colonial, then the term "postcolonialism" will only falsify the present situation and obscure its continuity with the past.[71] It will obscure the fact that some of us continue to enjoy the considerable privileges and benefits of the colonisers, obtained at the expense of Indigenous people. Thus, even when speaking of "post-colonialism", it is important to maintain recognition of continuing colonialism. Secondly, postcolonial thought has also not always been popular with those who see it as yet another use of Western academic theorising (whether conducted by expatriates or by inhabitants of post-independence states) to comprehend and appropriate the non-Western "other". Recognising this, as well as the multitude of different colonial situations and types of resistance to colonialism, it is important not to reduce the specificity of various experiences into one "postcolonial" experience.[72] (Having said that, what follows is of necessity a very simplified account.[73])

Postcolonial theory is associated with postmodernism (which will be the subject of Chapter 8), however, the critique of theoretical "meta-narratives" undertaken by postcolonialism specifically targets their Western, colonial and imperialistic nature. Ratna Kapur summarises postcolonialism as being concerned with three key themes. First, postcolonialism critiques the "linear, progressive narrative of history

---

70   See, for instance, the description offered by Ato Quayson, *Postcolonialism: Theory, Practice, or Process* (Polity Press, Cambridge, 2000), p 2.

71   Watson, "Indigenous Peoples' Law-Ways: Survival Against the Colonial State", p 56; Curthoys, "An Uneasy Conversation", pp 31-34.

72   See Quayson, *Postcolonialism*, p 10.

73   Three writers are generally regarded as "core" in postcolonial studies — Edward Said, Homi Bhabba, and Gayatri Chakravorty Spivak. Because of the difficulty of her work, I do not consider Spivak in this section, though I would not want this omission to be read as an underestimation of her ideas. See Spivak, *The Postcolonial Critic: Interviews, Strategies, Dialogues*, Harasym (ed) (Routledge, New York, 1990); Spivak, *A Critique of Postcolonial Reason: Toward a History of the Vanishing Present* (Harvard University Press, Cambridge Mass, 1999).

that occupies the citadel of liberal doctrine".[74] This narrative has frequently been deployed in the service of depicting the world's cultures and nations as existing on a linear continuum from the more primitive to the most advanced, with Western institutions and values representing the standard by which all others are measured. Second "is the relationship between power and colonial knowledge-production, and how assumptions about the Other have come to be produced". This second aspect of postcolonialism illustrates the ways in which power is exercised through discourse and cultural representation; in particular, how the West has constituted the "orient" or the non-Western world as a cultural "other". Thirdly, and perhaps most centrally, postcolonialism is concerned with the ways in which culture and subjectivity (that is, the condition of becoming positioned as a subject in language, under the law, in relation to regimes of "knowledge", and so on) are affected by the distinctive experiences of colonialism and its aftermath: these experiences always involve some clash of cultures, and the understanding of the self in relation to a colonial dynamic, either as colonised or as coloniser. The following paragraphs elaborate on the second and third of these themes.

In his famous work *Orientalism*, Edward Said considers the study of the Orient in European universities. He argues that the Orient *as an idea* is the product of this research agenda: it is "not an inert fact of nature. It is not merely *there*, just as the Occident itself is not just *there* either."[75] In other words, a massive European discourse (academic, literary, journalistic, political, religious) created a theoretical object out of an enormously disparate reality, labelled it the Orient, and opposed it to another idea, the Occident. Said's endeavour is not to describe the material facts of colonialism, but rather to consider the Western/colonial representation of the Orient as other, and the way that this discourse gave (and still gives) the West power over its object, justifying Western imperialism:[76]

> I myself believe that Orientalism is more particularly valuable as a sign of European-Atlantic power over the Orient than it is as a veridic discourse about the Orient (which is what, in its academic or scholarly form, it claims to be).

As an academic discourse, the European study of Orientalism was supposedly concerned with discovering some "truth" about the Orient. However, Said's point is that this "truth" is an exercise of Western power: a method in domination and control. In making this argument, Said is applying Foucault's conceptualisation of the relationship between power and knowledge: in appropriating to itself knowledge

---

74   Ratna Kapur, *Erotic Justice: Law and the New Politics of Postcolonialism* (Glasshouse Press, London, 2005), pp 20-28. This and the next quotation appear on p 21.

75   Said, *Orientalism* (Penguin, Harmondsworth, 1978), p 4.

76   Said, *Orientalism*, p 6.

about the "Orient" the West asserts its power over the Orient. It has power to tell the "truth" about its object, and Orientalism therefore becomes "a science of imperialism".[77]

Following this enormously influential text, which illustrated the ways in which colonial and imperial knowledges were produced by the West, numbers of thinkers in the postcolonial tradition have been engaged in unpacking the consequences of colonialism. And while Said focused upon the production of a *Western* knowledge of the Orient, others have considered how these colonial discourses impact upon the colonised people. Well before the advent of postcolonialism, theorists of race and colonialism had noticed that the racially oppressed person or the colonised person experiences a double consciousness — the colonised person takes on the construction of themselves promulgated by the colonisers, while continuing to relate to their own cultural setting or racial group.[78] Homi Bhabba is one theorist who has taken this insight a little further, drawing upon psychoanalysis (and hence I can give only the most simple of explanations here) to explain the effect of colonial discourse upon colonised people.

According to Bhabba, the effects of colonial discourse cannot merely be understood in terms of the separate spheres of the "mother culture" and the "alien culture":[79] it is not a matter of identifying two parties, self and other, who are held apart by colonialism. Rather, colonialism produces "hybridity" — identities which are not single, not stable, but rather in flux, caught in the opposition between colonising and colonised culture. (And this "hybridity" is not merely the fate of the colonised people, but also of the colonisers, who must constantly define themselves against the colonised "other", leaving a trace of this denied other in their own identity.) Moreover, Bhabba claims that recognition and exploitation of this hybridity can lead to subversion: the creation and celebration of new identities and new ways of being, which are resolutely anti-essentialist and cross-cultural. For instance, Ratna Kapur quotes Salman Rushdie's description of his *Satanic Verses* as a celebration of "hybridity, impurity, intermingling, the transformation that comes of new and unexpected combinations of human

---

77   Young, *White Mythologies*, p 127.

78   See Frantz Fanon, *Black Skin, White Masks* (McGibbon and Kee, London, 1968), p 197. Fanon says, for instance, "As I begin to recognize that the Negro is the symbol of sin, I catch myself hating the Negro. But then I recognize that I am a Negro." Edward Kamau Brathwaite, *The Development of the Creole Society in Jamaica 1770-1820* (Clarendon Press, Oxford, 1971), as extracted in Ashcroft, Griffiths and Tiffin (eds), *The Postcolonial Studies Reader*, p 202.

79   "Signs Taken for Wonders: Questions of Ambivalence and Authority Under a Tree Outside Delhi, May 1817" (1985) 12 *Critical Inquiry*, as reproduced in Ashcroft, Griffiths, and Tiffin (eds), *The Postcolonial Studies Reader*, pp 34-35. See also Colin Perrin, "Approaching Anxiety: The Insistence of the Postcolonial in the Declaration of the Rights of Indigenous People" (1995) 6 *Law and Critique* 55.

beings, cultures, ideas, politics, movies, songs."[80] Postcolonialism thus "focuses on the resistive subject — that is, one who produces resistance in coercive circumstances, a deeply layered and multifaceted subject."[81] One structuring principle for such subjects is their sex and sexuality. Kapur's wider project is the articulation of a postcolonial legal feminism which shows how colonialist laws and practices, historically and in their successor forms, produce "complex and ambivalent results for women and sexual subalterns."[82]

Postcolonial thought offers ways of thinking about racial and cultural identity which are not oppositional or based on the dualisms of self and other, subject and object. This is arguably an important subversion of Western philosophy and ideology and in particular of the liberal emphasis on the autonomous and unsituated subject. However, it is important to be cautious in applying the term "postcolonial" too broadly: as the example of Indigenous peoples in white settler societies indicates, colonialism is not necessarily a thing of the past.

Objectifying Whiteness

[785]   We may be on our way to genuine hybridity, multiplicity without (white) hegemony, and it may be where we want to get to — but we aren't there yet, and we wont get there until we see whiteness, see its power, its particularity and limitedness, put it in its place and end its rule. This is why studying whiteness matters.[83]

[790]   The power (and invisibility) of the white norm has been such that study of the concept of whiteness is a very recent phenomenon. While debate about race and racism is very well established in academic, social, and political discussion, critical reflection about the practical consequences and normative associations of whiteness only developed in the late 1980s. Remarkably, issues of "race" have been seen, especially by white people, to concern *non*-white people, as though the problem of inequality is of interest only to its victims.[84] Over the last 15 years, however, a number of studies on the concept of whiteness as a racial

---

80   Ratna Kapur, "'A Love Song to Our Mongrel Selves': Hybridity, Sexuality, and the Law" (1999) 8 *Social and Legal Studies* 353.

81   Ratna Kapur, *Erotic Justice*, p 26.

82   Ratna Kapur, *Erotic Justice*, p 28

83   Richard Dyer, *White* (Routledge, London, 1997), p 4.

84   See, for instance, Toni Morrison, *Playing in the Dark: Whiteness and the Literary Imagination* (Harvard University Press, Cambridge Mass, 1992), p 11.

identity have been published.[85] These studies have sought to highlight the fact that white is a racial identity (and thus to strip away its alignment with "race-neutrality"),[86] to unpack the social and normative power of whiteness, to illustrate how "white" is represented culturally (both by dominant white discourse, and within various non-white cultures), and to show its constructedness and fluidity as a concept.

The study of whiteness is undoubtedly useful in any attempt to understand systems of racial power. However, as others have noted, it carries certain dangers when undertaken by white people, which should at least be acknowledged. Those raised by Richard Dyer indicate the potential of white studies to result in the retention of a theoretical focus on whiteness. For instance, white studies may simply allow white people to continue to "write and talk about what in any case we have always talked about: ourselves".[87] Furthermore, he says that it may involve a certain level of "me-too-ism", that is, a need to be included in trendy new theories or the "poor us" perception that whites don't have a lot going for us culturally and are therefore also oppressed (can't dance, can't sing, no rhythm, no culture, tense, unfriendly, isolated, lacking "community", is it any wonder we are so dysfunctional?).[88] Even more frightening is the prospect that a reactionary strand of white studies could legitimate white supremacy by valorising white identity.[89] And finally, for white people engaging in critical white thought, there are the special issues raised by white guilt at the abuses perpetrated in the name of white supremacy: the presence of such guilt means that we are dealing with complex emotional factors as well as an intellectual

---

85 See especially Ruth Frankenburg, *White Women, Race Matters* (University of Minnesota Press, Minneapolis, 1993); Toni Morrison, *Playing in the Dark*; Richard Dyer, *White*; Jacobson, *Whiteness of a Different Color*; Ruth Frankenburg (ed), *Displacing Whiteness* (Duke University Press, Durham, 1997); Nakayama and Martin (eds), *Whiteness: The Communication of Social Identity* (Sage Publications, Thousand Oaks, 1999). In this last-mentioned collection, Parker Johnson gives an overview of the movement in "Reflections on Critical White(ness) Studies".

86 For an analysis of white race within the context of personality theory, see Robert Carter, "Is White a Race? Expressions of White Race Identity" in Fine, Weis, Powell and Wong (eds), *Off White: Readings on Race, Power, and Society* (Routledge, New York, 1997).

87 Dyer, *White*, p 10. For a critique of Dyer's approach, see Joe Pugliese, "Race as Category Crisis: Whiteness and the Topical Assignation of Race" (2002) 12 *Social Semiotics* 149. Pugliese argues that Dyer dissociates whiteness from its many different cultural and historical contexts, thus transforming it into something which is transcultural and transhistorical. For further discussion of the problems and possibilities of whiteness studies, see Jane Haggis, "Beyond Race and Whiteness: Reflections on the New Abolitionists and an Australian Critical Whiteness Studies" (2006) 3(2) *borderlands*.

88 Haggis, "Beyond Race and Whiteness". See also Joe Kincheloe and Shirley Steinberg, "Addressing the Crisis of Whiteness" in Kincheloe, Steinberg, Rodriguez, and Chennault (eds), *White Reign: Deploying Whiteness in America* (St Martin's Press, New York, 1997), pp 14-16.

89 Kincheloe and Steinberg, "Addressing the Crisis of Whiteness", p 10.

terrain.[90] Having said all of this, the fact that there are dangers in carrying out a particular type of analysis does not mean that it should not be attempted, especially when the social stakes are so high. In consequence, critical white studies have made enormous progress in recent times.

As I will explain shortly, whiteness carries with it many political and social consequences: most importantly, the fact of whiteness is often invisible in discussions about race (or any discussion for that matter), and this invisibility allows those of us who are white to speak authoritatively from a position of un-raced neutrality.[91] While whiteness was once explicitly celebrated as racial superiority, in a context where such racism is now unacceptable the power of whiteness has gone underground.[92] Because white racial identity is not evident to those of us who are white, and the race of "others" is, we see our position as the neutral and normal one, whereas "others" are often regarded as speaking from a perspective, or as a member of an interest group. (For instance, in this book, Chapters 2, 3, and 4, are not designated as white male jurisprudence, even though most of the views represented there have been developed by white males within a particular — established — jurisprudential tradition.) I will come back to these points. However, before considering these larger questions about the perception of normality and the white power to invent the world, it is important to point out that the privilege of whiteness does not merely manifest itself at the level of social power. The power of whiteness is also evident in the everyday symbolism of our language, religious beliefs, literature, and cultural representations.

For instance, Richard Dyer gives a number of examples in which whiteness is associated with moral goodness and purity, while darker shades (especially black) are associated with evil and moral degeneracy.[93] Perhaps the most obvious example in the Western context is the representation of Jesus as white. Although it is extremely unlikely that the historical Jesus was fair skinned, and although Christianity is by no means a religion followed only by white people, the figure of

---

90   For a subtle analysis of some of these factors in the Australian context see Sara Ahmed, "The Politics of Bad Feeling" (2005) 1 *Australian Critical Race and Whiteness Studies Association Journal* 72.

91   Thomas Nakayama and Robert Krizek, "Whiteness as a Strategic Rhetoric" in Nakayama and Martin (eds), *Whiteness: The Communication of Social Identity*; Moreton-Robinson, *Talkin' Up to the White Woman*.

92   The explicit celebration of whiteness was, according to Alistair Bonnett replaced by a celebration of Western cultural superiority, which is still with us in many forms: on some levels it still implicates whiteness, but less directly than the overt racism of white supremacist ideology. See "From the Crises of Whiteness to Western Supremacism" (2005) 1 *Australian Critical Race and Whiteness Studies Association Journal* 8.

93   For many examples, see also the famous 459-word sentence in Herman Melville, *Moby Dick*, reproduced in John Tehranian, "Performing Whiteness: Naturalization Litigation and the Construction of Racial Identity in America", pp 816-817.

Christ has been traditionally depicted as extremely white, often in contrast to some fallen or evil dark "other".[94] Such symbolism is not necessarily originally or directly a consequence of what we would in modern times call racism. As Dinesh D'Souza notes, colour associations within the English language (and other languages) are ancient, and certainly predate the modern consciousness of race, or even knowledge of non-white races:[95]

> All the familiar English metaphors — black sheep in the family, a black mark against one's name, black as the colour of death, to blackball or blackmail — evolved independently of racism. So did the religious symbolism of white as the colour of angels, and black as the colour of the devil.

Having said this, it is nonetheless true that the linguistic association of moral qualities with blackness and whiteness may reinforce modern notions of white supremacy which developed independently of language and cultural symbolism: although the cultural associations of whiteness with purity and goodness and blackness with the devil did not necessarily arise as a consequence of a white supremacist ideology, they may nonetheless strengthen and legitimise it.

As Dyer says, the association of whiteness with moral goodness and blackness with moral degeneracy is not invariable: we can think of many examples where the opposite is the case. However, what matters is the symbolism underlying such representations: "a white person who is bad is failing to be 'white', whereas a black person who is good is a surprise, and one who is bad merely fulfils expectations. However mixed up and varied the actual representations of black and white people are, the underlying regime of dualism is still in play."[96]

It is a privilege of being in a position of dominance that the social markers of dominance are both invisible *and* regarded as the benchmark of normality. Many commentators have noted that whiteness as a racial category is invisible or transparent,[97] meaning that those of us who are white tend on one level not to explicitly identify ourselves as such. In everyday language it is common for whites to identify non-white people by referring to their race. We do not refer to ourselves in this way.[98] At the same time and on another level, this whiteness is of the utmost importance to our identity, since we can take for granted the

94 Dyer, *White*, pp 66-68.

95 Dinesh D'Souza, "Ignoble Savages" from *The End of Racism*, p 60. D'Souza also cites Winthrop Jordan, *White Over Black: American Attitudes to the Negro, 1550-1812* (University of North Carolina Press, Chapel Hill, 1968), p 7. For further examples of the linguistic connotations of black and white, look in any thesaurus or dictionary.

96 Dyer, *White*, pp 63-64.

97 Thomas Nakayama and Robert Krizek, "Whiteness as a Strategic Rhetoric", pp 97-98.

98 See Dyer, *White*, p 2. Self-consciousness of whiteness as a racial identity was certainly greater in the late 19th and early 20th century than it was in the later 20th century when "race" came to mean "non-white". See Alistair Bonnett, "From the Crisis in Whiteness to Western Supremacism".

privilege it confers and are rarely forced to question it. One of the reasons that white feminism managed to pass as feminism itself (at least in the eyes of its practitioners), was that the whiteness of the theory was not explicit, but invisible. Early feminism was a product of the social struggles of relatively privileged women, whose race was an unidentified, but prevalent factor in the characterisation of patriarchal structures. In this extract, Barbara Flagg highlights the transparency of whiteness, and connects it to the perceived normality and naturalisation of the white norm.

Barbara J Flagg

"The Transparency Phenomenon, Race-Neutral Decisionmaking, and Discriminatory Intent"[99]

[795]   In this society, the white person has an everyday option not to think of herself in racial terms at all. In fact, whites appear to pursue that option so habitually that it may be a defining characteristic of whiteness: to be white is not to think about it. ...

...

White people externalise race. For most whites, most of the time, to think or speak about race is to think or speak about people of color, or perhaps at times, to reflect on oneself (or other whites) in relation to people of color. But we tend not to think of ourselves or our racial group as racially distinctive. Whites' "consciousness" of race is predominantly unconsciousness of whiteness. We perceive and interact with other whites as individuals who have no significant racial characteristics. In the same vein, the white person is unlikely to see or describe himself in racial terms, perhaps in part because his racial peers do not see him as racially distinctive. Whiteness is a transparent quality when whites interact with whites in the absence of people of color. Whiteness attains opacity, becomes apparent to the white mind, only in relation to, and contrast with, the "color" of non-whites.

I do not maintain that white people are oblivious to the race of other whites. As a powerful determinant of social status, race is always noticed, in a way that eye color, for example, is not. However, whites' social dominance allows us to relegate our own racial specificity to the realm of the subconscious. Whiteness is the racial norm. In this culture the black person, not the white, is the one who is different. Once an individual is identified as white, his distinctively racial characteristics need no longer be conceptualised in racial terms; he becomes effectively raceless in the eyes of other whites. Whiteness, once identified, fades almost instantaneously from white consciousness into transparency.

[7100] Flagg's point will probably be immediately familiar to many, if not all, white people. When was the last time I identified myself as "white"? Have I ever? If I have, it is certainly not something which is always present in my thoughts. Certainly I might have identified myself in ways

---

99   Barbara J Flagg, "'Was Blind But Now I See': White Race Consciousness and the Requirement of Discriminatory Intent" (1993) 91 *Michigan Law Review* 953 at 970-971.

which would in *most* cases describe a white person — pale skin, light hair (once chemistry, now age), blue-ish eyes — but such terms are neither specific to whiteness, nor descriptive of a white racial identity.[100]

Flagg asks white people (herself included) to question the transparency of our racial identities, and to challenge the concept of colour-blindness or race-neutrality: if we are not even conscious of our whiteness, let alone the social norms which might flow from it, how can we be so sure that any "race neutral" concept or decision is in fact race neutral, rather than simply being an expression of white dominance, the whiteness of which is invisible? Indeed, one of the objectives of the critical study of whiteness is to emphasise that whiteness is a perspective or "standpoint", as Ruth Frankenburg says, "a place from which white people look at ourselves, at others, and at society."[101] We whites may have the power to define our perspective as neutral, objective or rational, but strip away the power, and it remains a perspective.

Aligned with the transparency of whiteness is the social, economic, and legal privilege produced within a system of racial hierarchy, and the imperative that white people must let go of this exclusive privilege if racial justice is to be achieved. Clearly there are many advantages to being situated in a cultural position defined as the racial norm, where your race does not mark you (at least to other whites), and where you can comfortably presume that your values are universal (or should be), and your knowledge is the standard. As Michelle Fine has argued, it is important not only to notice the disadvantage of the victims of racial oppression, but also to acknowledge our own accumulation of privilege:[102]

> What if we took the position that racial inequities were not primarily attributable to individual acts of discrimination targeted against persons of color, but increasingly to acts of cumulative privileging quietly loaded up on whites? That is, what if by keeping our eyes on those who gather disadvantage, we have not noticed white folks, varied by class and gender, nevertheless stuffing their academic and social pickup trucks with goodies otherwise not as readily accessible to people of color?

Certainly there is a significant material advantage to whiteness, a fact that Cheryl Harris has characterised as the "property" of whiteness.[103] Whiteness is not only a place of privilege, it is a *protected and exclusive* place of privilege, to which non-white others have gained entry only on the terms and conditions of the white majority. In the past, of course,

---

100 As Dyer says, "A person is deemed visibly white because of a quite complicated interaction of elements, of which flesh tones within the pink to beige range are only one: the shape of nose, eyes, and lips, the colour and set of hair, even body shape may all be mobilised to determine someone's 'colour'". See Dyer, *White*, p 42.

101 Frankenburg, *White Women, Race Matters*, p 1.

102 Michelle Fine, "Witnessing Whiteness" in Fine, Weis, Powell and Wong (eds), *Off White: Readings on Race, Power, and Society*, p 57.

103 Cheryl Harris, "Whiteness as Property" (1993) 106 *Harvard Law Review* 1709.

whiteness has attracted formal legal rights: for instance, in Australia, the White Australia policy effectively precluded immigration by most non-Europeans until it was abolished in the late 1960s.[104] Under such a regime, whiteness is a valuable commodity, a right of passage which also carries with it the right to exclude. Most graphically, under current law in Australia property in land derived from white law is legally recognised and protected far more extensively than "native title".[105] There is no equal property where one type is valued far above another. And of course, as became clear in Chapter 6, the equalisation of legal rights does not automatically result in the equalisation of social position and power. If the world is still defined from a white perspective, then it is hardly surprising that what was once a legal "property in whiteness" has now become a social and cultural property, with less explicit, but equally powerful consequences.

Most of what I have said above concerns the structural aspects of whiteness: that it is invisible as a race, that it carries hierarchical power, that "property" value flows from whiteness and that it is associated with a power to define the world. However, a more specific content can be added to all of this, which is essentially the content of the Western liberal self, who is thought to be rational, autonomous, free, and — as such — the bearer of rights. Liberal individualism is a product of the European philosophies of early modernism (from 1600 onwards). It has taken hold in modern Western nations and the attributes of the liberal man have been typically associated with the Western self (male and, increasingly, female). At the same time and as a result of colonialism and later, cultural imperialism and globalisation, white liberal values are in the process of achieving global hegemony — that is, they are taken for granted, regarded as normal, rather than providing one alternative among several. This is not to suggest that there is nothing positive about liberal values, or that their adoption is always and necessarily problematic. However, the danger is that liberalism is often regarded as the default and preferred perspective. And, while its values are adopted throughout the world, the central example of the liberal rights holder remains the white male and non-Western discourse is either not heard or is appropriated by liberal discourse.

Race Consciousness and Critical Race Theory

[7105] Modern liberalism has taught us very effectively that explicit discrimination on the basis of race must be avoided. It has also, less effectively, counselled against indirect discrimination and racial stereotyping.

---

104 For a discussion of the application of the White Australia Policy to Italian people, see Joe Pugliese, "Race as Category Crisis".

105 Clarke, "Law and Race", pp 259-260; Janet Galbraith, "Processes of Whiteness and Stories of Rape" (2000) 14 *Australian Feminist Law Journal* 71 at 77-78.

The liberal outlook takes each person as an individual, who makes rational and free choices about every aspect of her life. Liberal thought therefore promotes "colour-blindness" in perception: that is, it advises all of us, regardless of our race, to ignore external appearance and to think of each person as essentially human. The educated liberal West has tried to eliminate race from its consciousness, as though race belonged to a primitive past, prior to the time when human beings were sufficiently enlightened to see past trivialities like skin colour. As Toni Morrison has noted "the habit of ignoring race is understood to be a graceful, even generous, liberal gesture ... According to this logic, every well-bred instinct argues against noticing, and forecloses adult conversation."[106]

Attractive as the philosophy may sound to modern sensibilities concerning universal rights, the notion of equality as colour-blindness has several flaws. First, in its insistence that people are essentially the same, it does not give sufficient recognition to actually existing differences. As Barbara Flagg says about the US context, "Blacks continue to inhabit a very different America than do whites".[107] The same could certainly be said of Indigenous people and other non-white minorities in most white-dominated societies, many of whom suffer social, political and economic disadvantage. The attempt to see all people as *ideally* equal masks the fact that people are *not* equal in their material conditions. Moreover, as we have seen, the position of Indigenous people does not merely concern the position of individuals under the law: it also concerns the *concept* of law which is brought to bear on Indigenous lives. As Michael Detmold has argued in relation to the Australian context,[108]

> Aboriginal and European are treated equally except in the matter of the law before which they are treated equally. It is no more justifiable to make Aborigines equal before European law than it is to make Europeans equal before Aboriginal law.

Equality may be nice for me under this law, but what if another does not accept my law? Her law is not equal to mine (because it is not recognised as law), so how can she then be equal to me?

Colour-blindness simply obscures the fact of white supremacy, because it permits officials, decision-makers, and ordinary people to believe in an illusion of equality and to operate in accordance with "universal" norms which are, in fact, designed for and skewed towards the white majority. (This is not to say that people should not be perceived as equal, but this must not be confused with a statement about the actual conditions under which people live.) Secondly, the liberal insistence

---

106 Morrison, *Playing in the Dark*, pp 9-10.

107 Barbara J Flagg, "'Was Blind But Now I See': White Race Consciousness and the Requirement of Discriminatory Intent", p 954.

108 Detmold, "Law and Difference: Reflections on Mabo's Case", p 163.

that people are rational atoms in a society of atoms assumes and promotes a very peculiar picture of the person — one typically associated with the adult white male.

In order to consider further the issue of race consciousness I am going to focus for the rest of this part on debate in the US legal academy, specifically the "critical race theory" movement. This movement has generated a substantial literature about race-consciousness and racial identity in the context of law. Angela Harris has described critical race theory as "the heir to both CLS and traditional rights scholarship".[109] As she says, critical race theory inherits from CLS the scepticism about legal objectivity and its attention to law's inbuilt ideologies, while it inherits from the civil rights movement a "commitment to a vision of liberation from racism through right reason."[110]

As was clear from the minority critiques of CLS considered in Chapter 5, mere rejection of the liberal concepts of equality and rights is problematic since it may remove the formal guarantees which secure basic legal identity for many people. The critical race theory response to liberalism has not been a call simply to eliminate rights. Rather, critical race theorists have attempted to highlight the ways in which formal equality can be indirectly discriminatory, to demystify the identity upon which rights (especially the right to equality) are premised, to focus upon minority racial identities as political agents, and to highlight alternative voices and perceptions.[111] Rather than erase colour in the name of equality, critical race theorists — attentive to the political nature of law — have in the first instance been motivated by a need to raise consciousness about race as a dimension of law. Like critical legal scholars, the critical race theorists have rejected the notion that law is a neutral arbiter: however, if law is political, it is imbued with the politics of race as much as with the politics of liberalism, capitalism, gender, and class.

As I explained above, the point of developing consciousness of whiteness is not to strengthen the concept of the white race, but rather to call it into question — to demystify white power, and to remove the certainty of the comfortable place white people occupy in the world. In contrast, the concept of non-white race consciousness is designed to strengthen and consolidate self-determining identities which have previously been stereotyped and erased by the dominant political discourse. For example, the Black Power movement in the United States arose as a direct response to the need to redefine the cultural symbolism

---

109 Angela Harris, "The Jurisprudence of Reconstruction" (1994) 82 *California Law Review* 741 at 743.

110 Harris, "The Jurisprudence of Reconstruction", p 743.

111 For an overview, see Anthony Alfieri, "Book Review: Black and White" (1997) 85 *California Law Review* 1647.

associated with African American people. As Kwame Ture and Charles Hamilton explained in 1967:[112]

> Black people must redefine themselves, and only they can do that. Throughout this country, vast segments of the black communities are beginning to recognize the need to assert their own definitions, to reclaim their history, their culture; to create their own sense of community and togetherness. ... When we begin to define our own image, the stereotypes — that is, lies — that our oppressor has developed will begin in the white community and end there.

In contrast to the Civil Rights Movement, which worked towards progressive law reform within the framework of a liberal legal system, the Black Power movement called for Black people to take control of their own identities, lives and communities. The construction of this identity was regarded as a political necessity — in particular, it aimed to preserve the distinct voices of African American people, threatened by liberal integrationism. In this way, the strategy of Black Power can be compared to that of other identity-based movements with a separatist dimension such as lesbian feminism and early radical feminism. Although it is now not very fashionable to advocate either separatism or the essentialised notion of identity upon which separatism is often based, the political motivation underlying such movements is convincing in many respects: advocates of forms of separatism wish to claim a space for marginalised peoples, and in doing so to remove the dominant culture's power to define and stereotype whole groups. Although it has been criticised as both simplistic and divisive, separatism is in my view an inevitable and useful method of challenging domination. However it can take contingent and strategic forms, and does not necessarily involve complete and permanent physical separation.[113]

Race consciousness as developed by critical race scholars in the United States has, at times, like the Black Power movement, involved a separatist element, inspired centrally by the thought that white institutions have not, do not, and arguably cannot, promote liberation from racial oppression. One important feature of the emergence of a subversive voice in legal scholarship has been the practice of "oppositional storytelling" — the idea that non-dominant truths can be heard through the telling of stories which counteract mainstream legal ideology.[114] Another strategy has been to use existing legal theory to analyse the position of African Americans in relation to the institutions

---

112 Kwame Ture and Charles Hamilton, "Black Power: Its Need and Substance" from *Black Power and the Politics of Liberation* (Vintage Books, New York, 1992), reproduced in Bulmer and Solomos (ed), *Racism*, p 236. As indicated above, whiteness theory also aims to end the lies.

113 See Maria Lugones, "Purity, Impurity and Separation" (1994) 19 *Signs* 458.

114 In particular see Richard Delgado, "Storytelling for Oppositionists and Others" (1989) 87 *Michigan Law Review* 2411.

of law. Derrick Bell, for instance, drawing upon the theory of legal realism, advocates "racial realism".[115] As I explained in Chapter 4, legal realism advocated a view of law unencumbered by abstraction, formalism, and circular reasoning. Realism aimed to demystify the law: rather than seeing law as a non-political system of formal principles which can be objectively applied, realists argued that law and politics are inseparable and that scholars should aim to present law in its *real* operation, not in the abstract. Bell applies aspects of legal realism to race: in particular, he argues that the racial realist approach must reject the promise of progress achieved through law. Bell argues that law only reinforces the racial status quo, and that it is important that Black people recognise this and do not have false hopes about an institution which has served them so poorly. Most controversially, Bell contends that racism is permanent:[116]

> Black people will never gain full equality in this country. Even those Herculean efforts we hail as successful will produce no more than temporary "peaks of progress", short-lived victories that slide into irrelevance as racial patterns adapt in ways that maintain white dominance. This is a hard-to-accept fact that all history verifies. We must acknowledge it and move on to adopt policies based upon what I call: "Racial Realism". This mind-set or philosophy requires us to acknowledge the permanence of our subordinate status. That acknowledgement enables us to avoid despair, and frees us to imagine and implement racial strategies that can bring fulfilment and even triumph.

As indicated above, Bell's thesis that racism is a permanent feature of law has been controversial although, as Richard Delgado pointed out at the time, it is possibly most distressing for white people for whom it is important to believe that progress is being made.[117] (If progress is being made, then white people like myself do not need to feel as guilty about the privilege of being white.)

Many critical race theorists have rejected monolithic notions of racial identity, arguing that they are essentialist and do not take account of diversity within particular racial groups.[118] It has also been argued that strategies designed to promote the political cause of one racially oppressed group can lead to the silencing of another. For instance, in recent years critical race theory has been criticised for operating under a "Black/White paradigm" to the exclusion of Asian identities, Latino/Latina identities, and multi-racial identities. This paradigm is said to

---

115 Derrick Bell, "Racial Realism" (1992) 24 *Connecticut Law Review* 363; see also the reviews — Richard Delgado, "Derrick Bell's Racial Realism: A Comment on White Optimism and Black Despair" (1992) 24 *Connecticut Law Review* 527; john powell "Racial Realism or Racial Despair?" (1992) 24 *Connecticut Law Review* 533; Willie Abrams, "A Reply to Derrick Bell's Racial Realism" (1992) 24 *Connecticut Law Review* 517.

116 Bell, "Racial Realism", pp 373-374.

117 Delgado, "Derrick Bell's Racial Realism".

118 See the commentary in Angela Harris, "The Jurisprudence of Reconstruction", pp 754-756.

neglect the distinctive forms of racism which have been applied to non-African American racial minorities.[119] Observation of this new form of dualism has led to the development of a further version of critical legal studies, "LatCrit" theory,[120] and consequential discussion over how the different forms of racial domination within US society intersect. In some ways, much of this debate is specific to the context of racism in the United States, where the history of widespread and institutionalised slavery was associated with a distinctive white supremacist attitude to African Americans.[121] However, the more general issues are common: in particular, it is important to be aware that racism is not monolithic, and that distinct experiences of racial oppression may lead to the need to base activism upon identities based on shared history and experience. That is not to say that essentialism prevails, as such political groupings may be contingently formed, open to redefinition, and operate where necessary in coalition with others.[122]

The concept of race consciousness, originally theorised as a method of claiming space in public discussion and asserting political agency, has led to broad questioning of identity as a construct. As we saw in Chapter 6, for many, "identity" is not a simple matter of identification with one group or community but is formed in relation to a number of "worlds".[123] Identity need not be seen as singular, or even as composed of several different strands related to culture, race, gender, sexuality. Identity can also be viewed as something which it not a stable essence, but rather in flux, dynamic, composed of insides and outsides.[124] This is not to say that people should not form political movements based

---

119 Juan Perea, "The Black/White Binary Paradigm of Race: The 'Normal Science' of American Racial Thought" (1997) 85 *California Law Review* 1213; Richard Delgado, "Derrick Bell's Toolkit — Fit to Dismantle that Famous House?" (2000) 75 *New York University Law Review* 283.

120 LatCrit Symposium (1997) 85 *California Law Review* 1647.

121 As Angela Harris comments in explaining, but not defending, the concept of "black exceptionalism": "Blackness is central to American white supremacy — Black people embody the nigger in the American imagination: a creature at the border of the human and the bestial, a being whose human form only calls attention to its subhuman nature. To be a nigger is to have no agency, no dignity, no individuality and no moral worth" in Leslie Espinoza and Angela Harris, "Embracing the Tar-Baby"; LatCrit, "Theory and the Sticky Mess of Race" (1997) 85 *California Law Review* 1585 at 1601-1602.

122 For instance, Richard Delgado says, "Minority groups in the United States should consider abandoning all binaries, narrow nationalisms, and strategies that focus on cutting the most favourable deal with whites, and instead set up a secondary market in which they negotiate selectively with each other.": "Derrick Bell's Toolkit", p 306.

123 See the discussion of Maria Lugones in Chapter 6.

124 Trinh T Minh-ha writes, "Differences do not only exist between outsider and insider — two entities. They are also at work within the outsider herself, or the insider herself — a single entity.": "Not You/Like You: Post-Colonial Women and the Interlocking Questions of Identity and Difference" in Gloria Anzaldúa, *Making Face, Making Soul, Haciendo Caras* (Aunt Lute Books, San Francisco, 1990), p 375.

around a shared identity, but rather that such shared identities respond to current political demands and are not necessarily inherent or essential. "Identity" can be an opportunity, not merely a limitation.

Conclusion: Beyond the Western Construct of Race

[7110] In Western jurisprudence, much of the debate concerning race takes place in response to the many forms of white supremacy, and the ways in which it has constructed, stereotyped, excluded, ignored, and practised violence upon various non-white "others". This focus is not surprising, given that there are urgent questions of political and social justice needing to be resolved. However, in different contexts, some voices are heard which either move beyond the dialogue of Western white supremacy, or aim to dismantle its concept of race in the name of achieving a new non-racialised concept of identity. I have already, for instance, mentioned Irene Watson, who writes of Western colonialism and imperialism from a position situated beyond their all-consuming discourse.[125] Such an approach is crucial, since it provides insight into how our Western legal paradigms and theory appear to those who have not been thoroughly drawn into their discursive net.

In the US context, and from the position of an African-American scholar, Reginald Leamon Robinson has argued that race consciousness, as a product of the social construction of race, reinforces racial division. In several detailed and subtle articles, he advocates the recovery of a human consciousness which moves beyond race. Such a non-racialised identity would not be the result of trying to ignore race in a "colour-blind" liberal pretence that race does not exist. Rather, I understand Robinson to be arguing for the recovery of a universal human identity in which the social construction of race has never existed, or has been transcended.

Reginald Leamon Robinson
"The Shifting Race-Consciousness Matrix and the Multiracial Category Movement"[126]

[7115] Although we socially, historically, and psychologically co-create racism and white supremacy, race is not biologically factual. It is not real. As such, race does not have any meaning that survives its social and historical context. Race exists, if ever, in our individual and cultural consciousness. If we do not constantly and consciously meditate on it, race cannot exist. Unfortunately, we fuel this social construct with our mental kindling and

---

125 See Chapter 6, and above at [745]-[780] under "Colonialism".

126 Reginald Leamon Robinson, "The Shifting Race-Consciousness Matrix and the Multiracial Category Movement: A Critical Reply to Professor Hernandez" (2000) 20 *Boston College Third World Law Journal* 231 at 232-236.

intellectual logs. Race, racism, and white supremacy exist because we — individually and collectively — create it, enforce it, and sustain it. Thus, it is our race consciousness and its attendant behaviour that remain the apt locus for racism and white supremacy. ...

Basically, if race arises from a consciousness matrix, does race necessarily have an essential meaning outside of how we think, use, and talk about race? I think not! Thinking, talking, and using give race its life force, content and meaning (eg racism). Without our thinking, talking, and using, race loses its practical, social function, and we need never experience the individual and collective pain that follows consciously or otherwise when we force people to separate unnaturally from each other.

[7.120] In a sense, Robinson is proposing something akin to what feminists have referred to as the "utopian moment" of theory,[127] that is, the point at which it is possible to envisage, if not achieve, a radical vision of the possibilities for liberation (which, incidentally, for some feminists, have involved envisaging the abolition of the category of sex, or the recognition of multiple sexes and sexualities[128]). For instance, Robinson argues that racial identities confer a kind of "expert knowledge" — that is, we (everyone) become experts about who we are through the meanings and constructions of the social world. Robinson argues that this expertise destroys our human potential.[129] He asks "[c]an blacks, whites, and others who have for hundreds of years immersed themselves in horror, pain, guilt, and fear of white supremacy and racial oppression transcend an expert knowledge about race and its consciousness?"[130] In the face of these destructive forces, Robinson favours the recovery of a "beginner's mind" or "human consciousness", that is, a mind which does not know of race (although it does know of culture and ethnicity).[131] Although it may be difficult to see how such a change can take place, Robinson points out that the way people think is constantly changing.[132] It may therefore be possible to eliminate consciousness of race, by deliberately refusing to act and think of it. Robinson argues that the "multiracial category movement" — the movement which denies unitary racial identities, and recognises the complexities in many people's racial heritages — can be one part of the transition between race-consciousness and its elimination.

---

127 See Nicola Lacey, *Unspeakable Subjects: Feminist Essays in Legal and Social Theory* (Hart Publishing, Oxford, 1997), p 208.

128 See the discussion of queer theory in Chapter 6.

129 Robinson, "'Expert Knowledge: Introductory Comments on Race Consciousness". For a critique of Robinson's position, see Robert Hayman, "Re-Cognizing Race: An Essay in Defense of Race Consciousness" (2000) 6 *Widener Law Symposium* 37.

130 Robinson, "'Expert Knowledge: Introductory Comments on Race Consciousness", p 170.

131 Robinson, "The Shifting Race-Consciousness Matrix and the Multiracial Category Movement", p 273.

132 Robinson, "The Shifting Race-Consciousness Matrix and the Multiracial Category Movement", p 256.

Frantz Fanon also envisioned a world in which skin colour was not a determining feature of identity, eloquently capturing the problems of the choice between colour-blind and race-conscious lives:

Frantz Fanon
Black Skin, White Masks[133]

[7125]   As I begin to recognize that the Negro is the symbol of sin, I catch myself hating the Negro. But then I recognize that I am a Negro. There are two ways out of this conflict. Either I ask others to pay no attention to my skin, or else I want them to be aware of it. I try then to find value for what is bad — since I have unthinkingly conceded that the black man is the color of evil. In order to terminate this neurotic situation, in which I am compelled to choose an unhealthy, conflictual solution, fed on fantasies, hostile, inhuman in short, I have only one solution: to rise above this absurd drama that others have staged round me, to reject the two terms that are equally unacceptable, and, through one human being, to reach out for the universal.

[7130] Robinson's humanity and Fanon's universal express the possibility of a world where race does not enforce division, hierarchy and all of the bloody and painful consequences which flow from it. It is important to distinguish this vision from the concept of colour-blindness, where race remains a submerged but active component of human consciousness and social organisation.

This is in many ways a compelling view, though I think myself I would prefer to speak of a "human potential" rather than the "universal", to signal that (for me) this identity is not an *essential* identity with a particular content, but may be expressed in numerous ways which still respect our individual and collective capacity for a dignified existence. The "universal" has been so strongly defined through whiteness and masculinity that an alternative term may be preferable. Further, it should be pointed out that white privilege, white power, and the presumption of the non-racial normality of whiteness at present offer strong resistance to envisioning a universal: critical examination of whiteness must lead not only to understanding of the white norm and white privilege, but also to an effective release or letting go of accumulated privilege. The property in whiteness must be *actively* dismantled — all the while white people insist upon maintaining privilege (ideological, physical, material), we dehumanise non-white people as well as ourselves.

---

133   Frantz Fanon, *Black Skin, White Masks* (MacGibbon and Kee, London, 1968), p 197.

EIGHT
POSTMODERNISM AND DECONSTRUCTION

Introduction

[805] This is probably the most difficult chapter of a book such as this, both from the point of view of the writer and of the reader. It is difficult to write because postmodernism is an elusive thing, if it exists at all. There are certainly some attitudes and arguments which are characteristic of what some have called "postmodernism", although the term has been used (and arguably abused) to denote a range of theoretical attitudes, which are philosophical to varying degrees, and transgressive of existing knowledge to varying degrees. For practical purposes I will use "postmodernism" as a generic name to refer to a range of theories I am going to describe. The difficulty will be in differentiating some of the fairly specific arguments and techniques of analysis from the plethora of vague and poorly theorised approaches which have also appropriated or been given that name.

Postmodern theory has a reputation for being difficult to read. It has to be said that most of the "primary" texts are written in a way which can discourage anyone, no matter what their philosophical background. But difficulty is something which depends not only upon the text we are reading, but also upon the expectations we have as readers. Lawyers are generally trained to distil reasonably clear meanings from the texts we read. We expect there to be an essential meaning and read with this in mind. Even if no such meaning is immediately evident, we expect one to emerge in time. In contrast, literary critics expect meanings to arise on many different levels and not to be reducible to a single thread or idea. This does not render our attempt to read literature futile, but it does make it rather open-ended, leaving the possibility for growth in the interpretation of any given work. If we attempt to read many of the works written in the postmodern tradition as though they were pieces of legislation, or reported cases, or academic papers, we will not very often succeed, because such works are not, on the whole, written with a single meaning in mind. They are written to disturb or subvert established meanings and assumptions, to unsettle us, and to make us actively reconsider what we have been taking for granted conceptually. If advice is in order then, I would say that we can and should relax about finding an absolute "meaning", and try to imagine or construct connections for ourselves. Having said this, I think it is also true that many of the ideas which have been developed in the postmodern tradition can be clearly stated and it is my purpose in this chapter to introduce these ideas with as much clarity as is possible in this context.

It can also be hard to see in the first instance what this particular type of theory has to do with law. Although there is an increasingly large literature which takes a postmodern approach to law[1] or criticises this approach,[2] my purpose in this chapter is not to describe this literature in any detail, but rather to consider the genesis of postmodernism, especially in its early theoretical manifestations. Thus, rather than concentrating on the legal theory inspired by postmodernism, I aim to explain some of its repeated themes, as they appear in some "core" postmodern writings. My own view about postmodernism and law, which I will be explaining later, is that postmodern thinking can be extremely valuable for legal theory, not only because it is about meaning, power, and the relation of individuals to systems, but also because it is about boundaries, limits, insides and outsides.[3] All of these issues are central to legal theory.

The difficulty of postmodern thought is exacerbated because "postmodern" approaches are not necessarily theories, nor even always critical methodologies, at least not in the conventional sense of these terms. "Deconstruction", for instance, does not rest on several basic principles which can be reduced to a set of theoretical axioms. It (if "it" exists) cannot simply be described as a configuration of general theoretical propositions, around which different theorists have constructed variations. It is perhaps best described (though this is already a cliché) as a practical intervention in established modes of

---

1   Some general works on postmodernism and law include Anthony Carty (ed), *Post-Modern Law: Enlightenment, Revolution, and the Death of Man* (Edinburgh University Press, Edinburgh, 1990); Costas Douzinas, Ronnie Warrington and Shaun McVeigh, *Postmodern Jurisprudence: The Law of Text in the Texts of Law* (Routledge, London, 1991); Joel Handler, "Postmodernism, Protest and the New Social Movements" (1992) 26 *Law and Society Review* 697; Alan Hunt, "The Big Fear: Law Confronts Postmodernism" (1990) 35 *McGill Law Journal* 507; Gary Minda, *Postmodern Legal Movements: Law and Jurisprudence at Century's End* (New York University Press, New York, 1995); Margaret Davies, *Delimiting the Law: "Postmodernism" and the Politics of Law* (Pluto Press, London, 1996); Douglas Litowitz, *Postmodern Philosophy and Law* (University Press of Kansas, Kansas, 1997); Helen Stacy, *Postmodernism and Law: Jurisprudence in a Fragmenting World* (Ashgate, Aldershot, 2001). Many articles written in a postmodern spirit are to be found in the UK journal *Law and Critique*. An in-depth (and somewhat critical) review of the ideas in this chapter is to be found in Suri Ratnapala, "Book Review" (1995) 16 *New Zealand Universities Law Review* 326.

2   For an overview of some of these criticisms see Stephen Feldman, "An Arrow to the Heart: The Love and Death of Postmodern Legal Scholarship" (2001) 54 *Vanderbilt Law Review* 2349.

3   I have begun to address some of these matters in Chapter 1: they will arise in this chapter specifically in the context of postmodern thought.

thinking, which destabilises the stereotypes, value-judgments, and categories upon which theories are inevitably constructed. An end-product, in the sense of a new world vision or a new legal system, is not available. The absence of such a unifying prescription from deconstruction does not make it politically incompetent, but rather the opposite, as I will attempt to demonstrate.[4] Exactly what this means and how (or if) it is achieved will be the main focus of this chapter.

One of the most problematic issues confronting readers is the confusing terminology used to describe these modern theoretical approaches to legal thought. Terms such as "postmodernism", "poststructuralism", and "deconstruction" are frequently used interchangeably, and it is true that they have emerged more or less in parallel as part of a general French-inspired philosophical movement. Given the fairly flexible usage of these terms, attempting to distinguish them may seem to be an artificial exercise. "Poststructuralism" and "postmodernism", in particular, do not necessarily describe separate intellectual domains, but are, in effect, words used to describe a particular intellectual climate. "Postmodernism" is generally used to refer generically to an entire cultural and scholarly climate (and is beyond what is called "modernism"), while "poststructuralism" refers to the reaction to a particular sort of linguistics (and is beyond what is called "structuralism"). A more direct genesis can be attributed to the term "deconstruction": it refers to a specific type of theoretical intervention to be found in the writings of the philosopher, Jacques Derrida. Again, however, the word has been appropriated for all sorts of purposes. For purely pragmatic reasons then, I will begin by explaining, as clearly as possible, some of the ways in which the terms have been used. These divisions should not, however, be taken as definitive of the possibilities: they are rather simply a guide to the terminology.

Modernism and Postmodernism

Modernism

[810] When (20 or so years ago) I was studying literature, "modernism" always referred to a particular literary period, that which occurred roughly between 1890 and 1930. "Modernist" writers were people like Yeats, Lawrence, Eliot, and Joyce who represented the end of literature as we then knew it, since a work had to be at least 50 years old to be put in a syllabus of "major" texts. Before "modernism" there was the Victorian Age, the Romantic poets, the rise of the novel, restoration drama, neo-classical poetry, Elizabethan drama, and so on, back to Old English. "Modernism", then, was presented as having already occurred, and we weren't to know what came afterwards because nobody really

---

4 See also Allan Hutchinson, "Inessentially Speaking (Is There Politics After Postmodernism?)" (1991) 89 *Michigan Law Review* 1549; and Handler, "Postmodernism, Protest, and the New Social Movements".

knew yet. Of course, "modernism" wasn't simply an era, it had defined characteristics, one of which was said to be the desire for order through the visual arts or literature. The basic idea of modernism was that art was a way of transcending the political and social chaos of the times and of attaining a higher significance than that which was apparent in the lived world. Art was a search for aesthetic unity, order, and universality — outside history, and outside social contexts. In "Tradition and the Individual Talent", TS Eliot argued that the literary tradition itself forms an ideal order, an order of great monuments, rather than a conglomeration of works which are valued according to the peculiarities of taste in a specific era. Beneath the chaos of texts, there is an underlying universal book.[5] The movement in early 20th century painting (for instance, cubism) to depict pure forms is another example of this attempt to transcend the particular events and images of everyday life.

In philosophy, "modernism" is understood in a similar way, though it is not tied to an ideal of artistic representation, nor to such a short historical period. In a philosophical sense "modernism" refers to the attempt to find absolute grounds for knowledge, to discover abstract, transcendent principles which would be the foundation for all philosophical questioning. One of the problems for philosophy has always been that relating to philosophical legitimation, or how to find a foundation which goes beyond particular situations, and is not reliant on assumptions requiring further demonstration. The method of Descartes, for instance, was to attempt to discover a rational ground for knowledge in the face of all possible doubt.[6] As we saw in Chapter 7, modernism produced both the scientific classification of races *and* the liberal discourse of equality which counteracted this biological concept of race.

In legal theory, legal philosophers have attempted to determine a universal basis for the concept of law — a grounding for legal systems which applies generally. Kelsen's *grundnorm* and Hart's rule of recognition are good examples of this attempt to fix the concept of legitimacy in an abstract and absolute principle.[7] As we shall see, philosophy, like jurisprudence (which has however, and, as usual, come to the party rather late), is no longer unified in its demand for an absolute ground of knowledge.

The problem of what is known as philosophical "modernity" is therefore essentially how a foundation for thought can be discovered which will not be subject to further scrutiny. And since a philosophical

---

5   This essay is readily available in critical anthologies, for instance in David Lodge (ed), *20th Century Literary Criticism, a Reader* (Longman, Harlow, Essex, 1972).

6   See René Descartes, *Meditations on First Philosophy* (2nd ed, Bobbs-Merrill, New York, 1960), especially the First Meditation.

7   Hans Kelsen, *General Theory of Law and State* (Russell, New York, 1961); HLA Hart, *The Concept of Law* (2nd ed, Clarendon Press, Oxford, 1994). See Chapter 3, above.

ground which originates outside the system cannot be demonstrated in terms of the system itself, there must be *self*-legitimation, that is, legitimation which can be contained within the system.[8] Faith in God as the author of the world and its meanings will not do, because God cannot be demonstrated in the terms of a philosophical system which relies on Her. She would always be an external intentional being. Descartes proposed that in order to resolve this problem of foundations, it was necessary to follow the correct philosophical method: method is etymologically "the way to truth".[9] One of the more famous methods, that of Hegel, the so-called "speculative dialectic" (the details of which are rather too complex to go into here), was presented as a way leading to such an absolute grounding, a self-legitimation.[10]

It is well known that one of the foundations which Descartes proposed in resolution of his radical doubt of everthing as simply perceived, was *cogito ergo sum* — "I think, therefore I am". *I* exist. The subject "I" is taken as the basis of cognition — the subject is unified, complete, and rational. Such an idea of subjectivity was also taken up by social contract theorists who used the concept of the individual free and rational subject who pre-existed political and social organisation as a basis for theories about the founding of society. The rational subject, in other words, could be used as a conceptual (though not empirical) foundation for theory, lifted out of its context and made into a universal principle. Thus one of the central concepts of modern philosophy is that the "subject", that is, the individual mind interacting with the world, pre-exists the world: the subject may be acted upon by the world, but is not created or constituted by it. As we have seen in previous chapters, this "subject" was never a politically or culturally neutral character: the ability to be a subject has been aligned closely with one's gender and race. I will come back to the idea of the subject in more detail later in the chapter.

The idea is also central to Kant's moral philosophy and epistemology. In the *Critique of Pure Reason*, Kant uses the concept of "unity of apperception", that is (basically) the pre-existent unity of subjective identity and consciousness (an autonomous and single "I"), to explain how a multitude of particular perceptions are synthesised and organised by the mind.[11] The unified subject is the precondition for seeing and interpreting the physical world. Similarly, in his moral

---

8   On this point see Rodolphe Gasché, *The Tain of the Mirror: Derrida and the Philosophy of Reflection* (Harvard University Press, Cambridge Mass, 1986), p 121. See also Gasché, *Inventions of Difference: On Jacques Derrida* (Harvard University Press, Cambridge Mass, 1994), Ch 6 "God, For Example".

9   Gasché notes that methods are roads to knowledge or truth. "Method" is derived from "hodos", meaning "way" or "road": *The Tain of the Mirror*, p 121.

10   The dialectical method is apparent in all of Hegel's major works. For legal philosophy the most relevent is *The Philosophy of Right* (Oxford University Press, London, 1967).

11   Immanuel Kant, *Critique of Pure Reason* (Macmillan, Hampshire, 1929) "Transcendental Analytic", s 16 "The Original Synthetic Unity of Apperception" (B132-B136).

philosophy, Kant presupposed as the basis for all moral thinking a free and independent rational subject: the subject who is self-contained, self-controlled and responsible for his own actions but not those of others, is the unit of moral thinking.[12] (Kant's subject, like Hegel's, is male,[13] and as we saw in Chapter 7, he is also white.) As I will explain, one of the central aspects of postmodern thought is the challenge to this idea of the subject.

This idea of a unified actor who is independent and rational forms the basis not only of many areas of substantive law, but also of the idea of law itself, as it has been traditionally presented. In substantive law, it is clearly a notion of the autonomous thinking and acting subject which underlies criminal law, contract, torts, and so on. The system is constructed as a coming together of these independent rational units, who simply act and react on each other. Each legal person has defined rights and responsibilities, and is — legally — independent from others. The corporation is merely an extrapolation of this notion of legal personality. And in the law of evidence, the witness is regarded as an individual speaking subject, one who expresses a pre-existing state of affairs. Thus, as Ngaire Naffine has demonstrated, the law holds out a concept of the legal actor, indeed puts this particular ideal of subjectivity at the very centre of law, based on the Enlightenment model of a rational and autonomous person.[14] An island. And typically a white man. (I should point out at this stage, that in case anyone is worried about what is coming next, a critique of the notion of subjectivity does not entail that we abandon it altogether. Rather, the point will be to show what remains unexpressed by this dominant idea of the subject and to indicate how subjectivity is constituted — the subject does not exist in isolation from her relationships, but is rather defined by them. "Independence" involves repression of "interdependence".)

In general then, philosophical modernity refers roughly to the attempt to formulate abstract universal principles which hold irrespective of historical era, or social context. There is also a desire for what is usually

---

12   See, for instance, Immanuel Kant, *Foundations of the Metaphysics of Morals* (2nd ed, Prentice-Hall, New Jersey, 1997), which is the shortest and most accessible of Kant's moral treatises.

13   See Genevieve Lloyd, *The Man of Reason: "Male" and "Female" in Western Philosophy* (Methuen, London, 1984); Carole Pateman, *The Sexual Contract* (Polity Press, Cambridge, 1988); and Luce Irigaray, "Any Theory of the 'Subject' Has Always Been Appropriated by the 'Masculine'" in *Speculum of the Other Woman* (Cornell University Press, Ithaca, 1985), p 133.

14   Ngaire Naffine, *Law and the Sexes* (Allen and Unwin, Sydney, 1990), Ch 5. For further development of Naffine's analysis of the legal person see "Who are Law's Persons: From Cheshire Cats to Responsible Subjects" (2003) 66 *Modern Law Review* 346. Michel Foucault puts it like this: "It is possible to suppose that the 'universal' intellectual, as he functioned in the nineteenth and early twentieth centuries was in fact derived from a quite specific historical figure: the man of justice, the man of law, who counterposes to power, despotisim, and the abuses and arrogance of wealth the universality of justice and the equity of an ideal law.": *Power/Knowledge* (Harvester Press, Brighton, 1980), p 128.

referred to as "closure", that is, completeness within philosophical systems — it must have no gaps and be a final account of the world. The idea of closure has also been important in philosophical ideas about law adopted by many writers, especially positivists. Our approach to law still tends to assume, under the positivist influence, that law is essentially something different from non-law and is internally coherent. Furthermore, the assumption of a rational and pre-existing individual identity is often foundational to such philosophical enquiries. This is a very simplified account, but one which will do for the time being.

Postmodernism

[815]   The term "postmodern" was apparently first coined by a British historian to refer to the post-World War II era of irrationalism and pessimism.[15] Subsequently "postmodernism" was used by literary critics to indicate that what had previously been called "modernism" was over, and that a new artistic culture had emerged which challenged the preconceptions of modernism. As a generic term, "postmodernism" has been used to refer to all sorts of cultural movements — in literature, painting, architecture, and philosophy, to name only the most obvious. Where modernists had been attempting to express order and pure form, outside context, postmodernists rejected the notion of artistic transcendence, integrated into their works attention to the way artistic media work (that is, artistic self-consciousness), and focused thematically on the fragmentary and complex nature of existence, rather than trying to reduce it to a manageable and orderly whole. As a cultural movement "postmodernism" is therefore simply what comes after modernism, reacting against it, and defining itself in contrast to it. Thus the dimensions of postmodernism are very much reliant on the idea of modernism.

The philosophical characteristics of postmodernism run parallel to these general cultural themes. I will explain some aspects of what is termed "postmodernism" here, and some in the section on "poststructuralism", as some linguistic theory needs to be explained before arguments about subjectivity and the formation of concepts can be properly understood.

In the late 1970s Jean-François Lyotard wrote an influential work, subsequently translated into English as *The Postmodern Condition*. Lyotard begins his argument by distinguishing two forms of knowledge: scientific and narrative. These forms bring to mind the two paradigms of evaluating evidence which have been proposed in evidence scholarship.[16]

---

15   Robert Pippin, *Modernism as a Philosophical Problem: On the Dissatisfactions of European High Culture* (Basil Blackwell, Cambridge Mass, 1991), p 156. The historian in question was Arnold Toynbee.

16   See John Leubsdorf, "Stories and Numbers" (1991) 13 *Cardozo Law Review* 455. For discussion of the related distinction between reason and emotion in the presentation of evidence see Luebsdorf, "Presuppositions of Evidence Law" (2006) 91 *Iowa Law Review* 1209.

On the one hand, in the "scientific" model evidence is evaluated according to its probability: an argument is composed of several essential components, each of which can be attributed a probability, and which are finally combined in a mathematical formula in order to determine what (according to the probabilities) happened. On the other hand, in the "storytelling" model, the trier of fact, after listening to all the evidence presented, attempts to formulate a narrative which best fits the evidence.

The precise characteristics of Lyotard's conception of the difference between narrative and scientific knowledge need not concern us here. I have outlined them in Chapter 2, in relation to the contrast between legitimation through time in classical common law theory and legitimation through an origin in post-Austinian jurisprudence. It is sufficient at this point to recognise that the dominant paradigm of knowledge in modern capitalist societies is scientific, and that the process of knowing in science relies on the idea that what is proposed theoretically must be susceptible to proof, which involves demonstrating that what is said corresponds to an actual state of affairs.

The central problem for Lyotard is that of the "legitimation" of knowledge. What methods do we use, or what assumptions do we need to make, in order to claim that something is scientifically correct or proven to the requisite degree? We can make scientific statements, just as we can make legal propositions, and we can show them to be justified, but what makes our means of justification justified? Who proves the proof? As I indicated above, this question is legal, because we are asking how we can justify what we claim to know. In fact, the question about foundations of knowledge is a problem which should also concern legal philosophers. This is clearly demonstrated in the following passage from Lyotard:

Jean-François Lyotard
The Postmodern Condition[17]

[820]   Take any civil law as an example: it states that a given category of citizens must perform a specific kind of action. Legitimation is the process by which a legislator is authorized to promulgate such a law as a norm. Now take the example of a scientific statement: it is subject to the rule that a statement must fulfil a given set of conditions in order to be accepted as scientific. In this case, legitimation is the process by which a "legislator" dealing with scientific discourse is authorized to prescribe the stated conditions (in general, conditions of internal consistency and experimental verification) determining whether a statement is to be included in that discourse for consideration by the scientific community.

---

17   Jean-François Lyotard, *The Postmodern Condition: A Report on Knowledge* (University of Minnesota Press, Minneapolis, 1984), p 8.

The parallel may appear forced. But as we will see, it is not. The question of the legitimacy of science has been indissociably linked to that of the legitimation of the legislator since the time of Plato. From this point of view, the right to decide what is true is not independent of the right to decide what is just, even if the statements consigned to these two authorities differ in nature. The point is that there is a strict interlinkage between the kind of language called science and the kind called ethics and politics: they both stem from the same perspective, the same "choice" if you will — the choice called the Occident.

[825] As Lyotard points out, knowledge and power (to legislate) are not separate.[18] We tend to regard knowledge as something which is independent of determination: it is just there, supported only by its truth, its correspondence with the way the world is. But in order to be worthy of the name, "knowledge", like law, must fulfil certain conditions of legitimacy. Scientific knowledge, for instance, must reach the required standards of verification and consistency. So who determines what counts as knowledge? In this case, those who have the institutional power to influence the conditions — the scientific community. There could be different conditions, more or less rigorous, more or less formal, for instance, but those that exist constitute scientific "legitimation". There are certain rules or standards of proof which must be adhered to before a statement will be accepted as scientifically proven. We can see a similar process at work in law. What counts as proof in a trial does not just appear, self-evidently: it is the product of the conditions of the trial — whether it is a civil or a criminal matter, the rules of evidence and procedure, what counts as fact and what as law, how the facts are interpreted, as well as certain socio-cultural norms such as who is likely to be seen as a credible witness. Justification of a claim that a state of affairs actually occurred is determined by a context of rules and norms, which needn't be in the form that they are, but which have been laid down or developed as the conditions and conventions of proof. They could be changed. What is eventually known cannot therefore be totally distinguished from the power of those who determine what constitutes proof or knowledge.

Science therefore attempts to legitimate itself, an attempt which places traditional science within the domain of what I described above as "modernism". Science even goes so far as to put itself at the pinnacle of all forms of knowledge, as the legitimating ground of, or universal standard for, evaluating other types of knowledge.[19] Lyotard argues that, in fact, science must always have recourse to what he calls a "metanarrative", that is, a higher set of principles which are not themselves scientific. Such a metanarrative provides the necessary

---

18 A similar point was made by Foucault, whose ideas about the relationship between truth and power will be discussed later in the chapter.

19 We should bear in mind that "science" in this context refers to general scientific practice and assumptions, and not the philosophies of science (for instance those of Kuhn and Feyerabend) which have focused upon the nature of scientific "truth". Lyotard identifies the latter philosophies as part of the postmodern movement in science.

framework to satisfy the desire for internal consistency and complete-ness. According to Lyotard, it is consensus among the community of scientists, not any absolute scientific principle, that forms the basis of scientific legitimacy. Consensus is part of the "metanarrative" of science. This is comparable to HLA Hart's emphasis on consensus among officials that the "rule of recognition" is valid, as the ultimate basis of legitimacy in law.[20] In fact, Lyotard argues that the idea of consensus is one of the dominant ideologies or narratives of the 20th century.

The point of all of this is that Lyotard argues that in the latter half of this century there has been a loss of faith in the idea of a "meta-narrative". Appeal to a higher, universal domain of thought is no longer seen as an effective or necessary way of validating knowledge. There has been a multiplication of methods, of forms of knowledge, and of technologies, as well as the collapse of the traditionally clear boundaries between areas of scientific investigation, giving us a glimpse of a potentially infinite number of new areas of thought. This has made the idea of a general unifying principle a practical impossibility. In addition, it has become clear that the ideal of scientific completeness is logically unattainable. Thought which is systematised necessarily relies upon assumptions which cannot be demonstrated in terms of the system itself. For instance, as I explained in Chapter 3, in the section on legal positivism, the positivist ideal of completeness and closure in the legal system can never be attained, because a higher term, like a sovereign, a rule of recognition, or a *grundnorm* (none of which can themselves be legitimated by the law) must always be posited. Thus we are left with making an assumption at what turns out to be the most crucial (central) point of the system. The same is said to be true of logical systems.[21]

The result of this loss of credibility of the metanarrative has been a splintering of scientific discourses and of discourses of knowledge.[22] There is an increasing recognition of the heterogeneity of discourses: what we see now is a multiplicity of what Wittgenstein calls language games,[23] which cannot be reduced to any overarching picture of discourse or knowledge. Generally speaking, this is what Lyotard

---

20 Hart, *The Concept of Law*, pp 100ff.

21 Lyotard refers to the work of Kurt Gödel, who demonstrated that mathematical systems necessarily contain a term which cannot be demonstrated in terms of the system itself. Logically then, no such system can be closed: *The Postmodern Condition*, pp 42-43.

22 The term "discourse" is one of those words which is frequently used but rarely explained in contemporary philosophical thought. I use it in a fairly loose way to designate an area of communication which can be either specific or general. So talking about discourse in general indicates the whole range of our practices of communication, while more specific areas could also be designated, such as legal discourse (simply, the sort of signifying practices used in relation to law).

23 The concept is used widely by Ludwig Wittgenstein in *Philosophical Investigations* (3rd ed, Basil Blackwell, Oxford, 1967). See, for instance, s 7.

identifies as the "postmodern condition". The postmodern, while not dispensing with legitimation, challenges pre-existing methods of legitimation and, in particular at the present time, the idea of universal, abstract principles of legitimation. The postmodern condition therefore describes an intellectual challenge to the assumptions and foundations of Western thought.

One thing that needs to be made absolutely clear is that post-modernism is not simply nihilism (as many legal writers have assumed). The point is not merely to destroy knowledge, nor even to demonstrate that any point of view is as good as any other. Rather, we are confronted with a reconstruction of what we regard as "true" or "real", and with the possibility of engaging with different language games, and formulating new positions. Traditional knowledge becomes dis-integrated, that is, questioned at its foundations, made specific to local contexts, and examined on a multiplicity of different levels, which interact, but do not necessarily form a whole. Knowledge is not just annihilated: indeed it cannot be annihilated. In speaking of social theories (but the argument can be generalised) Lyotard puts the point like this:[24]

> This breaking up of the grand Narratives ... leads to what some authors analyze in terms of the dissolution of the social bond and the disinte-gration of social aggregates into a mass of individual atoms thrown into the absurdity of Brownian motion. Nothing of the kind is happening ...
>
> A self does not amount to much, but no self is an island; each exists in a fabric of relations that is now more complex and mobile than ever before. Young or old, man or woman, rich or poor, a person is always located at "nodal points" of specific communication circuits, however tiny these may be. Or better: one is always located at a post through which various kinds of messages pass.

There is no absolute or total explanation of how the self interacts with society. Nor is there just, as the early critical legal studies writers thought, a "fundamental contradiction" which can be used to explain the tensions in the relationship between the individual and society.[25] Rather, there are many different effects of social organisation which form a fabric or network of relations. These influences can be described within their local contexts, but never totalised: that is, they can never be reduced to a theory which explains the fundamental properties of social relations.

The law provides a good example, since it so clearly operates on many levels, on many people and through many people, differently. We can try to describe an object called "the legal system" as the formal interaction of a number of different parts. Such a description will always be an inadequate account of the law, since what we cannot

---

24   Lyotard, *The Postmodern Condition*, p 15.

25   Duncan Kennedy, "The Structure of Blackstone's Commentaries" (1979) 28 *Buffalo Law Review* 205; Duncan Kennedy and Peter Gabel, "Roll Over Beethoven" (1984) 36 *Stanford Law Review* 1.

describe are the multitude of layers of the law. It is not a huge intellectual challenge to understand that things like the way the police operate, the position of victims of crime, what goes on in court, the experience of those undergoing family break-ups or those trying to gain political asylum, what we learn and teach in law school, the drudgery of practice as a solicitor, the workings of the Law Societies, the global structures of large businesses, and so on, all exist as layers or dimensions in the legal system, and could all be studied and described as local discourses. There may be regularities within each layer or "game", and some very complex interactions and tensions occurring between them but what we cannot do is form an overarching picture which explains everything consistently and in terms of a universal set of characteristics. As "selves" experiencing law, we exist at various "nodal points" or posts, receiving messages of varying types every day from the multitude of authorities, institutions, and other intellectual influences of the law. Any attempt to describe this situation from above or outside would simply amount to an imposition of a dominant (and falsely external) point of view.

Again, this does not mean knowledge is dead or that every perspective is equally defensible. It simply means that the boundaries and characteristics of what we know are being challenged and are, in the process, themselves changing. In terms of jurisprudence it means that the concept of legitimacy itself must be recognised to be a very complex one, reliant not only upon a single universal like a *grundnorm* or natural order, but is instead a product of the intricate relationships which make up the law, including community opinion, judicial decisions, legislative and bureaucratic acts, and, in general, the stories and narratives which circulate around, and in, every aspect of the legal system.[26] (Which is to say that we are never free from our social environment.)

The "postmodern", then, is a very general way of describing this fragmentation of our concepts of social interaction, and of the way we think about knowledge. What I will describe as "poststructuralism" offers some more specific arguments, which can be very useful in theoretical analysis. One more point needs to be mentioned, which may amount to a complication, but which is, I think, fairly important. There is a sense in which we can think of the present time, the early 21st century, as reflecting this "postmodern condition". We live in a postmodern age, in the sense that this questioning is, in fact, taking place around us, in the arts, in the human sciences, and other sciences and, even in law. But postmodernity, as Lyotard has described it, is much more than an era. It is potentially an ongoing state of affairs, one which positions itself as a challenge to any pre-existing modernity,[27]

---

26   This point will resurface later in the chapter in the discussion of Foucault.

27   That "modernity" still exists is well demonstrated by the ideas of Jurgen Habermas, who has formulated a theory of "communicative action" designed to counter arguments of indeterminacy in language.

and its accepted techniques of legitimation. Postmodernism is not just a break with modernism, nor is it simply a different period in the history of our culture and philosophy. It is that which does not merely seek to be innovative or novel, for its own sake; but to genuinely attempt to reconceptualise the forms or structures upon which our perceptions are based. This is one reason why the idea of postmodernism has become so important to feminist theorists: recognising the hold that a particular view of the world has, and why it is detrimental to women, it is important not only to strive for liberty within that system, but to begin to dismantle or question its foundations.

Structuralism and Poststructuralism

[830]   The act of naming, with all that we have seen it to imply in the way of solidifying and objectifying experience, becomes one of our most powerful suasive tools, enabling us to create entities practically out of nothing.

Bolinger *Aspects of Language*[28]

What's in a name? That which we call a rose

By any other name would smell as sweet.

Shakespeare *Romeo and Juliet*; II, ii.

[835]   Like modernism and postmodernism, the terms "structuralism" and "poststructuralism" have been used in a variety of ways, some more technical than others. Structuralism is something which can be identified as an intellectual approach to the question of how language relates to the world and how meaning works. "Poststructuralism" on the other hand is, as a term, rather more nebulous. It is basically also concerned with language and meaning, but moves beyond structuralist theory while nevertheless remaining distinctly reliant upon it.

Structuralism and semiotics

Ferdinand de Saussure

[840]   Structuralism is the term applied to the theory developed by the Swiss linguist, Ferdinand de Saussure and its many derivations in various intellectual disciplines.[29] Although Saussure's work was in linguistics,

---

28   Dwight Bolinger, *Aspects of Language* (2nd ed, Harcourt Brace, New York, 1975), p 259.

29   Apart from Ferdinand de Saussure's *Course in General Linguistics* (Philosophical Library, New York, 1966, c1959), there are a number of useful introductory works which explain structuralist thought generally: Catherine Belsey, *Critical Practice* (Methuen, London, 1980), pp 37-47; Terence Hawkes, *Structuralism and Semiotics* (Methuen, London, 1977); Kaja Silverman, *The Subject of Semiotics* (Oxford University Press, New York, 1983), pp 4-14; Jonathon Culler, *Saussure* (Fontana, Glasgow, 1976); Terry Eagleton, *Literary Theory: An Introduction* (Basil Blackwell, Oxford, 1983), Ch 3.

because of its importance for the understanding of how meaning is constructed in language and in other systems of signs, it has been influential in many fields, in particular the study of literature, anthropology, psychoanalysis, and certain strands of philosophy. Structuralism itself has not really made a significant impact on law, though some critical legal studies writers have used it.[30]

To understand why Saussure's linguistic theory has made such an impact on contemporary theory in many areas, and why it forms the basis for "post-structuralist" thought, it is first necessary to consider the conventional understanding of language and meaning expressed in it. When we think of a word, and typically a noun, like "summons", we think of it representing an object, in this case, a piece of paper with some words written on it designed to perform a specific function. There is a thing, a summons, which the word simply stands in for. A more sophisticated account of the process involves the interposition of a concept. A "summons" is a thing, but not just any thing: the object is a member of a group of things, which have certain things in common. The things they have in common form, on the abstract level, a concept, delineating what counts as a summons and what doesn't. Then there is the word, "summons" which represents the concept. The common idea is that there is a system of concepts or meanings (which may or may not correspond to actual things) which make up our thought processes, and language simply describes the meanings, it expresses or represents meanings. In other words, language works basically through a process of naming, that is, of giving names to meanings. Meanings are thought of as pre-existing language: language is a medium through which meanings can be communicated, just as conductors are mediums for electricity. As Jonathon Culler writes, "the ideal [in such a view of language] would be to contemplate thought directly. Since this cannot be, language should be as transparent as possible."[31] The ideal, in other words, would be to minimise the interference caused by language, so that expression can get as close as possible to reality.

Saussure proposed a totally different model of the way meaning in language works. In the first place he divided the study of language into diachronic and synchronic linguistics.[32] Diachronic (meaning through time) linguistics is concerned with the way words and their meanings evolve: the origin of words, and the way both their forms and meanings change, is the primary object of diachronic linguistics. However, Saussure also pointed out that the speaker of a language is not faced

---

30   For instance, Thomas Heller, "Structuralism and Critique" (1984) 36 *Stanford Law Review* 127.

31   Jonathon Culler, *On Deconstruction: Theory and Criticism After Structuralism* (Routledge Kegan Paul, London, 1983), p 92.

32   Ferdinand Saussure, *Course in General Linguistics*, Part 1, Ch 3 "Static and Evolutionary Linguistics". This work was compiled on the basis of Saussure's lectures after his death by several of his students. Saussure himself left no comprehensive record of his theory.

with its history, but rather with its present state.[33] Synchronic or static linguistics was therefore necessary to describe the structural properties of language as it exists at any particular moment. Language considered as a cross-section of time forms the basis for synchronic linguistics. The basic object of synchronic linguistics was to describe *langue*, or the underlying formal system of language, which Saussure contrasted with *parole*, everyday speech. To use a familiar metaphor, *langue* (language) is the underlying legal system of language — the formal rules — while *parole* (speech) is its everyday manifestation. *Langue* is conceptual, while *parole* is material. The emphasis on the formal static structure of language gave rise to the term "structuralism", which has been used loosely to refer to any intellectual study based on a description of the structure of the theoretical object. However the structuralist work which is derived more strictly from Saussure's linguistic theory is based on the view that certain systems of meaning which are *not* linguistic, can nevertheless be described through the characteristics of the structure of language. I will provide some examples shortly.

Saussure begins his famous discussion of the nature of the sign (which will be defined shortly) by rejecting the view that language is simply a nomenclature. Language is not "a list of words, each corresponding to the thing it names."[34] Quite apart from the obvious point that not all words are nouns, Saussure writes that such a view assumes that there is a system of ideas which pre-exist language. Whereas, according to Saussure:[35]

> Philosophers and linguists have always agreed in recognizing that without the help of signs we would be unable to make a clear-cut, consistent distinction between two ideas. Without language, thought is a vague, uncharted nebula. There are no pre-existing ideas, and nothing is distinct before the appearance of language.

Put like this, without the context of the rest of Saussure's theory, this certainly sounds like a very large claim which, if true, clearly has the potential to disrupt very seriously the common sense view that language is there to describe a pre-existent reality. Saussure is claiming that language comes first, then ideas. Thus if "reality" is to have any meaning, then it must be apprehended through language, or more precisely, through the distinctions and categories set up by language.

Before considering how language is seen by Saussure to be the precondition for conceptualisation, some basic terminology needs explaining. In rejecting the notion that language is composed of names which simply hook onto things, Saussure proposed a model of the sign which does not take as its primary motivation the physical object. The "concept" is called the "signified", and the "sound-image" (that is, the

---

33   Saussure, *Course in General Linguistics*, p 81.

34   Saussure, *Course in General Linguistics*, p 65.

35   Saussure, *Course in General Linguistics*, pp 111-112.

word which corresponds to the concept) is called the "signifier". Together the signified and the signifier make up the sign. The thing or object referred to, the "referent",[36] remains outside the system of language: it is not the referent which determines meaning. Rather, the sound or written trace which is a word, carries with it a concept (since it can be applied in an infinite number of situations). Because when we hear a word we invariably think of a concept, the illusion of transparency is maintained. Saussure's aim was to describe the systemic relationships between signifiers and signifieds which give rise to meaning.

The first principle of signification asserted by Saussure is not particularly controversial. It is that the relationship between the signified and the signifier is arbitrary. Put simply, there is no necessity, to use Saussure's example, that the French word "soeur" must signify the concept "sister". The very obvious demonstration of this point is that different languages use different words to signify the same concept. "Sister", "soeur" and "Schwester" all mean the same thing. Moreover different languages divide up the world differently and employ different schemes of categorisation, demonstrating that it is not pre-existent concepts which motivate language. Saussure's examples are well known. The French word "mouton" sometimes refers to the same thing as the English word "sheep". However, unlike "mouton", "sheep" cannot signify meat which is ready to be eaten. In English, what we eat is "mutton". The concept of "mouton" is therefore not the same as the concept of "sheep". Catherine Belsey offers another interesting example, contrasting the different ways that Welsh and English divide up the spectrum. The Welsh word "glas" (roughly blue) extends into what English speakers would call green or grey.[37] It is therefore not only the relationship between the signifier and the signified which is arbitrary, but also the system of concepts employed by a language.

"Arbitrary", however, does not mean that every speaker can choose for herself what words to use for which concepts. The fact that there is no natural connection between words and concepts does not mean that we can simply go around arbitrarily inventing words, or deliberately reassigning the conceptual structure of language. While this has certainly been the practice of some writers of literature, as well as some postmodern thinkers, such a practice works by using words in unusual or novel ways, but which nevertheless have resonances in the pre-existing structure of language. (Such "new" meanings are therefore never entirely new nor truly arbitrary.) Positing an entirely new order or arbitrarily inventing words will not work because the meaning of a sign is dependent on its having been established in language or adopted in some way by speakers of a language. It is not intention which

---

36   That is, to make it absolutely clear, the referent would be, for instance, the actual horse out there in the field, while the signified is the concept of horse and the signifier is the word "horse", whether written or spoken.

37   Belsey, *Critical Practice*, p 39; see also Culler, *Saussure*, pp 25-26.

establishes meaning, but convention.[38] Saussure uses the term "arbitrary" simply to indicate that the relationship between word and concept is unmotivated, that is, not natural.

The most important thing about Saussure's system is how he explains the way meaning is constructed. As I have said, he insisted that there are no pre-existent ideas, but that ideas arise from language. The different systems of conceptualisation specific to different languages indicate this point, but the crucial matter for consideration is exactly how meaning arises from a linguistic system. As indicated, the basic model of a sign in Saussure's system consists of a signified and a signifier, and the relationship between the two is signification. The signifier corresponds to the signified, and this, argues Saussure, is the unit of signification. But because the relationship is arbitrary, the existence of a sign cannot in itself give rise to meaning. Meaning is not just there in the sign. Rather the value (roughly what we call meaning) is the product of the relationship *between* signs.

In relation to the signified, argues Saussure, it is the difference between concepts which gives them the meaning they have. "Sheep" is defined in contrast to "mutton" and "lamb", and further, opposed to "cow", "dog", "hat", and so on. If the English word "mutton" did not exist, then we might use "sheep" to refer to what we eat. "Sheep" is limited as a concept by "mutton".[39] The concept associated with the word "sheep" is derived purely from all the things which it is not. If, without knowing English, I were to be given 50 sheep to look at and told in each case that the object is a "sheep", and I am then confronted with a duck, I might also call it a sheep, because I would not know which concept — animal or sheep — corresponds to the object.[40] Similarly, if confronted with 50 sheep and told they are all "animals" the duck might get called an "animal" or it might not. I would have no way of knowing whether this was the appropriate word. I will only know if the sheep is systematically contrasted with other animals, mammals contrasted with non-mammals, and animals contrasted with plants, or inorganic matter. The system of classifications arises from a system of contrasting uses of words. When I say "this is a sheep", I am also asserting, implicitly, that it is something distinct from other things which are not sheep. Thus concepts are a product of the oppositions in language, not of pre-existing ideas which just have names attached to them. As Saussure writes:[41]

---

38   Belsey, *Critical Practice*, p 42.

39   Saussure, *Course in General Linguistics*, p 116.

40   My example was suggested by a passage in Culler's *Saussure*, pp 24-26. Culler uses the colour brown as his example, but I thought it best to stick with sheep.

41   Saussure, *Course in General Linguistics*, p 117.

Instead of pre-existing ideas, then, we find ... values emanating from the system. When they are said to correspond to concepts, it is understood that the concepts are purely differential and defined not by their positive content but negatively by their relations with the other terms of the system. Their most precise characteristic is in being what the others are not.

... it is quite clear that initially the concept is nothing, that [it] is only a value determined by its relations with other similar values, and that without them the signification would not exist.

On the level of the signified then, value is determined through differences. Meaning is not positive, because whatever meaning is connected with a word, or a proposition, exists by virtue of the contrasts in language. Language is invested with the illusion of presenting pure positive concepts, but this is simply an effect of linguistic differences.

Saussure summarises the argument about differences in the following way:[42]

Everything that has been said up to this point boils down to this: in language there are only differences. Even more important: a difference generally implies positive terms between which the difference is set up; but in language there are only differences without positive terms. Whether we take the signified or the signifier, language has neither ideas nor sounds that existed before the linguistic system, but only conceptual and phonic differences that have issued from the system. The idea or phonic substance that a sign contains is of less importance than the other signs that surround it.

Now all of this might sound like a fairly benign set of claims. However, Saussurean linguistics has the potential to disrupt in a fairly major way how we think about the relationship between signs and the world.

In the first place, it becomes necessary to regard language as not only instrumental, but primary in the way we apprehend the world. Plato's view, for instance (upon which much of our philosophy is built), that there are ideal objects, or "forms" which make up an eternal reality — such as the form of a "table" or of an ideal "justice" — which pre-exist representation, is clearly rejected by these arguments.[43] The absolute distinction between a sensible world of change (simply, the world which is available to the senses) and an intelligible or ideal world of truth and "the good", simply cannot be sustained. Meanings, concepts, and ultimately "reality" are not simply "out there". They are not independent objects which language simply represents, rather they are constituted by language. If this sounds implausible, or limited in its significance, we need only to consider that even things which are very basic to most Western languages, like the division of time into past,

---

42   Saussure, *Course in General Linguistics*, p 120.

43   This distinction between a material world and an ultimate reality, the object of knowledge for philosophers, is most conveniently presented in Plato's *Republic* (Penguin, Harmondsworth, 1987), especially Book Six, 508-511 (the similes of the sun and divided-line), Book Seven, 514-521 (simile of the cave), and Book Ten, 595-608 (theory of art).

present, and future, and the presence of an individual speaking subject, an "I" totally distinct from its community and sovereign in the articulation of meaning, are not to be found in every language. This does not mean that the other languages are impoverished, or primitive in some ways, because frequently they incorporate elements not found in Western languages. However, it is clear that there can be no absolute "reality" common to all people. This certainly does not imply that there is no such thing as "reality". Rather, the way we think, and our comprehension of the world is situated in "discourse", and does not have a natural existence. Yet since much philosophy has been based on the attempt to discover a truth which is not specific to context and therefore should be totally translatable between languages, the impact of Saussure, and the philosophical resistance to his thought, has been significant.

Secondly, concepts are not positively existent, but always arise through a system of differences. Instead of always attempting to get at the core or essence of a concept, a process which neglects the contextuality of meaning, we should instead be asking how a concept is constituted in the system of which it forms a part, and how that system is itself constituted within a network of areas of knowledge. Structuralist-based thought requires us to go beyond thinking about unitary words and concepts to thinking in relational or differential terms. We typically learn to understand legal concepts as a series of definitions and distinctions, the latter being absolutely essential to the understanding of the former. (Thus what might elsewhere be seen as marginal, difference, ought to be understood at least by lawyers to be central.) The basic object of study in legal philosophy being law, legal philosophers in the Anglo-American tradition have often assumed that some positive definition of law could be obtained, a definition which would make clear exactly what law *is*. But in doing so it has always been necessary, for the sake of analytical clarity, to draw a boundary around law and distinguish it from not-law. In order to define what law is, we have to be able to define what it is not. There are reasons for arguing that such a project, for instance the one undertaken by the positivists to distinguish law from morality and other normative systems analytically, not only does, but must, fail. These arguments, however, go beyond structuralism into deconstruction, and will be explained later.

Semiotics

[845] I have dwelt on Saussure, because his thought is crucial to an understanding of the intellectual foundation and importance in modern philosophy of "post-structuralism" and "deconstruction". Before moving on to these topics though, something should be said about the general impact of structuralism. Saussure's major concern was with the way language operates as a signifying system. However, language is not the only system of signs used in society: others noted by Saussure are symbolic rites, etiquette, military signals, and sign language, to which

we could add things like stereotypes, advertising norms, political correctness, what we wear and how we wear it, any form of artistic representation, and so on. Saussure envisaged a science of signs extending beyond language into cultural phenomena:[44]

> A science that studies the life of signs within society is conceivable: ... I shall call it semiology ... Semiology would show what constitutes signs, what laws govern them. Since the science does not yet exist, no one can say what it would be; but it has a right to existence, a place staked out in advance. Linguistics is only a part of the general science of semiology; the laws discovered by semiology will be applicable to linguistics, and the latter will circumscribe a well-defined area within the mass of anthropological facts.

Saussure's prediction, or prescription, has indeed materialised, though the results would not perhaps qualify as a "science" and are more usually referred to as "semiotics". To take a legal example, we could ask what the significance of the judge's robes are. Clearly, in itself (and considered as part of the present structure, not one historically derived), court clothing has no inherent significance: if we were all to wear red gowns and long wigs, there would be no particular status or significance attached to these things. The significance is derived from the fact that only certain judges wear such attire, to distinguish themselves from other judges, and from legal practitioners, who themselves are traditionally clearly distinguished from non-lawyers. The system of court clothing is a system of signification — it is the expression of some very particular relationships, organised hierarchically.

Saussure's insights were used by the French psychoanalyst Jacques Lacan, in a re-formulation of Freudian theory. Lacan explained the structure of the psyche in linguistic terms, and specifically linked psychic development to the acquisition of language. His use of structuralism has had important consequences for the way the individual subject in its social environment (and in other contexts) is conceptualised. Rather than describing individuals simply as autonomous units (in the way I outlined above at [810] under the heading "modernism") Lacan theorised the subject as constructed in a way similar to the way signs are constructed, negatively. The subject has a relational, contextual, and constructed existence, not a naturally positive one. "I" am defined through my relations with others, through the complex fabric of discourses which surround me. Moreover, what is crucial to the Lacanian model of the subject is the element of "lack". For Lacan, entering language (and thus culture) involves dividing up the world, recognising oneself only through images and through relationships with others, and leaving behind the primordial state of infancy. The "subject" is therefore formed by a series of losses, and can never be the complete and separate individual posited by Enlightenment thought. "I" will have more to say about this in the next section, on "poststructuralism".

---

44   Saussure, *Course in General Linguistics*, p 16.

Structuralism has also been a source of great inspiration and controversy in anthropology. Claude Levi-Strauss used the methods and ideas of structural linguistics to study the structures of society. He interpreted cultural phenomena not as discrete independent entities, but rather as constituting an interlocking system, the parts of which are interdependent, and defined relationally. For instance, in *The Elementary Structures of Kinship* Levi-Strauss argued that the rules of kinship in a society and, in particular, rules relating to who may marry whom operate as a system of representation specific to a community. Levi-Strauss writes that women are typically the units of exchange in marriage, circulating between men just as words are exchanged or circulated. The exchange of women between families, and with it the system of meaning and values associated with women, sets up a sort of dialogue between families. Similarly, in the field of literary criticism, structuralism has been used to study the way in which literary meaning arises from systems of difference in a text.

Structuralism in this fairly strict sense gave way in time to the less clearly defined study of signifying systems. The work of Roland Barthes is a good example of the transition from structuralism to poststructuralism. In his early work, Barthes used structuralist methodology in a fairly formalistic way: for instance in *The Elements of Semiology* Barthes interpreted food as a signifying system in the following terms:[45]

> Let us now take another signifying system: food. We shall find there without difficulty Saussure's distinction [between language and speech]. The alimentary language is made of i) rules of exclusion (alimentary taboos); ii) signifying oppositions of units, the type of which remains to be determined (for instance the type savory/sweet); iii) rules of association, either simultaneous (at the level of a dish) or successive (at the level of a menu); iv) rituals of use which function, perhaps, as a kind of alimentary rhetoric ... . The menu ... illustrates very well this relationship between the language and speech: any menu is concocted with reference to a structure (which is both national — or regional — and social); but this structure is filled differently according to the days and the users, just as linguistic "form" is filled by the free variations and combinations which a speaker needs for a particular message.

If Barthes were not French one would readily suspect that he is being frivolous here. In his later writings Barthes continued the project of reading cultural systems of signification, but took a far less formalistic approach, in fact, making a scholarly virtue of frivolity. I will come back to Barthes in the section on poststructuralism.

Some of the better-known writers in semiotics have not really attempted to formulate meta-theories of signification, but have, in a postmodern spirit, taken local instances of the constitution of meaning. In this sense they might be considered in the context of poststructuralism, rather than structuralism, but an example of this

---

type of writing will be useful at this point, simply to demonstrate the type of thing which semioticians have been doing. Umberto Eco is a very well known Italian novelist and theorist. In the following extract from *Travels in Hyper-Reality*, he considers, in a not altogether frivolous way, the cultural and physical significance of jeans. (As with Barthes one can never be certain whether he is serious, but does it matter?) The basic presupposition here is that culture and society can be read: they form a text, and are subject to interpretation. In this extract we also see the impact of clothes on the body and indeed, on the conventional distinction between body and mind.

Umberto Eco
"Lumbar Thought"[46]

[850]   I began wearing blue jeans in the days when very few people did, but always on vacation. I found — and still find — them very comfortable, especially when I travel, because there are no problems of creases, tearing, spots. Today they are worn also for looks, but primarily they are very utilitarian. It's only in the past few years that I've had to renounce this pleasure because I've put on weight. True, if you search thoroughly you can find, an *extra large* (Macy's could fit even Oliver Hardy with blue jeans), but they are large not only around the waist, but also around the legs, and they are not a pretty sight.

Recently, cutting down on drink, I shed the number of pounds necessary for me to try again some *almost* normal jeans. I underwent the calvary described by Luca Goldoni, as the saleswoman said, "Pull it tight, it'll stretch a bit"; and I emerged, not having to suck in my belly (I refuse to accept such compromises). And so, after a long time, I was enjoying the sensation of wearing pants that, instead of clutching the waist, held the hips, because it is a characteristic of jeans to grip the lumbar-sacral region and stay up thanks not to suspension but to adherence.

After such a long time, the sensation was new. The jeans didn't pinch, but they made their presence felt. Elastic though they were, I sensed a kind of sheath around the lower half of my body. Even if I had wished, I couldn't turn or wiggle my belly *inside* my pants; if anything, I had to turn it or wiggle it *together with* my pants. Which subdivides so to speak one's body into two independent zones, one free of clothing, above the belt, and the other organically identified with the clothing, from immediately below the belt to the anklebones. I discovered that my movements, my way of walking, turning, sitting, hurrying, were *different*. Not more difficult, or less difficult, but certainly different.

As a result, I lived in the knowledge that I had jeans on, whereas normally we live forgetting that we're wearing undershorts or trousers. I lived for my jeans, and as a result I assumed the exterior behaviour of one who wears jeans. In any case, I assumed a *demeanor*. It's strange that the traditionally most informal and anti-etiquette garment should be the one that so strongly imposes an etiquette. As a rule I am boisterous, I sprawl in a chair,

46   Umberto Eco, *Travels in Hyper-Reality* (Pan Books and Secker and Warburg, London, 1987), pp 191-195.

I slump wherever I please, with no claim to elegance: my blue jeans checked these actions, made me more polite and mature. I discussed it at length, especially with consultants of the opposite sex, from whom I learned what, for that matter, I had already suspected: that for women experiences of this kind are familiar because all their garments are conceived to impose a demeanor — high heels, girdles, brassieres, pantyhose, tight sweaters.

I thought then about how much, in the history of civilization, dress as armor has influenced behaviour and, in consequence, exterior morality. The Victorian bourgeois was stiff and formal because of stiff collars; the nineteenth-century gentleman was constrained by his tight redingotes, boots, and top hats that didn't allow brusque movements of the head. If Vienna had been on the equator and its bourgeoisie had gone around in Bermuda shorts, would Freud have described the same neurotic symptoms, the same Oedipal triangles? And would he have described them in the same way if he, the doctor, had been a Scot, in a kilt (under which, as everyone knows, the rule is to wear nothing)?

A garment that squeezes the testicles makes a man think differently. Women during menstruation; people suffering from orchitis, victims of hemorrhoids, urethritis, prostate and similar ailments know to what extent pressures or obstacles in the sacroiliac area influence one's mood and mental agility. But the same can be said (perhaps to a lesser degree) of the neck, the back, the head, the feet. A human race that has learned to move about in shoes has oriented its thought differently from the way it would have done if the race had gone barefoot. — Not only did the garment impose a demeanor on me; by focusing my attention on demeanor, it obliged me to *live towards the exterior world*. It reduced, in other words, the exercise of my interior-ness. For people in my profession it is normal to walk along with your mind on other things: the article you have to write, the lecture you must give, the relationship between the One and the Many, the Andreotti government, how to deal with the problem of the Redemption, whether there is life on Mars, the latest song of Celentano, the paradox of Epimenides. In our line this is called "the interior life." Well, with my new jeans my life was entirely exterior: I thought about the relationship between me and my pants, and the relationships between my pants and me and the society we lived in. I had achieved heteroconsciousness, that is to say, an epidermic self-awareness.

I realized then that thinkers, over the centuries, have fought to free themselves of armor. Warriors lived an exterior life, all enclosed in cuirasses and tunics; but monks had invented a habit that, while fulfilling, *on its own*, the requirements of demeanor (majestic, flowing, all of a piece, so that it fell in statuesque folds), it left the body (inside, underneath) completely free and unaware of itself. Monks were rich in interior life and very dirty, because the body, protected by a habit that, ennobling it, released it, was free to think, and to forget about itself. The idea was not only ecclesiastic; you have to think only of the beautiful mantles Erasmus wore. And when even the intellectual must dress in lay armor (wigs, waistcoats, knee breeches) we see that when he retires to think, he swaggers in rich dressing-gowns, or in Balzac's loose, *drôlatique* blouses. Thought abhors tights.

But if armor obliges its wearer to live the exterior life, then the age-old female spell is due also to the fact that society has imposed armors on women, forcing them to neglect the exercise of thought. Woman has been enslaved by fashion not only because, in obliging her to be attractive, to maintain an ethereal demeanor, to be pretty and stimulating, it made her a sex object; she has been enslaved chiefly because the clothing counseled for her forced her psychologically to live for the exterior. And this makes us realize how intellectually gifted and heroic a girl had to be before she could become, in those clothes, Madame de Sévigné, Vittoria Colonna, Madame Curie, or Rosa Luxemburg. The reflection has some value because it leads us to discover that, apparent symbol of liberation and equality with men, the blue jeans that fashion today imposes on women are a trap of Domination; for they don't free the body, but subject it to another label and imprison it in other armors that don't seem to be armors because they apparently are not "feminine."

A final reflection — in imposing an exterior demeanor, clothes are semiotic devices, machines for communicating. This was known, but there had been no attempt to illustrate the parallel with the syntactic structures of language, which, in the opinion of many people, influence our view of the world. The syntactic structures of fashions also influence our view of the world, and in a far more physical way than the *consecutio temprum* or the existence of the subjunctive. You see how many mysterious paths the dialectic between oppression and liberation must follow, and the struggle to bring light.

Even via the groin.

1976

[855] What has always puzzled me about the ideas of structuralism and semiotics is why the basic unit of theorisation must be that of a sign, and not that of law. Why do we have to interpret phenomena through their signifying systems, rather than through their laws? It may be a highly unlikely scenario, but suppose a lawyer had been the one to propose a new and exciting way of interpreting legal systems, and proposed that this analysis could be applied to cultural phenomena generally. (Yes, it is very hard to imagine a lawyer doing this.) Why can't we analyse the system of clothing as a legal system — one which (perhaps) makes certain prescriptions, and imposes sanctions (being thrown out of a casino, being marginalised, patronised, or ostracised) if incorrectly performed? Don't clothes bring power? Isn't a law a form and a content, a letter and a spirit, a signifier and a signified? Can't we say that concepts are formed by certain laws, that is, by the process of drawing a boundary and excluding an outside? Isn't our conceptual system, in fact, a legal system? (Lawyers have thought for a long time that legal concepts are formed arbitrarily through differences and distinctions, but have perhaps been too short-sighted or too busy to extrapolate this insight.) Isn't what we study as "law" in law school actually continuous with all sorts of other normative systems in society? In the end, isn't a sign actually a law? Both signs and laws, in the end, operate as constraints, boundaries. Kelsen certainly seemed to recognise this when he wrote that the norm is a scheme of interpretation: norms operate on the world to give it legal meaning.[47] At the

47   Hans Kelsen, *Pure Theory of Law* (University of California Press, Berkeley, 1967), pp 3-4.

same time, both signs and laws are multi-dimensional and multi-conceptual (that is, susceptible to being conceptualised in many ways). Not only do we have a plurality of systems encompassing both signs and laws, as semiotics illustrates, but the idea of law itself is plural: law can be many things, as this book has attempted to illustrate.[48]

These questions are not presented as a criticism of structuralist thought, nor as a belated legal imperialism. I am simply trying to indicate something which may seem at once both to support and undercut structuralism — that the foundation of a system of thought is not an absolute, so (perhaps) it needn't be a sign. Surely there is nothing natural or necessary about the concept of the sign which would make it the only possible foundation for our analysis. It could be a legal system, an economy, social organisation, or a the concept of political institution. It is, moreover, clear that even such fundamental concepts are not themselves distinct, but overlap, and can be set to the task of interpreting the same territory. This is something which is important in poststructural thought, and I will return to it later.

Poststructuralism

[860]   Traditionally, as I indicated above, we have tended to regard the subject, an individual who writes, theorises, speaks, or acts, as an independent entity who is both self-contained and self-controlled. The idea is that as a theorist I simply perceive my object, and then express what I have seen through language. In theory, the subject is an external observer, who just reflects on the object. In society, the fully formed subject is an autonomous thinking unit who is in control of her or his destiny. I say "fully formed" because it is clear that this is an ideal, one which forms the basis of social thought (for instance, in social contract theory), but does not necessarily describe every person in society. Nevertheless, the assumption is that we strive to be as free from social determinations as possible (to have a sovereign identity), and as I have noted, much of our law is based on the assumption that this is our natural state.

The scientific division between system and subject is preserved by structuralist thought, since it relies on the concept of a formal underlying set of rules which the theorist can gain access to and explain fully. The underlying system of language, or *langue*, is presented as a unifiable, and universalisable whole which is available for objective interpretation. However, structuralism also contains within it the seeds

---

48   Although I have not specifically considered the question of legal pluralism, it is undoubtedly one of the more important issues to face legal theory in the 21st century. See Martha-Marie Kleinhans and Roderick MacDonald, "What is a Critical Legal Pluralism?" (1997) 12 *Canadian Journal of Law and Society/Revue Canadienne de droit et société* 25; Desmond Manderson, "Beyond the Provincial: Space, Aesthetics, and Modernist Legal Theory" (1996) 20 *Melbourne University Law Review* 1048; Brian Tamanaha, "A Non-Essentialist Version of Legal Pluralism" (2000) 27 *Journal of Law and Society* 296; Margaret Davies, "Pluralism and the Philosophy of Law" (2006) 57 *Northern Ireland Legal Quarterly* 577.

of its own contradiction, since what it makes clear is that the individual speaker is not free from language and is, in fact, caught within its fabric. So while structuralism posits the existence of a discrete system which becomes the object of theory, it also implies that this subject can never be free of the system.

The fundamental assumption then, would be that there is a subject and an external world which act upon each other, but which remain essentially and conceptually separate. Challenging this division between the subject and the system outside has been one of the major concerns of poststructural thought and, as I have already suggested in a preliminary fashion, how this challenge has been framed. For instance, we saw that Lyotard's conception of the self in society was as a "nodal point" or post which sends and receives increasingly complex cultural messages. And Jacques Lacan, in applying structural linguistics to psychoanalysis, saw the subject as the product of linguistic relations, a series of losses of the Other. On the other side of the system/subject divide, poststructuralism has also challenged the idea of the stable and fully determinate system: in part, this instability stems from the interaction of system and subject. Concentrating on the system itself (while retaining a reflective appreciation of it, since we are always *in* it) poststructuralist thought has questioned Saussure's concept of a *static* signifying environment.

Preserving the distinction between subject and system (since I can hardly reject it altogether), I am going to examine each of these elements in turn, briefly, before turning to deconstruction.

The subject

[865] It was probably Freud who first disrupted in a major way the view of total subjectivity, by theorising a fundamental and irreconcilable division in the individual between the conscious and unconscious sides of the psyche. What had previously been thought of as the totality of subjectivity, the conscious mind which simply needed development, was theorised by Freud as a product of certain relations. As Kaja Silverman writes: "The Freudian subject is above all a partitioned subject, incapable of exhaustive self-knowledge. Its parts do not exist harmoniously; they speak different languages and operate on the basis of conflicting imperatives."[49] According to Freud's early thought, the division between unconscious and conscious is formed primarily, though not exclusively, by repression. "Repression" does not involve merely ejecting something from the mind, but preventing it from entering the conscious mind.[50] Thus, at a very fundamental level, the subject is said to be not only a product of an environment, but one which is never whole, never internally consistent, and never quite stable.

---

49 Kaja Silverman, *The Subject of Semiotics* (Oxford University Press, New York, 1983), p 142.

50 Sigmund Freud, "The Unconscious" in *Freud: The Essentials of Psychoanalysis* (Penguin, Harmondsworth, 1986).

Since Freud, the notion of subjectivity has been questioned in a multitude of ways, the focal point of such controversies being how the subject functions in relation to the systems (of language, law, and society) which surround it. It is no longer possible to theorise the subject as a sovereign entity, since like the sign and, like concepts, it is defined relationally. What I am is a function of what I am not, what I repress, what I exclude, as well as of the various cultural messages which pass through me. (Perhaps "I" should not be feeling too bad if I seem to live a very fragmentary existence.)

One of the theorists who clearly defined the breakdown in the distinction between the supposedly external system of language and the speaker who uses it, is the linguist Emile Benveniste. Building upon the insight of structuralism that language is the condition of conceptualisation and operates through setting up oppositions between its terms, Benveniste argued that the subject, the "I", is nothing more than a position in language, defined in contrast to its other, "you". "I" implies a "you", and so the position of subjectivity is relational, not essential or original. Unlike other words, as Benveniste points out, "I" cannot be defined, except by reference to the person who is using it at a particular time.

Emile Benveniste
"Subjectivity in Language"[51]

[870]   Consciousness of self is only possible if it is experienced by contrast. I use *I* only when I am speaking to someone who will be a *you* in my address. It is this condition of dialogue that is *constitutive* of *person*, for it implies that reciprocally *I* becomes you in the address of the one who in his turn designates himself as *I*. Here we see a principle whose consequences are to spread out in all directions. Language is possible only because each speaker sets himself up as a *subject* by referring to himself as *I* in his discourse. Because of this, *I* posits another person, the one who, being, as he is, completely exterior to "me", becomes my echo to whom I say *you* and who says *you* to me. This polarity of persons is the fundamental condition in language, of which the process of communication, in which we share, is only a mere pragmatic consequence. It is a polarity, moreover, very peculiar in itself, as it offers a type of opposition whose equivalent is encountered nowhere else outside language. This polarity does not mean either equality or symmetry: "ego" always has a position of transcendence with regard to you. Nevertheless, neither of the terms can be conceived of without the other; they are complementary, although according to an "interior/exterior" opposition, and, at the same time, they are reversible ...

          ...

          Now these pronouns are distinguished from all other designations a language articulates in that *they do not refer to a concept or to an individual*.

---

51   In Emile Benveniste, *Problems in General Linguistics* (University of Miami Press, Florida, 1971), pp 224-227. See also "The Nature of Pronouns" in the same volume.

There is no concept "I" that incorporates all the *I*'s that are uttered at every moment in the mouths of all speakers, in the sense that there is a concept "tree" to which all the individual uses of "tree" refer ... Could it then be said that *I* refers to a particular individual? If that were the case, a permanent contradiction would be admitted into language, and anarchy into its use. How could the same term refer indifferently to any individual whatsoever and still at the same time identify him in his individuality? We are in the presence of a class of words, the "personal pronouns", that escape the status of all the other signs of language. Then, what does *I* refer to? To something very peculiar which is exclusively linguistic: *I* refers to the act of individual discourse in which it is pronounced, and by this it designates the speaker. It is a term that cannot be identified except in what we have called elsewhere an instance of discourse and that has only a momentary reference. The reality to which it refers is the reality of the discourse. It is in the instance of discourse in which *I* designates the speaker that the speaker proclaims himself as the "subject". And so it is literally true that the basis of subjectivity is in the exercise of language. If one really thinks about it, one will see that there is no other objective testimony to the identity of the subject except that which he himself thus gives about himself.

Language is so organised that it permits each speaker to *appropriate to himself* an entire language by designating himself as *I*.

[875] This last point is worth noting. By designating myself as "I", I thereby appropriate to myself the entire language. I speak only by adopting (often implicitly) the subject-position in language: speaking involves buying into the system.

We may feel inclined to reject Benveniste's arguments on the common sense (and empirical) ground that, after all, "I" do exist quite apart from language: "I" am a physical presence, if nothing else. But if I were really nothing other than a physical presence, I would only be a lump of flesh, not a subject, since a subject implies a system. The point is that I only come to know myself through contrast with other subjects, and therefore have an existence which is indissociable from the network of discursive relations in society.

A most interesting application of this type of analysis of the notion of subjectivity has been highlighted by Sarah Kofman, in a reading of a passage from Nietzsche (who anticipated many poststructuralist themes). What Nietzsche wrote was this:

Let us be more prudent than Descartes, who remained caught in the trap [*Fallstrick*] of words. *Cogito*, to tell the truth, is only a single word, but its meaning is complex. (There is no lack of complex things that we seize brutally, believing in good faith that they are simple.) In this famous *cogito* there is: (1) it thinks; (2) I believe that it is I who thinks; (3) but even admitting that this second point is uncertain, being a matter of belief, the first point — "it thinks" — also contains a belief that "thinking" is an activity for which one must imagine a subject, if only "it"; and the *ergo sum* signifies nothing more. But this is a belief in grammar: one supposes "things" and their "activities", and this puts us far from immediate certainty.[52]

---

52   Friedrich Nietzsche, *Nachgelassene Fragmente* (1885) quoted in Sarah Kofman, "Descartes Entrapped" in Eduardo Cadava, Peter Connor, and Jean-Luc Nancy (eds), *Who Comes After the Subject?* (Routledge, New York, 1991), p 178.

Far from thinking outside language, as he supposed he could do, Descartes is, as Nietzsche explains, trapped in language. To say *"cogito"*, I think, rather than "it thinks" already assumes, rather than proves, the existence of the subject. Against this assumption, Nietzsche pointed out that

> a thought comes when "it" wishes, and not when "I" wish, so that it is a falsification of the facts of the case to say that the subject "I" is the condition of the predicate "think". *It* thinks; but that this "it" is precisely the famous old "ego" is, to put it mildly, only a supposition, an assertion, and assuredly not an "immediate certainty".[53]

Because "I" am not in fact in control of my thoughts, argues Nietzsche, to say that "I" am the one doing the thinking is purely an indemonstrable assertion. Moreover, even to say "it thinks" is to be caught in the trap of grammar — the assumption that the activity "thinking" must have a cause which is a subject. So when Descartes says *ergo sum*, "therefore I am", all he is doing is asserting something which he assumed already. As Kofman puts it, what Descartes' argument amounts to is simply the assumption that if there is thought, there must be a subject who is thinking, and that this reflects merely our grammatical habits.[54] (Why am "I" in control of my thoughts? Isn't thought rather in control of me? Or is to say so simply to commit the same error, but to invert it, as though "thought" is the subject and "I" am the object? Either way, we are caught in the categories of language.)

The recognition of the linguistic constructedness of the concept of subjectivity has had a significant impact on literary criticism, since the "subject" who has traditionally been considered to be the origin (and therefore ultimate authority) of meaning in a work of literature is the Author. We have tended to think of the "meaning" of a text as being that which the Author intended: if something wasn't or couldn't have been intended, then it is not part of the meaning of the text. However if meaning is constructed in language, and not just intended outside and before language, then the Author has no particular authority over the ultimate or final interpretation of a text. She can tell us what she *meant* to achieve or to write, but there will always be meanings, or subtle resonances, which escape her control. There is in fact no such thing as an ultimate interpretation, since language, readers and contexts change. These ideas were presented in an essay by Roland Barthes in his "poststructuralist" phase.

---

53 Friedrich Nietzsche, *Beyond Good and Evil* (Gateway, Chicago, 1955), s 17. See Kofman, "Descartes Entrapped", p 185.

54 Kofman, "Descartes Entrapped", p 192.

Roland Barthes
"The Death of the Author"[55]

[880]   Linguistically, the author is never more than the instance writing, just as I is nothing other than the instance saying I: language knows a "subject", not a "person" and this subject, empty outside of the very enunciation which defines it, suffices to make language "hold together", suffices, that is to say, to exhaust it.

The removal of the Author ... is not merely an historical fact or an act of writing; it utterly transforms the modern text ... The temporality is different. The Author, when believed in, is always conceived of as the past of his own book: book and author stand automatically on a single line divided into a *before* and an *after*. The Author is thought to *nourish* the book, which is to say that he exists before it, thinks, suffers, lives for it ...

We know now that a text is not a line of words releasing a single "theological" meaning (the "message" of the Author-God) but a multi-dimensional space in which a variety of writings, none of them original, blend and clash. The text is a tissue of quotations drawn from the innumerable centres of culture ...

Once the Author is removed, the claim to decipher a text becomes quite futile. To give a text an Author is to impose a limit on that text, to furnish it with a final signified, to close the writing.

[885]   Several interesting issues arise from this passage. In the first place, as Barthes argues, the concept of the author, an intentional being who is the text's God, is dead. (Even if the person who wrote the text were to explain it fully, all we would get is more words, not the real thing.) Freed from the constraints of authorial intention, and the attempt to rediscover it, criticism can begin to untangle the complexities of the text. Secondly, the text is never a simple, unidimensional object. It is composed of a multitude of complex layers of meaning which often conflict and can never be reduced to a single complete meaning. Rather, as Barthes goes on to assert, any "unity" the text has is with the reader, not the author. It is the reader who holds together the complexities of the text.

Applying this sort of approach to law,[56] it should be clear (if it is not already, simply by application of a little common sense) that the intention of any Founding Fathers can never be the only criterion for the interpretation of a Constitution. Even if we could gain access to the minds of such people, and even if they were somehow of one mind, the authoritative thing is the text of the Constitution: if the meaning of the text is not so much a function of intention, but of context, of

---

55   In Roland Barthes, *Image Music Text* (Fontana, London, 1977), pp 145-146.

56   See Margaret Davies, "Authority, Meaning, Legitimacy" in Jeffrey Goldsworthy and Tom Campbell (eds), *Legal Interpretation in Democratic States* (Ashgate, Aldershot, 2002). See also William Conklin, "The Invisible Author of Legal Authority" (1996) 7 *Law and Critique* 173.

language and culture, then the attempt to limit meaning to the first and only understanding will always be futile. Perhaps, rather than ask what it "really" means, an inquiry which will only lead to endless debates about authenticity, we should be focusing on asking what a good (sensible, just) meaning would be, given the current social circumstances. Rather than attempt to reproduce the original meaning, even in our reading of precedents, we should regard legal texts as something to be read in a current context. This approach has been very clearly adopted by the Australian High Court, so it is probably not necessary to be too insistent about it.

Writings like those of Barthes have led to poststructuralism being stereotyped as nihilistic, or at least, as relativistic. Everything depends on where you are coming from. Each interpretation is as good as any other. We cannot know anything about meaning, or about anything at all for that matter, since the whole world is a text and subject to contradictory interpretations. So ethics, politics, and reality come to nothing, and we can simply destroy everything.

Now, it is certainly true that slogans like these have been picked up by both adherents and critics of the postmodern condition. "Postmodernism" has even been equated with such simplistic formulae. What I would like to point out, even if I have to adopt a purist stance to do it, is that such characterisations neglect entirely the philosophical complexities of this type of approach. As I explained above, saying that there is no original, pre-language meaning and that the subject is already constituted in relation to language and a cultural environment, does not mean that all we are left with is a free play of ideas. On the contrary. We can and do communicate, because we share a common signifying environment. What is being questioned is the "natural" and objective status of certain fundamental concepts. This, of course, does not mean that we can simply abandon them: intention, for instance, is a very useful concept, one which we use to explain how we get meaning into a sentence. To point out that it is perhaps not our own intention, but language, which is primary, does not mean that "intention" must be discarded. What must be discarded is the notion that the "real" and only legitimate meaning of the text is inside the author's head.

We have, therefore, to be careful about how we interpret the ideas being put forward by Barthes. Saying that the author is dead and that meaning is plural, does not mean that there is no such thing as communication from one person to another, or that any meaning is as good as any other.[57] In the first place, saying that the author is dead simply indicates that in many ways a text is not in the *absolute* control of the author: the author is not the text's God, though that does not

---

[57] It is true that at times Barthes does seems to suggest that textual interpretation is or can be quite free, and that a text can be interpreted in a multitude of ways, none of which has any particular authority over the others as an interpretation. To this extent, I would disagree.

mean that she has no control over it whatsoever. No matter what I intend to say in this book, despite the fact that I want to get certain points across with a reasonable degree of clarity, and notwithstanding that I think any text deserves to be treated with respect, I cannot determine totally how it is going to be interpreted. In fact, treating a text with respect may involve interpreting it in a way, or seeing things in it, which the author herself did not see or intend.

Secondly, saying that meaning is plural does not imply that any one of a multitude of interpretations of a text or a situation is as good as any other. As I have said, we do communicate: there can be substantial agreement about what a set of signs means. But there is never only *one* meaning, or an *absolute* meaning, or a meaning which will not change over time. This is not only a point about the nature of meaning itself: it is also important to realise that the insistence that there is only one meaning is a political strategy which reinforces the oppression of those who do not share the dominant view. Recognising that people speaking the same language can still see and interpret the world in radically different ways is one strategy for challenging this exclusion. Finally, we also need to remember that there are meanings which are socially dominant, such as those associated with gender differences. Such meanings cannot simply be interpreted away by arguing that, after all, meaning is plural, and if one person sees something one way, another may see it quite differently. The dominant meanings keep coming back: although they are contingent, they are nevertheless powerful, and manipulated and reinforced by those who wield power. The effects of such power do not just go away now that we have realised that meaning is not absolute. Nonetheless, saying that meaning is plural gives us a way of unsettling the dominant meanings, and showing that they are not natural, but contingent.

The claim that poststructuralism is basically about indeterminacy, and the destruction of meaning, can perhaps be best countered by an example. It is certainly true that language is indeterminate in a way more subversive than that envisaged by HLA Hart. (Hart said that language is "open-textured", meaning that there are "central" cases of a word like "vehicle" and "penumbral" cases, which exist on the boundaries of the word.[58]) It is not just the case that there comes a point where we don't know whether something falls into the category defined by one word or another. Such a view perpetuates the idea that there are essential meanings inherent in words, and that it is only the imperfection of language which leads to indeterminacy. But if words are only defined contextually, if there are no pure positive meanings, indeterminacy can be seen as a result of the complexity of the process of meaning, and of the various strata which form a meaning. This process should be especially evident in legal environments, where there are a multitude of different documents, statutes, decisions, various

---

58   Hart, *The Concept of Law*, pp 126-128.

formal things like interrogatories and statements of claim, and many discourses (as I noted above) all interacting at different stages and in diverse dimensions of the legal process. Law then, is a concrete demonstration of the heterogeneity of meaning. However, the heterogeneity of meaning does not necessitate its destruction in any given context: we should, as theorists, become more sensitive both to the contextual nature of meaning, and to the complex layers and resonances which constitute any discourse.

The basic arguments which form the critique of the subject can be summarised, though thereby simplified, reasonably clearly. First, the notion of subjective autonomy, which assumes independence, unity, sovereignty, rationality, and self-determination, is an assumption, or even a dogmatic assertion, which cannot be demonstrated. Secondly, this "subject" upon which we have pinned so much faith, is a product of differences: "I" am a negative product of what "I" am not. The subject can never therefore be one. Thirdly, as such, the "subject" and the "system" (of language, discourse, culture) are inextricably entangled. The subject cannot simply be the external observer, because she is already caught within the categories of language and thought. And reason itself, so vital to the concept of the subject, is also indissociable from the process of signification.

There is, of course, another dimension to the critique of the traditional notion of subjectivity: traditionally the rational subject is masculine and white, and philosophy itself, with its emphasis on universal rational knowledge, is conceptually centred on ideals drawn from the history of white male dominance. The feminist critique of the foundations of philosophy is concerned with precisely this theoretical bias. Rosi Braidotti, for instance, says:[59]

> It seems to me that the radical critique of philosophy unveils the power structures implicit in the theoretical processes and that it does so from a sexualised standpoint. In other words, all philosophical claims to universality are deconstructed by pointing out the complicity between the masculine and the rational. This implies that philosophical discourse, far from being universal, suffers from the most partial onesidedness: a sexual and conceptual bias in favour of the masculine.

I have discussed these matters in Chapters 6 and 7, and will not reiterate them here. However, an issue which I think is important to raise concerns the extent to which the male-centred "white mythology" of philosophy has been displaced as a result of the postmodern critique. I really only want to *raise* this as a question, not discuss it: my impression, however, is that an institution of postmodernity has arisen within academia, and that this institution is still largely dominated by its traditional class of men and, increasingly, white women like myself.

---

59   Rosi Braidotti, "Ethics Revisited: Women and/in Philosophy" in Pateman and Gross (eds), *Feminist Challenges: Social and Political Theory* (Allen and Unwin, Sydney, 1986), p 50.

The traditional values of philosophy are being questioned, but have not yet been significantly displaced. This is notwithstanding the fact that many male and white Western philosophers have taken up the questions of race, whiteness, masculinity and femininity in an attempt to reformulate traditional philosophical notions of the subject. In some instances, the ways in which the "feminine" has become an object for the male philosophical gaze, have not been at all helpful for feminism, and may indeed have only re-entrenched traditional stereotypical views of gender difference.[60]

The system

[890] Foucault is well known in jurisprudence for his work on the relationship between power and truth, and I will extract a relevant passage from his collection of essays, lectures and interviews, *Power/Knowledge*, shortly. Before doing so, however, it is necessary to explain a little about the general dimensions of Foucault's work.[61] One of the major themes of Foucault's work was the effect which the reformulation of the notion of the subject has on the understanding of theoretical objects. Challenges to the traditional notion of the subject, so that subjectivity as a pre-given, pre-social, rational and whole identity is radically questioned, has certain consequences for the way we regard our objects of theory. It is important to stress this point, since the critique of the subject is indissociable from "postmodern" or "poststructural" reconstructions of theoretical objects. (Do I need to say that "subject" and "object" are mutually interdependent terms? Traditionally the "subject" has been effaced in the name of "objectivity": bringing back the subject, and in a radically altered form, must have some effect on the "object".)

For instance, madness as a natural concept has been regarded simply as a pathological state opposed to reason. There are sound minds and unsound minds, sanity and insanity. Although early theorists of mental states did not have the conceptual apparatus to explain madness as a psychological phenomenon, it has always existed as something antithetical to the complete and rational individual. In *Madness and Civilisation* Foucault tells a different story. Madness and reason, he argues are, as categories of analysis, products of Enlightenment thought. Madness is the *effect* of the Age of Reason, the "other" which has been excluded and against which reason defines itself. If we are to insist upon our reason, our autonomy, our completeness, we *must not*

---

60 See generally: Margaret Whitford, *Luce Irigaray: Philosophy in the Feminine* (Routledge, London, 1991), pp 29-31; Gayatri Chakravorty Spivak, "Displacement and the Discourse of Woman" in Antony Easthope and Kate McGowan (eds), *A Critical and Cultural Theory Reader* (Allen and Unwin, Sydney, 1992).

61 A good collection of essays on Foucault is Timothy Armstrong, *Michel Foucault: Philosopher* (Harvester Wheatsheaf, Hemel Hempstead, 1992). See also Lois McNay, *Foucault and Feminism* (Polity Press, Cambridge, 1992); and Alan Sheridan, *Michel Foucault: The Will to Truth* (Tavistock Publications, London, 1980).

be mad.[62] We must protect what we are from what we are not. Foucault's argument takes the form of an analysis of the history of how certain marginalised people have been regarded and dealt with in society and, in particular, the process of confinement of the "mad", which was very suddenly accelerated in the mid-17th century. Foucault argues that it is no coincidence that this process of confinement developed in conjunction with the notion of reason. Rather, madhouses operated as the "other" or unconscious of reason. Alan Sheridan summarises the argument like this:[63]

> Madness did not wait, in immobile identity, for the advent of psychiatry to carry it from the darkness of superstition to the light of truth. The categories of modern psychiatry were not lying in a state of nature ready to be picked up by the perceptive observer: they were produced by that "science" in its very act of formation.

It is not possible to do justice to the detail of Foucault's argument here, but the clear implication is that reason and madness are reciprocal terms, defined in contrast to each other, necessary to the Enlightenment notion of the individual, and not naturally existing.

Foucault makes a similar point about historical analysis generally. Traditional history, he argues, has concentrated on what he calls "continuity".[64] "History" pretends that the past is a gradually unfolding story of progress, or of evolution. Or, which amounts to much the same thing, the past is regarded as linear, like time, and the purpose of history is to explain the underlying rationale of events; how things developed through the ages, what caused a particular event, how different events can be explained within a theory of an era, what the origin of a political or intellectual movement was. In general, the purpose of history, according to Foucault, is to accord an overall significance to events of the past, that is, to explain the past as a totality. Foucault saw this process of rationalisation of the past as attributing to history the reason and autonomy of the Cartesian subject: like "man" the past becomes total, rational, and explicable in terms of the larger movements which underlie the surface chaos of events. Moreover, "man" is seen as the central category and cause of historical events. In contrast to this "traditional" approach Foucault proposed an anti-humanistic analysis concentrating on the "discontinuities" and divisions of the past — events, practices, or periods which rupture the superficial smoothness of history. In this way we can see that the movement away from the

---

62 In the original French version of *Madness and Civilisation: A History of Insanity in the Age of Reason* (Tavistock, London, 1967), Foucault considers a passage in the *Meditations* where Descartes explicitly excludes the possibility of being mad from the process of thinking: *Histoire de la folie à l'âge classique* (Gallimard, Paris, 1976), pp 56-58; Descartes, *Meditations*, I.

63 Sheridan, *Michel Foucault: The Will to Truth*, p 26.

64 See generally the introduction to *The Archaeology of Knowledge* (Tavistock Publications, London, 1972), in which Foucault explains his view of "traditional" history and its Cartesian subject, and his own "archaeological" approach.

concept of sovereign theorising subjects who attempt to see their objects as totalities has had a profound effect on how analysis is conducted.

I have explained that one of the things which postmodern thinkers have been emphasising is that meaning is not simply a product of a single will, but is the effect of a complex set of relationships in language within the discursive practices of a culture. Overarching universal explanations, "metanarratives", have been replaced by some with an analysis of local systems of meaning. The Cartesian rational subject has been challenged. Many of these themes come together in the following extract from a series of two lectures given by Foucault in 1976, in which he considers the relationship between power and truth. Foucault starts by noting that traditionally the philosophical question has been how our appreciation of the truth can set appropriate limits to political power. How, for instance, can social contract theories help to regulate and control sovereignty? Foucault inverts this by asking how power produces truth in society.

It is important to note that the concept of "power" used by Foucault is reformulated in line with the poststructural challenges to subjectivity and meaning. Instead of being a commodity — something repressive which one individual (or institution) holds, and exercises over another individual — "power" for Foucault is like meaning in language: something which "circulates" (as he says) in the system, yet which can be appropriated for particular ends. This is, when we think about it, empirically convincing. Saying that I as a teacher have power over my students, that politicians are powerful, that men have power over women, and so on, neglects the way that power is only produced by the relations within a system. Thus the classical Marxist division of social relations into those who have power and those who don't, the oppressors and the oppressed, is discredited by this approach. "Domination" and "right" (including legal right) are not derived only from the power of a sovereign institution of subjects, but are the products of the lines of force arising from social relations. Subjects are not just determined from above, but constituted within the system. In this way, Foucault is attempting to direct the theoretical emphasis away from the conception of the sovereign will enshrined in a legislature or Leviathan (a conception which, as Foucault explains, is nothing more than a transcendent rational individual), towards the local relationships of power within society which constitute right, truth, and subjectivity.

Michel Foucault

"Lecture Two: 14 January 1976"[65]

[895]   My aim ... [has been] to give due weight ... to the fact of domination, to expose both its latent nature and its brutality. I then wanted to show not only how right is, in a general way, the instrument of this domination — which scarcely needs saying — but also to show the extent to which, and the

65   In Michel Foucault, *Power/Knowledge* (Harvester Press, Brighton, 1980), pp 93-102.

forms in which, right (not simply the laws but the whole complex of apparatuses, institutions and regulations responsible for their application) transmits and puts in motion relations that are not relations of sovereignty, but of domination. Moreover, in speaking of domination I do not have in mind that solid and global kind of domination that one person exercises over others, or one group over another, but the manifold forms of domination that can be exercised within society. Not the domination of the King in his central position, therefore, but that of his subjects in their mutual relations: not the uniform edifice of sovereignty, but the multiple forms of subjugation that have a place and function within the social organism.

...

Let us not, therefore, ask why certain people want to dominate, what they seek, what is their overall strategy. Let us ask, instead, how things work at the level of on-going subjugation, at the level of those continuous and uninterrupted processes which subject our bodies, govern our gestures, dictate our behaviours etc. In other words, rather than ask ourselves how the sovereign appears to us in his lofty isolation, we should try to discover how it is that subjects are gradually, progressively, really and materially constituted through a multiplicity of organisms, forces, energies, materials, desires, thoughts, etc. We should try to grasp subjection in its material instance as a constitution of subjects. This would be the exact opposite of Hobbes' project in Leviathan, and of that, I believe, of all jurists for whom the problem is the distillation of a single will — or rather, the constitution of a unitary, singular body animated by the spirit of sovereignty — from the particular wills of a multiplicity of individuals. Think of the scheme of Leviathan: insofar as he is a fabricated man, Leviathan is no other than the amalgamation of a certain number of separate individualities, who find themselves reunited by the complex of elements that go to compose the State; but at the heart of the State, or rather, at its head, there exists something which constitutes it as such, and this is sovereignty, which Hobbes says is precisely the spirit of Leviathan. Well, rather than worry about the problem of the central spirit, I believe that we must attempt to study the myriad of bodies which are constituted as peripheral *subjects* as a result of the effects of power.

... power is not to be taken to be a phenomenon of one individual's consolidated and homogeneous domination over others, or that of one group or class over others. What, by contrast, should always be kept in mind is that power, if we do not take too distant a view of it, is not that which makes the difference between those who exclusively possess and retain it, and those who do not have it, and submit to it. Power must by (sic) analysed as something which circulates, or rather as something which only functions in the form of a chain. It is never localised here or there, never in anybody's hands, never appropriated as a commodity or piece of wealth. Power is employed and exercised through a net-like organisation ...

The individual is not to be conceived as a sort of elementary nucleus, a primitive atom, a multiple and inert material on which power comes to fasten or against which it happens to strike, and in so doing subdues or crushes individuals. In fact, it is already one of the prime effects of power that certain bodies, certain gestures, certain discourses, certain desires, come to be identified and constituted as individuals. The individual, that is, is not the *vis-à-vis* of power; it is, I believe, one of its prime effects.

The individual is an effect of power, and at the same time, or precisely to the extent to which it is that effect, it is the element of its articulation. The individual which power has constituted is at the same time its vehicle.

...

By way of summarising ... I would say that we should direct our researches on the nature of power not towards the juridical edifice of sovereignty, the State apparatuses and the ideologies which accompany them, but towards domination and the material operators of power, towards forms of subjection and the inflections and utilisations of their localised systems, and towards strategic apparatuses. We must eschew the model of Leviathan in the study of power. We must escape from the limited field of juridical sovereignty and State institutions, and instead base our analysis of power on the study of the techniques and tactics of domination.

[8100] According to Foucault, power is dynamic and complex in a way not recognised by traditional political and legal accounts. Power is not just something which one individual holds, as a commodity, but arises within a system of meaning. Now, as I have said, I think that this is true: power, like meaning, is something which arises within a social context. Thus it is not pre-existing individuals who have power: power is not simply something which an autonomous person can aquire in the same way that one aquires a car.[66] People are powerful because of their place in a system: for instance because of their membership of a group (men, lawyers, white people, heterosexuals, able-bodied people) which is invested with social value, or because they can use social meanings to their own advantage. It is therefore a person's position in the social network which constitutes her or him as an individual with power. Thus, what I take Foucault to be saying is not that power can simply be re-interpreted, so that anyone can be seen to have it. The point is that we must recognise the complexity of power. It is not just a question of there being a hierarchy of persons who are more or less powerful: there is a complicated network of meanings and values which constitute us as individuals.

This analysis of power can be helpful for thinking about the structures which oppress women, and how we can fight them. Sneja Gunew explains:[67]

What remains important to the context of feminism ... is the idea that power does not necessarily reside only and always in a centre. It is not simply a question of storming a series of male citadels and of occupying the controls. And, to extend this, it is not merely a question of women taking over the controls: witness the rule of Margaret Thatcher ... It may

---

66 The cultural association of cars with power and masculinity is an unavoidable fact most obviously manifested in motor racing events. It is not possible to aquire power as one aquires a car, but that is not to say that cars have no place in the systems of meaning and value which surround us. Acquiring a car (of a certain sort, at any rate) is a way into this particular set of associations.

67 Sneja Gunew, "Feminist Knowledge: Critique and Construct" in Gunew (ed), *Feminist Knowledge: Critique and Construct* (Routledge, London, 1990), p 23.

well be quite misleading to think of power as consisting of a centre and a periphery and may be more productive to think of power as a network which operates everywhere in contradictory ways and can therefore be strategically resisted anywhere.

As I explained in Chapter 6, for instance, saying that men as a group oppress women as a group may be true in some instances, but cannot be taken to be an absolute statement of the power differentials involved. Indigenous women experience the effects of the distribution of power in Australian society in a very different way from non-Indigenous women. If power were simply a commodity it may be a relatively simple thing to appropriate it, or to hand it over to people. The point is, however, that subjection occurs within a context of persistent social meanings.

Foucault therefore suggests that we abandon the "juridical" analysis of power, which has emphasised the notion of sovereignty. If we think about law as something which is *in itself* powerful, something which supplies the answers to disputes and orders social behaviour according to the intentions of a powerful body of lawmakers and judges, we are, perhaps, missing an important point. This is simply that many other systems of power, many other systems of meaning and value in society, interact with the legal system. It is not just institutionalised law which says "no", or which orders behaviour, or which punishes us for our transgressions. There are, for instance, a multitude of social prescriptions (such as the one which says that women should shave our legs) which order behaviour and the way we think about the world.[68] The norms by which people order their lives are not merely legal norms but, more importantly, a plurality of social, religious, or moral conventions which emanate from a variety of discursive locations and deliver a range of imperatives and principles to each person. Law is one, but by no means the most important, of these sources of social "governance" or "discipline".

However, two further points might be made about this distinction of centralised, legal, sovereign power from more dispersed, material conceptions of power. First, bearing in mind contemporary approaches to legal theory, law is not actually separate from its social and political environments. As many 20th century legal theorists have argued, social norms cannot be distinguished ultimately from institutionalised law. The man or the woman with the wig (like every person) is also, to re-use Lyotard's metaphor, "a post through which various kinds of messages pass".[69] Similarly, the way that a law is applied depends on the interpretation of facts in a case, and therefore ultimately on the social values and assumptions which form such an interpretation. Power in the legal system cannot therefore be described simply in terms of a hierarchy of people with authority to make decisions, or of laws

---

68   I have discussed these matters in more detail in Chapter 1.

69   Lyotard, *The Postmodern Condition*, p 15.

with the potential to determine disputes: though both the hierarchy of people and that of laws certainly exist, they are shot through with social meanings and systems of relationships which cannot be reduced to one-dimensional descriptions. At the same time (and secondly), the distinction between legal and social forms of power/discipline is routinely made and acted upon. Law may not be conceptually or practically separate from the social context, and it may not itself entirely enshrine a top-down and commodity form of power. Nonetheless, the paradigm of law as a separate and centralised form of power remains influential and ethically significant. We cannot abandon a "juridical" notion of power because it is still normatively influential — in law and elsewhere. Most importantly, we cannot abandon it because, as the critical race theorists insist, legal power provides a mechanism for counteracting the other less transparent forms of social power.[70] Therefore, although Foucault's work provides a corrective to the simplistic notion that power is only located in defined structures and offices, that is not to say that such forms of power do not exist or are not still politically significant.

Deconstruction

Introduction

[8105] "Deconstruction" is a term which seems to have been fairly readily incorporated into everyday academic language. It is sometimes used simply as a substitute for the word "criticism", sometimes to mean what would more readily be identified as destruction or theoretical anarchy, and sometimes to indicate the process of exposing or undoing the assumptions implicit in an argument. The last use of the term is closest to the mark of the "deconstruction" I am going to describe. The other two senses appear to have arisen partly through consistent misunderstandings of the theoretical background of deconstruction, and partly through the normal process of assimilating a term into the categories with which we are already familiar.

"Deconstruction" is a term most frequently associated with the ideas of Jacques Derrida, and it is aspects of his early work which will be described here. Derrida's writings are "post-structuralist" in the sense that they are partly built upon, yet go beyond in some important ways, structuralist linguistics. What follows is only a summary of some of the basic ideas of Derridean deconstruction: the application of these ideas to legal philosophy will be considered in the next section of the chapter.

---

70   See Carole Smith, "The Sovereign State v Foucault: Law and Disciplinary Power" (2000) 48 *The Sociological Review* 283, Gary Wickham "Foucault, Law, and Power: A Reassessment" (2006) 33 *Journal of Law and Society* 596.

Foundations of philosophy

[8110] One of Derrida's constant arguments is that Western philosophy is a "metaphysics of presence". What this means is that we are always trying to make present (here and now) our objects of thought. Some examples of this emphasis on the notion of presence have already been implied in earlier sections of this chapter. One particularly clear manifestation of presence,[71] for example, occurs in the way we ordinarily think about language. Language has been thought of as a medium which makes thought present to the world. Language is the attempt to express in words a reality or something that we mean within ourselves. Language is therefore regarded as an imperfect medium: the ideal would be to get behind language to the real thing, the underlying thought, to strip away the layers until the true meaning is obtained. Similarly the desire of philosophy has usually been to attain truth — to make present and available now, that which has been hidden or obscured by error, ignorance, or language.[72] Theory aims at a knowledge which is final, right, and can be present to consciousness. The Cartesian "I", which as we saw remained certain in the face of every other doubt, is formulated as a "presence to self": because I am present, here and now, to myself, I cannot be doubted. Plato takes a direct, unmediated contemplation of ideals to be the essence of philosophical endeavour. The philosopher attempts to form a direct appreciation of the ideal of "justice", so that she has the concept present in the mind. When we attempt to give a defined or essential set of characteristics to a concept, for instance the idea of "femininity", what we are trying to do is to make present in the concept a positive essence of meaning so that the concept is fixed in its core meaning.[73]

Most importantly, according to Derrida, Western thought is "logocentric", meaning that it invariably attempts to put one term or word at the centre of theory. "In the beginning was the word, and the word was with God, and the word was God."[74] God is the origin and explanation of all things. We do not have to go very far to find an example of a logocentric theory. HLA Hart's concept of the "rule of recognition", Austin's sovereign, and Kelsen's *grundnorm*, are all formulated as foundational theoretical terms which inform the whole of a legal system. In the beginning (theoretically, if not temporally) there was the sovereign/rule/grundnorm, which is the origin and

---

71   As Ngaire Naffine has pointed out to me, another "clear manifestation" of presence is the use of visual metaphors like "clear manifestation" — which is an attempt to embody the concept in a physical form. The point also illustrates (another metaphorical term denoting presence) the way that language writes itself — I was quite unaware of this reference in my sentence until it was pointed out to me.

72   See the discussion on Coke's Error in Chapter 2, above.

73   See Jacques Derrida, *Of Grammatology* (Johns Hopkins University Press, Baltimore, 1974), p 12; Culler, *On Deconstruction*, pp 91-94.

74   *The Bible*, John i, 1.

explanation of all legal systems. Similarly, as we saw in Chapter 4, natural law theories elevate natural reason or some conception of the law of God to the status of the (ideal, if not actual) foundation of law.

The play of difference

[8115] Derrida undermines both the emphasis on presence and the ideal of a central organising term in philosophy, both by utilising and going beyond the conceptions of Saussurean linguistics. Meaning is constituted in language and by differences. That is, meaning is the effect of linguistic differences, and concepts are constituted by their place within a system of other concepts. They do not just exist alone. This means that no concept can be self-defining, or positive, or wholly present. Rather, concepts are determined by what they are not; by what is absent. "Presence" can therefore only ever be the effect of the differences between concepts. Beyond this, though, Derrida points out that since concepts are constituted within a philosophical system, they can never be pure: they will always contain within them the trace of otherness — the exclusion of which is necessary to their formation.[75]

> The play of differences supposes, in effect, syntheses and referrals which forbid at any moment, or in any sense, that a simple element be present in and of itself, referring only to itself. Whether in the order of spoken or written discourse, no element can function as a sign without referring to another element which itself is not simply present. This interweaving results in each "element" ... being constituted on the basis of the trace within it of the other elements of the chain or system.

Philosophical concepts then, can never simply be "present", in the sense of being just there, fully comprehensible. Nor can they be pure or completely distinguished from their contrasting concepts. Such a view already goes beyond Saussurean linguistics, which seems to emphasise the presence of the concept in the signifier. When we say the word, the concept is unavoidably present in our minds. True, but Derrida also points out that this "presence" is qualified by the constructedness of the concept through the things which are absent from it. These claims have consequences for legal philosophy which will be explained shortly.[76]

Rodolphe Gasché explains the impurity of concepts in the following terms:

> Philosophical concepts would be entirely homogeneous if they possessed a nucleus of meaning that they owed exclusively to themselves — if they were, in other words, conceptual atoms. Yet since concepts are produced within a discursive network of differences, they not only are what they are by virtue of other concepts, but they also, in a fundamental way, inscribe that Otherness within themselves.

---

75 Jacques Derrida, *Positions* (University of Chicago Press, Chicago, 1981), p 26.

76 Gasché, *The Tain of the Mirror: Derrida and the Philosophy of Reflection*, p 128.

The important thing to notice here is that Gasché says that the network of differences which is the condition of the formation of concepts, necessitates that in any given concept its "Other" (that is, what it is not) is inscribed in the concept. It cannot be exclusive, pure, or self-determined.

One important aspect of this conceptual impurity is what Derrida has called *différance*. *Différance* was said not to be a concept since the term refers to a process which is always ambivalent, rather than to something which can be fixed. For reasons which we do not need to go into here, Derrida coined a term which sounds the same as the French word *différence*, but looks different, being spelt with an *a*. The term, as Derrida uses it, is supposed to suggest two things (which need explaining in English, since the English terms are not identical to the French ones). The French verb *différer* means both to differ, and to defer (in time). *Différance* indicates the conceptual instability in language which a combination of differing and deferring produces. This obviously needs further explanation.

Saussure's linguistic theory was founded upon the idea that we can study language as a static system, that is, a system which does not move, at a particular cross-section of time. All of the elements are seen to be fixed both in relation to one another, and in that moment. "Difference" in this context just means the static set of differences which constitutes language. In contrast, Derrida's term *différance* — differing/deferring — is supposed to convey the essentially non-static nature of a signifying system. In the first place, the process of signification relies not only upon an already-existing set of formal differences, but on their ongoing *production*: language and conceptualisation require a continual process of exclusion and setting up of differences — rather than simply working according to a settled and passive set of differences, there is always some activity going on to maintain the differences and meaning.[77] *Différance* therefore names not just the thing, but the process. Secondly, meaning is deferred. That is, because of the structure of signification, we can never have a complete meaning right now. Any meaning we "have" is only there by virtue of the system of relations within which it was formed, its context. One meaning inevitably refers to another meaning which has either preceded it, or is yet to come.

There is, therefore, both temporal and spatial movement in any system of signification: no one concept can ever be pinned down so that it is present to the mind, here and now. This is not, however, to be taken as an imperfection in language, but rather its condition of existence. Language *necessarily* works like that. This is basically the type of textual indeterminacy, emphasised by deconstruction.

---

77 See Geoffrey Bennington and Jacques Derrida, *Jacques Derrida* (University of Chicago Press, Chicago, 1993), p 70; in my view Bennington's attempt to systematise Derrida's thought in this work easily constitutes the best exposition of Derrida's thought which has been written to date; see also Culler, *On Deconstruction*, p 97.

Thinking about law, we can see that this understanding of a signifying system has an interesting explanatory power. It is certainly true, as I explained briefly above, that as a system of categories, law works by setting up distinctions between certain areas and elements of itself. Yet at the same time, such a system can never be entirely fixed — we are continually working at defining the boundaries of an area of law, attempting to explain where it overlaps with another area, where the distinctions break down, what is "inside" and what is "outside" its limits. We can never contain the category of, say, torts, within itself — though in order to have an understanding of it we have to have made the attempt. Understanding law involves the continual process of distinguishing one thing from another: *applying* the law (which would be analogous to speaking a language) relies upon making this process concrete for individual cases. The application of a law is thus its deferred meaning. An abstract legal principle refers forwards to the possibility of its application in a particular case, and the case itself refers backwards to the abstract legal principle. Sometimes such a principle is indeed constructed retrospectively by the judges. The system itself therefore cannot be regarded as either spatially or temporally static. We cannot fix it into a stable set of meanings, and nor can we get it right now. The legal system, like other systems of signification, is inherently dynamic.

Arguments like these can help us see why essentialism, and not only in feminism, always assumes too much. The idea that we can fix a particular essence to a concept, like those of woman, law, tort or property, neglects the constructedness of such concepts within a system of differences. Moreover, the desire to have *now* a meaning which is complete, must be recognised as an ideal which would be, perhaps, theoretically satisfying, but is never attainable. In fact, insisting upon such an essence of meaning may be counter-productive, since — as feminists have discovered — essential definitions can always be turned against women, and they take the focus away from how our categories are constituted.

Dichotomy and hierarchy

[8120] What then, is deconstruction? How does one do it? This is not an easy question to answer, but some rough formulations may be useful. In *Positions*, Derrida explains:[78]

> in a classical philosophical opposition we are not dealing with the peaceful coexistence of a *vis-à-vis*, but rather with a violent hierarchy. One of the two terms governs the other (axiologically, logically, etc) or has the upper hand. To deconstruct the opposition, first of all, is to overturn the hierarchy at a given moment.

---

78 Derrida, *Positions*, p 41.

We have seen that conceptual organisation is not, according to structural and poststructural thought, natural, but constituted by difference. Many concepts are organised into oppositions or dichotomies, which purport to cover the field — something is either sensible or intelligible, inside or outside, positive or negative, nature or artifice, masculine or feminine, and so on. Derrida explains that in such oppositions, one term is philosophically regarded as superior, while the other term is marginal, a lesser version, or simply a negative. Thus, as feminists have made clear, "man" is typically taken to be the paradigm of humanity, while "woman" is an inferior version, something other. "Man" is the original term, and usually taken as naturally original (Adam was after all, supposedly here first), while "woman" is a deviation from "man". The opposition is violent because of the lack of equality, and because the dominant term is formed by the exclusion and repression of the subordinate term. To deconstruct the opposition, then, involves showing how the "lesser" term is in fact absolutely essential to the "higher" term: how, for instance, we cannot theorise "inside" without "outside", "man" without "woman", "true" without "false". Rather than being marginal then, the subordinated term in an opposition becomes central: rather than being a derivation, it *is* original.

Derrida says, in a seemingly innocuous phrase, that this deconstructive move occurs "at a given moment". This indicates an important point, which is that the deconstruction of a binary opposition can never destroy it. This can be a hard point to get across since, especially as lawyers, we tend to think that something either exists or it doesn't. It is either true or false. Such closures miss the point which is that the terms of the opposition are not conceptually distinct, even though they are generally presented as though they were. Deconstructing the opposition effects a disturbance of the apparent certainty of an opposition. The opposition still "exists", we can still use it, as indeed we must, but it is revealed to be non-natural, and operating by a logic of exclusion. This process of making central — "at a given moment" — that which in a dominant world-view has appeared to be marginal has been at times a crucial strategy for political activists.[79] Highlighting, for instance, the often hidden questions of race or gender in a discourse concentrating on equal rights is an illustration of such a strategy. Showing that man's self-identity and individualism is reliant on the oppression of women and on the erasure or naturalisation of this oppression, or that the official justification for causing thousands of civilian injuries in a war is reliant on the construction of the enemy as "other"[80] are instances of the political dimension of this type of critique.

---

79 See Handler, "Postmodernism, Protest and the New Social Movements".

80 Judith Butler has analysed the Gulf War in precisely these terms in "Contingent Foundations: Feminism and the Question of 'Postmodernism'" in Judith Butler and Joan W Scott (eds), *Feminists Theorize the Political* (Routledge, London, 1992).

The politics and ethics of deconstruction

[8125] Sometimes the term "deconstruction" is associated with annihilation or with criticism aimed at the destruction of a mode of thought. However, in its technical use as envisaged by Derrida, deconstruction does not eliminate or destroy: it undoes something, much like undoing a mechanism in order to see how it works (with the qualification that deconstruction is also an intervention — having seen the parts, you cannot simply put things back as they were). As Derrida explained in "Letter to a Japanese Friend": [81]

> But the undoing, decomposing, and desedimenting of structures — was not a negative operation. Rather than destroying, it was also necessary to understand how an "ensemble" was constituted and to reconstruct it to this end. However, the negative appearance was and remains much more difficult to efface than is suggested by the grammar of the word ... That is why this word, at least on its own, has never appeared satisfactory to me (but what word is), and must always be girded by an entire discourse.

Deconstruction, then, is not simply a "negative" gesture, despite the fact that this is certainly how it has frequently been understood: it aims in the first place to come to some understanding of how conceptual and linguistic structures are constituted, typically by concentrating on the "undecidability" evident at the limits of any conceptual system, and attempting to describe the effects of the theoretical repression of undecidability in the search for closure and certitude. Again, this may sound rather meaningless at this stage: I will give some examples shortly. The main point to be understood here is that deconstruction does not seek to annihilate established realities (an impossible project, since we would have to start again from absolutely nothing), but to work with whatever is already in place: deconstruction therefore generates altered understandings of dominant views.

This issue of the "political" in deconstruction has been the subject of some controversy. In my view, it is certainly the case that a deconstructive approach does not lay the groundwork for formulating a political position, a program of reform, or even a definite strategy. It does not tell us what to do about injustice, oppression, or reform, in the way that liberal theory (for instance) holds out concepts like "rights", "freedom", or "equality" as part of the solution to social and political inequities. But the fact that there is no universal formulation or plan, or idealisation of politically valued concepts does not necessarily mean that deconstruction, and other "postmodern" approaches, are politically incompetent.

The political and ethical element of deconstruction takes several different forms. In the first place, deconstruction involves an exposure of dogma — not a reckless destruction, but a careful and responsible

---

81   See Jacques Derrida, "Letter to a Japanese Friend" in Wood and Bernasconi (eds), *Derrida and Difference* (Northwestern University Press, Evanston, 1988), p 3.

questioning: it opens the founding assumptions of Western philosophy for critical examination. Far from being nihilistic, this self-reflectiveness is a necessary element of any ethical critique of knowledge. It also, in my view, helps us to understand how the physical violence of the world is related to the violence of discourse — that is, the fact that both language and Western philosophy operate through exclusion and hierarchy. Secondly, by virtue of exposing meanings, and the appreciation that concepts are not in themselves static or fixed but are rather made so by a philosophical tradition which favours fixity and origins, it is possible to envisage new meanings. Queer theory, discussed in Chapter 6, provides a concrete example of new meanings being imagined and theorised through deconstruction and postmodernism. This body of thought helps give expression to multiple sexes and sexualities, which for many constitutes a practical and conceptual escape from "heteronormativity". Finally, Derrida has recently spoken of an ethical imperative of hospitality.[82] Receptiveness to the other (whatever the axis of difference) is the logical consequence of deconstruction, since it not only challenges the fixity of abstractions, but also of fundamental philosophical oppositions such as that between subject and object, or self and other. Therefore, far from being a-political and nihilistic, deconstruction encourages purposeful and self-reflective intervention.

Deconstructing law's foundations[83]

[8130] When we start to think about jurisprudence in the light of some of the insights of deconstruction, we are immediately confronted with a range of difficulties associated with the idea of law itself. The very basis of jurisprudence must be that there is an object — "law" — which is in some sense distinct from other practical and intellectual pursuits.[84] In universities, for instance, law is considered to constitute a different intellectual discipline from history, politics, and physics. And as I explained in Chapter 3, positivists have tried to formalise these practical distinctions by arguing that there is something *necessary* about the distinction between law and not-law (and in particular morality). Law is seen to be in some way self-contained or self-defined, and closed as a system.

---

82   Jacques Derrida, *Of Hospitality* (Stanford University Press, Stanford, 2000).

83   The following exposition is based on part of an article of mine which explains in more detail the legal implications of Derrida's idea of "the law of genre". See Margaret Davies, "Pathfinding: The Way of the Law" (1992) 14 *Oxford Literary Review* 107 at 112-126; see also Margaret Davies, "Derrida and Law: Legitimate Fictions" in Tom Cohen (ed), *Jacques Derrida and the Humanities* (Cambridge University Press, Cambridge, 2001).

84   See David Sugarman, "Legal Theory, the Common Law Mind and the Making of the Textbook Tradition" in William Twining (ed), *Legal Theory and the Common Law* (Basil Blackwell, Oxford, 1986).

In positivist thinking the closure or self-identification[85] of the law is generally determined by an identifiable source which can take the form of a highest or founding principle, or (as in the case of Austin), a sovereign institution or person. The validity of a law depends on its having been determined within the framework laid down by such a foundation. So, to put it roughly, everything which is contained within the framework of a rule of recognition, is, according to the positivist thesis of HLA Hart, valid law. For Kelsen, if a rule or principle can be traced through the various levels of laws to the highest norm, then it is law. And for Austin, law "properly so called" is in essence the commands of a sovereign.[86] There must, in other words, be some general principle or standard which lays down the criteria of law, and allows it to be distinguished from non-law. Joseph Raz made the point very clearly and formalistically in an early article on the "limits of law", a (positivist) view of law which he explains as resting on "the position that there *is a test* which distinguishes what is law from what is not".[87] The argument is simply that law (conceptually and in practice) has a definable limit, and that it can be separated from non-law: as Raz explains, this view relies upon there being some fundamental test by which the limit of law can be identified:

> If the thesis of the limits of law is right, there must be a criterion of identity which sets necessary and sufficient conditions, satisfaction of which is a mark that a standard is part of a legal system.[88]

In other words, the basic positivist thesis (and we should bear in mind that this is not only a theoretical position but in fact represents the way lawyers tend to see law) is that what makes law "law", *the law of law*, is the existence of some limit, either conceptual or empirical, which is itself a principle of coherence and identity for law.

In "The Law of Genre" Derrida makes a similar initial point about how categories of thought, institutionally defined academic disciplines, and literary genres are defined. For instance, as I mentioned in Chapter 7, Lyotard attributes the scientificity of science to the existence of a set of criteria against which any proposition must be measured in order to determine whether it counts as a "scientific" statement.[89] Like law, scientific veracity is legitimated by an institutionalised set of conventions, principles and rules. Similarly, the philosophical nature of

---

85   I use the term "self-identification" simply to refer to the identification of law through law, and the perception that only through "legal" processes can the law be created and applied.

86   All of these matters have been explained in detail in Chapter 3, and, because of the difficulty of the issues arising here, I am assuming a basic knowledge of them.

87   Joseph Raz, "Legal Principles and the Limits of Law" (1972) 81 *Yale Law Journal* 823 at 842.

88   Raz, "Legal Principles and the Limits of Law", p 851.

89   In general, see Lyotard, *The Postmodern Condition*.

philosophy — what makes an argument "philosophical" — is determined by a certain set of criteria relating to coherence in argument,
political neutrality, and perhaps, most importantly, the specific
philosophical tradition within which any particular argument is made.
That there are different philosophical traditions of itself indicates
(though this would not count as a "philosophical" statement) that the
history of philosophy may be as important in formulating an
acceptable philosophical argument as the more usually cited desire for
truth (however it is defined). The existence of different philosophical
traditions might even be seen as a little embarrassing for philosophy,
which is supposedly universal in its inquiries, utilising a process of
natural, or at least common, reason transcending the boundaries of
nationality, culture, and language.[90]

Derrida makes some general comments about these matters in "The
Law of Genre", by pointing out that the definition of a genre, within
which we can include areas of knowledge, or any conceptual separation
of one intellecual terrain from any other, depends upon there being
some "mark" or "trait" which allows us to distinguish or recognise the
genre. (I will continue to use the literary term "genre" here, but it
should be read as including any of the sorts of intellectual domains
which I have been referring to.) There is then a "law of genre" —
basically that a "trait" sets the limits of any conceptual territory such
as science, philosophy or law, determining what falls within the genre,
and what falls outside.

Derrida goes on to explain (if that is ever an appropriate word to use
for Derrida) that there is a paradox which besets the definition of any
genre. And the paradox is another law, the "law of the law of genre",
since it applies generally. It is simply that the limit (or "mark" etc)
which defines the genre, can itself never be either inside or outside the
genre. Because it is itself a principle of definition and must inhere in
everything which forms a part of the genre, it cannot wholly be outside,
yet nor can it be wholly inside, since as a designation it is not itself one
of the objects of a genre. Whatever it is that makes a poem poetic, is
not itself a poem. Whatever it is that makes a philosophy philosophical,
is not itself a philosophy (but rather, in this case a certain set of institutionalised conventions). At the same time every "poem" must have
whatever it takes to be one, so the defining characteristic of poetry is
not wholly exterior to the genre. What this means, in essence, is that
there is no absolute "closure" or self-identification in any genre, or in
any intellectual discipline: there is always something other than the
genre inside it, and something essential to it outside.

---

90 See the opening remarks in Derrida, "Onto-Theology of National-Humanism
    (Prolegomena to a Hypothesis)" (1992) 14 *Oxford Literary Review* 3. Derrida points out
    here that the existence of different "philosophical idioms" is both a "scandal" — because
    philosophy is supposed to be universal — and the "chance" which is necessary to
    philosophical communication.

If this sounds difficult, that is probably because it is intellectually taxing to regard differently our understanding of, for instance, the (conventionally) mutually exclusive dichotomy between outside and inside. It is hard to imagine that this opposition may not be as clear as we assumed.[91] This is rather like the traditional division of the jurisprudential possibilities into natural law and positivism, anything else being regarded as not quite philosophy, or at least not affecting in any substantial way the territory of the major debate. We tend to think that law must be *either* "natural" *or* imposed (culturally, legally, socially, and so on). This obviously reflects a basic division in modern thought between "nature" and "culture" (or "society"). The distinction appears to account for all of the possibilities, in the manner of a simple *either/or*, a position which appeals to our senses of logic and coherence. Seeing the possibilities in a different way is very difficult, and one way to begin to do this is to show how the distinction is never absolute, and breaks down at a certain crucial point. This is essentially what is being done with the inside/outside dichotomy in "The Law of Genre". I think the point can be most clearly demonstrated with a jurisprudential example, which will also help to demonstrate the importance of questions of law and legitimation to the sort of contemporary thought I am describing.

One of the clearest expositions of the formal characteristics of a legal system is that of Hans Kelsen. Kelsen's grundnorm (or basic norm) is the foundation of validity in a legal system: anything ultimately validated by the basic norm is law, while anything not validated by it is not law. The last justification in any series of justifications, the first condition of the law, is to be found where there are no more justifications, merely a final norm. Thus the basic norm takes the place of the first and last criterion of law, the limit between law and non-law. But the basic norm is not itself simply part of the legal system: it is not a law in the same sense that other norms are laws because "it is not created in a legal procedure by a law-creating organ".[92] Nevertheless, it is part of every law: it is in a sense the *most* legal thing, because it is the essence of law. The basic norm must be at once both internal and external to law, legal and non-legal. And because it is at the heart of what it is to be law, and is reproduced in every law, there is a non-legal dimension of every law. The law cannot therefore simply be a closed or self-identifying structure, for this not-so-straightforward formal reason. The impurity of concepts discussed earlier appears in this way in the positivist idea of a legal system: whatever is "inside" the limit of law is there only because of the mark or "trace" left there by the "outside". In other words, the outside can not be kept entirely out, and nor is the inside ever entirely in.

As I explained in Chapter 3, Kelsen himself recognised the paradoxical nature of the basic norm, calling it first a "hypothesis", then a

---

91   A less technical explanation of these matters is to be found in Chapter 1.

92   Kelsen, *General Theory of Law and State*, p 116.

"presupposition", and finally a "fiction". The basic norm is a fiction not only because it contradicts reality (that is, does not exist), but also because it is self-contradictory.[93] It is self-contradictory because it represents an ultimate empowerment of the law, and thus implies that there is an even higher authority. To put this another way, the identity of law is reliant on a general principle, itself neither legal nor non-legal, representing a limit or finality which is, however, always requiring that more questions be asked.

A similar sort of paradox (though not the same one) has been highlighted in relation to Hart's "rule of recognition": as I explained in Chapter 3, the "rule of recognition" takes the place in Hart's theory of the defining characteristic of a developed legal system. The "rule of recognition" must be accepted as such by the officials of the system. As Matthew Kramer points out:[94]

> A rather obvious difficulty arises here: what Hart deems to be the foundation of any legal system turns out to presuppose that a legal regime exists already. In describing whose behaviour is given shape by the rule of recognition, Hart claims that the foundational rule is immanent in official practices. But "officials" can be identified as such only when a structure of laws has come into existence already.

The officials, in other words, recognise the rule of recognition, which recognises them as officials. There is therefore a problem of what Derrida often calls "undecidability" precisely at the line of demarcation between law and non-law, where positivist theory ought to be most certain. However, rather than think of undecidability as a failure of the theory or structure in question, Derrida regards it as a necessary condition: law cannot be understood as a definite thing, or even process, without this undecidability which constitutes it at its foundations and limits.

In part, "undecidability" refers to the tension or suspense between what might otherwise be seen as absolutes. It is not merely something like the loose sense of "indeterminacy" often alluded to in relation to the operation of language, for instance, the indeterminate reference of the word "reasonable". "Undecidability" involves a clash of imperatives: the grundnorm is absolutely legal and it is absolutely non-legal. This is an unresolvable contradiction, a point of "undecidability" in positivist theory. The "undecidability" of certain apsects of legal analysis is not confined to the positivist understanding of limitedness: more of these issues will be raised in the next section.

---

93 Kelsen is relying on the definition of fiction employed by Hans Vaihinger in *The Philosophy of As-If: A System of the Theoretical, Practical, and Religious Fictions* (Routledge Kegan Paul, London, 1965); see Kelsen, *General Theory of Norms* (Oxford University Press, Oxford, 1991), p 256.

94 Matthew Kramer, "The Rule of Misrecognition in the Hart of Jurisprudence" (1988) 8 *Oxford Journal of Legal Studies* 401 at 407; see also Iain Duncanson, "The Strange World of English Jurisprudence" (1979) 30 *Northern Ireland Legal Quarterly* 207.

Deconstruction and justice

[8135] As I indicated above, one of the most enduring criticisms of what has become known as deconstruction is that it is politically inept: the concern is simply that deconstruction does not enable a position to be adopted on ethical or political questions, because its major pre-occupations are seen as the indeterminacy of meaning, and the destruction of already existing structures of belief. Deconstruction is vaguely seen as involving a critique of everything (through its emphasis on the construction of meaning) and especially the critique of ethical and political prescriptions. In particular it is sometimes thought that deconstruction involves eliminating certainty about reality, so that, for instance, a statement like "women have always been oppressed" can simply be "deconstructed away"[95] (since it all depends on perspective) leaving no solid grounds for political action. The assumption under-lying such criticisms is that deconstruction is no more than a new version of relativism or nihilism.

It is certainly true that some writers who claim to be adopting a "postmodern" approach do, in fact, simply reproduce relativist points of view and, in particular, an emphasis on different perspectives. However, postmodernism, and deconstruction in particular, also (as I have indicated earlier) open the way for a politics of transformation achieved not through any simple critique and rebuilding, but through detailed and particular questioning and the reconstruction of fundamental modes of thought.

In October 1989, a symposium was held at the Benjamin J Cardozo School of Law in New York. The title of the symposium was "Deconstruction and the Possibility of Justice": most of the papers presented were subsequently published in (1991) 11 *Cardozo Law Review*.[96] The keynote address at the symposium was given by Derrida, and considered (among other things) the relationships between law and justice, law and deconstruction, law and force, and most interestingly, deconstruction and justice. I am not going to write a detailed exposition of Derrida's thoughts on these matters, but it will be helpful to explain some of the main issues in the light of what has already been

---

95 I am indebted to a very good friend for bringing this particular perception of deconstruction to my attention.

96 Many of the papers were also published in Drucilla Cornell, Michel Rosenfeld, David Gray Carlson (eds), *Deconstruction and the Possibility of Justice* (Routledge, New York, 1992). All references to Derrida's text, "Force of Law: The 'Mystical Foundation of Authority'", will be drawn from this work.

said in this chapter.[97] The text has become something of a classic, and much attention has been devoted to trying to work out its implications for legal theory.

Derrida begins by noting an English idiom: "to enforce the law". The expression, Derrida notes, is not adequately translated by the French expression "appliquer la loi" (to *apply* the law). In replacing "to enforce the law" with "to apply the law" in a translation, "one loses this direct or literal allusion to the force that comes from within to remind us that law is always an authorised force, a force that justifies itself or is justified in applying itself, even if this justification may be judged from elsewhere to be unjust or unjustifiable".[98] The explicit association of force with law made by Derrida is not one which has been particularly evident in traditional Anglo-American jurisprudence: both positivist and natural law theories attempt to explain law and particular legal systems as, in a sense, containing their own legitimacy, and not requiring any recourse to force or violence to maintain the system. (Or at least, mainstream legal theory does not highlight this — where contradiction, violence, or force are recognised within positivist theory they are not accorded central significance, but rather are relegated to the margins.) Law is supposed to be self-legitimating, or legitimate by appeal to a "natural" order, and not by virtue of something apparently as contingent and undemocratic as force. But, as Derrida goes on to explain, the very idea of law necessitates that there be force:

> The word "enforceability" reminds us that there is no such thing as law (droit) that doesn't imply, *in itself, a priori, in the analytic structure of its concept*, the possibility of being "enforced", applied by force. There are, to be sure, laws that are not enforced, but there is no law without enforceability, and no applicability or enforceability of the law without force, whether this force be direct or indirect, physical or symbolic, exterior or interior, brutal or subtly discursive and hermeneutic, coercive or regulative, and so forth.[99]

---

97   Nor am I going to explain the more complex ways in which Derrida's text has been interpreted and applied. The essay following Derrida's in 11 *Cardozo Law Review* by Drucilla Cornell, "The Violence of the Masquerade: Law Dressed Up as Justice", is a very good place to start. A more challenging work is Cornell's book *The Philosophy of the Limit*, especially chs 4 and 5. See also Louis Wolcher, "The Man in the Room: Remarks on Derrida's *Force of Law*" (1996) 7 *Law and Critique* 35; Weber, "Deconstruction Before the Name: Some Preliminary Remarks on Deconstruction and Violence" (1991) 13 *Cardozo Law Review* 1181; Seyla Benhabib, "Some Comments on Deconstruction, Justice, and the Ethical Relationship" (1991) 13 *Cardozo Law Review* 1219; Ben Mathews, "Why Deconstruction is Beneficial" (2000) 4 *Flinders Journal of Law Reform* 81; Davies, "Derrida and Law: *Legitimate Fictions*"; John McCormick, "Derrida on Law; Or, Poststructuralism Gets Serious" (2001) 29 *Political Theory* 395. For a recent extended discussion of law and its relationship to violence in the context of "Force of Law" see Costas Douzinas and Adam Geary, *Critical Jurisprudence: The Political Philosophy of Justice* (Hart Publishing, Oxford, 2005), 69-73.

98   Derrida, "Force of Law", p 5.

99   Derrida, "Force of Law", p 6.

Force is not of necessity something brutal (though it frequently does take that form) but may be the result of a complex discursive structure: for instance, there is force involved in attempting to cast a person's grievance in legal terms, a process which often ends with a sense of alienation experienced by the individual in relation to the law. The law re-casts, re-phrases, and re-views the experiences of lay people in the process of giving a "legal" interpretation to an event. It thus enforces its own meanings.

Derrida poses a series of questions on this basis, relating to the problem of distinguishing the "force of law" (which is, from within, a "justified" force) from unjust force or violence. Is there any absolutely clear distinction between unjust force and just (that is, lawful) force? The police "force" might provide an interesting case study, and indeed Derrida does use it as an example in the second half of this text. We could ask, for instance, why excess police "force" continues to be a problem — it may be that the line delimiting the degree of force necessary to preserve what we call "law and order" and the degree of force judged to be excessive is not all that clear. (I am certainly not suggesting that any such line ought to be abandoned or relaxed, rather that its precise position may be "undecidable", and that it is partly this undecidability which keeps the rigid structure of law as we understand it in place.)

Less controversially, Derrida mentions the "originary violence" of law. This is something which I have alluded to, but not explained in detail, in the discussions of positivism in Chapter 3, and earlier in this chapter. The positivist explanation of the origin of law is, of course, that the law of modern legal systems is "posited": law is essentially and originally laid down, by whatever mechanism. As I explained above, what this means is that the foundation of law (whether we are thinking about a historically first moment of the law, or a sort of conceptual limit to it) is never itself simply legal, and in order to be established as the origin and delimiting feature of law, the non-legality of this so-called foundation or essence must be excluded and repressed. But as Derrida asks:[100]

> How are we to distinguish between the force of law of a legitimate power and the supposedly originary violence that must have established this authority and that could not itself have been authorised by any anterior legitimacy, so that, in this initial moment, it is neither legal nor illegal ...

To take the easiest example, in a revolution, where one legal order is replaced with another, there will be a point where the new legal order is illegal, but will nevertheless provide the foundation for law (though that may not be known at the time). It is only by the rejection of the legality of the old order, and forcefully asserting a new legality, that any transition into a new system of law can be made. The origin of a legal

---

100   Derrida, "Force of Law", p 6.

order established in this way will therefore never be entirely legal nor illegal (but both at once): as I explained above, a proposition of this sort can be applied to any understanding of law as inherently limited or separated from non-law. The sense of closure of law is achieved through the forceful establishment and protection of the limit. One of the major potential contributions of deconstruction to legal theory relates to this "questioning of foundations", which as Derrida says "is neither foundationalist nor anti-foundationalist",[101] since although going back to origins it does not purport to posit a new set of immutable foundations, nor does it simply destroy those which are in place — as I have explained, it questions without annihilating.

What Derrida goes on to say is that the origin of law is therefore in some very strong sense "mystical": there will be a limit to our understanding of the legality of law, some point (in history, or simply in a "legal" analysis) will be reached where we will not be able to say that a proposition or norm is "legal", non-legal, or illegal. Law is in this way "essentially deconstructible".[102] (We encounter such points of indecision so frequently in the process of "applying the law" that it seems almost too obvious to make any philosophical capital out of. Nevertheless, there *is* a philosophical reason for this experience.) The following extract from "Force of Law" is a clear exposition of these ideas, culminating in what may at first sound like a rather surprising claim: that "deconstruction is justice". Derrida distinguishes law from justice, but not totally. Justice is not another normative order existing on a different plane from law: rather it becomes possible only through the existence of law and its deconstructible nature. Justice is possible because law is deconstructible.

Jacques Derrida
"Force of Law: The 'Mystical Foundations of Authority'"[103]

[8140]   Since the origin of authority, the foundation or ground, the position of the law can't by definition rest on anything but themselves, they are themselves a violence without ground. Which is not to say that they are in themselves unjust, in the sense of "illegal". They are neither legal nor illegal in their founding moment. They exceed the opposition between founded or unfounded, or between any foundationalism or anti-foundationalism. Even if the success of performatives that found law or right ... presupposes earlier conditions and conventions ... the same "mystical" limit will reappear at the supposed origin of said conditions, rules, or conventions, and at the origin of their dominant interpretation.

The structure I am describing here is a structure in which law (*droit*) is essentially deconstructible, whether because it is founded, constructed on interpretable and transformable textual strata ... or because its ultimate

---

101   Derrida, "Force of Law", p 8.

102   Derrida, "Force of Law", p 14.

103   Derrida, "Force of Law", pp 14-15.

foundation is by definition unfounded. The fact that law is deconstructible is not bad news. We may even see in this a stroke of luck for politics, for all historical progress. But the paradox that I'd like to submit for discussion is the following: it is this deconstructible structure of law (*droit*), or if you prefer of justice as *droit*, that also insures the possibility of deconstruction. Justice in itself, if such a thing exists, outside or beyond law, is not deconstructible. No more than deconstruction itself, if such a thing exists. Deconstruction is justice.

[8145] Law is "deconstructible" because it relies on rules and other sorts of standards, which, at some point, lose their determinacy or certitude, either because of the operation of language or because of the paradox of the foundation of law: law reaches a point of undecidability where a decision is required. (Mere calculation is not a decision, and it is not free since, in theory, it could be done by a machine.)

The important basis for these arguments is that because law reduces, simplifies, excludes otherness, and dominates the field of its operation, it is not the same as justice. Justice, rather, requires a reflective approach to the application of law: an approach which recognises the inability of law to distribute justice on a case-by-case basis. Law fails to recognise the particularity of cases, the otherness of one case to the next: instead it reduces them all to rules and variations on rules (analogies, precedents, distinctions, policies, and so on). It is important to understand that law is *necessarily* like this: it cannot recognise all differences, but simply provides a way of proceeding (without which we could not go anywhere). Justice, on the other hand, cannot be determined in advance: if it "exists", it is at the point where law fails. It is therefore not possible to lay down rules which will ensure justice — rather justice requires a recognition of the uniqueness of each case, and the "reinvention" of the law in its own application to the case. Justice therefore is "aporetic": it arises in the "aporia" of law, and it is always in the future.[104] ("Aporia" is another trendy word in postmodernism, meaning roughly "gap" or "silence". Derrida says "An aporia is a non-road",[105] meaning that an aporia does not lead anywhere in particular, as a rule does.) The relationship between law and justice is further expounded in the following short extracts.

---

104 Justice is always in the future because it cannot be normalised: it cannot be turned into a rule. This does not mean that there is no such thing as a just decision, but that the "justness" of the decision cannot simply be stated or grasped *now*. As Drucilla Cornell explains, in terms which are far too complex to reproduce here, this view of justice as always to come and never here and now, is part of Derrida's deconstruction of the the the philosophical emphasis on presence, which I explained in Chapter 7: Cornell, *The Philosophy of the Limit* (Routledge, New York, 1991).

105 Derrida, "Force of Law", p 16.

Jacques Derrida
"Force of Law: The 'Mystical Foundations of Authority'"[106]

[8150]   Every time that something comes to pass or turns out well, every time that we placidly apply a good rule to a particular case, to a correctly subsumed example, according to a determinant judgement, we can be sure that law (*droit*) may find itself accounted for, but certainly not justice. Law (*droit*) is not justice. Law is the element of calculation, and it is just that there be law, but justice is incalculable; and aporetic experiences are the experiences, as improbable as they are necessary, of justice, that is to say of moments in which the decision between just and unjust is never insured by a rule.

...

In short, for a decision to be just and responsible, it must, in its proper moment if there is one, be both regulated and without regulation: it must conserve the law and also destroy it or suspend it enough to have to reinvent it in each case, rejustify it, at least reinvent it in the reaffirmation and the new and free confirmation of its principle. Each case is other, each decision is different and requires an absolutely unique interpretation, which no existing, coded rule can or ought to guarantee absolutely. At least, if the rule guarantees it in no uncertain terms, so that the judge is a calculating machine, which happens, ... we will not say that he (sic) is just, free and responsible. But we also wont say it if he doesn't refer to any law, to any rule or if, because he doesn't take any rule for granted beyond his own interpretation, he suspends his decision, stops short before the undecidable or if he improvises and leaves aside all rules, all principles. It follows from this paradox that there is never a moment that we can say *in the present* that a decision is just (that is, free and responsible) ... Instead of "just", we could say legal or legitimate, in conformity with a state of law, with the rules and conventions that authorise calculation but whose founding origin only defers the problem of justice.

...

The undecidable, a theme often associated with deconstruction, is not merely the oscillation between two significations or two contradictory and very determinate rules, each equally imperative (for example respect for equity and universal right but also for the always heterogeneous and unique singularity of the unsubsumable example). The undecidable is not merely the oscillation or the tension between two decisions: it is the experience of that which, though heterogeneous, foreign to the order of the calculable and the rule, is still obliged ... to give itself up to the impossible decision, while taking account of law and rules. A decision that didn't go through the ordeal of the undecidable would not be a free decision, it would only be the programmable application or unfolding of a calculable process. It might be legal; it would not be just.

[8155] Note that Derrida says that a just, free and responsible decision cannot be made entirely without normative guidance. However, in order for a decision to be just it cannot be merely subsumption or calculation: it must take into account the newness and particularity of the case.

---

106   Derrida, "Force of Law", pp 16, 23 and 24.

In fact, what Derrida says here (in the second paragraph of the extract) about the making of a just decision reiterates precisely what I understand to be an ethical practice of deconstructive reading. Deconstruction, as I have repeatedly said, does not destroy, and nor does it pretend that there is a position simply outside its objects of analysis. It is, like the just decision, "both regulated and without regulation", suspending the imperatives of a theory, text, or mode of perception in order to reinvent it differently.

In her somewhat complex interpretation of this and other of Derrida's works, Drucilla Cornell argues that this view of the relationship between law and justice has clear implications for judges. The function of a judge or "justice" is to judge, not merely to calculate or apply the law formally. Calculation, or simple application of the law is an avoidance of the problem of judging, an easy way out:[107]

> the Derridean deconstruction of the privileging of the present reminds us of the responsibility of judges, lawyers, and law professors for what the law "becomes". Moreover, this responsibility is connected with the very idea of judgement. Judgement is only judgement and not mere calculation or recollection if it is "fresh". The judge is called upon to do just that, judge ... The unique Derridean contribution to legal interpretation is to show us why the act of memory in judging involves the seemingly contradictory notion that the judge, in his or her decision, remembers the future ...

It is not hard to understand why modern common law judges frequently seem to have lost this strong view of judicial responsibility. In the first place, we remain influenced by a fairly rigid distinction between making and applying the law: if the judge is not simply applying the law, then we think she must be "making" it, *before* applying it to the immediate case — such "judicial legislation" is seen to contravene the idea of the separation of powers. On the other hand, we could point out that every "application" is always a "creation", not only because the law must be interpreted (and this will always involve some original input) but also because the facts of the case must be given legal meaning, being entirely new. The application/creation distinction therefore cannot be seen as entirely explaining the range of possibilities. Furthermore, if "applying the law" *justly* is understood in the sense which Derrida proposes, judicial responsibility involves a continual (but not predetermined) process of rereading and reinventing the law. Even if we must use the making/applying distinction, we can still take "applying" to include a good deal of originality.

A second jurisprudential obstacle to the adoption of such a practice of judicial responsibility is the strict understanding of the doctrine of precedent, which encourages the view that any departure from binding precedents is an abdication of the judicial role. Again, this can be countered by pointing out that the judicial function is to decide particular cases, and a just decision can only be made if it *is* the

---

107 Cornell, *The Philosophy of the Limit*, p 120.

particular case which is decided. Finally, the influence of the positivist separation of law from morality cannot be underestimated. Although Derrida's point of departure is a positivist model of law, his analysis subverts it entirely, by establishing a relationship between law and justice which is not simple separation: justice is not a separate sphere or order, but appears in a contradictory way — it is reliant on the law, but also transgresses it. (Again, this "transgression" never takes the form of a simple rejection.)

Postscript

[8160] There are Law-Court offices in almost every attic, why should this be an exception?

Kafka, *The Trial*[108]

[8165] In some ways law is an end, and not only because it is perfectly possible to think that you've "made it" into law school or into the legal profession. As we (Westerners educated in the positivist tradition) understand it, law is an end because it imposes constraints — it tells us what to think, how to act, what to wear, and who to be. Before a judge thinks *anything* about the facts of a case, and well before she opens her mouth to give reasons for a particular interpretation or decision, a whole mess of laws — social, political, sexual, intellectual (etc) conventions, laws of thought, laws of language, and other personal constraints — have already shaped the way she perceives the issues, approaches a solution, and determines the case. Law gives us our identities — we live the law, it shapes our beings. This is important: as I explained in Chapter 2, the classical common law idea of law as custom suggests an understanding of law which is not simply outside the individual, but rather defines a community existence and identity. In contrast our modern conception of law has been that it is something outside. We see ourselves as free and rational individuals first. Thus the law is simply public, we are simply private, and organise our lives in relation to legal constraints as we wish.

One of the purposes of this book has been to challenge this perception: because the way we understand and order the world is itself defined by laws, it is not possible simply to distinguish so-called "positive" law from other types of norms. Or, at least, it may be possible to make such a distinction, but the line drawn will always be an arbitrary one, held in place only by convention. (Though we must not underestimate the strength of our conventions: even if arbitrary, they are incredibly resistant to change.) More importantly perhaps, the concept of law which predominates in Western thought is not the only concept of law: law is itself a plural concept, and cannot be reduced to a single perspective. Although I have concentrated upon what I believe are the

---

108   (Penguin, Harmondsworth, 1953), p 182.

various ways in which Western law can be understood and deconstructed, I hope also to have indicated that this concept is neither trans-historical nor universal.[109]

From all of this we can also conclude (yet not really "conclude") that there is *no end*. There is no end to the ways in which law influences us, and no end to the theoretical questions which can be debated, though this influence and these questions are themselves ends. There is no end to the concept of law — it is many things. More importantly, at this stage, there is no end to a book on legal theory, though there is an end to the time I can spend writing and rewriting it. Which proves the point about arbitrariness really. Law and books (like the areas of legal theory) are not things which can be confined to any particular territory, either intellectual, textual, or practical. In some ways writing a conclusion is futile. Everything the author has set out to write has already been written by that stage, much of it in the introduction: the book is a container which the conclusion is supposed to round off, complete, make sensible. Yet everything which has been written also leads outside the book to the world: it is not simply inside, despite the illusion of containment created by having words inside the covers. Thus: "Every limit is a beginning as well as an ending",[110] and the limits of law, as we know, are truly endless.

The End

---

109 See the critique made by Joelle Chenoweth, "Not the Law Question" (1994) 1 *Law/Text/Culture* 153. It is true that I believe the "law question" is far more extensive than the institutional and disciplinary constraints placed upon it. That is certainly not to deny the specificity of law and its historicity: as I hope to have shown, the concept of law which informs legal institutions and mainstream jurisprudence is extremely limited in terms of time and place.

110 George Eliot, *Middlemarch* [1872].

BIBLIOGRAPHY

Abel, Richard "A Critique of Torts" (1990) *University of Los Angeles Law Review* 785

Abel, Richard "Ideology and Community in the First Wave of Critical Legal Studies" (Book Review) (2003) 54 *Journal of Legal Education* 201

Abrams, Willie "A Reply to Derrick Bell's Racial Realism" (1992) 24 *Connecticut Law Review* 517

Adorno, Theodor and Max Horkheimer *Dialectic of the Enlightenment* (Verso, London, 1979)

Agamben, Giorgio "The Camp as Nomos of the Modern" translated by Daniel Heller-Roazen in Hent de Vries and Samuel Weber (eds) *Violence, Identity, and Self-Determination* (Stanford, Stanford University Press)

Ahmed, Sara "The Politics of Bad Feeling" (2005) 1 *Australian Critical Race and Whiteness Studies Association Journal* 72

Ahmed, Sara "Whose Counting?" (2000) 1 *Feminist Theory* 97

Alfieri, Anthony "Book Review: Black and White" (1997) 85 *California Law Review* 1647

Al-Hibri, Azizah "Islam, Law, and Custom: Redefining Muslim Women's Rights" (1997) 12 *American University Journal of International Law and Policy* 1

Allen, Theodore *The Invention of the White Race* (Verso, New York, 1994)

Allon, Fiona "Boundary Anxieties: Between Borders and Belongings" (2002) 1 *borderlands e-journal*

Anderson, James, Liam O'Dowd, and Thomas Wilson "Why Study Borders Now?" (2002) 12 *Regional and Federal Studies* 1

Anker, Kirsten "Law in the Present Tense: Tradition and Cultural Continuity in *Members of the Yorta Yorta Aboriginal Community v Victoria*" (2004) 28 *Melbourne University Law Review* 1

Anzaldúa, Gloria (ed) *Making Face, Making Soul: Haciendo Caras* (Aunt Lute Books, San Francisco, 1990)

Arblaster, Anthony *The Rise and Decline of Western Liberalism* (Basil Blackwell, Oxford, 1984)

Aristotle *The Ethics* (Penguin Books, Harmondsworth, 1976)

Aristotle *The Politics* (Penguin Books, Harmondsworth, 1981)

Arlen, Jennifer "Reconsidering Efficient Tort Rules for Personal Injury: The Case of Single Activity Accidents" (1990) 32 *William and Mary Law Review* 41

Armstrong, Timothy *Michel Foucault: Philosopher* (Harvester Wheatsheaf, Hemel Hempstead, 1992)

Ashman Keith and Phillip Baringer (eds) *After the Science Wars* (Routledge, New York, 2001)

Atiyah, Patrick "Justice and Predictability in the Common Law" (1992) 15 *University of New South Wales Law Journal* 448

Auchmuty, Rosemary "Out of the Shadows: Feminist Silence and Liberal Law" in Vanessa Munro and Carl Stychin (eds) *Sexuality and the Law: Feminist Engagements* (Routledge-Cavendish, Abingdon, 2007)

Austin, JL *How to Do Things With Words* (Harvard University Press, Cambridge Mass, 1962)

Austin, John *The Province of Jurisprudence Determined* (Weidenfeld & Nicholson, London, 1954)

Baghdadchi, Amir "On Academic Boredom" (2005) 4 *Arts and Humanities in Higher Education* 319

Baker, JH *An Introduction to English Legal History* (4th ed, Butterworths, London, 2002)

Balkin, JM "Deconstructive Practice and Legal Theory" (1987) 96 *Yale Law Journal* 743

Bankowski, Zenon "The Jury and Reality" in Nerhot (ed) *Law, Interpretation, and Reality: Essays in Epistemology, Hermeneutics, and Jurisprudence* (Kluwer Academic Publishers, Dordrecht, 1990)

Barthes, Roland "Le mort d'auteur", *Mantéia*, V, 1968 translated by Stephen Heath as "The Death of the Author" in Roland Barthes *Image Music Text* (Flamingo, London, 1984)

Barthes, Roland *Image Music Text* (Fontana, London, 1977)

Barzun, Charles "Common Sense and Legal Science" (2004) 90 *Virginia Law Review* 1051

Behrendt, Larissa "Black Women and the Feminist Movement: Implications for Aboriginal Women in Rights Discourse" (1993) 1 *Australian Feminist Law Journal* 27

Bell, Derrick "Racial Realism" (1992) 24 *Connecticut Law Review* 363

Belsey, Catherine "Disrupting Sexual Difference: Meaning and Gender in the Comedies" in John Drakakis (ed) *Alternative Shakespeares* (Methuen, London, 1985)

Belsey, Catherine *Critical Practice* (Methuen, London, 1980)

Bender, Leslie "A Lawyer's Primer on Feminist Theory and Tort" (1988) 38 *Journal of Legal Education* 3

Benhabib, Seyla "Some Comments on Deconstruction, Justice, and the Ethical Relationship" (1991) 13 *Cardozo Law Review* 1219

Benhabib, Seyla *Situating the Self: Gender, Community and Postmodernism in Contemporary Ethics* (Polity Press, Cambridge, 1992)

Benhabib, Seyla, Judith Butler, Drucilla Cornell and Nancy Fraser *Feminist Contentions: A Philosophical Exchange* (Routledge, New York, 1995)

Bennett, David "Introduction" in David Bennett (ed) *Multicultural States: Rethinking Difference and Identity* (Routledge, London, 1998)

Bennett, JAW and GV Smithers (eds) *Early Middle English Verse and Prose* (2nd ed, Clarendon Press, Oxford, 1968)

Bennett, Tony *Formalism and Marxism* (Methuen, London, 1979)

Bennington, Geoffrey and Jacques Derrida *Jacques Derrida* (University of Chicago Press, Chicago, 1993)

Benveniste, Emile *Problems in General Linguistics* (University of Miami Press, Florida, 1971)

Berger, Ben "Understanding Law and Religion as Culture: Making Room for Meaning in the Public Sphere" (2006) 15 *Constitutional Forum* 15

Berlin, Isaiah *Four Essays on Liberty* (Oxford University Press, Oxford, 1969)

Bernasconi, Robert (ed) *Race* (Blackwell Publishers, Oxford, 2001)

Bernasconi, Robert "Who Invented the Concept of Race?" in Robert Bernasconi (ed) *Race* (Blackwell Publishers, Oxford, 2001)

Berns, Sandra "Judicial Decision Making and Moral Responsibility" (1991) 13 *Adelaide Law Review* 119

Berns, Sandra *Concise Jurisprudence* (Federation Press, Sydney, 1993)

Beyleveld, Deryck and Roger Brownsword "The Practical Difference Between Natural-Law Theory and Legal Positivism" (1985) 5 *Oxford Journal of Legal Studies* 1

Bhabba, Homi "Signs Taken for Wonders: Questions of Ambivalence and Authority Under a Tree Outside Delhi, May 1817" in Bill Ashcroft, Gareth Griffiths, and Helen Tiffin (eds) *The Postcolonial Studies Reader* (Routledge, New York, 1995)

Bhavnani, Kum-Kum "Complexity, Activism, Optimism: An interview with Angela Y Davis" (1989) 31 *Feminist Review* 66

Bigongiari, Dino (ed) *The Political Ideas of St Thomas Aquinas: Representative Selections* (Hafner, New York, 1969, c1953)

Bjarup, Jes "The Philosophy of Scandinavian Legal Realism" (2005) 18 *Ratio Juris* 1

Blackstone, William *Commentaries on the Laws of England* (15th ed, T Cadell and W Davies, London, 1809)

Boland, Lawrence *Methodology for a New Microeconomics: The Critical Foundations* (Allen and Unwin, Boston, 1987)

Bolinger, Dwight *Aspects of Language* (2nd ed, Harcourt Brace, New York, 1975)

Bonnett, Alaistair "From the Crises of Whiteness to Western Supremacism" (2005) 1 *Australian Critical Race and Whiteness Studies Association Journal* 8

Bonnett, Alastair "Who Was White? The Disappearance of Non-European White Identities and the Formation of European Racial Whiteness" (1998) 21 *Ethnic and Racial Studies* 1029

Bottomley, Stephen and Simon Bronitt *Law in Context* (3rd ed, Federation Press, Sydney, 2006)

Bowring, John (ed) *The Works of Jeremy Bentham* (Russell and Russell, New York, 1962)

Boyd, Susan "Family, Law and Sexuality: Feminist Engagements" (1999) 8 *Social and Legal Studies* 370

Braidotti, Rosi "Ethics Revisited: Women and/in Philosophy" in Carole Pateman and Elizabeth Grosz (eds) *Feminist Challenges: Social and Political Theory* (Allen and Unwin, Sydney, 1986)

Brathwaite, Edward Kamau *The Development of the Creole Society in Jamaica 1770-1820* (Clarendon Press, Oxford, 1971) in Bill Ashcroft, Gareth Griffiths, and Helen Tiffin (eds) *The Postcolonial Studies Reader* (Routledge, New York, 1995)

Brown, Wendy "Suffering Rights as Paradoxes" (2000) 7 *Constellations* 230

Brown, Wendy Brown *States of Injury: Power and Freedom in Late Modernity* (Princeton University Press, Princeton, 1995)

Bulmer, Martin and John Solomos (eds) *Racism* (Oxford University Press, Oxford, 1999)

Burke, Anthony "Borderphobia: the politics of insecurity post 9/11" (2002) 1 *borderlands e-journal*

Burke, Carolyn, Naomi Schor, and Margaret Whitford (eds) *Engaging With Irigaray* (Columbia University Press, New York, 1994)

Burke, Edmund *Reflections on the Revolution in France and On the Proceedings in Certain Societies in London Relative to That Event* (Penguin Books, Harmondsworth, 1968)

Butler, Judith "Contingent Foundations: Feminism and the Question of 'Postmodernism'" in Judith Butler and Joan W Scott (eds) *Feminists Theorize the Political* (Routledge, London, 1992)

Butler, Judith *Antigone's Claim: Kinship Between Life and Death* (Columbia University Press, New York, 2000)

Butler, Judith *Bodies That Matter: On the Discursive Limits of Sex* (Routledge, New York, 1993)

Butler, Judith *Excitable Speech: A Politics of the Performative* (Routledge, New York, 1997)

Butler, Judith *Gender Trouble: Feminism and the Subversion of Identity* (Routledge, New York, 1990)

Cahn, C "Kropotkin and Law" in T Holterman and H van Maarseveen (eds) *Law and Anarchism* (Black Rose Books, Montreal, 1984)

Cahn, Naomi "Defining Feminist Litigation" (1991) 14 *Harvard Women's Law Journal* 1

Campbell, Tom and Jeffrey Goldworthy (ed) *Judicial Power, Democracy, and Legal Positivism* (Aldershot, Dartmouth, 2000)

Campbell, Tom *The Legal Theory of Ethical Positivism* (Aldershot, Dartmouth, 1996)

Campioni, Mia "Women and Otherness" (1991) 1 *Journal of Australian Lesbian Feminist Studies* 49

Carrigan, Frank "A Blast from the Past: The Resurgence of Legal Formalism" (2003) 27 *Melbourne University Law Review* 163

Carter, Angela *The Infernal Desire Machine of Doctor Hoffman* (Penguin, Harmondsworth, 1972)

Carter, Angela *The Sadeian Woman: An Exercise in Cultural History* (Virago, London, 1979)

Carter, April *The Political Theory of Anarchism* (Routledge and Kegan Paul, London, 1971)

Carter, Robert "Is White a Race? Expressions of White Race Identity" in Michelle Fine et al (eds) *Off White: Readings on Race, Power, and Society* (Routledge, New York, 1997)

Carty, Anthony (ed) *Post-Modern Law: Enlightenment, Revolution, and the Death of Man* (Edinburgh University Press, Edinburgh, 1990)

Cashman, Peter "Toxic Torts: The Bottom Line — How Corporate Counsel Condemn Consumers and Create New Forms of Forensic Farce for Litigation Lawyers" in Beerworth (ed) *Contemporary Issues in Product Liability Law* (Federation Press, Sydney, 1991)

Castles, Alex *An Australian Legal History* (Law Book Company, Sydney, 1982)

Chakrabarty, Dipesh "Modernity and Ethnicity in India" in David Bennett (ed) *Multicultural Studies: Rethinking Difference and Identity* (Routledge, London, 1998)

Chalmers, Alan *What Is This Thing Called Science?* (3rd ed, University of Queensland Press, St Lucia, 1999)

Chandra-Shekeran, Sangeetha "Challenging the Fiction of the Nation in the 'Reconciliation' Texts of *Mabo* and *Bringing Them Home*" (1998) 11 *Australian Feminist Law Journal* 107

Charlesworth, Hilary "Building Justice and Democracy After Conflict" (2007) 2 *Academy of the Social Sciences in Australia, Occasional Papers* 1

Charlesworth, Hilary "Feminist Methods in International Law" (1999) 93 *American Journal of International Law* 379

Charlesworth, Hilary "Martha Nussbaum's Feminist Internationalism" (2000) 111 *Ethics* 64

Chenoweth, Joelle "Not the Law Question" (1994) 1 *Law/Text/Culture* 153

Chow, Daniel "Trashing Nihilism" (1990) 65 *Tulane Law Review* 221

Chryssostalis, Julia "The Critical Instance 'After' the Critique of the Subject" (2005) 16 *Law and Critique* 3

Cicero *De Re Publica* (Harvard University Press, Cambridge Mass, 1928, 1977 reprint)

Cixous, Hélène "Sorties" in Elaine Marks and Isabelle de Courtivron *New French Feminisms* (Harvester Press, Sussex, 1981)

Cixous, Hélène and Mireille Calle-Gruber *Hélène Cixous, Rootprints: Memory and Life Writing* (Eric Prenowitz trans, Routledge, London, 1994)

Clark, Randall Baldwin "Love in a Colorado Courtroom: Martha Nussbaum, John Finnis, and Plato's *Laws* in *Evans v Romer*" (2000) 12 *Yale Journal of Law and the Humanities* 1

Clarke, Jennifer "Law and Race: The Position of Indigenous People" in Stephen Bottomley and Stephen Parker *Law in Context* (2nd ed, Federation Press, Sydney, 1997)

Coase, RH "The Problem of Social Cost" (1960) 3 *Journal of Law and Economics* 1

Code, Lorraine "Taking Subjectivity Into Account" in Linda Alcoff and Elizabeth Potter (eds) *Feminist Epistemologies* (Routledge, New York, 1993)

Coe, Paul "Mabo-Confirming Dispossession" (1993) *Broadside*, February 10

Cohen, Felix "Transcendental Nonsense and the Functional Approach" (1935) 35 *Columbia Law Review* 809

Coke, Edward *Institutes of the Laws of England* (15th ed, E and R Brooke, London, 1744)

Coleman, Jules "Economics and the Law: A Critical Review of the Foundations of the Economic Approach to Law" (1984) *Ethics* 649

Comte, Auguste *The Positive Philosophy* (AMS Press, New York, 1974)

Conaghan, Joanne "Reassessing the Feminist Theoretical Project in Law" (2000) 27 *Journal of Law and Society* 351

Conaghan, Joanne "Wishful Thinking or Bad Faith: A Feminist Encounter with Duncan Kennedy's Critique of Adjudication" (2001) 22 *Cardozo Law Review* 721

Conklin, William "The Invisible Author of Legal Authority" (1996) 7 *Law and Critique* 173

Cooper, Graeme "Inevitability and Use" (1989) 1 *Legal Education Review* 29

Cooter, Robert and Thomas Ulen *Law and Economics* (Harper and Collins, USA, 1988)

Copelon, Rhonda "A Crime Not Fit to be Named: Sex, Lies, and the Constitution" in Kairys (ed) *The Politics of Law: A Progressive Critique* (2nd ed, Pantheon Books, New York, 1990)

Cornell, Drucilla "Sexual Difference, the Feminine, and Equivalency: A Critique of MacKinnon's *Toward a Feminist Theory of the State*" (1991) 100 *Yale Law Journal* 2247

Cornell, Drucilla "The Violence of the Masquerade: Law Dressed Up as Justice" (1990) 11 *Cardozo Law Review* 1047

Cornell, Drucilla *At the Heart of Freedom: Feminism, Sex, and Equality* (Princeton University Press, New Jersey, 1998)

Cornell, Drucilla *Beyond Accommodation: Ethical Feminism, Deconstruction and the Law* (Routledge, New York, 1991)

Cornell, Drucilla *The Imaginary Domain: Abortion, Pornography, and Sexual Harassment* (Routledge, New York, 1995)

Cornell, Drucilla *The Philosophy of the Limit* (Routledge, New York, 1991)

Cornell, Drucilla, Michel Rosenfeld and David Gray Carlson (eds) *Hegel and Legal Theory* (Routledge, New York, 1991)

Cornell, Drucilla, Michel Rosenfeld, David Gray Carlson (eds) *Deconstruction and the Possibility of Justice* (Routledge, New York, 1992)

Corns, Chris "The Science of Justice and the Justice in Science" (1992) 10 *Law in Context* 7

Cotterrell, Roger "Power, Property, and the Law of Trusts" in Fitzpatrick and Hunt (eds) *Critical Legal Studies* (Basil Blackwell, Oxford, 1987)

Cotterrell, Roger *The Politics of Jurisprudence: A Critical Introduction to Legal Philosophy* (Butterworths, London, 1989)

Crenshaw, Kimberle "Demarginalizing the Intersection of Race and Sex: A Black Feminist Critique of Antidiscrimination Doctrine, Feminist Theory and Antiracist Politics" (1989) *University of Chicago Legal Forum* 139

Crespi, Gregory "Review Essay: Does the Chicago School Need to Expand its Curriculum?" (1997) 22 *Law and Social Inquiry* 149

Crozier, JB "Legal Realism and a Science of Law" (1984) 29 *American Journal of Jurisprudence* 151

Cudd, Ann "Objectivity and Ethno-Feminist Critiques of Science" in Keith Ashman and Philip Baringer (eds) *After the Science Wars* (London, Routledge, 2001)

Culler, Jonathan *On Deconstruction: Theory and Criticism After Structuralism* (Routledge Kegan Paul, London, 1983)

Culler, Jonathan *Saussure* (Fontana, Glasgow, 1976)

Curthoys, Ann "An Uneasy Conversation: The Multicultural and the Indigenous" in Docker and Fischer (eds) *Race, Colour, and Identity in Australia and New Zealand* (UNSW Press, Sydney, 2000)

D'Souza, Dinesh *The End of Racism: Principles for a Multiracial Society* (Free Press, New York, 1995)

Dale, Catherine "A Debate Between Queer and Feminism" (1997) 1 *Critical in Queeries* 145

Dalton, Harlon "The Clouded Prism" (1987) 22 *Harvard Civil Rights — Civil Liberties Law Review* 435

Dauvergne, Catherine "Making People Illegal" in Peter Fitzpatrick and Patricia Tuitt (eds) *Critical Beings* (Ashgate, London, 2004)

Davenport, Doris "The Pathology of Racism: A Conversation with Third World Wimmin" in Cherrie Moraga and Gloria Anzaldúa (eds) *This Bridge Called My Back: Writings By Radical Women of Color* (Kitchen Table, Women of Color Press, New York, 1981)

Davies, Margaret "Authority, Meaning, Legitimacy" in Jeffrey Goldsworthy and Tom Campbell (eds) *Legal Interpretation in Democratic States* (Ashgate, Aldershot, 2002)

Davies, Margaret "Derrida and Law: Legitimate Fictions" in Tom Cohen (ed) *Jacques Derrida and the Humanities* (Cambridge University Press, Cambridge, 2001)

Davies, Margaret "Legal Separatism and the Concept of the Person" in Tom Campbell and Jeffrey Goldsworthy (eds) *Judicial Power, Democracy and Legal Positivism* (Ashgate, Aldershot, 2000)

Davies, Margaret "Lesbian Separatism and Legal Positivism" (1998) 13 *Canadian Journal of Law and Society* 1

Davies, Margaret "Pathfinding: The Way of the Law" (1992) 14 *Oxford Literary Review* 107

Davies, Margaret "Pluralism and the Philosophy of Law" (2006) 57 *Northern Ireland Legal Quarterly* 577

Davies, Margaret *Property: Meanings, Histories, Theories* (Routledge-Cavendish, London, 2007)

Davies, Margaret "Queer Property, Queer Persons: Self-Ownership and Beyond" (1999) 8 *Social and Legal Studies* 328

Davies, Margaret "The Decapitation of a Discipline, Or How Legal Theory Lost Its Head" (2000) 4 *Flinders Journal of Law Reform* 127

Davies, Margaret "Towards the Common Law? The Limits of Law and the Problem of Translation" (1993) 2 *Asia Pacific Law Journal* 65

Davies, Margaret "Unity and Diversity in Feminist Legal Theory" (2007) 2 *Philosophy Compass* 650

Davies, Margaret *Delimiting the Law: "Postmodernism" and the Politics of Law* (Pluto Press, London, 1996)

Davies, Margaret and Nan Seuffert "Knowledge, Identity and the Politics of Law" (2000) 11 *Hastings Women's Law Journal* 259

Davies, Margaret and Ngaire Naffine *Are Persons Property? Legal Debates About Property and Personality* (Ashgate, Aldershot, 2001)

Davion, Victoria "Pacifism and Care" (1990) 5 *Hypatia* 90

de Lauretis, Teresa "Eccentric Subjects: Feminist Theory and Historical Consciousness" (1990) 16 *Feminist Studies* 115

de Saussure, Ferdinand *Course in General Linguistics* (Philosophical Library, New York, 1966, c1959)

Delacroix, Sylvie *Legal Norms and Normativity: An Essay in Genealogy* (Hart, Oxford, 2006)

Delanty, Gerard "Borders in a Changing Europe: Dynamics of Openness and Closure" (2006) 4 *Comparative European Politics* 183

DeLauretis, Teresa "The Essence of the Triangle or, Taking the Risk of Essentialism Seriously" (1988) 1 *differences: A Journal of Feminist Cultural Studies* 3

Delgado, Richard "Derrick Bell's Racial Realism: A Comment on White Optimism and Black Despair" (1992) 24 *Connecticut Law Review* 527

Delgado, Richard "Derrick Bell's Toolkit – Fit to Dismantle that Famous House?" (2000) 75 *New York University Law Review* 283

Delgado, Richard "Storytelling for Oppositionists and Others" (1989) 87 *Michigan Law Review* 2411

Delgado, Richard "The Ethereal Scholar: Does Critical Legal Studies Have What Minorities Want?" (1987) 22 *Harvard Civil Rights – Civil Liberties Law Review* 301

Delgado, Richard "Two Ways to Think about Race: Reflections on the Id, the Ego, and Other Reformist Theories of Equal Protection" (2001) 89 *Georgetown Law Journal* 2279

Derham, David, Francis Maher, and Louis Waller *An Introduction to Law* (7th ed, Law Book Company, NSW, 1995)

Derrida, Jacques "Force of Law: the 'Mystical Foundation of Authority'" in Drucilla Cornell, Michel Rosenfeld, and David Gray Carlson (ed) *Deconstruction and the Possibility of Justice* (Routledge, New York, 1992)

Derrida, Jacques "Letter to a Japanese Friend" in David Wood and Robert Bernasconi (eds) *Derrida and Difference* (Northwestern University Press, Evanston, 1988)

Derrida, Jacques "Onto-Theology of National-Humanism (Prolegomena to a Hypothesis)" (1992) 14 *Oxford Literary Review* 3

Derrida, Jacques "White Mythology: Metaphor in the Text of Philosophy" in *Margins of Philosophy* (University of Chicago Press, 1982)

Derrida, Jacques *Margins of Philosophy* (Harvester Press, Brighton, 1982)

Derrida, Jacques *Of Grammatology* (Johns Hopkins University Press, Baltimore, 1974)

Derrida, Jacques *Of Hospitality* (Stanford University Press, Stanford, 2000)

Derrida, Jacques *Positions* (University of Chicago Press, Chicago, 1981)

Desan Husson, Christine A "Expanding the Legal Vocabulary: The Challenge Posed by the Deconstruction and Defence of Law" (1986) 95 *Yale Law Journal* 969

Descallar, R "Anarchism and Legal Rules" in T Holterman and H van Maarseveen (eds) *Law and Anarchism* (Black Rose Books, Montreal, 1984)

Descartes, René *Meditations on First Philosophy* (2nd ed, Bobbs-Merrill, New York, 1960)

Detmold, Michael "Law and Difference: Reflections on Mabo's Case" (1993) 15 *Sydney Law Review* 158

Detmold, Michael *The Unity of Law and Morality: A Refutation of Legal Positivism* (Routledge Kegan Paul, London, 1984)

Dewey, John "Logical Method and Law" (1924) 10 *Cornell Law Quarterly* 17

Dickinson, John "The Law Beyond Law: Part 1" (1929) 29 *Columbia Law Review* 113

Didur, Jill and Teresa Heffernan "Revisiting the New Subaltern in the New Empire" (2003) 17 *Cultural Studies* 1

Dimock, Wai Chee "Rules of Law, Laws of Science" (2001) 13 *Yale Journal of Law and the Humanities* 203

Dorsett, Shaugnnagh and Shaun McVeigh "Just So: The Law Which Governs Australia is Australian Law" (2002) 13 *Law and Critique* 289

Douzinas, Costas "Oubliez Critique" (2005) 16 *Law and Critique* 47

Douzinas, Costas "The End(s) of Human Rights" (2002) 26 *Melbourne University Law Review* 445

Douzinas, Costas and Adam Geary *Critical Jurisprudence: The Political Philosophy of Justice* (Hart Publishing, Oxford, 2005)

Douzinas, Costas, Ronnie Warrington and Shaun McVeigh *Postmodern Jurisprudence: The Law of Text in the Texts of Law* (Routledge, London, 1991)

du Bois, Ellen et al "Feminist Discourse, Moral Values, and the Law — A Conversation" (1985) 34 *Buffalo Law Review* 11

Duncanson, Ian "Finnis and the Politics of Natural Law" (1989) 19 *University of Western Australia Law Review* 239

Duncanson, Ian "The Strange World of English Jurisprudence" (1979) 30 *Northern Ireland Legal Quarterly* 207

Dworkin, Andrea *Right-Wing Women: The Politics of Domesticated Females* (The Women's Press, London, 1983)

Dworkin, Andrea *Woman Hating* (EP Dutton, New York, 1974), Part 1 "The Fairy Tales"

Dworkin, Andrea "Woman-Hating Right and Left" in Leidholt and Raymond (eds) *The Sexual Liberals and the Attack on Feminism* (Pergamon Press, New York, 1990)

Dworkin, Ronald (ed) *The Philosophy of Law* (Oxford, Oxford University Press, 1977)

Dworkin, Ronald *A Matter of Principle* (Harvard University Press, Cambridge Mass, 1985)

Dworkin, Ronald *Law's Empire* (Fontana, London, 1986), pp 228-238

Dworkin, Ronald *Taking Rights Seriously* (Harvard University Press, Cambridge Mass, 1977)

Dyer, Richard *White* (Routledge, London, 1997)

Dyzenhaus, David "Why Positivism Is Authoritarian" (1992) 37 *American Journal of Jurisprudence* 83

Eagleton, Mary (ed) *Feminist Literary Theory: A Reader* (2nd ed, Basil Blackwell, Oxford, 1996)

Eagleton, Terry *Literary Theory: An Introduction* (Basil Blackwell, Oxford, 1983)

Easterbrook, Frank "The Inevitability of Law and Economics" (1989) 1 *Legal Education Review* 3

Eco, Umberto *Travels in Hyper-Reality* (Pan Books and Secker and Warburg, London, 1987)

Eisenstein, Zillah *The Radical Future of Liberal Feminism* (Longman, New York, 1981)

Elizabeth Landes and Richard Posner "The Economics of the Baby Shortage" (1978) 7 *Journal of Legal Studies* 323

Elliott, Terri "Making Strange What had Appeared Familiar" (1994) 77 *The Monist* 429

Enloe, Cynthia *Does Khaki Become You? The Militarization of Women's Lives* (Pluto Press, London, 1983)

Epstein, Richard "Law and Economics: Its Glorious Past and Cloudy Future" (1997) 64 *University of Chicago Law Review* 1167

Epstein, Richard "The Not So Minimum Content of Natural Law" (2005) 25 *Oxford Journal of Legal Studies* 219

Erlanger, Howard et al "Is it Time For a New Legal Realism" (2005) *Wisconsin Law Review* 335

Ermath, Elizabeth "What Counts as Feminist Theory?" (2000) 1 *Feminist Theory* 113

Espinoza, Leslie and Angela Harris "Embracing the Tar-Baby" LatCrit Theory and the Sticky Mess of Race" (1997) 85 *California Law Review* 1585

Eze, Emmanuel "The Color of Reason: The Idea of 'Race' in Kant's Anthropology" in Katherine M Faull (ed) *Anthropology and the German Enlightenment: Perspectives on Humanity* (Bucknell University Press, Lewisburg, 1995)

Fanon, Frantz *Black Skin, White Masks* (McGibbon and Kee, London, 1968)

Fanon, Frantz *The Wretched of the Earth* (McGibbon and Kee, London, 1965)

Feiwel, George (ed) *Issues in Contemporary Microeconomics and Welfare* (State University of New York Press, Albany, 1985)

Feldman, Stephen "An Arrow to the Heart: The Love and Death of Postmodern Legal Scholarship" (2001) 54 *Vanderbilt Law Review* 2349

Fenton, Steve *Ethnicity: Racism, Class and Culture* (Rowman and Littlefield, Lanham, 1999)

Ferguson, Kathy *The Man Question: Visions of Subjectivity in Feminist Theory* (University of California Press, Berkeley, 1991)

Fine, Michelle "Witnessing Whiteness" in Michelle Fine et al (eds) *Off White: Readings on Race, Power, and Society* (Routledge, New York, 1997)

Fineman, Martha "Challenging Law, Establishing Differences: The Future of Feminist Legal Scholarship" (1990) 42 *Florida Law Review* 25

Fineman, Martha "The Hermeneutics of Reason: A Commentary on Sex and Reason" (1993) 25 *Connecticut Law Review* 503

Finley, Lucinda "A Break in the Silence: Including Women's Issues in a Torts Course" (1989) 64 *Notre Dame Law Review* 886

Finley, Lucinda "Breaking Women's Silence in Law: The Dilemma of the Gendered Nature of Legal Reasoning" (1989) 41 *Yale Journal of Law and Feminism* 41

Finnis, John "Concluding Reflections" (1990) 38 *Cleveland State Law Review* 231

Finnis, John "Law, Morality, and 'Sexual Orientation'" (1994) 69 *Notre Dame Law Review* 1049

Finnis, John "On the Incoherence of Legal Positivism" (2000) 75 *Notre Dame Law Review* 1597

Finnis, John "The 'Natural Law Tradition'" (1986) 36 *Journal of Legal Education* 492

Finnis, John "The Good of Marriage and the Morality of Sexual Relations: Some Philosophical and Historical Observations" (1997) 42 *American Journal of Jurisprudence* 97

Finnis, John *Natural Law and Natural Rights* (Clarendon Press, Oxford, 1980)

Firestone, Shulamith *The Dialectic of Sex* (The Women's Press, London, 1979)

Fischl, Richard Michael "The Question That Killed Critical Legal Studies" (1992) 17 *Law and Social Inquiry* 779

Fisher, William, Morton Horwitz, and Thomas Reed (eds) *American Legal Realism* (Oxford University Press, New York, 1993)

Fitzpatrick, Peter "'No Higher Duty': Mabo and the Failure of Legal Foundation" (2002) 13 *Law and Critique* 233

Fitzpatrick, Peter and Patricia Tuitt (eds) *Critical Beings: Law, Nation and the Global Subject* (Ashgate, Aldershot, 2004)

Fitzpatrick, Peter *Modernism and the Grounds of Law* (Oxford University Press, Oxford, 2001)

Flagg, Barbara "'Was Blind But Now I See': White Race Consciousness and the Requirement of Discriminatory Intent" (1993) 91 *Michigan Law Review* 953

Forbath, William "Taking Lefts Seriously" (1983) 92 *Yale Law Journal* 1041

Ford, Richard T "Law's Territory (A History of Jurisdiction)" (1999) 97 *Michigan Law Review* 843

Forell, Caroline "The Reasonable Woman Standard" (1992) 11 *University of Tasmania Law Review* 1

Fortescue, John *De Laudibus Legum Angliae* (Sweet and Maxwell, London, 1917)

Foucault, Michel "What is an Author" in Josué Harari *Textual Strategies: Perspectives in Post - Structuralist Criticism* (London, Methuen, 1980)

Foucault, Michel *Madness and Civilisation: A History of Insanity in the Age of Reason* (Tavistock, London, 1967)

Foucault, Michel *Power/Knowledge: Selected Interviews and Other Writings, 1972-1977* (trans by Colin Gordon Harvester Press, Brighton, 1980)

Foucault, Michel *The Archaeology of Knowledge* (Tavistock Publications, London, 1972)

Foucault, Michel *The Order of Things: An Archaeology of the Human Sciences* (London, Routledge, 2001)

Fox Keller, Evelyn "Feminism and Science" in Richard Boyd, Philip Gaspar, and JD Trout (eds) *The Philosophy of Science* (MIT Press, Cambridge Mass, 1991)

Frank, Jerome *Law and the Modern Mind* (Bientano's, New York, 1930)

Franke, Katherine "Gendered Subjects of Transitional Justice" (2006) 15 *Columbia Journal of Gender and Law* 813

Frankenburg, Ruth (ed) *Displacing Whiteness* (Duke University Press, Durham, 1997)

Frankenburg, Ruth *White Women, Race Matters* (University of Minnesota Press, Minneapolis, 1993)

Franklin, Benjamin "Observations Concerning the Increase of Mankind and the Peopling of Countries" [1751] in Kenneth Silverman (ed) *Benjamin Franklin/Autobiography and Other Writings* (Penguin Books, New York, 1986)

Franklin, Sarah "Making Transparencies: Seeing Through the Science Wars" (1996) 46/47 *Social Text* 141-155

Fraser, David "The Owls Are Not What They Seem: David Lynch, The Madonna Question, and Critical Legal Studies" (1993) 18 *Queens Law Journal* 1

Fraser, David "Truth and Hierarchy: Will the Circle Be Unbroken?" (1984) *Buffalo Law Review* 729

Fraser, David "What a Long, Strange Trip Its Been: Deconstructing Law from Legal Realism to Critical Legal Studies" (1990) 5 *Australian Journal of Law and Society* 3

Freeman Alan "Truth and Mystification in Legal Scholarship" (1981) 90 *Yale Law Journal* 1229

Freeman, Alan and Elizabeth Mensch "The Public-Private Distinction in American Law and Life" (1987) 36 *Buffalo Law Review* 237

Freeman, MDA *Lloyd's Introduction to Jurisprudence* (7th ed, Sweet & Maxwell Ltd, London 2001)

Freud, Sigmund *The Essentials of Psychoanalysis* (Penguin, Harmondsworth, 1986)

Frug, Gerald "A Critical Theory of Law" (1989) 1 *Legal Education Review* 43

Frye Jacobson, Matthew *Whiteness of a Different Color* (Harvard University Press, Cambridge Mass, 1998)

Fuller, Lon "Positivism and Fidelity to Law — A Reply to Professor Hart" (1958) 71 *Harvard Law Review* 630

Fuller, Lon *Legal Fictions* (Stanford University Press, California, 1967)

Fuss, Diana (ed) *Inside/Out: Lesbian Theories, Gay Theories* (Routledge, New York, 1991)

Gabel, Peter "The Phenomenology of Rights-Consciousness and the Pact of the Withdrawn Selves" (1984) 62 *Texas Law Review* 1563

Gabel, Peter and Duncan Kennedy "Roll Over Beethoven" (1984) 36 *Stanford Law Review* 1

Gabel, Peter and Jay Feinman "Contract Law as Ideology" in David Kairys (ed) *The Politics of Law: A Progressive Critique* (rev ed, Pantheon Books, New York, 1990)

Galbraith, Janet "Processes of Whiteness and Stories of Rape" (2000) 14 *Australian Feminist Law Journal* 71

Gasché, Rodolphe *Inventions of Difference: On Jacques Derrida* (Harvard University Press, Cambridge Mass, 1994)

Gasché, Rodolphe *The Tain of the Mirror: Derrida and the Philosophy of Reflection* (Harvard University Press, Cambridge Mass, 1986)

Gava, John "Another Blast from the Past or Why the Left Should Embrace Strict Legalism: A Reply to Frank Carrigan" (2003) 27 *Melbourne University Law Review* 186

Gavison, Ruth "Natural Law, Positivism, and the Limits of Jurisprudence: A Modern Round" (1982) 91 *Yale Law Journal* 1250

George, Robert P (ed) *The Autonomy of Law: Essays on Legal Positivism* (Oxford, Clarendon Press, 1996)

Gerson, Gal "Liberal Feminism: Individuality and Oppositions in Wollstonecraft and Mill" (2002) 50 *Political Studies* 794

Gilligan, Carol *In a Different Voice: Psychological Theory and Women's Development* (Harvard University Press, Cambridge Mass, 1982)

Godden, Lee "Wik: Legal Memory and History" (1997) 6 *Griffith Law Review* 123

Golder, Ben "Law, History, Colonialism: An Orientalist Reading of Australian Native Title Law" (2004) 9 *Deakin Law Review* 41

Goldfarb, Phyllis "A Theory-Practice Spiral: The Ethics of Feminism and Clinical Education" (1991) 75 *Minnesota Law Review* 1599

Goodhart, CAE "Economics and the Law: Too Much One-Way Traffic" (1997) 60 *Modern Law Review* 1

Goodrich, Peter "Duncan Kennedy as I Imagine Him: The Man, the Work, his Scholarship and the Polity" (2001) 22 *Cardozo Law Review* 971

Goodrich, Peter "Sleeping With the Enemy: An Essay on the Politics of Critical Legal Studies in America" (1993) 68 *New York University Law Review* 389

Goodrich, Peter *Languages of Law: From Logics of Memory to Nomadic Masks* (Weidenfeld and Nicolson, London, 1990)

Goodrich, Peter *Oedipus Lex: Psychoanalysis, History, Law* (University of California Press, Berkeley, 1995)

Gordon, Robert "Historicism in Legal Scholarship" (1981) 90 *Yale Law Journal* 1017

Gordon, Robert "Critical Legal Histories" (1984) 36 *Stanford Law Review* 57

Gordon, Robert "Critical Legal Studies as a Teaching Method, Against the Background of the Intellectual Politics of Modern Legal Education in the United States" (1989) 1 *Legal Education Review* 43

Gordon, Robert "New Developments in Legal Theory" in Kairys (ed) *The Politics of Law: A Progressive Critique* (rev ed, Pantheon Books, New York, 1990)

Graycar, Regina and Jenny Morgan *The Hidden Gender of Law* (2nd ed, Federation Press, Annandale NSW, 2002)

Grbich, Judy "The Body in Legal Theory" (1992) 11 *University of Tasmania Law Review* 26

Greene, Gayle and Coppélia Kahn (eds) *Making a Difference: Feminist Literary Criticism* (Methuen, London, 1985)

Griffith, JAG *The Politics of the Judiciary* (Fontana, London, 1985)

Groenhout, Ruth "Essentialist Challenges to Liberal Feminism" (2002) 28 *Social Theory and Practice* 51

Gross, Paul and Norman Levitt *Higher Superstition: The Academic Left and Its Quarrels with Science* (Johns Hopkins University Press, Baltimore, 1994)

Grosz, Elizabeth "The Hetero and the Homo: The Sexual Ethics of Luce Irigaray" in Carolyn Burke, Naomi Schor, and Margaret Whitford (eds) *Engaging With Irigaray* (Columbia University Press, New York, 1994)

Guest, Stephen (ed) *Positivism Today* (Aldershot, Dartmouth, 1996)

Guillaumin, Collette *Racism, Sexism, Power and Ideology* (Routledge, London, 1995)

Gunew, Sneja (ed) *Feminist Knowledge: Critique and Construct* (Routledge, London, 1990)

Gunew, Sneja "Feminist Knowledge: Critique and Construct" in Gunew (ed) *Feminist Knowledge: Critique and Construct* (Routledge, New York, 1990)

Gunnarsson, Åsa "The Autonomous Taxpayer and the Dependent Caregiver: The Effects of the Division Between Tax Law and Social Law" in Kevät Nousiainen, Åsa Gunnarsson, Karin Lundström, Johanna Niemi-Kiesiläinen (eds) *Responsible Selves: Women in the Nordic Legal Culture* (Ashgate, Aldershot, 2001)

Gunnarsson, Åsa, Eva-Maria Svensson, and Margaret Davies (eds), *Exploiting the Limits of Law: Swedish Feminism and the Challenge to Feminism* (Ashgate, Aldershot, 2007)

Hadfield, Gillian "Flirting with Science: Richard Posner on the Bioeconomics of Sexual Man" (1992) 106 *Harvard Law Review* 479

Hadfield, Gillian "The Second Wave of Law and Economics: Learning to Surf" in Megan Richardson and Gillian Hadfield (eds) *The Second Wave of Law and Economics* (Federation Press, Sydney, 1999)

Hägerström, Axel *Inquiries into the Nature of Law and Morals* (CD Broad trans, Almqvist and Wiskell, Stockholm, 1953)

Haggis, Jane "Beyond Race and Whiteness: Reflections on the New Abolitionists and an Australian Critical Whiteness Studies" (2006) 3(2) *borderlands*

Haggis, Jane and Susanne Schech "Migrancy, Whiteness and the Settler Self in Contemporary Australia" in Docker and Fischer (eds) *Race, Colour and Identity in Australia and New Zealand* (UNSW Press, Sydney, 2000)

Hale, Matthew "Reflections by the Lord Chiefe Justice Hale on Mr Hobbes his Dialogue of the Lawe" in Holdsworth *A History of English Law*, Volume V, Appendix III (Methuen, London, 1924)

Hale, Matthew *History of the Pleas of the Crown* (rev ed, T Payne et al, London, 1778)

Hale, Matthew *The History of the Common Law of England* (Edited and with an Introduction by Charles M Gray, University of Chicago Press, Chicago, 1971)

Halperin, David M *Saint Foucault: Towards a Gay Hagiography* (Oxford University Press, New York, 1995)

Handler, Joel "Postmodernism, Protest and the New Social Movements" (1992) 26 *Law and Society Review* 697

Handsley, Elizabeth "The Reasonable Man: Two Case Studies" (1996) 1 *Sister in Law* 53

Hanks, Bryan, and Peter Keon-Cohen (eds) *Aborigines and the Law: Essays in Memory of Elizabeth Eggleston* (Allen and Unwin, Sydney, 1984)

Haraway, Donna "Situated Knowledges: The Science Question in Feminism and the Privilege of Partial Perspective" (1988) 14 *Feminist Studies* 575

Haraway, Donna *Simians, Cyborgs and Women: The Reinvention of Nature* (Routledge, New York, 1991)

Harding, Sandra "Comment on Walby's 'Against Epistemological Chasms: The Science Question in Feminism Revisited': Can Democratic Values and Interests Ever Play a Rationally Justifiable Role in the Evaluation of Scientific Work" (2001) 26 *Signs* 511

Harding, Sandra "Rethinking Standpoint Epistemology: 'What Is Strong Objectivity?'" in Linda Alcoff and Elizabeth Potter (eds) *Feminist Epistemologies* (Routledge, New York, 1993)

Harding, Sandra *The Science Question in Feminism* (Milton Keynes, Open University Press, 1986)

Harding, Sandra *Whose Science? Whose Knowledge? Thinking From Women's Lives* (Cornell University Press, Ithaca NY, 1991)

Harford, Barbara and Sarah Hopkins (eds) *Greenham Common: Women at the Wire* (The Women's Press, London, 1984)

Harris, Adrienne and Ynestra King (eds) *Rocking the Ship of State: Toward a Feminist Peace Politics* (Westview Press, Boulder, 1989)

Harris, Angela "Categorical Discourse and Dominance Theory" (1989) 5 *Berkeley Women's Law Journal* 181

Harris, Angela "Equality Trouble: Sameness and Difference in Twentieth Century Race Law" (2000) 88 *California Law Review* 1923

Harris, Angela "Race and Essentialism in Feminist Legal Theory" (1990) 42 *Stanford Law Review* 581

Harris, Angela "The Jurisprudence of Reconstruction" (1994) 82 *California Law Review* 741

Harris, Cheryl "Whiteness as Property" (1993) 106 *Harvard Law Review* 1709

Harris, JW *Legal Philosophies* (2nd ed, Oxford University Press, Oxford, 2004)

Harris, JW "Unger's Critique of Formalism in Legal Reasoning: Hero, Hercules, and Humdrum" (1989) 52 *Modern Law Review* 42

Harrison, Jeffrey "Piercing Pareto Superiority: Real People and the Obligations of Legal Theory" (1997) 39 *Arizona Law Review* 1

Hart, HLA "Positivism and the Separation of Law and Morals" in Ronald Dworkin (ed) *The Philosophy of Law* (Oxford University Press, Oxford, 1977)

Hart, HLA *Law, Liberty and Morality* (Oxford University Press, Oxford, 1963)

Hart, HLA *The Concept of Law* (2nd ed, Clarendon Press, Oxford, 1994)

Hawkes, Terence *Structuralism and Semiotics* (Methuen, London, 1977)

Hawkesworth, Mary "Knowers, Knowing, Known: Feminist Theory and Claims of Truth" (1989) 14 *Signs* 533

Hayman, Robert "Re-Cognizing Race: An Essay in Defense of Race Consciousness" (2000) 6 *Widener Law Symposium* 37

Heath, Mary "Catharine MacKinnon: Toward a Feminist Theory of the State?" (1997) 9 *Australian Feminist Law Journal* 45

Hegel, GWF *The Philosophy of Right* (Knox trans, Oxford University Press, London, 1967)

Hekman, Susan "Beyond Identity" (2000) 1 *Feminist Theory* 289

Hekman, Susan "Truth and Method: Feminist Standpoint Revisited" (1997) 22 *Signs* 341

Heller, Thomas "Structuralism and Critique" (1984) 36 *Stanford Law Review* 127

Hemmings, Clare "Telling Feminist Stories" (2005) 6 *Feminist Theory* 115

Herman, Didi "'An Unfortunate Coincidence': Jews and Jewishness in Twentieth-century English Judicial Discourse" (2006) 33 *Journal of Law and Society* 277

Herman, Didi "A Jurisprudence of One's Own? Ruthann Robson's Lesbian Legal Theory" in Wilson (ed) *A Simple Matter of Justice? Theorising Lesbian and Gay Politics* (Cassell, London, 1995)

Hird, Myra "Gender's Nature" (2000) 1 *Feminist Theory* 347

Hoagland, Sarah Lucia *Lesbian Ethics: Toward New Value* (Institute of Lesbian Studies, Palo Alto, 1988)

Hobbes Thomas *A Dialogue Between a Philosopher and a Student of the Common Laws of England* (University of Chicago Press, Chicago, 1971)

Hobbes, Thomas *Leviathan* (Cambridge University Press, Cambridge, 1991)

Hoeflich, MH "Law and Geometry: Legal Science from Leibniz to Langdell" (1986) 30 *American Journal of Legal History* 95

Holmes, Oliver Wendell "Law in Science and Science in Law" in Holmes *Collected Legal Papers* (Harcourt, Brace and Howe, New York, 1920)

Holmes, Oliver Wendell "The Path of the Law" (1897) 10 *Harvard Law Review* 457

Holmes, Oliver Wendell "The Path of the Law" in *Collected Legal Papers* (Harcourt, Brace and Howe, New York, 1920)

Holmes, Oliver Wendell *The Common Law* (Little, Brown, Boston, 1881)

Holmlund, Christine "The Lesbian, the Mother, the Heterosexual Lover: Irigaray's Recodings of Difference" (1991) 17 *Feminist Studies* 283

Holterman, T "Anarchist Theory of Law and the State" in T Holterman and H van Maarseveen (eds) *Law and Anarchism* (Black Rose Books, Montreal, 1984)

Holterman, T and H van Maarseveen (eds) *Law and Anarchism* (Black Rose Books, Montreal, 1984)

hooks, bell "Theory as Liberatory Practice" (1991) 4 *Yale Journal of Law and Feminism* 41

Horkheimer, Max *Critical Theory: Selected Essays* (Continuum, New York, 1968)

Horwitz, Morton "The Historical Contingency of the Role of History" (1981) 90 *Yale Law Journal* 1057

Horwitz, Morton "Why Is Anglo-American Jurisprudence Unhistorical?" (1997) 17 *Oxford Journal of Legal Studies* 551

Hudson, Barbara "Beyond White Man's Justice: Race, Gender and Justice in Late Modernity" (2006) 10 *Theoretical Criminology* 29

Hughes, Graham "Validity and the Basic Norm" (1971) 59 *California Law Review* 695

Hume, David *A Treatise of Human Nature* (Penguin, Middlesex, 1969)

Hunt, Alan "The Big Fear: Law Confronts Postmodernism" (1990) 35 *McGill Law Journal* 507

Hunt, Alan "The Critical Legal Studies Movement" in Fitzpatrick and Hunt (eds) *Critical Legal Studies* (Basil Blackwell, Oxford, 1987)

Hunt, Alan "The Theory of Critical Legal Studies" (1986) 6 *Oxford Journal of Legal Studies* 1

Hutchinson, Allan *Evolution and the Common Law* (Cambridge University Press, Cambridge, 2005)

Hutchinson, Allan "Inessentially Speaking (Is There Politics After Postmodernism?)" (1991) 89 *Michigan Law Review* 1549

Hutchinson, Allan and Patrick Monahan "Law, Politics and Critical Legal Scholars: The Unfolding Drama of American Legal Thought" (1984) 26 *Stanford Law Review* 199

Hutchinson, Allan and Patrick Monahan "The 'Rights' Stuff: Roberto Unger and Beyond" (1984) 62 *Texas Law Review* 1477

Hutchinson, Allan *Dwelling on the Threshold* (Carswell Company, Toronto, 1988)

Irigaray, Luce *I Love to You: Sketch of a Possible Felicity in History* (Routledge, New York, 1996)

Irigaray, Luce *Je, Tu, Nous: Toward a Culture of Difference* (Routledge, London, 1993)

Irigaray, Luce *Speculum of the Other Woman* (Cornell University Press, Ithaca NY, 1985)

Irigaray, Luce *This Sex Which is Not One* (Cornell University Press, Ithaca NY, 1985)

Irigaray, Luce *To Be Two* (Monique Rhodes and Marco Cocito-Monoc trans, Athlone, London, 2000)

Irigaray, Luce *Why Different? A Culture of Two Subjects* (Interviews) (Semiotext(e), New York, 2000)

Jabbari, David "From Criticism to Construction in Modern Critical Legal Theory" (1992) 12 *Oxford Journal of Legal Studies* 507

Jaggar, Alison *Feminist Politics and Human Nature* (Rowman and Littlefield, New Jersey, 1983)

Jagose, Annamarie *Queer Theory* (Melbourne University Press, Carlton, 1996)

James, William *Pragmatism* (first published 1907, Harvard University Press, Cambridge Mass, 1975)

Jeffreys, Sheila "The Queer Disappearance of Lesbians in the Academy: Sexuality in the Academy" (1994) 17 *Women's Studies International Forum* 459

Johnson, Parker "Reflections on Critical White(ness) Studies" in Thomas Nakayama and Judith Martin (eds) *Whiteness: The Communication of Social Identity* (Sage Publications, Thousand Oaks, 1999)

Johnson, Pauline "Feminism and Liberalism" (1991) 14 *Australian Feminist Studies* 57

Johnson, Samuel *Rasselas, Poems, and Selected Prose* (Holt Rinehart and Winston, New York, c1958)

Jones, Harry "Legal Inquiry and the Methods of Science" in Harry Jones (ed) *Law and the Social Role of Science* (Holt, Rinehart and Winston, New York, 1958)

Kairys, David "Legal Reasoning" in David Kairys (ed) *The Politics of Law: A Progressive Critique* (Pantheon Books, New York, 1990)

Kamali, Maryam "Accountability for Human Rights Violations: A Comparison of Transitional Justice in East Germany and South Africa" (2001) 40 *Columbia Journal of Transnational Law* 89

Kant, Immanuel "On the Use of Teleological Principles in Philosophy" (1788) reprinted in Robert Bernasconi (ed) *Race* (Blackwell Publishers, Oxford, 2001)

Kant, Immanuel "Prolegomena to any Future Metaphysics" in Lewis White Beck (ed) *Kant: Selections* (Scribner/MacMillan, New York, 1988)

Kant, Immanuel *Critique of Judgement* (Oxford University Press, Oxford, 1957)

Kant, Immanuel *Critique of Pure Reason* (Macmillan, Hampshire, 1929)

Kant, Immanuel *Foundations of the Metaphysics of Morals* (2nd ed, Prentice-Hall, New Jersey, 1997)

Kapur, Ratna "'A Love Song to Our Mongrel Selves': Hybridity, Sexuality, and the Law" (1999) 8 *Social and Legal Studies* 353

Kapur, Ratna *Erotic Justice: Law and the New Politics of Postcolonialism* (Glasshouse Press, London, 2005)

Katona, Jacqui "'If Native Title Is Us, It's Inside Us': Jabiluka and the Politics of Intercultural Negotiation" (1998) 10 *Australian Feminist Law Journal* 1

Keen, Steve *Debunking Economics: The Naked Emperor of the Social Sciences* (Pluto Press and Zed Books, NSW and London, 2001)

Keener, William "Methods of Legal Education" (1892) 1 *Yale Law Journal* 143

Kelley, Patrick "Holmes, Langdell and Formalism" (2002) 15 *Ratio Juris* 26

Kellogg, Frederic "Legal Scholarship in the Temple of Doom: Pragmatism's Response to Critical Legal Studies" (1990) 65 *Tulane Law Review* 15

Kelly, JM *A Short History of Western Legal Theory* (Clarendon Press, Oxford, 1992)

Kelman, Mark "Trashing" (1984) 36 *Stanford Law Review* 293

Kelsen, Hans "On the Theory of Interpretation" (1990) 10 *Legal Studies* 127

Kelsen, Hans "Professor Stone and the Pure Theory of Law" (1965) 17 *Stanford Law Review* 1128

Kelsen, Hans "The Pure Theory of Law: Its Method and Fundamental Concepts, Part 1" (1934) 200 *Law Quarterly Review* 474

Kelsen, Hans *General Theory of Law and State* (Russell, New York, 1961)

Kelsen, Hans *General Theory of Norms* (Michael Hartney trans, Oxford University Press, Oxford, 1991)

Kelsen, Hans *Introduction to the Problems of Legal Theory* (Translation of the First Edition of the Reine Rechtslehre or Pure Theory of Law) [1934] (Bonnie Litschewski Paulson and Stanley Paulson trans, Clarendon Press, Oxford, 1992)

Kelsen, Hans *Pure Theory of Law* (University of California Press, Berkeley, 1967)

Kennedy, Duncan "Legal Education As Training For Hierarchy" in David Kairys (ed) *The Politics of Law: A Progressive Critique* (rev ed, Pantheon Books, New York, 1967)

Kennedy, Duncan "Psycho-Social CLS: A Comment on the Cardozo Symposium" (1985) 6 *Cardozo Law Review* 1013

Kennedy, Duncan "The Structure of Blackstone's Commentaries" (1979) 28 *Buffalo Law Review* 205

Kennedy, Duncan "Two Globalizations of Law and Legal Thought: 1850-1968" (2003) *Suffolk University Law Review* 631

Kennedy, Duncan *Critique of Adjudication [Fin de Siecle]* (Harvard University Press, Cambridge Mass, 1997)

Kerruish, Valerie "At the Court of the Strange God" (2002) 13 *Law and Critique* 271

Kerruish, Valerie "Philosophical Retreat: A Criticism of John Finnis' Theory of Natural Law" (1983) 15 *University of Western Australia Law Review* 224

Kerruish, Valerie "Responding to Kruger: The Constitutionality of Genocide" (1998) 11 *Australian Feminist Law Journal* 65

Kerruish, Valerie and Colin Perrin "Awash in Colonialism" (1999) 24 (1) *Alternative Law Journal* 3

Keyser, Cassius "On the Study of Legal Science" (1929) 38 *Yale Law Journal* 413

Kierkegaard, Søren "Rotation of Crops" in *Either/Or Part I* (Princeton University Press, Princeton, 1987)

King, Deborah "Multiple Jeopardy, Multiple Consciousness: The Context of a Black Feminist Ideology" (1988) 14 *Signs* 42

Kingdom, Elizabeth "Citizenship and Democracy: Feminist Politics of Citizenship and Radical Democratic Politics" in Susan Millns and Noel Whitty (eds) *Feminist Perspectives on Public Law* (Cavendish, London, 1999)

Kingdom, Elizabeth "Gendering Rights" in Arnaud and Kingdom (eds) *Women's Rights and the Rights of Man* (Aberdeen University Press, Aberdeen, 1990)

Kingdom, Elizabeth *What's Wrong With Rights? Problems for Feminist Politics of Law* (Edinburgh University Press, Edinburgh, 1990)

Kirby, Michael "In Praise of Common Law Renewal" (1992) 15 *University of New South Wales Law Review* 462

Kleinhans, Martha-Marie and Roderick MacDonald 'What is a Critical Legal Pluralism?' (1997) 12 *Canadian Journal of Law and Society/Revue Canadienne de droit et société* 25

Kofman, Sarah "Descartes Entrapped" in Eduardo Cadava, Peter Connor, and Jean-Luc Nancy (eds) *Who Comes After the Subject?* (Routledge, New York, 1991)

Kornstein, Daniel *Kill All the Lawyers? Shakespeare's Legal Appeal* (Princeton University Press, New Jersey, 1994)

Kramer, Matthew "The Rule of Misrecognition in the Hart of Jurisprudence" (1988) 8 *Oxford Journal of Legal Studies* 26

Kramer, Matthew *In Defence of Legal Positivism: Law Without Trimmings* (Clarendon Press, Oxford, 1999)

Kramer, Matthew *Legal Theory, Political Theory, and Deconstruction: Against Rhadamanthus* (Indiana University Press, Bloomington, 1991)

Kropotkin, Peter "Law and Authority" in Roger N Baldwin (ed) *Kropotkin's revolutionary pamphlets: a collection of writings* (Dover Publications, New York, 1970 c1927)

Kruks, Sonia "Simone de Beauvoir and the Politics of Privilege" (2005) 20 *Hypatia* 178

Krygier, Martin "Ethical Positivism and the Liberalism of Fear" in Tom Campbell and Jeffrey Goldworthy (ed) *Judicial Power, Democracy, and Legal Positivism* (Aldershot, Dartmouth, 2000)

Kuhn, Thomas *The Structure of Scientific Revolutions* (3rd ed, University of Chicago Press, Chicago, 1996)

Kyambi, Sarah "National Identity and Refugee Law" in Peter Fitzpatrick and Patricia Tuitt (eds) *Critical Beings* (Ashgate, London, 2004)

Lacey, Nicola "Analytical Jurisprudence Versus Descriptive Sociology Revisited" (2006) 84 *Texas Law Review* 945

Lacey, Nicola "Feminist Perspectives on Ethical Positivism" in Tom Campbell and Jeffrey Goldworthy (eds) *Judicial Power, Democracy, and Legal Positivism* (Aldershot, Dartmouth, 2000)

Lacey, Nicola *A Life of HLA Hart: The Nightmare and the Noble Dream* (Oxford University Press, Oxford, 2004)

Lacey, Nicola *Unspeakable Subjects: Feminist Essays in Legal and Social Theory* (Hart Publishing, Oxford, 1998)

Lancaster, Jane *Primate Behaviour and the Emergence of Human Culture* (New York, Holt, Rinehart and Winston, 1975)

Landauer, Carl "Deliberating Speech: Totalitarian Anxieties and Postwar Legal Thought" (2000) 12 *Yale Journal of Law and the Humanities* 171

Lane, Bernard "Mutually Assured Boredom" *The Australian* 14 December 2005, 25

Langdell, Christopher Columbus "Harvard Celebration Speeches"(1997) 9 *Law Quarterly Review* 123

Langford Ginibi, Ruby "Aboriginal Traditional and Customary Law" (1994) 1 *Law/Text/Culture* 8

Larrabee, Mary Jeanne (ed) *An Ethic of Care: Feminist and Interdisciplinary Perspectives* (Routledge, New York, 1993)

Laski, Harold Joseph *The Rise of European Liberalism* (Allen and Unwin, London, 1936)

Lawrence, DH *Study of Thomas Hardy and Other Essays* (Cambridge, New York, 1985)

Leonard, Leigh Megan "A Missing Voice in Feminist Legal Theory: The Heterosexual Presumption" (1990) 12 *Women's Rights Law Reporter* 39

Leubsdorf , John "Presuppositions of Evidence Law" (2006) 91 *Iowa Law Review* 1209

Leubsdorf, John "Stories and Numbers" (1991) 13 *Cardozo Law Review* 455

Levit, Nancy "Listening to Tribal Legends: An Essay on Law and the Scientific Method" (1989) 58 *Fordham Law Review* 263

Lewis, John Underwood "Sir Edward Coke: His Theory of 'Artificial Reason' as a Context for Modern Basic Legal Theory" (1968) 84 *Law Quarterly Review* 330

Liddington, Jill *The Long Road to Greenham: Feminism and Anti-Militarism in Britain since 1820* (Virago, London, 1989)

Litowitz, Douglas *Postmodern Philosophy and Law* (University Press of Kansas, Kansas, 1997)

Llewellyn, Karl "Roscoe Pound" in Llewellyn *Jurisprudence: Realism in Theory and Practice* (University of Chicago Press, Chicago, 1962)

Llewellyn, Karl "Some Realism about Realism — Responding to Dean Pound" (1931) 44 *Harvard Law Review* 1222

Llewellyn, Karl "The Theory of Legal Science" (1931) 44 *Harvard Law Review* 697

Lloyd, Dennis *The Idea of Law* (Penguin, London, 1964)

Lloyd, Genevieve "The Man of Reason" (1979) 10 *Metaphilosophy* 19

Lloyd, Genevieve *The Man of Reason*: *"Male" and "Female" in Western Philosophy* (2nd ed, Routledge, London, 1993)

Locke, John *Two Treatises of Government*, Second Treatise (Cambridge University Press, Cambridge, 1967)

Lodge, David (ed) *20th Century Literary Criticism, a Reader* (Longman, Harlow, Essex, 1972)

Louis Wolcher, "The Man in the Room: Remarks on Derrida's *Force of Law*" (1996) 7 *Law and Critique* 35

Lücke, HK "The Common Law: Judicial Impartiality and Judge-Made Law" (1982) 98 *Law Quarterly Review* 29

Lugones, María "Hispaneando y Lesbiando: On Sarah Hoagland's *Lesbian Ethics*" (1990) 5 *Hypatia* 139

Lugones, María "Playfulness, 'World'-Travelling, and Loving Perception" (1987) 2 *Hypatia* 3

Lugones, María "Purity, Impurity and Separation" (1994) 19 *Signs* 458

Lyotard, Jean-François *The Differend: Phrases in Dispute* (Manchester University Press, Manchester, 1988)

Lyotard, Jean-François *The Postmodern Condition: A Report on Knowledge* (University of Minnesota Press, Minneapolis, 1984)

Lyotard, Jean-François and Jean-Loup Thébaud *Just Gaming* (University of Minnesota Press, Minneapolis, 1985)

MacCormick, Neil "Ethical Positivism and the Practical Force of Rules" in Tom Campbell and Jeffrey Goldworthy (eds) *Judicial Power, Democracy, and Legal Positivism* (Aldershot, Dartmouth, 2000)

MacCormick, Neil "Natural Law and the Separation of Law and Morals" in Robert P George (ed) *Natural Law Theory: Contemporary Essays* (Clarendon Press, Oxford, 1992)

MacCormick, Neil "Natural Law Reconsidered" (1981) 1 *Oxford Journal of Legal Studies* 99

MacCormick, Neil "Reconstruction After Deconstruction: A Response to CLS" (1990) 10 *Oxford Journal of Legal Studies* 539

MacCormick, Neil *Questioning Sovereignty: Law, State, and Nation in the European Commonwealth* (Oxford University Press, Oxford, 1999)

MacKinnon, Catharine "Feminism, Marxism, Method and the State: Toward Feminist Jurisprudence" (1983) 8 *Signs* 635

MacKinnon, Catharine "Feminism, Marxism, Method, and the State: An Agenda for Theory" (1983) 7 *Signs* 515

MacKinnon, Catharine "From Practice to Theory, or What is a White Woman Anyway?" (1991) 41 *Yale Journal of Law and Feminism* 13

MacKinnon, Catharine "Points Against Postmodernism" (2000) 75 *Chicago-Kent Law Review* 687

MacKinnon, Catharine *Feminism Unmodified: Discourses on Life and Law* (Harvard University Press, Cambridge Mass, 1987)

MacKinnon, Catharine *Only Words* (Harvard University Press, Cambridge, Mass, 1993)

MacKinnon, Catharine *Toward a Feminist Theory of the State* (Harvard University Press, Cambridge Mass, 1989)

Mahmood, Saba *Politics of Piety: The Islamic Revival and the Feminist Subject* (Princeton University Press, Princeton, 2005)

Maine, Henry *Ancient Law* (Murray, London, 1888)

Maitland, Frederic William "Outlines of English Legal History 560-1600" in HAL Fisher (ed) *The Collected Papers of Frederic William Maitland* (Cambridge University Press, Cambridge, 1911)

Malkin, Ian and Joan Wright "Product Liability under the Trade Practices Act — Adequately Compensating for Personal Injury?" (1993) 1 *Torts Law Journal* 63

Malloy, Robin and Christopher Braun (eds) *Law and Economics: New and Critical Perspectives* (Peter Lang, New York, 1995)

Malloy, Robin *Law in a Market Context: An Introduction to Market Concepts in Legal Reasoning* (Cambridge University Press, Cambridge, 2004)

Manderson, Desmond "Beyond the Provincial: Space, Aesthetics, and Modernist Legal Theory" (1996) 20 *Melbourne University Law Review* 1048

Manger, Tara "A Less than 'Pacific' Solution for Asylum Seekers in Australia" (2004) 16 *International Journal of Refugee Law* 53

Manji, Irshad *The Trouble with Islam: A Muslim's Call for Reform in Her Faith* (Random House, NSW, 2003)

Marcus, Julie *Australian Race Relations, 1788-1993* (Allen and Unwin, Sydney, 1994)

Markey, Howard "Jurisprudence or 'Juriscience'?" (1984) 25 *William and Mary Law Review* 525

Markus, Andrew *Race: John Howard and the Remaking of Australia* (Allen and Unwin, Sydney, 2001)

Marmor, Andrei "Legal Positivism: Still Descriptive and Morally Neutral" (2006) 26 *Oxford Journal of Legal Studies* 683

Marotta, Vince "The Ambivalence of Borders: The Bicultural and the Multicultural" in Docker and Fisher (eds) *Race, Colour and Identity in Australia and New Zealand* (UNSW Press, Sydney, 2000)

Martin, Biddy "Sexualities Without Genders and Other Queer Utopias" (1994) 24.2 *diacritics* 104

Martin, Brian "Eliminating State Crime by Abolishing the State" in Ross (ed) *Controlling State Crime: An Introduction* (Garland, New York, 1995)

Martin, Robyn "A Feminist View of the Reasonable Man: An Alternative Approach to Liability in Negligence for Personal Injury" (1994) 23 *Anglo-American Law Review* 334

Mason, Anthony "Future Directions in Australian Law" (1987) 13 *Monash University Law Review* 149

Mathews, Ben "Why Deconstruction is Beneficial" (2000) 4 *Flinders Journal of Law Reform* 81

Matsuda, Mari "Public Response to Racist Speech: Considering the Victim's Story" (1989) 87 *Michigan Law Review* 2320

Matsuda, Mari "When the First Quail Calls: Multiple Consciousness as Jurisprudential Method" (1988) 11 *Women's Rights Law Reporter* 7

Maxwell, Anne "Ethnicity and Education: Biculturalism in New Zealand" in David Bennett (ed) *Multicultural Studies: Rethinking Difference and Identity* (Routledge, London, 1998)

McCormick, John "Derrida on Law; Or, Poststructuralism Gets Serious" (2001) 29 *Political Theory* 395

McGlade, Hannah and Jeannine Purdy "From Theory to Practice: Or What is a Homeless Yamatji Grandmother Anyway?" (1998) 11 *Australian Feminist Law Journal* 137

McHugh, Michael "The Law-making Function of the Judicial Process — Part 2" (1988) 62 *Australian Law Journal* 116

McNay, Lois *Foucault and Feminism* (Polity Press, Cambridge, 1992)

McRae, Heather, Garth Nettheim, and Laura Beacroft *Indigenous Legal Issues: Commentary and Materials* (3rd ed, Lawbook Co., Pyrmont NSW, 2003)

Menkel-Meadow, Carrie "Feminist Legal Theory, Critical Legal Studies, and Legal Education or 'The Fem-Crits Go to Law School'" (1988) 38 *Journal of Legal Education* 61

Mensch, Elizabeth "The History of Mainstream Legal Thought" in David Kairys (ed) *The Politics of Law: A Progressive Critique* (rev ed, Pantheon Books, New York, 1990)

Merchant, Carolyn *The Death of Nature: Women, Ecology, and the Scientific Revolution* (Harper and Rowe, San Francisco, 1980)

Mercuro, Nicholas and Steven Medema *Economics and the Law: From Posner to Post-Modernism and Beyond* (2nd ed, Princeton University Press, Princeton, 2006)

Merry, Sally Engle "New Legal Realism and the Ethnography of Transnational Law" (2006) 31 *Law and Social Inquiry* 975

Mill, John Stuart "On Liberty" in Mill *Utilitarianism* (12th ed, Routledge, London 1895)

Millet, Kate *Sexual Politics* (Abacus, London, 1972 c1970)

Mills, Charles W *The Racial Contract* (Cornell University Press, Ithaca NY, 1997)

Minda, Gary *Postmodern Legal Movements: Law and Jurisprudence at Century's End* (New York University Press, New York, 1995)

Minh-ha, Trinh T "Not You/Like You: Postcolonial Women and the Interlocking Questions of Identity and Difference" in Anne McClintock, Aamir Mufti, and Ella Shohat (eds) *Dangerous Liaisons: Gender, Nation, and Postcolonial Perspectives* (University of Minnesota Press, Minneapolis, 1997)

Mir-Hosseini, Ziba "The Construction of Gender in Islamic Legal Thought and Strategies for Reform" (2003) 1 *HAWWA: Journal of Women in the Middle East and the Islamic World* 1

Mirza, Qudsia "Islam, Hybridity and the Laws of Marriage" (2000) 14 *Australian Feminist Law Journal* 1

Mitrophanous, Eleni "Soft Positivism" (1997) 17 *Oxford Journal of Legal Studies* 621

Modood, Tariq "'Difference', Cultural Racism and Anti-Racism" in Pnina Werbner and Tariq Modood (eds) *Debating Cultural Hybridity: Multi-Cultural Identities and the Politics of Anti-Racism* (Zed Books, London, 1997)

Moles, Robert "Law and Morality — How to Do Things With Confusion" (1986) 37 *Northern Ireland Legal Quarterly* 29

Moraga, Cherrie and Gloria Anzaldúa (eds) *This Bridge Called My Back: Writings By Radical Women of Color* (Kitchen Table, Women of Color Press, New York, 1981)

Moran, Leslie J, Daniel Monk and Sarah Beresford (eds) *Legal Queeries: Lesbian, Gay and Transgender Legal Studies* (Cassell, London, 1998)

Moreton-Robinson, Aileen "Troubling Business: Difference and Whiteness Within Feminism" (2000) 15 *Australian Feminist Studies* 343

Moreton-Robinson, Aileen *Talkin' Up to the White Woman: Indigenous Women and Feminism* (University of Queensland Press, St Lucia, 2000)

Morgan, Robin (ed) *Sisterhood is Powerful: An Anthology of Writings from the Women's Liberation Movement* (Vintage Books, New York, 1970)

Morgan, Wayne "Queer Law: Identity, Culture, Diversity, Law" (1995) 5 *Australian Gay and Lesbian Law Journal* 1

Morrison, Toni *Playing in the Dark: Whiteness and the Literary Imagination* (Harvard University Press, Cambridge Mass, 1992)

Motha, Stewart "The Sovereign Event in a Nation's Law" (2002) 13 *Law and Critique* 311

Motha, Stewart "Veiled Women and the Affect of Religion in Democracy" (2007) 34 *Journal of Law and Society* 138

Moya, Paula "Chicana Feminism and Postmodernist Theory" (2000) 26 *Signs* 441

Munger, Frank and Caroll Seron "Critical Legal Studies versus Critical Legal Theory: A Comment on Method" (1984) 6 *Law and Policy* 257

Munro, Vanessa and Carl Stychin (eds) *Sexuality and the Law: Feminist Engagements* (Routledge-Cavendish, Abingdon, 2007)

Munt, Sally (ed) *Butch/Femme: Inside Lesbian Gender* (London, Cassell, 1998)

Murphy, Jay Wesley "John Dewey — A Philosophy of Law for Democracy" (1960) 14 *Vanderbilt Law Review* 291

Murphy, Mark "Natural Law Jurisprudence" (2003) 9 *Legal Theory* 241

Naffine, Ngaire "Possession: Erotic Love and the Law of Rape" (1994) 57 *Modern Law Review* 10

Naffine, Ngaire "Who are Law's Persons: From Cheshire Cats to Responsible Subjects" (2003) 66 *Modern Law Review* 346

Naffine, Ngaire "Windows on the Legal Mind: The Evocation of Rape in Legal Writings" (1992) 18 *Melbourne University Law Review* 741

Naffine, Ngaire *Law and the Sexes: Explorations in Feminist Jurisprudence* (Allen and Unwin, Sydney, 1990)

Nagel, Thomas *The View from Nowhere* (Oxford University Press, Oxford, 1986)

Nain, Tang "Black Women, Sexism and Racism: Black or Antiracist Feminism?"; Chandra Mohanty "Under Western Eyes: Feminist Scholarship and Colonial Discourses" (1988) 30 *Feminist Review* 61

Nakayama, Thomas and Judith Martin (eds) *Whiteness: The Communication of Social Identity* (Sage Publications, Thousand Oaks, 1999)

Nakayama, Thomas and Robert Krizek "Whiteness as a Strategic Rhetoric" in Thomas Nakayama and Judith Martin (eds) *Whiteness: The Communication of Social Identity* (Sage Publications, Thousand Oaks, 1999)

Neacsu, E Dana "CLS Stands for Critical Legal Studies, If Anyone Remembers" (2000) 8 *Journal of Law and Policy* 415

Newman, David and Anssi Paasi "Fences and Neighbours in the Postmodern World: Boundary Narratives in Political Geography" (1998) 22 *Progress in Human Geography* 186

Ní Aoláin, Fionnuala "Political Violence and Gender During Times of Transition" (2006) 15 *Columbia Journal of Gender and Law* 829

Nicholson, Linda (ed) *Feminism/Postmodernism* (Routledge, New York, 1990)

Nicholson, Linda "Interpreting Gender" (1994) 20 *Signs* 79

Nietzsche, Friedrich *Beyond Good and Evil* (Gateway, Chicago, 1955)

Nietzsche, Friedrich *Human, All Too Human* (Russell & Russell, New York, 1964)

Nietzsche, FW "On Truth and Lies in a Nonmoral Sense" in FW Nietzsche *Philosophy and Truth: Selections from Nietzsche's Notebooks of the Early 1870s* Breazeale (ed) (London, Humanities Press, 1979)

Nousiainen, Kevät Åsa Gunnarsson, Karin Lundström, and Johanna Niemi-Kiesiläinen (eds) *Responsible Selves: Women in the Nordic Legal Culture* (Ashgate, Aldershot, 2001)

Nunn, Kenneth "Law as a Eurocentric Enterprise (1997) 15 *Law and Inequality* 323

Nussbaum, Martha "Platonic Love and Colorado Law: The Relevance of Ancient Greek Norms to Modern Sexual Controversies" (1994) 80 *Valparaiso Law Review* 1515

Nussbaum, Martha "The Feminist Critique of Liberalism" in Martha C Nussbaum *Sex and Social Justice* (Oxford University Press, New York, 2000)

Nussbaum, Martha "The Professor of Parody: The Hip Defeatism of Judith Butler" (1999) 22 *The New Republic*

Nussbaum, Martha "Women and Equality: The Capabilities Approach" (1999) 138 (3) *International Labour Review* 227

O'Connell, Rory "Do We Need Unicorns When We Have Law" (2005) 18 *Ratio Juris* 484

O'Donnell, Therese "Executioners, Bystanders and Victims: Collective Guilt, the Legacy of Denazificaiton and the Birth of Twentieth-Century Transitional Justice" (2005) 25 *Legal Studies* 627

O'Donovan, Katherine *Sexual Divisions in Law* (Weidenfeld and Nicolson, London, 1985)

O'Driscoll, Sally "Outlaw Readings: Beyond Queer Theory" (1996) 22 *Signs* 30

O'Hear, Anthony *Introduction to the Philosophy of Science* (Clarendon Press, Oxford, 1989)

O'Shane, Pat "Is There Any Relevance in the Women's Movement for Aboriginal Women?" (1976) 12 *Refractory Girl* 31

Okin, Susan Moller "Is Multiculturalism Bad for Women?" in Joshua Cohen and Matthew Howard (eds) *Is Multiculturalism Bad For Women?* (Princeton University Press, New Jersey, 1999)

Olivecrona, Karl *Law as Fact* (2nd ed, Stevens and Sons, London, 1971)

Oloka-Onyango, J and Sylvia Tamale "'The Personal is Political,' or Why Women's Rights are indeed Human Rights: an African Perspective" (1995) 17 *Human Rights Quarterly* 691

Parkinson, Patrick *Tradition and Change in Australian Law* (3rd ed, Lawbook Co., Pyrmont NSW, 2005)

Parsons, Keith (ed) *The Science Wars: Debating Scientific Knowledge and Technology* (Prometheus Books, Amherst NY, 2003)

Pateman, Carole *The Sexual Contract* (Polity Press, Cambridge, 1988)

Patterson, Edwin "The Case Method in American Legal Education: Its Origins and Objectives" (1951) 4 *Journal of Legal Education* 1

Patterson, Rachel "The Minimum Content of Law: A Critique of Hart's Descriptive Theory of Positive and Natural Law" (2005) 8 *Canberra Law Review* 9

Paulson, Stanley "Four Phases in Hans Kelsen's Legal Theory? Reflections on a Periodization" (1998) 18 *Oxford Journal of Legal Studies* 153

Paulson, Stanley and Bonnie Litschewski Paulson (eds) *Normativity and Norms: Critical Perspectives on Kelsenian Themes* (Clarendon Press, Oxford, 1998)

Pavlich, George "Experiencing Critique" (2005) 16 *Law and Critique* 95

Perea, Juan "The Black/White Binary Paradigm of Race: The 'Normal Science' of American Racial Thought" (1997) 85 *California Law Review* 1213

Perera, Suvendrini "What Is a Camp...?" (2002) 1 (1) *borderlands e-journal*

Perrin, Colin "Approaching Anxiety: The Insistence of the Postcolonial in the Declaration of the Rights of Indigenous People" (1995) 6 *Law and Critique* 55

Phillips, Anne "Feminism and Liberalism Revisited: Has Martha Nussbaum Got It Right?" (2001) 8 *Constellations* 249

Piercy, Marge "The Grand Coolie Damn" in Robin Morgan (ed) *Sisterhood is Powerful: An Anthology of Writings from the Women's Liberation Movement* (Vintage Books, New York, 1970)

Pippin, Robert *Modernism as a Philosophical Problem: On the Dissatisfactions of European High Culture* (Basil Blackwell, Cambridge Mass, 1991)

Plato *The Republic* (Penguin, Harmondsworth, 1987)

Plucknett, TFT *Legislation of Edward I* (Clarendon Press, Oxford, 1949)

Pocock, Frederick *The Ancient Constitution and the Feudal Law* (Norton, New York, reprinted 1967 c1957)

Pollock, Frederick "Oxford Law Studies" (1886) 8 *Law Quarterly Review* 453

Popper, Karl *Conjectures and Refutations: The Growth of Scientific Knowledge* (3rd ed, Routledge Kegan Paul, London, 1969)

Popper, Karl *Logic of Scientific Discovery* (Unwin Hyman, London, 1959)

Posner, Richard *Economic Analysis of Law* (3rd ed, Little, Brown, Boston, 1986)

Posner, Richard *Sex and Reason* (Harvard University Press, Cambridge Mass, 1992)

Posner, Richard *The Problems of Jurisprudence* (Harvard University Press, Cambridge Mass, 1990)

Post, Robert "Law and Cultural Conflict" (2003) 78 *Chicago-Kent Law Review* 485

Postema, Gerald "Some Roots of our Notion of Precedent" in Goldstein (ed) *Precedent in Law* (Clarendon Press, Oxford, 1987)

Postema, Gerald *Bentham and the Common Law Tradition* (Clarendon Press, Oxford, 1989)

Pound, Roscoe "Law and the Science of Law in Recent Theories" (1934) 43 *Yale Law Journal* 525

Pound, Roscoe "Mechanical Jurisprudence" (1908) 8 *Columbia Law Review* 605

Pound, Roscoe "The Call for a Realist Jurisprudence" (1930) 44 *Harvard Law Review* 697

powell, john "Racial Realism or Racial Despair?" (1992) 24 *Connecticut Law Review* 533

powell, john a "The Multiple Self: Exploring Between and Beyond Modernity and Postmodernity" (1997) 81 *Minnesota Law Review* 1481

Priest, George "The New Scientism in Legal Scholarship: A Comment on Clark and Posner" (1981) 90 *Yale Law Journal* 1284

Proudhon, PJ *General Idea of the Revolution in the Nineteenth Century* (John Beverley Robinson trans, Haskell House Publishers, New York, 1969)

Pryor, Judith "Reconciling the Irreconcilable? Activating the Differences in the Mabo Decision and the Treaty of Waitangi" (2005) 15 *Social Semiotics* 81

Pugliese, Joe "Race as Category Crisis: Whiteness and the Topical Assignation of Race" (2002) 12 *Social Semiotics* 149

Pulkkinen, Tuija *The Postmodern and Political Agency* (SoPhi, Jyväskylä, 2000)

Putnam, Hilary "The 'Corroboration' of Theories" in Boyd, Gaspar, and Trout (eds) *The Philosophy of Science* (MIT, Cambridge Mass, 1991)

Pylkkänen, Anu "The Responsible Self: Relational Gender Construction in the History of Finnish Law" in Kevät Nousiainen, Åsa Gunnarsson, Karin Lundström, and Johanna Niemi-Kiesiläinen (eds) *Responsible Selves: Women in the Nordic Legal Culture* (Ashgate, Aldershot, 2001)

Quayson, Ato *Postcolonialism: Theory, Practice, or Process* (Polity Press, Cambridge, 2000)

Quraishi, Asifa "Her Honour: An Islamic Critique of the Rape Laws of Pakistan from a Woman-Sensitive Perspective" (1997) 18 *Michigan Journal of International Law* 287

Ratnapala, Suri "Book Review" (1995) 16 *New Zealand Universities Law Review* 326

Rattansi, Ali and Sallie Westwood *Racism, Modernity and Identity: On the Western Front* (Polity Press, Oxford, 1994)

Raz, Joseph "Legal Principles and the Limits of Law" (1972) 81 *Yale Law Journal* 823

Razack, Sherene "Imperilled Muslim Women, Dangerous Muslim Men, and Civilised Europeans: Legal and Social Responses to Forced Marriages" (2004) 12 *Feminist Legal Studies* 129

Reid "The Judge as Lawmaker" (1972) 12 *Journal of the Society of Public Teachers of Law* (ns) 22

Rich, Adrienne "Compulsory Heterosexuality and Lesbian Existence" (1980) 5 (4) *Signs: Journal of Women in Culture and Society* 631

Richardson, Megan and Gillian Hadfield (eds) *The Second Wave of Law and Economics* (Federation Press, Sydney, 1999)

Robinson, Reginald Leamon "'Expert' Knowledge: Introductory Comments on Race Consciousness" (2000) 20 *Boston College Third World Law Journal* 145

Robinson, Reginald Leamon "The Shifting Race Consciousness Matrix and the Multiracial Category Movement: A Critical Reply to Professor Hernandez" (2000) 20 *Boston College Third World Law Journal* 231

Robson, Ruthann *Lesbian (Out) Law: Survival Under the Rule of Law* (Firebrand Books, Ithaca, 1992)

Robson, Ruthann *Sappho Goes to Law School: Fragments in Lesbian Legal Theory* (Columbia University Press, New York, 1998)

Roithmayr, Daria "Left Over Rights" (2001) 22 *Cardozo Law Review* 1113

Rothfield, Philipa "Alternative Epistemologies, Politics and Feminism" (1991) 30 *Social Analysis* 54

Rouse, Joseph *Knowledge and Power: Toward a Political Philosophy of Science* (Cornell University Press, Ithaca NY, 1987)

Rudy, Kathy "Radical Feminism, Lesbian Separatism, and Queer Theory" (2001) 27 *Feminist Studies* 191

Said, Edward *Orientalism* (Penguin, Harmondsworth, 1978)

Sardar, Ziauddin "Above, Beyond, and at the Center of the Science Wars: A Postcolonial Reading" in Keith Ashman and Philip Baringer (eds) *After the Science Wars* (London, Routledge, 2001)

Sartre, Jean-Paul "Colonialism is a System" (2001) 3 *Interventions* 127

Sartre, Jean-Paul *Existentialism and Human Emotions* (Philosophical Library, New York, 1957)

Scavone, Robert "Natural Law, Obligation and the Common Good: What Finnis Can't Tell Us" (1985) 43 *University of Toronto Faculty of Law Review* 90

Schlegel, John Henry "Notes Toward an Intimate, Opinionated, and Affectionate History of the Conference on Critical Legal Studies" (1984) 35 *Stanford Law Review* 391

Schmutz, Set Lee "No Longer Mute" (1997) 3 *Law/Text/Culture* 7

Schofield, Philip "Jeremy Bentham and Nineteenth-Century English Jurisprudence" (1991) 12 *Journal of Legal History* 58

Schroeder, Jeanne "Abduction from the Seraglio: Feminist Methodologies and the Logic of Imagination" (1991) 70 *Texas Law Review* 109

Schroeder, Jeanne "Just So Stories: Posnerian Methodology" (2001) 22 *Cardozo Law Review* 351

Schroeder, Jeanne "Rationality in Law and Economics Scholarship" (2000) 79 *Oregon Law Review* 147

Schwartz, Louis "With Gun and Camera Through Darkest CLS-Land" (1984) 36 *Stanford Law Review* 413

Scott, Joan "Symptomatic Politics: The Banning of Islamic Head Scarves in French Public Schools" (2005) 23 *French Politics, Culture and Society* 106

Scutt, Jocelyn *Women and the Law: Commentary and Materials* (Law Book Company, Sydney, 1990)

Sebok, Anthony *Legal Positivism in American Jurisprudence* (Cambridge University Press, New York, 1998)

Sen, Amartya "Rational Fools: A Critique of the Behavioural Foundations of Economic Theory" (1977) *Philosophy and Public Affairs* 317

Shachar, Ayelet "Group Identity and Women's Rights in Family Law: The Perils of Multicultural Accommodation" (1988) 6 *Journal of Political Philosophy* 285

Shah, Prakash *Legal Pluralism in Conflict: Coping with Cultural Diversity in Law* (Glasshouse Press, London, 2005)

Sharpe, Andrew "Institutionalizing Heterosexuality: The Legal Exclusion of 'Impossible' (Trans)sexualities" in Leslie J Moran, Daniel Monk and Sarah Beresford (eds) *Legal Queeries: Lesbian, Gay and Transgender Legal Studies* (Cassell, London, 1998)

Shearmur, Jeremy "Natural Law Without Metaphysics? The Case of John Finnis" (1990) 38 *Cleveland State Law Review* 123

Sheehan, Katherine "Caring for Deconstruction" (2000) 12 *Yale Journal of Law and Feminism* 85

Sheridan, Alan *Michel Foucault: The Will to Truth* (Tavistock Publications, London, 1980)

Shiva, Vandana *Biopiracy: The Plunder of Nature and Knowledge* (Green, Dartington, 1997)

Showalter, Elaine (ed) *The New Feminist Criticism: Essays on Women, Literature, and Theory* (Virago, London, 1986)

Showalter, Elaine *A Literature of Their Own: British Women Novelists from Brontë to Lessing* (rev ed, Virago, London, 1982)

Siegel, Neil "Sen and the Hart of Jurisprudence: A Critique of the Economic Analysis of Judicial Behaviour" (1999) 87 *California Law Review* 1581

Silverman, Kaja *The Subject of Semiotics* (Oxford University Press, New York, 1983)

Simmonds, Neil *Central Issues in Jurisprudence: Justice, Laws and Rights* (Sweet and Maxwell, London, 1986)

Simpson, Brian "The Common Law and Legal Theory" in William Twining (ed) *Legal Theory and the Common Law* (Basil Blackwell, Oxford, 1986)

Singer, Barbara "The Reason of the Common Law" (1983) 37 *University of Miami Law Review* 797

Singer, Joseph "The Player and the Cards: Nihilism and Legal Theory" (1984) 94 *Yale Law Journal* 1

Smart, Carol *Feminism and the Power of Law* (Routledge, London, 1989)

Smith, Barbara "Racism and Women's Studies" in Anzaldúa (ed) *Making Face, Making Soul: Haciendo Caras* (Aunt Lute Books, San Francisco, 1990)

Smith, Barbara "Toward a Black Feminist Criticism" in Showalter (ed) *The New Feminist Criticism: Essays on Women, Literature, and Theory* (Virago, London, 1986)

Smith, Carole "The Sovereign State v Foucault: Law and Disciplinary Power" (2000) 48 *The Sociological Review* 283

Smith, George "*Dr Bonham's Case* and the Modern Significance of Lord Coke's Influence" (1966) 41 *Washington Law Review* 297

Snowden, Frank *Before Color Prejudice: The Ancient View of Blacks* (Harvard University Press, Cambridge Mass, 1983)

Soifer, Aviam "Confronting Deep Strictures: Robinson, Rickey, and Racism" (1985) 6 *Cardozo Law Review* 865

Sokal, Alan "Transgressing the Boundaries: Toward a Transformative Hermeneutics of Quantum Gravity" (1996) 46-47 *Social Text* 217

Sokal, Alan and Jean Bricmont *Fashionable Nonsense: Postmodern Intellectuals Abuse of Science* (Picador, New York, 1998)

Sollers, Werner "Who Is Ethnic?" from Sollers *Beyond Ethnicity: Consent and Descent in American Culture* (Oxford University Press, New York, 1986) extract reprinted in Bill Ashcroft, Gareth Griffiths, and Helen Tiffin (eds) *The Postcolonial Studies Reader* (Routledge, London, 1995)

Sophocles *The Theban Plays* "Antigone" (Penguin, Baltimore, 1947)

Spelman, Elizabeth *Inessential Woman: Problems of Exclusion in Feminist Thought* (Beacon Press, Boston, 1988)

Spiegel, Stephen "John Chipman Gray and the Moral Basis of Classical Legal Thought" (2001) 86 *Iowa Law Review* 1513

Spivak, Gayatri Chakravorty "Can the Subaltern Speak?" in Cary Nelson and Laurence Grossberg (eds) *Marxism and the Interpretation of Culture* (University of Illinois Press, 1988)

Spivak, Gayatri Chakravorty "Displacement and the Discourse of Woman" in Antony Easthope and Kate McGowan (eds) *A Critical and Cultural Theory Reader* (2nd ed, University of Toronto Press, Buffalo, Toronto, 2004)

Spivak, Gayatri Chakravorty *A Critique of Postcolonial Reason: Toward a History of the Vanishing Present* (Harvard University Press, Cambridge Mass, 1999)

Spivak, Gayatri Chakravorty *The Postcolonial Critic: Interviews, Strategies, Dialogues,* Sarah Harasym (ed) (Routledge, New York, 1990)

St German, Christopher *Doctor and Student* (The Selden Society, London, 1974)

Stacy, Helen *Postmodernism and Law: Jurisprudence in a Fragmenting World* (Ashgate, Aldershot, 2001)

Standen, Jeffrey "Critical Legal Studies as an Anti-Positivist Phenomenon" (1986) 72 *Virginia Law Review* 983

Stang Dahl, Tove *Women's Law: An Introduction to Feminist Jurisprudence* (trans by Ronald L Craig, Norwegian University Press, Oslo, 1987)

Stanley, Liz and Sue Wise "But the Empress Has No Clothes!" (2000) 1 *Feminist Theory* 261

Steinberg, Shirley "Addressing the Crisis of Whiteness" in Joe Kincheloe et al (eds) *White Reign: Deploying Whiteness in America* (St Martin's Press, New York, 1997)

Stewart, Iain "Closure and the Legal Norm: An Essay in Critique of Law" (1987) 50 *Modern Law Review* 908

Stewart, Iain "Kelsen Tomorrow" (1998) 51 *Current Legal Problems* 181

Stewart, Iain "The Critical Legal Science of Hans Kelsen" (1990) 17 *Journal of Law and Society* 273

Stick, John "Can Nihilism be Pragmatic?" (1986) 100 *Harvard Law Review* 332

Stigler, George "Law or Economics?" (1992) 35 *Journal of Law and Economics* 455

Stokes, Geoffrey "Citizenship and Aboriginality: Two Conceptions of Identity in Aboriginal Political Thought" in Geoffrey Stokes (ed) *The Politics of Identity in Australia* (Cambridge University Press, Cambridge, 1997)

Stone, Julius "Mystery and Mystique in the Basic Norm" (1963) 26 *Modern Law Review* 34

Stone, Julius "The Ratio of the Ratio Decidendi" (1959) 22 *Modern Law Review* 597

Stychin, Carl *Law's Desire: Sexuality and the Limits of Justice* (Routledge, London, 1995)

Stychin, Carl and Didi Herman (eds) *Sexuality in the Legal Arena* (Athlone Press, London, 2000)

Sugarman, David "Legal Theory, the Common Law Mind, and the Making of the Textbook Tradition" in William Twining (ed) *Legal Theory and the Common Law Mind* (Basil Blackwell, Oxford, 1986)

Susan Arndt "African Gender Trouble and African Womanism: An Interview With Chikwenye Ogunyemi and Wanjira Muthoni" (2000) 25 *Signs* 709

Svensson, Eva-Maria, Anu Pylkkänen and Johanna Niemi-Kiesiläinen (eds) *Nordic Equality at a Crossroads: Feminist Legal Studies Coping with Difference* (Ashgate, Aldershot, 2004)

Swift, Jonathon *Gulliver's Travels* (Harmonsworth Penguin, 1967)

Tamanaha, Brian "A Non-Essentialist Version of Legal Pluralism" (2000) 27 *Journal of Law and Society* 296

Tamanaha, Brian *General Jurisprudence of Law and Society* (Oxford University Press, Oxford, 2001)

Tan, Seow Hon "Validity and Obligation in Natural Law Theory: Does Finnis Come Too Close to Positivism" (2003) 15 *Regent University Law Review* 195

Tang Nain, Gemma "Black Women, Sexism and Racism: Black or Antiracist Feminism?" (1991) 37 *Feminist Review* 1

Taub, Nadine and Elizabeth Schneider "Women's Subordination and the Role of Law" in David Kairys (ed) *The Politics of Law: A Progressive Critique* (Pantheon Books, New York, 1990)

Taylor Mill, Harriet *Enfranchisement of Women*, and John Stuart Mill *The Subjection of Women* (Virago, London, 1983)

Tehranian, John "Performing Whiteness: Naturalization Litigation and the Construction of Racial Identity in America" (2000) 109 *Yale Law Journal* 816

Thompson, Denise "The Sex/Gender Distinction: A Reconsideration" (1989) 10 *Australian Feminist Studies* 23

Thornton, Margaret "Embodying the Citizen" in *Public and Private: Feminist Legal Debates* (Oxford University Press, Melbourne, 1995)

Thornton, Margaret "Feminism and the Contradictions of Law Reform" (1991) 19 *International Journal of the Sociology of Law* 453

Thornton, Margaret "Feminist Jurisprudence: Illusion or Reality" (1986) 3 *Australian Journal of Law and Society* 5

Thornton, Margaret *Portia Lost in the Groves of Academe Wondering What to Do about Legal Education* (La Trobe University Legal Studies, Melbourne, 1991)

Töllborg, Dennis "Law as Value" (1998) 4 *Archiv für Rechts und Sozialphilosophie* 489

Tolstoy, Leo "The Slavery of Our Times" in Tolstoy *Essays from Tula* (Sheppard Press, London, 1948)

Trebilcock, Michael "The Value and Limits of Law and Economics" in Megan Richardson and Gillian Hadfield (eds) *The Second Wave of Law and Economics* (Federation Press, Sydney, 1999)

Trubeck, David "Where the Action Is: Critical Legal Studies and Empiricism" (1984) 36 *Stanford Law Review* 575

Tuori, Kaarlo *Critical Legal Positivism* (Ashgate, Aldershot, 2002)

Ture, Kwame and Charles Hamilton "Black Power: Its Need and Substance" from *Black Power and the Politics of Liberation* (Vintage Books, New York, 1992) reproduced in Bulmer, Martin and John Solomos (eds) *Racism* (Oxford University Press, Oxford, 1999)

Tushnet, Mark "An Essay on Rights" (1984) 62 *Texas Law Review* 1363

Tushnet, Mark "Critical Legal Studies: A Political History" (1991) 100 *Yale Law Journal* 515

Tushnet, Mark "Critical Legal Theory (Without Modifiers) in the United States" (2005) 13 *Journal of Political Philosophy* 99

Tushnet, Mark "Post-Realist Legal Scholarship" (1980) 15 *Journal of the Society of Public Teachers of Law* 20

Twining, William "The Bad Man Revisited" (1973) 58 *Cornell Law Review* 275

Twining, William *Karl Llewellyn and the Realist Movement* (Weidenfeld and Nicolson, London, 1973)

Ulen, Thomas "Book Review: Law's Order: What Economics Has to Do With Law and Why it Matters" (2001) 41 *Santa Clara Law Review* 643

Unger, Roberto Mangabeira *The Critical Legal Studies Movement* (Harvard University Press, Cambridge Mass, 1983)

Vaihinger, Hans *The Philosophy of As-If: A System of the Theoretical, Practical, and Religious Fictions* (Routledge Kegan Paul, London, 1965)

van Krieken, Robert et al *Sociology: Themes and Perspectives* (3rd ed, Pearson Longman, NSW, 2006)

van Maarseveen, H "Anarchism and the Theory of Political Law" in Holterman and van Maarseveen (eds) *Law and Anarchism* (Black Rose Books, Montreal, 1984)

Veitch, Scott (ed) *Law and the Politics of Reconciliation* (Ashgate, Aldershot, 2007)

Veljanovski, Cento "The Economic Approach to Law: A Critical Introduction" (1980) 7 *British Journal of Law and Society* 158

Veljanovski, Cento *Economic Principles of Law* (Cambridge University Press, Cambridge, 2007)

Wacquant, Loïc "Critical Thought as Solvent of *Doxa*" (2004) 11 *Constellations* 97

Waithe, Mary Ellen (ed) *A History of Women Philosophers* (Martinus Nijhoffs, Dordrecht, 1987 c1995)

Walby, Sylvia "Against Epistemological Chasms: The Science Question in Feminism Revisited" (2001) 26 *Signs* 485

Walters, Suzanna Danuta "From Here to Queer: Radical Feminism, Postmodernism, and the Lesbian Menace (Or, Why Can't a Woman Be More Like a Fag?" (1996) 21 *Signs* 830

Waluchow, WJ "Herculean Positivism" (1985) 5 *Oxford Journal of Legal Studies* 187

Waluchow, WJ "The Many Faces of Legal Positivism" (1998) 48 *University of Toronto Law Journal* 387

Waluchow, WJ "The Weak Social Thesis" (1989) 9 *Oxford Journal of Legal Studies* 23

Waluchow, WJ *Inclusive Legal Positivism* (Oxford, Clarendon Press, 1994)

Ward, Ian "When Mercy Seasons Justice: Shakespeare's Woman Laywer" in Claire McGlynn (ed) *Legal Feminisms: Theory and Practice* (Ashgate, Aldershot, 1998)

Waring, Marilyn *Counting for Nothing: What Men Value and What Women Are Worth* (Allen and Unwin, Wellington NZ, 1988)

Watson, Irene "Aboriginal Laws and the Sovereignty of Terra Nullius" (2002) 1 *borderlands e-journal*

Watson, Irene "Buried Alive" (2002) 13 *Law and Critique* 253

Watson, Irene "Indigenous People's Law-Ways: Survival Against the Colonial State" (1997) 8 *Australian Feminist Law Journal* 39

Watson, Irene "Kalsowinyeri — Munaintya — In the Beginning" (2000) 4 *Flinders Journal of Law Reform* 3

Watson, Irene "Power of the Muldarbi, The Road to Its Demise" (1998) 11 *Australian Feminist Law Journal* 28

Weaver, Russell "Langdell's Legacy: Living with the Case Method" (1991) 36 *Villanova Law Review* 517

Weber, Sam "Deconstruction Before the Name: Some Preliminary Remarks on Deconstruction and Violence" (1991) 13 *Cardozo Law Review* 1181

Weed, Elizabeth and Naomi Schor (eds) *Feminism Meets Queer Theory* (Indiana University Press, Bloomington, 1997)

Weinrib, Ernest "Legal Formalism: On the Immanent Rationality of Law" (1988) 97 *Yale Law Journal* 949

Weinrib, Ernest "Natural Law and Rights" in Robert George (ed) *Natural Law Theory: Contemporary Essays* (Clarendon Press, Oxford, 1992)

Weinrib, Ernest "Why Legal Formalism" in Robert George (ed) *Natural Law Theory: Contemporary Essays* (Clarendon Press, Oxford, 1992)

Wendell, Susan "A (Qualified) Defense of Liberal Feminism" (1987) 2 *Hypatia* 65

Wesley-Smith, Peter "Theories of Adjudication and the Status of Stare Decisis" in Laurence Goldstein (ed) *Precedent in Law* (Clarendon Press, Oxford, 1987)

West, Robin "Deconstructing the CLS-Fem Split" (1986) 2 *Wisconsin Women's Law Journal* 85

West, Robin *Caring for Justice* (New York University Press, New York, 1997)

Westmoreland, Robert "Dworkin and Legal Pragmatism" (1991) 11 *Oxford Journal of Legal Studies* 174

White, TH *The Book of Beasts: Being a Translation From a Latin Bestiary of the Twelfth Century* (Cape, London, 1954)

Whitehead, Jason "From Criticism to Critique: Preserving the Radical Potential of Critical Legal Studies Through a Reexamination of Frankfurt School Critical Theory" (1999) 26 *Florida State University Law Review* 701

Whitford, Margaret "Reading Irigaray in the Nineties" in in Carolyn Burke, Naomi Schor, and Margaret Whitford (eds) *Engaging With Irigaray* (Columbia University Press, New York, 1994)

Whitford, Margaret *Luce Irigaray: Philosophy in the Feminine* (Routledge, London, 1991)

Wickham, Gary "Foucault, Law, and Power: A Reassessment" (2006) 33 *Journal of Law and Society* 596

Wiegers, Wanda "Economic Analysis of Law and 'Private Ordering': A Feminist Critique" (1992) 42 *University of Toronto Law Journal* 170

Wievorka, Michel "Is It So Difficult to Be Anti-Racist" in Pnina Werbner and Tariq Modood (eds) *Debating Cultural Hybridity: Multi-Cultural Identities and the Politics of Anti-Racism* (Zed Books, London, 1997)

Williams, Patricia "Alchemical Notes: Reconstructing Ideals from Deconstructed Rights" (1987) 22 *Harvard Civil Rights — Civil Liberties Law Review* 401

Williams, Patricia "On Being the Object of Property" (1988) 14 *Signs* 5

Williams, Robert "Documents of Barbarism: The Contemporary Legacy of European Racism and Colonialism in the Narrative Traditions of Federal Indian Law" (1989) 31 *Arizona Law Review* 237

Williams, Robert *The American Indian in Western Legal Thought* (Oxford University Press, New York, 1990)

Williams, Susan "Feminism's Search for the Feminine: Essentialism, Utopianism, and Community" (1990) 75 *Cornell Law Review* 700

Winter, Bronwyn "Who Counts (Or Doesn't Count) What as Feminist Theory? An Exercise in Dictionary Use" (2000) 1 *Feminist Theory* 105

Winterson, Jeanette *Sexing the Cherry* (Vintage, London, 1989)

Wittgenstein, Ludwig *Philosophical Investigations* (3rd ed, Basil Blackwell, Oxford, 1967)

Wittgenstein, Ludwig *Tractatus Logico-Philosophicus* (Routledge and Kegan Paul, London, 1922)

Wittig, Monique *Les Guerillères* (Owen, London, 1971)

Wittig, Monique *The Straight Mind and Other Essays* (Harvester Wheatsheaf, New York, 1992)

Wolf, Naomi *The Beauty Myth* (Vintage, London, 1990)

Wollstonecraft, Mary *Vindication of the Rights of Women* (2nd ed, Penguin, Harmondsworth, 1978)

Woodmansee, Martha "The Genius and the Copyright: Economic and Legal Conditions of the Emergence of the 'Author'" (1984) 17 *Eighteenth-Century Studies* 425

Wright, Shelley "Human Rights and Women's Rights" (1993) 18 *Alternative Law Journal* 113

Yablon, Charles "Forms" in Drucilla Cornell, Michel Rosenfeld, and David Gray Carlson (eds) *Deconstruction and the Possibility of Justice* (Routledge, New York, 1992)

Yale, DEC "Hobbes and Hale on Law, Legislation, and the Sovereign" (1972) 31 *Cambridge Law Journal* 121

Yilmaz, Ihsan "The Challenge of Postmodern Legality and Muslim Legal Pluralism in England" (2002) 28 *Journal of Ethnic and Migration Studies* 343

Yntema, Hessel "The Rational Basis of Legal Science" (1931) 31 *Columbia Law Review* 925

Young, Claire and Susan Boyd "Losing the Feminist Voice? Debates on the Legal Recognition of Same Sex Partnerships in Canada" (2006) 14 *Feminist Legal Studies* 213

Young, Robert *White Mythologies: Writing History and the West* (Routledge, London, 1990)

Zamboni, Mauro "Legal Realisms: On Law and Politics" (2006) 12 *Res Publica* 295

Zetlein, Sarah "Lesbian Bodies Before the Law: Chicks in White Satin" (1995) 5 *Australian Feminist Law Journal* 49

Zizek, Slavoj "The Spectre of Ideology" in Slavoj Zizek (ed) *Mapping Ideology* (Verso, London, 1994)

INDEX

[References are to paragraph numbers]